Disorders of Volition

Disorders of Volition

edited by Natalie Sebanz and Wolfgang Prinz

A Bradford Book
The MIT Press
Cambridge, Massachusetts
London, England

MIT Press books may be purchased at special quantity discounts for business or sales promotional use. For information, please email special_sales@mitpress.mit.edu or write to Special Sales Department, The MIT Press, 55 Hayward Street, Cambridge, MA 02142.

This book was set in Stone sans and Stone serif by SNP Best-set Typesetter Ltd., Hong Kong, and was printed and bound in the United States of America.

Library of Congress Cataloging-in-Publication Data

Disorders of volition / edited by Natalie Sebanz and Wolfgang Prinz.
    p. ; cm.
"A Bradford book."
Includes bibliographical references and index.
ISBN 0-262-19540-2 (hc : alk. paper)
1. Schizophrenia. 2. Will. 3. Mental illness. I. Sebanz, Natalie. II. Prinz, Wolfgang, 1942–.
[DNLM: 1. Mental Disorders. 2. Volition. 3. Depressive Disorder. 4. Prefrontal Cortex—injuries. 5. Schizophrenia. 6. Substance-Related Disorders. WM 140 D612 2006]

RC514.D56 2006
616.89—dc22

                                                                          2005056188

10 9 8 7 6 5 4 3 2 1

Contents

20   A Dynamic Model of the Will with an Application to Alcohol-Intoxicated Behavior   439
Jay G. Hull and Laurie B. Slone

1 Toward a Science of Volition

Wolfgang Prinz, Daniel Dennett, and Natalie Sebanz

This book aims at improving our understanding of the processes supporting voluntary action by looking at conditions in which the will is impaired or even breaks down. We use this introductory chapter to prepare the ground for contributions by philosophers, psychologists, neuroscientists, and psychiatrists that tackle the experience of acting intentionally, the ability to make decisions and implement one's goals, and the many ways in which the experience and the exertion of willful behavior can be disturbed. In the first part of this introduction, we describe the status of the will as we see it in present and past thinking. In the second part of the chapter, we provide an overview of the contributions in this book.

1.1 Studying the Will

When trying to decipher the forbidding complexity of the mind/brain, the standard simplifying assumption is that it is an "input–output system" in which perception goes in and (control of) action eventually comes out. We experimenters then work from the outside in, first getting control and understanding of the peripheral input systems, and postponing difficult questions about the center, which is shrouded in fog and mystery. This makes sense but risks distorting our vision of the whole, since we seldom if ever find ways of even posing questions about the requirements for the more central components that must eventually get transformed into the highest levels of outbound or "inside-out" traffic.

This potential for distortion is exacerbated by two further sources of distraction: introspection and the demands of free will. Introspection seems at first to be a godsend: Just as our inbound journey through the brain gets hopelessly beset with uncertainty and confusion, along comes introspection, the "first-person point of view," a well-positioned insider who can cut through the fog with a near-miraculous "access" to these central goings-on. The price we pay is that it is far from clear how to translate the mind-talk of introspection into the language of cognitive neuroscience. Nor is it clear when the deliverances of this embedded spy in terra incognita are reliable. The other perhaps even more serious source of distortion is the ideological conviction that we need to preserve, somewhere and somehow in this foggy center, a radical disconnect of some sort that will leave elbow room for free will.

This is often described as a philosophical concern, but it is not just the preoccupation of philosophers. The undertaking of science itself apparently calls for it: When investigators take themselves to be able to manipulate an input variable independent of the phenomenon being studied, they presume, do they not, that they are the origin of the manipulations or choices, not causally coupled with the phenomenon or a mere way station being driven (by some other phenomenon) to choose the manipulations they choose. Scientific investigation in any field thus apparently depends on the autonomy or freedom of the investigator, and this idea that some human actions have to be causally insulated or privileged in some special way has motivated a variety of speculative theories of how this might be accomplished, science-fictional at best and often simply incoherent. Infinite regress threatens at every turn. As Gilbert Ryle (1949) pointed out long ago, if what makes an action voluntary is that it is caused by an act of will, we need to ask if that act of will was itself voluntary and, hence, the effect of a prior act of will—and if not, how could an act of will that was not itself voluntary endow the action it causes with voluntariness?

Beset by such high-stakes theoretical demands, and such experimental intractability, it is small wonder that research on volition has lagged behind research on other aspects of the mind. However, intrepid forays into this long-shunned territory are at last under way, and as one might expect, even in advance of a clear theory, hard-won empirical details have a way of illuminating the theoretical prospects so that the imponderables do not look so unmanageable after all. When we look more closely at what is going on, the "extensionless point" of the self (Nagel 1979) expands into a spatially and temporally distributed self that can work its "miracles" with less than miraculous means. Some philosophers will probably continue to prefer their fantasies about "agent causation" and quantum amplifiers hiding in the convenient fog in the center of the brain, but the science of volition is poised to march past them and secure a theory that can finally make sense of the recursive, reflective control systems that make voluntary human action so deserving of credit and blame.

1.2 Action

Throughout centuries, science has approached human action in two major contexts—cognition and volition. In the context of *cognition*, researchers study how action is planned, controlled, and modulated *in response to conditions encountered in the environment*. Hence, cognitive approaches view actions from an outside-in perspective, examining how they are formed and informed by external conditions. Conversely, in the context of *volition*, researchers study how action is planned, controlled, and modulated *in the service of the agent's needs, motives, desires, or goals*. Hence, volitional approaches view actions from an inside-out perspective, examining how they are formed and informed by internal conditions.

Cognitive approaches to action have always been more elaborate and better developed than volitional approaches. Some reasons for this bias are rooted in the history, methodology, and theory of cognitive studies. Historically, the scientific study of the mind and the brain has emerged from epistemology, and epistemology has, of course, always been a lot more concerned with the outside-in rather than the inside-out perspective. Yet, later on, when the sciences of the mind and the brain had long broken away from philosophy and forgotten all about their epistemological roots, they still continued to prefer the outside-in over the inside-out perspective. One of the reasons why this bias was preserved, if not strengthened, is related to the methodology of experimental research. In experimental settings, where external stimulus conditions can be manipulated in a straightforward way, it is easy and natural to study action as a consequence of foregoing stimulation. This is not true of internal conditions like goals, or impulses of the will, which are, by their very nature, less accessible to such manipulations. Furthermore, this difference in methodology goes along with a related difference in theory: When it comes to theoretical accounts of action, external conditions, such as stimuli, may take the innocent role of *causa efficiens* for the action to follow, whereas internal conditions, such as goals, come close to the more precarious role of *causa finalis*.

Yet, science has not only preferred cognition but also avoided volition. Ever since, the will has been a sensitive subject. In some ages, it has been venerated as the incarnation of personhood and autonomy, whereas in other ages it has been disdained as an indecent faculty of the mind. As concerns *veneration*, take a look at *free will* as it appears illustrated in Cesare Ripa's iconology (Ripa 1709; see fig. 1.1). In this picture volition appears to be closely intertwined with notions of personal autonomy and freedom—notions that are deeply rooted in the ideological underpinnings of ethical, legal, and political systems (at least in modern Western civilization). Some even believe that these notions are too crucial for establishing these ideologies to be delivered to scientific discourse and enquiry. For instance, philosophers often claim that science has nothing to say about issues of personhood and autonomy: Addressing these issues is just their business. And the guardians of law and jurisdiction often contend that science may shake the legal system to its foundations and thus jeopardize our society altogether when it starts questioning free will, the Holy Grail of law and constitution.

As concerns *disdain*, take a look at the maid *Volition* as she appears illustrated in Ripa's iconology (see fig. 1.2). In a somewhat rough exterior, we see a person with loose hair, clothed in beggar's garments. As she walks about, haunting the air with her huge wings, in search of whatever high-flying goal, she is blind to her surroundings,

Figure 1.1
The notion of Free Will as illustrated in Cesare Ripa's (1709) iconology. We see a young and active nobleman, a sovereign vested with the power to take decisions and to reign accordingly. The tip of the scepter is split—a symbol for the option of having to choose between virtue versus vice. (Source: Ripa, C. [1709]. *Iconologia or moral emblems*. London. Online: http://emblem.libraries.psu.edu/Ripa/Images/ripatoc.htm/.)

Figure 1.2
Maid Volition. Taken from the same source as figure 1.1.

always running the risk of losing grip of the ground. This picture suggests that volition may be a harmful malfunction of mental life that may indicate an inappropriate
power of the will. In any case we cannot fail to see that Maid Volition enjoys much
less esteem than Prince Free Will.

As these contrasting views suggest, the will is not just a neutral and innocent faculty
of the mind. Rather, discussions about the nature of volition have always been deeply
intertwined with discussions about ethical and political issues. Historically speaking,
the will started its career in theology and ethics, and then from there it made its way
into law and politics. Only very recently has it arrived in scientific theory as well, yet
leaving traces of its long nonscientific history. In medieval Christian theology and
philosophy, human will was considered a derivative of the Will of God—to the effect
that the will would never choose Evil, but always Good (i.e., resist desire and follow
reason; cf., e.g., Taylor 1989; Romano 2004). In postmedieval times, the will became
secularized and was now considered the faculty of making choices—choices that were
now no longer intrinsically directed toward the good. Accordingly, since the good was
no longer inherent in that faculty itself, that faculty now had to become the locus in
individual minds at which all sorts of external regulations of human conduct had to
be addressed. These could be regulations about Right and Wrong, or good and bad
choices, about ways of dealing with conflicts between incompatible choices, or even
about the inclusion/exclusion of individuals with respect to the right of making
choices. For instance, at certain ages, it may have been appropriate for priests and
princes to make choices and decisions of their own, but not for servants and slaves to
do so—appropriate for Prince Free Will, but not for Maid Volition. In this sense, the
will is the psychological counterpart of ethics, law, and politics. The will has two faces
to it. From the inside, it is a faculty of individual minds. From the outside, it serves
as a theater for the impact of external regulation of individuals' conduct.

1.3 Volition

For the scientific study of volition we may, as a first step, turn to William James's treatise on the will in chapter 26 of *The Principles of Psychology*, which appeared more than
a hundred years ago. James's treatise, which is an elegant piece of armchair psychology, is in fact a suitable starting point, because it absorbed, as it were, decades, if not
centuries, of foregoing philosophical discussion and cast it in a convenient conceptual framework. That framework can still be used today as a guideline for sorting out
major empirical issues that have to be addressed, as well as major theoretical problems that have to be resolved.

According to James's account, voluntary actions require that two conditions be met:
(1) There must be an idea, or representation, of what is being willed, and (2) any conflicting ideas must be absent or removed. When these two conditions are fulfilled,

those ideas, or representations of intended goal states, have the power to generate the action. On this account, cognitive representations are in their very nature impulsive—to the effect that volition can be partly reduced to cognition. This is particularly true of those representations that refer to movements and actions. To these representations, a principle applies that James christened the ideomotor principle of voluntary action: *"Every representation of a movement awakens in some degree the actual movement which is its object; and awakens it in a maximum degree whenever it is not kept from doing so by an antagonistic representation present simultaneously in the mind"* (James 1890, vol. II, p. 526).

James believed that the volitional nature of cognition arises from learning. Whenever a motor act is performed, it goes along with perceivable effects. Some are close to the action in the sense of being accompaniments of the act itself, like kinesthetic proprioception of ongoing movements. Some others may be more remote, like a bell ringing at a distance when one's finger operates a doorbell knob. Such regular connections between motor acts and their ensuing effects can then be functional in two ways. One is to generate forward models, that is, *anticipate appropriate effects, given certain acts.* The other is to create inverse models, that is, *select appropriate acts, given intentions to achieve certain effects.* This latter relationship, which leads from intended effects to acts, forms the functional basis of the ideomotor principle: Any representation of an event of which individuals have learned that it follows from a particular action will henceforward exhibit the power to call forth that action.

The ideomotor principle has received support from a great number of experimental studies (see Hommel et al. 2001 for an overview). Nevertheless, the Jamesian framework leaves us with a number of *issues for empirical research.* Major research issues concern, for example, the content and realization of intentions, the relation between processes of cognition and volition, the relation between making choices and implementing decisions, and the role of the temporal aspects of intended goals. These issues can be characterized in terms of distinctions like What/How, Mechanics/Dynamics, Selection/Implementation, and Acting/Planning.

1.3.1 What/How

First, empirical research needs to address What issues and How issues. Research directed at What issues tries to determine *what* people intend to do under given circumstances, how the contents of their intentions depend on internal and external conditions, and how they may change over time (i.e., *issues of motivation*). Conversely, research directed at How issues tries to determine *how* people realize given goals through actions. How does internal goal-related information interact with external environment-related information to generate appropriate action and bring forth intended effects (i.e., *issues of volition*)?

1.3.2 Mechanics/Dynamics

Second, one of the major dimensions on which volition differs from cognition refers to what may be called temperature: We may distinguish between "hot volition" and "cold cognition." Entities like motives, goals, impulses of the will, desires, and temptations are but insufficiently characterized by the mere contents they refer to. Rather, they have to be characterized in energetic terms as well and require functional architectures specifying both the cold mechanics of cognitive operations and the hot dynamics of volitional forces.

1.3.3 Selection/Implementation

A third aspect worthy of empirical investigation is the relation between volition as a faculty for decision making and goal selection, and volition as a faculty for the implementation of previously made decisions. Given that the question of free will is a central issue in the psychological and philosophical discussion of volition, it is not surprising that these and other disciplines have mainly focused on the decision-making role of volition. However, many disorders of volition are characterized by an impairment related to the implementation of decisions. Investigating the relation between the selective and the dynamic role of volition is thus an important issue for scientific investigation.

1.3.4 Acting/Planning

Finally, it may be useful to distinguish between volition with versus without a direct executional component. Processes underlying the will-in-action are often short-term operations, whereas processes underlying the will-in-planning are long-term. The processes underlying the will-in-action can be regarded as supporting action control, whereas the processes underlying the will-in-planning are of particular importance to self-control.

Yet, the Jamesian framework not only provides us with issues for empirical research but also confronts us with *theoretical puzzles and paradoxes* that pose severe challenges—partly to commonsense intuitions, partly to scientific theories.

1.3.5 Agency and Authorship

One such puzzle refers to agency and authorship. Central to our commonsense intuitions about the workings of the will is the notion that voluntary action, whatever the mechanics and dynamics of its underlying machinery may be, is ultimately directed, controlled, and—for that matter—*authored by a personal agent* within, or perhaps behind, that machinery. However, if one takes a closer look at it, the Jamesian framework has no role whatsoever for personal agents and authors. Instead, voluntary action is thought to emerge from, and be fully determined by, the mechanics and dynamics of a subpersonal machinery. In a way, we lose the agent while trying to explain her actions. Should we be concerned about this loss or should we perhaps be relieved about it?

1.3.6 Mental Causation

A further puzzle relates to mental causation—a notion the Jamesian framework shares with folk psychology. Here the idea is that *mental kinds* such as intentions *have the power to cause physical kinds* such as bodily movements. This notion seems to entail a dualistic stance—at least as long as mental representations are considered as being incommensurate with the physical entities to which they refer. In everyday life we may be successful practitioners of such dualism, but in our scientific theories we should perhaps be concerned about it. Here it may be useful to distinguish between real and apparent mental causation (Wegner 2003).

1.4 Disorders of Volition

In this book we focus on ways in which volition can be impaired. Such impairments can be observed in a number of psychiatric and neurological disorders. While some of them—such as schizophrenia and prefrontal lobe damage—are clearly established as disorders of volition, others, such as depression or substance abuse, are perhaps less commonly regarded from this viewpoint. Still, we believe that investigating ways in which the will can be impaired or break down across different pathologies is a promising means to gain a better understanding of the nature of voluntary action.

As always, there are two ways to approach impairments and disorders. One goes from regular function to disorders. The other goes from disorders to regular function. We have planned the conference that provided the basis for this book in an attempt to go either way. These two approaches are reflected in the volume. On the one hand, we discuss the will and its pathologies from a more general point of view across different disorders. In that part, we mainly explore what is known about the nature of voluntary action in general, and how this knowledge can inform our understanding of disorders of volition. On the other hand, we focus on specific neurological and psychiatric disorders and discuss how they can be understood as disorders of volitional functions. We have decided to focus on four specific disorders rather than covering the neurological and psychiatric conditions that can be regarded as disorders of volition in an all-embracing way. We explore what is known about the nature of schizophrenia, depression, prefrontal lobe damage, and substance abuse and discuss how this knowledge can inform our understanding of the regular functioning of volition.

If it is true that the will is the psychological counterpart of ethics, law, and politics and serves as the psychological theater for the impact of the social environment on individuals' conduct, it will even more be true that notions concerning "disorders" and "regular functions" of volition will reflect moral, legal, and political conditions.

This once more brings us back to Maid Volition. Her somewhat bizarre appearance reminds us that the dividing line between regular function and malfunction is, at least partially, a matter of cultural construction and may be subject to historical change. What the picture suggests is that volition and agency—which are nowadays considered respected functions of healthy mental life—were in her time regarded as malfunctions, indicating perhaps an indecent preponderance of self-governance over compliance with the divine and worldly order.

Accordingly, talking about disorders may easily turn into talking about exclusion—exclusion from those who are entitled to make choices of their own—and talking about exclusion may eventually turn into practicing exclusion in one or the other way. At this point, we should remind ourselves of the abhorrent examples of pushing exclusion to its extremes that took place at Kloster Irsee, the site of the conference from which this book emerged.[1] The conclusion to be drawn from this is simple enough: Since much of our intuitions about the divide between "good" and "bad" functioning reflects cultural—and even political—constructs rather than natural facts, we need to avoid any ontologizing of this divide—not only for the sake of preventing discriminations against those who suffer from bad functioning but also in the interest of scientific theory. Therefore, it may perhaps be wiser to speak of *varieties* rather than *disorders* of volition.

1.5   Approaches to Disorders of Volition

The contributions in this book are grouped into five parts. The first part presents different conceptual frameworks that identify the experience of agency, decision making, and goal pursuit as central components of volition (Metzinger; Bayne and Levy; Haggard; Proust; Ainslie; Cohen and Gollwitzer). The remaining four parts explore the question of how impairments in these and other aspects of volition manifest themselves as "disorders of volition." The second part is concerned with the link between volition and certain symptoms in schizophrenia (Jeannerod; Liddle; Spence and Parry; Frith). The third part addresses impairments in the formation and implementation of intentions in depression (Nitschke and Mackiewitz; Schneider; Jouvent, Dubal, and Fossati). The fourth part deals with changes in action planning and decision making following prefrontal lobe damage (Owen; Grafman and Krueger; Burgess, Gilbert, Okuda, and Simons). The last part explores the relationship between decision making and substance abuse (Bechara; Sayette; Hull and Slone). In the following, we provide an overview of the contributions in each of the five parts.

1.5.1   Part I: Conceptual Foundations

The first four chapters in this part analyze the experience of agency. The authors of these chapters agree that the feeling of acting intentionally is "thin" and "evasive" but merits theoretical analysis as well as empirical study because it is a fundamental component of volition.

In the opening chapter, Thomas Metzinger develops a model that accounts for the phenomenology of agency and describes the transition from willing to acting intentionally. Metzinger argues that for an understanding of volition, it is crucial to take into account the self-representational character of agency. Individuals not only form representations of goals but also form a representation of themselves as having goals. Metzinger suggests that a phenomenal model of the self is the causal mediator connecting a goal representation to the motor system, enabling the transformation of intentions into actions. In the final part of the chapter, he discusses akinetic mutism, a condition in which patients are awake but show no indication of intentionality in terms of this model: Metzinger argues that what these patients are missing is a representation of self in relation to action goals.

In the next chapter, Tim Bayne and Neil Levy "deconstruct" the phenomenology of agency. They assume that "there is no single experience of agency" and analyze different representational contents that contribute to the feeling of acting intentionally. In particular, Bayne and Levy discuss the phenomenology of mental causation, the phenomenology of authorship, and the phenomenology of effort. They propose that the experience of mental causation is neither necessary nor sufficient for the experience of will and place a form of experienced authorship—agent causation—at the heart of the experience of acting intentionally. The feeling of mental effort is assumed to support the experience of authorship.

The following chapter, by Patrick Haggard, shows that the analysis of the experience of agency is not restricted to theoretical deliberation but can benefit from experimental investigation. Haggard reviews laboratory studies in which he and his colleagues investigated the effects of intentions on the perceived time of actions and their effects. These studies demonstrate a strong temporal compression surrounding intentional action. Subjects perceive their intentional actions and corresponding action effects as closer in time than they really are, providing evidence for a strong link between intention and agency. Haggard discusses these findings in terms of motor control theory. He suggests that there is a specific conscious experience of preparing an action, emerging as a consequence of preparatory brain activity, whose phenomenal content is the anticipated action effect. Thus, prediction lies at the heart of the experience of conscious intention and agency.

In the contributions by Metzinger, Bayne and Levy, and Haggard, the experience of agency is analyzed with respect to physical actions. The last contribution on the experience of agency, by Joëlle Proust, adds a new perspective by raising the question of whether there is a sense of agency that is common to bodily and mental actions. Drawing on principles of hierarchical control theories, Proust sketches a theory of volition that accounts not only for willful bodily actions but also for willful thinking processes. She proposes that simulation operates at different levels of control to allow for the evaluation of actions from various perspectives. This theory allows her to explain two ostensibly disparate symptoms in schizophrenia in a unified framework, namely, the experience that one is not the author, or owner, of one's actions (delusion of control) and the experience that thoughts are inserted in one's mind and are not one's own (thought insertion).

Beside the experience of agency, another important component of volition is the ability to choose between competing goals and the ability to pursue goals over longer time spans. The last two contributions in the section on conceptual foundations are dedicated to these issues. George Ainslie presents a conceptual framework that allows him to explain principles of choice and to derive implications for self-control. Ainslie argues that choice is shaped by reward and is the result of a competition between behaviors that are associated with motivational states. He provides evidence that spontaneous choice in humans and animals is best described by a hyperbolic shape, where value stands in inverse proportion to delay, rather than by hierarchies of preference as proposed by traditional rational choice theory. Ainslie discusses how recursive self-prediction can account both for a surge in willpower when a current choice is seen as a decisive instance and for lapses in willpower when there is a one-time occasion to indulge.

What happens once an intention is formed? In the following chapter, Anna-Lisa Cohen and Peter Gollwitzer argue that the intention to achieve a certain goal is not a good predictor for goal attainment, as assumed by traditional goal-striving theories. They claim that "a second act of willing" is necessary, helping people to resume goals in the presence of competing alternatives. Cohen and Gollwitzer review a wide range of empirical findings to support the claim that forming a certain type of intention is an efficient means to forestall the second act of willing. They show that implementation intentions, which create a mental link between a specified future situation and actions to be performed in this situation, effectively facilitate goal attainment. The authors discuss the use of implementation intentions to ameliorate problems in goal pursuit observed in patients with frontal lobe damage, schizophrenia, and depression, thus providing a transition to the following parts of this volume that deal with specific disorders of volition.

1.5.2   Part II: Disorders of Volition in Schizophrenia

The contributions in part 2 discuss volitional impairments in schizophrenia from a behavioral and a brain perspective. Impairments in agency, which have been considered from a more theoretical perspective in part 1, are discussed in detail in the first chapter in part 2. The next two chapters in this part are dedicated to two other categories of symptoms, disorganization and psychomotor poverty, and explore how these symptoms are related to impairments in volition. The last chapter discusses some new ways of thinking about volitional impairments in schizophrenia.

Following the conceptual approaches to agency in the first part, Marc Jeannerod proposes that feeling authorship of one's actions is crucial for the experience of intentional action. He reviews studies in which the origin of an observed action was rendered ambiguous or a systematic mismatch between performed actions and observed actions was introduced to investigate the cognitive and neural mechanisms involved in action attribution. These studies indicate that the inferior parietal lobe plays an important role in detecting discordance between observed and executed movements. In schizophrenic patients who show impairments in action attribution, activation in this area does not correlate with the amount of discrepancy between observed and performed actions. This suggests that these patients lack the cues for recognizing their own actions that are normally provided by changes in parietal activity. Jeannerod speculates that the origin of the action attribution impairments may be found in prefrontal areas that exert inhibitory control over areas involved in motor and sensorimotor processing.

In the following chapter, Peter Liddle present an account of symptoms of disorganization, which may lead to serious impairments in volition. He proposes that the brain engages in different states of activity that are associated with charateristic patterns of distributed neural activities. Two of these brain states are the "default state," a state of introspective awareness of oneself, and the "motivated attention state," a state in which one is engaged in attending to salient information in order to perform a mental or physical act. Liddle provides evidence from brain imaging studies to support the claim that the recruitment of this motivated attention system is impaired in schizophrenia. He suggests that the recruitment problem arises from an impairment of the mechanism by which low-frequency oscillatory activity in the brain is generated.

Avolition, the lack of voluntary behavior, is in the focus in the following chapter by Sean Spence and Chris Parry. They review brain imaging studies from their own and other labs showing that the prefrontal cortex plays a key role in the generation of actions that are chosen and executed spontaneously. Spence and Parry provide evidence that psychomotor poverty, which incorporates avolition, not only exhibits a correlation with reduced activity in prefrontal cortex but is also associated with structural changes in prefrontal cortex. Given the possibility that plastic changes over time may modulate prefrontal function and structure, the authors discuss how certain therapeutic interventions might ameliorate volitional impairments in schizophrenia.

In the final chapter on schizophrenia, Chris Frith argues that some schizophrenic symptoms, such as delusions of control, thought insertion, and psychomotor poverty can only be understood by taking into account the social nature of cognition. In line with other contributions on agency, Frith proposes that delusions of control and thought insertion involve a failure in action attribution. However, he suggests that this failure not only may result from impaired forward models in the motor system but could also be related to impairments in the intentional binding mechanism proposed by Patrick Haggard in part I. Such an impairment implies that the ability to understand others' intentions may be reduced. A further novel idea is that poverty of will and disorganization could result from difficulties in generating actions that are appropriate in a given social context. The proposal that volition and its disorders can only be fully understood when taking into account the social context also provides a new way of thinking about top-down action control.

1.5.3 Part III: Disorders of Volition in Depression

Symptoms of avolition not only appear in schizophrenia but are an important characteristic of impaired volition in depression. Accordingly, the three contributions in part 3 all discuss how impairments in the formation and execution of action plans lead to avolition.

Jack Nitschke and Kristen Mackiewicz propose that individuals suffering from depression have a desire to act but lack the ability to form and implement an action plan. They review findings showing that the dorsolateral prefrontal cortex plays a major role in the formation and implementation of action plans. Nitschke and Mackiewicz suggest that the inability of patients with depression to override established behaviors and initiate new goal-directed behaviors may be explained by reduced activity in left dorsolateral prefrontal cortex. An asymmetric pattern of frontal activity with more activity on the right may be related to withdrawal, negative emotions, and threat perception. Decreased activity in the anterior cingulate cortex is assumed to lead to impaired conflict monitoring and the selection and implementation of action plans. The authors discuss how treating volition as a central feature of depression may affect the understanding of volition as well as the treatment of depression.

In the following contribution by Werner Schneider, depression is also regarded as a misregulation of action control. In the first part of his chapter, Schneider outlines a framework for action control, specifying how goals compete, how an action goal is selected and implemented, and how the outcome of actions is monitored and evaluated. In the second part, he proposes that in depression, a chronic stress response due to repeated failures in pursuing action goals may lead to short-term and long-term changes in the brain structures supporting action planning. Schneider argues that the onset phase of depression is related to damage of the prefrontal cortex, with successive damage of the anterior cingulate cortex due to chronic stress leading to more severe forms of depression.

In the last chapter of this part, Roland Jouvent, Stéphanie Dubal, and Philippe Fossati focus on the role of cognitive flexibility and the ability to mobilize cognitive resources in volitional impairments observed in depression and anhedonia. They present evidence that faced with tasks that require cognitive effort, depressed patients and anhedonics recruit more cognitive resources than controls. Jouvent, Dubal, and Fossati suggest that volitional impairments in depression and the loss of pleasure in anhedonia could reflect the exhaustion of cognitive resources.

1.5.4 Part IV: Disorders of Volition in Patients with Prefrontal Lobe Damage

The three contributions in this part analyze the volitional impairments observed in patients with prefrontal lobe damage. Although differing in the approach taken to identify the function of areas of the prefrontal lobe and the investigation of volitional impairments, these contributions provide converging empirical evidence that the prefrontal cortex plays a crucial role in the formation and implementation of intentions, as well as in decision making.

Adrian Owen reviews neuropsychological data to suggest that damage to the frontal lobes impairs the formation and implementation of conscious intention, whereas more automatic, stimulus-driven processes remain unaffected. Drawing on brain imaging and neurophysiological studies, Owen proposes that the midventrolateral cortex is especially important for intentional action. He presents data suggesting that activity in midventrolateral frontal cortex is associated with the intentional encoding of stimuli. However, this area does not seem to be restricted to intentional mnemonic processing, as it is also involved in other intentional processes such as the shifting of stimulus–reward associations and inhibition.

The observation that patients with lesions in prefrontal cortex are impaired in their ability to form and implement self-generated actions, whereas their ability to decide to perform actions elicited by external cues remains relatively unimpaired, is also the starting point of Jordan Grafman and Frank Krueger's contribution. The patient studies they report demonstrate that patients with lesions in prefrontal cortex have particular difficulty with planning problems that extend into the future, and they are impaired at advice taking and using foresight. Furthermore, the authors describe a case study showing that the ability to make rational decisions in personal and social matters may be impaired while general cognitive decision-making abilities remain intact. Grafman and Krueger interpret these findings within a framework based on the assumption that aspects of episodic and semantic knowledge are represented in the form of structured event complexes in prefrontal cortex.

Paul Burgess, Sam Gilbert, Jiro Okuda, and Jon Simons discuss the role of a specific part of prefrontal cortex, the rostral prefrontal cortex, in supporting intentional behavior. They review brain imaging, neurophysiological, and patient studies to suggest that rostral prefrontal cortex acts as a gateway that biases the relative influence of stimulus-oriented and stimulus-independent thought. This account offers an explanation of why patients with lesions in rostral prefrontal cortex have specific difficulties with situations requiring multitasking and carrying out intended actions after a delay.

1.5.5   Part V: Disorders of Volition in Substance Abuse

The last part is dedicated to volitional impairments that give rise to or accompany addiction and substance abuse. The three contributions provide a multifaceted discussion of issues of willpower and self-control and relate closely to the conceptual contributions by Ainslie and by Cohen and Gollwitzer in part 1.

Antoine Bechara argues that the ability to forego immediate rewards to obtain future benefits is the result of a balance between an impulsive system, signaling pain or pleasure of immediate events, and a reflective system, signaling positive or negative future prospects. He suggests that the amygdala provides the neural basis for the first system, whereas orbitofrontal cortex plays an important role in the latter system. Bechara provides empirical evidence from patient studies to support his claim that addiction is characterized by a dysfunctional reflective system, which does not provide necessary control over the impulsive system, as well as a hyperactive impulsive system, which biases the somatic signals associated with immediate prospects.

Michael Sayette addresses issues of self-control by reviewing findings on craving in smokers. He demonstrates that craving is linked to changes in perception and decision making and presents studies suggesting that craving may take different forms depending on individuals' intentions. These findings shed light on the relationship between craving and addiction.

Jay Hull and Laurie Slone discuss volitional impairments that arise as a result of alcohol intoxication. They review findings demonstrating that alcohol affects processes crucial for supporting controlled actions, including conflict detection and conflict resolution. These results inform their dynamic system model of volition, in which disorders are conceptualized as a failure in overriding automatic behavior based on the comparison of an action representation with an internal standard of behavior.

We hope that the collection of contributions in this book will inspire those interested in understanding the processes underlying voluntary action and those striving to explain and treat volitional impairments. The majority of the contributions originate from the talks and discussions at the conference "Disorders of Volition" in Irsee, Germany, in December 2003. A few chapters were invited later to complete the picture emerging from the conference contributions. The conference was made possible by the generous support of the Volkswagen-Stiftung and was part of an interdisciplinary research project on the nature and culture of volition, also funded by the Volkswagen-Stiftung.

Notes

1. In Nazi times, the monastery was a psychiatric hospital and formed part of Nazi Germany's so-called euthanasia program. The ideology behind it was that psychiatric disorders serve as

markers for genetic disorders that are immune to any treatment and threaten the integrity of the gene pool. Through the killing of a vast number of hospitalized psychiatric patients, this program in fact practiced exclusion-to-death (von Cranach 2003). Nowadays, the monastery serves as a center for various scientific conferences, political meetings, and cultural events.

References

Hommel, B., J. Muesseler, G. Aschersleben, and W. Prinz. 2001. The Theory of Event Coding (TEC): A framework for perception and action planning. *Behavioral and Brain Sciences, 24,* 849–937.

James, W. 1890. *The Principles of Psychology.* New York: Holt.

Nagel, T. 1979. *Mortal Questions.* Cambridge: Cambridge University Press.

Ripa, C. 1709. *Iconologia or Moral Emblems.* London. Available online at http://emblem .libraries.psu.edu/Ripa/Images/ripatoc.htm.

Romano, C. 2004. Volonté. In B. Cassin (dir.), *Vocabulaire Européen des Philosophies, Dictionnaires des Intraduisibles.* Paris: Editions du Seuil/Editions Robert.

Ryle, G. 1949. *The Concept of Mind.* London: Hutchinson.

Taylor, C. 1989. *Sources of the Self: The Making of the Modern Identity.* Cambridge, Mass.: Harvard University Press.

von Cranach, M. 2003. The killing of psychiatric patients in Nazi Germany 1939–1945. *Israel Journal of Psychiatry, 40,* 8–28.

Wegner, D. 2003. *The Illusion of Conscious Will.* Cambridge, Mass.: MIT Press.

I Conceptual Foundations

2 Conscious Volition and Mental Representation: Toward a More Fine-Grained Analysis

Thomas Metzinger

Two projects are central for any serious theory of volition: describing the *phenomenology of will* more precisely and analyzing the *functional fine structure* of its physical substrate in a more accurate manner. Both projects have difficult empirical aspects, and both generate their own conceptual problems. Here, I will try to contribute to the first project by proposing a model of how the phenomenology of conscious volition could be described on the representationalist level of analysis, yielding an almost universal deep structure. This representational deep structure can hopefully help us to understand standard configurations as well as disorders of volition. Being a philosopher, I will be mostly interested in conceptual issues. However, to test the model here proposed, I will also present one empirical case study and a number of empirical predictions at the end of this chapter.

2.1 The Phenomenology of Volition

"Phenomenal content" is what philosophers call the specific experiential content of conscious states, as tied to an individual subjective perspective. The first difficulty in describing the phenomenal content of volition is perhaps the biggest and most fundamental one, and it is very rarely made explicit: The phenomenology of volition is *thin* and it is *evasive*.

"Thin" means that the conscious experience of willing something is not as crisp and vivid as, say, the conscious experience of seeing colors or of feeling pain. First, it lacks the sensory concreteness typically going along with stimulus-correlated states. Second, ongoing volitional processing can certainly be globally available and bound into short-term memory (and therefore conscious; see Metzinger 2003a, chap. 3), but actual access is intermittent and not functionally stable. What we are subjectively aware of are *stages* in the middle of a chain, not a stable end product (Haggard 2003, p. 126). Therefore, willing something, consciously, can be a rather subtle and vague inner process, and at times the fact that one is currently willing something can even be introspectively overlooked. Third, even in maximally simple, nonconflict situations, it is often not quite clear at what point in subjective time an experience of will begins and when exactly it ends. From a phenomenological point of view, episodes of will are not *temporally segmented* in a clear-cut way. Finally, not only are the temporal borders of episodes of will fuzzy but the object component of volition—*what* one is currently willing, the goal state itself—may often be less than clear. Frequently, the mental representation of what philosophers call the "intentional object" is much less salient and reliable than, for instance, the emotional sensations going along with an experience of will. Just think of certain moods, diffuse longings, and urges, or the states of mild confusion preceding difficult decisions.

"Evasive" means that attempts to deliberately focus one's introspective attention on the different steps and stages of conscious will formation often lead to a state in which the target of introspection—will "itself"—seems to *recede* or to *dissolve*. Let me give an example of how this phenomenological fact could affect the interpretation of highly relevant data. Recent empirical findings show how in certain simple paradigms attending to one's own intention enhances the blood-oxygenation-level-dependent (BOLD) signal in the presupplementary motor area (pre-SMA; see Lau et al. 2004). The relevant specific task for subjects was to "report . . . the time at which they felt the intention to move" (Lau et al. 2004, p. 1208). However, what we do not know is how exactly this heightened neural activity in the pre-SMA, should it turn out to be a *general* effect in intentional action, translates into the processing of representational content: What is the actual relation between this enhancement and the unstable, weakly segmented, and evasive nature of introspected volition? After all, attending to a mental representation should be attending to its *content*. But in what time window? What time slice of the overall continuous dynamics of mentally "containing" the process, which today we call "intending," are we actually targeting? Is the observed BOLD-signal enhancement simply the correlate of a momentary "urge to respond" or rather of a more extended process of monitoring and/or stabilizing volitional mental content? If, given the recessive nature of volitional content, introspective attention were to be sustained, would it rather have to count as an early stage in a process of *disintegration*? The phenomenological fact to be accommodated is that in longer time windows the experience of will, if introspectively attended to, often recedes and dissolves. It may recede by losing phenomenal saliency, by losing introspectively perceived intensity, or simply by coming to an end more quickly as soon as one decides to observe it more carefully. It may dissolve, for instance, by suddenly coming apart into its hitherto unnoticed proprioceptive, emotional, and motor subcomponents.

In this context, it may possibly be interesting to note how precisely this evasive character of the phenomenology of will, has been, for centuries, functionally exploited by more serious practitioners of meditation: They make the will go away by effortless attention, by simply observing it unfold, without any judgment. However, for the scientific and philosophical project of constructing a comprehensive *theory* of conscious volition, this functional property of "evasiveness," together with the shallowness or "thinness" mentioned before, amounts not to an advantage, but to a very serious obstacle: It is hard to arrive at a first-person description of the *explanandum* that exhibits a methodological minimum of potential for consensus. Let us coin a technical term for this fact, by calling it the problem of "phenomenological indeterminacy."[1]

I have no direct solution to this problem. However, I believe that considerable progress in our understanding of conscious volition can still be made. The conclusion of this first section is that, given the current stage of this field of research, it is important to complement first-person descriptions of our target phenomenon with a more rigorous third-person representationalist analysis, which can later function as a logical bridge between bottom-up, data-driven, and microfunctional analyses of volition and top-down, introspective, and phenomenological descriptions. What we can do is to conceptually describe the contents of experience in a way that, at least in principle, allows us to tie specific phenomenal properties to specific causal roles realized by certain parts and dynamical subcomponents of the brain, thereby generating testable hypotheses. For now, the fundamental epistemological problem remains. Nevertheless, the strategic hope is that through developing an interdisciplinary, multilevel research program and by tying fine-grained phenomenological descriptions to data-driven models, we may discover as yet unknown aspects of the problem of phenomenological indeterminacy. These aspects could eventually allow us to solve or at least to circumvent it.

2.2   The Representational Content of Volition

Phenomenologically, volition precedes action. Functionally, willed actions are a specific subset of goal-directed bodily movements: A series of movements that are functionally integrated with an explicit and currently active representation of a goal state constitute an action. Therefore, conceptually, an action is not isomorphic to a particular bodily movement or any specific behavioral pattern, because many different movements can constitute the same goal-directed action. It is the goal state that makes an action what it is. This is our first defining characteristic for the concept of a "willed action." For example, in unlocking and opening a door, what makes this action an "opening the door" action is not whether you turn the key with your left or with your right hand but the fact that your behavior is aimed at a specific goal state—namely, the open door. What individuates an action is the set of *satisfaction conditions* defining the representational content of its goal component, plus the special way in which this goal-representation is causally linked to the actual event of overt movement generation. In particular, an action results from a selection process (which may or may not be conscious) and a representation of the system as a whole as now standing in a certain relation to a specific goal state (which is phenomenally represented, e.g., globally available via short-term memory). I call this conscious model of the system as a whole its "phenomenal self-model" (PSM; see Metzinger 2003a). From now on I will use "PSM" and "conscious self-model" interchangeably. The satisfaction conditions defining the goal state are those conditions that would make the action count as *successfully terminated*. Consciously experienced volition then becomes a process of transiently integrating the PSM with an active representation of these satisfaction conditions. Please note how this standard model assumes some sort of high-level binding. It is important to note how there exists not only the logical possibility but also empirical evidence that a representation of satisfaction conditions, the "goal component," can at times be activated in an isolated fashion, lacking any integration with the self-model. As Jeannerod and Pacherie (2004, pp. 139ff.; see also Marc Jeannerod's contribution to this volume) have pointed out, we can also be consciously aware of what these authors call " 'naked' intentions" ("unbound goal components" in the present terminology), by leaving the agent parameter in our mental representation unspecified, without being by the same token aware of *whose* intention it is. The main point I want to make in this chapter is that, because of the automatic inclusion of a self-representational component in nonpathological standard configurations, volitional states are functionally characterized by a "principle of relational coding." This principle is reflected in the structure of phenomenal experience itself.

The second defining characteristic is that any consciously willed action involves not only an explicit and conscious self-representation but also a representation of the *perspective* the system now takes onto the world. That is, the motor selection process may well be unconscious (and depend on abstract premotor processing; see Haggard and Eimer 1999, p. 131; Metzinger and Gallese 2003), but in consciously willed actions it typically leads to a more global final stage resulting in a phenomenal representation of the system as a whole—as *having* an intention, as initiating and executing its own bodily movements. In other words, on the phenomenal level we always find a corresponding global state in which the system as a whole is itself represented as an agent by standing in relation to a *specific* action. Of course, unconscious, subpersonal selection processes can drive behavior as well, and we may well choose the terminological option of calling these processes "unconscious volition." Given our initial definition of the term, it would also be conceptually coherent to speak of "subjectively unwilled actions."[2] Here, I am only concerned with the structure of phenomenal volition. The two central issues are these: How can a system represent itself *to* itself as "having an intention," and how can we understand the special causal linkage between an active goal representation and the overt motor output? I will propose that both are simultaneously mediated through a single and specific representational structure, namely, the "phenomenal model of the intentionality relation" (PMIR) (see fig. 2.1). This structure will be explored in the next section.

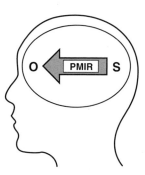

Figure 2.1

The *phenomenal model of the intentionality relation* (PMIR): A subject component (S; the PSM, an internal, conscious model of the system as a whole,) is phenomenally represented as directed at an object component (O; the "intentional object"). In conscious volition, O always is a *goal component*, for example, an allocentric representation of a successfully terminated bodily action.

2.2.1 The Concept of a PMIR: A Short Representationalist Analysis

What is the phenomenal model of the intentionality relation? (For further details, see Metzinger 2003a, chap. 6; for some ideas about its unconscious functional precursors in the monkey brain, see Metzinger and Gallese 2003.) It is a conscious mental model,[3] and its content is an ongoing, episodic subject–object relation. Here are four different examples, in terms of typical phenomenological descriptions of the class of phenomenal states at issue: "I am someone who is currently visually attending to the color of the book in my hands," "I am someone currently grasping the content of the sentence I am reading," "I am someone currently hearing the sound of the refrigerator behind me," "I am someone now deciding to get up and get some more juice." The central defining characteristic of phenomenal models of the intentionality relation is that they depict a certain *relationship* as currently holding between the system as a whole, as transparently represented to itself, and an object component. The content of consciousness never is a mere object, it always is a *relation*. Phenomenologically, a PMIR typically creates the experience of a self in the act of knowing, of a self in the act of perceiving—or of a *willing* self in the act of intending and acting. In the latter case, a goal representation is transiently integrated into an ongoing action simulation. This class of phenomenal mental models (the class of "volitional PMIRs") is particularly rich, because the number of possible object components is almost infinitely large. Please also note how subjectively experienced volition now becomes an important special case of the more general phenomenon of consciously possessing a first-person perspective: To experience oneself as a willing self, as a volitional *subject*, means to consciously take on a specific, individual perspective on the world. In particular, it means to generate a perspective on those actual and possible states of the world that

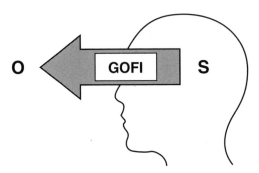

Figure 2.2
Good old-fashioned intentionality (GOFI): A subject component (S; the "mental act") is directed at an object component (O; the "intentional object"). As O does not necessarily exist, GOFI is a non-physical relation.

are perceived or represented as possessing *value*, as being goal states to which the system as a whole is currently *directed*. We may therefore also speak of the constitution of a "volitional first-person perspective."

The notion of a PMIR must be clearly separated from the *classical* concept of intentionality as it can be found in Brentano 1874. Good old-fashioned intentionality (GOFI) is a relation between a mental act and an object component, which is mentally contained in the mode of "intentional inexistence" (see fig. 2.2).

What I want to draw attention to is a point which has been frequently overlooked in the past: The classical intentionality relation can *itself* form the content of a conscious mental representation. In beings like us, there exists a phenomenal model *of* the intentionality relation (see fig. 2.3). We have, as it were, the capacity to "catch ourselves in the act": At times we have higher-order conscious representations of ourselves *as* representing. Maybe phenomenal content and representational content[4] could even be dissociated; maybe a brain in a vat could lack GOFI but still have a PMIR (e.g., by nonrepresentationally hallucinating it; see footnote 4). On the other hand, from an empirical point of view, it is highly plausible to assume that many nonhuman animals are intentional systems, but that their nervous systems do not allow them to ever become aware of this fact. In any case, it is important to note how, for *Homo sapiens* in ordinary waking states, GOFI can itself be a form of phenomenal content: My central point is that we do not only represent but that we also corepresent the *representational relation* itself—and that this fact is relevant for understanding the architecture of volition.

In this context, it may be interesting to note how the originally philosophical concept of a conscious model of the intentionality relationship (Metzinger 1993, 2000, 2003a) currently surfaces at a number of places in the cognitive neurosciences. Jean

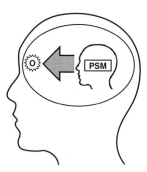

Figure 2.3
The *phenomenal model of the intentionality relation* (PMIR): In humans, the subject-component is a phenomenal self-model (PSM), an internal, conscious model of the system *as a whole*. Because the PSM is phenomenally transparent, it is not experienced *as* an internal model. Therefore no homunculus problem arises, and an infinite regress is avoided. In conscious volition, O, the goal component, is represented in a *phenomenally opaque* manner. This means that we are able to phenomenally experience it *as* a self-generated mental simulation, plus to consciously represent the additional fact that we, the organism as a whole, are currently *directed* to it.

Delacour, in an excellent review of current ideas about possible neural correlates of conscious experience, explicitly introduces the notion of an "intentionality-modelling structure" (Delacour 1997, p. 138). LaBerge (1997, pp. 150, 172) elucidates how important an understanding of the self-representational component present in attentional processing will have to be for a full-blown theory of conscious attention. Craik and colleagues (1999) point out how episodic memory, of course, is a process of reconstructing what was here termed a PMIR, because one necessary constituent of memory retrieval is not simply the simulation of a past event, but an association of this simulation with a self-representation (Craik et al. 1999, p. 26). Building an autobiographic memory is a process of self-related encoding, and conscious, episodic memory retrieval is a process necessarily involving the self-model, because reactivating a PMIR inevitably means reactivating a PSM. Most notable, of course, is Antonio Damasio's conception of a "juxtaposition" of self and object (see Damasio and Damasio 1996a, 1996b, pp. 172, 24) and the general framework of a fully embodied "self in the act of knowing" (Damasio 1994, 1999).

PMIRs typically consist of a transparent subject component and varying object components. Those can be transparent as well as opaque, transiently being integrated into an overarching, comprehensive representation of the system as standing in a specific relation to a certain part of the world. What is a "phenomenally transparent" representation, as opposed to an "opaque" one? First, please note that transparency in the sense here intended is a property of conscious representations *only*: Unconscious representations are neither transparent nor opaque. Second, a transparent representation is one that the subject cannot phenomenally experience *as* a representation. A phenomenally opaque representation is one where (like in conscious thought, visual illusions, or pseudo-hallucinations) we consciously experience the fact that all of this *is* a representation, that it is something in our minds, something self-constructed, something that could always turn out to be a *mis*representation. Transparent content (like the book in your hands) is experienced as given, in a naively realistic fashion; opaque content (like your conscious critical thoughts about my argument) is something that is "made" and may even be false or hallucinatory.[5]

The overall picture now emerging is that of the human self-model continuously integrating the mechanisms functionally subserving the attentional, cognitive, and volitional availability of information into a stable background, which is formed by the transparent representation of the bodily self (Metzinger 2000, 2003, chap. 6). If one then takes the step from a representationalist level of description to the actual phenomenological changes inherent in the emergence of a full-blown conscious first-person perspective, it is easy to see how for the first time it allows a system to consciously experience itself as not only being a part of the world but as being fully immersed in it through a dense network of causal, perceptual, cognitive, attentional, and agentive relations.

Of further particular interest is the fact that the brain models the relationship between subject and object as an *asymmetric* relationship. Whenever it catches itself in the act, whenever it corepresents the representational relation with the help of a PMIR, then it also generates the consciously experienced "arrow of intentionality," paradigmatically experienced in having the feeling of "projecting" visual attention outward, as it were, or in attentionally "tracking" objects in the environment. *Intendere arcum*, to bend the bow of the mind and point the arrow of knowledge toward parts of the world, is an intuitively plausible and popular philosophical metaphor, especially in combination with the notorious idea of "direct," magical intentionality.

We can now understand why such an idea will strike beings like us as intuitively plausible: It is *phenomenally* possible, because there is a directly corresponding structural element in our conscious model of reality. Many theoretical models of the representational relationship are implicitly inspired by the phenomenal experience of visual attention, of the directedness inherent in the phenomenal model of the intentionality relation. Frequently, the theoretical model we design about ourselves as cognitive agents is one of organisms, which, *ad libitum*, direct the beam of their "epistemic flashlight" at parts of the external world or their own internal lives, of beings, which generate the representational relation as subjects of experience. This can lead to the kind of fallacy which Daniel Dennett has described as "Cartesian materialism" (Dennett 1991, p. 333). As Dennett has pointed out, many of the different forms of Cartesian materialism, the assumption of a final inner stage, can also be generated in the context of representationalist theories of mind by mistakenly transporting what he called the "intentional stance" (Dennett 1987a) into the system (see Dennett 1991, p. 458). The model here proposed, of course, does not make this mistake; it is rather aimed at an empirically plausible extension of the idea of a "second-order intentional system" (Dennett 1987b), a system that applies the intentional stance to itself—but in a stronger sense—namely, in a phenomenally transparent manner.

A related hypothesis is that over the centuries philosophical theorizing about the intentionality relation has generally been influenced by that aspect of our phenomenal model of reality which we generate by our strongest sensory modality. If the process of mental representation in general is internally modelled in accordance with our dominant sensory modality (i.e., vision), it may automatically reproduce structural features of our transparent, visual model of reality—for example, a type of scene segmentation that leads to clear-cut, distal objects. Imagine how different things could have been if the sense of smell had been our strongest perceptual module! For beings like us, seeing is the paradigm for what it means to know the world, and visual attention, the conscious experience of being visually directed at an object, is the paradigm of having a first-person perspective. Not only may this fact influence the way in which the brain later models itself as an epistemic engine, but it also carries over into *theoretical* attempts to describe ourselves as epistemic agents, as knowledge-seeking cognitive subjects directed at cognitive objects. If the object component of a phenomenally modeled intentionality relation is of an opaque nature (i.e., experienced as *not* directly given)—as is the case in genuinely cognitive, that is, abstract contents or as in goal representation—then a conceptual interpretation of such mental contents as nonphysical, "intentionally inexistent" objects in the sense of Brentano (1874) becomes almost inevitable. However, we must now return to the relevant special case, the emergence of a *volitional* PMIR.

2.2.2 The Phenomenal Representation of Volition

Given the notion of a PMIR, we can now begin to develop a more fine-grained analysis for the phenomenological target properties of volitional subjectivity and agency. Volition and agency are two distinct types of phenomenal content: Conscious volition can be experienced passively, without executive control—just "willing without acting," as it were. The experience of bodily agency, on the other hand, additionally involves feedback, complex sensorimotor loops, and various echoes of these on the level of phenomenal representation. Of course, we also have to accommodate the obvious functional/phenomenological fact of "spontaneous action." Imagine snatching a child away from a fastly approaching car. We have a full-blown experience of agency, but no subjective experience of any preceding volitional process. The first conclusion is that both forms of phenomenal content can clearly be active in isolation. In my view, the most interesting and pressing theoretical issue now consists in developing an empirically plausible and conceptually convincing model describing the *transition* from volition to agency. But let us first begin with phenomenal volition, as we can now give a simple and straightforward analysis.

Conscious volition is generated by integrating abstract goal representations—which, as I propose for basic bodily actions, are constituted by allocentric motor simulations of successfully terminated behaviors—into the current model of the intentionality relation as object components. This process is subjectively experienced as decision or selection. Obviously, a longer period of deliberation, a period of trying out different mentally simulated goal states before settling into a stable state, may precede this integration process. Two features are special in the volitional PMIR: first, the phenomenal opacity of the object component (it is not experienced as *given*, but as a self-constructed internal representation) and, second, the fact that the subject component is a PSM, a transparent whole-organism model (not just a subsystemic "mental act," as in GOFI[6]).

Let us now differentiate a number of cases. If we contemplate a certain action goal, for example, when we ask ourselves whether we should get up and walk over to the refrigerator, we experience ourselves as cognitive subjects. This kind of occurrent, phenomenally represented subject–object relationship can be analyzed as one in which the object component is phenomenally opaque: Experientially, we know that we now take a certain attitude toward a self-generated *representation* of a goal. We are introspectively aware that all this is only a mental *simulation* of a certain possible end state of a particular bodily behavior. A completely different situation ensues if we integrate a long-term goal representation into the phenomenally transparent *self-model* (the PSM), thereby making it a part of ourselves by representationally identifying with it. Obviously, goal representations and goal hierarchies can also be important components of self-models that are based not on transient subject–object relations, but on enduring internal reorganizations of the self-model, of its emotional and motivational structure, and so forth, and which may possibly last for a lifetime. These two possibilities should not be confounded. I am here only concerned with the first reading.

Second, please note how a similar distinction can be made for the sense of agency: There is what I will from now on call "executive consciousness" or "online agency," and there are long-term components in the conscious self-model, developed in parallel with concrete actions, due to long-term learning and socialization. These are distinct target phenomena. Again, I am here only concerned with the first variant, with the question how phenomenal online agency develops over short periods of time.

I will now offer a speculative model of the transition from conscious volition to conscious agency. Please note that this model is disjunct from the theory of volition proposed above or the self-model theory in general (Metzinger 2003a). If it is incoherent or false, this does not influence the rest of the framework. The transition from volition to agency—the phenomenal experience of practical intentionality—emerges if two conditions are satisfied. First, the object component must be constituted by a particular self-simulation, by a neural simulation of a concrete behavioral pattern, for example, like getting up and walking toward the refrigerator, and its end state. Second, the relationship depicted on the level of conscious experience is one of the subject currently *selecting* this particular behavioral pattern and its end state, as simulated. If an action now takes place, we can usefully illustrate this by describing it as "representational identification": The moment following volition, the moment at which concrete bodily behavior actually ensues, is the moment in which the already active motor simulation is integrated into the currently active bodily self-model and, thereby, causally coupled to the rest of the motor system and the effectors. It is precisely the moment in which we *functionally* identify with a particular action, transforming it from a possible into an actual pattern of behavior and thereby functionally *as well* as phenomenologically enacting it. Simulation becomes execution. Embodiment leads to enaction—via the PSM, the phenomenal self-model. It is the causal mediator connecting a goal representation to the motor system.

Interestingly, the moment of online agency also seems to be the moment when the phenomenal model of the intentionality relation *collapses*. An extravagant, but possibly attractive, idea is that this may also be the moment at which "volitional binding" (the construction of a PMIR) is seamlessly followed by what Haggard and Clark (2003, p. 697) have termed "intentional binding" (a process that integrates representations of actions with those of their effects). So what precisely do I mean by "collapsing" the PMIR, the phenomenal model of the intentionality relation? We can now proceed to describe the experience of being a volitional subject and the experience of being an agent more precisely. Their temporal succession, the transition from volition to agency, can be described as a transition of representational content from an allocentric frame of reference into an egocentric one, from an abstract action representation in the premotor cortex to an increasingly specific one. If all stages are conscious, it can be analyzed as one from opacity to transparency, and as a process in which the object component of the PMIR is integrated into the PSM. By the time I have arrived at the refrigerator, what was before a simulated goal state has now become a part of my own (phenomenal) self; I *am* in the desired position. What is most interesting is the period *between* deliberation and goal achievement, because it includes the phenomenology of *becoming* an agent.

To see the difference between simple volition and full-blown agency more clearly, let us briefly return to the conscious experience of will. Phenomenal volition is a form of conscious mental content. It can be analyzed as representational content as follows (phenomenal content in brackets, embedded representational content in parentheses):

[I myself (= the currently active transparent model of the self) am currently present (= the *de-nunc*-character of the overall PMIR, as integrated into a virtual window of presence generated by short-term memory) in a world (= the transparent, global model of reality currently active), and I am just about to select (= the type of relation depicted in the PMIR) a possible way to walk around the chairs toward the refrigerator (= the object component, constituted by an allocentric goal representation of the successfully terminated action)].

Now let us again look at my speculative model of the transition process. The experience of full-blown online agency emerges briefly before the moment in which the internal "distance" created between phenomenal self-representation and phenomenal self-simulation in the previously mentioned structure collapses to zero: I *realize* a possible self-state, by enacting it, by integrating it into an egocentric frame of reference, into an ongoing executive control loop. Not all stages of this process have to be conscious or possess a vivid phenomenology (for instance, explicit motor patterns will only rarely reach the level of subjective awareness). However, something else is conscious. As I experience myself walking around the chairs and toward the refrigerator, proprioceptive and kinesthetic feedback (which is itself unconscious but indirectly determines the content of my PSM) allows me to feel the degrees to which I have already identified with the sequence of bodily movements I have selected in the previous moment. In successful bodily action, there is a convergence, an unfolding congruence or goodness of fit between two representational states (goal/object component and conscious self-model). The temporal development of this congruence is what we can consciously feel as *becoming* an agent. In executive consciousness, experiential agency is not an all-or-nothing phenomenon—with every individual action it flowers and then it disappears. The idea is that we can do justice to this more subtle phenomenological constraint by saying that there is a high-dimensional distance between the activation vector describing the currently active goal representation and the path of the PSM, the trajectory describing ongoing changes in the conscious self-model of the organism. As this distance decreases, the sense of agency increases. I metaphorically refer to this temporal dynamics when I speak of "appropriating a goal" or "collapsing the PMIR."

Please recall how phenomenally transparent representations are precisely those representations the existence of whose content we cannot doubt. They are those the content of which we experience as real, whereas opaque representations are those which we experience as thoughts, as imagination, or as pseudo-hallucinations. "Realizing" a simulated self-state means developing a functional strategy of making it the content of a transparent self-model, of a self that really exists—on the level of phenomenal experience. Phenomenologically, volition is an attempt to realize a new phenomenal self.

Ongoing agency, the conscious experience of sustained executive control, can therefore be representationally analyzed according to the following pattern:

[I myself (= the content of the transparent self-model) am currently present (= the *de-nunc*-character of the PMIR as integrated into a virtual window of presence generated by short-term memory) in a world (= the transparent, global model of reality), and I am currently experiencing myself as carrying out (= continuously integrating into the transparent self-model) an action which I have previously imagined and selected (= an opaque self-simulation forming the object component, which is now step-by-step assimilated into the subject component)].

Under this analysis, volition and action become two stages of a unitary process by which we phenomenally *appropriate* a goal state. Of course, there can be all sorts of additional functional and representational complications—for example, if multiple goals compete or if the proprioceptive and kinesthetic feedback integrated into the internal model of the body does not match with the forward model. Also, as already noted above, it is not necessary that the object component be formed by an explicit, consciously constructed motor pattern (this will only rarely be the case). Both types of phenomenologies exist. But it is interesting to see how agency conceived of as online, executive consciousness can be analyzed as an ongoing representational dynamics collapsing a model of the practical intentionality relationship into a new transparent self-model. In every single action, phenomenal agency emerges at some point, peaks, and then disappears. As the whole structure is embedded into a virtual window of presence, the transparent, untranscendable experiential state for the system as a whole is one of *now* being a full-blown volitional subject, currently being present in a world, and successfully acting in it.

Finally, we have to do justice to the fact that the PMIR has a phenomenally experienced *direction*: PMIRs are like arrows pointing from self-model to object component. As soon as one has understood the arrowlike nature of the PMIR, two special cases can be much more clearly described. First, the arrow can point not only outward, but also inward, namely, in cases in which the object component is formed by the PSM itself (as in introspective attention or in thinking about oneself). Here, the second-order PMIR internally models a system–system relationship instead of a system–object relationship. Furthermore, in consciously experienced social cognition, the object component can now be formed either by a phenomenal model of another agent or an arrow in the other agent's head (as in observing another human being observing another human being). Such ideas are appealing, because they show how the relevant representational domain is an open domain: In principle, many layers of complexity and intersubjective metacognition (i.e., cognition about cognitive processing in *another* individual) can be added through a process of social/psychological evolution. As the elementary representational building block, the PMIR, gets richer and more abstract, an ascending and cognitively continuous development from the simple portrayal of body-centered subject–object relations to full-blown self–other modeling becomes conceivable. More about this in section 2.4.

2.3 The Case of Akinetic Mutism: Is the Volitional PMIR a Functionally Distinct Representational Module?

Bilateral anterior damage to the cingulate and bilateral medial parietal damage lead to a situation which can be described by, first, the absence of the PMIR, while, secondly, a coherent conscious model of the world centered by a phenomenal self is still retained. To give a prominent example, Antonio Damasio has introduced a widely known conceptual distinction, which is simple and straightforward: Patients suffering from such damage exhibit wakefulness, but not what he calls "core consciousness." Core consciousness is the minimal form of phenomenal experience constituted by what he calls a "second-order mapping" and what, for the purposes of this chapter, simply *is* the basic phenomenal model of the intentionality relation in terms of the representationalist analysis here proposed. Let us look at how Damasio describes such cases:

Just as is the case with patients with bilateral cingulate damage, patients with bilateral medial parietal damage are awake in the usual sense of the term: their eyes can be open, and their muscles have proper tone; they can sit or even walk with assistance; but they will not look at you or at any object *with any semblance of intention* [emphasis mine]; and their eyes may stare vacantly or orient toward objects with no discernable motive. These patients cannot help themselves. They volunteer nothing about their situation and they fail to respond to virtually all the examiner's requests. Attempts to engage them in conversation are rarely successful, the results being erratic at best. We can coax them into looking briefly at an object, but the request will not engender anything else in terms of productive reaction. These patients react no differently to friends and family than they do to physicians and nurses. The notion of Zombie-like behavior could perfectly well have come from the description of these patients, although it did not. (Damasio 1999, p. 263)

This well-documented condition is akinetic mutism (AM), the absence of volition following ventromedial damage or the bilateral anterior lesions of the cingulate just mentioned. A number of diverging etiologies exist. AM is a silent immobility, with the only behavioral manifestation being gaze following related to the examiner's movements and, in some cases, monosyllabic speech (for three further cases studies, plus a brief review of the literature, see Ure et al. 1998).

What we learn from disorders of volition such as AM is how phenomenal volition can deviate in two directions. There is hypervolitionalism, as, for instance, in obsessive–compulsive disorder. There are also hypovolitional states, in which the ability to generate the experience of conscious will is greatly diminished. AM belongs to the second class, as it is a state of wakefulness, combined with the absence of speech, emotional expression, or any movement. Obviously, for such patients there is an impoverished but integrated functional self-model, because they are able to briefly track objects, to pull a bed cover, or, if forced, to say their own name (see Damasio 1999, p. 101). Obviously, these patients still have an integrated self-representation, making self-related information globally available for the control of action or guided attention. If pinched (hard enough), they would experience the pain as their *own* pain. They can spatially locate its cause in their body image, and they possess autobiographical memory for the relevant periods of time. However, there is no *volitional subject* that could exert control. As these examples show, the use of globally available system-related information can be forced or triggered from the outside, to a limited degree, but what is missing is an *autonomous* phenomenal representation of a self in relation to possible action goals. "Autonomy" is here used in a weak sense, not referring to a homunculus but to the agent-free, subpersonal self-organization of more complex and flexible control structures. The integration of the subject component with what can be described as volitional object components—abstract, allocentric goal representations or mental simulations of possible, successfully terminated, and concrete actions in an egocentric frame of reference—is missing. This demonstrates how you can have phenomenal ownership (e.g., the ability to locate a pain experience in your *own* body and to later autobiographically remember it as an episode in your *own* life) without being able to consciously represent a *representational relation* between you and this pain, or a goal state, or another person. The arrow is missing. The model of reality of such patients is still functionally centered; they are awake and embodied selves; but what they do not possess precisely is a phenomenal first-person perspective. They certainly have phenomenal experience and low-level selfhood, but—this is my proposal—no conscious representation of the "arrow of intentionality" (see fig. 2.4).

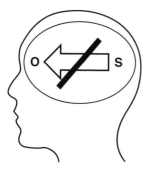

Figure 2.4
Akinetic mutism (AM): Disruption of the phenomenal model of the intentionality relation? Is AM a condition functionally characterized by the brain's being unable to support the organism as a whole in representing Good old-fashioned intentionality to itself on the level of global availability? O, object component; S, subject component.

Patients suffering from AM are phenomenally embodied beings, but their conscious reality is not an *enacted, lived* reality in the full sense of the term. They are not *directed*. What the outside observer experiences as a vacuous stare or emotional neutrality is the complete absence of any willed action or communicative intention, is the absence of a globally available model of subject–object relations (and of the goal to establish subject–*subject* relations as well, as can be seen from the lack of desire to talk). Functionally and phenomenologically centered but aperspectival models of reality, therefore, are not only conceptual possibilities but, in some tragic cases, actually occurring representational configurations. They very clearly demonstrate what it means to say that the phenomenal first-person perspective is the decisive factor in turning a mere biological organism into an agent, into a willing subject. Consciousness and self-awareness are not enough. You can have a phenomenal self without having a consciously experienced first-person perspective.

To sum up, the clinical picture of AM includes wakefulness, absence of volition, absence of bodily motion, absence of emotional expression, absence of speech, absence of future planning, and gaze following. A phenomenological analysis finds embodiment, but no *volitional* subject, no experience of *agency*, no emotional internal context, no *cognitive* subject, no high-level attention plus the fact that the subject is not *phenomenally situated*. On the representational level of description, I have analyzed this situation as the absence of any phenomenal modeling of subject–object relations, the absence of any phenomenal modeling of subject–subject relations, as a selective loss of the emotional layer in the PSM (see Metzinger 2003a), and, in particular, as a selective loss of the PMIR.

I am aware that the phenomenology of AM is not as clear-cut and simple as the single case study presented above may make it look. In cases of much more extended damage like persistent vegetative state (PVS), we find a clinical picture which may look similar at first sight, but here there is little evidence for conscious experience at all, because large-scale integrational functions seem to be inoperative, and distant cerebral areas are functionally disconnected, making the emergence of a global, unified model of reality highly unlikely (see, e.g., Laureys et al. 2000, pp. 1590, 1598; for a discussion of the globality constraint for phenomenal representation, cf. Metzinger 2003a, section 3.2.3). It is interesting to note how in PVS, as well as in anencephalic infants and possibly in many nonhuman animals, there may exist low-level tracking mechanisms triggered by subcortical and brainstem structures (like turning the head toward a sound or a moving object), which we then often intuitively misinterpret *as* the existence of a PMIR, *as* the intitiative of a conscious, actively directed, attending self (probably because, in beings like us, they falsely trigger unconscious intentionality detectors and social cognition modules). Exceptional cases do exist in AM as well—for instance, of patients suddenly uttering whole sentences once or twice (von Cramon, personal communication). My point, however, is that this class of disorders makes it highly plausible to assume that there is a single functional factor—namely, the dynamical integration mechanism transiently binding the phenomenal self and varying volitional object components into a unified structure—that can be selectively lost and dissociated from all other functional factors underlying the emergence of phenomenal experience in standard situations. You can be conscious without being directed. You can have a phenomenal self without having a phenomenal perspective. If there is a distinct functional module, then there should be a distinct entity corresponding to it in our theory of volition. This theoretical entity is the PMIR. On the phenomenological/representationalist level of analysis, this entity appears as a specific form of mental content, that is, "the willing self" or "the organism as a whole as currently directed toward a certain goal state." I will now offer a brief functional analysis of the PMIR and then conclude by making some empirical predictions.

2.4 What Is the Function of a PMIR?

Phenomenal mental models are instruments used to make a certain subset of information currently active in the system globally available for the control of action, for focal attention and for cognitive processing. A phenomenal model of transient subject–object relations makes an enormous amount of new information available for the system: all information related to the fact that it is currently perturbed by perceptual objects, to the fact that certain cognitive states are currently occurring in itself, or to the fact that certain abstract goal representations are currently active. This might be the information that there are a number of concrete self-simulations connecting the current system state with the state the system would have if this goal state was to be realized, in turn allowing for selective behavior, or the information that it is a system capable of manipulating its own sensory input, for example, by turning its head and directing its gaze to a specific visual object. A PMIR makes a specific type of information *globally available*. Globally available information enables *selective* and *flexible* control of behavior. From an evolutionary point of view, one can offer a teleofunctionalist analysis of the PMIR as high-level *virtual organ*. The function of this organ is to realize new layers of complexity, to enhance selectivity and flexibility in behavioral autoregulation. If it is not needed, the organism can turn it off, and the conscious first-person perspective disappears.

A PMIR also contributes to the overall intelligence of the system. It allows for a dynamical representation of transient subject–object relations and thereby makes a new class of facts globally available. If the capacity to iterate the construction of a PMIR is given (i.e., to point a second-order arrow at a first-order arrow, to turn one PMIR into the object component of another one), two entirely new forms of intelligence emerge, because the system can now flexibly and selectively react to two entirely new classes of facts:

- *Introspective intelligence* (see fig. 2.5a)

Agency   The system can become aware of the fact that it *has* a will and that it *is* an agent (= selectively directed at goal states). Please note that, in philosophy, the capacity for higher order volition is a traditional criterion for ascribing personhood (Frankfurt 1971).

Attentional subjectivity   The system can become aware of the fact that it *has* selective, high-level attention. This enables more complex forms of learning and epistemic autoregulation.

Reflexive self-consciousness   If it has the capacity for conceptual thought, the system can mentally represent the fact *that* it has a first-person perspective. This makes the transition from phenomenal to cognitive subjectivity possible.

- *Social intelligence* (see fig. 2.5b)

Other-agent modeling   The system can become aware of the fact that other systems have a first-person perspective too. This permits action coordination and cooperative behavior.

Mind-reading   The system can internally simulate external PMIRs. It can develop an empathic understanding of other agents, and consciously experience this fact.

High-level intersubjectivity   Systems with *cognitive* PMIRs can mutually acknowledge each other as persons. This enables the emergence of *normative* intersubjectivity and complex societies.

First, please note that the PMIR theory as such takes no position on whether—genetically as well as conceptually—social intelligence came first and introspective intelligence is only a secondary specialization within social cognition. It may well be that babies first understand *other* people and even physical events according to the PMIR coding principle, and only much later develop inward-directed, introspective forms of conscious intentionality. I regard this as an empirical issue, not to be decided by philosophers. Rather, my aim is to shed some light on potentially universal aspects of the representational architecture underlying the phenomenology of will. The possession of a PMIR as such does not imply full-blown capacities for mentalizing or the possession of a theory of mind. In principle, we could imagine a class of systems unable to make the intentional states of conspecifics or other agents in their environment the object component of their own PMIR. To give an example, such systems could already possess the capacity to consciously represent the fact that they currently direct their attention toward certain perceptual objects or to subjectively experience their own capacity to direct volitional processes toward internally represented goal states. In our new terminology, we might then say that such beings possess an "attentional first-person perspective" or a "volitional first-person perspective." They have the capacity to experience themselves as attending and willing selves. What this would *not* yet imply is the ability to verbally report this very fact or to even mentally form a concept of themselves *as* being an organism of this type. Furthermore, such beings

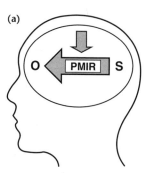

Figure 2.5a

Introspective intelligence: A second-order phenomenal model of the intentionality relation (PMIR) is directed at a first-order PMIR as its object component. The underlying principle of relational coding is iterated. In the special case of conscious second-order volition, the first-order PMIR is an ongoing representation of the system as currently directed at a goal component. The volitional second-order PMIR, within certain temporal boundary conditions, can allow you to *terminate* the initiation of an action, or to consciously represent the fact that you *want to want* something.

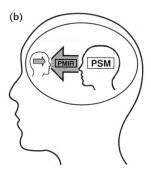

Figure 2.5b

Social intelligence: A second-order phenomenal model of the intentionality relation (PMIR) is directed at a first-order PMIR, which has been *integrated into the model of another agent*. The underlying principle of relational coding is now iterated in the social domain. In the special case of consciously experienced sociovolitional cognition, the second-order PMIR is an ongoing representation of the system as currently directed at *the intention of another agent*. The brain integrates a volitional first-order PMIR into a model of another agent, either as currently perceived in the environment or as mentally simulated. Again, the functional significance of this architecture is that a *new class of facts* can be consciously integrated, facts having to do with the actual or potential existence of other goal-directed beings, other intentional agents in the environment.

might not yet have the capacity to emulate the existence of a PMIR in another agent and to make it the object component of a second-order PMIR pointing at it (as described above). Their range of possible object components would only include goal states in themselves, but not in others. Such beings could then never consciously experience the fact that there are other attending and willing phenomenal selves in their environment at all. Maybe it could be fruitful to analyze certain types of autism as related to deficits in iterating the PMIR in the social domain (e.g., Frith and Happé 1999). To use a PMIR as a differential representational mechanism for modeling goal-directed activity and belief–desire attribution in others is a second step, which demands taking it offline, as it were, of applying the same coding strategy in another domain. It is important to note that the theory here proposed must satisfy the "acquisition constraint," that is, it must allow us to understand how the respective capacity has gradually evolved in nonhuman agents and how it develops in human infants. Very obviously, some of the basic features of phenomenal volition must already exist in the animal kingdom. Elsewhere, we have therefore discussed potential unconscious precursors of the PMIR in the monkey brain (Metzinger and Gallese 2003). Please note how social intelligence and goal detection in other agents could well work without being conscious: Low-level resonance mechanisms in the motor system might (e.g.) achieve unconscious mind reading by automatically simulating perceived agent–object relations in an allocentric format. This might functionally guide the animal's behavior by extracting an abstract property, namely, the goal state of the visually observed behavior of another agent. Plausibly, there are many situations in which human beings do not exhibit the full phenomenological spectrum described above, because we "drop back" into functional stages shared with our biological ancestors and other animals. Just think of a mass panic in a football stadium or combat situations. What conscious experience adds, however, are all the new functional properties that come along with metarepresentation in a single, unified model or reality, with integration into the extended "Now" of working memory, and with the global availability of information to many different processing systems at the same time: flexibility in action coordination, selectivity in response generation, and enhanced learning.

In order to develop a differentiated research program for the phylo- and ontogenetic history of what today we call "conscious volition," the transient activation of a PMIR, we should ask the following questions: What *object components* are available to the relevant target system (perceptual objects, goal states, abstract conceptual content, PMIRs in other agents)? How rich is the *subject component* (precisely which cognitive, emotional, volitional, and interoceptive layers does the organism's self-model contain and which of them participate in generating the PMIR)? What types of subject–object *relations* can the organism grasp by internally representing them (selection of motor patterns, attention, volition, concept formation, subject–subject relations, subject–group relations, group–group relations, etc.)? If these basic components have been determined, we may proceed to ask which of these forms of representational content are at all elevated to the level of conscious experience, and at what stage of their overall processing history does this happen? It is interesting to note how exactly the same questions could also guide cognitive neuropsychiatry toward a more systematic and fine-grained diagnosis of disorders of volition—or of neurological/ psychiatric disorders generally.

As is obvious from this brief sketch, possessing a PMIR brings about new functional properties, and it is therefore conceivable how the human PMIR plus the capacity to mentally iterate the underlying principle may actually have been the decisive neuro- computational tool to enable the transition from biological to cultural evolution. Therefore, the PMIR is an interesting interdisciplinary research target. However, return- ing to disorders of volition, it is now obvious how a deeper understanding of the *voli- tional* PMIR will be central for making progress in this domain.

2.5 Empirical Predictions

Let me make two kinds of empirical predictions, one about the many different forms of PMIRs generally and one about the *volitional* PMIR specifically. Being a philosopher, I will not engage in any amateurish speculation about anatomical substrates. However, let me at least state my intuition: The crucial form of conscious content, which I have described as the phenomenal model of the intentionality relation in the preceding sections of this chapter, will only be weakly localized. I conceive of it as a high-level binding operation, a transient dynamic process, which must be highly distributed— simply because it can be directed at such a great variety of object components. If, as an empirical researcher, I had to "nail down" the area of highest invariance, then I would certainly start with the self-model: There should be aspects of the *subject com- ponent* achieving its continuity, coherence, and functional stability over time, and these aspects should be present in all or most PMIRs.

If my speculative argument is sound, then it should in principle be possible to *tran- siently block or neutralize* the dynamical integration mechanism I have introduced as a theoretical entity above. Possibly this could be done by transcranial magnetic stimu- lation (TMS) or some future neurotechnological descendant of this and related tech- niques. What would be needed is a risk-free and noninvasive form of influencing brain dynamics in a highly selective manner. "Selective" means that such a technique would not search for the anatomical location of the PMIR's neural substrate but would target the distinct causal role played by it in the overall dynamics of the brain. The predic- tion would be that the subjects' phenomenology changes in a way that—while temporarily dissolving the consciously experienced first-person perspective—leaves basic layers of the phenomenal self, the capacity for autobiographical memory, and perceptual world model coherent and fully intact. "Dissolving" means that various components of the first-person perspective would still exist, but they would no longer be unified. This effect would necessarily have to be accompanied by specific functional deficits.

Let us proceed in two steps. Before moving on to conscious volition, let us take the attentional and the cognitive PMIR as general examples of what a consciously experienced first-person perspective is. My assumption here is that they can be functionally dissociated: If the dynamical binding of subject and object component in attentional processing could be selectively inhibited, the prima facie phenomenological prediction would be that subjects retain their stable sense of selfhood, an integrated experience of the world as a whole, plus the ability to later report the content of their experience, given that autobiographical memory remains intact. Let us call this imagined paradigm Experiment 1a: It consists in selectively inhibiting the integration process underlying the phenomenal representation of subject–object relationships in attention, and *only* this process. The idea is that the attending self can be dissociated from the thinking self. What subjects should lack is, first, any retrospective experience of having attended to either the external world or aspects of their inner mental life. Second, and in particular, they should now lack the phenomenal property of *attentional agency*:[7] Not only should they be incapable of experiencing themselves as *initiating* actual shifts in attention (including any active form of non-conceptual introspection) but they should also be unable to become aware of the fact that they *have* selective, high-level attention, resp. that they have *had* this capacity in the past. The interesting question now is whether such subjects could, on a purely cognitive level, exclusively as thinking subjects, and under the influence of an intervention with TMS, still represent the autobiographical fact that in the past they actually *were* attentional agents. If not, two aspects of my prediction are falsified: First, autobiographical memory would not remain intact and could therefore not count as functionally dissociable from the attentional PMIR. Maybe the attentional PMIR is a necessary coding principle for episodic memory, because memory retrieval necessarily involves the reconstruction of a PMIR. Second, it is perhaps plausible to assume that in such a situation the phenomenal self as a whole would actually be in great danger of disintegration: Attentional agency could turn out to be an essential ingredient for the stability of self-consciousness, a necessary condition for the phenomenal property of *being someone*. Does functionally blocking the attentional PMIR lead to depersonalization? It goes without saying that, as even transitory episodes of depersonalization could be traumatizing to some subjects, issues of this kind would also be central for ethics committees having to assess the risk-free character of any such experiment.

What are the *functional* predictions for selectively blocking the attentional PMIR? As noted above, it enables more complex forms of learning and epistemic autoregulation. All these forms of learning should be absent, including all forms of perception involving focused attention. It would be easy to test this using standard neuropsy-chological methods. Second, all tasks depending on what was termed "introspective intelligence" above should create major difficulties for subjects in experiments of this type. Examples would be all tasks that involve becoming introspectively aware of changes in one's own emotional or bodily states, but also those critically involving the capacity to become aware of the simple fact that high-level cognitive faculties like thought and memory are at all currently *available*. Maybe it would be helpful to term this second set of functional predictions "introspective neglect." Third, all forms of social cognition which are nonconceptual and nonlinguistic, that rely on consciously attending to another human being's motor behavior, its *own* directed attention, and so forth should be absent. A more specific prediction would be that even many so-called "purely" conceptual or linguistic forms of social interaction would immediately disappear as well. This could be the case because they are actually anchored in the attentional PMIR, or at least in the capacity to introspectively *discover* the results of unconscious and automatic processes of social cognition that have been going on in the background all the time (Metzinger and Gallese 2003).

Let us turn to Experiment 1b now. What about the cognitive PMIR? The consciously experienced cognitive first-person perspective allows us to become *thinking subjects* (Metzinger 2003b). It permits us subjectively to experience ourselves as beings con-structing, searching for, and recombining abstract conceptual contents by operating on mental representations of this content. The phenomenological prediction for selec-tively blocking the cognitive PMIR—that is, the capacity to form an integrated mental representation of oneself as currently being directed at and selectively operating on *conceptual* forms of mental content—is that we would simply not be able to experi-ence ourselves as thinkers of thoughts any more. Thoughts would perhaps keep on appearing, but the subject in our hypothetical experiment would later report a phe-nomenology closely resembling an extended daydream: Conscious thoughts would be there, like clouds drifting in the sky, appearing and disappearing from time to time, but with no one actively *thinking* them. Such thought contents could well be *owned*, but they would not be *intended*. The missing phenomenal property would be a paral-lel to attentional agency (see note 7), which I would like to call "cognitive agency." In particular, an experience very dear to philosophers should be entirely absent, namely, the subjective experience of *grasping a concept*.[8]

Again, this leads to a series of functional and therefore empirically testable predic-tions for selectively blocking the generation of a cognitive PMIR: All forms of high-level intelligence based on stabilizing and manipulating abstract forms of conceptual mental content in working memory should be entirely absent. Reflexive self-consciousness should be entirely absent as well—plus another capacity that, again, has been very dear specifically to philosophers in past and present (Baker 1998; Metzinger 2003b). It is the capacity not only to *have* a first-person perspective but to be able to mentally ascribe this very fact to oneself, to form and grasp a concept of oneself *as* a thinking subject, *as* a possessor of a cognitive first-person perspective. Third, the empirically testable effects in all tasks involving high-level social intelligence should be obvious: All abstract and future-directed forms of other-agent modeling, of conceptually—and not only empathically—grasping the fact that other systems have a first-person perspective too, and consequently all forms of action coordination and cooperative behavior relying on this capacity should simply disappear. High-level mind reading in terms of internally simulating external PMIRs on a conceptual level should be absent, and consequently all complex forms of intersubjectivity implying mutually acknowledging each other as persons and the abstract understanding of a normative context should be absent. After having looked at some phenomenological and functional predictions for selectively disrupting the binding process underlying the formation of an attentional/cognitive model of the intentionality relation, let us now finally return to volition.

Readers may already have started to think that the empirical predictions I am making basically have the consequence of creating an artificial model of AM. But I think the PMIR theory should allow us to describe not only different aspects of AM more precisely but different forms of volitional disorders generally—and also how these may underlie deficits traditionally not conceived of as *volitional* in nature. Let us ask what would happen if we could selectively block the generation of a volitional PMIR, and *only* the volitional PMIR, in the brain of a subject? This would be Experiment 2 then, transiently dissolving the consciously experienced volitional·first-person perspective. Let us this time begin with the functional deficits to be expected. They are rather clear-cut and have already been described in section 2.3. There should be all signs of wakefulness, but no self-initiated overt behavior. Given that gaze following rests on an involuntary, subpersonal mechanism, it should be preserved.

Phenomenologically, the prima facie prediction is that this subject would later report having been a thinker of thoughts (as opposed to typical AM patients). The subject should also describe his or her own phenomenology as having had the capacity to initiate shifts in attention (as opposed to typical AM patients), and as having possessed introspective capacities—but as not having had any desires or long-term goals. The subject would report wakefulness, but a complete absence of volition in terms of being consciously directed at any goals at all, and *therefore* no interest in bodily motion, *therefore* an absence of specific emotions,[9] *therefore* a lack of interest in verbal communication and future planning.

The difficult question here is if the lack of interest in the future, of interest in social interaction, and of intrinsic motivation generally would not at the same time have prevented such a subject from even exerting his or her powers of introspection that, ex hypothesi, have been there all along. To be sure, I do not want to claim that *every* subject perturbed in his or her volition would necessarily become anosognostic, lacking insight into his or her being so perturbed. I am just pointing to the possibility that a representational deficit might systematically lead to an executive deficit, but this time a deficit in generating certain *inner* actions: Would such subjects start directing their inward attention to the fact that they suddenly do not have any desires and goals any more, to the fact that they have become emotionally flat? Would they start to *think* about the nature of their current state? Could introspective discoveries of this type happen *by chance*, in a nonintended way? Or is what I have provisionally termed "introspective neglect" above a stable, self-sustaining condition? If so, autobiographical memory might remain rather empty for the period in question, and it could be hard to verify the phenomenological prediction.

Moreover, the deeper and more interesting problem seems to lie in developing an empirical research strategy allowing one to dissociate those general deficits in attentional and cognitive processing predicted in the first five paragraphs of this section from a genuine volitional core disorder. Maybe the volitional PMIR turns out to be fundamental in that many of those functional deficits really stem from a disruption of the volitional PMIR, while leaving the actual mechanisms of high-level attention and cognition fully intact. One way of categorically dividing the empirical material would be by saying that there could be two classes of attentional and cognitive deficits: those resting on specific functional deficits preventing the stabilization of attentional and cognitive PMIRs in the human brain and those originating in a selective loss of the volitional PMIR only. For instance, many cases of introspective neglect might actually be disorders of volition, and not of attention or cognition at all. If my terminological proposals are not completely misguided, if they point at least vaguely in the right direction, then it would be a rewarding aim for empirical research to determine how distinct and exclusive these two classes of phenomena actually are.

Acknowledgments

This chapter has profited from four unusually substantial and particularly constructive reviews. I want to thank two anonymous referees, Timothy Bayne, and Wolfgang Prinz for the care and concentrated work they have put into their criticism. It goes without saying that they are in no way responsible for remaining problems with the current version of my proposal.

Notes

1. The problem of phenomenological indeterminacy has additional epistemological aspects, which I have deliberately not mentioned in the main text (in order not complicate matters too much right at the beginning). These aspects emerge if we look at the way in which we later *linguistically represent* our first-order target phenomenon itself. On the first, folk-phenomenological,

level of linguistic representation we find what philosophers would call the "theory ladenness" of introspection: In transforming introspective experience into verbal reports, subjects inevitably reproduce the implicit theoretical/conceptual background assumptions they have had before. In particular, if one then reacts to this difficulty by deciding to generate truly systematic and uni-vocal descriptions by first *training* introspectors for scientific experiments, the training process itself introduces new labels and systematic relations between these labels—basically it offers a whole new ontology. What we would then—on the second level, which is already driven by explicitly articulated scientific theories—lose is the original "folk phenomenology" of will, which formed our initial research target. A third important aspect is that there may even be dissocia-ble and more cognitive aspects of the phenomenology of will, exhibiting a strong dependence on a specific *metatheoretical* background. That is, phenomenological descriptions may even be contaminated by *philosophical* background assumptions. The prime example here is "the ability to do otherwise": Is the possibility of alternative courses of action *all other conditions remaining the same* really a necessary component of the phenomenal experience of will (as philosophical libertarians would frequently claim), or is this simply a misdescription of the actual content? For a clear recent exposition of these problems, see, for instance, Nahmias, Morris, Nadelhoffer, and Turner 2004.

2. Please recall how willed actions were defined as a specific subset of goal-directed bodily move-ments: a series of movements that are functionally integrated with an explicit and currently active representation of a goal state. A behavior that is preceded by an unconscious selection process operating on just these types of explicit representations and then appropriately caused by it could still count as an action but lack considerable parts of the phenomenology of will. It would be individuated by its satisfaction conditions and, therefore, have intentionality. However, from a first-person perspective, much of its causal history would remain in the dark, and it would therefore lack phenomenality. I believe that a scientific, third-person analysis should attempt to describe a fine-grained *continuum* leading from behavior to full-blown action (e.g., in terms of explicitness of goal representation, of the number of layers in the self-model causally active, and of degrees of the introspective availability/flexibility of the functional mechanisms involved). At the same time, I predict that many of us would initially find such a fine-grained conceptual con-tinuum counterintuitive: Our traditional folk-phenomenological image of ourselves demands a maximum of conscious access.

3. The concept of a "phenomenal mental model" (Metzinger 2003a, chap. 3) is loosely connected to a theory of mental representation developed by Philip Johnson-Laird (see, e.g., 1983, 2001), which it extends to the phenomenological domain by imposing an additional set of constraints. Models are representational entities, but the fact that they are models *of* something does not emerge on the phenomenal level. Unconscious self-models and nonphenomenal precursors of a representation of the intentionality relation could exist. However, *phenomenal* models possess a number of special functional/neurocomputational features which are relevant for understanding the volitional process (and its disorders) as a whole.

4. Let me add a short terminological clarification for my nonphilosophical readers here. The rep-resentational (or intentional) content of a representation is what it is directed at. An entirely unconscious structure or process in the brain could have this first sort of content—for instance,

by being directed at a certain goal state. The goal state would be its representational content. The second sort of content, often called "phenomenal content" by philosophers, is determined by how it *feels* to you, from a subjective, first-person perspective, to have this specific representational/intentional content. Only conscious representations have phenomenal content. The author of the present chapter (like many other philosophers today) holds a representationalist theory of consciousness: He believes that there exist intentional properties and phenomenal properties in our world, and that phenomenal properties are simply a special sort of intentional properties. For instance, phenomenal content could be a special form of intentional content, which only appears if it is additionally available for attentional processing, bound into a unified, global model of reality, integrated into working memory, etc. However, another philosopher could say that there is no such thing as mental representation at all, but that consciousness nevertheless exists: He would deny the existence of intentional properties and offer us a completely different, nonrepresentational explanation for the existence of phenomenal properties. Such a philosopher might say that all of us (not only brains in a vat) are never representing anything, are never in this way intentionally directed at any objects of knowledge or desire at all, but that we only *hallucinate* intentionality, that we only consciously experience ourselves *as if* there actually was something like a representational relationship between ourselves and the world—or between us and our own goal states.

5. One can further illustrate the crucial difference by drawing on a conceptual distinction, which is well-known in psychiatry: "Complex hallucinations" are those in which the patient does not have any introspective access to the fact that he or she is currently hallucinating; "pseudo-hallucinations" are those for which the patient has access to the fact. In the first case, we have phenomenal transparency; in the second case we find a paradigmatic case of opacity. Today, a standard philosophical strategy to conceptually analyze phenomenal transparency in general would be to say that, in all relevant cases, we only have introspective access to the *content* of a conscious mental representation, but not to the *carrier* (or construction process, as I would add). Therefore we necessarily experience ourselves as being in direct contact with this content. A further phenomenological constraint for any modern theory of mind is that there exists a *continuum* between transparency and opacity. For more on this continuum and the notions of phenomenal transparency and opacity, see Metzinger 2003a, 2003b.

6. I would rather like to look at the phenomenal self-model as a single complex act. Let me add another terminological clarification, which may be helpful for those readers who are not philosophers. It is important not to read "act" as some sort of mental action, with some sort of hidden agent behind it ("the transcendental thinker of the self-thought"), but simply as referring to an occurrent, active mental representation. Following a long line in the history of ideas starting with Aristotle, an "act" is something that realizes an implicit "potentiality," an abstract possibility. For instance, it could be something that transiently actualizes a certain form of self-representational content, makes it explicit on the level of conscious experience, and endows it with new functional properties. Maybe a (very) modern way to describe the difference would be to say that a mental act can be conceptually analyzed as a point or trajectory in an *activation vector space* describing the underlying neural network, whereas the corresponding psychological potential would be a point in *weight space*.

7. So far, I have defined the concept of "agency" only for bodily behavior. It is important to note that a parallel form of phenomenal content exists for high-level attention. It is the subjective experience of deliberately directing one's attention at a certain (inner or outer) object component and of sustaining it for a certain period of time. The frequently overlooked phenomenological fact, which must be accommodated by any modern theory of mind, is that attention is often experienced as an inner form of action, as something that includes a sense of effort, explicit goal representation, and a selection process. In my view, finding a functional-level explanation for the sense of effort could constitute the most rewarding research target. Losing this sense of effort or one's capacity for attentional agency generally means losing a *major*—and likely central—component for what it means to be a conscious self.

8. "Grasping a concept" here refers to the phenomenal experience going along with the transient activation of a cognitive PMIR, i.e., the emergence of an integrated representation of the subject as now being (typically, for the first time) related to some abstract, conceptual, and phenomenally opaque content. If the underlying integration process is disturbed, the subject could neither consciously experience itself as a "thinker of a thought" (in cognitive agency) any more nor as an "interpreter of another subject's thought" (in communicative situations). However, the isolated conceptual contents might still be conscious. Please note how the first variant, possibly in schizophrenia, could lead to a confabulatory/delusional attempt to reconstruct the PMIR via the second one: If these thoughts are not my own, they *must* be someone else's. This inference to the best explanation may be exactly what happens in some types of schizophrenic delusion.

9. I do not want to exclude certain mood states or body-state-related background emotions here, which can also emerge in passive encounters with a situation and are not directly associated with an explicitly represented goal state. Please also note that, given the terminological proposals developed above (e.g., "subjectively unwilled actions"), we may well speak of intermediate-level action programs triggered without a full-blown PMIR's being available on the level of conscious experience.

References

Baker, L. 1998. The first-person perspective: A test for naturalism. *American Philosophical Quarterly*, 35, 327–346.

Brentano, F. 1874. *Psychologie vom empirischen Standpunkt*. Erster Band. Hamburg: Meiner.

Brentano, F. 1973 (1874). *Psychology from an Empirical Standpoint*. Edited by O. Kraus. English edition edited by L. McAlister. Translated by A. C. Rancurello, D. B. Terrell, and L. McAlister. London and New York: Routledge and Kegan Paul, and Humanities Press.

Craik, F. I. M., T. M. Moroz, M. Moscovitch, D. T. Stuss, G. Winocur, E. Tulving, and S. Kapur. 1999. In search of the self: A positron emision tomography study. *Psychological Science*, 10, 26–34.

Damasio, A. R. 1994. *Descartes' Error*. New York: Putnam/Grosset.

Damasio, A. R. 1999. *The Feeling of What Happens: Body and Emotion in the Making of Consciousness*. New York: Harcourt Brace.

Damasio, A. R., and H. Damasio. 1996a. Images and subjectivity: Neurobiological trials and tribulations. In *The Churchlands and Their Critics*, ed. R. N. McCauley, pp. 163–175. Cambridge, Mass.: Blackwell.

Damasio, A. R., and H. Damasio. 1996b. Making images and creating subjectivity. In *The Mind–Brain Continuum*, ed. R. Llinás and P. S. Churchland, pp. 19–27. Cambridge, Mass.: MIT Press.

Delacour, J. 1997. Neurobiology of consciousness: An overview. *Behavioral Brain Research, 85,* 127–141.

Dennett, D. C. 1987a. *The Intentional Stance.* Cambridge, Mass.: MIT Press.

Dennett, D. C. 1987b. Intentional systems in cognitive ethology: The Panglossian Paradigm defended. In Dennett 1987a. (First published in *Brain and Behavioral Sciences 6*, 343–390.)

Dennett, D. C. 1991. *Consciousness Explained.* Boston: Little, Brown.

Frankfurt, H. 1971. Freedom of the will and the concept of a person. *Journal of Philosophy, 63,* 5–20.

Frith, U., and F. Happé. 1999. Theory of mind and self-consciousness: What is it like to be autistic? *Mind and Language, 14,* 1–22.

Haggard, P. 2003. Conscious awareness of intention and of action. In *Agency and Self-awareness,* ed. J. Roessler and N. Eilan, pp. 111–127. Oxford: Clarendon Press.

Haggard, P., and S. Clark. 2003. Intentional action: Conscious experience and neural prediction. In *Grounding Selves in Action*, ed. G. Knoblich, B. Elsner, G. von Aschersleben, and T. Metzinger, special issue of *Consciousness and Cognition, 12,* 695–707.

Haggard, P., and M. Eimer. 1999. On the relation between brain potentials and the awareness of voluntary movements. *Experimental Brain Research, 126,* 128–133.

Jeannerod, M., and E. Pacherie. 2004. Agency, simulation, and self-identification. *Mind and Language, 19,* 113–146.

Johnson-Laird, P. N. 1983. *Mental Models: Towards a Cognitive Science of Language, Inference, and Consciousness.* Cambridge: Cambridge University Press.

Johnson-Laird, P. N. 2001. Mental models and deduction. *Trends in Cognitive Science, 5,* 434–442.

LaBerge, D. 1997. Attention, awareness, and the triangular circuit. *Consciousness and Cognition, 6,* 149–181.

Lau, H. C., R. D. Rogers, P. Haggard, and R. E. Passingham. 2004. Attention to intention. *Science, 303,* 1208–1210.

Metzinger, T. 2000. The *subjectivity* of subjective experience: A representationalist analysis of the first-person perspective. In *Neural Correlates of Consciousness—Empirical and Conceptual Questions,* ed. T. Metzinger, pp. 285–306. Cambridge, Mass.: MIT Press.

Metzinger, T. 2003a. *Being No One: The Self-Model Theory of Subjectivity.* Cambridge, Mass.: MIT Press.

Metzinger, T. 2003b. Phenomenal transparency and cognitive self-reference. *Phenomenology and the Cognitive Sciences, 2,* 353–393.

Metzinger, T. 2004. Why are identity-disorders interesting for philosophers? In *Philosophy and Psychiatry,* ed. T. Schramme and J. Thome, pp. 311–325. Berlin: de Gruyter.

Metzinger, T., and V. Gallese. 2003. The emergence of a shared action ontology: Building blocks for a theory. In *Grounding Selves in Action,* ed. G. Knoblich, B. Elsner, G. von Aschersleben, and T. Metzinger, special issue of *Consciousness and Cognition, 12,* 574–576.

Nahmias, E., S. Morris, T. Nadelhoffer, and J. Turner. 2004. The phenomenology of free will. *Journal of Consciousness Studies, 11,* 162–179.

Ure, J., E. Faccio, H. Videla, R. Caccuri, F. Giudice, J. Ollari, and M. Diez. 1998. Akinetic mutism: A report of three cases. *Acta Neurologica Scandinavica, 98,* 439–444.

3 The Feeling of Doing: Deconstructing the Phenomenology of Agency

Tim Bayne and Neil Levy

3.1 Introduction

One of the most exciting developments in the cognitive sciences in recent years has been a rediscovery of the phenomenology of agency (see, e.g., Hohwy 2004; Horgan et al. 2003; Nahmias et al. 2004). That the phenomenology of agency has received renewed attention is due in no small part to claims that it is at odds with what the cognitive sciences are revealing about the structure of agency itself: in short, that the manifest or phenomenological image of ourselves as agents is inconsistent with the image emerging from the cognitive sciences. Wegner speaks for many when he writes as follows:

it seems to each of us that we have conscious will. It seems we have selves. It seems we have minds. It seems we are agents. It seems we cause what we do. Although it is sobering and ultimately accurate to call all this an illusion, it is a mistake to conclude that the illusion is trivial. On the contrary, the illusions piled atop apparent mental causation are the building blocks of human psychology and social life. (Wegner 2002, p. 342)

One response to will skeptics—as we shall call them—is to challenge their interpretations of the data derived from the cognitive sciences. This is a project that we have pursued in other work (Levy and Bayne 2004), but it is not the one we will pursue here. Instead, we will concentrate on the task of examining the phenomenology of agency. We suspect that much of the motivation for the current wave of will skepticism derives from rather naive models of the phenomenology of agency. A more nuanced account of the phenomenology of agency might fit rather better with what the cognitive sciences are telling us about ourselves.

Clarifying both the content of the phenomenology of agency and its relationship to the scientific image of ourselves as it is being revealed by the cognitive sciences is essential to a full understanding of disorders of volition, for many disorders of volition manifest themselves in the form of abnormal experiences of volition. Sometimes these abnormalities are reflections of the fact that the actual structure of agency itself has been disrupted, but in other cases it may be only that the mechanisms responsible for the phenomenology of agency are disrupted.

There are many components within the experience of first-person agency. Or, as we can also put it, the experience of first-person agency includes many other experiences as components. (Assume from now on that by "the phenomenology of agency" we mean "the phenomenology of *first-person* agency.") We will focus on just three components: the experience of *mental causation*, the experience of *authorship*, and the experience of *effort*.[1] These experiences have representational content. That is, they present the world—in this case, the agent and his or her actions—as being a certain way. Our main aim in this chapter is to examine the ways in which these experiences represent agents and their actions.

3.2   The Phenomenology of "Mental Causation"

We typically experience our actions as purposive. We do not simply find ourselves walking toward a door and, on the basis of this, form the belief that we must be intending to open it; instead, we experience ourselves as walking toward the door in order to open it. This sense of goal-directedness can operate at a number of levels. For example, one might experience oneself: walking toward a door in order to open it; opening the door in order to feed the dog; and feeding the dog in order to keep him quiet. The phenomenology of a single action can include the nested purposes for which the action is being performed.

How should we understand the experience of purposiveness? Is it the central component of the phenomenology of agency? Perhaps experiencing a movement as an action *just is* to experience it as implementing an intention that one experiences as one's own. Call this the *purposiveness thesis*. The purposiveness thesis suggests that disorders in the phenomenology of agency can arise either from failures to accurately track the contents of one's intentions or from failures to track the fact that one's intentions are one's own (Wegner 2002; Frith 2002, this volume).

An obvious objection to the purposiveness thesis is that we perform many actions without experiencing these actions as being performed on the basis of a specific intention (Marcel 2003). To give an example of Searle's (1983), when deep in thought one might suddenly get up and start pacing around the room. Actions of this kind—what, following Bach (1978), we will call *minimal actions*—might be caused by intentions, but that is not how they are experienced. It seems possible to experience oneself as performing an action without experiencing that action as the result (or implementation) of an intention. Call this the objection from *minimal actions*.[2]

There are a number of ways in which a proponent of the purposiveness thesis might respond to this objection. We will mention three. First, one might deny that minimal actions are accompanied by a sense of agency. Minimal actions, on this line of thought, might be actions, but they do not feel like actions. We think the proponent of the purposiveness thesis would be unwise to adopt this position: Minimal actions sure seem like actions to us! There seems a marked phenomenological difference between feeling one's arm go up in the context of an automatic action and feeling one's arm being raised by a friend. The former feels like an action; the latter does not.

A second response to the objection from minimal actions is to claim that minimal actions are accompanied by an awareness of intentions. The proponent of the purposiveness thesis might admit that minimal actions are not accompanied by an awareness of what Searle (1983) calls *prior intentions*, but he or she might insist that there is an intentional component—what Searle calls an *intention in action*—to all experiences of agency. In fact, this seems to be Searle's view. Searle holds that the content of an experience of agency *just is* the content of an intention in action (Searle 1983, p. 91).

We grant that there are fine-grained intentions that do not merely trigger actions but govern their evolution in a dynamic way. And we grant that we can be—and often are—aware of their role in shaping our movements. But is the presence of such intentions essential to the phenomenology of agency? Can we not experience a movement as an action without experiencing it as implementing an intention-in-action? We think so, although the elusiveness of the phenomenology of agency makes this a difficult point to confirm.

A third response on the part of the purposiveness theorist to the minimal actions objections is to modify the view. The original idea with which we began is that the experience of agency involves an awareness of the *content* of the intention that is implemented in the target action. A weaker and more plausible view is to hold that the experience of agency involves an experience of the action as having a certain intention, without necessarily involving an awareness of the content of that intention. On this view, to experience a movement as one's action involves an experience of it as implementing an intention (which one experiences as one's own). This view seems plausible, but it is a long way from the original purposiveness theory.

We turn now to a different set of issues raised by talk of the experience of purposiveness. What is involved in experiencing an action as being performed in virtue of a certain intention? What is involved in experiencing a movement as implementing a certain intention? One view, which seems to be widely endorsed, adopts a causal approach to the phenomenology of purposiveness. According to what we call the *mental causation thesis*, experiencing oneself as opening a door involves an experience of the intention to open the door as causing one's movements.

Note two important points about the mental causation thesis. First, it is a claim about the phenomenology of agency, not the structure of agency. One can reject the mental causation thesis without rejecting the causal theory of agency itself (and vice versa). Second, the mental causation thesis should not be confused with the claim that we experience our *experiences* of agency as causing our movements, a view that Searle (1983) advocates. We find this Searlean view implausibly strong.

Is the mental causation thesis plausible? There is room for skepticism. As Horgan et al. write: "Your phenomenology presents your own behavior to you as having yourself as its source, rather than (say) presenting your own behavior to you as having your own occurrent mental events as its source" (Horgan et al. 2003, p. 225). It is doubtful whether the phenomenology of purposeful agency involves an experience with causal content, at least if by "cause" one means anything more than counterfactual dependence. We do not, it seems, experience our intentions as sufficient conditions for our movements. In making these claims we are not relying on a skepticism about the phenomenology of causation; unlike Hume, we grant that causal relations can be experienced. We simply doubt that, in the usual run of things, the experience of first-person agency involves an experience of mental causation as such.

In fact, the experience of one's movements being caused by one's intentions seems to be characteristic of some disorders of volition. It is sometimes suggested that one of the pathological features of the phenomenology of addiction and obsessive–compulsive spectrum disorders is that the individuals concerned experience their actions as caused by their desires and urges rather than as having their source in *them*.[3] We suspect that as one begins to experience one's movements as caused by one's mental states, one no longer experiences them as one's own actions. That is, one no longer experiences the action as an instance of *first-person* agency.

A further problem for proponents of the mental causation thesis is that it seems possible to experience one's movements as being caused by one's intentions without experiencing the movements in question as actions. Consider the following variant on a classic thought experiment from the action theory literature (Davidson 1973, p. 153):

A climber might want to rid himself of the weight and danger of holding another man on a rope, and he might know that by loosening his hold on the rope he could rid himself of the weight and danger. This belief and want might lead him to form the intention to loosen his hold on the rope, and this intention might so unnerve him as to cause him to loosen his hold, and yet it might be the case that he never *chose* to loosen his hold, nor did he do it intentionally.

The climber experiences the loosening of his hold as caused by his intention to loosen his hold, but he does not experience the loosening of his hold as an action. Davidson introduced the case of the unfortunate climber in order to demonstrate that causal accounts of action face a problem of deviant causal chains. His point was that even though the loosening of the climber's hold was caused by the climber's beliefs and desires, a causal theorist shouldn't say that the climber's loosening of his hold was an action. Causal accounts of action have to say when the causal relation between beliefs and desires (and intentions) and movement generates agency and when it is merely deviant. Our motivation for referring to the unfortunate climber is to point out that causal accounts of the phenomenology of agency face a parallel problem. They have to say when the experience of a causal relation between an agent's intentions generates the experience of agency and when it does not. We will leave the task of exploring possible solutions to this problem for another occasion.

3.3   The Phenomenology of Authorship

We turn now from the experience of mental causation to the experience of ourselves as agents—what we will call the *phenomenology of authorship*. We begin by asking how the experience of authorship might be related to two other experiences mentioned in connection with the phenomenology of agency: the experience of self as source (Horgan et al. 2003) and the experience of agent causation (O'Connor 1995).

Talk of an experience of "self as source" seems to capture certain features of the experience of agency. As Horgan and coauthors say, we experience our actions as deriving from ourselves rather than deriving from our mental states. But how exactly should we understand this relation of being a source? Should we understand it in causal terms? Horgan and coauthors don't want to commit themselves to a causal reading of this notion, but it is unclear how to read it if not in causal terms.

As the term suggests, agent causal theorists adopt an explicitly causal conception of the phenomenology of being an agent. According to O'Connor, "[agent causation] is appealing because it captures the way we experience our own activity. It does not seem to me (at least ordinarily) that I am caused to act by the reasons which favour doing so; it seems to be the case, rather, that I produce my own decisions in view of those reasons. . . ." (O'Connor 1995, p. 196). Ginet also gives an agent causal gloss on the phenomenology of agency, although he does not himself endorse agent causation: "My impression at each moment is that I at that moment, and nothing prior to that moment, determine which of several open alternatives is the next sort of bodily exertion I voluntarily make" (1990, p. 90). Agent causation is the thesis that agents are, or at least can be, primitive causes of their movements, where the force of the "primitive" indicates that the causal relation between the agent and the movement cannot be reduced to relations between events (Chisholm 1982; O'Connor 1995; Taylor 1966). Proponents of agent causation typically claim that the causal relation between the agent and his or her movements is not necessitated by prior states of the agent. On this view, agents are the ultimate source of their actions, unmoved movers of an ontologically distinct kind.

Is it plausible to suppose that we could experience ourselves in agent causal terms? Note that the question is not whether our normal, everyday experience of ourselves as agents should be understood in agent causal terms; rather, the question is whether agent causation is something that could be experienced.

There are two issues that should give us pause before answering this question in the affirmative. First, it is not clear whether the very notion of agent causation is coherent. Searle claims that "It is a constraint on the notion of causation that wherever some object x is cited as a cause, there must be some feature or property of x or some event involving x that functions causally. It makes no sense to say, *tout court*, that object x caused such and such an event" (Searle 2001, p. 82). Searle's comment concerns the concept of causation, but there is some reason to think that a similar constraint holds for experiences of causation. We are by no means convinced that Searle's objection is sound; we advance it simply as a claim that any development of an agent causal account of the phenomenology of agency must address. Second, even if it is possible to experience oneself as a mover, it does not follow that it is possible to experience oneself as an *unmoved* mover. It is hard to see how one could experience an agent causal relation as undetermined by prior states.

We turn now from the question of how the experience of authorship might be understood to the question of whether such experiences are reliable. Is our experience of ourselves as agents veridical, or is it systematically misleading?

Wegner, among others, has recently argued that there is reason to think that it is misleading (Wegner and Wheatley 1999; Wegner 2002; see also Halligan and Oakley 2000). Wegner's argument rests on the claim that it is possible to create illusions of agency: We can experience ourselves as doing things that we are not doing, and we can experience ourselves as not doing things that we are doing. Wegner takes such dissociations to show that experiences of agency "may only map rather weakly, or perhaps not at all, onto the actual causal relationship between the person's cognition and action" (Wegner and Wheatley 1999, p. 481).

Consider one of Wegner's examples of a dissociation between agency and the experience thereof: his *I-spy* experiment (Wegner and Wheatley 1999). In this experiment participants and an experimental confederate had joint control of a computer mouse that could be moved over any one of a number of images on a board (e.g., a swan). On certain trials the confederate forced the pointer to land on a target image while participants were primed with the name of the image via headphones at a certain temporal interval either after or before the pointer landed on the image. When the prime occurred immediately before the pointer landed on the target image, participants showed an increased tendency to self-attribute the action, that is, to claim that they had intended to land on the image. Wegner and Wheatley argue that the prime creates an experience of agency in the absence of an exercise of agency.

The *I-Spy* experiment does suggest that priming can modulate experiences of agency, but it does not, we suggest, provide much support for *general* skepticism about the reliability of our experience of agency. Indeed, the lengths to which one has to go in order to create a nonveridical experience of agency demonstrates just how reliable those mechanisms that generate the experience of agency are. That they are *fallible* should not be surprising, for all monitoring mechanisms are fallible. Think of visual perception! People do, of course, confabulate their intentions (see Wilson 2002), but there is no reason to think that the confabulation of intentions is more common than perceptual error. Indeed, Wegner's own account of the experience of mental causation suggests that such experiences are generally reliable, for his model predicts that one is likely to experience oneself as acting on the basis of a certain intention only when one is acting on the intention in question (see, further, Bayne forthcoming).

Wegner also offers the indirectness of experiences of agency as evidence against their veridicality. But the mere fact that the relationship between an experiential state and the state of the world that it is monitoring is theoretically mediated gives us no reason to regard the resulting experiences as unreliable. Visual phenomenology is also theoretically mediated, for it relies on assumptions about the structure of the perceptual environment, but this is no reason to assume that visual experience misrepresents the world.

Another possibility is that Wegner is conceiving of the experience of authorship in agent causal terms. Perhaps he is assuming that we experience ourselves as Cartesian selves—agents who lie outside the causal nexus of the physical world. But agent causal accounts of authorship are not committed to endorsing a Cartesian conception of the self. Rather than conceive of the agent causal relation as holding between a Cartesian self and its actions, it is open for agent causationists to think of the agent causal relation as holding between an organism and its actions (see, e.g., Bishop 1983). That is, one can think of the acting self as identical to the animal. Arguments against Cartesian conceptions of the self would have no impact on this version of agent causation.

A second response to Wegner's position (as here understood) is to allow that experiences of agent causation are nonveridical but to insist that there are other components of the experience of authorship that are unscathed by the attack on agent causation. As we have seen, it is an open question whether the experience of agent causation is a component of the experience of authorship, and even if it is, it is doubtful that it is the sole component of the experience of agency. We suggest that much of the content of our normal, everyday experience of authorship would survive the discovery that there is no primitive causal relation between the self and its actions.

A further possibility is that Wegner is building certain claims about consciousness or deliberation into what it is for an action to be authored. Certain passages in his writings suggest that Wegner holds that our experiences of authorship are illusory because our actions are generated by unconscious and nondeliberative processes rather than conscious, deliberative processes. On this view, the only actions that are truly our own would be those that originate from processes of conscious deliberation.

We think that this account of the content of the experience of authorship should be rejected. For one thing, it is highly restrictive. Few of our actions derive from processes of conscious deliberation, and there is no reason to think that those actions that are nondeliberative are any less authored than those that are. Of course, it may be that conscious deliberation brings in additional kinds or forms of authorship—it is certainly true that self-consciousness creates new levels and layers of control within an organism—but there is no reason to think that the content of the quotidian experience of authorship refers to authorship by an essentially conscious deliberator.

But rejecting Wegner's attack on the experience of authorship is far from settling all of the issues raised by such experiences. One question that deserves some attention is how common such experiences are. Do they occur only in some contexts—such as those involving deliberation, decision making or self-control—or are they a component of all experiences of agency, even those involving stimulus-driven (or automatic) actions? We are inclined towards the latter view. Although it seems to be true that experiences of authorship are recessive or dampened in the context of automatic actions (or, at least, actions which we experience as automatic), we doubt that the phenomenology of authorship is entirely lacking from such experiences (see also Haggard, this volume). There seems to be a stark contrast between the phenomenology of stimulus-driven actions, such as accelerating in response to a green light, and the phenomenology of pathologies of agency, such as the anarchic hand syndrome and Penfield actions (actions produced by direct neural stimulation, by the American neurosurgeon Wilder Penfield). It is tempting to think that this difference is at least in part a difference in the experience of authorship: In the former case one has an experience of authorship (albeit recessive), while in the latter cases one has no experience of authorship. Indeed, it is not unlikely that the experience of authorship is essential to the experience of agency—that to experience a movement as one's own action necessarily involves an experience of oneself as the author of the movement.

We turn now to consider anarchic hand (Della Sala et al. 1991; Goldberg and Bloom 1990) and Penfield actions in more detail (Penfield and Welch 1951; Penfield 1975), for both syndromes raise acute questions about the content of the experience of authorship. The phenomenology of anarchic hand appears to be one of alienation authorship—anarchic hand patients fail to experience their actions as their own. Patients will often describe the anarchic hand as having a will of its own, and this description appears to reflect the phenomenology of the syndrome. It is intuitively plausible to suppose that the experience of alienated authorship in the anarchic hand is veridical: Anarchic hand patients are not the authors of "their" anarchic actions (see Peacocke 2003; Levy and Bayne 2004). Penfield's patients produced a number of actions, such as movements of the hand or vocalizations—but they did not experience a sense of authorship of the actions; in fact, they experienced their actions as alien and unowned. And again, there is some temptation to judge that this experience of alienated agency is veridical: Penfield patients are not the agents of their actions.

But although intuitively plausible, the thought that the phenomenology of alienated authorship in these cases is veridical can be challenged by considering another pair of disorders of volition: utilization behavior (Lhermitte 1983; Estlinger et al. 1991) and Delgardo actions (Delgardo 1969). Patients with utilization behavior engage in stimulus-driven behavior which looks rather similar to that seen in the anarchic hand. Both syndromes involve an inability to inhibit prepotent movements. (In the anarchic hand the movements are both endogenously and exogenously triggered, while in utilization behavior the triggers are solely exogenous.) Yet despite these similarities, the two syndromes appear to differ phenomenologically: Whereas anarchic hand patients have an experience of alienated authorship, patients with utilization behavior appear to experience their utilization actions as their own.[4] Now, the similarities in the generation of behavior in these two syndromes puts pressure on what we should say about the phenomenology of the two conditions. There is a prima facie case for thinking that if the phenomenology of the anarchic hand is veridical, then that of utilization actions is not. If, on the other hand, we insist that the experience of authorship in utilization behavior is veridical, then there is some reason to think that we should judge experiences of nonauthorship in the anarchic hand as nonveridical.

Consider now Delgardo actions. Delgardo (1969) also elicited "actions" by direct neural stimulation, but unlike Penfield's patients, Delgardo's patients seem to have experienced the resultant actions as their own. Perhaps it is the phenomenology of Delgardo's patients, rather than Penfield's patients, which is veridical. Again, there is a prima facie case for thinking that if the phenomenology of authorship in Delgardo actions is veridical, then the phenomenology of nonauthorship in Penfield actions is nonveridical, and vice versa.

We take no stand here on which of these experiences of agency might be veridical. It is difficult to make a judgment about these cases without knowing more about the disorders and their etiology. It could, of course, turn out that there are relevant differences between (say) Delgardo and Penfield actions, such that the respective experiences of agency and nonagency are both veridical. We present these pairs of cases to draw attention to some of the challenges one faces in giving an account of the experience of authorship and to the need to consider a full range of cases in addressing those challenges.

3.4   The Phenomenology of Effort

A third component of the experience of agency is the sense of effort. The world's resistance to our actions, coupled with our limited success in changing it, may give rise to the feeling of effort—the experience of needing to invest energy and willpower in our actions. This experience is perhaps most pronounced in the context of physical agency, but it also occurs in the context of mental agency. We shall focus largely on the effort associated with mental acts.

The experience of effort raises a number of questions. How prevalent is it? Is it a feature of human mental life generally, or is it restricted to a relatively few specific circumstances? What is the relationship between the experience of mental effort and the experience of physical effort? Does the experience of effort have representational content? If so, what is the nature of that content? We examine these questions in turn.

Some theorists suggest that the experience of mental effort is restricted to situations of motivational conflict (Holton 2003). On this view, we exert mental effort only when we attempt to resist the pull of our desires. This might be described as the experience of exerting *willpower*, which can be identified with the capacity for reflective choice against the momentum of the impulsive system (Bechara, this volume). We suggest, however, that the experience of mental effort extends beyond cases of motivational conflict. Mental effort is also experienced when we actively direct our thoughts. Anyone who has struggled with a difficult conceptual issue has experienced the effort involved in thinking a problem through. It gives rise to characteristic feelings of tiredness and a growing urge to stop. When we do stop for a break, it seems to require real effort to return to the task.

Of course, we might try to assimilate this kind of case to the experience of motivational conflict. As we grow tired, we experience both a desire to rest as well as a desire to continue to work on the puzzle, and it is the conflict between these two desires that leads to the experience of mental effort. However, it seems better to understand the mental effort involved here as distinct from the effort involved in resisting a desire. Effort seems to be involved not only in motivating the urge to stop but also in *causing* this urge: Tasks that involve concentration, for instance, are more tiring than tasks that don't, other things being equal, and it is plausible to suggest that this is because they are more effortful.

Clear and vivid experience of mental effort is perhaps restricted to cases of motivational conflict and active direction of thought. However, there is some reason to think that a recessive experience of effort accompanies a very wide range of mental actions: Hard decisions are experienced as requiring effort, perhaps as a consequence of the cognitive resources we need to devote to them. There is also some plausibility to the idea that even easy decisions might require *some* degree of effort (Mele 1987).[5] Consider in this respect the following question: Do we experience a sense of effort only for physically demanding actions, or do we experience a sense of effort in proportion to the demands of the action (and the tiredness of our muscles)? There seem to be plausible grounds for asserting the latter: Someone feels a great sense of effort when lifting 60 kilograms, a lesser but still clearly perceptible sense of effort when lifting 15 kilograms, and less still when lifting 5 kilograms. Perhaps it is generally true that the sense of effort dwindles proportionally as the resources—be they mental or physical—needed for the task decrease. However, it does seem to be true that there are some actions that are experienced as effortless (Marcel 2003).

We turn now to the relationship between the experience of physical and mental effort. In both cases, the experience of effort seems to be the experience of resisting a force: usually an external force in the physical case, internal in the mental case. Despite the apparent difference in the nature of the force being resisted, it may seem that the experience of resisting it is very similar.

Some theorists argue that physical and mental forces cause human movements in very different ways. They point out that a physical force can act directly on my body—the wind can lift me off my feet, for instance—but mental forces cannot. Instead, mental forces operate on our minds by *motivating* actions rather than *compelling* them. And since physical forces compel but mental forces do not, mental forces can be resisted indefinitely. As Feinberg puts it, "Human endurance puts a severe limit on how long one can stay afloat in an ocean, but there is no comparable limit to our ability to resist temptation" (Feinberg 1970, p. 283). It may be that this alleged difference gives rise to differences in the phenomenology of resisting a mental as opposed to a physical force.

Consider the experience of giving in to a mental force, when, for instance, we find ourselves breaking a resolution in the face of temptation. In these cases, we don't experience ourselves as compelled by mental forces. Instead, we seem to have an experience of authorship. This experience is characteristic both of cases of giving in to a temptation and of successfully resisting temptation, and it is especially vivid in the latter case. As Holton remarks of such cases, "It certainly doesn't feel as though in employing will-power one is simply letting whichever is the stronger of one's desires or intentions have its way. It rather feels as though one is actively doing something, something that requires effort" (2003, p. 49).

Watson (2004) suggests that the experience of resisting mental forces in cases of motivational conflict is not an experience of *compulsion*—as in the case of physical effort—but an experience of *seduction*. Whereas a physical force can *bypass* someone's will—overcoming his or her muscular strength, for example—desires work *through* our will. In cases of motivational conflict, we are unable to make a wholehearted effort to resist mental forces. We do not try as hard as we might to resist the desires in question because they are our own; we are divided against ourselves. Watson claims that this difference between mental and physical effort is reflected in the phenomenology of giving in to temptation: "one who is defeated by appetite is more like a collaborationist than an unsuccessful freedom fighter. This explains why it can feel especially shameful" (Watson 2004, pp. 65–66).

There are at least two problems with Watson's suggestion. First, although seduction (and therefore reduced effort) might be characteristic of motivational conflict, it does not seem to characterize all instances of mental effort. Watson's account does best in contexts in which one struggles to overcome a desire that one clearly identifies as one's own. It works less well in contexts in which agents resist desires that they experience as alien to themselves, such as certain cases of Tourette's syndrome and obsessive–compulsive disorder. In such cases agents can experience intense urges to engage in self-destructive actions—such as punching themselves—that they take themselves to have no reason at all to perform. It seems unlikely that there is *any* element of seduction in these cases. Although the force being resisted is (in some sense) internal to the agent, it is plausible to suppose that it is experienced as no less alien or external to the agent than physical forces.

Second, we doubt that the phenomenon of seduction is restricted to contexts involving mental effort. Arguably, many cases of being overwhelmed by physical forces also involve some degree of seduction. As a physical effort becomes increasingly difficult, we experience a temptation to stop. As a result, we are likely to experience motivational conflict when engaged in physical effort; if motivational conflict prevents us from making a wholehearted effort, as Watson suggests, then this is likely to be a regular feature of resistance to physical forces.

More generally, the experience of being overcome by a physical force is typically quite unlike the experience of being lifted off one's feet by the wind. Consider the experience of muscular fatigue—for instance, the experience of jogging until you are too exhausted to continue. We suggest that most of us experience succumbing to physical exhaustion as a matter of voluntarily giving in to external forces—that is, we do not experience ourselves as literally unable to continue at the task.

Sometimes, however, people push themselves beyond the point at which giving in feels voluntary. Professional athletes, for instance, sometimes exert themselves to the point where their legs will no longer support their weight. This experience is very different from the experience of resisting a mental force, but it may well resemble the experience of mental collapse, when we feel as though our minds are no longer under our control. (If legs can collapse, minds can become delusional.) Both the normal and the extreme cases seem to support a general parallelism between the experiences of mental and physical effort.

We turn now to the representational content of the experience of effort. One might be tempted to think that the experience of effort has no representational content at all. Perhaps it is a mere feeling—a brute sensation that has no veridicality conditions. Although we are certainly happy to grant that experiences of effort have a phenomenal character that outruns their representational content, we think that it would be a mistake to deny that the experience of effort has *any* representational content. In exerting effort it feels as though one is exerting a power of one's own against a force. (Whether or not this force feels alien or merely unwanted differs from case to case, with motivational conflict tending toward the unwanted end of the spectrum and pathologies such as Tourette's syndrome and obsessive–compulsive disorder tending toward the alien end.) Moreover, it feels as though the power one is drawing on becomes progressively weaker as effort is exerted. In the physical case, we know (or think we know) the nature of that power: It is muscular strength. We suggest that one is drawing on an analogous power in exercising mental effort, and that the experience of mental effort involves a representation of the utilization and progressive fatigue of *mental muscles*—what Baumeister and colleagues call *will power* (Baumeister et al. 1998; Muraven et al. 1998; Baumeister 2002). Moreover, we suggest that our experiences of effort are broadly consistent with what Baumeister et al. have discovered about willpower.

First, willpower is depletable over the short term. Subjects required to perform a task which requires the application of willpower perform worse at subsequent tasks requiring willpower. Moreover, the effect seems independent of (physical) fatigue: Controls who are required to perform tiring tasks which do not require willpower do not suffer the same degree of impairment at subsequent willpower tasks.

We have also suggested that mental effort is experienced in cases of motivational conflict, as well as in decision making more generally, and that the experience is of utilizing a mental muscle. Ego-depletion studies seem to support all three claims. First, they provide evidence that there is a depletable resource—akin to a mental muscle—used in resisting temptation. This evidence takes the following forms:

Behavioral evidence   Ego-depleted individuals quit tasks requiring persistence earlier than do nondepleted individuals. Of course, there may be alternative explanations of why they quit, but it seems plausible to suggest that the effort of the task is an important factor.

Physiological evidence   Subjects engaged in ego-depletion tasks exhibit the same kinds of physiological arousal which accompany physical effort, such as a rise in pulse rate, blood pressure, and skin conductance (Muraven et al. 1998).

Self-reports   Though subjects in ego-depletion experiments report no more fatigue than controls after the initial ego-depletion task, they report greater levels of fatigue after performing the common task at which they persist for a shorter time than controls (Vohs et al. unpublished). This is consistent with their having exerted greater effort than controls.

This evidence seems to suggest that persistence in some tasks does indeed take effort, and that the ability to exert this effort diminishes with continuous use. This goes some way to showing that the experience of mental effort as the experience of progressive exhaustion of a depletable resource is veridical.

Second, ego-depletion studies also seem to indicate that the experience of effort in decision-making is veridical, inasmuch as it depletes the same resource used in resisting temptation. Close-call decisions seem to be ego-depleting (Vohs et al.

unpublished). Further evidence for this claim comes from the self-reports of subjects in introspectionist studies of decision making (Nahmias et al. 2004). At least when decisions are not routine, there seems to be an experience of effort, and this experience may accurately represent the fact that these mechanisms are more energy expensive than those which implement automatic decision making.[6] Third, as already noted, the ego-depletion hypothesis seems to suggest that the resources utilized are progressively weakened by continuous use, in a manner akin to the way muscular strength is depleted.

However, although ego-depletion experiments go some way toward establishing the veridicality of experiences of mental effort, other studies seem to suggest that some experiences of fatigue are nonveridical. (The research we draw on here involves the perception of muscular fatigue, but it is entirely possible that similar results can be obtained for experiences of mental fatigue.) Research by St. Clair Gibbon and colleagues seems to indicate that the degree of fatigue we experience is "teleoanticipative"—that is, it is influenced by unconscious representations of the amount of muscular effort that will be required in the near future rather than merely being a response to the depletion of a physical resource. Whereas traditional theories explain muscular exhaustion in terms of the total depletion of a physical resource, the teleoanticipation view suggests that exhaustion is the product of neural mechanisms designed to preserve physical resources in case of emergencies (Hampson et al. 2001; Noakes et al. 2004).

The teleoanticipation explanation of the experience of fatigue suggests that its content is nonveridical, if, as seems plausible, the experience of fatigue represents ourselves as having entirely "run out of gas." On this view, the mechanisms causing the perception of fatigue are designed to preserve resources well above the critical level, and it seems natural to think of them as generating systematically misleading representations of our energy levels.

But perhaps the experience of exhaustion does not represent the complete depletion of resources needed for mental and physical effort. Perhaps, instead, the experience represents an inability to make the effort in the precise circumstances in which we believe ourselves to be. And, on the teleoanticipation view, this experience may well be veridical, for the view suggests that the resources we have when exhausted can be accessed only when needed.

The research supporting the teleoanticipation view of fatigue has been restricted to the experience of muscular fatigue. However, we suggest that the demonstration that physical fatigue is not the veridical perception of a catastrophic muscular event provides some indirect support for our claim that the experiences of mental and physical effort and fatigue are closely analogous. The temptation to believe that there is a deep gulf between the two kinds of experiences seems to be the product of the belief that although physical forces are subject to total depletion, mental forces are not. The demonstration that physical fatigue is not normally a product of running too low on physical resources goes some way toward making the view that mental fatigue is analogous to physical fatigue more palatable. Though it is probably true that people typically give in to mental forces while still possessing enough mental resources to hold out longer, this is normally the case with regard to physical effort as well. In both cases, agents do not experience themselves as able to draw upon (or perhaps as possessing) resources which are nevertheless present.[7]

We speculate that ego-depletion triggers the same kind of mechanisms that give rise to the perception of physical fatigue, prompting the subject to desist from a task in order to save energy for emergencies. Perhaps in mental effort a mediating role is played by the inhibition mechanism that prevents internal and external stimuli from leading to action (the frontal lobe mechanisms damaged in both utilization behavior and anarchic hand syndrome). We suggest that operating this inhibiting mechanism takes energy and is therefore experienced as effortful. Evidence that it is the energy utilized by the inhibitory mechanism that is depleted comes from the behavior of ego-depleted subjects. They do not lapse into passivity when they are ego-depleted—as we would expect if ego-depletion used up a general-purpose energy supply—but instead act on their strongest desires, whether these are for rest or for something else. For instance, ego-depleted dieters eat more than do ego-depleted nondieters (Vohs and Heatherton 2000).

A final question: How does the experience of effort relate to the experience of authorship and mental causation? Although the experience of authorship is, we have suggested, a central component of the phenomenology of agency generally, it appears to be particularly vivid in experiences of effort. The experience of effort involves an experience of the self as a source of force. Arguably, if the experience of agency were limited to experiences of mental causation, we would not experience ourselves as playing an active role in endorsing or resisting our urges. We might experience conflict between competing desires and intentions, but we would not experience ourselves as allied with some desires and opposed to others. If the experience of authorship ever takes the experience of agent causation, we suggest that it is in contexts in which the experience of effort is particularly vivid.

3.5   The Phenomenology of Agency and Disorders of Volition

In this final section we return to the connection between the phenomenology of agency and disorders of volition. There are two perspectives one can adopt on this connection. The first perspective considers the ways in which disorders of volition involve departures from the normal phenomenology of agency. Such departures can involve the absence of content that is usually present in the phenomenology of agency, and they can involve the presence of content that is usually absent from the phenomenology of agency. The experience of being caused to act by one's desires—which might occur in some cases of addiction and obsessive–compulsive disorder—would be an example of the latter form of abnormality, and the lack of the experience of authorship in the anarchic and Penfield cases would be an example of the former. Of course, not all unusual experiences of agency ought to count as disorders in the phenomenology of agency. Flow experiences, which seem to involve a departure from the normal phenomenology of agency, do not seem to count as disorders of volition.

A second perspective on the relationship between the phenomenology of agency and disorders of volition is in terms of the operation of those mechanisms responsible for generating the phenomenology of agency. Here, it is useful to distinguish two ways in which unusual experiences of agency can arise. On the one hand, abnormal experiences of agency might be a reflection of the fact that the agent's actions are themselves abnormal in etiology and structure. If a person's action generation system is abnormal and his or her phenomenology of agency generating system is normal, then we would expect that person to have abnormal experiences of agency—at least, so long as the system that generates the phenomenology of agency is designed to track the structure of the agent's actions. On the other hand, the etiology and structure of the agent's actions might be perfectly normal, and the abnormality in the agent's experiences of phenomenology might be due solely to the malfunctioning of those mechanisms responsible for generating such experiences. (A third possibility is that the mechanisms responsible for generating actions and those responsible for generating the experience of agency are both malfunctioning.) Of course, this tidy distinction between pathologies of action generation and pathologies in the generation of the phenomenology of agency is complicated by the fact that there are undoubtedly intimate feedback loops between the phenomenology of agency and the generation of actions: Abnormalities in the experience of agency are likely to change the structure of agency itself.

Consider this distinction as it applies to hypnotic actions. It could turn out that the mechanisms governing hypnotically suggested actions are functioning entirely normally and that the only pathology here is in the patients' experience of their movements (Kirsch and Lynn 1997; Haggard et al. 2004). Alternatively, it might be the case that the mechanisms that are disrupted are those governing the production of the hypnotically suggested actions themselves and that the patient's experiences of involuntariness are an accurate reflection of the fact that the actions in question are not produced by those mechanisms governing the voluntary production of behavior (Woody and Bowers 1994). And, of course, a third possibility is that the mechanisms responsible for the generation of the movements and the phenomenology of agency are both malfunctioning.

There is much about the phenomenology of agency that is obscure. Perhaps this reflects the relative neglect of the topic; perhaps it arises from the fact that the phenomenology of agency appears to be less vivid and stable than the phenomenology of perception. In this chapter we have attempted to fill in some of the structure of experience of agency. As we have seen, much remains to be done before we know, in the relevant sense, what it is like to be an agent.

Acknowledgments

The authors gratefully acknowledge David Chalmers, George Graham, Peter Menzies, Elisabeth Pacherie, Kathleen Vohs, and audiences at the Department of Philosophy, Melbourne University, and the Department of Philosophy (RSSS), The Australian National University, for helpful comments on this chapter and the issues discussed therein. The research was partially funded by Australia Research Council Discovery Grant DP0452631.

Notes

1. Other putative experiences involved in the phenomenology of agency include the experience of *freedom*, the experience of *trying*, and the experience of *deliberation* or *decision making*. Although these experiences are closely related to the experiential states we discuss, we lack the space to address the connections here.

2. A related objection derives from Hécaen et al.'s data (Hécaen et al. 1949; reported in Marcel 2003). Hécaen and colleagues stimulated the central thalamus, which produced contralateral hand clenching and unclenching. Hécaen's patients seem to have experienced these movements as their actions, despite having no idea why they had made them. These data suggest that one can experience a movement as an action without experiencing it as implementing an intention.

3. It is often thought that such disorders as Tourette's syndrome involve an experience of being caused to act by one's urges, but individuals with Tourette's report experiencing their tics as having their source in themselves (Bliss 1980; Cohen and Leckman 1992).

4. The phenomenological differences are nicely illustrated by a case in which a patient exhibited utilization behavior with his right hand and anarchic agency with his left hand: The patient was unconcerned about the former but troubled by the latter (Marcel 2003)!

5. Note that it is important not to confuse a weak (recessive, peripheral) experience of effort with an experience of weak effort. The content of an experience is one matter, its phenomenal saliency is another.

6. Many studies have shown that the prefrontal cortex and the anterior cingulate cortex are highly active in close-call decision making, but not in more automatic tasks (Paus et al. 1998). As subjects become proficient at a task, the degree of activation of the anterior cingulate cortex, in particular, decreases. See Zhu 2004 for a review. The experience of effort may be a reflection of the extent to which certain tasks are energy intensive.

7. We note one further implication of the claim that the sensation of effort, including the sense that exhaustion is overwhelming, is a product of teleoanticipation: The popular method of ascertaining ability or capacity by a straightforward appeal to counterfactuals will give the wrong result in many cases. We cannot infer from the fact that subjects would find the reserves to persist in a task in some counterfactual circumstances that they can persist in the actual circumstances.

References

Bach, K. 1978. A representational theory of action. *Philosophical Studies, 34*, 361–379.

Baumeister, R. F. 2002. Ego depletion and self-control failure: An energy model of the self's executive function. *Self and Identity, 1*, 129–136.

Baumeister, R. F., E. Bratslavsky, M. Muraven, and D. M. Tice. 1998. Ego-depletion: Is the active self a limited resource? *Journal of Personality and Social Psychology, 74*, 1252–1265.

Bayne, T. Forthcoming. Phenomenology and the feeling of doing: Wegner on the conscious will. In *Does Consciousness Cause Behavior? An Investigation of the Nature of Volition*, ed. S. Pockett, W. P. Banks, and S. Gallagher. Cambridge, Mass.: MIT Press.

Bishop, J. 1983. Agent Causation. *Mind, 92*, 61–79.

Bliss, J. 1980. Sensory experience of Gilles de la Tourette syndrome. *Archives of General Psychiatry, 37*, 1343–1347.

Chisholm, R. 1982. Human freedom and the self. In *Free Will*, ed. G. Watson, pp. 24–35. Oxford: Oxford University Press.

Cohen, A., and J. F. Leckman. 1992. Sensory phenomena associated with Gilles de la Tourette's syndrome. *Journal of Clinical Psychiatry, 53*, 319–323.

Davidson, D. 1973. Freedom to act. In *Essays on Freedom of Action*, ed. T. Honderich, pp. 137–156. London: Routledge.

Delgardo, J. M. R. 1969. *Physical Control of the Mind: Toward a Psychocivilized Society*. New York: Harper and Row.

Della Sala, S., C. Marchetti, and H. Spinnler. 1991. Right-sided anarchic (alien) hand: A longitudinal study. *Neuropsychologia, 29*, 1113–1127.

Estlinger, P. J., G. C. Warner, L. M. Grattan, and J. D. Easton. 1991. Frontal lobe utilization behavior associated with paramedian thalamic infarction. *Neurology, 41*, 450–452.

Feinberg, J. 1970. *Doing and Deserving*. Princeton: Princeton University Press.

Frith, C. 2002. Attention to action and awareness of other minds. *Consciousness and Cognition, 11*, 481–487.

Ginet, C. 1990. *On Action*. Cambridge: Cambridge University Press.

Goldberg, G., and K. K. Bloom. 1990. The alien hand sign: Localization, lateralization, and recovery. *American Journal of Physical Medicine and Rehabilitation, 69,* 228–238.

Haggard, P., P. Cartledge, M. Dafydd, and D. A. Oakley. 2004. Anomalous control: When "free-will" is not conscious. *Consciousness and Cognition, 13,* 646–654.

Halligan, P., and D. A. Oakley. 2000. Greatest myth of all. *New Scientist, 168,* 35–39.

Hampson, D. B., A. St. Clair Gibbon, E. V. Lambert, and T. D. Noakes. 2001. The influence of sensory cues on the perception of exertion during exercise and central regulation of exercise performance. *Sports Medicine, 31,* 935–952.

Hécaen, H., J. Talairach, M. David, and M. B. Dell. 1949. Coagulations limitées du thalamus dans les algies du syndrome thalamique: Résultats thérapeutiques et physiologiques. *Revue de Neurologie, 81,* 917–931.

Hohwy, J. 2004. The experience of mental causation. *Behavior and Philosophy, 32,* 377–400.

Holton, R. 2003. How is strength of will possible? In *Weakness of Will and Practical Irrationality,* ed. S. Stroud and C. Tappolet, pp. 39–67. Oxford: Clarendon Press.

Horgan, T., J. Tienson, and G. Graham. 2003. The phenomenology of first-person agency. In *Physicalism and Mental Causation: The Metaphysics of Mind and Action,* ed. S. Walter and H.-D. Heckmann, pp. 323–340. Exeter, U.K.: Imprint Academic.

Kirsch, I., and S. J. Lynn. 1997. Hypnotic involuntariness and the automaticity of everyday life. *American Journal of Clinical Hypnosis, 40,* 329–348.

Levy, N., and T. Bayne. 2004. A will of one's own: Consciousness, control and character. *International Journal of Law and Psychiatry, 27,* 459–470.

Lhermitte, F. 1983. Utilization behavior and its relation to lesions of the frontal lobes. *Brain, 106,* 237–255.

Marcel, A. 2003. The sense of agency: Awareness and ownership of action. In *Agency and Self-Awareness: Issues in Philosophy and Psychology,* ed. J. Roessler and N. Eilan, pp. 48–93. Oxford: Oxford University Press.

Mele, A. 1987. *Irrationality: An Essay on Akrasia, Self-Deception, and Self-Control.* New York: Oxford University Press.

Muraven, M., D. M. Tice, et al. 1998. Self-control as limited resource: Regulatory depletion patterns; *Journal of Personality and Social Psychology, 74,* 774–789.

Nahmias, E., S. Morris, et al. 2004. The phenomenology of free will. *Journal of Consciousness Studies, 11,* 162–179.

Noakes, T. D., A. St. Clair Gibbon, et al. 2004. From catastrophe to complexity: A novel model of integrative central neural regulation of effort and fatigue during exercise in humans. *British Journal of Sports Medicine, 38,* 511–514.

O'Connor, T. 1995. Agent causation. In *Agents, Causes, Events*, ed. T. O'Connor, pp. 173–200. New York: Oxford University Press.

Paus, T., L. Koskl, Z. Caramanos, and C. Westbury. 1998. Regional differences in the effects of task difficulty and motor output on blood flow response in the human anterior cingulate cortex: A review of 107 PET activation studies. *Neuroreport, 9*, R37–R47.

Peacocke, C. 2003. Action: Awareness, ownership, and knowledge. In *Agency and Self-Awareness: Issues in Philosophy and Poychology*, ed. J. Roessler and N. Eilan, pp. 94–110. Oxford: Oxford University Press.

Penfield, W. 1975. *The Mystery of Mind*. Princeton: Princeton University Press.

Penfield, W., and K. Welch. 1951. The supplementary motor area of the cerebral cortex. *Archives of Neurology and Psychiatry, 66*, 289–317.

Searle, J. R. 1983. *Intentionality: An Essay in the Philosophy of Mind*. Cambridge: Cambridge University Press.

Searle, J. R. 2001. *Rationality in Action*. Cambridge, Mass.: Harvard University Press.

Taylor, R. 1966. *Action and Purpose*. Englewood Cliffs, N.J.: Prentice-Hall.

Vohs, K. D., R. F. Baumeister, J. M. Twenge, D. M. Tice, and J. Crocker. Unpublished. Self-regulation and choice.

Vohs, K. D., and T. F. Heatherton. 2000. Self-regulatory failure: A resource-depletion approach. *Psychological Science, 11*, 249–254.

Wakefield, J., and H. Dreyfus. 1991. Intentionality and the phenomenology of action. In *John Searle and His Critics*, ed. E. Lepore and R. van Gulick, pp. 259–270. Oxford: Blackwell.

Watson, G. 2004. Disordered appetites: Addiction, compulsion, and dependence. In *his Agency and Answerability: Selected Essays*, pp. 59–87. Oxford: Clarendon Press.

Wegner, D. M. 2002. *The Illusion of Conscious Will*. Cambridge, Mass.: MIT Press.

Wegner, D. M., and T. Wheatley. 1999. Apparent mental causation: Sources of the experience of will. *American Psychologist, 54*, 480–491.

Wilson, T. 2002. *Strangers to Ourselves: Discovering the Adaptive Unconscious*. Cambridge, Mass.: Harvard University Press.

Woody, E. Z., and K. S. Bowers. 1994. A frontal assault on dissociated control. In *Dissociation: Clinical and Theoretical Perspectives*, ed. S. J. Lynn and J. W. Rhue, pp. 52–79. New York: Guilford Press.

Zhu, J. 2004. Locating volition. *Consciousness and Cognition, 13*, 302–322.

4 Conscious Intention and the Sense of Agency

Patrick Haggard

4.1 Introduction

For the purpose of this chapter, I will define an "intention" as a conscious state generated as part of the chain of information processing in the motor system that translates desires and goals into motor behavior and events in the external world. This definition has some important consequences. First, purely reflex behaviors which are driven by a stimulus and are not linked to any preceding goal of the organism do not involve intentions. Second, intentions occupy a middle range of the motor hierarchy, located between the motivational drivers which cause us to initiate any behavior at all and the behaviors themselves. Third, conscious intentions do not directly correspond to the philosophical concept of libertarian free will. From a neuroscientific perspective, a conscious intention cannot be the ultimate cause of our actions, since that would imply mind–body causation. Rather conscious intentions occur as part of the long-range causation of present behavior by the combination of previous experience, present motivation, and innate or acquired dispositions.

Following the definition above, conscious intentions typically occur in the middle section of the temporal evolution of action. Within the broad range of neural information processing between goal and action, a number of quite different mental processes and conscious experiences have been given the label "intention." Searle (1983), for example, has proposed a hierarchical distinction between *prior intentions* and *intention-in-action*. Prior intentions resemble the planning aspect of executive function (Shallice 1978). Intention-in-action refers to the conscious experience one has at the point of initiating a goal-directed action. Most experimental studies of human voluntary action are focused more on intention-in-action than on prior intention, including the studies described here. A major difficulty in interpreting experimental results in this area is the fact that most studies use a unitary concept of "intention," whose precise content is difficult to locate within the motor processing chain. Improved methodology might generate useful dissociations between different levels of intention in both psychological and neural studies.

In this chapter I wish to explore three main features of conscious intention. First, I will argue that the phenomenal content of conscious intention is principally the sense of agency, that is, of being able to cause and influence events in the world. Second, I will show how implicit measures of conscious intention, based on comparing the perceived time of intentional actions with that of involuntary movements, reinforce the connection between intention and agency. Third, I will review the relatively small number of neuroscientific studies that have directly focused on the conscious experience of intending. In particular, I will use these studies to investigate the neural substrate and informational content of conscious intention. This investigation suggests that the experience of intention is not an illusory post hoc reconstruction, but a perceptual experience generated at specific points of the neural elaboration of an action plan.

4.2 Phenomenal Content of Intention

The phenomenology of intentional action is thin and evasive. We often have no specific, vivid, or focal experience of actions which we would definitely accept as intentional, such as switching a light switch. Put another way, actions are controlled "automatically," with little conscious experience or directed attention. Some psychologists have suggested that only a very small part of our behavioral life is conscious (Wegner 2002). This view implies that our manual actions, for example, might often have no phenomenology at all. I feel this is a mistake: The thin phenomenology of our actions is phenomenally quite distinct from the *absence* of any phenomenology. Most of the time we do not feel the heart beating or the stomach churning. But we do have an awareness that we are switching the light, whereas we may not have any awareness at all that the heart is beating. My awareness of my hand when I switch the light is quite different from my awareness of my heart or gut at the same moment.

There is, then, a background level of sensorimotor experience that characterizes intentional actions and that involuntary movements do not have. The content of this background experience seems strongly linked to the "sense of agency" (Gallagher 1995). "Sense of agency" refers to the feeling that we are in control of our own actions and of their effects on the external world. Put another way, I feel that my voluntary actions are caused *by me*, and *by my intentions*. In normal circumstances, this feeling seems to be a matter of matching what actually happens against what I intended to happen. The normal phenomenology of switching on a light is a rather vague feeling of a set of linked perceptual events (realizing it is dark, reaching out, feeling pressure on the finger, hearing a click, experiencing increased luminance). These percepts occur in a predicted, coherent order, and at appropriate times.

The link between intention, agency, and prediction has been developed using computational models originally applied to human movement control (Frith, Blakemore, and Wolpert 2000; Frith, this volume). In these models, efference copy of a motor command is used to anticipate the somatic or external consequences of intentional action before delayed sensory feedback about the progress of the action becomes available. This allows rapid updating of the motor command. This prediction has a second, quite distinct advantage: The actual sensory feedback can be compared to the prediction. If the two match, then detailed sensory processing of the feedback becomes unnecessary and can be gated out. The common finding that sensory perception and processing are reduced during voluntary movement is generally taken as evidence for such predictive sensorimotor suppression (Frith, this volume). I would like to make a further, less widely accepted point: Predictive sensorimotor suppression could also explain *why* the phenomenology of intention and agency is so thin. Most of the perceptual events surrounding intentional action are highly predictable. Both our body movements and their effects in the world normally match our intentions and are thus largely suppressed. Therefore, the resulting phenomenology involves a tightly coupled chain of faint, elusive perceptual content. Only when the effects of action do not match our intention do we have vivid experience, in the often unpleasant form of an action error (James 1890; Reason 1990; Haggard 2001).

Unfortunately, this sense of predictable structure in intentional action is difficult to test in laboratory experiments. Several studies have focused on matching action outcomes to action predictions, known as the "self-recognition" or "attribution" test (Sirigu et al. 1999). In this task, subjects perform an intentional hand action while watching a visual display. The display may show either the action that they themselves make or an action simultaneously made by an experimenter in a separate room. The subjects' task is to judge whether the display shows their action or not. Most authors have assumed that subjects do this by predicting the visual appearance of the action they are currently making and matching this prediction against the visual signal they see on the display. Only if the match seems good will subjects decide that the display shows their own hand performing the action.

The self-recognition task suffers from two limitations as an experimental tool for investigating conscious intention. First, it makes the matching process underlying awareness of intentional action very explicit. Subjects are explicitly asked to evaluate and judge the match between intention, action, and feedback. We have already seen that, in everyday life, this matching process seems to operate in the background, without focal directed attention, and in phenomenal silence. Making the matching process itself the object of attention seems to miss both its normal phenomenology and its evolutionary purpose. Second, the classic self-recognition task does not clearly distinguish the role of intention in the phenomenology of action. To decide whether they see their own action or another's, subjects could match the visual feedback either against their intention to perform a specific action or against the proprioceptive sensation when they actually acted. These two components of the matching process have to be dissociated if the self-recognition task is to clarify the process of conscious intention.

A recent experiment by Tsakiris et al. (2005) attempted precisely this dissociation. On each trial, the subject's right index finger was passively lifted by a lever. In one condition, the subject moved the lever by an intentional action of the left hand, while in the control condition the subject made no intentional action, and an experimenter moved the lever in a similar way. Subjects viewed either their own or someone else's right index finger being passively lifted and judged whether they saw their own action or not. The results showed that self-recognition was at chance level when the experimenter imparted the passive movement to the subject's right index finger. This implies that the match between passive proprioceptive information and visual feedback was poor. Self-recognition was significantly improved when subjects made intentional actions to impart the passive movement to the right index finger. This implies that efferent information contributes significantly to a matching process which is used to attribute actions and events to the self. Thus, intentional action may make an important contribution to self-awareness. This finding contrasts with the conventional view that proprioception is the key sensory modality underlying self-consciousness (Bermudez 1998).

However, self-recognition experiments such as this focus on the effects of intentional action on other perceptual states. They cannot clarify either the phenomenology of intentional action or of agency nor the specific neural processes that give rise to an experience of intention. Implicit measures have been much more successful in this connection, as the next section will discuss.

4.3   The Perceived Time of Intentional Actions: An Implicit Measure of Agency

The time at which an event is perceived to occur may differ from the time at which it actually occurs. The discrepancy between the two, or temporal judgment error, can be extremely informative about the mental representation of the event. This approach was used by Libet, Gleason, Wright, and Pearl (1983) in what may have been the first quantitative study of conscious intention. Libet et al. asked subjects to watch a dot rotating on a screen in the manner of a clock hand. The subjects made a simple intentional action at a time of their own choice and later reported the time on the clock at which they had first experienced conscious intention (or the "the urge to move," as Libet called it). On average, this occurred some 206 ms before the actual onset of movement measured in the muscles of the forearm. Libet et al.'s interest focused on the fact that conscious intention occurred much later than the onset of brain activity linked to the preparation of the movement. This recalls the view elaborated much earlier by Michotte (1963) that the processes giving rise to conscious intentional action seem to operate autonomously and automatically. It is as if one is informed of one's volition more or less as an afterthought.

Most reaction to this result has argued over whether it does or does not constitute good experimental evidence against libertarian free will. That doctrine requires that the conscious mind can control the body, via the brain, and would thus require that conscious intention precede neural preparation rather than follow it. I wish to avoid the "free will" debate entirely and concentrate instead on what the perceived time of events can tell us about the processes of intentional action. Briefly, I argue that Libet-type studies provide strong evidence that conscious intention is generated as part of the tightly linked predictive chain described in the previous section, which associates our goals, movements, and effects. We do not normally have several distinct conscious experiences corresponding to each element in the chain, such as desire, plan, intention, movement, feedback, and consequence. Rather, we tend to have a rapid, condensed experience of the whole sequence of events. Studies of perceived time of events have shown a strong temporal compression surrounding intentional action, which recalls the predictive nature of the psychomotor chain.

A first example of this compression occurs in Libet's original results, though he appears not to have remarked on it. Libet's main interest centred on the perceived time of conscious intention. We have already seen that this so-called *W judgment* averaged 206 ms before movement onset. But in a further control condition, Libet asked his subjects to judge the actual time of movement onset, which he called *M judgment*. On average, his subjects thought they began to move 86 ms before the onset of electrical activity in relevant muscles. The interval between these two values implies that the conscious experience of preparing an action—namely, the interval between awareness that the action will shortly happen and awareness that it is happening—is restricted to a narrow window of time, lasting only 120 ms. This short subjective experience corresponds to the much longer neural interval between the beginning of the preparation for action and the action itself. The onset of the readiness potential may be taken as an indicator of the start of neural preparation for action. This begins several hundred milliseconds (Libet et al. 1983), and sometimes over 1 s (Haggard and Eimer 1999), before action. Taken together, these values indicate that the phenomenal experience of intentional action is temporally compressed relative to the underlying neural events.

We recently discovered that the temporal compression surrounding voluntary action occurs for judgments of the effects of actions also and is specifically linked to predicting the consequences of our intentional actions (Haggard, Clark, and Kalogeras 2002). In the main experiment of that study, subjects made voluntary key presses, which were followed 250 ms later by a brief auditory tone. The tone may be considered the effect of the subject's action in the external world. Subjects used a Libet-type clock to judge either the time of their key press or the time of the tone. These were compared to estimates obtained in two blocks of control trials. In one of these blocks, subjects estimated the time of a voluntary key press which did not produce any tone. In the other, subjects did not make voluntary actions but estimated the onset of a

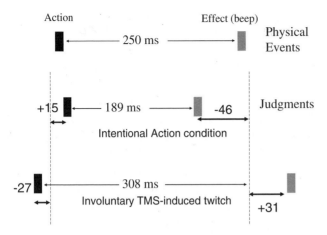

Figure 4.1
Schematic results of the intentional binding experiment of Haggard, Clark, and Kalogeras (2002). Subjects judged the perceived time of a voluntary action, an involuntary twitch induced by transcranial magnetic stimulation (TMS), or an auditory tone in three control blocks. The average perceived time of these events, which typically does not coincide with their actual onsets, is schematized by a dashed vertical line. In further blocks, the action or the TMS-induced twitch are paired with the tone. Subjects judged either the time of the action or the tone, or the twitch. The association between the action and the auditory tone causes a binding or perceptual attraction between the perceived times of these events, implying a perceptual compression of subjective time. When the action is replaced by a TMS-induced twitch, a perceptual repulsion in the opposite direction is observed.

tone which occurred randomly. A schematic representation of the results is shown in figure 4.1.

We found that actions that caused a tone were perceived to occur 15 ms later than the actions in the control block that were not followed by a tone. Conversely, when subjects were asked to judge the time of the tone, an effect in the opposite direction was found. Tones that the subjects caused by their own voluntary actions were perceived to occur 46 ms earlier than tones in the control block that occurred without being caused by voluntary actions. This pattern of results gives a clear temporal compression: Subjects perceive their intentional actions and their effects as closer in time than they really are. This study also includes an important methodological advantage over previous uses of the Libet technique. Any individual numerical estimate in a Libet experiment is subject to numerous well-known biases and should be interpreted with extreme caution. These biases include large individual differences in cross-modal synchronization, the division of attention between the subject's internal stream of consciousness and the clock, the perceptual center of any physical event judged (Morton,

Marcus, and Frankish 1976), and the prior entry phenomenon (Shore, Spence, and Klein 2001). If, however, the subject judges the time of an identical physical event in two different contexts, then these factors should be held constant. Therefore, a *difference* between Libet estimates of the same event in two different conditions is a much more reliable guide to the conscious perception of time than a single numerical value.

This binding between the subjective experiences of action and effect emphasizes the association between them. The binding effect could therefore underlie the sense of agency, as long as two further conditions were satisfied. First, the binding effect should occur only for truly intentional actions. Second, it should occur only when the intentional action is indeed the cause of the tone. We investigated the first question by using transcranial magnetic stimuluation (TMS) to produce involuntary movements and pairing these with the tone in the same way as for the intentional key presses. TMS over the primary motor cortex was used to produce involuntary twitches of first dorsal interosseus muscle. This muscle flexes the index finger and was the prime mover in the voluntary key press action. The muscle activity evoked by TMS thus has the same anatomical specificity as the intentional action, though the temporal pattern of muscle contraction differs. When subjects judged the perceived time of these involuntary twitches followed by the identical auditory tone, they judged the twitch to occur 27 ms *earlier* than in a control condition when no tone occurred. When they judged the time of a tone which followed a TMS-induced twitch, they perceived the tone to occur 31 ms *later* than the same tone in a control condition where no TMS was delivered. That is, the subjective experience of twitch and tone showed a perceptual repulsion, in contrast to the binding effect found for voluntary action. The perceptual compression of time was thus specific to intentional actions. We accordingly used the term "intentional binding" to designate this effect.

I suggested earlier that perceptual compression of a sequence of events surrounding voluntary action might reflect the internal mental process of prediction within the motor system. If this view is correct, intentional binding should occur only when the relation between intentional action and external effect is close and predictable. We tested this hypothesis in a second experiment, by adjusting the interval between key press and effect (Haggard, Clark, and Kalogeras 2002). When the interval was increased across blocks between 250, 450, and 650 ms, we found that the perceptual shift of the tone toward the intentional action that caused it decreased monotonically. This finding recalls previous results that the sense of agency is greater over shorter time windows than over longer intervals (Wegner and Wheatley 1999). However, when the same intervals were tested in a random order, so that subjects could no longer predict on each trial when the tone would occur, the intentional binding effect disappeared. Predictability is a necessary condition for intentional binding, as it is for the sense of agency (Gallagher 1995).

The clear link between intentional binding and prediction could arise in several ways. First, a "weak" prediction might be based on statistical regularity in the relation between action and effect, such as Hume's "constant conjunction between events" (Hume 1748). A process similar to instrumental conditioning in animals might associate the mental representation of action and effect, so that activation of the action representation would activate the effect representation by association, bringing forward the perceived time of the effect. Alternatively, a "strong" prediction might be based on predictive processes within the motor system. The conscious perception of action and effect might reflect the timing of specific computational events within an internal motor model, for example (Wolpert 1997). To compare these two possibilities, we performed a further experiment in which either an intentional key press or a TMS-induced twitch might lead to an auditory tone (Haggard and Clark 2003).

In the key condition, subjects prepared and made intentional actions to produce a tone 250 ms later. Their preparation was interrupted on some trials by a randomly timed TMS pulse to the motor cortex, evoking an involuntary twitch in the same muscles they had been preparing to move voluntarily. The TMS pulse was followed by an identical tone, in the same way that the incompleted intentional action would have been. Thus, on each trial, both intention and tone were always present. However, on some trials the tone was produced by the normal, intentional process, while on other trials the tone was produced involuntarily, by an external agent. We found that the time of the TMS-evoked tone was no earlier when it had been preceded by an uncompleted intentional preparation·than in a control block in which subjects made no intentional actions at all. Conversely, on those trials in which the subject's intentional preparation for action was completed, and was not disrupted by TMS, the previous finding of intentional binding of the tone toward the action was replicated. That is, the mere conjunction of an intention and an effect is not sufficient for the subjective experience of binding. Rather, the intention, action, and effect must all be linked together in an appropriate temporal pattern. This finding suggests that a strong prediction within the motor system precisely estimates the timing of the various elements of action and, accordingly, constructs a conscious experience that associates these elements to give a sense of agency.

4.4 Neural Correlates and Informational Content of Judgments about Intention

The first section of this chapter argued that the phenomenology of intention consists chiefly in agency or authorship of action. The second section has shown that even implicit measures of intention show a strong link between conscious intention and the sense of agency. This third section will review the relatively few neuroscientific studies that have asked at what stage in the motor processing chain between motivation and action the conscious experience of intention may arise. Identifying the neural circuits and the type of motor information associated with the conscious experience of intention would be important for three reasons. First, it would represent a major step in the experimental analysis of human intention, by giving a measurable basis to a formerly metaphysical concept. Second, it could guide the diagnosis and treatment of disorders of volition (see. Prinz, Dennett, and Sebanz, this volume). Finally, it could be relevant to the moral and legal issue of whether an individual has moral responsibility for an action or not, since conscious intention, or mens rea, is normally considered necessary for responsibility.

Libet et al.'s (1983) original experiment implicitly identified the frontal motor circuits of the brain as the cause of conscious intention. This argument was based on the temporal relation between the readiness potential, a gradual increase in frontal negativity thought to originate in the supplementary motor area (SMA), and the W judgment. The spatial precision for localizing the readiness potential is, however, poor at best. Therefore, a much more convincing pointer toward the SMA as the correlate of conscious intention comes from a study by Fried et al. (1991), in which conscious patients received direct electrical stimulation from a grid of subdural electrodes positioned over the frontal cortex, as part of a localization procedure prior to neurosurgical operations for epilepsy. One relatively neglected result in their study comes from the verbal reports of the patients following stimulation of the SMA. When the SMA was stimulated at low current, the patients reported feeling an urge to move their arm. When higher currents were used at the same stimulating electrode, complex arm movements were evoked. Taken as a pair, these results suggest that the SMA participates in the conscious experience of volition and that this experience is a normal part of the neural mechanisms of action generation. Interestingly, Fried et al.'s (1991) result is also relevant to another key debate in the modern discussion of intention. Wegner (2002), following Hume's skeptical line, has suggested that the experience of conscious intention may involve a post hoc explanation of our apparently purposive movements. That is, we perceive our own movement to the light switch, and, to explain why this occurred, we subsequently attribute to ourselves a conscious intention, which we retrospectively insert into our stream of consciousness just prior to the action. Fried et al.'s (1991) results show that the experience of intention can occur prior to action, as a part of the construction of action, and not purely as a post hoc reconstruction.

Two further recent studies have suggested that the SMA and the parietal cortex together form a circuit underlying conscious intention. Lau, Rogers, Haggard, and Passingham (2004) performed an event-related functional magnetic resonance imaging study of Libet's original W and M judgment conditions. Subtracting the brain activations in the M condition from those in the W condition revealed significant differences in just two brain areas. These were the pre-SMA and the intraparietal sulcus. Several functional imaging and primate studies suggest that these areas play a key role in the planning of actions (Jenkins, Jahanshahi, Jueptner, Passingham, and Brooks

2000) and in updating perceptual systems to track the ongoing development of action (Duhamel, Colby, and Goldberg 1992; Wolpert, Goodbody, and Husain 1998). However, Lau et al.'s result by itself does not clarify why requirement to judge intentions influenced these circuits. On the one hand, the increased attention to intention in the W condition might increase the cognitive effort and planning preceding the movement. The increased neural activations would then be linked to the effects of attention on motor preparation rather than to conscious intention per se. Alternatively, the M and W conditions might be completely equivalent from an attentional and motoric point of view, in which case the additional neural activations for W judgment could be thought of as the neural correlates of judging conscious intention. That is, the pre-SMA and parietal areas might form part of a parallel processing loop for monitoring the development of intentional actions, and activity in this loop might be associated with elaboration of conscious experience (Johnson-Laird 1983). It is difficult to see how these two possible interpretations could be dissociated in future experiments.

Sirigu et al. (2004) found convergent evidence for an involvement of the parietal cortex in a neuropsychological study of the W and M judgments in small groups of parietal patients, cerebellar patients, and matched healthy control subjects. The three groups did not differ in the perceived time of their actions (M condition). However, the parietal patients showed a significant delay in the W judgment compared to the other two conditions (see fig. 4.2). Whereas the cerebellar patients and the normal controls showed W judgments that preceded M judgments by a few hundred milliseconds, the parietal patients appeared to perceive their intentions and their actions almost simultaneously.

This result confirms that the parietal cortex participates in the conscious experience of intention, but again, it does not conclusively show what role it plays. The parietal cortex might merely monitor the planning and preparation processes in the frontal motor areas. This monitoring could involve an internal model for predicting the consequences of a planned action (Frith, Blakemore, and Wolpert 2000; Frith, this volume). The conscious experience of intention would be provided by the operation of the predictive model (Tsakiris and Haggard 2005). However, the performance of parietal patients in the Sirigu et al. study does not suggest a pure monitoring deficit: In addition to delayed W judgments, the patients also showed reduced amplitudes of the frontal readiness potential preceding action, in comparison to the healthy control subjects. The delayed W judgment might therefore reflect a delayed or compromised process of preparation for action rather than a failure to monitor an intact frontal preparation system. The reason for the reduced readiness potential in the parietal patients therefore becomes highly important. The reduced readiness potential could be merely a secondary frontal consequence of lesions that have their foci more posteriorly. However, the lack of other cognitive deficits in the patients suggests that no

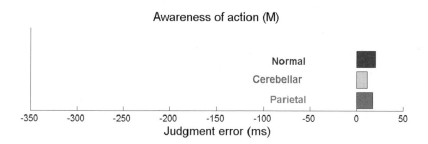

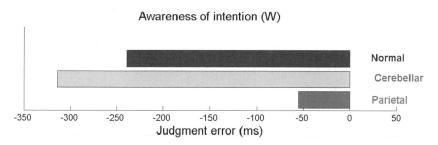

Figure 4.2

The perceived time of intentions and of voluntary actions in patients with cerebellar or parietal lesions and in healthy control subjects. Data from Sirigu et al. 2004.

such frontal damage was present. A more interesting possibility is that the parietal areas are actively involved in the preparation of action, via a reciprocal circuit with the frontal areas. Activity in the frontal–parietal circuit would both generate actions and simultaneously generate the conscious content of intentions. A key question for future research would be to distinguish between the contributions that the frontal and parietal poles of this circuit make to conscious intention. For example, do patients with focal lesions of the SMA exhibit W judgments similar to those of parietal patients? If they do, one would conclude that conscious experience of intention is a consequence of neural preparation within a frontoparietal network. If, on the other hand, frontal patients show normal W judgments, one would conclude that the frontal lobes plan actions, while the parietal lobes monitor the development of the plan, eliciting conscious experience as a by-product of the monitoring process.

While the above studies clarify the neural correlates of conscious intention, they do not particularly explain its information content. For example, knowing that conscious intentions are linked to activity in the parietal or frontal lobe does not, of itself, identify which *informational processes* in the motor chain between motivation and effect generate the conscious experience of intention. Does the conscious experience of intention reflect initiating an action, deciding which action to make, deciding not to veto the action, or indeed a "point of no return" where the motor command is passed to a final execution stage? Phenomenal content and neural localization (see the first section of this chapter) can only give partial clues about information processing. Haggard and Eimer (1999) investigated the informational content of W judgments. They asked subjects to judge the time of conscious intention in a free-choice version of the Libet task, in which subjects chose on each trial whether to make a movement of the left or right hand. The readiness potential recorded in this task can be divided into two clear phases, based on its scalp distribution. The earliest portion of the readiness potential is maximal over midline frontal electrodes and has similar amplitudes over both hemispheres. Shortly before movement, however, the readiness potential begins to lateralize, becoming larger contralateral to the hand that the subject will move than over the ipsilateral hemisphere. This second phase is known as the lateralized readiness potential (LRP). By the serial logic of cognitive psychology, many studies have argued that the mental process of selecting which response to make have has completed by the time of LRP onset (Eimer 1998). The informational processes preceding movement can thus be divided into a general preparation phase, prior to movement selection, and a second, specific preparation phase which generates the selected action. The LRP onset forms an objective marker of the division between these two phases.

Haggard and Eimer (1999) investigated which of these two phases of preparation gave rise to the W judgment using a correlational approach. Each subject's trials were divided at the median time of W judgment into trials showing awareness of intention long before the time action and others where W preceded action by a much shorter interval. A generalized readiness potential was then calculated for each of these groups of trials separately.

Interestingly, the readiness potential for trials with early W awareness lagged behind rather than leading that for trials with later W awareness. By Mill's (1843) method of concomitant variation, this finding rules out the possibility that the general readiness potential causes the conscious awareness of intention. They then repeated the same procedure with the LRP. Trials with early W awareness were found to have significantly earlier LRPs than trials with late W awareness (see table 4.1). This suggests the possibility that the conscious awareness of intention is caused by the lateralization of the readiness potential toward the hemisphere contralateral to the hand that the subject selects to move on each particular trial.

This finding has two important consequences for our present purposes. First, the point in the motor processing chain at which conscious intentions are formed is surprisingly late. In the Haggard and Eimer (1999) experiment, subjects' W judgments

Table 4.1
Lateralized readiness potential (LRP) onsets and mean W judgments (ms), relative to the time of key press, from Haggard and Eimer (1999).

	Early W trials	Late W trials
Mean W	−530	−179
LRP onset	−906	−713

corresponded not to the earliest initiation or decision to perform an action but to the much later stage when the specific form of movement to be used is selected. In the terminology of Searle (1983), the experience of intention corresponds to intention-in-action rather than prior intention or willing. Second, the point at which conscious intentions are formed corresponds to a critical processing stage in computational motor control (Wolpert 1997). There are generally an infinite number of possible movement patterns which will all achieve a given action goal, and there is normally no algorithmic solution for selecting a particular one. The fact that conscious intention emerges at the computationally intensive stage of movement selection fits with the view that conscious experience is linked to the most advanced executive functions of the human brain (Jack and Shallice 2001). In summary, the Haggard and Eimer (1999) experiment suggests that conscious intention is tied to a specific element in the information expansion required for control of movement.

4.5   Conclusion

Much of the data reviewed in this chapter has been based on the perceived time of intentions and other aspects of intentional actions. This approach, pioneered by Libet, has attracted a great deal of attention, together with a welter of criticism. For example, many of the replies to Libet's (1985) target article in *Behavioural and Brain Sciences* were overtly hostile to his experimental approach. This seems an appropriate place to make three general comments about what this method can and cannot tell us about intention.

First, the Libet task obviously captures only a small part of what we mean by conscious intention. It focuses on the perceived time of conscious intention and not directly on the *content* of conscious intention. However, we have seen that perceived time can be used as an implicit measure to investigate both the phenomenal contents (e.g., agency) and the informational contents (e.g., selection) of intentions. Direct verbal reports about the content of intentions are easily mediated by cognitive strategies, by the subjects' understanding of the experimental situation, and by their folk psychological beliefs about intentions. For these reasons an implicit measure is highly desirable.

Second, a single numerical value obtained from a Libet experiment is not particularly informative in itself. For example, the fact that W judgments typically lag behind the onset of neural preparation of action, rather than anticipate it, is only weak evidence against mind–body causation. The large number of biases inherent in cross-modal synchronization tasks means that the perceived time of a stimulus may differ dramatically from its actual onset time. There is every reason to believe that purely internal events, such as conscious intentions, are at least as subject to this bias as perceptions of external events. A much stronger inference can be drawn by *comparing* the perceived time of an identical event occurring in two different contexts. Then, the factors causing bias in time judgment are common to both contexts and can be subtracted out.

Third, the process of volition seems to vanish in a laboratory setting. Subjects, by the fact of their participation, seem to align their normal process of volition with the experimenter's instructions. Thus, when the experimenter asks them to make a voluntary key press, or to make an action when they "feel the urge" to do so (Libet et al. 1983), the psychological process entailed seems rather different from normal volition. Subjects' behavior may be guided partly by a feeling that they should behave randomly (Jahanshahi et al. 1998) or by their assessment of what the experimenter wants them to do (Frith, this volume). A skeptic might ask whether enough remains of the normal process of volition to make such experiments scientifically useful. I would argue that such experiments can be scientifically illuminating once one accepts that they are not studies of libertarian free will. Instead, they are studies of how actions may be prepared, selected, and initiated when the environment does not directly specify this information. Humans have evolved a capacity for long-range actions in which their responses are only partly and indirectly related to a preceding stimulus. Conscious intention is an element in the process whereby the cognitive and motor systems generate the additional information required to guide such underdetermined actions.

To summarize, this chapter has argued that conscious intentions may be studied experimentally. A number of studies, beginning with the work of Libet, have shown that the perceived time of conscious intention is among the most promising experimental approaches. However, studying the effects of intentions on the perceived time of other events, such as actions and their consequences, is methodologically more robust. Moreover, such studies have clearly identified the strong link between conscious intention and agency. This key aspect of the phenomenology of intention has been largely ignored because of an almost exclusive focus on the link between conscious intention and "free will." Recent studies have implicated a network of frontal and parietal regions in the judgment of conscious intention. However, it is at least as important to identify which neural processes are associated with the experience of conscious intention. In this connection, the selection of specific movement patterns, and the predictive monitoring of anticipated consequences of our actions, may be particularly important elements of conscious intention. These processes occur relatively late in the motor processing chain. There is little evidence that the experience of conscious intention is linked to the very earliest initiation of that chain, as the philosophical concept of free will might suppose. Finally, all these comments relate to the highly artificial case of manual actions, performed repeatedly and in the absence of any broad functional context, in a laboratory setting. There are many other aspects of our experience of volition in the real world. Some of these aspects undoubtedly involve Conscious experience, such as strategic forward planning, goal setting, mental rehearsal, and so forth. These seem close to Searle's concept of prior intention.

Despite these caveats, I would like to end with the assertion that there is a specific conscious experience of preparing an action, or of being about to make it. This experience arises in large part before the action occurs. Its phenomenal content is largely given by the effect that our action will have in the outside world, and it thus underlies a sense of agency. This might seem like a curious combination: The content of intention is generated *before* action, but the content is *about* the effects or goals of action. These, by definition, can only occur after the action itself. Put another way, prediction lies at the heart of conscious intention. It is difficult but possible to capture conscious intention in laboratory experiments. The behaviorist tradition in psychology has traditionally been very hostile to the concept of intention (Skinner 1953). Since intentional action is both a key element of human intelligence and one of the most fascinating aspects of our nature, this hostility has done psychology as a whole a disservice. The present renaissance of scientific research in this area is to be strongly welcomed. Moreover, it is now widely accepted that many psychopathological and neurological conditions involve failures of neural prediction (Frith, this volume). Understanding the altered experiences of conscious intention in such cases may be an important part of understanding and treating such disorders of volition.

References

Bermudez, J. L. 1998. *The Paradox of Self-Consciousness*. Cambridge, Mass.: MIT Press.

Duhamel, J. R., C. L. Colby, and M. E. Goldberg. 1992. The updating of the representation of visual space in parietal cortex by intended eye movements. *Science, 255,* 90–92.

Eimer, M. 1998. The lateralized readiness potential as an on-line measure of central response activation processes. *Behavior Research Methods, Instruments, and Computers, 30,* 146–156.

Fried, I., A. Katz, G. McCarthy, K. J. Sass, P. Williamson, S. S. Spencer, and D. D. Spencer. 1991. Functional organization of human supplementary motor cortex studied by electrical stimulation. *Journal of Neuroscience, 11,* 3656–3666.

Frith, C. D., S. J. Blakemore, and D. M. Wolpert. 2000. Abnormalities in the awareness and control of action. *Philosophical Transactions of the Royal Society of London B: Biological Sciences, 355,* 1771–1788.

Gallagher, S. 1995. Body schema and intentionality. In *The Body and the Self,* ed. J. L. Bermudez, and A. J. Anthony, pp. 225–244. Cambridge, Mass.: MIT Press.

Haggard, P. 2001. The psychology of action. *British Journal of Psychology, 92,* 113–128.

Haggard, P., and S. Clark. 2003. Intentional action: Conscious experience and neural prediction. *Consciousness and Cognition, 12,* 695–707.

Haggard, P., and M. Eimer. 1999. On the relation between brain potentials and the awareness of voluntary movements. *Experimental Brain Research, 126,* 128–133.

Haggard, P., S. Clark, and J. Kalogeras. 2002. Voluntary action and conscious awareness. *Nature Neuroscience, 5,* 382–385.

Hume, D. 1748. *An Enquiry Concerning Human Understanding.* In *Enquiries Concerning Human Understanding and Concerning the Principles of Morals.* Ed. L. A. Selby-Bigge, 3rd edition revised by P. H. Nidditch. Oxford: Clarendon Press, 1975.

Jack, A. I., and T. Shallice. 2001. Introspective physicalism as an approach to the science of consciousness. *Cognition, 79,* 161–196.

Jahanshahi, M., P. Profice, R. G. Brown, M. C. Ridding, G. Dirnberger, and J. C. Rothwell. 1998. The effects of transcranial magnetic stimulation over the dorsolateral prefrontal cortex on suppression of habitual counting during random number generation. *Brain, 121,* 1533–1544.

James, W. 1890. *The Principles of Psychology,* 2 vols. New York: Henry Holt.

Jenkins, I. H., M. Jahanshahi, M. Jueptner, R. E. Passingham, and D. J. Brooks. 2000. Self-initiated versus externally triggered movements. II. The effect of movement predictability on regional cerebral blood flow. *Brain, 123,* 1216–1228.

Johnson-Laird, P. N. 1983. *Mental Models.* Cambridge: Cambridge University Press.

Lau, H. C., R. D. Rogers, P. Haggard, and R. E. Passingham. 2004. Attention to intention. *Science, 303,* 1208–1210.

Libet, B. 1985. Unconscious cerebral initiative and the role of conscious will in voluntary action. *Behavioral and Brain Sciences, 8,* 529–566.

Libet, B., C. A. Gleason, E. W. Wright, and D. K. Pearl. 1983. Time of conscious intention to act in relation to onset of cerebral activities (readiness potential): The unconscious initiation of a freely voluntary act. *Brain, 106,* 623–642.

Michotte, A. 1963. *The Perception of Causality.* Oxford, England: Basic Books.

Mill, J. S. 1843. *A System of Logic.* London.

Morton, J., S. Marcus, and C. Frankish. 1976. Perceptual centers (P-centers). *Psychological Review, 83*, 405–408.

Reason, J. 1990. *Human Error.* New York: Cambridge University Press.

Searle, J. R. 1983. *Intentionality: An Essay in the Philosophy of Mind.* Cambridge: Cambridge University Press.

Shallice, T. 1978. *From Neuropsychology to Mental Structure.* New York: Cambridge University Press.

Shore, D. I., C. Spence, and R. M. Klein. 2001. Visual prior entry. *Psychological Science, 12,* 205–212.

Sirigu, A., E. Daprati, S. Ciancia, P. Giraux, N. Nighoghossian, A. Posada, and P. Haggard. 2004. Altered awareness of voluntary action after damage to the parietal cortex. *Nature Neuroscience, 7,* 80–84.

Sirigu, A., E. Daprati, D. P. Pradat, N. Franck, and M. Jeannerod. 1999. Perception of self-generated movement following left parietal lesion. *Brain, 122,* 1867–1874.

Skinner, B. F. 1953. *Science and Human Behavior.* Oxford: Macmillan.

Tsakiris, M., P. Haggard, N. Franck, N. Mainy, and A. Sirigu. 2005. A specific role for efferent information in self-recognition. *Cognition, 96,* 215–231.

Tsakiris, M., and P. Haggard. 2005. Experimenting with the acting self. *Cognitive Neuropsychology, 22,* 387–407.

Wegner, D. M. 2002. *The Illusion of Conscious Will.* Cambridge, Mass.: MIT Press.

Wegner, D. M., and T. Wheatley. 1999. Apparent mental causation: Sources of the experience of will. *American Psychology, 54,* 480–492.

Wolpert, D. M. 1997. Computational approaches to motor control. *Trends in Cognitive Sciences, 1,* 209–216.

Wolpert, D. M., S. J. Goodbody, and M. Husain. 1998. Maintaining internal representations: The role of the human superior parietal lobe. *Nature Neuroscience, 1,* 529–533.

5 Agency in Schizophrenia from a Control Theory Viewpoint

Joëlle Proust

There does not seem to be a consensus as to the components of and processes underlying willful activity, or on the functional structures that are engaged in voluntary action. What makes the problem still more intractable is the difficulty, in the present state of the art, in offering an account of voluntary action that applies both to physical and to mental kinds of actions. In what sense can imagining, remembering, or planning be seen as voluntary mental actions rather than something that happens to the thinker? Is there a sense of agency that is common to physical actions, such as opening a door, and mental actions, such as focusing on a problem?

The importance in studying impairments of willful activity lies in the fact that the scope of possible action-related states and feelings turns out to be wider than what our folk-psychological intuitions suggest. There is more to voluntary action than a simple "yes" or "no" answer to the question "Is this action *my* action?" As many authors have observed, some subjects with schizophrenia, as well as brain-lesioned patients with alien hand syndrome, present a strange dissociation between the feeling that their own body is moving—an experience of *ownership* related to the fact that something happens to the self—and the feeling that their body is moved by a foreign intention, rather than by their own will. For example, patients complain that their hands are moved by some irresistible external force. Although they do not acknowledge the action as theirs, they do identify the hand as their own. Thus *ownership* can be experienced while *agency* is not.

A fact that makes this dissociation all the more remarkable and relevant to the study of volitional states is that it extends to bodily as well as to mental actions. Patients who experience a lack of control of their bodily actions sometimes also have the feeling that their thoughts do not belong to them; these are experienced as "inserted" in the patients' heads, a sensation that is different from, although related to, more classical forms of auditory–verbal hallucinations: Inserted thoughts are perceived "internally," while auditory hallucinations are referred to an external speaker.

Some philosophers are insisting that there is nothing to be learned about normal function from psychopathology (Ricoeur 1986). Some also maintain that patients with schizophrenia only display their irrationality in denying self-evident facts, of a kind that is taken to be "immune to error of misidentification" (Coliva 2002). In other words, it seems impossible to believe that an action is performed by me, but not as a consequence of my intentions; nor is it apparently possible to be mistaken as to who I am, because in both cases the thinker does not need to identify herself as an agent or as a self but enjoys a form of direct, "nonobservational" knowledge.

If it is recognized, however, that brain states and processes form a highly modular structure, evolved in steps, the view that the self offers a single unified model of the whole mind/brain's ongoing states tends to lose its appeal. A widely held claim in cognitive science is that there are different levels of selfhood, from sensorimotor integration in an egocentric frame of reference to more complex levels of self-attribution in a social context (Rochat 2003). The separation of these levels can benefit from the study of dissociations exhibited by patients with lesions or delusions. Specific functional disconnections are associated with phenomenological changes in patients' experiences of agency, which may help us expand our understanding of the dimensions of self-awareness. As many authors have observed, any functional change of this kind will retroact on other functions, bring new emotions into play, call for compensatory mechanisms, and so forth. But this may not prevent us from distinguishing crucial features reflected in patients' reports and cognitive performances.

We will therefore focus on schizophrenic impairments of the sense of volition with a dual motivation: first, in order to better understand the dissociation between sense of ownership and sense of agency, a dissociation that defies folk-psychological intuitions, and second, to use this specific problem as an opportunity to scrutinize the notion that the mind is a set of nested control structures.

The structure of my argument will be as follows. I will first describe clinical facts related to the ownership/agency dissociation that have to be accounted for (section 5.1); I will then discuss the metarepresentational view of delusions of control as developed by Tim Shallice and Chris Frith in their classical studies (section 5.2). In section 5.3, I will consider more recent views of the disorders of volition in schizophrenia. Section 5.4 will introduce proposals for relating the control and monitoring view of the mind/brain to metacognitive capacities engaged in volition. Finally, section 5.5 will offer a revised picture of the impairments of volition in schizophrenia. According to the proposed hypothesis, three different control loops are engaged in the senses of ownership, of agency, and of explicit social attribution of actions.

5.1   Four Intriguing Features of Impaired Will in Patients with Schizophrenia

5.1.1   The Ownership/Agency Asymmetry

We saw above that experience of agency in patients with schizophrenia involves a dissociation where none exists in a normal subject; these patients demonstrate that one can have a thought or perform an action consciously—in the sense that they have the characteristic impression of having a thought or of executing an action—without being conscious of thinking or acting as the motivated agent or author of that thought or of that action. Phenomenology thus splits up into two different dimensions whose relationship is distinctively asymmetrical. *Whereas there is no case of an impression of agency without an impression of subjectivity, a sense of subjectivity can survive when the sense of agency is lost.* It is one of the aims of a proper theory of conscious experience to explain such an asymmetry.

5.1.2   The Parallel Phenomena of Thought Insertion and Delusion of Control

Another challenge to a theory of volition (and of its disorders) has to do with its scope: Is a single theory able to deal with willful thinking processes *and* willful bodily actions? It seems quite natural to require that a theory of volition provide a common theory of agency in both kinds of cases, as the phenomenologies in hallucinating patients with schizophrenia are very similar: An idea is entertained, an action is performed accompanied by a subjective impression, but both are sensed as having an externally generated, motivationally incongruent intentional content. This analogy has been spelled out either by taking thoughts to be actions of some sort, or by considering both thought and action as involving a common metarepresentational format, which would be disrupted in schizophrenia. We will explore these avenues below, and I will provide a third explanation that builds on both ideas.

5.1.3   The External Attribution Puzzle

The puzzle can be summarized in this way: Supposing that a patient with schizophrenia is impaired in monitoring her own intentions, actions, and thoughts, why does she not simply recognize that something is wrong with her ability to keep track of what she does and thinks? Why does she instead come up with odd judgments, such as that her neighbour, or some unknown person she met in the street, has taken control of her brain/body? What is the cognitive basis of "extraneity," one of the major symptoms in schizophrenia?

5.1.4   The Occasionality Problem

This problem presents an additional difficulty to the preceding puzzle. Patients deny being the author of an action or of a thought only in certain cases; they seem to be able to have an irregular disposition to "project" their mental contents onto others. The disposition is irregular in the sense that no general property of the projected content (such as its emotional significance) seems to explain why the patient attributes it to another thinker or agent.

My goal in this chapter will be to discuss accounts of schizophrenic cognitive impairments that lead to an integrated explanation of the first two features. Although the last two would well deserve an extensive discussion, it cannot be conducted within the confines of the present chapter.

5.2 Frith's Metarepresentational View on Self-Monitoring

Chris Frith published in 1992 an influential book—*The Cognitive Neuropsychology of Schizophrenia*—in which the view that schizophrenia is essentially related to an impaired will was carefully presented and documented. Although Frith's theory was not meant to account for our first feature above (the asymmetry between sense of ownership and sense of agency), his 1992 theory contains the seeds of an explanation for it. There is an asymmetry between sense of ownership and sense of agency because first-order thoughts as well as routine intentions and actions are preserved in patients; therefore, the phenomenology of perception and action is unchanged. Metarepresentations are impaired, however, which affects selectively the sense of agency as well as the explicit representations of the self. Let us first examine how volition is affected in schizophrenia according to this classical account.

5.2.1 Classes of Volitional Processes Impaired in Schizophrenia

According to Frith (1992), there are three major processes engaged in willful action that seem to be crucially involved in schizophrenic symptoms.

(A) The generation of intentions to act is massively impaired in patients who exhibit a "poverty of will": Patients with negative symptoms, in particular, may exhibit a reduced activity, a lack of persistence in their work, poor personal hygiene, and difficulties communicating with others.

(B) The monitoring of intentions is also often impaired: Patients have difficulties selecting an appropriate action schema; they also often have the feeling that the intentions driving their actions are not their own and that their thoughts are inserted into their heads by other agents. The patients' impaired sense of agency seems to lead them to misattribute intentions to others: They may, for example, believe that other people are watching them (delusion of reference), are plotting against them (delusion of persecution), or are having an emotional attachment to them (erotomania). In some cases, however, the patients attribute to themselves agency of others' actions. They feel responsible for other people's actions or even for large-scale world events, such as the war in Iraq.

(C) Finally, patients with schizophrenia monitor their actions in an abnormal way; they seem to be able to correct failed actions only if they have access to unambiguous visual feedback, in contrast to normal subjects, who seem to also rely on internal forms of monitoring (Frith and Done 1989; Malenka et al. 1982).

In addition to these symptoms, which are directly involved in the sense of agency, two more symptoms have been mentioned by other authors as having an indirect relationship with action processes. One is the ability to *refer to self*, which seems disrupted in particular with respect to the use of personal pronouns such as "I" (a patient is reported to have told other patients in the ward "I am you, you, and you," pointing to three different individuals);[1] the other is the related capacity to construct *an identical self* over time.

5.2.2 The Metarepresentational Theory of Impaired Intention, Action, and Self-Monitoring

Frith (1992) builds on the work of Shallice (1988) to offer a simple explanation for the three main kinds of symptoms, which provides a parallel account for action and thought monitoring (our second feature above). Shallice's model for the control of action contrasts two functional levels. One is the "contention scheduling system" (CSS), which activates effectors on the basis of environmental affordances. It is taken to be a "low-level" system that can perform routine or complex actions; it is regulated by mutual inhibition (winner takes all). However, according to this model, there is a higher-level form of control, called the "supervisory attentional system" (SAS). The latter is able to trigger nonroutine actions or actions that do not involve stimuli presently perceived. When SAS is active, it can invoke CSS-stored motor programs in an endogenous way (action is no longer under the control of external stimuli). Various channels can be used to harness CSS programs to SAS, in particular natural language—which allows for the storage of plans of action and delayed commands in working memory—and episodic memory (in which a variety of situations are stored with their respective affordances).

Now, what is the functional difference between SAS and CSS? Shallice hypothesizes that the SAS has access to a representation of the environment and of the organism's intentions and cognitive capacities, whereas CSS only performs stimulus-driven, routine action programs.[2] Thus the main feature of SAS that allows it both to provide an agent with a conscious access to her actions and to control routine actions is a metarepresentational capacity, that is, a capacity to represent oneself as having representations. An agent becomes able to act on her plans, instead of reacting to the environment, when that agent can form the conscious thought that she has such and such an intention.

Frith's (1992) theory works from Shallice's model to argue that an impaired metarepresentational capacity might account for distinctive features of patients' intentions and actions. "Specific features of schizophrenia," Frith writes, "might arise from specific abnormalities in metarepresentation. This is the cognitive mechanism that enables us to be aware of our goals, our intentions, and the intentions of other people."[3] If metarepresentation is disrupted, a patient not only will be unable to select actions endogenously and to monitor them (for lack of a conscious representation of her own intentions) but also will be impaired in attributing an action or an intention to herself (or to others). Furthermore, impaired metarepresentation will disrupt conscious access to the contents of one's mental states.[4] If metarepresentation is malfunctioning, an "imbalance" occurs between higher-level conscious processes and lower-level unconscious processes. As a result, patients become aware only of the contents of propositions, not of the metarepresentations in which they are embedded. Having had metarepresentations in the past, they are still able to attempt forming them. But they end up grasping only the embedded contents: When trying to form the thought that someone thinks about P, they might only think "P." This same process would occur in inserted thought and in the sense of a loss of agency in action. Instead of considering some form of action, they will mistake the thought of a possible action for an order to act.[5]

5.2.3   Discussion

This unifying theory, Frith (1992) admits, runs the risk of being "overinclusive,"[6] in that it predicts that every form of metarepresentation should be the possible target of a symptom, whether in language, in social attribution, and so on, which is not the case. On the contrary, Frith and his colleagues have observed that dissociations do occur in tasks supposed to tax metarepresentational capacity. For example, a patient can have trouble monitoring her intentions while being capable of inferring the intentions of others in indirect speech (Corcoran and Frith 1995). Furthermore, patients with schizophrenia do not appear, as a rule, to be unable to report on their own mental states; rather, they are considered to be hyperreflexive (Parnas and Sass 2001). An additional difficulty is that the model fails to account for the fact that patients who have lost the sense of agency never admit that they do not know why they act but infer that *someone else* is acting through their own mind or body. Extraneity remains a mysterious feature of schizophrenic experience.

5.3   Alternative Accounts of the Parallel between Action Control and Thought Insertion: The Motor Control View (Frith, Campbell, Jeannerod)

5.3.1   Frith's Comparator Model

In addition to the metarepresentational account summarized above, Chris Frith (1992) also sketches a motor-control explanation of delusions of agency, an explanation that turns out to be independent from the metarepresentational view and has since become the dominant view in the field, to the detriment of Frith's own former hypothesis. Patients' specific difficulty in monitoring their actions might be a consequence of a faulty or irregular efference mechanism of efference copy. In a normal subject, each time an action is launched, a copy of the intended movement is generated to compare it with the observed feedback. Such a comparator cuts down the amount of feedback required to check whether the action is successful and makes control of action in normal subjects smooth and quick. In schizophrenia, the comparator might be faulty,[7] thus depriving the agent both of the capacity to anticipate on the observed feedback and to consciously take responsibility for her actions.

How does this view deal with the parallel between action and thought? Frith invokes Irwin Feinberg's (1978) idea that thinking might also involve a "sense of effort and deliberate choice": "If we found ourselves thinking without any awareness of the sense of effort that reflects central monitoring, we might well experience these thoughts as alien and, thus, as being inserted in our minds" (p. 81). It is not clear, however, in what a "sense of effort" might consist when no motor output is apparent. Furthermore, it is not clear whether the sense of effort presumably involved in thinking should be tagged as ownership (having a subjective feeling that one has a thought) rather than agency (the feeling that one is producing "deliberately" that thought).

5.3.2   The Frith–Campbell View on Agency in Thought

In a series of papers (1998, 1999, 2002), John Campbell attempts to answer these two questions. According to him, the preserved sense of ownership in thought is dependent on what he calls "introspective knowledge," whereas the sense of agency in thought stems from a mechanism similar to efferent copy of action signals. Campbell hypothesizes that a *motor instruction* might normally mediate between background beliefs and desires, on the one hand, and the formation of a thought, on the other: "the background beliefs and desires cause the motor instruction to be issued," which "causes the occurrent thought" (Campbell 1999, p. 617). This explains "how the ongoing stream of occurrent thoughts can be monitored and kept on track" (Campbell 1999, p. 617).

There are several problems raised by the Frith–Campbell "control" model, in particular by the motor picture of thought formation.[8] It has been observed that imagining performing action A (a particular kind of thought), activates motor-related brain structures that are normally active when A is performed.[9] Some inserted thoughts have an imperative form, which might be interpreted as a failure to attribute intentions to self. But many cases of inserted thought do not include any reference to an action and thus cannot be explained by misattributed agency. Why should motor activity be involved in thinking, for example, about the Pythagorian theorem? It seems implausible, prima facie, to speculate that symbol activation and sentence generation "in the head" actually involve "manipulating" items, which would in turn require an efference copy mechanism.

A second objection is that many thoughts come to mind without a prior intention (or even without any "intention-in-action") that would make current ideation under

immediate intentional control. Indeed if every thought presupposed a former intention, we would embark on an infinite regress.[10] It does not seem that we normally
intend to move from one thought to the next. The process of thinking does not seem
to be constrained, in general, by former intentions. Furthermore, many of our ideas
are not experienced as ours; for example, in a conversation, we process thoughts that
are conveyed to us; we have no trouble both having the sense that we entertain a
thought, understand it, process its consequences, and so forth and attributing its
source to another thinker.[11] The motor view, therefore, seems to deal rather poorly
with the parallel between action and thought.

5.3.3 Simulation and Naked Intentions

A different way of bringing action and thought closer is to consider action in its covert
as well as overt aspects. This is the way in which Jeannerod and Pacherie (2004)
approach the problem: They propose that the existence of overt behavior should not
be a prerequisite for the sense of agency. They agree with Frith that the degree of mismatch between predicted and observed feedback modulates activation in the right
inferior parietal lobule and is responsible for external attributions of action (see also
Jeannerod, this volume, and Farrer et al. 2003); the feeling of control is indeed
inversely related to the activation level in this structure. However, they attempt to
understand why covert actions, such as those performed in imagination, are also susceptible to being attributed to self or to other. Their solution consists in emphasizing
two facts. First, simulatory mechanisms are elicited when observing as well as imagining and executing actions: intentions to act are thus represented impersonally, that
is, independently from the representation of an agent's having formed that intention
and/or executed that action (such impersonal intentions are nicely labeled "naked
intentions"). Second, patients with schizophrenia have a general difficulty in
(covertly) simulating actions. Evidence from subjects with auditory hallucination suggests that they do not expect feedback from their own inner speech—another form of
covert, simulatory activity.[12] A defective simulation mechanism, rather than a defective action-monitoring mechanism, could therefore be responsible for an impaired
sense of agency in patients with schizophrenia. Unable to simulate the covert operations needed for attribution, these patients fail to identify some of their own actions
and thus may misattribute them to others as well as misattribute others' actions to
themselves.

Jeannerod and Pacherie's claim that there exists a neurally identified representational level that is common to overt and to covert behavior is clearly of major importance for understanding not only the nature of schizophrenic impairments but also
the sense of agency in normal subjects; their view implies that simulatory mechanisms
have to be functional even before a comparator comes into play. Their account,
however, raises several new and interesting questions. First and foremost, does

impaired simulation per se underlie the patients' deficits? How is it that a person with schizophrenia has no problem simulating *her own movements* but has difficulty simulating goal-directed actions in the context of *attribution*? Is self-identity affected by impaired self-attribution of actions, and how so? How is the asymmetry between the sense of subjectivity and the sense of agency to be explained? Finally, why is it that attribution of action and of thought are both impaired if the patients' primary disorder has to do with simulating bodily actions?

In order to answer these questions, we need to be more explicit about the architecture of representations of action and to better understand their dynamic relations with self–other representations. The present proposal explores the possibility that there is a functional connection between thought and action, which explains why extraneity (delusions of control and of influence) applies to thoughts as well as to actions. This proposal is compatible with a view such as Jeannerod and Pacherie's, in which simulation is at the core of the generation and understanding of action.

5.4 An Alternative Proposal: Clearing the Theoretical Background

We take the main contributions of Frith and Jeannerod's groups to be the following. Frith had two important but very different hypotheses. One was that very different symptoms in schizophrenia can be accounted for by an impaired metarepresentational capacity, whose links with executive competence have been emphasized by Shallice. The second was that patients with schizophrenia fail to identify and to self-attribute their intentions as a result of a failure in a comparator device. Jeannerod proposed that the main impairment is not related to the monitoring of action but rather involves the simulatory mechanisms that make feedback prediction possible.

The present proposal aims to retain the advantages of a theory that accounts for a disturbance of thought as well as of action, as in Frith's metarepresentational view, while also trying to understand the specificity of the delusional experience in schizophrenia in control terms, in a way compatible with some aspects of Jeannerod and Pacherie's proposal. In short, I want to show that the parallel between thought insertion and impaired volition is grounded in the very control structure of mental activity, a structure that is common to thought and action. My claim is built on three assumptions that must be made explicit before I attempt to articulate my hypothesis on the phenomenology of volition in schizophrenia. First, simulation occurs in the brain as part of a control-monitoring sequence. Second, control levels are embedded, such that lower-level processing can be reused (redescribed for other goals) at higher levels. Third, metacognition, rather than metarepresentation, is used in many contexts requiring insight about one's own competencies and informational states. Recent results show that metacognition is present in animals with no metarepresentational capacity.

5.4.1 Ubiquity of Simulation and Mental Architecture

Simulation occurs because the essential structure of the mind is a control structure. Simulating a sequence of action, or a sequence of external events, amounts to building a dynamic model of the internal or external environment. This dynamic model is constructed covertly (in an implicit, nonconscious way) on the basis of prior learning. It helps produce internal feedback that provides detailed anticipations of reafferences in the absence of any actual engagement in the world. This simulatory process has been shown to be involved both in the production and the observation of actions by others (Decety and Chaminade 2003; Grezes et al. 2004).

Given that negative feedback control introduces intrinsic delays in the sensorimotor loop, a useful simulation must combine a feedforward dynamic model of an effector with an internal negative feedback loop to reduce such delays (Miall et al. 1993). Such a "Smith Predictor" is a two-loop structure: The inner loop provides a prediction of the outcome of each motor command sent to the effector, whereas the outer loop provides a prediction of the feedback synchronous with the actual feedback. Thus, it is an internal feedback mechanism that operates in a feed-forward mode. As has been shown by Miall et al. (1993), this type of model might be multiply realized in the cerebellum and underly a number of predictions concerning the timing or the sensory reafference of a variety of action signals (Miall and Wolpert 1996).

Now a consequence of the present proposal is that, as far as control is concerned, there is no real contrast between mental and bodily action. Indeed, a familiar claim in metacognitive studies is that thought as well as bodily action can be controlled (Nelson and Narens 1990). Metacognition refers to the kind of *knowledge* that a cognitive organism has of its own cognitive functioning and to the various *processes* that are involved in controlling and monitoring its own informational states. From this perspective, there is no fundamental difference whether control applies to external or to internal actions.[13] In both cases, the brain uses its own internal states and stored reafferences to simulate and regulate its own processes. In both cases, the brain must model dynamically one or several sequences of potential activity, launch the execution of one of these sequences—overtly or only covertly—and compare the observed to the predicted outcome. These forms of control indeed require the same kind of predicted and observed feedback; they all develop through the same kind of monitoring processes. If this view holds, it could help us understand impaired intentions, actions, and occurrent thoughts in one fell swoop, in the spirit of Shallice (1988) and Frith (1992), although metarepresentation would no longer play a role in the new model; as will be shown below, the unifying feature of the various processes impaired in schizophrenia involves metacognition rather than metarepresentation.

It may be objected that bodily action brings with it rich reafferences about the world (that may later be covertly simulated), while mental activity apparently does not. What are the reafferences, say, of searching one's memory or appreciating whether a plan is feasible? Furthermore, overt action engages not only the brain but also the body, in particular the hands, limbs, and posture. The feedback in bodily action thus seems to be inherently nonmental, but rather corporeal–environmental, in contrast to the kind of feedback one has in situations involving metamemory such as the feeling of knowing, or the "tip of the tongue" phenomenon, and so forth. Is there a true distinction between these two types of feedback?

Let us first observe that bodily experience plays a role in bodily action insofar as it represents an action in progress and related external events; *bodily sensations* help us recognize whether the action being performed is coherent with our intention; these sensations are useful only insofar as they are *reafferences*, that is, perceptions that depend on former commands and are anticipated by internal feedback (conscious perceptual imagery and nonconscious dynamic models). The same structure operates in mental actions. For example, a subject who tries to remember a proper name expects that she will have a specific experience prior to any actual remembering; she will either have the feeling of knowing, or the feeling of not-knowing the name in question. In the first case, the distinctive feeling might be triggered by the propagation of activation in the subject's memory network. In the second, the absence of this expected level of activation might trigger a distinct state. Insofar as it correlates with actual success, this feeling of knowing is obviously of crucial epistemic relevance: It allows the subject to be confident in her memory, and to launch a search only (or mostly) when potentially successful. But this epistemic property may be based on a reafferent signal associated with the activation level of a specific structure.

Another sort of metacognitive feeling is the sense of something being "feasible by me." When planning to execute a new task—for example, lift a heavy object—one has to simulate how to grip it and so forth. Predicted reafferences based on prior experience with similar tasks help the agent decide whether she is able to handle the task at hand.

To summarize, although the word "reafference" is usually applied to perception, it may have a broader applicability. The feeling of knowing, just as the feeling of being able, or other metacognitive feelings, can also be counted as a reafference insofar as (i) it is collected on the basis of a prior command; (ii) it is the dynamic properties of a specific brain/mental process, that is, properties relevant for action, that are collected; and (iii) its function is to help the perceiving agent predict whether or not her action will be successful. If this is correct, there is no real contrast, from a control viewpoint, between "internal" and "external" reafferences. In both cases, the information collected represents an objective state of affairs: in the case of a bodily action, the expected/observed content of a perception, for example, "that some external goal state is (about to be) reached," and in the case of a mental action, "that some internal goal state is (about to be) reached," for example, "that the retrieved name is correct." Obviously, modeling the external world and modeling internal processes have different functions. The former kind of information processing has to do with coping with a changing world, the second with the limitations of internal resources and with the feasability of the operations required by various mental processes.[14] But the forms of control might nevertheless be quite similar and involve in part the same anatomical structures. The idea that these two forms of control have the very same structure whether the reafferences are internal, proximal, or distal can be illustrated with two recent results in neuroscience.

First, Miguel Nicolelis and his collaborators have shown that a monkey can learn to control a robot to which it is connected in a "closed-loop brain–machine interface" (BMIc)—the robot is directly wired to neurons in the frontal and parietal areas (Nicolelis 2000). Using visual feedback, monkeys are indeed able to reach and grasp objects using the robot's arms, without moving their own limbs. As learning develops, a functional reorganization in cortical areas takes place: The function of this reorganization is to incorporate the dynamic properties of the BMIc into sensory and motor cortical representations. The important point for our present discussion is that monkeys learn to reach and grasp virtual objects with a robot *in the absence of overt or covert arm movements*. They can also learn to move a robot arm separated from their own body. This "mechanical actuator" is acting out the subject's motor intentions in the absence of any proprioceptive feedback: Vision provides all the necessary feedback for the cortical mapping of new commands. This fascinating experiment shows that there is more to external action than goal-directed behavior using one's body. It suggests a more general view of action in which an agent acts anytime she applies a command and monitoring sequence, in order to reach an outcome. Whether or not bodily movements are used in this sequence is a secondary matter.

A second example demonstrates human subjects' ability to use visual information to control brain activity. A study by Bock et al. (2003) has shown that human subjects are able to control regional brain activity using a form of feedback still further removed from ordinary perceptual reafferences, that is, real-time functional magnetic resonance imaging "neuro-feedback." Subjects in this experiment were provided visual access (through a brain–computer interface; BCI) to the blood-oxygenation-level-dependent (BOLD) responses of two preselected brain areas (supplementary motor area and parahippocampal place area) and were able within a few sessions to accomplish a given "mental" task, that is, to reach a preselected (de)activation level in these areas. This study offers a very good example of how metacognitive activity is engaged in reaching preestablished goals—here, to produce a given BOLD response—in a way that applies indiscriminately to various brain areas (whether purely informational, like memory, or executive, like motor areas). In this type of approach, the very distinction between bodily and mental action becomes murky.

These two types of studies suggest that, contrary to prima facie intuitions, the experimental setting of a BCI or BMIc is in some sense perfectly ecological: The brain indeed interfaces the present states of the world and the past interactions of the organism with it, in order to better cope with future situations. In such an interface, there is no "internal state" that is not meant to reflect external states, and there is no perception of the environment that is not meant to potentially influence future actions and motivations; command and monitoring are the two dimensions of plasticity that the brain uses to adjust itself to the world dynamics. In all these cases, the controlling brain might be simulating its own processes in order to extract from the simulated dynamics the relevant potential reafferences and the final outcome of the projected action.

5.4.2 Diversity of Simulation Levels: Control Hierarchy across Dynamical Units

Let us then come back to our prior question: Is simulation per se the site of the deficit in patients with schizophrenia, as is claimed by Jeannerod and Pacherie? These authors defend their view by emphasizing that there is a specific level at which actions are represented (retrieved, recognized, identified, imagined, planned) that is independent of the process of social attribution ("who did it?").[15] This representational level is engaged when covertly simulating actions, whether overt (in acting) or covert (in observing actions in others or in planning and imagining one's own). What would be impaired in patients with schizophrenia is the very experience of agency (rather than the level of conscious control of action). Patients would have difficulty attributing overt *or covert* actions to themselves or others due to an impaired ability to simulate actions in general. As Jeannerod further explains in the present volume, changes in patterns of cortical connectivity might disrupt either the networks mediating different representations or the relative intensity of activation in the areas constituting these networks.

But simulating action by invoking various representations of action is not the only process involved in metacognitive evaluation and in attribution of action. There are various ways in which an action—or any dynamic event, internal or external—can be evaluated; accordingly there should be different functional control loops at play, interacting in a semihierarchical way.[16] The diversity of control levels is a direct consequence of the fact that a dynamic, flexible control structure such as a human mind must monitor sequences developing on various time scales and dealing with various environmental properties. An event can be judged *for its sensorimotor adequacy, for its instrumental adequacy, for its present and future social consequences, and finally for its resonance with long-term values and life goals.* Corresponding to these various time scales and interests, we find a succession of embedded control-evaluative schemas: At the *motor level*, the move is judged as correct or incorrect at a postural spatio-temporal level; at the *action output level*, the successful completion of the intended action is evaluated; at the *agency level*, the action is attributed to its author, whether the self or another individual; at the *social level*, it is deemed whether the action, executed by self or by another, is compatible with a set of values that the agent is attempting to realize in her behavior, in line with her status, life projects, and so forth.[17]

If there is such an embedding of control levels, as seems to be the case, then the notion of simulation becomes a generic term that might apply at each control level, but each time *in a different way*. Some forms of simulation might involve the effectors (muscles, joints, proximal limbs), some might involve perceptual memories of the external world, whether physical (object positions, events to be reached) or social (forming bonds, gaining influence, etc.). Finally, emotional properties should play a crucial role in retrieving the scenarios involved in specific plans or social attributions.

Given the existence of such a control hierarchy, the question remains how the brain manages to regulate the informational flow across the various levels. For example, once an action is simulated, an additional task involves sending the relevant information to another structure in charge of executing the desired higher-level task: Is this representation to be used as an internal command to act, as a piece of evidence to be factored into a prediction of what another person will do, as a cue to understand hidden goals and specific (true or false) beliefs, as a key move in a value-laden larger scheme? These various ways of using a given motor representation may look similar. But evidence from evolutionary biology suggests that they are in fact different: Each one functionally builds on the former; they are acquired successively in phylogeny and in ontogeny (at least in humans, the only beings who normally possess them all in adulthood). Thus, a major task that the brain has to carry out is not only to simulate actions but also to dispatch the output of a simulation to the specific contextually adequate control center. This task typically requires metacognitive processing.

5.4.3   From Metarepresentation to Metacognition

An important and distinctive feature of schizophrenic delusions, independent of their specific themes, is that patients fail to appreciate the extent to which their thoughts are deviant with respect to norms. Most patients with delusions seem to lack insight into how others will evaluate their utterances and react to them. This symptom has often been taken to involve an abnormal capacity to represent others' mental states. It might be tempting indeed to interpret this fact, as well as those discussed at the end of the preceding section, as supporting the metarepresentational view; the various capacities distinguished above may seem to differ from each other only in that some are invoked directly while others are imbedded in metarepresentations such as "He desires X to do Y," "She evaluates that X will help her get O," "she sees herself as being good at Y-ing," and so on. In this section, I want to show why metacognitive processes can be understood in a way that does not necessarily involve such a metarepresentational format.

The functional difference between metacognition and metarepresentation is obviously of major relevance to our present discussion. Whereas metarepresentation is a theoretical (language-based) capacity for reporting (explicitly) on the contents of mental representations, metacognition is a practical (implicit) capacity for guiding mental activity (Proust 2003a). As we saw in section 5.4.1, metacognition includes all the processes through which primary mental functions are subjected to evaluation and control on the basis of their informational features. A key example of metacognition is metamemory, which determines what is accessible in memory and triggers memory searches when appropriate (Koriat 1993); another example is perceptual attention, which determines priorities and thresholds in information intake. The type of metacognitive competence involved in agency encompasses control, monitoring, and self-attribution of thought, of intention, and of action (planning, e.g., relies heavily on appreciating contextually one's own ability to perform various tasks).

In the Shallice–Frith model, summarized in section 5.2.2, the metacognitive realization that an action is being performed or that an intention is being entertained by the self or another agent is required to be in a specific metarepresentational format. It has recently been found, however, that this is not the case. Recent findings in animal cognition indeed suggest that animals without a theory of mind (i.e., unable to metarepresent their own states in any explicit way), such as monkeys and dolphins, are able to evaluate their present ability to perform a particular task; they can judge which of two tasks (e.g., visual density discrimination tasks; Smith et al. 2003) they are more competent to perform. It is plausible that a more basic capacity to mentally simulate a process (running a forward model to collect internal feedback) allows for an implicit form of (metacognitive) self-knowledge, which cannot be made explicit in nonverbal animals. Thus, metarepresentational capacity might crucially depend on existing metacognitive skills for its normal functioning.[18]

5.5   A Control View of Impaired Volition in Schizophrenia

It should be clear by now that the distinction between overt and covert simulation does not carry much functional weight. The core of the present proposal is that impaired volition should affect bodily as well as mental actions. As we saw in section 5.4.2, simulation is part of a control structure that also involves other processing steps. We now need to identify which processing steps are affected when a specific intention to act is "disowned" and thus misattributed. A way of addressing this question in control terms consists in trying to reconstruct the various control loops that are involved in the experience of agency and in the attribution of action.

5.5.1   Step 1: "Mineness" of Phenomenal Experience

Step 1 involves a control loop that is responsible for an elementary feeling of "mineness"—ownership—experienced when a perception (or action) cycle is developing. This feeling corresponds to the sense of the current experience being one's own. A perception cycle refers to the programming of a certain pattern of exploration of the world and the reafferences produced as a result, which in turn yield a new cycle. The sense of ownership associated with all forms of phenomenal consciousness is generally analyzed as including two types of representations: (i) that the perception (intention, memory) is about some event and (ii) that the perception (intention, memory) is mine. Should a given perceptual event be divided into what is seen and the fact that it is seen by [me]?[19] What is often disregarded in such an analysis is the fact that the sense of ownership is generally *not* explicitly reflexive; in Perry's (2000) terms a conscious experience reflexively "concerns" a subject, but this relation of an experience—or of a thought—to the thinker does not have to be explicitly represented as an "articulated" constituent. The self does not need to be represented as such in this elementary form of experience—a form arguably present in "selfless" animals. What then is the correct analysis of the sense of mineness associated with perception or thought in general?

From a control theory viewpoint, what makes an experience mine is that it involves a set of (monitored) reafferences of a specific kind. A plausible hypothesis is that the feature of the reafferences that carries the implicit reflexive value of *mineness* is a specific *emotional* marker:[20] Only perception-cum-emotion can trigger the appropriate motivation to respond to the world in a self-relevant way without the need for a representation of self. In this light, the sense of subjectivity can be seen as a primitive metacognitive feeling, analogous to a feeling of knowing. This feeling applies to bodily states, as well as to thoughts and experiences. It allows the organism to distinguish, on the basis of the reafferences, what "concerns itself," that is, how the affordances present in the environment relate to its own fitness.

An alternative hypothesis is to take the sense of mineness as essentially associated with body-centered spatial content.[21] This does not seem to be a solution, however, as it begs the question of how bodily sensations feel like they are mine; furthermore, the sense of mineness applies to thoughts as well as to bodily sensations; it is not clear why the latter should be taken as more primitive or more substantial than the former.

To make the case that emotion is a crucial factor in mineness, let us articulate what conditions have to be present for an experience to be sensed as one's own; they should include three types of clauses:

1. The experience has a certain phenomenological intensity and categorical content that covaries with a state of the world.
2. Its phenomenology refers to a specific source (usually a given modality) that carries metacognitive information about the experience.
3. The phenomenology includes a marker of emotional value to the organism itself. This emotional value is associated with specific motivations and dispositions to act.

These three properties of a phenomenological state help clarify the kind of reflexivity that the sense of mineness entails. Clause 1 relates to the representational aspect of a (monitored) reafference (experiences carry content, i.e., they have intentionality). Clause 2 articulates the metacognitive constituent implicit in phenomenology (as Brentano 1924 observed, perceiving a red thing involves an awareness that this thing is seen rather than heard, but this awareness is "implicit," so it can lead to further control operations without being explicit and metarepresentational). Clause 3 explains why a subject treats reflexivity as self-*concern*: Emotional perspective stems directly from the innate capacity to evaluate perceptual input and to exploit the affordances in goal-directed actions.

In bodily action, emotions are normally associated with perceptual and, in particular, with somatosensory and proprioceptive reafferences; in thought, there might be at least two sources of emotional content. One is the content of thoughts, which is associated with prior emotional responses to external events; the other is the metacognitive value of thoughts as reafferences: For example, subjects can be worried about (proud of, ashamed of, etc.) their cognitive performances.[22]

It is important to observe that reafferences carry an emotional marker of mineness whether a willed action or a passive movement is performed. This observation leads us to make a distinction between the sense of agency and the sense of ownership, in contrast with Thomas Metzinger (2003; this volume), who takes the former to be a subcategory of the latter. The fact that the two phenomenal dimensions of experience may coalesce should not lead one to ignore their functional difference (possibly associated with different phylogenetic origins). The very fact that the sense of ownership is unimpaired in patients with schizophrenia, whose sense of agency is impaired, might thus be accounted for by the fact that the sense of ownership belongs to a primary functional/phenomenal loop that feeds into higher-level loops, for example, the agency loop. This question will be addressed below in section 5.5.2.4.

It is likely, however, that other pathologies might directly affect the sense of ownership, which should in turn disturb higher-level control loops; if the present hypothesis is on the right track, an impaired emotional system might fail to trigger a feeling of self-concern, which should in turn massively disturb the agency-control loop and the attribution-of-agency loop. This might be the case in patients with Cotard syndrome: Gerrans (1999) argues that the absence of affective processing in these patients might explain that perception and cognition have no emotionally significant bodily consequences and thus are not accompanied by feelings of ownership. We might speculate that the first level in our control system—underlying the sense of ownership—engages the primary somatosensory cortex, the cerebellum as well as the thalamus and the amygdala (the latter structures providing a sense of mineness to the associated sensorimotor feature detected by the former; Damasio 1994; LeDoux 1996; Leube et al. 2003; Ruby and Decety 2003).

In brief: The sense of ownership is prereflexive. It does not take a metarepresentation and the resulting self-attribution for an experience to feel like mine. Indeed ownerhip is implicitly experienced in the subject's emotional reafferences when he or she has this perception, performs this action or has this thought.[23]

5.5.2 Step 2: Sense of Agency

A sense of agency does not amount to sensing that one's body is moving or that thoughts are rolling in one's head: Such a feeling belongs to the experience of ownership; the proper locus of the sense of agency is the feeling that the movement, or the thought process currently performed, are performed intentionally. The capacity to develop contrasting phenomenologies for passive and active movement is a major condition of survival. The metacognitive model sketched above provides an account of this capacity.

5.5.2.1 Challenging the classical "motor" view   According to the "motor theory" view presented in section 5.3, the agent recognizes herself as acting when observed and predicted sensory reafferences are delivering congruent messages. This requires (i) that an efferent copy of a motor command has been used as input by a specific forward model to generate a state estimate and (ii) that the latter is used to compare in another forward output model the predicted with the observed sensory consequences of motor commands. In this section, what I will argue is the following: (i) Such a comparison proceeds on the basis of specific instructions as to which sensory afferences to take into account. (ii) These instructions already depend on a metacognitive understanding of the task being performed. The agent might thus metacognize her being active (in thought or in action) by relying on a task-specific signal selectively perturbed in patients with schizophrenia. This proposal is still speculative, but it seems compatible with classical data and indeed finds support in recent studies.

5.5.2.2 Deluding the motor system   To introduce the proposal, I will discuss work by Sarah Blakemore and colleagues (Blakemore et al. 2003; Blakemore 2003) in which an interesting parallel is developed between a hypnosis-induced and a schizophrenic form of delusion of passive movement. In order to understand what distinguishes self-generated from externally generated sensory events in normal subjects, Blakemore et al. used an experimental paradigm based on hypnotic suggestion. All subjects were hypnotized prior to test. In an active movement condition, subjects were instructed to raise their left arm. In the passive movement condition, subjects were told that their arm would be moved by a pulley (the pulley did not actually move it). Highly hypnotizable subjects moved their arm as suggested but reported no feeling of agency (they took their arm to be raised by the device). The cerebellum and the parietal operculum were found to be more active in the passive condition.

Interpreting these data in terms of the dual loop forward model discussed above, Sarah Blakemore hypothesizes that the forward output model is specifically involved in the sense of agency, while the forward dynamic model regulating the movement itself is not (because the execution of the movement was unchanged, whether sensed as active or passive by the subjects). She thus explains agency in classical terms, through congruency with expected feedback and input cancellation. Lack of congruency (experienced in the Passive condition) would trigger cerebellar error messages to the posterior parietal cortex on the right side, gradually promoting the impression that the action was under foreign control (Spence et al. 1997; Farrer et al. 2003).

Interestingly, Blakemore (2003) offers two other possible accounts of the sense of agency in an attempt to explain why a lack of congruency should be felt by the hypnotized subjects. (The latter actually did send a motor command to the arm, which presumably triggered an efferent copy signal. So why is a noncongruency signal delivered?) The first possibility is that there might be a frontal route to the sense of agency; referring to evidence that hypnotic suggestion results in an increase in regional cerebral blood flow in left frontal cortical areas,[24] she speculates that hypnotic suggestion might prevent motor intentions to reach the forward output model. The second explanation draws from work on attention. Attention to a particular stimulus is well known to enhance its sensory processing. Indeed, it has been shown recently that preparing to attend to an anticipated stimulus can modulate activity in sensory brain areas *before* stimulus onset (Driver and Frith 2000). The brain can covertly prepare a template of what it is supposed to detect by making appropriate "baseline shifts" in sensory activation. It is thus plausible that one of the main effects of hypnotic suggestion might consist in restricting the subject's attention to part of the stimulus (its passive component). Given this top-down influence of attention, the comparator would ignore stimuli that have to do with willful activity. This shows that the comparator might not be the decisive structure for attributing the source of an action to self or other. The forward output model on which the comparator bases its predictions might already be preselected or filtered by attentional mechanisms.

Blakemore suggests that a similar mechanism might underlie delusions of control in schizophrenia. However, this mechanism has to be spelled out in more detail. We will see that, upon closer scrutiny, the proposal appears to contradict the classical view on one main point.

If hypnotic suggestion prevents motor intentions from reaching the forward output model in normal subjects, does it help us understand why patients with schizophrenia are misattributing their actions to external agents? Presumably, a feature common to Blakemore's subjects and to patients with schizophrenia is that, in both cases, an instruction is sent to the cerebellum to ignore the fact that the movement is indeed voluntary; in other words, the cerebellum selects a normal feed-forward dynamic model while failing to associate it with the appropriate feed-forward output model, which triggers right parietal activation.[25]

This account has to be refined, however, for in fact the induced delusions are different: Patients with schizophrenia attribute their movements to an *external* agency, whereas hypnotized subjects are simply experiencing their movement as *passive*. Blakemore suggests that this difference might be explained by the contrast between being aware and being unaware of one's intention: The patient with delusion of control would know her intention, then misattribute it to an external source for lack of congruence in the comparator; the hypnotized subject would not know her intention, and thus would not attribute it to an external agency, but rather would feel the movement as passive. However ingenious and promising, this reasoning is incomplete: How does, in this account, a patient with delusions come to be aware of having an intention (before she acts)? This is a crucial question indeed, one that needs to be asked to fully understand the sense of agency. Only a theory that relies on the covert part of intentional action, such as Jeannerod and Pacherie's or the present proposal, can offer a noncircular answer to that question.

Let us now briefly explore the second route. Here, the idea is that both hypnotized subjects and patients with delusion of control fail to use their *attention* in a normal way. Focusing their attention on sensations associated with passive movement, they accordingly report having no sense of agency. But here again, we need to understand why patients *ignore* the willful component of the reafferences in the output model. It seems clear that the attentional account also jeopardizes the classical view, which is shown to be crucially incomplete: If the comparator is indeed under attentional influence, then it only plays a secondary role in the impairment of the sense of agency. What needs to be examined is no longer the comparator but the attentional commands that are sent to it.

5.5.2.3 A metacognitive interpretation of the alternative accounts The two kinds of explanation sketched in Blakemore (2003) can easily be made to merge into one unifying metacognitive framework. Metacognition is the capacity to regulate brain activity on the basis of incoming internal and external information. Attention allocation and task selection are essential components of this regulatory system. The top-down effect of a frontal inhibitory command (preventing the relevant intention to influence the output model) can be redescribed in attentional terms. Under hypnotic suggestion, or in a schizophrenic delusion of control, attention can be restricted to the passive features of the executed movement. Whether the specific attentional baseline shift documented by Driver and Frith (2000) is under prefrontal control is not indicated. But other studies have emphasized that a system exerting a top-down influence on the selection for stimuli and responses involves the superior frontal cortex and its projections to the dorsal posterior parietal cortex. This system might integrate top-down and bottom-up information, in order to form and update the "salience maps," that is, to determine which objects should be selected for recognition and action even before they are perceived (Corbetta and Shulman 2002). It is plausible to speculate that the attentional restriction in hypnotized subjects and in patients is triggered by biased or impaired frontal signals, respectively, which fail to induce correct predictions of sensory reafferences in the parietal area (in the output forward model).

This explanation is compatible with traditional views on impaired executive memory in schizophrenia: In patients with schizophrenia, it may be that insufficient gain is allotted to a course of mental action, namely, an intention to act physically or to develop a train of thoughts. The inhibitory/gain component of selective attention, usually taken to belong to control processes (Umiltà and Stablum 1998) and likely a prefrontal lobe function, has been shown to be impaired in patients with schizophrenia (Franzen and Ingvar 1975; Goldman-Rakic 1991). Patients have a general problem discriminating familiar from new information, and maintaining their goals in "working memory." Both types of problems are well-documented manifestations of prefrontal malfunction. In Goldman-Rakic's terms, the disorder comprises "a breakdown in the processes by which representational knowledge governs behavior."[26]

More recent work lends additional support to the metacognitive component of impaired agency in schizophrenia. It has been shown that the rostral prefrontal cortex (Brodmann Area 10) might be involved in prospective memory when task coordination is required (Koechlin et al. 1999; Burgess et al., this volume). The evidence suggests that this capacity is impaired in patients with schizophrenia (Elvevåg et al. 2003). More generally, the function of this area might be to produce, recall and evaluate internally generated information; it would contribute to the establishment of a task set before actual task performance (Christoff et al. 2003). Liddle (this volume) also develops an approach compatible with our metacognitive hypothesis, observing an abnormal activation of a supramodal "motivated attention system" in patients with schizophrenia.

These findings suggest the need to introduce a significant change in the comparator story. It is not so much that the schizophrenic patient with delusions has an impaired output forward model, as the classical view proposes. Rather, she is impaired in the ability to keep track of her intention to act over time and to inform the comparator of that intention. Shifting the main causal role to the intention to act implicates the capacity of a patient to use implicit metacognitive goals to monitor and further control his or her actions.

We are now in a position to account for the parallel between delusion of control in thought and in action The problem common to both symptoms might not primarily consist in a poor simulating capacity (a cerebellar–parietal function) but rather involves initiating and maintaining the proper simulation over time (a prefrontal top-down influence on the cerebellar–parietal function). The sense of agency, that is, the feeling associated with actively thinking and moving, might thus originate primarily in a prefrontal–parietal metacognitive reafference rather than from a parietal–cerebel-lar one.

5.5.2.4 The asymmetry between sense of ownership and sense of agency In the revised picture, the asymmetry between sense of ownership and sense of agency is an automatic consequence of an idea introduced in section 5.4.2 of *a semi-hierarchy of controlled processes*.[27] The basic idea is as follows: The control and monitoring system used to generate the sense of ownership is linked to the *hic et nunc* of perception and action in a given context; it feeds back into upper loops, such as the intentional agency or the social attribution loops, which have longer time spans, and whose content depends critically on the output of lower loops. Thus, although higher and lower loops can influence each other's activity (an example was offered above by baseline sensory shifts in attention), one can speculate that only lower loop output can be inherited by higher level representations.[28] More concretely, if a perceptual or behavioral event is not treated as mine through relevant emotional marker(s), it should fail to trigger further processing by the brain. Indeed an organism deprived of the emotions associ-ated with a "mine" feeling in a given context would not have the necessary motiva-tion to carry out further processing.

5.5.3 Step 3: Explicit Agency Attribution: A Social Control Level
Various authors, in particular philosophers, have based the feeling of agency in thought on the whole set of epistemic constraints that shape the attibution of agency.[29] According to most, it involves accessing the *content* of the thoughts involved; some even require identifying the *kind of thought* being entertained (believing, imag-ining, etc.).[30] Much research devoted to the feeling of agency in action such as Daprati et al. (1997) and Jeannerod and Pacherie (2004), as well as Blakemore (2003) has tended to identify the feeling of agency in action as a full-blown attributional mech-anism, through which the experience of action is explicitly referred to an author, whether the self or another person. One thus tends to blur the distinction between two types of attribution: The feeling of agency is the automatic, often implicit sense that an action was performed willfully; this feeling—or at least its functional equiva-lent—has to be present in one form or another in every behaving organism. The attri-bution of agency, on the other hand, is a process that requires the concept of an agent (as the source of an intentional action). The capacity to categorize goal-directed actions performed by others is a precursor of such an attribution. The animal has a primitive way of recognizing agency in others, which probably relies in part on the same neural structures as involved in action.[31] While this attributional capacity obviously could not evolve in beings with no sense of agency, there are organisms that have a feeling of agency but no attributional capacity, however primitive. An explicit attributional capacity might be necessary to identify stable agents in a social group, while a sense

of agency only plays a role in an agent's own engagement in goal-directed behavior. How should we characterize, then, the functional difference between implicit (or action-level) and explicit (or social-level) attribution of agency?

5.5.3.1 Social-level attribution and self-identity In Proust 2003b, arguments were made in favor of the view that the kind of control and monitoring involved in representing oneself as a stable entity, responsible for her deeds, and permanently engaged in corrective metacognition, occurs at a level distinct both from control loops involved in ownership and from mechanisms involved in the feeling of agency. A *third* level of control is needed to form dynamic models of one's own self as well as of others in a social group. In a nutshell, it is argued that such a representation emerges from a capacity to attribute and to keep track of one's long-term goals and values and to revise them when needed. The same capacity can also be used to simulate observed agents engaged in individual, competitive, or cooperative tasks, with possibly conflicting intentions or selfish goals. Recent work in neuroimaging is indeed compatible with this view (Decety and Chaminade 2003; Grèzes et al. 2004).

We saw above that, in schizophrenic delusions of control, the sense of agency is impaired, whereas the sense of ownership is spared. The clash between conflicting reafferences (the movement is mine but I did not execute it) is solved, at level 3, in the explicit attributional style that is characteristic of human cultures: The subject attributes her actions to another agent (or attributes other agents' actions to herself). She accordingly feels herself either as diminished and enslaved to others' wills or as amplified and extended to other agents. The emergent disorder of attribution is located at the social level; it results from a complex control structure (Adolphs 2003), which obviously exerts a top-down influence on other loops by creating an expectation of extraneity in incoming reafferences. As was shown by Decety and Sommerville (2003), executive inhibition (i.e., possibly the right lateral prefrontal cortex) plays a major role in this control structure by suppressing the prepotent self-perspective in order to understand another person.[32] This control structure for social attribution also involves external controllers: As emphasized by Frith (this volume), individual volition is also influenced at that level by exogenous constraints imposed on the subject by social partners. The susceptibility of the social control structure to external influence might account for the involvement of highly diverse areas across tasks.

5.5.3.2 Simulating one's actions versus simulating others' The present account provides a tentative answer to a question that we raised in section 5.3.3: Why does a person with schizophrenia have a specific difficulty simulating goal-directed actions in the context of *attribution* rather than *execution*? In the present analysis, the two capacities are functionally distinct. Simulating one's actions, or simulating others', relies in part on the same structures. But using a simulation to explicitly attribute an observed action to an agent requires a higher-order control loop, which integrates self-representations as well as motivational and emotional judgments. Given that this control loop requires the inhibition of self-simulatory processes and disengagement from routine evaluations (a "prefrontal" capacity), it is plausible that patients with schizophrenia fail to attribute actions in contexts which require adjustment and fine-tuning. This explains why patients are much better in executing than in attributing actions.

5.6 Conclusion

The present proposal is an attempt to account for the fact that patients suffering from delusions of control exhibit an impaired sense of agency while their sense of subjectivity both in thought and in action remains intact. The theory draws from studies showing the wide range of control structures in the mind/brain, as well as the important metacognitive apparatus through which these structures operate. It was suggested that three different comparators have to be distinguished: the sense of subjectivity relies on a "local" comparator. Motivation and emotion play a structuring role in the "mineness" of the reafferences collected by this comparator. The sense of agency emerges in a different system: cerebellar, parietal, and prefrontal structures deliver a rough categorization of self-generated—as opposed to other-generated—actions and mental activities, a competence closely related to source judgment, present in many nonhuman animals. A third system specializes in the social evaluation of the effects of an action, intention, or other thought process, given certain goals in self or in others. It seems to be present only in humans (and maybe in other primates and dolphins). It involves many structures, in particular the limbic system and the orbitofrontal and medial frontal lobe. The full-blown "human" understanding of agency results from our capacity to plan our mental and physical engagements, a second-order kind of control structure that reinterprets the output of the feeling of agency.

This type of control is necessarily exerted on local control structures responsible for the sense of subjectivity. The resulting experience normally fuses agency, ownership, and attribution in one single stream. It is not necessary, however, for a system endowed with a sense of subjectivity to maintain a sense of agency or an explicit social attribution capacity; when the higher-level control structure breaks down, the lower level can still persist, although the phenomenology changes as it operates in an uncontrolled (or abnormally controlled) mode.

There may be different grades of loss of higher-level control, from cases of patients with schizophrenia whose moderate executive difficulties translate into impressions of occasional xenopathy to patients with severe forms of dementia who have lost any capacity to act autonomously. From this perspective, action and thought are similarly organized as controlled processes, and there is no a priori reason to treat them separately: The solution offered here works in the same way for inserted thoughts and xenopathic actions.

Clearly, this proposal opens up new questions, whose relevance goes beyond purely theoretical considerations: What are the relative contributions of innate and acquired factors in the attributional system? In particular, what is the impact of exogenous social demands on attribution of agency and controlled action? How can the motivational top-down influence of the social level on the sense of agency be functionally understood? How does a theory of mind interact with this system? Does theory of mind form an essential part of the human attributional system, or does it build upon it? And finally, how, more generally, does (implicit) human metacognition benefit from an (explicit) attribution of agency? Answering these questions will not only shape social brain science but it will also deeply influence social development and education.

Acknowledgments

The research presented in this chapter has been supported by the European Science Foundation EUROCORES program *The Origin of Man, Language, and Languages*. The author expresses her gratitude to Sliman Bensmaïa for his linguistic help.

Notes

1. Grivois 1995.

2. See Shallice 1988, p. 335.

3. Frith 1992, p. 134.

4. For a philosophical elaboration of metarepresentation as a key to consciousness, see Rosenthal 1993.

5. Frith suggests that the underlying anatomical structures that might realize metarepresentational capacity consist in projections between various brain sites where primary representations are built (e.g., in the temporal lobe) to the orbitofrontal cortex, which effects the secondary embedding.

6. Frith 1992, p. 133.

7. As already shown in Frith and Done 1989, Malenka et al. 1982; see also Mlakar, Jensterle, and Frith 1994, Wolpert et al. 1995; Blakemore, Rees, and Frith 1998.

8. For a detailed discussion of this view by a philosopher, see Gallagher 2000.

9. See, e.g., Blakemore and Decety 2001.

10. This objection was articulated in Gallagher 2000. See Ryle 1949 for a general presentation of this argument, and see Proust 2001 for a line of response.

11. A third difficulty is that this model does not deal with the problem of occasionality (Gallagher's term): Why does a patient only experience certain thoughts as inserted? A fourth difficulty is that the model fails to account for the fact that patients who have lost the sense of agency never admit that they do not know why they act but infer that someone else is acting through their own mind or body.

12. Blakemore et al. 2000.

13. On "internal," i.e., "mental" actions, see Proust 2001 and Proust 2006.

14. See Proust 2006 for an analysis of "informational quality" as a crucial parameter in metacognitive prediction.

15. On this question, see Jeannerod's chapter in the present volume.

16. See Proust 2003b.

17. In this general picture, the construction of a self retaining its identity over time refers to a dedicated control structure; such a structure comprises a set of commands and feedback monitoring systems which allow one to project value in future actions, and to select from among possible goals (and associated desires) those that are compatible with certain values and global preferences. See Proust 2003b.

18. For an analysis of a possible evolutionary scenario, see Proust 2006.

19. *Me* is written in brackets to emphasize the fact that self-reference is being made in an implicit way, which does not presuppose the mastery of a concept of self.

20. See Damasio 1994, 1999.

21. As claimed by Martin (1995), "In having bodily sensations, it appears to one as if whatever one is aware of through having such sensation is a part of one's body" (p. 269); but the question remains why we sense events within our boundaries as owned by ourselves.

22. Some authors attribute to thoughts an original kind of subjective feeling (Goldman 1993; Peacocke 1998); others invoke the auditory, internal speech component of thinking as involved in the sense of subjectivity (Hoffman 1986).

23. Peacocke (1998) defends a similar view on the notion of subjective feeling. When thinking, you are trying to do something with your thought: "A specification of whether the subject's attention is occupied in trying to do something must also be included in an account of what it is like for him" (Peacocke 1998, p. 69).

24. Rainville et al. 1999.

25. As reported in section 3.3, a mismatch bertween observed and predicted feedback activates the right inferior parietal lobule, a structure involved in external attribution of actions.

26. Goldman-Rakic 1991, p. 17. Goldman-Rakic further hypothesizes that "the most likely focus of a 'lesion' in this disorder may be the corticocortical processing networks by which the prefrontal cortex 'accesses' and holds 'on line' representational knowledge of the outside world through its connections with parietal and limbic centers."

27. This hierarchy also plays a role in Stephens and Graham's (2001) model, as well as in Frith's use of Shallice's model of action; however, it is absent from a general view on the experience of acting which incorporates the sense of subjectivity.

28. See Jackendoff 1987.

29. Campbell (1997) and Stephens and Graham (2000), for example, base the sense of agency in thought on the felt coherence of an occurrent thought with long-standing dispositions. In other words, a patient denies having one particular thought because it does not fit his or her conception of himself or herself.

30. Currie and Ravenscroft (2002) relate an impaired sense of agency to mistaking one's own imaginings for beliefs (according to them, imaginings are a kind of action). In their view, a patient with a delusion of control does not realize that he or she is imagining P, believing instead that he or she believes P (while in fact he or she has no first-order belief that P).

31. Rizzolatti and Craighero 2004.

32. For an analysis of how simulation theory must be articulated to include a decoupling ability, see Proust 2002.

References

Adolphs, R. 2003. Cognitive neuroscience of human social behavior. *Nature Reviews Neuroscience, 4*, 165–178.

Blakemore, S. 2003. Deluding the motor system. *Consciousness and Cognition, 12*, 647–655.

Blakemore, S.-J., and J. Decety. 2001. From the perception of action to the understanding of intention. *Nature Reviews Neuroscience, 2*, 561–567.

Blakemore, S. J., D. A. Oakley, and C. D. Frith. 2003. Delusions of alien control in the normal brain. *Neuropsychologia, 41*, 1058–1067.

Blakemore, S.-J., G. Rees, and C. D. Frith. 1998. How do we predict the consequences of our actions? A functional imaging study. *Neuropsychologia, 36*, 521–529.

Blakemore, S.-J., J. Smith, R. Steel, E. C. Johnstone, and C. D. Frith. 2000. The perception of self-produced sensory stimuli in patients with auditory hallucinations and passivity experiences: Evidence for a breakdown in self-monitoring. *Psychological Medicine, 30*, 1131–1139.

Bock, S. W., N. Weiskopf, F. Scharnowski, K. Mathiak, R. Goebel, and N. Birbaumer. 2003. Differential neuro-feedback using a brain–computer interface (BCI) based on real-time fMRI. Posted communication, Meeting of the European Society for Cognitive Science, Osnabruck, 2003.

Brentano, F. 1924–1928. *Psychologie vom Empirischen Standpunkt*, 3 vols. Leipzig: Felix Meiner Verlag.

Campbell, J. 1998. Le modèle de la schizophrénie de Christopher Frith. In *Subjectivité et conscience d'agir, Approches cognitive et clinique de la psychose*, ed. H. Grivois and J. Proust, pp. 99–113. Paris: Presses Universitaires de France.

Campbell, J. 1999. Schizophrenia, the space of reasons, and thinking as a motor process. *Monist, 82*, 609–625.

Campbell, J. 2002. The ownership of thoughts. *Philosophy, Psychiatry, and Psychology, 9*, 35–39.

Christoff, K., L. P. T. Geddes, J. T. Ream, and J. D. E. Gabrieli. 2003. Evaluating self-generated information: Anterior prefrontal contributions to human cognition. *Behavioral Neuroscience, 117*, 1161–1168.

Coliva, A. 2002. Thought insertion and immunity to error through misidentification. *Philosophy, Psychiatry, and Psychology 9*, 41–46.

Conant, R. C., and W. R. Ashby. 1970. Every good regulator of a system must be a model of that system. *International Journal of Systems Science, I* (2), 89–97.

Corbetta, M., and G. L. Shulman. 2002. Control of goal-directed and stimulus-driven attention in the brain. *Nature Reviews Neuroscience, 31*, 201–215.

Corcoran, R., and C. D. Frith. 1996. Conversational conduct and the symptoms of schizophrenia. *Cognitive Neuropsychiatry, 1*, 305–318.

Corcoran, R., G. Mercer, and C. D. Frith. 1995. Schizophrenia, symptomatology, and social inference: Investigating "theory of mind" in people with schizophrenia. *Schizophrenia Research, 17*, 5–13.

Currie, G., and I. Ravenscroft. 2002. *Recreative Minds*. Oxford: Oxford University Press.

Damasio, A. 1994. *Descartes' Error*. New York: Harper Collins.

Damasio, A. 1999. *The Feeling of What Happens*. San Diego: Harcourt.

Daprati, E., N. Franck, N. Georgieff, J. Proust, E. Pacherie, J. Dalery, and M. Jeannerod. 1997. Looking for the agent: An investigation into self-consciousness and consciousness of the action in patients with schizophrenia. *Cognition, 65*, 71–86.

Decety J., and T. Chaminade. 2003. Neural correlates of feeling sympathy. *Neuropsychologia, 41*, 127–138.

Decety J., and J. A. Sommerville. 2003. Shared representations between self and other: A social cognitive view. *Trends in Cognitive Science, 7*, 527–533.

Desmurget, M., and S. Grafton. 2000. Forward modeling allows feedback control for fast reaching movements. *Trends in Cognitive Science, 4*, 423–431.

Driver, J., and C. D. Frith. 2000. Shifting baselines in attention research. *Nature Reviews Neuroscience, 1*, 147–148.

Elvevåg, B., E. A. Maylor, and A. L. Gilbert. 2003. Habitual prospective memory in schizophrenia. *BMC Psychiatry, 3*, 1–9.

Farrer, C., N. Franck, N. Georgieff, C. D. Frith, J. Decety, and M. Jeannerod. 2003. Modulating the experience of agency: A positron emission tomography study. *NeuroImage, 18*, 324–333.

Farrer, C., and C. D. Frith. 2002. Experiencing oneself vs. another person as being the cause of an action: The neural correlates of the experience of agency. *NeuroImage, 15*, 596–603.

Feinberg, I. 1978. Efference copy and corollary discharge: Implications for thinking and its disorders. *Schizophrenia Bulletin, 4*, 636–640.

Fourneret, P., and M. Jeannerod. 1998. Limited conscious monitoring of motor performance in normal subjects. *Neuropsychologia, 36*, 1133–1140.

Franzen, G., and D. H. Ingvar. 1975. Absence of activation in frontal structures during psychological testing of chronic schizophrenics. *Journal of Neurological and Neurosurgical Psychiatry, 38*, 1027–1032.

Frith, C. D. 1992. *The Cognitive Neuropsychology of Schizophrenia.* Hillsdale, N.J.: Lawrence Erlbaum.

Frith, C. D. 1994. Theory of mind in schizophrenia. In *The Neuropsychology of Schizophrenia*, ed. A. David, pp. 147–161. Hillsdale, N.J.: Lawrence Erlbaum.

Frith, C. D., S.-J. Blakemore, and D. M. Wolpert. 2000. Explaining the symptoms of schizophrenia: Abnormalities in the awareness of action. *Brain Research Reviews, 31*, 357–363.

Frith, C. D., and D. J. Done. 1989. Experiences of alien control in schizophrenia reflect a disorder of central monitoring of action. *Psychological Medicine, 19*, 353–363.

Gallagher, S. 2000. Self reference and schizophrenia. In *Exploring the Self*, ed. D. Zahavi, pp. 203–239. Amsterdam: John Benjamins.

Gerrans, P. 1999. Delusional misidentification as subpersonal disintegration. *Monist, 82*, 590–608.

Goldman-Rakic, P. 1991. Prefrontal cortical dysfunction in schizophrenia: The relevance of working memory. In *Psychopathology and the Brain*, ed. B. J. Carroll and J. E. Barrett, pp. 1–23. New York: Raven Press.

Grèzes, J., C. D. Frith, and R. E. Passingham. 2004. Inferring false beliefs from the actions of oneself and others: An fMRI study. *NeuroImage, 21*, 2, 744–750.

Grivois, H. 1995. *Le fou et le mouvement du monde.* Paris: Grasset.

Hoffman, R. 1986. Verbal hallucinations and language production processes in schizophrenia. *Behavioral and Brain Sciences, 9*, 503–517.

Jackendoff, R. 1987. *Consciousness and the Computational Mind.* Cambridge, Mass.: MIT Press.

Jeannerod, M. 1999. To act or not to act: Perspectives on the representation of actions. *Quarterly Journal of Experimental Psychology, 52A*, 1–29.

Jeannerod, M., and E. Pacherie. 2004. Agency, simulation, and self-identification. *Mind and Language, 19*, 113–146.

Koechlin, E., G. Basso, P. Pietrini, S. Panzer, and J. Grafman. 1999. The role of the anterior prefrontal cortex in human cognition. *Nature, 13*, 148–151.

Koechlin, E., G. Corrado, P. Pietrini, and J. Grafman. 2000. Dissociating the role of the medial and lateral anterior prefrontal cortex in human planning. *Proceedings of the National Academy of Sciences, 97*, 7651–7656.

Koriat, A. 1993. How do we know that we know? The accessibility model of the feeling of knowing. *Psychological Review, 100*, 609–639.

Kristoff, K., L. P. T. Geddes, J. M. Ream, and J. D. E. Gabrieli. 2003. Evaluating self-generated information: Anterior prefrontal contributions to human cognition. *Behavioral Neuroscience, 117*, 1161–1168.

LeDoux, J. 1996. *The Emotional Brain*. New York: Simon and Schuster.

Leube, D. T., G. Knoblich, M. Erb, W. Grodd, M. Bartels, and T. J. Kircher. 2003. The neural correlates of perceiving one's own movements. *Neuroimage, 20*, 2084–2090.

Malenka, R. C., R. W. Angel, B. Hampton, and P. A. Berger. 1982. Impaired central error-correcting behavior in schizophrenia. *Archives of General Psychiatry, 39*, 101–107.

Martin, M. G. F. 1995. Bodily awareness: The sense of ownership. In *The Body and the Self*, ed. J. Bermudez, A. J. Marcel, and N. Eilan, pp. 267–289. Cambridge, Mass.: MIT Press.

Maruff, P., P. Wilson, and J. Currie. 2003. Abnormalities of motor imagery associated with somatic passivity phenomena in schizophrenia. *Schizophrenia Research, 60*, 229–238.

Metzinger, T. 2003. *Being No One*. Cambridge, Mass.: MIT Press.

Miall, R. C., D. J. Weir, D. M. Wolpert, and J. F. Stein. 1993. Is the cerebellum a Smith predictor? *Journal of Motor Behavior, 25*, 203–216.

Miall, R. C., and D. M. Wolpert. 1996. Forward models for physiological motor control. *Neural Networks, 9*, 1265–1279.

Mlakar, J., J. Jensterle, and C. D. Frith. 1994. Central monitoring deficiency and schizophrenic symptoms. *Psychological Medicine, 24*, 557–564.

Nelson, T. O., and L. Narens. 1990. Metamemory: A theoretical framework and new findings. *Psychology of Learning and Motivation, 26*, 125–141. Reprinted in *Metacognition: Core Readings*, ed. T.O. Nelson, pp. 117–130 (Boston: Allyn and Bacon, 1992).

Parnas, J., and A. Sass. 2001. Self, solipsism, and schizophrenic delusions. *Philosophy, Psychiatry, and Psychology, 8*, 101–120.

Peacocke, C. 1998. Conscious attitudes and self-knowledge. In *Knowing Our Own Minds*, ed. C. Wright, B. C. Smith, and C. MacDonald, pp. 63–98. Oxford: Clarendon Press.

Perry, J. 2000. *The Problem of the Essential Indexical and Other Essays*. Stanford: Center for the Study of Language and Information.

Proust, J. 2000. Awareness of agency: Three levels of analysis. In *The Neural Correlates of Consciousness*, ed. T. Metzinger, pp. 307–324. Cambridge, Mass.: MIT Press.

Proust, J. 2001. A plea for mental acts. *Synthese, 129*, 105–128.

Proust, J. 2002a. A critical review of G. Lynn Stephens and G. Graham's *When Self-Consciousness Breaks*. *Philosophical Psychology, 15*, 543–550.

Proust, J. 2002b. Can "radical" theories of simulation explain mental concept acquisition? In *Simulation and Knowledge of Action*, ed. J. Dokic and J. Proust, pp. 201–228. Amsterdam: John Benjamins.

Proust, J. 2003a. Does metacognition necessarily involve metarepresentation? *Behavior and Brain Sciences, 26*, 352.

Proust, J. 2003b. Thinking of oneself as the same. *Consciousness and Cognition, 12*, 495–509.

Proust, J. 2006. Rationality and metacognition in non-human animals. In *Rational Animals?*, ed. S. Hurley and M. Nudds. Oxford: Oxford University Press.

Ricoeur, P. 1986. *Fallible Man*. New York: Fordham University Press.

Rizzolatti, G., and L. Craighero. 2004. The mirror-neuron system. *Annual Reviews Neuroscience, 27*, 169–192.

Rochat, P. 2003. Five levels of self-awareness as they unfold early in life. *Consciousness and Cognition, 12*, 717–731.

Rosenthal, D. 1993. Thinking that one thinks. In *Psychological and Philosophical Essays*, ed. M. Davies and G. W. Humphreys, pp. 197–223. Oxford: Blackwell.

Ruby, P., and J. Decety. 2003. Effect of perspective taking during simulation of action: A PET investigation of agency. *Nature Neuroscience, 4*, 546–550.

Ryle, G. 1949. *The Concept of Mind*. London: Hutchinson.

Shallice, T. 1988. *From Neuropsychology to Mental Structure*. Cambridge: Cambridge University Press.

Shallice, T., and P. Burgess. 1991. Higher-order cognitive impairments and frontal lobe lesions in man. In *Frontal Lobe Function and Dysfunction*, ed. H. S. Levin, H. M. Eisenberg, and A. L. Benton, pp. 125–138. Oxford: Oxford University Press.

Smith, J. D., W. E. Shields, and D. A. Washburn. 2003. The comparative psychology of uncertainty monitoring and metacognition. *Behavioral and Brain Sciences, 26*, 317–373.

Spence, S. A., D. J. Brooks, S. R. Hirsch, P. F. Liddle, J. Meehan, and P. M. Grasby. 1997. A PET study of voluntary movement in patients with schizophrenia experiencing passivity phenomena (delusions of alien control). *Brain, 120,* 1997–2011.

Stephens, G. L., and G. Graham. 2000. *When Self-Consciousness Breaks: Alien Voices and Inserted Thoughts.* Cambridge, Mass.: MIT Press.

Umiltà, C., and F. Stablum. 1998. Control processes explored by the study of closed-head injury patients. In *Metacognition and Cognitive Neuropsychology: Monitoring and Control Processes,* ed. G. Mazzoni and T. O. Nelson, pp. 37–52. Mahwah, N.J.: Lawrence Erlbaum.

Wolpert, D. M., Z. Ghahramani, and J. R. Flanagan. 2001. Perspectives and problems in motor learning. *Trends in Cognitive Sciences, 5,* 487–494.

Wolpert, D. M., Z. Ghahramani, and M. I. Jordan. 1995. An internal model for sensorimotor integration. *Science, 269,* 1880–1882.

Wolpert, D. M., R. C. Miall, and M. Kawato. 1998. Internal models in the cerebellum. *Trends in Cognitive Sciences, 2,* 338–347.

6 A Selectionist Model of the Ego: Implications for Self-Control

George Ainslie

Behavioral science offers a smorgasbord of principles describing how people make choices (Mellers et al. 1998), but where actual social planning is necessary, as in economics and law, these principles are winnowed down to the refinement of utility theory that was initiated by Samuelson (1937) and has come to be called "expected utility theory," or, more generally, "rational choice theory" (RCT; Boudon 1996; Korobkin and Ulen 2000; Sugden 1991). In this theory a person with enough information and time to assimilate it will arrive at hierarchies of preference that are internally consistent (transitive, commensurable, etc.), that maximize her probability of getting what she prefers, and that do not shift as the perspective of time changes. Lawyers and economists are well aware of evidence from all the behavioral sciences of how people violate RCT. Jolls et al. (1998) summarized these violations as bounded willpower (a failure to follow your own plans), bounded rationality (failure to correctly interpret environmental contingencies), and bounded self-interest (a tendency to invest altruism where it will not bring returns), but the violations have seemed haphazard (Posner 1998), and RCT offers at least a coherent system. Admired for its "unique attractiveness . . . [because] we need ask no more questions about it" (Coleman 1986), it is demonstrably the norm for competitions in marketplaces, where anyone who violates it puts herself at a competitive disadvantage.

The adaptiveness of RCT is so obvious that many authors make the subtle leap from viewing it as a norm to viewing it as *descriptive* of normal behavior. Its tenets become "assumptions about how people respond to incentives" (Korobkin and Ulen 2000, p. 1055). Volition is just what passes the incentives through to the responses, and violations are due to either errors in evaluating the incentives or "disorders of volition." This way of thinking has spread from the policy-making disciplines to individual psychology, where "how people create actions from intentions and desires" and how "they stay on course" are matters of information processing (e.g., Carver and Scheier 2000, and other authors in Boekaerts et al. 2000). A lower principle such as Plato's passion or Freud's id has historically been seen as a competing mechanism of choice, but the lower principle is now seen as mere noise that sometimes obscures the clear signal of RCT. On the contrary, I will argue that the observed deviations from RCT are coherent, that they motivate coherent strategies for dealing with them, and that the competition of these strategies with the deviations that they target generates familiar complexities of choice that RCT has not begun to contemplate.

6.1 The Problem of Lower Mental Processes

Outside of RCT, people have always divided mental life into lower and higher processes. Lower processes appear at an early age, are spontaneous and strongly motivated, tend to seek goals that are obviously useful to organisms in evolution, and are often thought of as the animal part of our nature. Higher processes develop later, often seem arbitrary, are less connected with biological need, and are often thought of as transcending our animal nature. They are not refined versions of lower processes but respond to them and often conflict with them in asymmetrical combats, in which the weapon of the lower processes is superior force and the weapon of the higher processes is superior organization and foresight. Ancient thinkers often held that higher processes should simply replace lower ones, as in the Buddhist and stoic ideals of escaping from desire, the Zoroastrian goal of light replacing darkness, and the Judeo-Christian practice of mortifying the flesh. However, it became evident that the relationship of these processes is not one of good versus evil. As Freud pointed out, "The substitution of the reality principle for the pleasure principle implies no deposing of the pleasure principle, but only a safeguarding of it" (1911, p. 223). Conversely, psychotherapies often attribute patients' miseries to overgrown higher processes—"cognitive maps (Gestalt)," "conditions of worth (client-centered)," "musturbation (rational–emotive)," and, of course, the punitive superego (summarized in Corsini 1984). To be truly higher, a principle must keep lower principles healthy, but it has never been clear how such a relationship works.

Most theories have had what has been called in this conference a top-down approach to the topic. An autonomous faculty—the Vedic *tapas*, St. Augustine's *temperance*, Plato's *reason*—imposes logical consistency and stability over time on the lower process. In top-down theories this faculty is not governed by the same determinants as the lower process, which is the slave of reward and—if this is something different—of passion.[1] Perhaps attributing the same determinants would make theorists expect the same results; in any case, hypothesized dependence on lawful principles that make "the human person a closed system" is said to reduce people to "powerless victims of mechanism" (Miller 2003, p. 63). The higher principle is held to be the "you-noun" (Miller 2003, p. 63), the ego, that must be and perhaps should be impenetrable.

It is always possible that our higher processes are inexplicable as the interaction of relatively simple mechanisms, that is, by a bottom-up approach, but it is also possible that the right mechanisms simply have not been discerned. Certainly many authors have leapt from the discovery of a new atom of learning or motivation to an encompassing theory in which these atoms are merely multiplied or writ large, making the world into a procrustean Skinner box that fails to fit the subtleties of human experience. However, the science of motivation has finally become a cumulative one, in which the current generation stands on the shoulders of previous generations rather than rediscovering the same phenomena in different frames. I will argue that developments during the last four decades in behavioral research, bargaining theory, and the philosophy of mind permit an explicit explanatory model that comes significantly closer than previous models to fitting the subtleties of human character. In particular, I will show how it improves on a currently dominant atom-writ-large, RCT.

Of the three kinds of deviation from RCT catalogued by Jolls et al., the most attention has been paid to bounded rationality and bounded self-interest. I will not discuss them here.[2] A far more serious problem is bounded willpower—the widespread violation of temporal consistency. People regularly express a preference for one course of action and then take the opposite course when they actually choose. This is sometimes a minor foible, mere fickleness, but often immerses the person in substance abuse, pathological gambling, destructive rage—indeed, a large part of the psychiatric diagnostic manual (American Psychiatric Association 1994). An even larger number of "bad habits" never reach the level of diagnosis: smoking, overeating, credit card abuse, rash personal attachments, impatience for pleasant things and procrastination of unpleasant ones—all the activities that you plan to avoid when you are at a distance from them, and regret after you have done them.

RCT holds, against all intuition, that insight alone should prevent these lapses. Consistent choice implies an exponential discount curve of the value of delayed goals, such that they lose a constant proportion of their remaining value for every additional unit of delay. Financial transactions are universally conducted on the basis of the exponential discount curve, for any curve more bowed than this would cause a good to change its value relative to alternatives simply as it drew closer, an irrational instability. People regularly make their investment choices on the basis of exponential curves, so it makes sense to think that these curves are part of attainable insight. According to RCT, the choice between dessert now and fitness down the road should be reduceable to a graph like figure 6.1a (given that an extended reward like fitness can be represented as an equivalent momentary event—Mazur 1986; Ainslie 1992, pp. 147–152, 375–385).

Confronted with the prevalence of temporary preferences, utility theorists have borrowed a mechanism from popular culture, a sudden surge of preference for the less valued alternative when an evocative reminder appears. Spirit possession was popular in more superstitious times, and you can still hear, "The Devil made me do it." However, since the surge often follows a cue that has been associated with the bad

(a)

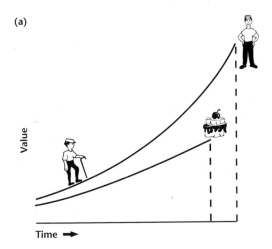

(b)

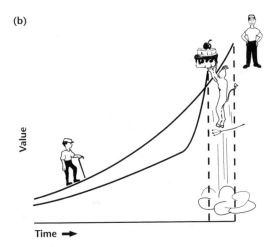

Figure 6.1
In rational choice theory, the values of larger-later fitness and smaller-sooner dessert keep the
same proportion at all times (a), unless a special mechanism (here, a demon) creates a surge in
the dessert's value (b).

option, psychology has attributed it to classical conditioning: Appetite is assumed to be an unmotivated response transferred from a hardwired stimulus, and its sudden appearance makes the prospective reward from the bad option jump above that of the good option—hence the effect seen in figure 6.1b.

The problem with this model, aside from serious questions about whether classical conditioning represents a selective principle separate from reward (see below, and Ainslie 1992, pp. 39–48 and 2001, pp. 19–22), is that most, if not all, rewards are preceded by predictive cues. Almost all rewards must be "conditioned," even the rewards that seem to be discounted rationally. Cues merely tell us the likeliness of occurrence and probable delay of whatever rewards they predict. A cue that regularly precedes a reward should become predictable in turn, and if it makes the bad reward more valuable it should soon raise the height of the discount curve for its entire length, causing it to be revalued as a straightforwardly better reward (fig. 6.2a). Thus the conditioning theory of impulses has to assume that you cannot learn the connection between cues and the kind of rewards that get temporarily preferred, or at least that you cannot learn the hedonic implications of this cue/reward pair. The "visceral rewards" that are frequent offenders in impulsive choice (Loewenstein 1996) must thus stay surprising and jump out at an unwary person however often she has previously lapsed and chosen the bad reward in the same circumstances (fig. 6.2b).

This would be a somewhat anomalous occurrence, given that animals evaluate the prospect of the same visceral rewards with great accuracy (Herrnstein 1969), and human addicts often anticipate lapses enough to take precautions against them. The experience of suddenly developing an overwhelming appetite is common and requires explanation in its own right, but it is not an adequate mechanism for temporary changes of preference in general.

6.2   Theoretical Models of the Will

In RCT the person continually maximizes her future prospective reward; higher processes involve only estimating what means will do this (Becker and Murphy 1988). If we graft unpredictable conditioned appetites and consequent temporary preferences onto this model, we add the task of forestalling these temporary preferences. Most people would say that the tool they use for this task is willpower or some synonym—resolve, intentionality, or the exercise of volition, the topic of this symposium. However, this has not been a robust concept, rather a will-o'-the-wisp, which has eluded definition and study to the point where some authors deny its existence. Part of the problem has been that the term refers to at least three distinct processes—not only (1) the maintenance of long-range plans but also (2) the simple initiation of any behavior—the sense in which Ryle (1949/1984) found the concept unnecessary—and (3) the integration of specific plans with the whole self, the "ownership" process, the

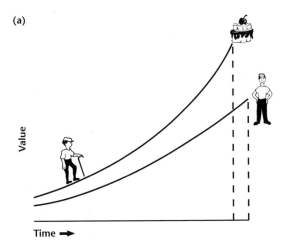

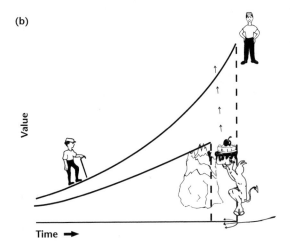

Figure 6.2
After several surges like that in figure 6.1a, the person should come to anticipate them and simply
revalue dessert (a), unless the surge cannot be anticipated and thus stays surprising (b).

well-described flaws in which led Wegner to call the will illusory (2002; see Ainslie 2004). It is only in the first sense of maintaining long-range plans that the concept of willpower is relevant, and there is no generally accepted mechanism for how this happens. The will can serve as an exemplar of the higher processes that are often held to be impenetrable.

Although a mechanism has been lacking, there has been agreement about several properties of willpower. First, gimmicks are excluded. Seeking external means of control, like taking appetite-spoiling drugs, committing your funds to money managers, or joining social groups that will exert pressure, would not be called will. Positive properties were well defined by Victorian psychologists. Willpower was said to

- come into play as "a new force distinct from the impulses primarily engaged" (Sully 1884, p. 669);
- "throw in its strength on the weaker side . . . to neutralize the preponderance of certain agreeable sensations" (Sully 1884, p. 669);
- "unite . . . particular actions . . . under a common rule," so that "they are viewed as members of a class of actions subserving one comprehensive end" (Sully 1884, p. 631);
- be strengthened by repetition (Sully 1884, p. 633);
- be exquisitely vulnerable to nonrepetition, so that "every gain on the wrong side undoes the effect of many conquests on the right" (Bain 1886, p. 440); and
- involve no repression or diversion of attention, so that "both alternatives are steadily held in view, and in the very act of murdering the vanquished possibility the chooser realizes how much in that instant he is making himself lose" (James 1890, vol. 2, p. 534).

Three internal mechanisms have been proposed that are at least roughly compatible with these properties: building "strength," making "resolute choices," and deciding according to principle. However, we need to ask each of these hypotheses both whether its mechanism is complete or requires another will-like faculty to guide it and whether it recruits adequate motivation to govern the decision. If the motivational structure is made up of exponential (consistent) discount curves and conditioned cravings, these models all have problems.

1. Strength   Baumeister and others have proposed an organ of self-control, the main property of which is that, like a muscle, it gets stronger with use in the long run but can be exhausted in the short run (Baumeister and Heatherton, 1996; Muraven and Baumeister 2000). Presumably it adds motivation to what is otherwise the weaker side (fig. 6.3a), pushing it above the temporary surge of motivation (fig. 6.3b). The principal problem with this kind of model is it has to be guided by some evaluation process outside of motivation, since it has to act counter to the most strongly motivated choice at the time. On what basis does this process choose? What keeps this strength from being co-opted by the bad option? Even granting a homunculus that governs from

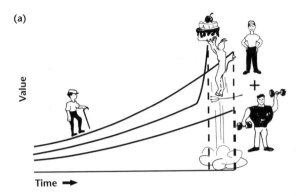

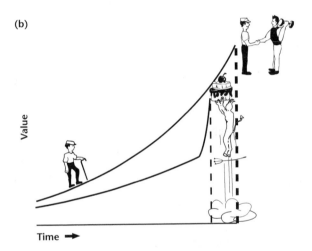

Figure 6.3
In the *strength* model of will, there is an additional faculty that can add its own value to that of fitness (a), leading to a combined value that overcomes the attraction of dessert (b). It is not clear why this strength can be absent when there is a different kind of temptation (here, smoking—c).

above, what lets a person's strength persist in one modality, say, overeating, when it has fallen flat in another such as smoking (fig. 6.3c)? The strength concept merely elevates one of the experiential properties of will into a mechanism in its own right, without grounding it in any robust source of motivation.

2. Resolute choice   Philosophers of mind favor the idea of "resolute choice" (e.g., McClennen 1990; Bratman 1999). When they venture to specify a mechanism, it mostly involves not reexamining choices, at least not while you expect the bad choice to be dominant. There have been a number of experiments suggesting how children learn to do this: Mischel and his collaborators sometimes refer to a combination of controlling attention and avoiding emotionally "hot" thoughts as willpower (e.g., Metcalf and Mischel 1999), essentially a use of mental blinders (fig. 6.4).

However, I have argued that diverting attention and nipping emotion in the bud are distinct and less powerful mechanisms than will is of committing your behavior in advance (Ainslie 1992, pp. 133–142). The ability to control yourself in such a way that "both alternatives are steadily held in view" requires something more. Metcalfe and Mischel describe a growing interconnectedness of a child's "cool" processes, which does imply more than just diversion of attention. Mere diversion after all is an act of holding your breath, usable, as hypnosis has demonstrated, against very short-range urges like panic and the affective component of pain, but not against addictions (McConkey 1984), the urge for which unavoidably weighs in against your original valuation at some point over the hours or days that the diversion must be maintained. The philosophers, too, sense the need for a more complex mechanism: McClennen

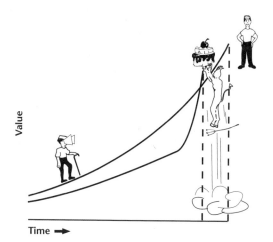

Figure 6.4
In *resolute choice*, the person may avoid reevaluating the options (blinders)—or there may be more to it.

refers to "a sense of commitment" to previously made plans (1990, pp. 157–161), which sounds like more than diversion of attention, and Bratman refers to "a planning agent's concern with how she will see her present decision at plan's end" (1999, pp. 50–56), which suggests that self-prediction is a factor. They seem to be invoking an additional device, deciding according to principle, which I will now examine.

3. Principle   Since ancient times keeping your attention away from tempting options has been the main folk ingredient of self-control, but a subtler technique is just as venerable: deciding according to principle. Referring to dispositions to choose as "opinions," Aristotle said, "We may also look to the cause of incontinence [*akrasia*] scientifically in this way: One opinion is universal, the other concerns particulars" (*Nichomachean Ethics* 1147a24–28). Deciding according to universals made you more continent. Many authors have repeated this advice (some listed in Ainslie 2001, pp. 79–81) but mostly without speculating as to how people can maintain their motivation to narrow their range of choice in this way. Simply summing series of exponentially discounted rewards together does nothing per se to change their relative values (fig. 6.5).

However, Howard Rachlin has written extensively about how people come to choose in "molar," overall patterns rather than making "molecular" decisions, by which he means going case by case (Rachlin 2000). He believes that there comes to be an aesthetic factor in molar choice itself, just as, with learning, a whole symphony comes to be more rewarding than the sum of its parts. Thus, a recovering addict might avoid lapses because of the aversiveness of spoiling her pattern of sobriety. In this model the strength or resolve that feels like the active ingredient in willpower is hypothesized to come from a specific mechanism, molar appreciation of an overall pattern, leading to distaste for options that break the pattern. This model has the advantage of specifying the extra motivation to overcome temptations that choosing in categories seems to supply.

However, this aesthetic factor does not seem robust enough; most people would not say that their temptations had become distasteful or irritating, even after they have learned to avoid them. Nevertheless, without this additional motive, there seems to be no way that bundling exponentially discounted options together could be expected to shift the direction of choice.

I have argued that no satisfactory theory of impulsiveness or impulse control can be based on exponential discount curves—that a priori, without data about the actual shape of the curves, there is a need to hypothesize curves more bowed than exponential ones (Ainslie 1975, 2001, pp. 117–140). Highly bowed curves can account for both temporary preferences and the motivation to forestall them, as figure 6.6 demonstrates.

A hyperbolic discounter who faces a choice between smaller-sooner (SS) and larger-later (LL) rewards will evaluate them roughly in proportion to their objective

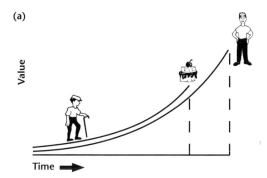

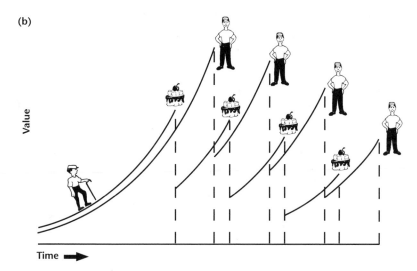

Figure 6.5
Using *principled choice*, membership in a larger category of larger-later rewards must increase the relative value of individual larger-later rewards. This does not happen with *exponential curves*; a prospective series of reward (b) keep the same relative values as a single choice (a).

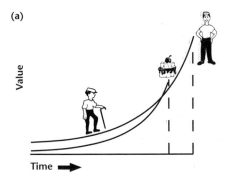

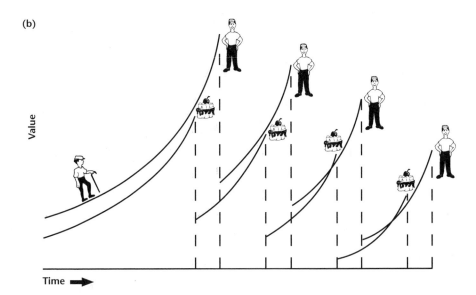

Figure 6.6
Principled choice boosts larger-later reward values only when discount curves are *hyperbolic* or otherwise deeply bowed. Such curves from a series of paired smaller-sooner and larger-later rewards may come never to cross (b), with the same amounts that cause curves from a single pair to cross (a, = last pair in b).

size—their values at zero delay—when both are distant but will value the SS reward disproportionately when it is close (fig. 6.6a). Thus she will have an innate tendency to form temporary preferences for SS rewards, purely as a function of elapsing time. Furthermore, if she makes a whole series of choices at once—for instance, a class of choices united by a principle—the slower decline of the curves at long delays will make her aggregate valuation of the LL rewards much higher (fig. 6.6b).

Hyperbolic discount curves are a radical theoretical departure and lead to converse problems with how choice becomes stable, but they are not an outrageous leap. The degree of most psychophysical changes—from one intensity of warmth or brightness or heaviness to another—is experienced proportionately to the original intensity, a relationship expressed by a hyperbolic rather than an exponential curve (Gibbon 1977). The accepted formula describing how foraging animals make prey and patch choices, Holling's "disc equation" (1959), is also hyperbolic (see Green and Myerson 1996). It does not strain our beliefs about nature that amounts of reward might be experienced proportionally to their immediacies.

6.3 Empirical Evidence about the Shape of the Discount Curve

Fortunately, the shape of the discount curve can be studied by controlled experiment, with at least four different methods and in both people and nonhuman animals. A large body of such research has occurred in the thirty years since I first proposed the hyperbolic shape (Ainslie 1974, 1975); this research has found a robust and apparently universal tendency to discount delayed events in a curve more bowed than an exponential curve. Where the method has permitted estimation of the exact shape, the shape that has best fit the data produced by that method has been a hyperbola. I will summarize the findings briefly:

1. Given choices between rewards of varying sizes at varying delays, both human and nonhuman subjects express preferences that by least squares tests fit curves of the form

$$V = A/(1 + kD),$$

a hyperbola, better than the form

$$V = A\, e^{kD},$$

an exponential curve (where V is motivational value, A is amount of reward, D is delay of reward from the moment of choice, and k is a constant expressing impatience; Grace 1996; Green, Fry, and Myerson 1994; Kirby 1997; Mazur 2001). It has also been observed that the incentive value of small series of rewards is the sum of hyperbolic discount curves from those rewards (Brunner and Gibbon 1995; Mazur 1986; Mitchell and Rosenthal 2003).

2. Given choices between SS rewards and LL ones available at a constant lag after the SS ones, subjects prefer the LL reward when the delay before both rewards is long but switch to the SS reward as it becomes imminent, a pattern that would not be seen if the discount curves were exponential (Ainslie and Herrnstein 1981; Ainslie and Haendel 1983; Green et al. 1981; Kirby and Herrnstein 1995). Where anticipatory dread is not a factor, subjects switch from choosing LL relief from aversive stimuli to SS relief as the availability of the SS relief draws near (Navarick 1982; Solnick et al. 1980).

3. Given choices between SS rewards and LL ones, nonhuman subjects will sometimes choose an option available in advance that prevents the SS alternative from becoming available (Ainslie 1974; Hayes et al. 1981). The converse is true of punishments (Deluty et al. 1983). This design has not been run with human subjects, but it has been argued that illiquid savings plans and other choice-reducing devices serve this purpose (Laibson 1997). Such a pattern is predicted by hyperbolic discount curves, while conventional utility theory holds that a subject has no incentive to reduce her future range of choices (Becker and Murphy 1988).

4. When a whole series of LL rewards and SS alternatives must be chosen all at once, both human and nonhuman subjects choose the LL rewards more than when each SS versus LL choice can be made individually. Kirby and Guastello (2001) reported that students who faced five weekly choices of a SS amount of money immediately or a LL amount one week later picked the LL amounts substantially more if they had to choose for all five weeks at once than if they chose individually each week. These authors reported an even greater effect for different amounts of pizza. Ainslie and Monterosso (2003) reported that rats made more LL choices when they chose for three trials all at once than when they chose between the same contingencies separately on each trial. The effect of such *bundling* of choices is predicted by hyperbolic but not exponential curves: As I described above, exponentially discounted prospects do not change their relative values however many are summed together (fig. 6.5); hyperbolically discounted SS rewards, although disproportionately valued as they draw near, lose this differential value insofar as the choices are bundled into series (fig. 6.6).

Thus, hyperbolic discounting seems to be an elementary property of the reward process. The resulting implication that our choices are intrinsically unstable is obviously disturbing and requires a fair amount of theoretical retooling. Several counterproposals have attempted to account for temporary preference phenomena as variants of exponential discounting. The simplest possibility is that different kinds of reward are discounted at different rates, so that the prospect of sobriety, say, might be discounted more slowly than that for intoxication. Such an explanation could account for temporary preferences, precommitment, and the effect of summing series of choices, as long as the SS rewards were of a different modality than the LL rewards. However, in all of the above experiments the SS rewards were of the same kind as the LL.

Other proposals have included the following:

• Noise in the valuation process, such that discount curves wobble randomly across one another (Strotz 1956; Skog 1999). However, since exponential curves draw further apart as delay decreases (fig. 6.1a), this wobble should create fewer changes of preference, or at least no more, when the SS is near than when it is distant. The opposite is regularly observed.

• A step function in which immediate events are valued disproportionately and events at all delays are discounted exponentially (Simon 1995); the most prominent example is Laibson's (1997) "hyperboloid" discount function. This accounts grossly for the incentive for precommitment, but this function, not seen elsewhere in nature, is contradicted by the smooth curve that describes the available data (Ainslie and Monterosso 2004).

• An exponential discount rate whose exponent itself varies as a function of amount (Green and Myerson 1993). However, to explain changes of preference as a function of delay, the exponent would have to be determined only by the value at delay zero, the very objection that makes hyperbolic discounting inconvenient for utility-based analysis (Laibson 1997). Even accepting this convention, Green et al. (1997) have found that hyperbolic curves fit the data substantially better than amount-dependent exponential curves.

• The summation of separate exponential discount rates for association and valuation (Case 1997). However, the association component that gives the necessary bowing to the overall curve should affect only new learning, not choice between the familiar alternatives that confronted subjects in most of the above research.

None of these proposals contradicts hyperbolic discounting except in the precise fitting of the curve itself, and in this respect, the data for best least squares fit overwhelmingly support the hyperbola.

6.3.1 Importance of Nonhuman Data

The finding of evidence for hyperbolic discounting in nonhumans as well as humans is crucial, because social psychology experiments are notoriously vulnerable to unprogrammed incentives, not the least of which is compliance with perceived experimenter demand (Orne 1973). Phrasing a choice one way or another can reverse the direction of the findings (Tversky and Kahneman 1981), and subjects are apt to express what they believe to be rational rather than what their spontaneous preference is; thus, six- to ten-year-olds are actually poorer at some kinds of reward-getting tasks than four-year-olds, because they rigidly hold to what they believe the right strategy should be (Sonuga-Barke et al. 1989). Furthermore, human subjects learn to compensate for their tendencies to form temporary preferences, and they express valuations that have this compensation already factored in; I am still surprised that people reveal hyperbolic preferences for future money to the extent that they do, given its demonstrable irrationality. Of course, nonhuman animals have their own behavioral foibles (Breland and Breland 1961), but we can be sure that these do not include social demand or theoretical notions.

6.3.2 Range of Implications

Hyperbolas can obviously account for reversals of preference as SS rewards become imminently available. At first glance, they do not explain the stimulus-driven quality often reported for these reversals: A switch in preference is often experienced as happening not simply when a reward can be had soon, but when a stimulus induces a "conditioned" surge of appetite for it, much like the surges of emotion that also lead to changes of preference. However, I will argue presently that reward-based hyperbolic curves govern both kinds of surge by the same mechanism that leads to the willpower phenomenon. Hyperbolic curves also suggest rationales for many other phenomena that RCT fails to predict, including but not limited to anomalies of investment (Thaler 1991), the value of emotion, and the most important occasion for emotion, the vicarious experience of other people. I will discuss willpower and sudden appetite/emotion here and refer the reader elsewhere for the other topics (Ainslie 2001, pp. 161–197; 2003).

6.4 Will as Intertemporal Bargaining

The most basic consequence of hyperbolic discounting is that we cannot be sure of our own future choices. Neither cognitive theory nor popular imagination has revised the renaissance image of the person as an internal hierarchy, with an ego as king over obedient agents (muscles) and passive support organs (viscera; Tillyard 1959). At best this image has been modernized to a corporation controlled by a CEO, or an army controlled by a general. By contrast, if our preferences tend to change as one reward and then another get close, we are more like a marketplace in which any plan we make at one moment must be sold to ourselves at future moments if it is to have any chance of succeeding. This, indeed, is what even corporations and armies look like when the motives of the individuals who "serve" in them are examined closely (Brunsson 1982, chaps. 1 and 2; Brennan and Tullock 1982, p. 226). Memos and orders by leaders have to be supported by a great deal of tacit bargaining in order to motivate followers to follow.

What bargaining within individuals can make a future self obey the plan of the present self? Of course, there is sometimes external or physiological commitment, as when the present self takes an appetite-altering medication, makes a promise to a friend, limits the information that will come to future selves, or just starts a behavior that will affect motivation in the immediate future (Ainslie 2001, pp. 73–78). However, these methods are often unavailable or are too costly or restricting. A more adaptable method is suggested by hyperbolic curves' property of increasingly favoring LL rewards when they are drawn from whole series of rewards, as demonstrated in the fourth kind of experiment, above. This property may be the basis for what authors from Aristotle to Rachlin have suggested: that self-control increases when you decide according to principle—that is, when you choose whole series of similar options instead of just "particular" or "molecular" cases. But how do you make yourself choose according to principle in the face of individual short-range temptations? To explain this, we need to invoke a process that would make no sense for the continual reward maximizers envisioned by RCT, *intertemporal bargaining*.

Future selves partially share the goals of the present self—the LL rewards that it values at a discount—and partially have different goals—the SS rewards that only momentary selves value highly. This defines a relationship of limited warfare (Schelling 1960, pp. 53–80), the incentives for which, in inter*personal* bargaining, form repeated prisoners' dilemmas (RPDs). Among individuals, such dilemmas can be solved by finding clear, albeit often tacit, criteria for what constitutes cooperation or defection, as long as mutual cooperation will benefit each player more than mutual defection will. Within an individual, the limited warfare between, say, eating to satiety and staying thin can also be brought to a truce by RPD logic. Classical RPDs cannot occur among successive selves within an individual because a later self can never literally retaliate against an earlier one; however, if your expectation of getting a whole series of LL rewards depends on seeing yourself pick LL rewards in current choices, you have effectively created the outcome matrix of an RPD (Ainslie 2001, pp. 90–104). If you see yourself violate your diet today, you reduce your expectation that your diet will succeed, and tomorrow's self will have that much less at stake in choosing. The resulting expectation that tomorrow's self will violate your diet in turn, and precipitate subsequent violations, in effect constitutes retaliation against today's defector.

The incentive structure of intertemporal bargaining can replace not only Rachlin's supplementary reward from love of principle but also faculties like a transcendent self or overriding ego that have long been assumed to be inborn. The process is analogous to the inter*personal* bargaining through which small, stable markets come to regulate themselves by "self-enforcing contracts" (Klein and Leffler 1981)—self-enforcing in that the incentive for cheating in a given transaction is continuously less than the expected gain from continuing mutual trust. By the same logic, an individual has incentives to develop self-enforcing cooperative arrangements with her future selves. Such higher mental functions can develop by trial and error on the basis of the heavily discounted long-range rewards that shape foresight. A person's cognitive machinery need not be run by an autonomous part of the person herself, an ego that stands apart from its gears and power trains; the internal factory itself is autonomous, the ultimate bottom-up mechanism that Dennett envisions (see Prinz, Dennett, and Sebanz, this volume).

6.4.1   An Illustration

The contingencies of the intertemporal RPD were illustrated by a demonstration at this conference: I asked the audience to imagine that I was running a game show. I announced that I would go along every row, starting at the front, and give each member a chance to say "cooperate" or "defect." Each time someone said "defect," I would award a euro only to her. Each time someone said "cooperate," I would award ten cents to her and to everyone else in the audience. And I asked that they play this game solely to maximize their individual total score, without worrying about friendship, politeness, the common good, and so forth. I said that I would stop at an unpredictable point after at least 20 players had played. Like successive motivational states within a person, each successive player had a direct interest in the behavior of each subsequent player and had to guess her future choices somewhat by noticing the choices already made. If she believed that her move would be the most salient of these choices for the next players right after she made it, she had an incentive to forego a sure euro, but only if she thought that this choice would be both necessary and sufficient to make later players do likewise.

In this kind of game, knowing the other players' thoughts and characters—whether they are greedy or devious, for instance—will not help you choose, as long as you believe them to be playing to maximize their monetary gains. This is so because the main determinant of their choices will be the pattern of previous members' play at the moment of these choices. Retaliation for a defection will not occur punitively—a current player has no reason to reward or punish a player who will not play again[3]—but what amounts to retaliation will happen through the effect of this defection on subsequent players' estimations of their prospects and their consequent choices. These would seem to be the same considerations that bear on successive motivational states within a person, except that in this interpersonal game the reward for future cooperations is flat (ten cents per cooperation, discounted negligibly), rather than discounted in a hyperbolic curve depending on each reward's delay.

Perceiving each choice as a test case for the climate of cooperation turns the activity into a positive feedback system—cooperations make further cooperations more likely, and defections make defections more likely. The continuous curve of value is broken into dichotomies by volitions that either succeed or fail. Proximity to temptation still influences the outcome of choices, but much less so than before choices served as test cases with whole series of expectations riding on them. The interpretation of cases as tests or not, that is, as members or not of this particular RPD, becomes more important in determining whether a temptation is worth resisting. If you ignore your diet on a special day like Thanksgiving, or if a single conspicuous outsider like the only child in the game show audience defects, the next choice makers will be much less likely to see it as a precedent. The importance of interpretation creates incentive for what Freudians call "rationalization," or Sayette calls "motivated reasoning" (this volume). Making resolutions more explicit forestalls impulsively motivated reasoning and increases their chances of being carried out (Cohen and Gollwitzer, this volume), but at the risk of compulsive side effects, as we shall see.

6.4.2 Evidence for Intertemporal Bargaining

The similar incentive structures of interpersonal and intertemporal bargaining might make it seem like a good idea to use the former to study the properties of the latter. In full-blown form, however, this turns out to be a daunting undertaking. John Monterosso, Pamela Toppi Mullen, and I have tried out the game show experiment with repeated trials for real money in a roomful of recovering addicts, but it was evident that social pressure was more of a factor than the announced rewards (unpublished data). Practical use of this method would require subjects sitting at 30 or 40 separate terminals, enough trials to make them familiar with the logic of choice, and enough payoff to make it worth their time—obvious material for a well-funded Internet study. Meanwhile it has been possible to model some of the logic of intertemporal cooperation in a two-person RPD: Subjects at computer terminals given false feedback about their partners' responses have shown that damage done by defections is greater and more long lasting than is damage repair following cooperations (Monterosso et al. 2002)—the same asymmetry described for lapses of will (Bain 1886, p. 440).

Experimental analogues are a noisy way to study intertemporal bargaining, but direct experimentation on this recursive, internal process is even less practical. There are suggestive data. For instance, when Kirby and Guastello (2001) compared separate and bundled choices in their college subjects they found an intermediate degree of self-control if they suggested to the separate-choice subjects that their current choice might be an indicator of what they would choose on subsequent occasions. However, nothing short of imaging techniques would allow direct observation of the separate steps of recursive choices within individuals; I will describe some beginnings presently, but these techniques are in their infancy. Meanwhile, the most convincing evidence for the dependence of will upon self-observation comes from thought experiments of the kind that have been finely honed by the philosophy of mind (Kavka 1983; Sorensen 1992). Monterosso's problem is tailored to self-control:

Consider a smoker who is trying to quit, but who craves a cigarette. Suppose that an angel whispers to her that, regardless of whether or not she smokes the desired cigarette, she is destined to smoke a pack a day from tomorrow on. Given this certainty, she would have no incentive to turn down the cigarette—the effort would seem pointless. What if the angel whispers instead that she is destined never to smoke again after today, regardless of her current choice? Here, too, there seems to be little incentive to turn down the cigarette—it would be harmless. Fixing future smoking choices in either direction (or anywhere in between) evidently makes smoking the dominant current choice. Only if future smoking is in doubt does a current abstention seem worth the effort. But the importance of her current choice cannot come from any physical consequences for future choices; hence the conclusion that it matters as a precedent. (Monterosso and Ainslie 1999)

6.5   Recursive Self-Prediction in Will and "Conditioned Craving"

Sometimes resolutions are deliberate, and a person monitors her serial cooperation systematically. However, less deliberate resolutions that still depend on recursive self-observations are apt to be more widespread. We intend to donate blood or dive into a cold lake, and we notice no loss besides a certain uneasiness if we do not; but if we do not, it will be harder to intend similar acts the next time. Resolutions and intentions shade into the kind of self-predictions that merely forecast the immediate future, are made according to no principle, and may well occur in nonhuman animals. Such "James–Lange" phenomena were described in the nineteenth century, actually first by Darwin:

The free expression by outward signs of an emotion intensifies it. On the other hand, the repression, as far as this is possible, of all outward signs softens our emotions. He who gives way to violent gestures will increase his rage; he who does not control the signs of fear will experience fear in greater degree. (1872/1979, p. 366)

The role of this mechanism has been controversial, but it is believable that a dog, say, predicts its own panic when it sees itself backing away from a danger and thereby helps bring the panic on. It seems much less likely that the dog will become aware of this effect and for that reason be motivated to avoid backing away—to "control the signs of fear." Such awareness represents the progression from simple self-prediction to will and produces in its most elementary form the kind of experience that Russell describes:

I suspect that I may be getting seasick so I follow someone's advice to "keep your eyes on the horizon . . ." The effort to look at the horizon will fail if it amounts to a token made in a spirit of desperation . . . I must look at it in the way one would for reasons other than those of getting over nausea . . . not with the despair of "I must look at the horizon or else I shall be sick!" To become well I must pretend I am well. (1978, pp. 27–28)

Anxiously hovering over your own performance is common in behaviors that you recognize to be only marginally under voluntary control: summoning the courage to perform in public (vs. what comedians call "flop sweat") or face the enemy in battle, recalling an elusive memory, sustaining a penile erection, or, for men with enlarged prostates, voiding their bladders. To seem to be succeeding increases the likelihood of actual success. I suspect that it was not just to account for fate, but to deal with the tenuous process of succeeding in just such behaviors, that ancient polytheists discerned the sometime interventions of such gods as Mars, Venus, and Aesculapius. Will in the sense of willpower is a refinement of this recursive self-prediction; its targets are behaviors that are more controllable than the above examples in the short run but that become unreliable when they must be sustained over long periods. People pray to gods for success against temptations, too.

6.5.1 Neuroimaging

Neuroimaging technology may soon be able to add information about the components of will, perhaps even including intertemporal bargaining. As Bechara (this volume) discusses, parts of the prefrontal cortex are clearly involved in foresight and can influence activity in reward centers[4] (see also Davidson et al. 2000; Rolls 1999, pp. 124–144). It is too early to tell whether the prefrontal area competes against "lower" areas, as a person would wrestle with a bear (McClure et al. 2004), or whether it *exploits* them strategically from a position of relative weakness, as a person would ride a horse (in Paul McLean's classic image; Ainslie and Monterosso 2004)—or arranges "to set affection against affection and to master one by another: even as we use to hunt beast with beast" (Francis Bacon, quoted in Hirschman 1977, p. 22). The latter models have the advantage of being expandable to multiple ranges of impulsiveness and control, as when drinking alcohol may be a way of controlling an urge to panic, while at the same time representing an addiction that invites controls (Ainslie 1992, pp. 119–122). The multiple reciprocal connections among the centers involved in appetite/emotion and foresight suggest that at least the process of choice can be recursive (Lewis 2005), a necessary feature of the model of will that I have presented.

6.5.2 Sudden Craving

Recursive self-prediction is a likely mechanism for the frequent suddenness of emotions and "conditioned" craving—processes that arise from the appearance of a stimulus associated with a reward rather than simple proximity to the reward. In the reward-based view I am presenting, craving is an example of appetite, a goal-directed preparatory behavior that increases the effect of relevant rewards, given adequate biological need (or deprivation, or "drive"; Ainslie 2001, pp. 67–69). That is, an appetite is rewarded by the object consumed just as consumption behavior is; but while consumption itself is a muscle behavior subject to being willed, appetite is one of the many processes, often including the direction of thought itself, that occur too rapidly to be controlled by will. Furthermore, since the role of appetite is to increase the effect of a reward, its occurrence also makes choice of the reward more likely. If we intend not to eat dessert—or take a drug—we evaluate our future choices without the relevant appetite. The sudden appearance of a dessert cart, or drug works, gives our appetite an occasion to see if it can overturn our intention. Generating an appetite does not take much energy; unless our resolve is such that there is really no chance that we will choose consumption, a trial of appetite may be worth the effort. It is like having a pet that eats when we eat and will beg under circumstances where we have even occasionally eaten in the past.

"Begging"—an increase in appetite—raises our anticipated reward for consumption, which increases the odds that we will choose it; but this further encourages our appetite, which increases our anticipated reward for consumption. It looks like another

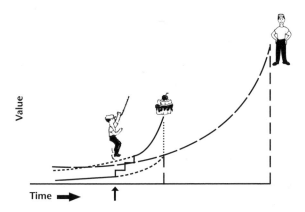

Figure 6.7
With *hyperbolic curves*, sudden craving may occur not only from proximity but also in recursive, Darwin–James–Lange fashion (steps), when appetite and the person's prediction of taking a nearby smaller-sooner reward feed back positively to each other. Unless the person is sure of not indulging, a suggestive cue (arrow) makes incentive move from the lower curve (value without appetite) to the upper curve (value with appetite).

Darwin–James–Lange positive feedback cycle. If we never consume the reward in a particular circumstance, we do not generate appetite there, just as orthodox Jews are said not to crave cigarettes on the Sabbath (Schachter et al. 1977). At the opposite pole, if we accept that we usually consume the reward in this circumstance, we will develop appetite smoothly as the rewarding event gets closer, and the full effect of reward with appetite will be discounted in a simple hyperbolic curve. But between these extremes, if we intend, without certainty, not to consume the reward, we will be prone to sudden increases in appetite that may change the preference that was based on our previous anticipation (fig. 6.7). The notorious dessert cart phenomenon occurs only in people who intend weakly not to have dessert. Furthermore, if we add to our resolve and stop ever consuming the reward in this circumstance, it will still take many, many repetitions for our trials of appetite to extinguish there.

6.5.3 Negative Appetites

I have argued elsewhere that the category of appetites should include emotions—that emotions are appetites that do not require an object of consumption but are rewarding in their own right (Ainslie 2001, pp. 65–67, 164–171). That is, both emotions and other appetites are reward-based processes that are usually subjectively involuntary but that are not selected by conditioning. The principle obstacle that such a model encounters is the question of whether negative emotions/appetites can compete with positive ones. It is counterintuitive that experiences like pain, anger, fear, and grief, which seemingly have to be imposed by conditioning, are actually chosen for their rewardingness.

The difficulty comes largely from a linguistic tendency to equate "reward," that which selects for the choices it follows, and "pleasure," that which is subjectively desirable. Ample evidence that organisms often engage in activities that are not pleasurable, but for which there is no apparent incentive, has led Berridge (2003) to distinguish "liking," finding pleasure in, from "wanting," having a "nonhedonic" tendency to choose an unliked activity. His exemplar is the strong tendency of both patients and nonhumans with indwelling electrodes to self-stimulate in certain brain centers while evincing scant pleasure and even irritation, but he lists many other examples as well.

Berridge suggests conditioning as the nonhedonic mechanism. However, the subjects were responding with muscles that are subject to voluntary control. Even when responses are outside of voluntary control, modern research on conditioning has shown it to be "not the shifting of a response from one stimulus to another [but] the learning of relations among events" (Rescorla 1988, p. 158). Thus the hypothesis that actions like pressing for self-stimulation are nonhedonic leaves them without a principle of selection. An action that is "wanted" really has to have hedonic value, that is, has to trade in the marketplace of goal-directed processes—be rewarded—whether or not it is "liked." The distinction between pleasure and the kind of nonpleasurable urge that could motivate negative emotions/appetites, as well as unwanted behaviors like tics and nailbiting, can permit a quantum leap in the parsimony of motivational theory (Ainslie 1992, pp. 244–249), but only if this distinction can itself be explained.

Hyperbolic discounting again comes to the rescue. It predicts how activities that are subjectively aversive and are avoided from a distance become almost irresistible at very close range, the experience described as vividness or urgency (Ainslie 2001, pp. 48–70). Briefly, aversions may be rapid cycles of short, intense reward and relatively longer suppression of reward—the same pattern as recurrent binges followed by hangovers or, more rapidly, repeatedly scratching an itch and being distracted from richer activities—but condensed into so short a period that the rewarding and unrewarding components fuse in perception. This model makes it possible to see unconditioned stimuli as selecting for the behaviors they follow in exactly the same way as acknowledged pleasures do.[5] Hyperbolic discounting theory renders a separate selective principle based on conditioning unnecessary, even to account for the participation of apparently unwilling subjects in aversive experiences. Even when craving or emotions are unwelcome, they can be seen as arising only insofar as they are rewarding in the very short run.

The brain site(s) that reward in the very short run could well be different from sites that subtend pleasure. Berridge (2003) implicates the lateral hypothalamus, but the amygdalar activity reported by Bechara (this volume) to accompany "primary inducers" would also be a good candidate. He describes primary inducers as "innate or learned stimuli that cause pleasurable or aversive states." Certainly both positive and negative emotional imagery has been found to elicit amygdalar activity (Hamann and Mao 2002), and an intact amygdala is necessary to a core process common to initiating both positive and negative emotions, although the exact nature of this process is unclear (Berridge 1999). Bechara describes the "somatic states" (emotions) occasioned by primary inducers as obligatory, but also as subject to selection such that "stronger ones gain selective advantage over weaker ones," as modified by reflective processes. It seems that even primary inducers have to trade in some kind of marketplace; I am suggesting that instead of being conditioned reflexes, they are selected by very short-term reward and are thus experienced as difficult—though not always impossible—to resist.

6.6 Implications for Well-Being

What the theories of choice that have evolved into RCT describe is the general application of what is actually one particular solution to intertemporal inconsistency. The recursive intertemporal bargaining that generates willpower is especially suited to the needs of long-term planning and the conditions of competitive interpersonal markets, but it has a cost. Because of the inescapable ambiguities in these bargains, a person is fated to achieve "rationality" only imperfectly. Furthermore, insofar as these bargains are all that protect her from her own nature, red in tooth and claw, she is their prisoner. I have argued elsewhere that extensive or unskilled reliance on the perception of intertemporal RPDs for self-control will motivate the development of four side effects (Ainslie 2001, pp. 143–160):

• When an option is worth more as a test case than as an event in its own right, you are less able to experience it in the here-and-now and your choice making becomes lawyerly.
• A lapse that you see as a precedent reduces your hope for self-control in similar situations in the future, a reduction that recursively reduces your power of self-control in those situations. This explains why a successful dieter may be "helpless" against smoking, and how other encapsulated symptoms persist.
• The incentive not to recognize a lapse may lead to gaps in your awareness of your own behavior, a process that creates a motivated unconscious à la Freud.
• Explicit criteria for defining lapses will tend to replace subtle ones, so that what might be your richest plans get replaced by the most enforceable ones.

Clinically, these side effects manifest themselves as compulsive symptoms, in the extreme as obsessive–compulsive personality disorder (Villemarette-Pittman et al. 2004).[6] When particular kinds of test cases assume exceptional importance, they may produce modality-specific syndromes like anorexia nervosa (Gillberg and Rastam 1992) or narrow character traits like miserliness. Thus, if rationality is maximizing experienced reward over time, strengthening volition by making extensive intertemporal bargains may be rational only up to a point. The limitations of intertemporal bargaining are analogous to the social problems that arise where society uses laws to control inter*personal* bargaining (Sunstein 1995, pp. 991–996).

6.7 Conclusions

I have proposed that volition (willpower) involves a pattern of recursive self-prediction that extends an individual's basic ability to use her own current behaviors as cues. This extended ability would not be important if people evaluated choices with the exponential discount curves that are integral to RCT; it becomes crucial in the limited warfare engendered by hyperbolic discount curves. Recursive self-prediction can account for both the recruitment of willpower when you see current choices as test cases and the sudden evaporation of willpower when there is a discrete occasion for a weakly opposed appetite.

This approach provides a bottom-up rationale for the growth and selection of higher functions. Higher literally means more farsighted, for they will be selected according to how well they can anticipate and influence future motivational factors, in particular their own future interpretations of choices as moves in an intertemporal RPD. Higher functions do not depend upon an independent organ of reason. Rather, they are selected by long range reward itself, an invisible hand like that of Adam Smith's marketplace. However, higher does not necessarily mean wiser, since they are prone, like agents in interpersonal marketplaces, to fall into overly rigid patterns through the demands of the bargaining situation itself. Although these emergent higher functions are necessary for achieving the reward-seeking priorities that are defined by RCT, they can only approximate what we would call rational.

Acknowledgments

I thank Lynne Debiak for artwork and John Monterosso and the editors and referees for comments.

Notes

1. Departing from the long stoic tradition, authors are beginning to equate "emotion" with its cognate, "motivation"—e.g., "It is useful to consider under the umbrella of emotion those neural processes by which an animal judges and represents the value of something in the world, and responds accordingly" (Cardinal et al. 2002, p. 332), or "emotional processes must also always

involve an aspect of affect, the psychological quality of being good or bad" (Berridge 2003, p. 106).

2. Much of bounded rationality seems to arise from pure cognitive error (Kahneman and Tversky 2000). However, some reported examples probably arise form strategic motives, either serving self-control (as when people pay a premium to keep money in an illiquid account; Harris and Laibson 2001) or evading it (for instance, if the sunk cost fallacy evades a personal rule for recognizing loss; Ainslie 1992, pp. 291–293). The strategic approach presented here also provides a rationale for vicarious experience as a primary good, which can explain the apparent boundedness of self-interest (Ainslie 1995, 2001, pp. 179–186).

3. In actual play subjects often sacrifice their ostensible interests to punish others (Thaler 1988), but in the intertemporal game being modeled the programmed contingencies encompass all incentives.

4. Preliminary evidence suggests that the medial prefrontal (orbitofrontal) cortex "establishes a motivational value based on estimation of potential reward" (London et al. 2000) but may be implicated in either temptation or longer range planning, depending on the method of observation (Davidson et al. 2000; McClure et al. 2004; Rolls 1999, pp. 124–144; Volkow and Fowler 2000).

5. Other models could also do this, as long as they somehow posited the ability of aversive events to attract attention in a competitive internal marketplace.

6. This disorder is not the same entity as obsessive–compulsive disorder (without the "personality"), which involves rapidly recurring dysphoric urges to wash, check things, or perform other small behaviors, and is associated with low brain serotonin (Thomsen and Mikkelsen 1994). These seem to be another set of "wanted" but not "liked" behaviors (Berridge 2003).

References

Ainslie, G. 1974. Impulse control in pigeons. *Journal of the Experimental Analysis of Behavior, 21,* 485–489.

Ainslie, G. 1975. Specious reward: A behavioral theory of impulsiveness and impulse control. *Psychological Bulletin, 82,* 463–496.

Ainslie, G. 1992. *Picoeconomics: The Strategic Interaction of Successive Motivational States within the Person.* Cambridge: Cambridge University Press.

Ainslie, G. 1995. A utility-maximizing mechanism for vicarious reward. *Rationality and Society, 7,* 393–403.

Ainslie, G. 2001. *Breakdown of Will.* Cambridge: Cambridge University Press.

Ainslie, G. 2003. Uncertainty as wealth. *Behavioural Processes, 64,* 369–385.

Ainslie, G. 2004. The self is virtual, the will is not illusory. *Behavioral and Brain Sciences, 27,* 659–660.

Ainslie, G., and V. Haendel. 1983. The motives of the will. In *Etiology Aspects of Alcohol and Drug Abuse*, ed. E. Gottheil, K. Druley, T. Skodola, and H. Waxman, pp. 119–140. Springfield, Ill.: Charles C. Thomas.

Ainslie, G., and R. Herrnstein. 1981. Preference reversal and delayed reinforcement. *Animal Learning and Behavior, 9,* 476–482.

Ainslie, G., and J. Monterosso. 2003. Building blocks of self-control: Increased tolerance for delay with bundled rewards. *Journal of the Experimental Analysis of Behavior, 79,* 83–94.

Ainslie, G., and J. Monterosso. 2004. Towards a marketplace in the brain. *Science, 305,* 5695.

American Psychiatric Association. 1994. *Diagnostic and Statistical Manual of Mental Disorders,* 4th edition. Washington, D.C.: APA Press.

Bain, A. 1859/1886. *The Emotions and the Will.* New York: Appleton.

Baumeister, R. F., and T. Heatherton. 1996. Self-regulation failure: An overview. *Psychological Inquiry, 7,* 1–15.

Becker, G., and K. Murphy. 1988. A theory of rational addiction. *Journal of Political Economy, 96,* 675–700.

Berridge, K. C. 1999. Pleasure, pain, desire, and dread: Hidden core processes of emotion. In *Well-Being: The Foundations of Hedonic Psychology*, ed. D. Kahneman, E. Diener, and N. Schwartz, pp. 525–557. Thousand Oaks, Calif.: Sage.

Berridge, K. C. 2003. Pleasures of the brain. *Brain and Cognition, 52,* 106–128.

Boekaerts, M., P. R. Pintrich, and M. Zeidner. 2000. *Handbook of Self-Regulation.* New York: Academic Press.

Boudon, R. 1996. The "rational choice model": A particular case of the "cognitive model." *Rationality and Society, 8,* 123–150.

Bratman, M. E. 1999. *Faces of Intention: Selected Essays on Intention and Agency.* Cambridge: Cambridge University Press.

Breland, K., and M. Breland. 1961. The misbehavior of organisms. *American Psychologist, 16,* 681–684.

Brennan, G., and G. Tullock. 1982. An economic theory of military tactics: Methodological individualism at war. *Journal of Economic Behavior and Organization, 3,* 225–242.

Brunner, D., and J. Gibbon. 1995. Value of food aggregates: Parallel versus serial discounting. *Animal Behavior, 50,* 1627–1634.

Brunsson, N. 1982. *The Irrational Organization.* Stockholm School of Economics.

Cardinal, R. N., J. A. Parkinson, J. Hall, and B. J. Everitt. 2002. Emotion and motivation: The role of the amygdala, ventral striatum, and prefrontal cortex. *Neuroscience and Biobehavioral Reviews, 26,* 321–352.

Carver, C. S., and M. F. Scheier. 2000. On the structure of behavioral self-regulation. In *Handbook of Self-Regulation*, ed. M. Boekaerts, P. R. Pintrich, and M. Zeidner, pp. 41–84. New York: Academic Press.

Case, D. A. 1997. Why the delay-of-reinforcement gradient is hyperbolic. Paper presented at the 20th Annual Conference of the Society for the Quantitative Analyses of Behavior. Chicago, May 22.

Coleman, J. 1986. *Individual Interests and Collective Action: Selected Essays*. Cambridge: Cambridge University Press.

Corsini, R. J. 1984. *Current Psychotherapies*, 3rd edition. Itasca, ILL: Peacock.

Darwin, C. 1979 (1872). *The Expressions of Emotions in Man and Animals*. London: Julian Friedman.

Davidson, R. J., K. M. Putnam, and C. L. Larson. 2000. Dysfunction in the neural circuitry of emotional regulation: A possible prelude to violence. *Science, 289*, 591–594.

Deluty, M. Z., W. G. Whitehouse, M. Mellitz, and P. N. Hineline. 1983. Self-control and commitment involving aversive events. *Behavior Analysis Letters, 3*, 213–219.

Freud, S. 1911/1956. Formulations on the two principles of mental functioning. In *The Standard Edition of the Complete Psychological Works of Sigmund Freud*, vol. 12, ed. J. Strachey and A. Freud. London: Hogarth.

Gibbon, J. 1977. Scalar expectancy theory and Weber's law in animal timing. *Psychological Review, 84*, 279–325.

Gillberg, C., and M. Rastam. 1992. Do some cases of anorexia nervosa reflect underlying autistic-like conditions? *Behavioural Neurology, 5*, 27–32.

Grace, R. 1996. Choice between fixed and variable delays to reinforcement in the adjusting-delay procedure and concurrent chains. *Journal of Experimental Psychology: Animal Processes, 22*, 362–383.

Green, L., E. B. Fisher, Jr., S. Perlow, and L. Sherman. 1981. Preference reversal and self-control: Choice as a function of reward amount and delay. *Behaviour Analysis Letters*, 143–151.

Green, L., A. Fry, and J. Myerson. 1994. Discounting of delayed rewards: A life-span comparison. *Psychological Science, 5*, 33–36.

Green, L., and J. Myerson. 1993. Alternative frameworks for the analysis of self-control. *Behavior and Philosophy, 21*, 37–47.

Green, L., and J. Myerson. 1996. Exponential versus hyperbolic discounting of delayed outcomes: Risk and waiting time. *American Zoologist, 36*, 496–505.

Green, L., J. Myerson, and E. McFadden. 1997. Rate of temporal discounting decreases with amount of reward. *Memory and Cognition, 25*, 715–723.

Hamann, S., and H. Mao. 2002. Positive and negative emotional verbal stimuli elicit activity in the left amygdala. *NeuroReport, 13*, 15–19.

Harris, C., and D. Laibson. 2001. Dynamic choices of hyperbolic consumers. *Econometrica, 69*, 535–597.

Hayes, S. C., J. Kapust, S. R. Leonard, and I. Rosenfarb. 1981. Escape from freedom: Choosing not to choose in pigeons. *Journal of the Experimental Analysis of Behavior, 36*, 1–7.

Herrnstein, R. J. 1969. Method and theory in the study of avoidance. *Psychological Review, 76*, 49–69.

Hirschman, A. 1977. *The Passions and the Interests*. Princeton: Princeton University Press.

Holling, C. S. 1959. Some characteristics of simple types of predation and parasitism. *Canadian Journal of Entomology, 91*, 385–398.

James, W. 1890. *Principles of Psychology*. New York: Holt.

Jolls, C., C. R. Sunstein, and R. Thaler. 1998. A behavioral approach to law and economics. *Stanford Law Review, 50*, 1471–1550.

Kahneman, D., and A. Tversky, eds. 2000. *Choices, Values, and Frames*. Cambridge: Cambridge University Press.

Kavka, G. 1983. The toxin puzzle. *Analysis, 43*, 33–36.

Kirby, K. N. 1997. Bidding on the future: Evidence against normative discounting of delayed rewards. *Journal of Experimental Psychology: General, 126*, 54–70.

Kirby, K. N., and B. Guastello. 2001. Making choices in anticipation of similar future choices can increase self-control. *Journal of Experimental Psychology: Applied, 7*, 154–164.

Kirby, K. N., and R. J. Herrnstein. 1995. Preference reversals due to myopic discounting of delayed reward. *Psychological Science, 6*, 83–89.

Klein, B., and K. B. Leffler. 1981. The role of market forces in assuring contractual performance. *Journal of Political Economy, 89*, 615–640.

Korobkin, R., and T. S. Ulen. 2000. Law and behavioral science: Removing the rationality assumption from law and economics. *California Law Review, 88*, 1051–1144.

Laibson, D. 1997. Golden eggs and hyperbolic discounting. *Quarterly Journal of Economics, 62*, 443–479.

Lewis, M. D. 2005. Bridging emotion theory and neurobiology through dynamic systems modeling. *Behavioral and Brain Sciences, 28*, 169–245.

Loewenstein, G. 1996. Out of control: Visceral influences on behavior. *Organizational Behavior and Human Decision Processes, 35*, 272–292.

London, E. D., M. Ernst, S. Grant, K. Bonson, and A. Weinstein. 2000. Orbitofrontal cortex and human drug abuse: Functional imaging. *Cerebrol Cortex, 10*, 334–342.

Mazur, J. E. 1986. Choice between single and multiple delayed reinforcers. *Journal of the Experimental Analysis of Behavior, 46*, 67–77.

Mazur, J. E. 2001. Hyperbolic value addition and general models of animal choice. *Psychological Review, 108,* 96–112.

McClennen, E. F. 1990. *Rationality and Dynamic Choice.* Cambridge: Cambridge University Press.

McClure, S. M., D. I. Laibson, G. Loewenstein, and J. D. Cohen. 2004. The grasshopper and the ant: Separate neural systems value immediate and delayed monetary rewards. *Science, 305,* 5695.

McConkey, K. M. 1984. Clinical hypnosis: Differential impact on volitional and nonvolitional disorders. *Canadian Psychology, 25,* 79–83.

Mellers, B. A., A. Schwartz, and A. D. J. Cooke. 1998. Judgment and decision making. *Annual Review of Psychology, 49,* 447–477.

Metcalfe, J., and W. Mischel. 1999. A hot/cool-system analysis of delay of gratification: Dynamics of willpower. *Psychological Review, 106,* 3–19.

Miller, W. R. 2003. Comments on Ainslie and Monterosso. In *Choice, Behavioural Economics, and Addiction,* ed. R. Vuchinich and N. Heather, pp. 62–66. Amsterdam: Pergamon.

Mitchell, S. H., and A. J. Rosenthal. 2003. Effects of multiple delayed rewards on delay discounting in an adjusting amount procedure. *Behavioural Processes, 64,* 273–286.

Monterosso, J., and G. Ainslie. 1999. Beyond discounting: Possible experimental models of impulse control. *Psychopharmacology, 146,* 339–347.

Monterosso, J. R., G. Ainslie, P. Toppi Mullen, and B. Gault. 2002. The fragility of cooperation: A false feedback study of a sequential iterated dilemma. *Journal of Economic Psychology, 23*(4), 437–448.

Muraven, M., and R. Baumeister. 2000. Self-regulation and depletion of limited resources: Does self-control resemble a muscle? *Psychological Bulletin, 126,* 247–259.

Navarick, D. J. 1982. Negative reinforcement and choice in humans. *Learning and Motivation, 13,* 361–377.

Orne, M. T. 1973. Communication by the total experimental situation: Why it is important, how it is evaluated, and its significance for the ecological validity of findings. In *Communication and Affect: Language and Thought,* ed. P. Pliner, L. Krames, et al. New York: Academic Press.

Posner, R. 1998. Rational choice, behavioral economics, and the law. *Stanford Law Review, 50,* 1555–1556.

Rachlin, H. 2000. *The Science of Self-Control.* Cambridge, Mass.: Harvard University Press.

Rescorla, R. A. 1988. Pavlovian conditioning: It's not what you think it is. *American Psychologist, 43,* 151–160.

Rolls, E. T. 1999. *The Brain and Emotion.* Oxford: Oxford University Press.

Russell, J. M. 1978. Saying, feeling, and self-deception. *Behaviorism, 6,* 27–43.

Ryle, G. 1984 (1949). *The Concept of Mind.* Chicago: University of Chicago Press.

Samuelson, P. A. 1937. A note on measurement of utility. *Review of Economic Studies, 4,* 155–161.

Schachter, S., B. Silverstein, and D. Perlick. 1977. Psychological and pharmacological explanations of smoking under stress. *Journal of Experimental Psychology: General, 106,* 31–40.

Schelling, T. C. 1960. *The Strategy of Conflict.* Cambridge, Mass.: Harvard University Press.

Simon, J. L. 1995. Interpersonal allocation continuous with intertemporal allocation: Binding commitments, pledges, and bequests. *Rationality and Society, 7,* 367–430.

Skog, O.-J. 1999. Rationality, irrationality, and addiction. In *Getting Hooked: Rationality and Addiction,* ed. J. Elster and O.-J. Skog, pp. 173–207. Cambridge: Cambridge University Press.

Solnick, J., C. Kannenberg, D. Eckerman, and M. Waller. 1980. An experimental analysis of impulsivity and impulse control in humans. *Learning and Motivation, 2,* 61–77. Review, 217–225.

Sonuga-Barke, E. J., S. E. Lea, and P. Webley. 1989. The development of adaptive choice in a self-control paradigm. *Journal of the Experimental Analysis of Behavior, 51,* 77–85.

Sorensen, R. A. 1992. *Thought Experiments.* Oxford: Oxford University Press.

Strotz, R. H. 1956. Myopia and inconsistency in dynamic utility maximization. *Review of Economic Studies, 23,* 166–180.

Sugden, R. 1991. Rational choice: A survey of contributions from economics and philosophy. *Economic Journal, 101,* 751–785.

Sully, J. 1884. *Outlines of Psychology.* New York: Appleton.

Sunstein, C. R. 1995. Problems with rules. *California Law Review, 83,* 953–1030.

Thaler, R. 1991. *Quasi Rational Economics.* New York: Russell Sage.

Thomsen, P. H., and H. U. Mikkelsen. 1994. Development of personality disorders in children and adolescents with obsessive–compulsive disorder: A 6 to 22 year follow-up study. *Acta Psychiatrica Scandinavica, 87,* 456–462.

Tillyard, E. M. 1959. *The Elizabethan World Picture.* New York: Knopf.

Tversky, A., and D. Kahneman. 1981. Framing decisions and the psychology of choice. *Science, 211,* 453–458.

Villemarette-Pittman, N. R., M. S. Stanford, K. W. Greve, R. J. Houston, and C. W. Matthias. 2004. Obsessive–compulsive personality disorder and behavioral inhibition. *Journal of Psychology, 138,* 5–22.

Volkow, N. D., and J. S. Fowler. 2000. Addiction, a disease of compulsion and drive: Involvement of the orbitofrontal cortex. *Cerebral Cortex, 10,* 318–325.

Wegner, D. M. 2002. *The Illusion of Conscious Will.* Cambridge, Mass.: MIT Press.

7 If–Then Plans and the Intentional Control of Thoughts, Feelings, and Actions

Anna-Lisa Cohen and Peter Gollwitzer

Over a century ago, Baldwin (1897, as cited in Olson, Astington, and Zelazo 1999, p. 2) defined intentional action as "the emergence of desire, deliberation, and effort: the conscious representation of a goal, the active consideration of alternative means and ends, and the feeling accompanying the selection and execution of a plan." The term "goal" or "intention" is used to refer to the idea that a mental representation has been formed to accomplish a task or direct behavior to achieve some desired state in the world. This concept of intention is central in human goal striving (e.g., Bandura 1991; Gollwitzer and Moskowitz 1996; Locke and Latham 1990; Wicklund and Gollwitzer 1982). In traditional theories of goal striving, the intention to achieve a certain goal is seen as an immediate determinant (or at least predictor) of goal-directed action. A related concept is the term "volition," which is described as the power of choosing or determining and is assumed to be a necessary component of conscious goal-directed action. Based on these descriptions of intention, goal, and volition, one would expect that the strength of an intention (i.e., how much one wants to realize it) determines whether it is implemented or not (Ajzen 1991; Godin and Kok 1996; Sheeran 2002). However, intention–behavior relations are modest, largely due to the fact that people, despite having formed strong intentions, fail to act on them (Orbell and Sheeran 1998). Given this paradox, one wonders what people can do to facilitate the translation of intentions into successful goal attainment.

Over time, evidence accumulated showing that forming strong intentions does not guarantee goal attainment, as there are a host of subsequent implementation-related problems that have to be solved successfully (Gollwitzer 1996). For instance, after having set a goal, people may procrastinate in acting on their intentions and thus fail to initiate goal-directed behavior. Furthermore, in everyday life people often strive for multiple or even competing goals, many of which are not simple short-term goals but rather long-term projects that require repeated efforts (e.g., buying a new house). Also, in order to meet their goals, people have to seize viable opportunities to act, a task which becomes particularly difficult when attention is directed elsewhere (e.g., one is absorbed by competing goal pursuits, wrapped up in ruminations, gripped by intense emotional experiences, or simply tired) and when these opportunities are not obvious at first sight or only present themselves briefly.

In the current chapter, it is suggested that people need to engage in a second act of willing that can help them circumvent these potential breakdowns in voluntary action. In many cases, goal pursuit may come to an early halt because competing projects have temporarily gained priority and the individual fails to successfully resume the original project. Automatic action control can be useful as established routines linked to a relevant context release the critical goal-directed behavior immediately, efficiently, and often without a conscious intent. Frequently, however, such routines are not established and the goal-directed behavior is not part of an everyday routine. Gollwitzer (1993, 1999) suggested that forming a certain type of intention called an "implementation intention" is a powerful self-regulatory strategy that alleviates such problems and thus promotes the execution of goal-directed behaviors. Implementation intentions take the format of "If Situation X is encountered, then I will perform Behavior Y!" In an implementation intention, a mental link is created between a specified future situation and the anticipated goal-directed response. Forming an implementation intention commits the individual to perform a certain goal-directed behavior once the critical situation is encountered.

Implementation intentions are to be distinguished from goal intentions (goals). Goal intentions have the structure of "I intend to reach Z!" whereby Z may relate to a certain outcome or behavior to which the individual feels committed. Goal intentions are the type of intentions with which the majority of theories of motivation are concerned. Implementation intentions, on the other hand, are formed in the service of goal intentions and specify the when, where, and how of goal-directed responses. For instance, a possible implementation intention in the service of the goal intention to eat healthy food would link a suitable situational context (e.g., one's favorite restaurant) to an appropriate behavior (e.g., order a vegetarian meal). In other words, implementation intentions link anticipated opportunities with goal-directed responses and thus commit a person to respond to a certain critical situation in a stipulated manner.

Forming implementation intentions is expected to facilitate goal attainment on the basis of psychological processes that relate to both the anticipated situation and the specified behavior. Because forming implementation intentions implies the selection of a critical future situation (i.e., a viable opportunity), it is assumed that the mental representation of this situation becomes highly activated and thus more easily accessible (Gollwitzer 1999). This heightened accessibility should, in turn, make it easier to detect the critical situation in the surrounding environment and readily attend to it, even when one is busy with other ongoing activity. Moreover, this heightened accessibility should facilitate the recall of the critical situation because a strong link had been formed between the two components (situation cue + response).

Forming implementation intentions also involves the selection of an effective goal-directed behavior, which is then linked to the selected critical situation. The mental act of linking a critical situation to an intended behavior in the form of an if–then plan leads to automatic action initiation in the sense that action initiation becomes swift and efficient and does not require conscious intent once the critical situation is encountered. Thus, by forming implementation intentions, people can strategically switch from conscious and effortful action initiation (guided by goal intentions) to having their goal-directed actions directly elicited by the specified situational cues.

We argue that such plans produce automatic action control by intentionally delegating the control of one's goal-directed thoughts, feelings, and behaviors to specific situational cues. We use the word "automatic" in terms of John Bargh's (1994) definition. Bargh argues that "mental processes at the level of complexity studied by social psychologists are not exclusively automatic or exclusively controlled but are in fact combinations of the features of each" (p. 3). He suggests that there are three ways in which a person may be unaware of a mental process. First, individuals may be unaware of the stimuli itself (e.g., subliminal perception). Second, individuals may be unaware of the way in which they categorize a stimulus event (e.g., stereotyping). And third, individuals may be unaware of the way in which their judgments or subjective feeling states are determined or influenced. For example, one may feel ease when completing a task requiring perceptual categorization and misattribute this feeling of ease to an incorrect cause because it is readily available as an explanation. Therefore, when forming an implementation intention, a single act of will or volition results in the formation of an if–then plan that reduces the need for continued conscious control for attaining the desired outcome as soon as the previously specified cue is encountered. Thus, by forming implementation intentions, people can strategically switch from conscious and effortful control of their goal-directed behaviors to being automatically controlled by selected situational cues. We understand this type of automatic action control as *strategic automaticity* or *instant habits* (Gollwitzer 1999), as it originates from a single act of will rather than being produced by repeated and consistent selection of a certain course of action in the same situation (i.e., principles of routinization, Anderson 1987; Fitts and Posner 1967; Newell and Rosenbloom 1981).

7.1 Empirical Evidence for Automation of Action Initiation

This postulated automation of action initiation (also described as strategic "delegation of control to situational cues") has been supported by the results of various experiments that tested immediacy, efficiency, and the presence/absence of conscious intent (Brandstätter, Lengfelder, and Gollwitzer 2001; Gollwitzer and Brandstätter 1997, Study 1; Lengfelder and Gollwitzer 2001). Given that implementation intentions facilitate attending to, detecting, and recalling viable opportunities to act toward goal attainment, and in addition, automate action initiation in the presence of such opportunities, people who form implementation intentions should show higher goal attainment rates as compared to people who do not furnish their goal intentions with implementation intentions. This hypothesis is supported by the results of a host of studies examining the attainment of various different types of goal intentions. As a general research strategy, goal intentions were selected for analysis that are not easily attained for various reasons (e.g., distractions, unpleasantness).

For instance, Gollwitzer and Brandstätter (1997, Study 2) analyzed a goal intention that had to be performed at a bad time (e.g., writing a report about Christmas Eve during the subsequent Christmas holiday). Students were asked to write a report about how they spent Christmas Eve and send it back to the experimenters as soon as possible. Half of the participants formed implementation intentions about where (e.g., father's desk) and when (e.g., after attending church) they intended to sit down and start writing; participants in the control condition did not form such plans. Results showed that 71 percent of the participants in the implementation intention condition wrote the report in the specified time, whereas only 32 percent of the control participants did so. The authors concluded that the higher success in the implementation intention condition was not due to participants' having their motivation increased. Rather, it was due to the fact that forming if–then plans helped them to meet their goal by facilitating action initiation, as measures that would indicated higher motivation (e.g., length of reports) did not differ between groups.

Other studies have examined the effects of implementation intentions on goal attainment rates with goal intentions that are somewhat unpleasant to perform. For instance, the goal intentions to perform regular breast examinations (Orbell, Hodgkins, and Sheeran 1997), cervical cancer screenings (Sheeran and Orbell 2000), resumption of functional activity after joint replacement surgery (Orbell and Sheeran 2000), and physical exercise (Milne, Orbell, and Sheeran 2002) were all more frequently acted upon when people had furnished these goals with implementation intentions. Furthermore, implementation intentions facilitated the attainment of goal intentions in patient populations that are known to have problems with the control of goal-directed behaviors (e.g., heroin addicts during withdrawal; Brandstätter et al. 2001, Study 1).

Evidence presented by Jordan Grafman and Frank Krueger (this volume) demonstrates that special populations such as frontal lobe lesion (FLL) patients have particular difficulty in tasks with ill-structured environments. They make a distinction between volition (ability to make a conscious choice or decision) and autonomy (ability to choose among viable alternatives), as volition may be intact in FLL individuals but autonomy is impaired. That is, FLL individuals have little difficulty making decisions on a more local level but decisions on a global level are more difficult. Grafman and Krueger (this volume) concluded based on their findings that almost all FLL patients have some preserved volitional ability. Impaired performance arises most in situations in which choices are more ambiguous and autonomy is required to choose among alternatives. In line with this analysis, Lengfelder and Gollwitzer (2001) reasoned that patients with frontal lobe damage may be a population who would especially benefit from forming implementation intentions. Implementation intentions help to automate the link between a situational cue and a response, which decreases the need to rely on making choices on a higher or global level. Results by Lengfelder and Gollwitzer (2001) showed improved task performance on a go/no-go task in frontal lobe patients who had formed respective implementation intentions, and these benefits were even observed under conditions of high cognitive load.

The method involved having three groups of participants (patients with frontal lobe lesions, patients with nonfrontal lobe lesions, university students) perform a dual task (tracking task, go/no-go task) on the computer. In the tracking task, subjects had to enclose a wandering circle within a square (controlled by moving the mouse) requiring continuous attention allocation; the simultaneous go/no-go task required subjects to press the left mouse button each time that a number appeared within the circle and to not press the button when a letter appeared. Therefore, this second task required intermittent attention. All participants were told that they should try to press the mouse button especially fast when the number "3" appeared on the computer screen, thereby establishing a critical cue that could be compared to noncritical cues (i.e., other numbers between 1 and 9). Then, all participants were told that certain mental strategies can aid with their performance. Those in the familiarization condition (control group) were told that an efficient mental strategy was to familiarize themselves with the number 3 by writing it down several times. Participants in the implementation intention condition formed an implementation intention: "If the number 3 appears, I will press the button particularly fast!" The control condition (i.e., familiarization) was expected to control for priming the number 3 and potential experimenter demand. The prediction was that all three groups of participants would show a stronger speed-up effect and less interference in the implementation intention condition. This prediction was confirmed with both lesion groups and university students showing significant speed-up responding in the implementation intention condition as compared to the familiarization condition. Furthermore, this speed-up effect was not at a cost to overall performance in responding to noncritical numbers.

As Peter Liddle (this volume) emphasizes, schizophrenic patients experience both disorganized volition (e.g., disordered thought, bizarre thought) and diminished volition (flat affect, poverty of speech). Liddle outlines the challenges faced by schizophrenics as the difficulty of selecting among a set of possible responses. His results show that schizophrenics exhibit difficulty compared to controls in attending to relevant stimuli and ignoring irrelevant stimuli. Not surprisingly, therefore, schizophrenic patients could also be shown to benefit in their action control from forming implementation intentions (Brandstätter, Lengfelder, and Gollwitzer 2001, Study 2). The method involved asking a group of schizophrenics and a group of matched controls to perform a go/no-go task (similar to the one used in the Lengfelder and

Gollwitzer study with frontal lobe patients) in which they had to respond by pressing a button when a number appeared on the computer screen and to not press the button if a letter appeared. There were two conditions: a control condition in which participants familiarized themselves with the number 3 and an implementation intention condition in which they formed the if–then plan "If number 3 appears, I will press the button particularly fast!" Overall, results demonstrated that both controls ($M = 43$ ms) and schizophrenics ($M = 34$ ms) were significantly faster in responding to critical stimuli in the implementation intention condition versus the familiarization condition.

Even though the positive effects of implementation intentions on action initiation seem easy to come by, there are a number of moderators to these effects that need to be taken in account. Various studies have observed that the strength of commitment to the respective goal intention matters. For instance, Orbell et al. (1997) report that the beneficial effects of implementation intentions on compliance in performing a health-protecting behavior (i.e., regular breast self-examination) were observed only in those women who strongly intended to perform such self-examinations to begin with. This finding suggests that implementation intentions do not work when the respective goal intention is weak. A study by Sheeran, Webb, and Gollwitzer (2005, Study 2) points to a further moderator. Goals either related or unrelated to the implementation intention were primed, with the result that implementation intentions then facilitated goal-directed behavior only when the respective superordinate goal had been activated. This finding suggests that implementation intention effects are moderated by the situational activation of the respective superordinate goal. In support of this hypothesis, a recent experiment (Cohen, Bayer, Jaudas, and Gollwitzer submitted) using the Rogers and Monsell (1995) task-switch paradigm demonstrated that implementation intentions only affect a person's task performance if the task at hand is relevant to the superordinate goal in the service of which the implementation intention was formed.

7.2 Shielding Ongoing Goal Pursuits

Whereas past research on implementation intentions has focused almost exclusively on getting started with moving toward a desired goal, recent research analyzes how implementation intentions can be used to control unwanted derailing of an ongoing goal pursuit (summary by Gollwitzer, Bayer, and McCulloch 2002). The latter can be achieved in two different ways. As long as people are in a position to anticipate what could potentially make them stray off course (the relevant hindrances, barriers, distractions, and temptations), they can specify these critical situations in the "if" part of an implementation intention and link them to responses that facilitate goal attainment. The response specified in the "then" part of an implementation intention can be geared at either ignoring disruptive stimuli, suppressing the impeding responses to them, or blocking obstructions to goal pursuit by engaging in it all the more.

This way of using implementation intentions to protect goal pursuit from straying off course necessitates that people know what kind of obstacles and distractions have to be watched for. Moreover, people need to know what kind of unwanted responses are potentially triggered (so that people can attempt to suppress them) or what kind of goal-directed responses are particularly effective in blocking these unwanted responses (so that people can engage in these goal-directed activities). In other words, using such implementation intentions to control unwanted straying off course requires much cognitive, clinical, and social-psychological knowledge. Otherwise no effective "if" and "then" components can be specified.

However, an alternative solution to protecting oneself from getting derailed is also available. Instead of concentrating on potential obstacles and various ways of effectively dealing with them, people may exclusively concern themselves with the intricacies of implementing the goal pursuit at hand. That is, an individual can plan out the goal pursuit by forming implementation intentions that determine how the various steps of goal attainment are to be executed. Such careful planning encapsulates goal pursuit, protecting it from the adverse influence of potential obstacles and distractions, whether internal or external. This use of implementation intentions allows the attainment of goals without having to change a noncooperative self (e.g., being in a state of irritation) or an unfavorable environment (e.g., disruptive intrusions). Critically, one does not need to possess any psychological knowledge on how to effectively deal with adverse self-states or situational contexts because it suffices if the person is aware of the demands of the current goal being pursued.

Research on how to use implementation intentions to shield an ongoing goal pursuit has thus analyzed two major strategies to control unwanted derailing: (a) directing one's implementation intentions toward the suppression of anticipated unwanted responses and (b) blocking all kinds of unwanted influences (even non-anticipated ones) from inside or outside the person by directing one's implementation intentions toward spelling out the wanted goal pursuit.

The first strategy of forming suppression-oriented implementation intentions can be executed in various different ways. If, for instance, a person wants to avoid being unfriendly to a friend who is known to make outrageous requests, she can protect herself from showing the unwanted unfriendly response by forming suppression-oriented implementation intentions that may take one of the following three different formats. The suppression-oriented implementation intention may focus on reducing the intensity of the unwanted response by intending not to show the unwanted response: "And if my friend approaches me with an outrageous request, then I will not respond in an unfriendly manner!" But it may also try to reduce the intensity of the unwanted response by specifying the initiation of the respective antagonistic response: "And if my friend approaches me with an outrageous request, then I will respond in a friendly manner!" Finally, a suppression-oriented implementation intention may focus a person away from the critical situation: "And if my friend approaches me with an outrageous request, then I'll ignore it!"

Two lines of experiments analyzed the effects of suppression-oriented implementation intentions. The first line looked at the control of unwanted spontaneous attending to tempting distractions (Gollwitzer and Schaal 1998). Participants had to perform an intellectual task (i.e., perform a series of arithmetic problems) while being bombarded with attractive distractive stimuli (e.g., video clips of award-winning commercials). Whereas control participants were asked to form a mere goal intention ("I will not let myself get distracted!"), experimental participants in addition formed one of two implementation intentions: "And if a distraction arises, then I'll ignore it!" or "And if a distraction arises, then I will increase my effort at the task at hand!" The "ignore" implementation intention always helped participants to ward off the distractions (as assessed by the level of task performance), regardless of whether the motivation to perform the tedious task (as manipulated at the beginning of the task) was low or high. The effort-increase implementation intention, in contrast, was effective only when motivation to perform the tedious task was low. Apparently, when motivation is high to begin with, effort-increase implementation intentions may create overmotivation that hampers task performance. It seems appropriate therefore to advise motivated individuals who suffer from being distracted (e.g., ambitious students doing their homework) to resort to "ignore" implementation intentions, rather than to implementation intentions that focus on the strengthening of task effort.

The second line of experiments analyzing suppression-oriented implementation intentions studied the control of the automatic activation of stereotypical beliefs and prejudicial evaluations (Gollwitzer and Schaal 1998; Gollwitzer, Achtziger, Schaal, and Hammelbeck 2002). In various priming studies using short stimulus-onset asynchronies of less than 300 ms between primes (presentations of members of stigmatized groups) and targets (adjectives describing relevant positive/negative stereotypical attributes or neutral positive/negative adjectives), research participants using implementation intentions inhibited the activation of stereotypical beliefs and prejudicial evaluations about women, the elderly, the homeless, and soccer fans. The implementation intentions described a scenario of being confronted with a member of the critical group in the "if" part, and a "then I won't stereotype" (respectively: "then I won't evaluate negatively"), or a "then I will ignore the group membership" response in the "then" part. Regardless of which formats were used, both types of suppression-oriented implementation intentions were effective in suppressing the activation of stereotypical beliefs and prejudicial evaluations.

Suppression implementation intentions specify a critical situation or problem in the "if" part, which is then linked to a "then" part that describes an attempt at suppressing the unwanted response. This type of self-regulation by implementation intentions implies that the person needs to anticipate potential hindrances to achieving the goal, and what kind of unwanted responses these hindrances elicit. However, implementation intentions can also be used to protect oneself against unwanted derailing of a goal pursuit by taking a quite different approach. Instead of directing one's implementation intentions toward anticipated potential hindrances and the unwanted responses triggered thereof, the person may form implementation intentions directed at stabilizing the goal pursuit at hand. Consider again the example of a tired person who is approached by her friend with an outrageous request and who will likely respond in an unfriendly manner: If this person has stipulated in advance in an implementation intention what she will converse about with her friend, the critical interaction should simply run off as planned, and the self-state of feeling provoked and angry should fail to affect the person's responding to the outrageous request in a negative, unwanted way. As is evident from this example, the present self-regulatory strategy should be of special value whenever the influence of detrimental self-states (e.g., being angry and irritated) on derailing one's goal-directed behavior has to be controlled. This should be true no matter whether such self-states and/or their influence on behavior reside in the person's consciousness or not.

Gollwitzer and Bayer (2000) tested this hypothesis in a series of experiments in which participants were asked to make plans (i.e., form implementation intentions) regarding their performance on an assigned task or not. Prior to beginning the task, participants' self-states were manipulated so that the task at hand became more difficult (e.g., a state of self-definitional incompleteness prior to a task that required perspective taking; Gollwitzer and Wicklund 1985; a good mood prior to a task that required evaluating others nonstereotypically; Bless and Fiedler 1995; a state of ego-depletion prior to solving difficult anagrams; Baumeister 2000; Muraven, Tice, and Baumeister 1998). The results suggested that the induced critical self-states negatively affected task performance (i.e., goal attainment) only for those participants who had not planned out working on the task at hand via implementation intentions (i.e., had only set themselves the goal to come up with a great performance). In other words, implementation intentions that spelled out how to perform the task at hand were effective in protecting the research participants from the negative effects associated with the induced detrimental self-states.

This research provides a new perspective on the psychology of self-regulation. Commonly, effective self-regulation is understood in terms of strengthening the self, so that the self can meet the challenge of being a powerful executive agent (Baumeister, Heatherton, and Tice 1994). Therefore, most research on goal-directed self-regulation focuses on strengthening the self in such a way that threats and irritations become less likely, or on restoring an already threatened or irritated self. It is important to recognize that all of these maneuvers focus on changing the self so that the self becomes a better executive. The findings of Gollwitzer and Bayer (2000) suggest a perspective on goal-directed self-regulation that focuses on facilitating action control without changing the self. It assumes that action control becomes easier if a person's behavior is directly controlled by situational cues and that the forming of implementation intentions achieves such direct action control. As this mode of action control circumvents the self, it no longer matters if the self is threatened or secure, agitated or calm, because the self is effectively disconnected from its influence on behavior. The research by Gollwitzer and Bayer (2000) supports this line of reasoning by demonstrating that task performance (i.e., taking the perspective of another person, judging people in a nonstereotypical manner, solving difficult anagrams) does not suffer any impairment from the respective detrimental self-states (e.g., self-definitional incompleteness, mood, and ego-depletion) if performing these tasks has been planned in advance via implementation intentions.

People's goal pursuits, however, are threatened not only by detrimental self-states but also by adverse situational contexts. There are many situations that have negative effects on goal attainment unbeknownst to the person who is striving for the goal. A prime example is the social loafing phenomenon, where people show reduced effort in the face of work settings that produce a reduction of accountability (i.e., performance outcomes can no longer be checked at an individual level). As people are commonly not aware of this phenomenon, they cannot form implementation intentions that specify a social loafing situation as a critical situation, thereby rendering an implementation intention that focuses on suppressing the social loafing response as an unviable self-regulatory strategy. As an alternative, however, people may resort to forming implementation intentions that stipulate how the intended task is to be performed and thus effectively block any negative situational influences.

Supporting this contention, Endress (2001) performed a social loafing experiment that used a brain storming task (i.e., participants had to find as many different uses for a common knife as possible). She observed that implementation intentions ("And if I have found one solution, then I will immediately try to find a different solution!") but not goal intentions ("I will try to find as many different solutions as possible!") protected participants from social loafing effects. Findings reported by Trötschel and Gollwitzer (2003) also support the notion that goal pursuits planned by forming implementation intentions become invulnerable to adverse situational influences. In their experiments on the self-regulation of negotiation behavior, loss-framed negotiation settings failed to unfold their negative effects on fair and cooperative negotiation outcomes when the negotiators had in advance planned out their goal intentions to be fair and cooperative with if–then plans. Similarly, Gollwitzer (1998) reports experiments in which competing goal intentions (i.e., goal intentions contrary to an ongoing goal pursuit) were activated outside of a person's awareness using goal-priming procedures (Bargh 1990; Bargh, Gollwitzer, Lee-Chai, Barndollar, and

Troetschel 2001). In these studies, furnishing the ongoing goal pursuit with implementation intentions protected it from the intrusive influences of the primed competing goals.

It appears, then, that the self-regulatory strategy of planning out goal pursuit in advance via implementation intentions allows the person to reap the desired positive outcomes without having to change the environment from an adverse to a facilitative one. There are many situations in which it is impossible to influence the environment because environmental change may sometimes be very cumbersome (e.g., it takes the costly interventions of mediators to change the loss frames adopted by conflicting parties into gain frames) or not under the person's control. Moreover, people are often not aware of the adverse influences of the current environment (e.g., a deindividuated work setting or a loss-framed negotiation setting) or they do not know what alternative kind of environmental setting is actually facilitative (e.g., an individualized work setting or a gain-framed negotiation setting). In these situations, the self-regulatory strategy of specifying critical situations in the "if" part of an implementation intention and linking them to a coping response in the "then" part does not qualify as a viable alternative self-regulatory strategy. Rather, people need to resort to the strategy of planning out goal pursuit in advance via implementation intentions, thereby protecting it from adverse situational influences.

7.3 Remembering to Execute Intentions: Prospective Memory

Research on goal pursuit and implementation intentions is thematically similar to another related research domain known as prospective memory. Prospective memory focuses more on the memory aspect of carrying out intentions and is defined as the ability to remember to execute a delayed intention. An interesting conundrum frequently occurs in daily life in which we intend to remember to take some medication, keep an appointment, or mail a letter but find ourselves forgetting to carry out this previously encoded intention. Despite the strong intent or will or volition to remember to do something, these types of memory errors are reported as the most frequent form of memory failures. In recent years, this aspect of human cognition has been the focus of an increasing number of experimental paradigms.

Researchers McDaniel and Einstein (1992) proposed that successful prospective memory is supported by two related component processes. The prospective component is defined as the realization that some prospective action is to be performed when an appropriate cue is encountered. The retrospective component is defined as the ability to recall an intention when the prospective cue is detected. Thus, we must remember at an appropriate moment that we must do something (prospective component), and we have to recall what is to be done (retrospective component). For example, if an individual has to remember to give a friend a message, successful prospective memory requires that the appearance of the friend trigger the memory that a message has to be given (prospective component). Successful prospective memory also requires that the individual remember the content of the message (retrospective component). Despite one's best intentions, prospective memory often fails in one of two ways. A person may completely forget upon seeing the friend that there is a message to give (failure of the prospective component) or may remember that there is a message to give but forget what the actual message is (failure of the retrospective component).

Implementation intentions can be decomposed into components similar to those specified in the McDaniel and Einstein (1992) distinction. For example, when participants form an implementation intention, they say: "If situation X arises, then I will perform response Y." Therefore, the first portion of the implementation intention, "if situation X arises," is focused on specifying a situational cue that will eventually be linked with the goal-directed behavior. It focuses on the "I will have to do *something* when I encounter X." Therefore, this first half of the implementation intention may serve to establish the noticing process or prospective component of prospective memory. The second part of the implementation intention, "I will perform response Y," may serve to establish or strengthen memory for the content of the intention. This enables the individual to remember what that "something" actually is; therefore, it strengthens the search process or retrospective component of prospective memory. By forming an implementation intention, participants establish a link between both components, and it may be this association that leads to a benefit in performance.

According to a model of prospective memory known as the automatic associative module model (McDaniel et al. 1998; see also Moscovitch 1994), successful prospective remembering occurs when there is sufficient interaction between a prospective cue and an associated memory trace. A module (subserved by the hippocampus) is thought to respond reflexively to cues. This results in the memory trace for the intended action being delivered automatically to consciousness (McDaniel et al. 1998). Thus, successful prospective remembering is determined by the strength of association between the cue and associated memory trace. If the cue does not automatically interact with a memory trace, then that memory trace is not retrieved unless another memory module (prefrontal component) initiates a strategic memory search. In this model, the planning and encoding stage of prospective memory is critical for successful performance because an association between a cue and an intention must be made to ensure successful prospective remembering. It is at this point that descriptions of prospective memory become conceptually similar to discussions of implementation intentions. Earlier in the chapter, we stated that forming an implementation intention causes the mental representation of the situational cue to become highly activated and thus more easily accessible (Gollwitzer 1999). And it is this heightened accessibility that makes it easier to detect the critical situation in the surrounding environment and readily attend to it even when one is busy with other ongoing activity. Moreover, this heightened accessibility should facilitate the recall of the critical situation because a strong link had been formed between the two components (situation cue + response).

Findings from research on implementation intentions provide evidence that is consistent with predictions made by the automatic associative model. For example, the automatic associative model suggests that a cue must automatically interact with a memory trace for a prospective memory intention to be retrieved. In line with this claim, results from several studies on implementation intentions showed that successful goal completion was accomplished by establishing strong mental links between anticipated environmental cues and behaviors (Gollwitzer 1999). Furthermore, results from Lengfelder and Gollwitzer (2001) demonstrated that behavior was reflexive and did not require conscious deliberation once the critical situation cue is encountered. These studies showed that goal-directed behavior is initiated through links that are established between intended situations and goal-directed behavior. It may be that successful prospective remembering can be accomplished through similar reflexive associations between cues and previously encoded intentions. For example, in a study by Guynn, McDaniel, and Einstein (1998), participants were given various types of reminders during the retention interval of a prospective memory task. Based on their results, the authors concluded that the most effective reminders were those that served to improve both the prospective memory cues and the intended activity itself. According to their findings, reminders that activated this association were most beneficial for prospective memory performance.

We have discussed the various similarities between the domains of prospective memory and implementation intentions, but there are some significant differences between them as well. For example, implementation intentions are always formed within the context of serving a respective higher-order goal. Furthermore, the relationship between the implementation intention and the respective goal can determine the outcome—for example, it matters whether the person is strongly committed to the goal. Prospective memory, in contrast, has never been considered within the context of some higher order goal. Rather, successful retrieval and execution of the intention *itself* is the goal at issue.

When goals or intentions must be postponed or set aside temporarily, successful memory retrieval and execution of the intention can be especially difficult with increasing age. The ability to perform well in prospective memory tasks (e.g., remembering to take medication) is obviously essential for independent living.

The frontal lobes are assumed to play a critical role in cognitive activities such as planning actions, monitoring one's behavior, and keeping information active in working memory (Baddeley 1986; West 1996). There is neuropsychological and neuroanatomical evidence that changes in the aging brain are particularly pronounced in the frontal areas (West 1996). The frontal lobe hypothesis posits that mental functions that rely on the frontal lobes will be particularly susceptible to declines with aging. However, results pertaining to age differences in prospective memory performance are mixed, with some studies reporting no deficits for older adults (e.g., Einstein and McDaniel 1990; Einstein, Holland, McDaniel, and Guynn 1992) and others observing significant age-related differences (e.g., Dobbs and Rule 1987; Einstein, McDaniel, Smith, and Shaw 1998; West and Craik 1999).

Paul Burgess, Sam J. Gilbert, Jiro Okuda, and Jon S. Simons (this volume) report results indicating that the rostral prefrontal cortex (PFC) supports delayed intention performance. More specifically, their findings showed that the lateral rostral PFC (Brodmann Area 10) seems to be involved in maintaining an intention (i.e., while engaged in an ongoing task) and medial Brodmann Area 10 is more involved when one is concentrating on the ongoing task alone. When maintaining an intention in mind, one must periodically switch conscious attention to one's internal representation of the intention, and the lateral regions appear to subserve this attention switch. In contrast, the medial region plays a role when one wants to put attentional focus on some external stimuli and minimize attention that is allocated to maintaining the intention. It may be that age differences in prospective memory are due to older adults' difficulty with switching attention between the ongoing activity of the primary task and the internal representation of the intention.

If we think of the retention interval in prospective memory as an effortful undertaking in which one must maintain the content of an intention in mind while continuing ongoing activities, one would predict that such cognitive operations may be vulnerable to age-related decline. Maylor (1996) claimed that prospective memory is inherently effortful because an intention must be retrieved when one is in the midst of some other competing activity. That is, retrieval of the intention must interrupt the ongoing flow of thought and activity in order to be properly executed. The person must disengage from an ongoing activity in order to carry out the action or intention at the appropriate time (Einstein and McDaniel 1990).

Despite the striking similarities between ideas elaborated within research on implementation intentions and prospective memory, few empirical investigations have examined how these two domains interact. It may be that the use of compensatory self-regulatory techniques such as implementation intentions could help alleviate the burden for older adults by causing intention-related behavior to become reflexive. Indeed, several studies (e.g., Cohen, Dixon, Lindsay, and Masson 2003; Cohen, West, and Craik 2001) have shown that older adults have particular difficulty with performance on the prospective component of prospective memory (ability to detect the prospective memory cue) as compared to the retrospective component (recalling the associated intention). Thus, implementation intentions that involve specifying in advance a cue that will elicit a desired response may be especially helpful in such prospective memory contexts.

There is one published study within the prospective memory literature that explicitly tests whether forming implementation intentions provides a benefit to an older adult population. Chasteen, Park, and Schwarz (2001) showed that forming implementation intentions significantly enhanced older adults' prospective memory performance. The authors concluded that implementation intentions benefited older adults' prospective memory functioning by allowing them to take advantage of the fact that this technique recruits automatic rather than effortful controlled memory processes. Their results showed that creating an implementation intention allowed behavior to become reflexive, thus eliminating the need for conscious control once the prospective memory cue target was encountered. Therefore, encoding an implementation intention sets stored action schemas into a state of readiness, and when the appropriate trigger conditions are satisfied, the intention can be executed without mediation of a conscious recollection of the intention. This research demonstrated that implementation intentions facilitated the attainment of goal intentions in a situation where it was easy to forget to act on them.

7.4 Conclusion

Much of the evidence reviewed in the current chapter suggests that implementation intentions help not only to promote initiation of goal pursuits but also to protect goal pursuits from being thwarted by various forms of distractions. As long as we are in a position to anticipate what could potentially make us stray off course (barriers, interruptions, distractions, and temptations), we can specify these critical situations in the "if" part of an implementation intention and link it to a response that facilitates goal attainment. The response specified in the "then" part of an implementation intention can then be geared at either ignoring disruptive stimuli, suppressing the impeding responses to them, or blocking obstructions to goal pursuit by engaging in it all the more. Alternatively, people may simply focus on spelling out the critical goal pursuit by forming respective implementation intentions, thus blocking it even from unanticipated distractions and disruptions.

Furthermore, while these plans can be formed instantly by an act of will, no such conscious effort is needed to carry out the planned goal-directed action. As goals are mentally represented as knowledge structures, these encapsulated plans too have a specific structure. Implementation intentions create cognitive links between select situational cues and intended goal-directed behaviors. Once this cue is actually encountered, the planned behavior runs off automatically, overriding and defying any habits or divisive spontaneous attentional responses. If we consider if–then plans in the context of Prinz, Dennett, and Sebanz's (this volume) vision of a bottom-up mechanisim, we would have to conclude that implementation intentions involve aspects of both top-down and bottom-up processing. For example, it can be thought of as a top-down approach in terms of the selection and purposeful formation of a plan, but then the plan runs off in a bottom-up automatic fashion when the previously specified situational cue is encountered.

The potential strength of implementation intentions can also be considered in the context of the self-model theory described by Metzinger (this volume). Implementation intentions can be thought of as a representational coding strategy that allows them to be integrated into a person's unconscious self model. Therefore, a goal is formed and incorporated into the self model, but future action initiation (carrying out the implementation intention) does not take place in the phenomenal self-model, which is highly sensitive to a multitude of overlapping contexts. Rather, implementation intentions can be thought of as "functionally encapsulated," allowing the system to be automatically driven via the self-generated cue–action association. Therefore, conscious effortful processing occurs when the implementation intention is encoded. But when the previously specified situational cue is encountered, the associated response is triggered automatically. We would hesitate to say that action initiation is unconscious per se; rather, it is obligatory once the associated cue is recognized.

The potential benefit of implementation intentions is important not only for the average individual's everyday goal-directed activities but for other populations such as brain-injured patients (e.g., Lengfelder and Gollwitzer 2001), opiate addicts, schizophrenics (e.g., Brandstätter et al. 2001), and older adults (e.g., Chasteen et al. 2001) who experience symptoms that interfere with goal attainment. A perfect testing ground for the effectiveness of implementation intentions on a difficult-to-implement behavior would be with individuals who are attempting to quit smoking. As Sayette (this volume) states, in the United States smoking remains the leading preventable cause of premature death with 25 percent of the population being identified as smokers. That is, a large proportion of people persist in the destructive behavior of smoking, despite the known risks. A smoking habit is a very repetitive, well-defined behavior for which one could easily establish a situational cue and response that would serve the higher goal of helping individuals quit smoking and ultimately improving their health. As Sayette reports, many aspects of smokers' cognitions about their smoking behavior are inaccurate (e.g., time perception, anticipated urge duration), and thus a self-regulatory strategy that relies on automatic action initiation should benefit smokers more so than consciously controlled strategies. Because the act of taking a cigarette out of its pack, lighting it, and taking the first drag is a well-practiced and familiar behavior, it would be fairly simple to set up an implementation intention that would establish a situational cue and response serving to help reduce smoking behaviors. For example, a potential suppression-oriented implementation intention could be "If I light a cigarette, then I will think of my favourite uncle who died of lung cancer."

Other populations such as depressed patients may also benefit from the use of a strategy that improves goal-directed activity. As the contributions on depression in this volume show (Jouvent, Dubal, and Fossati, this volume; Nitschke and Mackiewicz, this volume; Schneider, this volume), the impact of depression on behavior results in loss of drive, decreased interest, and lower levels of overall activity. Furthermore, depression appears to reduce overall goal-directed behavior. Thus, there is a need for ameliorative techniques such as implementation intentions to facilitate goal-directed activity. Given the limited resources for conscious self-regulation in depressed individuals (given the burden produced by ruminative thought), delegating control to situational cues by one express act of will should be a particularly welcome way to bridge the gap that exists between good intentions and the successful attainment of them.

Acknowledgments

This essay was funded by a postdoctoral fellowship awarded to the first author, Anna-Lisa Cohen, from the Social Sciences and Humanities Research Council of Canada: 756-2003-0105.

References

Ajzen, I. 1991. The theory of planned behavior. *Organizational Behavior and Human Decision Processes, 50*, 179–211.

Anderson, J. R. 1987. Skill acquisition: Compilation of weak-method problem solutions. *Psychological Review, 94*, 192–210.

Baddeley, A. D. 1986. *Working Memory*. Oxford: Oxford University Press.

Baldwin, J. M. 1897. *Social and Ethical Interpretations in Mental Development: A Study in Social Development*. London: Macmillan.

Bandura, A. 1991. Self-regulation of motivation through anticipatory and self-reactive mechanisms. In *Nebraska Symposium on Motivation: Perspectives on Motivation*, vol. 38, ed. R. A. Dienstbier, pp. 69–164. Lincoln: University of Nebraska Press.

Bargh, J. A. 1990. Auto-motives: Preconscious determinants of social interaction. In *Handbook of Motivation and Cognition: Foundations of Social Behavior*, vol. 2, ed. E. T. Higgins and R. M. Sorrentino, pp. 93–130. New York: Guilford Press.

Bargh, J. A. 1994. The four horsemen of automaticity: Awareness, intention, efficiency, and control in social cognition. In *Handbook of Social Cognition, vol. 1: Basic Processes*, 2nd ed., ed. R. S. Wyer, Jr., and T. K. Srull, pp. 1–40. Hillsdale, N.J.: Erlbaum.

Bargh, J. A., P. M. Gollwitzer, A. Lee-Chai, K. Barndollar, and R. Troetschel. 2001. The automated will: Nonconscious activation and pursuit of behavioral goals. *Journal of Personality and Social Psychology, 81,* 1014–1027.

Baumeister, R. F. 2000. Ego-depletion and the self's executive function. In *Psychological perspectives on self and identity,* ed. A. Tesser, R. B. Felson, and J. M. Suls, pp. 9–33. Washington, D.C.: American Psychological Association.

Baumeister, R. F., T. F. Heatherton, and D. M. Tice. 1994. *Losing Control: How and Why People Fail at Self-Regulation.* San Diego: Academic Press.

Bless, H., and K. Fiedler. 1995. Affective states and the influence of activated general knowledge. *Personality and Social Psychology Bulletin, 21,* 766–778.

Brandstätter, V., A. Lengfelder, and P. M. Gollwitzer. 2001. Implementation intentions and efficient action initiation. *Journal of Personality and Social Psychology, 81,* 946–960.

Chasteen, A. L., D. C. Park, and N. Schwarz. 2001. Implementation intentions and facilitation of prospective memory. *Psychological Science, 12,* 457–461.

Cohen, A.-L., U. C. Bayer, A. Jaudas, and P. M. Gollwitzer. Submitted. Self-regulatory strategy and executive control: Implementation intentions modulate task switching and Simon Task performance.

Cohen, A.-L., R. A. Dixon, D. S. Lindsay, and M. E. J. Masson. 2003. The effect of perceptual distinctiveness on the prospective and retrospective components of prospective memory for young and older adults. *Canadian Journal of Experimental Psychology, 57,* 274–289.

Cohen, A.-L., R. West, and F. I. M. Craik. 2001. Modulation of the prospective and retrospective components of memory for intentions in younger and older adults. *Aging, Neuropsychology, and Cognition, 8,* 1–13.

Craik, F. I. M. 1986. A functional account of age differences in memory. In *Human Memory and Cognitive Capabilities: Mechanisms and Performances,* ed. F. Klix and H. Hagendorf, pp. 409–422. Amsterdam: Elsevier.

Craik, F. I. M., and S. A. Kerr. 1996. Prospective memory, aging, and lapses of intention. In *Prospective Memory: Theory and Applications,* ed. M. Brandimonte, G. O. Einstein, and M. A. McDaniel, pp. 227–237. Mahwah, N.J.: Erlbaum.

Dobbs, A. R., and B. G. Rule. 1987. Prospective memory and self-reports of memory abilities in older adults. *Canadian Journal of Psychology, 41,* 209–222.

d'Ydewalle, G., D. Bouckaert, and E. Brunfaut. 2001. Age-related differences and complexity of ongoing activities in time- and event-based prospective memory. *American Journal of Psychology, 114,* 411–423.

Einstein, G. O., L. J. Holland, M. A. McDaniel, and M. J. Guynn. 1992. Age-related deficits in prospective memory: The influence of task complexity. *Psychology and Aging, 7,* 471–478.

Einstein, G. O., and M. A. McDaniel. 1990. Normal aging and prospective memory. *Journal of Experimental Psychology: Learning, Memory, and Cognition, 16*, 717–726.

Einstein, G. O., M. A. McDaniel, R. Smith, and P. Shaw. 1998. Habitual prospective memory and aging: Remembering instructions and forgetting actions. *Psychological Science, 9*, 284–288.

Endress, H. 2001. *Die Wirksamkeit von Vorsätzen auf Gruppenleistungen. Eine empirische Untersuchung anhand von brainstorming.* (Implementation intentions and the reduction of social loafing in a brain storming task.) Unpublished master's thesis. University of Konstanz, Germany.

Fitts, P. M., and M. I. Posner. 1967. *Human Performance.* Monterey, Calif.: Brooks-Cole.

Glisky, E. L. 1996. Prospective memory and the frontal lobes. In *Prospective Memory: Theory and Applications*, ed. M. Brandimonte, G. O. Einstein, and M. A. McDaniel, pp. 249–266. Mahwah, N.J.: Erlbaum.

Godin, G., and G. Kok. 1996. The theory of planned behavior: A review of its applications in health-related behaviors. *American Journal of Health Promotion, 11*, 87–98.

Gollwitzer, P. M. 1993. Goal achievement: The role of intentions. *European Review of Social Psychology, 4*, 141–185.

Gollwitzer, P. M. 1996. The volitional benefits of planning. In *The Psychology of Action: Linking Cognition and Motivation to Behavior*, ed. P. M. Gollwitzer and J. A. Bargh, pp. 287–312. New York: Guilford Press.

Gollwitzer, P. M. 1998. Implicit and explicit processes in goal pursuit. Paper presented at the Symposium "Implicit vs. Explicit Processes" at the Annual Meeting of the Society of Experimental Social Psychology, Atlanta, Georgia.

Gollwitzer, P. M. 1999. Implementation intentions: Strong effects of simple plans. *American Psychologist, 54*, 493–503.

Gollwitzer, P. M., A. Achtziger, B. Schaal, and J. P. Hammelbeck. 2002. Intentional control of stereotypical beliefs and prejudicial feelings. Unpublished manuscript. University of Konstanz, Germany.

Gollwitzer, P. M., and U. C. Bayer. 2000. Becoming a better person without changing the self. Paper presented at the Self and Identity Pre-conference of the Annual Meeting of the Society of Experimental Social Psychology, Atlanta, Georgia.

Gollwitzer, P. M., U. Bayer, and K. McCulloch. 2005. The control of the unwanted. In *The New Unconscious*, ed. R. Hassin, J. Uleman, and J. A. Bargh, pp. 485–515. Oxford: Oxford University Press.

Gollwitzer, P. M., and V. Brandstätter. 1997. Implementation intentions and effective goal pursuit. *Journal of Personality and Social Psychology, 73*, 186–199.

Gollwitzer, P. M., and G. B. Moskowitz. 1996. Goal effects on action and cognition. In *Social Psychology: Handbook of Basic Principles*, ed. E. T. Higgins and A. W. Kruglanski, pp. 361–399. New York: Guilford.

Gollwitzer, P. M., and B. Schaal. 1998. Metacognition in action: The importance of implementation intentions. *Personality and Social Psychology Review, 2*, 124–136.

Gollwitzer, P. M., and R. A. Wicklund. 1985. Self-symbolizing and the neglect of others' perspectives. *Journal of Personality and Social Psychology, 56*, 531–715.

Guynn, M. J., M. A. McDaniel, and G. O. Einstein. 1998. Prospective memory: When reminders fail. *Memory and Cognition, 26*, 287–298.

Huppert, F. A., and L. Beardsall. 1993. Prospective memory impairment as an early indicator of dementia. *Journal of Clinical and Experimental Neuropsychology, 15*, 805–821.

Lengfelder, A., and P. M. Gollwitzer. 2001. Reflective and reflexive action control in patients with frontal brain lesions. *Neuropsychology, 15*, 80–100.

Locke, E. A., and G. P. Latham. 1990. *A Theory of Goal Setting and Task Performance.* Englewood Cliffs, N.J.: Prentice Hall.

Maylor, E. A. 1996. Does prospective memory decline with age? In *Prospective Memory: Theory and Applications*, ed. M. Brandimonte, G. O. Einstein, and M. A. McDaniel, pp. 173–197. Mahwah, N.J.: Erlbaum.

McDaniel, M. A. 1995. Prospective memory: Progress and processes. In *The Psychology of Learning and Motivation*, ed. D. L. Medin, pp. 191–222. San Diego: Academic Press.

McDaniel, M. A., and G. O. Einstein. 1992. Aging and prospective memory: Basic findings and practical applications. *Advances in Learning and Behavioral Disabilities, 7*, 87–105.

McDaniel, M. A., and G. O. Einstein. 2000. Strategic and automatic processes in prospective memory retrieval: A multiprocess framework. *Applied Cognitive Psychology, 14*, S127–S144.

McDaniel, M. A., B. Robinson-Riegler, and G. O. Einstein. 1998. Prospective remembering: Perceptually driven or conceptually driven processes? *Memory and Cognition, 26*, 121–134.

Milne, S., S. Orbell, and P. Sheeran, P. 2002. Combining motivational and volitional interventions to promote exercise participation: Protection motivation theory and implementation intentions. *British Journal of Health Psychology, 7*, 163–184.

Moscovitch, M. 1994. Memory and working-with-memory: Evaluation of a component process model and comparisons with other models. In *Memory Systems*, ed. D. L. Schacter and E. Tulving, pp. 269–310. Cambridge, Mass.: MIT Press.

Muraven, M., D. M. Tice, and R. F. Baumeister. 1998. Self-control as a limited resource: Regulatory depletion pattern. *Journal of Personality and Social Psychology, 74*, 774–789.

Newell, A., and P. S. Rosenbloom. 1981. Mechanisms of skill acquisition and the law of practice. In *Cognitive Skills and Their Acquisition*, ed. J. R. Anderson, pp. 1–55. Hillsdale, N.J.: Erlbaum.

Olson, D. R., J. W. Astington, and P. D. Zelazo. 1999. Introduction: Actions, intentions, and attributions. In *Developing Theories of Intention: Social Understanding and Self-Control*, ed. P. D. Zelazo, J. W. Astington, and D. R. Olson, pp. 1–13. Mahwah, N.J.: Lawrence Erlbaum.

Orbell, S., S. Hodgkins, and P. Sheeran. 1997. Implementation intentions and the theory of planned behavior. *Personality and Social Psychology Bulletin, 23*, 945–954.

Orbell, S., and P. Sheeran. 1998. "Inclined abstainers": A problem for predicting health-related behavior. *British Journal of Social Psychology, 37*, 151–165.

Orbell, S., and P. Sheeran. 2000. Motivational and volitional processes in action initiation: A field study of the role of implementation intentions. *Journal of Applied Social Psychology, 30*, 780–797.

Park, D. C., C. Hertzog, D. P. Kidder, and R. W. Morell. 1997. Effect of age on event-based and time-based prospective memory. *Psychology and Aging, 12*, 314–327.

Rogers, D., and S. Monsell. 1995. Costs of a predictable switch between simple cognitive tasks. *Journal of Experimental Psychology: General, 124*, 207–231.

Sheeran, P. 2002. Intention–behavior relations: A conceptual and empirical review. *European Review of Social Psychology, 12*, 1–30.

Sheeran, P., and S. Orbell. 1999. Implementation intentions and repeated behavior: Augmenting the predictive validity of the theory of planned behavior. *European Journal of Social Psychology, 29*, 349–369.

Sheeran, P., and S. Orbell. 2000. Using implementation intentions to increase attendance for cervical cancer screening. *Health Psychology, 19*, 283–289.

Sheeran, P., T. L. Webb, and P. M. Gollwitzer. 2005. The interplay between goal intentions and implementation intentions. *Personality and Social Psychology Bulletin, 31*, 87–98.

Smith, R. E. 2003. The cost of remembering to remember in event-based prospective memory: Investigating the capacity demands of delayed intention performance. *Journal of Experimental Psychology: Learning, Memory, and Cognition, 29*, 347–361.

Ste-Marie, D. M., and L. L. Jacoby. 1993. Spontaneous versus directed recognition: The relativity of automaticity. *Journal of Experimental Psychology: Memory, Learning, and Cognition, 19*, 777–778.

Trötschel, R., and P. M. Gollwitzer. 2003. *Implementation Intentions and the Control of Framing Effects in Negotiations.* Manuscript under review.

West, R. 1996. An application of prefrontal cortex function theory to cognitive aging. *Psychological Bulletin, 120*, 272–292.

West, R., and F. I. M. Craik. 1999. Age-related decline in prospective memory: The roles of cue accessibility and cue sensitivity. *Psychology and Aging, 14*, 264–272.

West, R., and F. I. M. Craik. 2001. Influences on the efficiency of prospective memory in younger and older adults. *Psychology and Aging, 16*, 682–696.

Wicklund, R. A., and P. M. Gollwitzer. 1982. *Symbolic Self-Completion.* Hillsdale, N.J.: Erlbaum.

II Disorders of Volition in Schizophrenia

8 From Volition to Agency: The Mechanism of Action Recognition and Its Failures

Marc Jeannerod

8.1 Introduction: What Is Volition?

A brief semantic analysis of the word "volition" seems in order before the reader is introduced to this chapter of a book on "disorders of volition." To this aim, I have used a computerized semantic atlas which analyzes the sense of English words into clusters of contexonyms, that is, words which lie within the same semantic field (Ji et al. 2003; the semantic atlas can be consulted at http://www.isc.cnrs.fr/). Take, for example, the word "will." A large cluster of words within the semantic field of "will" refers to the "force of will" (e.g., "willpower," "strength of will," "mind"). The word "volition" is included within a smaller cluster of words which overlaps with "pleasure." The semantic field of the word "volition" itself includes words like "discretion," "option," "choice," or "preference." It also includes "will" and "free will." Thus, it appears that volition is associated with the notion of willing or considering to do something in relation to a deliberate and free choice but is clearly dissociated from the transfer of this choice into an intention or an executive force. Indeed, the semantic field of the word "intention," which is intuitively related to the anticipation of an action, includes neither "volition" nor "will."

Considering the meaning of volition in the above strict sense, the expression "disorders of volition" should only refer to those pathological conditions in which the ability to make choices, to express preferences, or possibly to experience pleasure and freedom in making these choices or expressing these preferences is affected. Many of these disorders are described in other chapters of this book (see Bechara, this volume; Nitschke and Mackiewicz, this volume). An extreme example of what could be a pathological condition of "avolition" has been described clinically under the term of "athymhormia": Such patients show loss of drive and search for satisfaction, lack of curiosity, lack of taste and preferences, and flattened affect. This condition, clearly distinct from depression, can be observed in schizophrenia and may also be caused by multiple lacunar lesions in the basal ganglia (Habib and Poncet 1988).

One major aspect of volition is its conscious nature. We experience a sense of conscious will when we execute an action or a sense of freedom when we express a preference. We feel and we strongly believe that our thoughts have a causal influence on our behavior. This feeling, Wegner suggests, is an illusion that results from our tendency to perceive ourselves as causal, while we actually ignore the cause from which our actions originate. Conscious free choice, like conscious will, is not a direct perception of a causal relation between a thought and an action, but rather a feeling based on the causal inference one makes about the data that do become available to consciousness—the thought and the observed action. The illusion arises from the fact that the thought and the observed action are consistently associated, even though they are not causally related (Wegner 2002).

Now consider pathological conditions in which this regularity of the association between a thought and an action disappears, or the perception that arises from this regularity is altered. In such a situation a subject should rapidly become convinced that the movements he produces were not caused by his conscious will and did not result from his free choice. In other words, the subject should lose the normal experience of agency, itself a constituent of the experience of volition, which allows an agent to feel responsible of his own actions and to attribute them to himself.

In this chapter, I will first describe experiments designed for testing the factors that contribute to the sense of agency in normal subjects. These experiments are based on a substitution paradigm borrowed from Nielsen (1963). This same paradigm will be subsequently used for examining the changes in brain activity related to different degrees of the experience of agency, both in normal subjects and in subjects where the sense of agency is pathologically affected.

8.2   The Nielsen Substitution Paradigm for Studying the Recognition of Self-Generated Actions

Pioneer experiments investigating the sense of agency were undertaken in the 1960s by Torsten Nielsen working at the Psychological Laboratory of the University of Copenhagen. One of the phenomena Nielsen thought of great importance for self-awareness was the volitional experience, that is, the experience of volitional or intentional control of perceived events, as opposed to the experience of no control of those events. Nielsen considered that an essential task for approaching this problem was to create situations in which the experiences of intentional control versus lack of control could be experimentally manipulated. To this aim, he created several varieties of a *substitution* paradigm, where the subjects received a false feedback from their own actions: In fact, what the subjects perceived was the effect of the actions of another person which was substituted for their own.

In one of Nielsen's experiments (Nielsen 1963), the subject was facing a box placed on a tabletop. He placed his hand holding a pencil on the table below the box and looked at it through the box. The box was equipped with a mirror which could be displaced by the experimenter between trials, unknown to the subject, so that the subject either saw his own hand or the hand of another person (the alien hand) through the mirror. The mirror was placed in such a way that the subject experienced that he was looking directly at his own hand while in reality he was presented with the alien hand, lying at the same location on the table as his own. Finally, to ensure that the subject had no cues to identify the hand he saw, the two hands were made undistinguishable by wearing identical gloves. During the experiment itself, the subject was requested to draw a straight line in the sagittal direction on a piece of paper. In those trials where the subject saw the alien hand, the alien hand was also doing the same task at about the same rate. In some trials, however, the alien hand carried out a movement that diverged from that which the subject was carrying out at the same time. The latter condition generated a conflict between what the subject saw and what he kinesthetically felt from what he was doing. In order to solve this conflict, the subjects tended to deviate the trajectory of their own (unseen) hand in the direction opposite to that of the alien hand, so as to fulfill the instruction they had received to draw a straight line (see Jeannerod 2004 for details on Nielsen's experiments).

According to Nielsen, all subjects experienced, in the conflict trials, that they saw their own hand moving involuntarily in the wrong direction. They remained unaware of having themselves performed a movement departing from the instruction by erring in the direction opposite to that of the alien hand to compensate for the conflict produced by the movement they saw: When shown their own deviant performance, they tried to explain it by factors independent of their volition, such as fatigue or inattention. In Nielsen's terms, some subjects reported impressions of loss of voluntary control, as if driving one's car on an icy road. Thus, this experiment revealed that subjects were poor at recognizing their own hand movements and tended to misattribute to themselves movements that were not theirs. The cues arising from the visual perception of the hand of the other person dominated the kinesthetic cues arising from the subject himself in determining self-awareness.

Nielsen's experiments were embedded into a conceptual framework aiming at a formal description of how human beings can act and reflect on their acts. His main idea was to present an alternative to psychological theories which are based on a deterministic and objectified view of human action. Human beings, rather than the psychologist, he thought, must provide themselves answers to the question of how they understand their own actions. By placing subjects in situations where everyday life activities become suddenly incomprehensible and infeasible, Nielsen thought that they would feel compelled to ask themselves questions on their own actions and that these spontaneous questions "would generate a useful and inspiring material for [his] efforts to constitute some basic concepts concerning action..." (Nielsen 1978, p. 258).

Although Nielsen's experiment dealt with recognition of action and with the degree of awareness that a subject can gain from his own movements, it said little about the cues that can be used for conscious determination of agency. This has been the objective of another set of experiments initiated by Daprati et al. (1997), which explored the factors of self-attribution of a moving hand. A substitution situation close to that designed by Nielsen (1963) was created where the subjects were shown movements of a hand of an uncertain origin, that is, a hand that could equally likely belong to them or to someone else. Subjects were instructed to explicitly determine whether or not they were the author of the hand movements they saw. In order to give such a response, they had to use all available cues for comparing the current movement of their unseen hand with the movement that was displayed to them. The task for the subjects was to perform a requested movement with their right hand and to monitor its execution by looking at the image in the mirror. At the beginning of each experimental trial, a blank screen was presented. An instruction to perform a movement was given, and the subject and the experimenter had to execute the requested movement at an acoustic signal. Once the movement was performed and the screen had returned to blank, a question was asked to the subject about whether the hand that he just saw was his or not. One of three possible images of the hand could be presented to the subjects in each trial: (1) their own hand (condition: Subject), (2) the experimenter's hand performing a different movement (condition: Experimenter Different), or (3) the experimenter's hand performing the same movement (condition: Experimenter Same).

Subjects were able to unambiguously determine whether the moving hand seen on the screen was theirs or not, in two conditions. First, when they saw their own hand (trials from the condition Subject), they correctly attributed the movement to themselves. Second, when they saw the experimenter's hand performing a movement which departed from the instruction they had received (condition Experimenter Different), they denied seeing their own hand. By contrast, their performance degraded in the condition Experimenter Same, that is, in those trials where they saw the experimenter's hand performing the same movement as required by the instruction: In this condition, they misjudged the hand as theirs in about 30 percent of cases. Subjects' judgment had to rely on slight differences in timing and kinematics between their intended movement and that which they perceived on the screen. This result therefore indicates that the threshold for action recognition must be relatively high and that small differences tend to be neglected.

8.3   The Mechanism of Action Recognition

There are several ways of conceiving the mechanisms involved in the recognition of one's actions. In the following paragraphs, two empirically based hypotheses of action recognition will be examined. The first hypothesis relies on the idea that executed actions generate signals which are centrally monitored and compared: Action recognition arises as the outcome of this comparison (the central monitoring hypothesis). The other hypothesis relies on the idea that actions, whether or not they come to execution, are centrally simulated by the neural network, and that this simulation is the basis for action recognition and attribution (the simulation hypothesis). These two theories will appear to be largely complementary (see Jeannerod 2003).

8.3.1 The Central Monitoring Hypothesis of Action Recognition

The first hypothesis to be considered, that which holds that the comparison between efferent signals at the origin of an action and those which arise from its execution (the reafferent signals) provides cues about where the action originates, is deeply rooted in physiological thinking. Let us first rephrase its basic principles. The original idea, inherited from the cybernetic era and still operational nowadays, is that each time the motor centers generate an outflow signal for producing a movement, a copy of this command (the "efference copy") is retained. The reafferent inflow signals generated by the movement (e.g., visual, proprioceptive) are compared with the copy. If a mismatch arises between the two types of signals, new commands are generated until the actual outcome of the movement corresponds to the desired movement (Sperry 1950; von Holst and Mittelstaedt 1950).

This model of the control of action can be directly applied to the problem of self-recognition. Self-recognition can be based on the concordance between a desired (or intended) action and its sensory consequences, which can be used to assess attribution of action to the self (see Wolpert et al. 1995; see Frith, this volume, for a more complete formulation of this idea). This hypothesis can be tested experimentally. Haggard et al. (2002), using a paradigm initiated by Libet et al. (1983), instructed subjects to make a simple voluntary movement (a key press) at a time of their choice. The action of pressing the key caused an auditory signal to appear after a fixed delay of 250 ms. The subjects were asked to report the position of a clock hand either at the time they thought they had pressed the key or at the time when they heard the auditory signal. Haggard et al. found that the time interval between the two estimated events was shorter than what it should be, that is, it was shorter than 250 ms. Subjects tended to perceive their key press as occurring later, and the auditory signal as occurring earlier, than was actually the case. This shrinkage of perceived time between the two events did not happen in a control situation where the finger movement was not voluntary but was produced by a magnetically induced stimulation of motor cortex. The authors conclude that intentional action binds together the conscious representation of the action and its sensory consequences. This binding effect would thus account for the self-attribution of their own actions shown by normal subjects.

A further step in identifying the mechanism of action recognition and attribution is to compare brain activity during the processing of externally produced stimuli and stimuli resulting from self-produced movements. Blakemore et al. (1999), using positron-emission tomography (PET), found that the presentation of externally produced tones resulted in an activity in the right temporal lobe greater than when the tones were the consequence of self-produced movements. This result suggests that, in the self-produced condition, the sensory signals reaching the recipient cortical area in the temporal lobe are modulated by the central command signals originating from the volitional system. This mechanism thus represents a powerful means of determining whether a sensory event is produced by one's own action or by an external agent (and, ultimately, whether an action is self-produced or not). Another PET experiment (Fink et al. 1999) explored the effect of a conflict between finger movements executed by a subject and the visual feedback given to the subject about his movements. When the executed finger movements no longer correlated with the seen ones, an increased activity was observed in the posterior parietal cortex (Areas 40 and 7) bilaterally. Activation of dorsolateral prefrontal cortex on both sides was also found.

A new experiment using a similar paradigm was undertaken by Farrer et al. (2003). In this study, it was conjectured that processes underlying the sense of agency or the consciousness of action should not be all-or-none states but should rather be based on the continuous monitoring of the different action-related signals, from sensory (kinesthetic, visual) and central (motor command) origin. To test this hypothesis, Farrer et al. devised an experimental situation where the visual feedback provided to the subjects about their own movements could be either congruent or distorted to a variable degree. The degree of distortion went up to the point where the seen movements were completely unrelated to the executed ones. Thus, in the congruent condition, the subjects were likely to feel in full control of their own movements, whereas in the maximally distorted condition, they were likely to feel that they were not in control, but rather being overridden by the influence of another agent. During the experiments, the subjects were instructed to continuously move a joystick with their right hand. The hand and the joystick were hidden from subjects' view. Instead, the subjects saw the electronically reconstructed image of a hand holding a joystick appearing at the precise location of their own hand. When the subject moved, the electronic hand also moved by the same amount and in the same direction: Subjects rapidly became acquainted with this situation and felt the movements of the electronic hand as their own. Distortions were introduced in this system, such that the movements seen by the subjects could be rotated with respect to those they actually performed. A graded rotation was produced by using a 25° rotation, a 50° rotation, and finally a situation where the movements appearing on the screen had no relation with those of the subjects (they were actually produced by an experimenter). Subjects were instructed to concentrate on their own feelings of whether they felt in control of the movements they saw.

Introducing a discordance between executed movements and the visual reafference from these movements produced an activation in several brain areas: The rostral part of the dorsal premotor cortex, the pre–supplementary motor area (pre-SMA), and the right anterior cingulate gyrus were involved. The most interesting result, however, was an activation at the level of the inferior parietal lobule on the right side (fig. 8.1A). A decreasing feeling of control due to larger and larger distortions was associated with an increased activation in the right inferior parietal lobule and, to a lesser extent, in a symmetrical zone on the left side. Interestingly, the peak activation in the right inferior parietal lobule (in Area 39) was modulated as a function of the feeling experienced by the subject of being in control of the action. This graded activation thus related to the increased degree of discordance between central signals arising from the motor command and visual and kinesthetic signals arising from movement execution. The mismatch between normally congruent sets of movement-related signals is likely to have resulted in an increased level of processing of these action-related signals.

The role of the right inferior parietal lobule, which is demonstrated by the above experiments, is consistent with the effects of lesions in this area. Patients suffering from such lesions frequently deny ownership of the left side of their body. They may even report delusions about their left body half by contending that it belongs to another person in spite of contradictory evidence from touch or sight (Bisiach and Berti 1987; Daprati et al. 2000). Conversely, a transient hyperactivity of a similar area of the parietal lobe (during epileptic fits, e.g.) may produce impressions of an alien phantom limb (see Spence et al. 1997). The conflict between sensory cues from different modalities produced by the substitution of an alien hand for the subject's hand has been proposed as a model for explaining the denial of the effects of stroke in some patients (Sullivan 1969). Patients experiencing an impaired integration of visual and somatosensory cues following a stroke are likely to believe that their senses still provide them with veridical information about their body, as this was the case before the stroke. During the initial poststroke period, these patients presumably rely on visual cues to test out their perception. Because they can see, for example, their arm, they will assume that it is not impaired and will finally come to deny their illness.

8.3.2   The Simulation Hypothesis

The problem raised by these results is to determine how the modulation of activity for different degrees of discordance between an intended and an executed action, mainly in the posterior parietal cortex and in the dorsolateral prefrontal cortex, can be at the origin of the feelings of being in control of an action and attributing an action to oneself. The action monitoring model capitalizes on peripheral signals

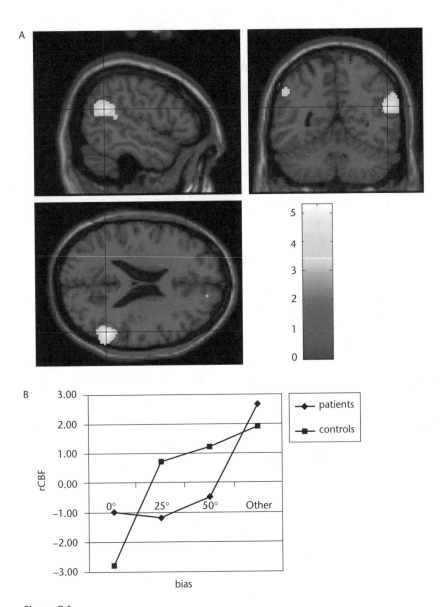

Figure 8.1

A. Activation of posterior parietal area 39 in subjects experiencing a mismatch between the movements they perform and the visual reafference of their movements. B. Amplitude of parietal activation for different degrees of mismatch. 0°, no mismatch; 25°, 50°, increasing mismatch; Other, complete mismatch. Subjects see the effect of movements performed by another agent. Squares: normal subjects. Note the progressive increase in parietal activation. Diamonds: schizophrenic patients. Note the poor correlation between activation and degree of mismatch. rCBF, regional cerebral blood flow. See plate 1. Data from Farrer et al. 2004.

produced by the subject's motor activity. It postulates that these signals are used for comparison with the internal model of the action. There are many situations, however, in which an action representation is formed but no movement is executed. In such situations, no output signals to the muscles, no reafferent (e.g., visual) signals from the outside world, no proprioceptive signals (and therefore, no possibility for comparing execution with a desired output) exist. Yet, the attribution of the representation is clearly made to the self.

The simulation hypothesis postulates that covert actions are in fact actions in their own right, except for the fact that they are not executed. Covert and overt stages represent a continuum, such that every overtly executed action implies the existence of a covert stage, whereas a covert action does not necessarily turns into an overt action. As will be argued below, most of the neural events which lead to an overt action already seem to be present in the covert stages of that action. The theory therefore predicts a close similarity, in neural terms, of the state where an action is internally simulated and the state which precedes execution of that action (Jeannerod 1994).

Specific methods, partly based on introspection but also relying on changes of physiological variables, have been designed to experimentally access these mental states characterized by absence or paucity of overt behavior. One of the most extensively studied of these representational aspects of action is mental motor imagery. Behavioral studies of motor imagery have revealed that motor images retain the same temporal characteristics as the corresponding real action when it comes to execution. For example, it takes the same time to mentally "walk" to a prespecified target as it takes to actually walk to the same place (Decety et al. 1989; see also Sirigu et al. 1996; Frak et al. 2001). This indication of a similar temporal structure for executed and nonexecuted actions by a biological system is reinforced by a similarity at the level of physiological indicators. Examining autonomic activity in subjects imagining an action at different effort rates reveals changes in heart rate and respiration frequency proportional to the imagined effort, in the absence of any metabolic need. These results (Decety et al. 1993; see the review in Jeannerod 1995) reveal the existence of a central patterning of vegetative commands during covert actions, which would parallel the preparation of muscular commands. Autonomic changes occurring during motor imagery are closely related to those observed during central preparation of an effortful action (Krogh and Lindhart 1913). Those are mechanisms that anticipate forthcoming metabolic needs, with the function of shortening the intrinsic delay required for heart and respiration to adapt to effort.

8.3.3 The Concept of Shared Representations: A Neural Basis for the Simulation Theory

Mental imagery is only one of the forms an action representation can take. Another form is the representation created by the observation of the actions performed by other people. Little is known concerning the biological effects of observing someone's actions. However, extending the simulation theory to understanding the representations underlying actions of other people requires that a continuity be established between the embodiment of representations of the observer and those of the agent being observed.

Consider a simple experiment with normal subjects observing the action of an actor. The subjects are equipped for recording their respiration rate and sit in front of a large screen on which they see an actor performing an effortful action. The actor stands on a treadmill that either is motionless or moves at a constant velocity (2.5, 7, or 10 km/h) or progressively accelerates from 0 to 10 km/h over 1 minute. The main result of this experiment (Paccalin and Jeannerod 2000) was that the respiration rate increased during the observation of the actor walking or running at an increasing speed. Typically, the average increase during observation of the actor running at 10 km/h is about 25 percent above the resting level. Further, the increase in respiration frequency correlates with running velocity. Watching an action is thus different from watching a visual scene with moving objects. During watching an action, the observer is not only seeing visual motion but he is also internally (and nonconsciously) simulating (or rehearsing) the action. Simulating an accelerated running implies an increase of the breathing rate, because, if the running movements were actually executed, they would require an anticipatory increase in metabolic needs. This finding substantiates the hypothesis that perceiving an action triggers a neural state in which the neural structures potentially involved in executing that action are facilitated.

A critical condition for assigning motor images and observed actions the status of covert and simulated actions is that they should activate brain areas known to be devoted to executing actions. Early work by Ingvar and Philipsson (1977) using measurement of local cerebral blood flow had shown that "pure motor ideation" (e.g., thinking of rhythmic clenching movements) produced a marked frontal activation and a more limited activation in the area of motor cortex. More recent brain mapping experiments using PET or functional magnetic resonance imaging (fMRI) have led to the conclusion that represented actions involve an activation of the motor system (see Jeannerod 2001 for a review). They show the existence of a cortical and subcortical network activated during both motor imagery and action observation. This network involves structures directly concerned with motor execution, such as motor cortex, dorsal and ventral premotor cortex, lateral cerebellum, and basal ganglia; it also involves areas concerned with action planning, such as dorsolateral prefrontal cortex and posterior parietal cortex. Concerning primary motor cortex itself, fMRI studies unambiguously demonstrate that voxels activated during contraction of a muscle are also activated during imagery of a movement involving the same muscle (Roth et al. 1996). During action observation, the involvement of primary motor pathways was demonstrated by a direct measurement of corticospinal excitability using transcranial magnetic stimulation. Fadiga et al. (1995) found that subjects observing an actor executing hand-grasping movements showed an increase in responsivity to stimulation in their own hand motor area. The area involved during observation of the hand movements was superimposed with that activated while the subjects themselves actually performed the movement.

In principle, a theory that postulates that both actions of the self and actions of another can be distinguished on the basis of their central representations should predict separate representations for these two types of actions. At the neural level, one should expect the existence of different networks devoted to action recognition whether the action originates from the self or not. One network would be in relation to recognizing actions as belonging to the self, another should correspond to attributing actions to another person. We know from the results described above that brain areas activated during representing self-produced actions (executed or not) and observing actions of other people partly overlap: This is the basis for the concept of shared representations (Georgieff and Jeannerod 1998), according to which different mental states concerning actions (e.g., intending an action or observing it from another person) share the same neural representations and yet still have distinct patterns of neural activity.

To clarify this concept, let us briefly describe experimental results obtained from monkeys. A dramatic illustration of what a shared representation is, is offered by the finding of mirror neurons (Rizzolatti et al. 1995). Mirror neurons were identified in the monkey premotor cortex. They are activated in two conditions: First, they fire when the animal is involved in a specific motor action, like picking up a piece of food with a precision grip; second; they also fire when the immobile animal watches the same action performed by an external agent (another monkey or an experimenter). In other words, mirror neurons represent one particular type of action, irrespective of the agent who performs it. At this point, it could be suspected that the signal produced by these neurons, and exploited by other elements downstream in the information-processing flow, would be the same for an action performed by the self and by another agent: The two modalities of that action (executed and observed) would thus completely share the same neural representation. The problem of action identification, however, is solved by the fact that other premotor neurons (the canonical neurons), and presumably many other neuron populations as well, fire only when the monkey performs the action and not when it observes it from another agent. This is indeed another critical feature of the shared representations concept: They overlap only partially, and the nonoverlapping part of a given representation can be the cue for attributing the action to the self or to another person. The same mechanism operates in humans. Brain activity during different conditions in which subjects were simulating actions (e.g., intending actions and preparing for execution, imagining actions, or observing actions performed by other people) was compared (Decety et al. 1994,

1997; Grafton et al. 1996; Rizzolatti et al. 1996; Gérardin et al. 2000). The outcome of these studies is twofold: First, there exists a cortical network common to all conditions, to which the inferior parietal lobule (Areas 39–40), the ventral premotor area (ventral Area 6), and part of the SMA contribute; second, motor representations for each individual condition are clearly specified by the activation of cortical zones which do not overlap between conditions (Ruby and Decety 2001).

8.4 Failure of Action-Recognition Mechanisms in Pathological States

In this section, we investigate the effects of pathological conditions as another potential source of information concerning the mechanisms of self-recognition and recognition of others. Pathological conditions offer many examples of misidentification of the self: a typical case is that of schizophrenia. A detailed analysis of the relevant symptomatology in schizophrenic patients is provided in the chapters by Frith and Liddle in this volume. According to Liddle's description, the difficulties shown by these patients for self-identification would fall into the reality distortion cluster of symptoms.

The pattern of self-misidentification in schizophrenic patients is twofold. First, patients may attribute their own actions or thoughts to others rather than to themselves (underattributions); second, patients may attribute the actions or thoughts of others to themselves (overattributions). According to the French psychiatrist Pierre Janet (1937), these false attributions reflect the existence in each individual of a representation of others' actions and thoughts, in addition to the representation of one's own: False attributions were thus due to an imbalance between these two representations. A typical example of underattributions is hallucinations. Hallucinating schizophrenic patients may show a tendency to project their own experience onto external events. Accordingly, they may misattribute their own intentions or actions to external agents. During auditory hallucinations, the patient will hear voices that are typically experienced as coming from an external powerful entity but which in fact correspond to subvocal speech produced by the patient (Gould 1949; David 1994). The voices often consist of comments where the patient is addressed in the third person and include commands and directions for action (Chadwick and Birchwood 1994). The patient may declare that he or she is being acted upon by an alien force, as if his or her thoughts or acts were controlled by an external agent. The so-called mimetic behavior observed at the acute stage of psychosis also relates to this category.

The reverse pattern of misattribution can also be observed. Overattributions were earlier described by Janet (1937): What this author called "excess of appropriation" corresponds for the patient to the illusion that actions of others are in fact initiated or performed by him or her and that he or she is influencing other people (the clinical picture of megalomania). In this case, patients are convinced that their intentions or actions can affect external events, for example, that they can influence the thought and the actions of other people. Accordingly, they tend to misattribute the occurrence of external events to themselves. The consequence of this misinterpretation would be that external events are seen as the result expected from their own actions. More recently, impairments of other- and self-recognition in schizophrenia have been categorized, together with other manifestations of this disease, among the so-called first rank symptoms. According to Schneider (1955), these symptoms, which are considered critical for the diagnosis of schizophrenia, refer to a state in which patients interpret their own thoughts or actions as being due to alien forces or to other people and feel being controlled or influenced by others.

One possible explanation for these impairments in self-recognition could be the dysfunction of the system normally used for perceiving, recognizing and attributing actions that has been partly identified in the above section. This hypothesis is supported by the fact that schizophrenic patients with delusion of influence make frequent errors in experimental situations in which they have to attribute a movement to its author. We compared a group of patients with delusion of influence with nondelusional patients and normal controls in the alien hand experiment already described in section 8.2. In this situation, schizophrenic patients with delusions tended to massively attribute these movements to themselves (Daprati et al. 1997). Similarly, patients with delusions were also impaired in the joystick task described in section 8.3.1. Unlike normal subjects, patients with delusions could still attribute to themselves movements of the artificial hand rotated by up to 40° with respect to the actually executed movements (Franck et al. 2001). Such a gross misrecognition of the direction of a movement must be deleterious for self-recognition. Perceiving the direction of a movement is indeed useful information for an observer to understand the action of the agent of this movement: During a movement, the arm points to the goal of the action and its direction may reveal the intention of the agent. It is thus not surprising that a patient deprived of this information will misinterpret the intention displayed by others in their movements, and that this will have consequences on attributing actions to their agent and ultimately understanding interactions between people.

Finally, the difficulties in correct attribution of actions by schizophrenic patients with delusions is reflected at the level of their brain metabolism. An experiment in which brain activity was measured with PET during the same joystick task was performed in a group of such patients. As in normal subjects, a right posterior parietal focus of activation was observed in the patients (see section 8.3.1). Unlike in normal subjects, however, the level of activity in this area did not correlate with the amount of discordance between the executed and the seen movements. Instead, the activity level during the normal situation (i.e., full control of the movement) was higher than in normal subjects and did not increase further in the discordant situation until the situation with complete loss of control was reached (fig. 8.1B). This finding (Farrer et al. 2004) is consistent with other findings showing a higher-than-normal level of activity in this area in schizophrenic patients during voluntary movements (Spence et al. 1997), or even during rest (Franck et al. 2002). In the context of the present discussion, this finding suggests that these patients may lack the cues for recognizing their own movements normally provided by the changes in activity of their parietal cortex. A similar explanation has been used to account for verbal hallucinations: Patients would not recognize their own internal speech and attribute it to external sources (see Frith, this volume).

8.5   Conclusion

In this chapter, I have laid down a framework for integrating self-recognition to the neural substrate. This conception of action recognition is based on the existence of neural networks subserving the various forms of representation of an action. According to the simulation hypothesis, simulation of one's own actions or of others' actions produces an activation of some of the areas normally devoted to action execution (Jeannerod 2001). These networks, although clearly distinct from one form of representation to another (e.g., the representation of a self-generated action vs. the representation of an action observed or predicted from another agent), partly overlap. When two agents socially interact with one another, this overlap creates what has been referred to as "shared representations," that is, activation of neural structures that are common to several modalities of representations. In normal conditions, however, the existence of nonoverlapping parts, as well the existence of possible differences in intensity of activation between the activated zones, allows each agent to discriminate between representations activated from within (for a self-generated intention) from those activated from the outside (by an action displayed by another agent). This process would be the basis for correctly attributing a representation to the proper agent or, in other words, for answering the question of "who" is the author of the act of communication (Georgieff and Jeannerod 1998; Jeannerod 1999).

This conception allows us to make hypotheses about the nature of the dysfunction responsible for misattribution of actions by schizophrenic patients. Changes in the pattern of cortical connectivity could alter the shape of the networks corresponding to different representations, or the relative intensity of activation in the areas composing these networks. Although little is known about the functional aspects of cortical connectivity underlying the formation of these networks and, a fortiori, about their dysfunction in schizophrenia, several studies have pointed to the prefrontal cortex as one of the possible sites for perturbed activation (e.g., Weinberger and Berman 1996). Because prefrontal areas are known to normally exert an inhibitory control on other areas involved in various aspects of motor and sensorimotor processing, an alteration of this control in schizophrenic patients might result in aberrant representations and interpretations of intersubjective events (Spence et al. 1998).

References

Bisiach, E., and A. Berti. 1987. Dyschiria: An attempt at its systemic explanation. In *Neurophysiological and Neuropsychological Aspects of Spatial Neglect*, ed. M. Jeannerod, pp. 183–201. Amsterdam: Elsevier North Holland.

Blakemore, S. J., C. Frith, and D. Wolpert. 1999. Spatio-temporal prediction modulates the perception of self-produced stimuli. *Journal of Cognitive Neuroscience, 11*, 551–559.

Chadwick, P., and M. M. Birchwood. 1994. The omnipotence of voices. A cognitive approach to auditory hallucinations. *British Journal of Psychiatry, 164*, 190–201.

Daprati, E., N. Franck, N. Georgieff, J. Proust, E. Pacherie, J. Dalery, and M. Jeannerod. 1997. Looking for the agent: An investigation into consciousness of action and self-consciousness in schizophrenic patients. *Cognition, 65*, 71–86.

Daprati, E., A. Sirigu, P. Pradat-Diehl, N. Franck, and M. Jeannerod. 2000. Recognition of self produced movement in a case of severe neglect. *Neurocase, 6*, 477–486.

David, A. S. 1994. The neuropsychological origin of auditory hallucinations. In *The Neuropsychology of Schizophrenia*, ed. A. S. David and J. C. Cutting, pp. 269–313. Hove: Lawrence Erlbaum.

Decety, J., M. Jeannerod, and C. Prablanc. 1989. The timing of mentally represented actions. *Behavioural Brain Research, 34*, 35–42.

Decety, J., D. Perani, M. Jeannerod, V. Bettinardi, B. Tadary, R. Woods, J. C. Mazziotta, and F. Fazio. 1994. Mapping motor representations with PET. *Nature, 371*, 600–602.

Decety, J., J. Grezes, N. Costes, D. Perani, M. Jeannerod, E. Procyk, F. Grassi, and F. Fazio. 1997. Brain activity during observation of action: Influence of action content and subject's strategy. *Brain, 120*, 1763–1777.

Decety, J., M. Jeannerod, D. Durozard, and G. Baverel. 1993. Central activation of autonomic effectors during mental simulation of motor actions in man. *Journal of Physiology, 461*, 549–563.

Fadiga, L., L. Fogassi, G. Pavesi, and G. Rizzolatti. 1995. Motor faciulitation during action observation: A magnetic stimulation study. *Journal of Neurophysiology, 73*, 2608–2611.

Farrer, C., N. Franck, N. Georgieff, C. D. Frith, J. Decety, T. d'Amato, and M. Jeannerod. 2004. Neural correlates of action attribution in schizophrenia. *Psychiatry Research: Neuroimaging, 131*, 31–44.

Farrer, C., N. Franck, N. Georgieff, C. D. Frith, J. Decety, and M. Jeannerod. 2003. Modulating the experience of agency: A PET study. *Neuroimage, 18*, 324–333.

Fink, G. R., J. C. Marshall, P. W. Halligan, C. D. Frith, J. Driver, R. S. J. Frackowiack, and R. J. Dolan. 1999. The neural consequences of conflict between intention and the senses. *Brain, 122*, 497–512.

Frak, V. G., Y. Paulignan, and M. Jeannerod. 2001. Orientation of the opposition axis in mentally simulated grasping. *Experimental Brain Research, 136*, 120–127.

Franck, N., C. Farrer, N. Georgieff, M. Marie-Cardine, J. Daléry, T. D'Amato, and M. Jeannerod. 2001. Defective recognition of one's own actions in schizophrenic patients. *American Journal of Psychiatry*, *158*, 454–459.

Franck, N., D. S. O'Leary, M. Flaum, R. D. Hichwa, and N. C. Andreasen. 2002. Cerebral blood flow changes associated with Schneiderian first-rank symptoms in schizophrenia. *Journal of Psychiatry and Clinical Neuroscience*, *14*, 277–282.

Georgieff, N., and M. Jeannerod. 1998. Beyond consciousness of external reality: A "who" system for consciousness of action and self-consciousness. *Consciousness and Cognition*, *7*, 465–477.

Gérardin, E., A. Sirigu, S. Lehéricy, J.-B. Poline, B. Gaymard, C. Marsault, Y. Agid, and D. Le Bihan. 2000. Partially overlapping neural networks for real and imagined hand movements. *Cerebral Cortex*, *10*, 1093–1104.

Gould, L. N. 1949. Auditory hallucinations in subvocal speech: Objective study in a case of schizophrenia. *Journal of Nervous and Mental Diseases*, *109*, 418–427.

Grafton, S. T., M. A. Arbib, L. Fadiga, and G. Rizzolatti. 1996. Localization of grasp representations in humans by PET: 2. Observation compared with imagination. *Experimental Brain Research*, *112*, 103–111.

Habib, M., and M. Poncet. 1988. Loss of vitality, of interest and of the affect (athymhormia syndrome) in lacunar lesions of the corpus striatum. *Revue Neurologique*, *144*, 571–577. (In French.)

Haggard, P., S. Clark, and J. Kalogeras. 2002. Voluntary action and conscious awareness. *Nature Neuroscience*, *5*, 282–285.

Ingvar, D., and L. Philipsson. 1977. Distribution of the cerebral blood flow in the dominant hemisphere during motor ideation and motor performance. *Annals of Neurology*, *2*, 230–237.

Janet, P. 1937. Les troubles de la personnalité sociale. *Annales Médico-Psychologiques*, *2*, 149–200.

Jeannerod, M. 1994. The representing brain: Neural correlates of motor intention and imagery. *Behavioral and Brain Sciences*, *17*, 187–245.

Jeannerod, M. 1995. Mental imagery in the motor cortex. *Neuropsychologia*, *33*, 1419–1432.

Jeannerod, M. 1999. To act or not to act: Perspectives on the representation of actions. *Quarterly Journal of Experimental Psychology*, *52A*, 1–29.

Jeannerod, M. 2001. Neural simulation of action: A unifying mechanism for motor cognition. *Neuroimage*, *14*, S103–S109.

Jeannerod, M. 2003. The mechanism of self-recognition in humans. *Behavioural Brain Research*, *142*, 1–15.

Jeannerod, M. 2004. From self-recognition to self-consciousness. In *The Structure and Development of Self-Consciousness: Interdisciplinary Perspectives*, ed. D. Zahavi, T. Grünbaum, and J. Parnas, pp. 65–87. Amsterdam: John Benjamins.

Ji, H., S. Ploux, and E. Wehrli. 2003. Lexical knowledge representation with contexonyms. In *Proceedings of the 9th MT Summit*, pp. 194–201. New Orleans.

Krogh, A., and J. Lindhart. 1913. The regulation of respiration and circulation during the initial stages of muscular work. *Journal of Physiology, 47,* 112–136.

Libet, B., C. A. Gleason, E. W. Wright, and D. K. Perl. 1983. Time of conscious intention to act in relation to cerebral activities (readiness potential): The unconscious initiation of a freely voluntary act. *Brain, 102,* 193–224.

Nielsen, T. I. 1963. Volition: A new experimental approach. *Scandinavian Journal of Psychology, 4,* 225–230.

Nielsen, T. I. 1978. *Acts: Analyses and Syntheses of Human Acting, Concerning the Subject and from the Standpoint of the Subject.* Copenhagen: Dansk Psykologisc Forlag.

Paccalin, C., and M. Jeannerod. 2000. Changes in breathing during observation of effortful actions. *Brain Research, 862,* 194–200.

Rizzolatti, G., L. Fadiga, V. Gallese, and L. Fogassi. 1995. Premotor cortex and the recognition of motor actions. *Cognitive Brain Research, 3,* 131–141.

Rizzolatti, G., L. Fadiga, M. Matelli, V. Bettinardi, E. Paulesu, D. Perani, and G. Fazio. 1996. Localization of grasp representations in humans by PET: 1. Observation versus execution. *Experimental Brain Research, 111,* 246–252.

Roth, M., J. Decety, M. Raybaudi, R. Massarelli, C. Delon-Martin, C. Segebarth, S. Morand, A. Gemignani, M. Décorps, and M. Jeannerod. 1996. Possible involvement of primary-motor cortex in mentally simulated movement: A functional magnetic resonance imaging study. *Neuroreport, 7,* 1280–1284.

Ruby, P., and J. Decéty. 2001. Effect of subjective perspective taking during simulation of action: A PET investigation of agency. *Nature Neurosciences, 4,* 546–550.

Schneider, K. 1955. *Klinische Psychopathologie.* Stuttgart: Thieme Verlag.

Sirigu, A., J.-R. Duhamel, L. Cohen, B. Pillon, B. Dubois, and Y. Agid. 1996. The mental representation of hand movements after parietal cortex damage. *Science, 273,* 1564–1568.

Spence, S. A., D. J. Brooks, S. R. Hirsch, P. F. Liddle, J. Meehan, and P. M. Grasby. 1997. A PET study of voluntary movement in schizophrenic patients experiencing passivity phenomena (delusions of alien control). *Brain, 120,* 1997–2011.

Spence, S. A., S. R. Hirsch, D. J. Brooks, and P. M. Grasby. 1998. Prefrontal cortex activity in people with schizophrenia and control subjects: Evidence from positron emission tomography for remission of "hypofrontality" with recovery from acute schizophrenia. *British Journal of Psychiatry, 172,* 376–393.

Sperry, R. W. 1950. Neural basis of the spontaneous optokinetic response produced by visual inversion. *Journal of Comparative and Physiological Psychology, 43,* 482–489.

Sullivan, R. 1969. Experimentally induced somatagnosia. *Archives of General Psychiatry, 20,* 71–77.

von Holst, E., and H. Mittelstaedt. 1950. Das Reafferenzprinzip. Wechselwirkungen zwischen Zentralnervensystem und Peripherie. *Naturwissenschaften, 37,* 464–476.

Wegner, D. 2002. *The Illusion of Conscious Will.* Cambridge, Mass.: MIT Press.

Weinberger, D. R., and K. F. Berman. 1996. Prefrontal function in schizophrenia: Confounds and controversies. *Philosophical Transactions of the Royal Society, B, 351,* 1495–1503.

Wolpert, D. M., Z. Ghahramani, and M. I. Jordan. 1995. An internal model for sensorimotor integration. *Science, 269,* 1880–1882.

9 Motivated Attention and Schizophrenia

Peter F. Liddle

9.1 Introduction

According to Emil Kraepelin, the clinician who first delineated the illness we now call schizophrenia, the essence of the condition was

that destruction of conscious volition . . . which is manifest as a loss of energy and drive, in disjointed volitional behavior. This rudderless state leads to impulsive instinctual activity: there is no planned reflection which suppresses impulses as they arise or directs them into proper channels. (Kraepelin 1920)

More recent examination of the symptoms of schizophrenia reveals that the characteristic symptoms of the illness segregate into three groups: psychomotor poverty, which includes blunted affect, poverty of speech, and decreased spontaneous movement; disorganization, which includes formal thought disorder, inappropriate affect, and bizarre behavior; and reality distortion, which includes delusions and hallucinations (Arndt, Alliger, and Andreasen 1991; Bilder, Mukherjee, Rieder, and Pandurangi 1985; Liddle 1984, 1987a). Symptoms from within each cluster tend to coexist frequently, implying that symptoms within a cluster arise from a shared pathophysiological mechanism, while the clusters themselves coexist more often than would be expected by chance, implying that the pathophysiological mechanisms underlying the different clusters are related. Thus, these symptom clusters form distinguishable dimensions within a single illness. Typical cases of schizophrenia exhibit at least some evidence of all three clusters of symptoms at some stage during the illness.

The psychomotor poverty symptoms appear to correspond to the loss of energy and drive referred to by Kraepelin. The neural mechanisms underlying this loss of drive are described elsewhere in this book (Spence and Parry, this volume). The symptoms of reality distortion reflect an impaired ability to evaluate self-generated mental activity. Frith has proposed that hallucinations, and also some specific types of delusion, such as delusions of alien control of behavior, reflect a failure of the internal monitoring of self-generated mental activity (Frith, this volume). In this chapter we examine the evidence regarding the psychological and neuronal abnormalities associated with the disorganization syndrome.

9.2   Psychological Impairment Associated with Disorganization

In an early study, Liddle (1987b) found that severity of disorganization symptoms was associated with impaired ability to focus attention, as assessed by a letter cancellation task, in which each occurrence of a target letter must be identified in a text string, and the Corsi block test, in which the participant is required is a register and reproduce the sequential touching of a series of locations in a random spatial array. In a later study, Liddle and Morris (1991) demonstrated that disorganization is associated with slower performance of the Trails B test, in which the participant is required to trace a path connecting a set of sites labeled with numbers and alphabet letters, switching between ascending numbers and letters on alternate trials. The common feature of all of these tasks is an ability to direct attention to stimuli relevant to the current goal and respond to those stimuli while ignoring competing responses. Subsequently, numerous studies have demonstrated that disorganization symptoms in schizophrenia are associated with impaired ability to select appropriate responses while inhibiting inappropriate responses. For example, Frith et al. (1991) demonstrated an association between disorganization symptoms and false alarms to distractor stimuli in a continuous performance test, in which the participants were required to respond only to specified target stimuli.

9.3   Cerebral Activity Associated with Disorganization

In a positron-emission tomography (PET) study of brain activity associated with persistent schizophrenic symptoms, Liddle et al. (1992) found that the disorganization syndrome was associated with aberrant activity in anterior cingulate cortex, medial frontal cortex, and thalamus and with decreased activity in ventrolateral prefrontal cortex and contiguous insula, extending into the temporal pole, and temporoparietal cortex. The finding of increased anterior cingulate and medial frontal activity was replicated by Ebmeier et al. (1993) and by Yuasa et al. (1995), while the finding of decreased activity in temporoparietal cortex was replicated by Szechtman et al. (1988).

In a PET study of brain activity associated with the generation of thought-disordered speech, one of the cardinal features of the disorganization syndrome, McGuire et al. (1998) found reduced activity in ventrolateral prefrontal cortex, insula, and superior temporal gyrus. In a subsequent functional magnetic resonance imaging (fMRI) study, Kircher et al. (2001) replicated the finding that the generation of thought-disordered speech is accompanied by decreased activity in the left superior temporal gyrus. In addition, Kircher et al. (2001) found some evidence for a disturbance of the normal hemispheric asymmetry of specialization for language processing, insofar as they observed aberrant activation of right lateral temporal cortex.

Overall, despite some differences in details between the various studies, the evidence indicates that disorganization symptoms are associated with aberrant activity in a distributed set of cerebral sites embracing association cortex of the frontal, temporal, and parietal lobes; paralimbic cortex (anterior cingulate and insula); and the thalamus.

9.4   The Coordination of Basic Brain States

What kind of pathophysiological process might give rise to disorganization of mental activity within domains as diverse as thought, emotion, and voluntary action? The evidence from functional imaging studies indicates that this putative abnormal pathophysiological process involves a distributed array of cerebral sites, involving association cortex, paralimbic cortex, and thalamus. The fact that the clinical features represent diverse aspects of mental activity suggests that the essential defect is not an impairment of the function of specialized neural populations but rather in the mechanism by which the activities of discrete specialized neural populations are harnessed to meet the overall goals of the individual.

Consistent with this speculation based on the observation of patients with schizophrenia, a large body of evidence indicates that in healthy individuals the processes mediating cognition and volition entail nonlocal cooperative integration of the activities of spatially distributed local neuronal populations (John 2002). I propose that a core feature of schizophrenia, manifest most clearly in the clinical features of the disorganization syndrome, is a disruption of the mechanism by which this cooperative integration is achieved.

In particular, I propose that the brain engages in various discrete states of activity, each characterized by a pattern of distributed neural activity, and each providing a foundation for mobilizing specialized neural populations required to meet the immediate needs of the individual. Two of these putative states are the default state and the motivated attention state.

The default state is an introspective state of awareness of oneself. The pattern of brain activity associated with this state can be demonstrated by comparing brain activity (assessed by imaging regional perfusion, or metabolism) in the resting state or in a cognitively undemanding state with that during states of engagement in a demanding goal-orientated task. Such comparisons reveal greater activity during the resting state in medial frontal cortex, posterior cingulate, and precuneus, largely irrespective of the nature of the active comparison state (Raichle et al. 2001).

The motivated attention state is a state in which the individual attends to salient information for the purpose of preparing a voluntary motor act or drawing a goal-oriented conclusion. Imaging studies in our own laboratory, reviewed in more detail below, indicate that this state entails activity in a distributed brain system involving areas of multimodal association cortex, limbic and paralimbic structures, and related subcortical nuclei. This system is supramodal in the sense that the core pattern of activity is largely independent of the source of information that is being processed, whether it be from any of the external senses or from interoception, and also independent of the modality of the output, whether it be a voluntary motor action or an internally registered conclusion. After reviewing evidence from studies of healthy subjects that identify the cerebral regions involved in motivated attention, we will demonstrate that the recruitment of this motivated attention system is impaired in schizophrenia. In general, the system is underengaged in schizophrenia, though under some circumstances, the evidence suggests that some components of the system are inappropriately overengaged.

9.5   The Motivated Attention System in Healthy Individuals

To test the hypothesis that there is a supramodal neural system that evaluates information from diverse sensory modalities in light of current goals, and facilitates the selection of appropriate responses, my colleagues and I performed a series of fMRI studies of brain activity during various target detection tasks, employing diverse types of stimuli, and requiring various different types of response, in the presence of varying levels of distraction. The stimuli, distractors, and required responses for these tasks are summarized in table 9.1.

Four of the tasks were classic oddball target detection tasks in which rare targets and also novel distractors occurred unpredictably in a series of repeated background stimuli. Target stimuli and novel stimuli each occurred with a probability of .125. In the first task, the stimuli were auditory and the participant was required to make a button press in response to target stimuli. The second task employed the same auditory stimuli but the participant was required to count each stimulus rather than press a button. In the third task the stimuli were visual and the participant made a button-press in response to targets. The fourth task also employed visual stimuli and the participant counted targets.

The remaining three tasks also entailed the detection of target stimuli but should be described as go/no-go tasks insofar as the emphasis was on responding rapidly to targets while withholding a response to the distractor stimuli, rather than on detecting rare targets as in the oddball tasks. In the fifth task, either a target or distractor visual stimulus occurred with equal probability at a predictable time, following a series of warning stimuli presented at 1-second intervals (five asterisks, followed by four asterisks in a descending series down to one asterisk), designed to heighten the readiness to make a response. Participants were required to make a button press in response to target stimuli (letter X) and to refrain from responding to distracter stimuli (letter

Table 9.1

Design details for seven tasks used in fMRI studies of the motivated attention system in healthy participants.

No.	Study type	Baseline stimuli	Target stimuli	Distractor stimuli	Response	Reference
1	Auditory oddball	1000 Hz tones	1500 Hz tones	Synthetic novel sounds	Press button	Kiehl et al. (2001b)
2	Auditory oddball (counting)	1000 Hz tones	1500 Hz tones	Synthetic novel sounds	Count targets	Liddle et al. (2004)
3	Visual oddball	Small, white squares	Larger white squares	Colored geometric shapes	Press button	Kiehl et al. (2001a)
4	Visual oddball (counting)	Small, white squares	Larger white squares	Colored geometric shapes	Count targets	Unpublished
5	Visual go/no go	Series of asterisks	X	K	Press button	Liddle et al. (2001)
6	Visual go/no go	None	X or K	K or X	Press button	Laurens et al. (2005)
7	Auditory go/no go	None	1500 Hz or 1000 Hz tones	1000 Hz or 1500 Hz tones	Press button	Laurens et al. (2005)

K). In the sixth task, the only stimuli were visual target stimuli (e.g., X) or distracter stimuli (e.g., K) presented in random order at a rate of one stimulus per second. In this task, circumstances were not manipulated so as to enhance the propensity to respond rapidly, and hence there was no intrinsic bias favoring responding rather than withholding of a response. The seventh task was an auditory analogue of task 6, identical in all respects except that the stimuli were presented in the auditory modality (e.g., target stimulus: 1500 Hz tone burst, distractor: 1000 Hz tone burst, or vice versa).

In all seven tasks, very similar patterns of activation were observed when target stimulus processing was contrasted with the baseline condition, apart from expected differences in primary sensory cortex according to sensory modality, and in primary sensorimotor cortex in those tasks requiring a button press response. In all tasks, activation was observed in lateral prefrontal cortex, parietal lobe in the vicinity of the intraparietal sulcus, and also in the supramarginal gyrus near the temporoparietal junction. In addition activation was observed in thalamus, basal ganglion, and cerebellum, and in limbic/paralimbic sites including amygdala, entorhinal cortex, temporal pole, and insula, and anterior and posterior cingulate cortex.

Although activation at similar sites in association cortex, limbic/paralimbic cortex, and subcortical nuclei were observed in all tasks, there were some systematic differences in relative magnitude of activation of the various sites. For example, a comparison of activation associated with oddball target processing when the participants were required to make a button press response with that when they were required to count the target stimuli revealed a similar magnitude of activation in neocortical areas but substantially greater activation in limbic/paralimbic sites when participants were required to make a button press response (Liddle, Laurens, Das, and Kiehl 2004). It appears that the greater time pressure when a button press response was required led to greater engagement of limbic/paralimbic sites.

Distractor stimuli tended to produce activation at similar sites in association cortex, limbic/paralimbic cortex, and subcortical sites, though for all tasks except task 5, the activation associated with distractor stimuli was much less than for target stimuli. In the case of task 5, in which the warning stimuli (descending numbers of asterisks) heightened the propensity to make a rapid button press, the activation associated with distractor stimuli was greater than that associated with target stimuli at most sites, apparently because withholding a response to a distractor stimulus was a more demanding task than making a response to a target stimulus.

The similarity in the pattern of brain activation, despite differences in stimulus modality, response modality, and contextual features such as relative frequency of stimuli, in all seven tasks, suggests that the set of brain sites engaged during all of these tasks composes an integrated brain system which serves the task of detecting, evaluating, and directing processing resources to behaviorally salient stimuli. It is probable that each node in this network of regions makes a specialized contribution to the overall process. For example, it is probable that parietal sites play a special role in the orienting of attention (Corbetta and Shulman 2002), while limbic sites play a special role in evaluating the stimuli in light of current motivation and past experiences. It is probable that anterior cingulate sites play a role in the detection of conflict between the neural representations of competing responses (van Veen and Carter 2002). The fact that all of these sites are engaged during a diverse range of tasks indicates that these sites should be regarded as an integrated system. This proposed motivated attention system is represented schematically in figure 9.1.

It should be noted that the proposal that there is a supramodal system engaged in directing attention to behaviorally salient stimuli, evaluating them in light of motivational state, and mobilizing resources for a response does not contradict the abundant evidence that there are brain regions specialized for identification of specific types of stimuli, such as faces or speech sounds. In fact, by employing an oddball target detection paradigm in which the targets include different classes of stimuli, it is possible to identify such specialized brain areas. For example, if targets consist of either speech sounds or nonlinguistic sounds carefully matched with the speech sounds on

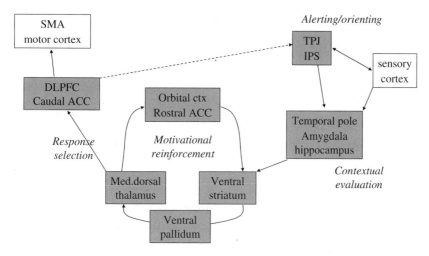

Figure 9.1

Diagrammatic illustration of the motivated attention system. The brain regions comprising this system (shown in shaded boxes) exhibited significant activation during seven target detection tasks that differed in the nature of the target objects, the background circumstances, and the responses required. TPJ, temporoparietal junction; IPS, intraparietal sulcus; ACC, anterior cingulate cortex; DLPFC, dorsolateral prefrontal cortex; SMA, supplementary motor area

other acoustic properties, contrast between the pattern of activation elicited by speech target sounds with that elicited by nonspeech target sounds reveals that speech sounds elicit more activity in the posterior superior temporal gyrus (Vouloumanos, Kiehl, Werker, and Liddle 2001), a brain area that is specialized for the comprehension of speech. However, in comparison with baseline, both types of stimuli elicit activation throughout the motivated attention system illustrated in figure 9.1. It is likely that the deficit relevant to the pathophysiological mechanism common to disorganization in the diverse domains of speech, affect, and voluntary motor behavior lies in a supramodal system rather than in a specialized system.

9.6 The Function of the Motivated Attention System in Schizophrenia

My colleagues and I have performed a series of fMRI studies of cerebral activity during auditory oddball target detection tasks (Kiehl and Liddle 2001) and go/no-go tasks (Laurens, Ngan, Bates, Kiehl, and Liddle 2003; Laurens, Ngan, and Liddle 2004) in patients with schizophrenia and in healthy control subjects. In general, these studies have revealed that patients with schizophrenia exhibit a reduced degree of activation of the motivated attention system when responding to target stimuli in both types of task.

For example, in the study of auditory oddball target detection reported by Kiehl and Liddle (2001), patients with schizophrenia exhibited significantly less activation than healthy control subjects in virtually all of the brain loci identified as components in the motivated attention system depicted in figure 9.1. These sites include association cortex areas such as lateral intraparietal sulcus, temporoparietal junction, and dorsolateral prefrontal cortex; paralimbic areas such as anterior and posterior cingulate and temporal pole, and subcortical sites such as the thalamus (Kiehl and Liddle 2001). The decreased activity in the motivated attention system was not merely part of a generalized failure to activate the brain, as the patients produced a normal level of activation in primary sensorimotor cortex, consistent with the observation that the patients correctly responded to the target stimuli on more than 97 percent of trials. The patients exhibited a slower reaction time than healthy controls, indicating that the lower level of activity in the motivated attention system was accompanied by a slower rate of information processing. Nonetheless, the variation in reaction time accounted for only a small portion of the variance in activation in the motivated attention system.

The contrast of the pattern of brain activity elicited by target stimuli with that elicited by novel stimuli provides some insight into the recruitment of the motivated attention system by stimuli that differ in their behavioral relevance. In healthy subjects, novel stimuli tend to elicit activation in most of the sites involved in the motivated attention system, but the magnitude of activation tends to be less than that elicited by target stimuli. The increase in activation elicited by targets relative to that elicited by novel stimuli tends to be especially pronounced in limbic and paralimbic sites (see fig. 9.2), possibly reflecting the greater motivational impact of target stimuli relative to the task-irrelevant novel stimuli. However, in patients with schizophrenia, the difference between the activation elected by target and novel stimuli is small at these limbic and paralimbic sites (fig. 9.2).

Furthermore, in auditory processing areas in the lateral temporal lobe, the activation elicited by task-irrelevant novel stimuli is even greater than that elicited by target stimuli in patients with schizophrenia, whereas in healthy controls there is little difference in the activity elicited by target and novel stimuli. This observation indicates that the patients with schizophrenia devote greater resources to processing novel stimuli, even though these stimuli are irrelevant to the current task, implying a decreased ability to allocate resources in accord with current goals.

9.7 Conclusions and Speculations

The studies by Liddle et al. (1992), McGuire et al. (1998), and Kircher et al. (2001) of the patterns of brain activity associated with the occurrence of disorganized mental activity revealed a complex pattern of overactivity and underactivity at a distributed array of sites in association cortex, paralimbic cortex, and thalamus. This set of sites

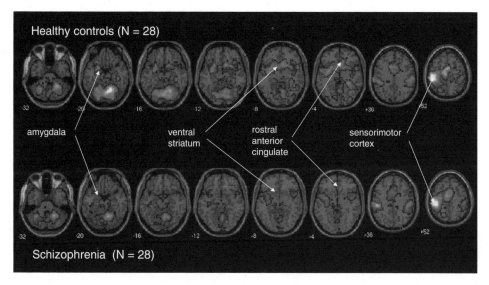

Figure 9.2
Functional magnetic resonance imaging study of auditory oddball target detection in 28 patients with schizophrenia and 28 healthy controls. Outlined regions denote clusters of voxels in which activation was greater during processing of target stimuli than novel stimuli (cluster significance $p < .05$ corrected for multiple comparisons). The patients exhibit less activation than controls in the motivated attention system, especially in limbic/paralimbic areas (amygdala, ventral striatum, rostral anterior cingulate) despite a normal level of activity in sensorimotor cortex. See plate 2.

overlaps with the supramodal motivated attention system delineated in our studies of healthy individuals performing various simple goal-orientated tasks, such as oddball target detection or go/no-go tasks. Furthermore, when patients with schizophrenia perform oddball target detection or simple go-no go tasks, they fail to activate the motivated attention system to the normal degree (Kiehl and Liddle 2001; Laurens et al. 2003; Laurens et al. 2004). In general, the patients exhibit lesser activation of the motivated attention system in response to target stimuli, despite correct detection of virtually all of the targets and a normal level of activation of primary sensorimotor cortex. However, the abnormality is not simply a generalized failure to activate this brain system under all circumstances. In limbic and paralimbic areas, the patients exhibit less differentiation between the response to target stimuli and novel stimuli. The evidence suggests impaired ability to allocate processing resources according to current goals.

In light of this evidence for impaired recruitment of the motivated attention system, it is pertinent to speculate on the mechanism by which this distributed system is recruited. In general, a substantial body of evidence suggests that coordination of neural activity at spatially remote cerebral sites is achieved by means of oscillatory fluctuations in transmembrane potential which ensure that neurons throughout the network are primed to generate action potentials in a temporally coordinated manner (Engel, Fries, and Singer 2001). Oscillatory activity in the CNS occurs at frequencies spanning from the delta band (frequency range 1–4 Hz) up to the gamma band (25–60 Hz). In particular, a growing body of evidence indicates that activity in the theta band (4–7 Hz) generated in limbic and paralimbic regions plays an important role in coordinating goal-orientated activity in animals and in humans.

Recent studies in our own laboratory (Golembo, 2004) reveal that during a go/no-go task, in which trials are presented with an intertrial interval varying in the range of 2–3 seconds, feedback regarding performance on the preceding trial generates oscillatory activity in the theta band, with a frontocentral spatial distribution suggesting an origin in cingulate cortex, and furthermore, the amplitude of this theta activity predicts the likelihood of correct performance in the subsequent trial. Furthermore, we have recently shown that patients with schizophrenia exhibit a decreased amount of event-related theta and delta activity in a simple go/no-go task similar to those employed in the studies reported above (Bates, Kiehl, Laurens, Ngan, and Liddle 2004). Thus it is plausible that the impairment of recruitment of the motivated attention system in schizophrenia arises from an impairment of the mechanism by which low-frequency oscillatory activity is generated. Further studies employing both electroencephalograph techniques and fMRI are required to test this hypothesis.

fMRI studies assess the contrast of brain activity during a state of interest with a reference state. In the oddball target detection studies, the reference state, against which both the processing of both target stimuli and novel stimuli was compared, was exposure to regularly repeated 1000-Hz nontarget tones. In the go/no-go studies comparing patients with controls, the reference state was rest. In the studies in which we observed a reduction in activation in patients relative to healthy controls, during target stimulus processing relative to the reference state, we cannot exclude the possibility that the abnormality lies in the level of brain activity during the reference condition, rather than during goal-oriented task performance. The fact that we observed abnormal activation of the motivated attention system elicited by target stimuli relative to that elicited by novel stimuli does imply that the abnormality lies, at least in part, in the recruitment of the motivated attention system. On the other hand, the observed association between severity of disorganization and overactivity of medial frontal cortex, anterior cingulate cortex, and thalamus in the resting state (Ebmeier et al. 1993; Liddle et al. 1992; Yuasa et al. 1995) raises the possibility that the disorganization syndrome is associated not only with reduced engagement of the motivated attention system during goal-directed activity but also with aberrant cerebral activation during the default state. Indeed, it is possible that the deficit in schizophrenia is not so much an inability to engage the motivated attention system but a difficulty in engaging it appropriately during goal-directed activity and disengaging it appropriately during introspective states.

Acknowledgments

I am grateful for the contribution of my colleagues, Karl Friston, Chris Frith, Philip McGuire, Kristin Laurens, Kent Kiehl, Elton Ngan, Alan Bates, Tina Patel, and Nicole Golembo for helping collect and analyze the data presented in this chapter and for stimulating discussions about its meaning.

References

Arndt, S., R. J. Alliger, and N. C. Andreasen. 1991. The distinction of positive and negative symptoms—The failure of a 2-dimensional model. *British Journal of Psychiatry, 158*, 317–322.

Bates, A., K. Kiehl, K. Laurens, E. Ngan, and P. Liddle. 2004. Inefficient coordination of slow oscillations in schizophrenia. *Schizophrenia Research, 67/*1S, 127.

Bilder, R. M., S. Mukherjee, R. O. Rieder, and A. K. Pandurangi. 1985. Symptomatic and neuropsychological components of defect states. *Schizophrenia Bulletin, 11*, 409–419.

Corbetta, M., and G. L. Shulman. 2002. Control of goal-directed and stimulus-driven attention in the brain. *Nature Reviews Neuroscience, 3*, 201–215.

Ebmeier, K. P., D. H. R. Blackwood, C. Murray, V. Souza, M. Walker, N. Dougall, et al. 1993. Single-photon emission computed tomography with Tc-99m-exametazime in unmedicated schizophrenic patients. *Biological Psychiatry, 33*, 487–495.

Engel, A. K., P. Fries, and W. Singer. 2001. Dynamic predictions: Oscillations and synchrony in top-down processing. *Nature Reviews Neuroscience, 2*, 704–716.

Frith, C. D., J. Leary, C. Cahill, et al. 1991. Disabilities and circumstances of schizophrenic patients—A follow-up study. IV. Performance on psychological tests. *British Journal of Psychiatry, 159* (suppl. 13), 26–29.

Golembo, N. 2004. Pre-existing oscillatory activity in the theta band predicts the likelihood of error committal: An ERP study. Thesis, University of Nottingham: Nottingham.

John, E. R. 2002. The neurophysics of consciousness. *Brain Research Reviews, 39*, 1–28.

Kiehl, K. A., K. R. Laurens, T. L. Duty, B. B. Forster, and P. F. Liddle. 2001a. An event related to fMRI study of visual and auditory oddball tasks. *Journal of Psychophysiology, 15*, 221–240.

Kiehl, K. A., K. R. Laurens, T. L. Duty, B. B. Forster, and P. F. Liddle. 2001b. Neural sources involved in auditory target detection and novelty processing: An event-related fMRI study. *Psychophysiology, 38*, 133–142.

Kiehl, K. A., and P. F. Liddle. 2001. An event-related functional magnetic resonance imaging study of an auditory oddball task in schizophrenia. *Schizophrenia Research*, *48*, 159–171.

Kircher, T. T. J., P. F. Liddle, M. J. Brammer, S. C. Williams, R. M. Murray, and P. K. McGuire. 2001. Neural correlates of formal thought disorder in schizophrenia: An fMRI study. *Archives of General Psychiatry*, *58*, 769–774.

Kraepelin, E. 1920. Die Ercheinungsformen des Irreseins. *Zeitschrift fur Neurologie und Psychiatrie*, *62*, 1–29.

Laurens, K. R., K. A. Kiehl, and P. F. Liddle. 2005. A supramodal network encompassing limbic, paralimbic, and frontal and parietal association cortices mediates goal-directed attention. *Human Brain Mapping*, *24*, 35–49.

Laurens, K. R., E. T. C. Ngan, A. T. Bates, K. A. Kiehl, and P. F. Liddle. 2003. Rostral anterior cingulate cortex dysfunction during error processing in schizophrenia. *Brain*, *126*, 610–622.

Laurens, K. R., E. T. C. Ngan, and P. F. Liddle. 2004. Limbic–paralimbic dysfunction in schizophrenia during goal-directed stimulus processing. *Neuroimage*, *22*/S1, abstract TH 214.

Liddle, P. F. 1984. Chronic schizophrenic symptoms, cognitive function, and neurological impairment. Membership thesis, Royal College of Psychiatrists, London.

Liddle, P. F. 1987a. The symptoms of chronic schizophrenia—A reexamination of the positive–negative dichotomy. *British Journal of Psychiatry*, *151*, 145–151.

Liddle, P. F. 1987b. Schizophrenic syndromes, cognitive performance, and neurological dysfunction. *Psychological Medicine*, *17*(1), 49–57.

Liddle, P. F., K. J. Friston, C. D. Frith, S. R. Hirsch, T. Jones, and R. S. J. Frackowiak. 1992. Patterns of cerebral blood-flow in schizophrenia. *British Journal of Psychiatry*, *160*, 179–186.

Liddle, P. F., K. R. Laurens, D. Das, and K. A. Kiehl. 2004. Attention to behaviorally relevant stimuli: An event-related fMRI study of the effect of task demands on the hemodynamic response to auditory oddball target stimuli. *Neuroimage*, *22*/S1, abstract TH 77.

Liddle, P. F., and D. L. Morris. 1991. Schizophrenic syndromes and frontal-lobe performance. *British Journal of Psychiatry*, *158*, 340–345.

Liddle, P. F., A. J. Smith, and K. A. Kiehl. 2001. An event related fMRI study of response inhibition. *Human Brain Mapping*, *12*, 100–109.

McGuire, P., D. J. Quested, S. A. Spence, R. M. Murray, C. D. Frith, and P. F. Liddle. 1998. Pathophysiology of "positive" thought disorder in schizophrenia. *British Journal of Psychiatry*, *173*, 231–235.

Raichle, M. E., A. M. MacLeod, A. Z. Snyder, W. J. Powers, D. A. Gusnard, and G. L. Shulman. 2001. A default mode of brain function. *Proceedings of the National Academy of Sciences USA*, *98*, 676–682.

Szechtman, H., C. Nahmias, E. S. Garnett, G. Firnau, G. M. Brown, R. D. Kaplan, et al. 1988. Effect of neuroleptics on altered cerebral glucose-metabolism in schizophrenia. *Archives of General Psychiatry, 45,* 523–532.

van Veen, V., and C. S. Carter. 2002. The anterior cingulate as a conflict monitor: fMRI and ERP studies. *Physiology and Behavior, 77,* 477–482.

Vouloumanos, A., K. A. Kiehl, J. F. Werker, and P. F. Liddle. 2001. Detection of sounds in the auditory stream: Event-related fMRI evidence for differential activation to speech and nonspeech. *Journal of Cognitive Neuroscience, 13,* 994–1005.

Yuasa, S., M. Kurachi, M. Suzuki, Y. Kadono, M. Matsui, O. Saitoh, et al. 1995. Clinical symptoms and regional cerebral blood-flow in schizophrenia. *European Archives of Psychiatry and Clinical Neuroscience, 246,* 7–12.

10 Schizophrenic Avolition: Implications from Functional and Structural Neuroimaging

Sean A. Spence and Chris Parry

10.1 Introduction: Two Perspectives on Avolition

(i) "Avolition manifests itself as a characteristic lack of energy and drive. Subjects are unable to mobilise themselves to initiate or persist in completing many different kinds of tasks. Unlike the diminished energy or interest of depression, the avolitional symptom complex in schizophrenia is usually not accompanied by saddened or depressed affect. The avolitional symptom complex often leads to severe social and economic impairment" (Andreasen 1983).

(ii) Ulysses never knew his father and saw little of his mother, as she was often confined to psychiatric hospitals. He grew up in a number of institutions, intermittently fostered but never adopted. At the age of seventeen Ulysses was discharged from local authority care and spent the next twenty years roofless on the streets. He never claimed state benefits and lived off the food he found in rubbish bins. He moved from city to city, recognized by police but not subject to assessment until he came to the notice of a psychiatric team treating the homeless. After following Ulysses around the city and attempting to engage with him, they detained him for assessment under the United Kingdom's Mental Health Act.

When seen on the ward, Ulysses appeared to be a young man. Initially, his ethnicity could not be determined because he was so unkempt, his long hair matted into dreadlocks. His clothes and shoes needed to be cut from him. It emerged that he is Caucasian. Ulysses said little, but when he spoke he reported voices commenting upon his behavior. He had lived without social contact for most of his adult life, and his only desire was to "keep walking." He did not use or understand denominations of money. He was edentulous, his gums lined with dental abscesses. Blood tests revealed low serum folate (consistent with malnutrition).

Ulysses exhibited marked executive deficits on formal neuropsychological assessment. His verbal fluency was particularly reduced. He made only minimal response to antipsychotic medications: olanzapine, risperidone, amisulpiride, and clozapine. While waiting (over a year) for a rehabilitation placement, he continued to exhibit avolition and alogia, needing to be reminded to change his clothes and wash his hair. He displayed a stereotypical pattern of behavior. He always sat in the same place in the television room (among others, though not speaking to them). He rocked to and fro on his chair. Over a year, many chairs were replaced, as he broke them through rocking. Indeed, there are two holes in the TV room carpet where he rocked on the chair's back legs, to and fro. He still described voices, though they were "quieter now." When taken to see the rehabilitation unit, he walked back four miles rather than stay. He wanted to live on the acute ward.

Though the "positive" symptoms of Ulysses' schizophrenic illness (i.e., third-person auditory verbal hallucinations) were those most responsive to antipsychotic medication, it was his "negative" symptoms, his lack of volition and speech, that most incapacitated him. These respond less well to treatment. Foremost of these is avolition.

10.2   Volition and Its Absence

If the concept of volition attempts to describe the purposeful behaviors that humans undertake (Jeannerod, this volume), then "avolition" describes their absence, in particular, the failure of the subject/agent to initiate spontaneous action. Such a failure of initiation is incorporated into Andreasen's definition (1983, above, i). It is also apparent in Ulysses (ii); though he might occasionally carry out goal-directed behaviors (as he did when he left the rehabilitation unit), in general, his self-care was stymied by a failure to act. Hence, he was disheveled and generally "stuck," performing repetitive, purposeless activities (stereotypies), such as rocking on his chair.

In this short account we posit that the choosing and/or initiation of spontaneous acts in health is subserved by brain systems incorporating (though by no means confined to) prefrontal cortex, and that disorder of these same systems is evident in avolition.

10.3   Basic Anatomy

The frontal lobes comprise approximately one-third of the adult human brain and may be seen as pivotal to the control of purposeful behavior. At their most posterior limit, they include the primary motor cortices (Brodmann Area, BA 4), essentially motor relay stations, engaged in the execution of demonstrable movements (e.g., by contralateral limbs; Spence and Frith 1999). The familiar homunculus describes the representation of motor regions along the convexity of motor cortex, from the lower limb represented medially, to the arm and facial musculature more laterally. Motor cortical activation is particularly necessary when the movement to be performed requires skill or dexterity (as might occur in musical performance, below).

Anterior to the primary motor cortices lie the premotor cortices (PMC, BA 6), regions particularly implicated in the programming of movements and speech (Passingham 1993). These regions also exhibit an interesting lateral/medial distinction, so that lateral areas may be most engaged in movements programed in response to environmental cues, while medial PMC (the "supplementary motor area"; SMA) is more involved when movements are internally determined by subjects (either with respect to their identity, e.g., which finger to move, or their timing, i.e., when to move it). Such distinctions may be defended on the basis of animal data, human neuropsychological case material (Passingham 1993), and, in more recent years, the results of *in vivo* functional neuroimaging experiments (below). An accessible overview of frontal anatomy is provided by Bradshaw (2001, especially pp. 13–34).

Anterior to the PMC lie the frontal eye fields (concerned with control of eye movements, BA 8) and prefrontal cortices (PFC), also exhibiting regional functional specificities (Stuss and Knight 2002; Goldberg 2001). While lateral regions (such as the dorsolateral prefrontal cortex; DLPFC) are involved in working memory (holding information transiently in consciousness, such as the telephone number to be implemented), selection of action, and spontaneous speech (see Spence and Frith 1999; Spence et al. 2002), more inferior regions (ventrolateral and orbitofrontal cortex; OFC) have been implicated in the inhibition of responses and their reversal (as in some forms of conditioning). This is a grossly simplified distinction but serves as a general framework: The lateral PFC engages in response generation while inferior, ventral regions are more involved in response inhibition (Goldberg 2001). A more detailed account of the regional specifications of certain PFC foci can be found in Shallice (2002).

While the left DLPFC (BA 9/46) has been particularly implicated in response selection ("sculpting the response space"; Fletcher et al. 2000) and the encoding of working memory contents, right DLPFC is implicated in self-monitoring, particularly in the context of mnemonic retrieval (when data are checked for their accuracy; Shallice 2002). Right inferolateral PFC (BA 47) is implicated in response reversal and inhibition (Aron et al. 2004) and hence may be activated when prepotent responses are withheld by the organism (Spence et al. 2001, 2004). It is also implicated in retrieval of information from memory (Shallice 2002; and see Owen, this volume). At the frontal poles (BA 10) there are regions activated when subjects hold "intentions" in their minds—plans for the future, which have been termed "prospective memory" (Burgess et al. 2001; Burgess, Gilbert, Okuda, and Simons, this volume). Regions activated during the performance of speech include Broca's area and anterior insula on the left (Wise et al. 1999), the former being seen by some as an extension of PMC (Passingham 1993). As the requirements of the speech task develop beyond mere word repetition toward self-generated speech, as in discourse, then more anterior regions are implicated (e.g., Wise et al. 1999; Spence et al. 2000; Blank et al. 2002).

As well as contributing to the behaviour of the organism *as an individual* (choosing what to do and when to do it) the PFC is pivotal to their social interactions, among others. Key areas include the OFC, which may be engaged in modulating behaviors according to the hierarchical relationships pertaining to those present (Blair 2004), and ventromedial PFC, implicated in "theory of mind" or understanding another person's point of view (e.g., Farrow et al. 2001; Frith and Frith 1999). Damage to such regions may be associated with radical changes of personality and moral conduct (see Grafman and Kreuger, this volume; Bechara, this volume). Also on the medial surface of PFC, the anterior cingulate cortex (ACC) is a multimodal region pivotally implicated in attention and response monitoring (and perhaps error correction; Carter et al. 1998). This area is richly interconnected with lateral regions (DLPFC) engaged in action planning, and posterior regions (PMC and motor cortices) engaged in action execution, and it receives ascending autonomic and limbic projections, impacting upon arousal and motivation. ACC has been conceptualized as helping to translate "intentions into actions" (Paus 2001).

10.4 Action and the Prefrontal Cortex

There are many experiments demonstrating that when healthy subjects initiate *spontaneous* acts or choose *which* acts to perform, they activate regions of PFC. By contrasting such behavior with baseline/comparator states, in which initiation or selection is not required, investigators have demonstrated that PFC is necessary (though not sufficient) for action generation (Spence and Frith 1999). Regions of PFC contribute to neural architectures involving other cortical regions (e.g., SMA and parietal cortex) and subcortical foci (e.g., within the basal ganglia, thalamus, and cerebellum). These latter systems may be sufficient to execute routine motor procedures/behaviors, such as those composing stereotypical sequences. However, generally, novel acts require the contribution of PFC. Such a conceptualization is consistent with at least one model of human cognitive control, provided by Shallice (1988, p. 334), in which a higher, executive system exerts a supervisory/modulatory influence upon "lower" brain systems. Figure 10.1 outlines a simplified version of Shallice's model, adapted to illustrate the roles of PFC and subordinate regions in the generation of novel and routine motor behaviors (and also the influence of distal causes, such as genes and early environment).

10.5 A Simple Choice

By way of illustration, let us consider a very simple experiment demonstrating the functional anatomical consequences of asking subjects to choose a response or follow a prespecified pattern. In Spence et al. 1998, we asked healthy subjects to perform a

DEVELOPMENT   **ANATOMY**   **BEHAVIOR**

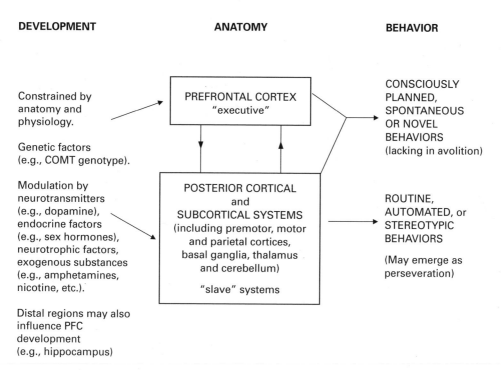

Constrained by
anatomy and
physiology.

Genetic factors
(e.g., COMT genotype).

Modulation by
neurotransmitters
(e.g., dopamine),
endocrine factors
(e.g., sex hormones),
neurotrophic factors,
exogenous substances
(e.g., amphetamines,
nicotine, etc.).

Distal regions may also
influence PFC
development
(e.g., hippocampus)

PREFRONTAL CORTEX
"executive"

POSTERIOR CORTICAL
and
SUBCORTICAL SYSTEMS
(including premotor, motor
and parietal cortices,
basal ganglia, thalamus
and cerebellum)

"slave" systems

CONSCIOUSLY
PLANNED,
SPONTANEOUS
OR NOVEL
BEHAVIORS
(lacking in avolition)

ROUTINE,
AUTOMATED, or
STEREOTYPIC
BEHAVIORS

(May emerge as
perseveration)

Figure 10.1

Schematic illustrating the neural basis of behavioral control. Prefrontal systems (center,
"Anatomy") are implicated in control of complex and novel behavioral patterns (right, "Behavior"), modulating "lower" brain systems (center, "Anatomy"). However, lower brain systems
are necessary for the performance of both complex and routine behaviors. Thus, "cognitive
subtractions" yielding those brain regions *specifically* activated during complex behaviors (as in
fig. 10.3) reveal prefrontal cortex (PFC; the contribution of the lower centers having been "subtracted" away). Constraints are imposed by prior genetic and neurodevelopmental factors (left,
"Development"), and function continues to be modulated by neurotransmitters (see text). These
constraints impose limits on the envelope of possible responses emitted by the organism (right,
"Behavior," and see fig. 10.9). COMT, catechol-O-methyltransferase.

simple verbal (oro-bucco-lingual) task involving three conditions. In this positron-emission tomography (PET) study, subjects lay in a scanner and heard a pacing tone at a rate of 1 pulse every 3 seconds. The task conditions were the following:

1. Rest, in which the subjects listened to the tone but did not respond.
2. Stereotypical (externally specified) responding, in which the subjects enunciated the syllables "la" or "bah" in a repetitive sequence (la, bah, bah, la, la, bah, bah, la) one response per tone.
3. Freely selected (internally specified) responding, in which the subjects enunciated the same two syllables in a sequence of their own choosing (the stipulation being that they make the sequence as random as possible).

From a cognitive perspective we should posit that the second condition engages those systems necessary to maintain "online" the task demands ("keep to the sequence la, bah, bah, la etc."), perceive the stimulus tone, engage in a speech act, and perceive one's own voice upon speaking. However, from the perspective of a model such as that of Shallice (1988), or our simplified version (fig. 10.1), it is important to note that this task engages "lower" motor centers, sufficient to execute stereotypy. Figure 10.2 shows those brain regions activated in the second condition relative to the first, that

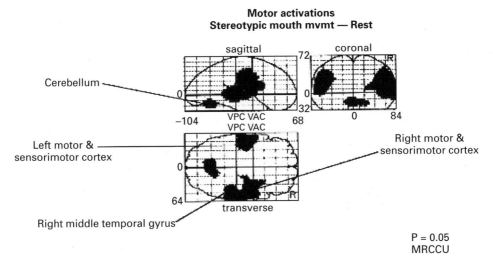

Figure 10.2
Activations in subjects performing a stereotypical (externally specified) sequence of mouth movements compared with the resting state. There is significantly greater activation of bilateral sensorimotor regions and cerebellum. The figure shows statistical parametric maps thresholded for display purposes at $p < .05$ (data reported in Spence et al. 1998). The labels VAC and VPC indicate a standard vertical reference plane passing through the anterior and posterior commissures (AC and PC), respectively.

is, following the "cognitive subtraction" stereotypical movement "minus" rest. The regions we found to be activated were primarily in the motor and premotor cortices, their corresponding sensory cortices, and cerebellum (the sensitivity of our technique did not allow us to image the requisite basal ganglia activity; Spence et al. 1998). It is also interesting (in light of later work by Wise and colleagues, 1999), that this stereotypical task did not significantly activate/engage Broca's area (consistent with a view that anterior insula and other "lower" motor centers are sufficient for vocal articulation).

Turning to the third condition, in which the subjects *chose* the sequence of their responses, we may posit that by subtracting away those activations associated with stereotypical responding (in condition 2), we should reveal those brain regions implicated in choice. Figure 10.3 shows the brain regions maximally activated in the free-selection condition ("minus" stereotypical responding). Clearly the regions implicated are those in left PFC (particularly BA 9), though there is also increased activity in Broca's area and regions adjacent (Spence et al. 1998).

This and similar experiments support the hypothesis that PFC is involved in the generation of chosen acts (e.g., Goldman-Rakic 1987; Frith et al. 1991a, 1991b; Goldman-Rakic et al. 1992; Ingvar 1994; Passingham 1996; Desmond et al. 1998; de Zubicaray et al. 1998; Jahanshahi et al. 1998, 2000), at least in the case of healthy subjects. However, these findings do not exist in isolation, and there is also considerable

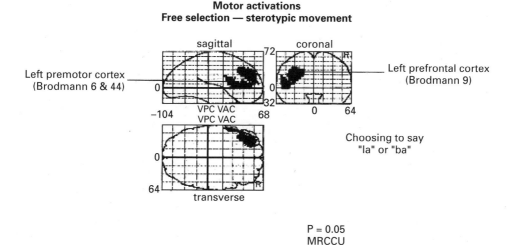

Figure 10.3

Activations in subjects performing a freely selected (internally specified) sequence of mouth movements compared with performing a stereotypic sequence. There is significantly greater activation of left prefrontal regions (in particular Brodmann Area 9). Shown are statistical parametric maps thresholded for display purposes at $p < .05$ (data reported in Spence et al. 1998).

evidence from the neuropsychological literature that humans with lesions in these PFC areas exhibit deficits in their ability to initiate action (e.g., Milner 1963; Perret 1974; Petrides and Milner 1982; Dolan et al. 1993; Petrides 1996; de Zubicaray et al. 1997). Hence, though PFC is not sufficient to initiate purposeful chosen acts, it does seem to be *necessary*.

10.6   Choosing When

As well as choosing which action to perform, it is clearly crucial that, as agents, humans choose *when* to act. Again, avolition appears to impact upon a patient's ability to act spontaneously, to move or care for the self or to interact with others (above, ii). Recently, in a series of studies using event-related functional magnetic resonance imaging (fMRI), we have been interested in discovering the neural correlates of acts which the agent initiates "spontaneously" (Hunter et al. 2003, 2004; Ganesan et al. 2005).

In the first study, healthy subjects lay in a magnetic resonance scanner and were scanned for epochs of 10 minutes. During these periods, they were instructed to push buttons with either their right index or right middle finger, *whenever* they wished. Clearly, this is a less constrained task than that of Spence et al. (1998), but the point is that we deliberately wished to allow subjects a degree of "freedom." We recorded the choices that subjects made and the times of their actions. Using these recordings, we were able to analyze the imaging data to show those brain regions active at the *moment* of action (and, by reverse modeling, those regions activated prior to action; Hunter et al. 2004). The important finding here (fig. 10.4) is that at the instant of action a coherent network of related brain regions is activated (incorporating PFC, SMA, and motor cortex), consistent with our simple model of those systems necessary

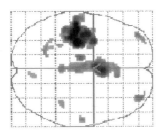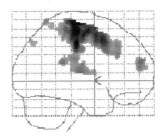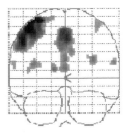

Figure 10.4
Activations in subjects performing spontaneous actions using two fingers of the right hand. There is significantly greater activation of bilateral prefrontal, premotor (supplementary motor area), and left motor cortices. The figure shows statistical parametric maps thresholded for display purposes at $p < 0.05$ (data reported in Hunter et al. 2003). See plate 3.

for the initiation of spontaneous behavior (fig. 10.1). Such a brain map does not allow one to infer a cognitive hierarchy, in terms of PFC supervening upon "lower regions" (SMA and motor cortex), but this is a consequence of the analytic method used. Here, we see the network functioning in concert, as a whole (i.e., we have not "subtracted away" subordinate components, as in fig. 10.3).

However, we were also able to explore the temporal, dynamic characteristics of the signal detected in each of those brain regions identified. We found that left PFC (BA 10) and SMA (BA 6) responses occurred significantly earlier than that of motor cortex (BA 4), a finding consistent with the thesis that "higher" centers are indeed superordinate to the latter (Hunter et al. 2003).

In subsequent studies, focusing on the antecedents of action, we have replicated the above findings and also demonstrated that prior to the activation of BA 10, 6, and 4, there is activation of left DLPFC (BA 9; Hunter et al. 2004). Our hypothesis is that even within the cognitive executive there is a dynamic hierarchy, according to task demands, and that on this task left DLPFC may be superordinate to all the other foci detected. The relationships we described between discrete PFC foci were also revealed through an even simpler (though similarly unconstrained) protocol: requiring subjects to move only one finger whenever they wished, but making the timing as random as possible (Hunter et al. 2004). Here the challenge to subjects is to vary their response solely in terms of time: to avoid stereotypical, fixed interresponse intervals. When we have used this protocol to study people with chronic schizophrenia, we have found that the magnitude of left DLPFC activity correlates with performance, that is, the variance patients exhibit in the timing of their actions (Ganesan et al. 2005). These data suggest that left DLPFC plays a pivotal role in controlling action in time, at least in people with schizophrenia. Finally, performance on this task and activity in left DLPFC are inversely correlated with severity of attentional impairments (Ganesan et al. 2005), another finding consistent with our model (fig. 10.1), that is, those patients exhibiting impaired attention are less able to modulate their behavior in time and are more stereotypical in their response patterns.

Taken together, these simple studies illuminate the key role of prefrontal systems in the generation of behaviors that are chosen and executed spontaneously. What is their relevance to avolition? Their relevance is that they prompt the hypothesis that patients who exhibit avolition will also exhibit deficits (functional and/or structural) in their prefrontal cortices (as is implied in the Ganesan et al. 2005 data). The findings of several other neuroimaging studies support this view.

10.7 Psychomotor Poverty

In a PET study of 30 patients with chronic schizophrenia, scanned while they were at rest, Liddle and colleagues (1992) utilized a within-group correlational design to

Psychomotor poverty syndrome

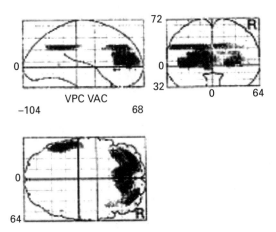

Negative correlations

Figure 10.5
Areas where relative resting state activity in people with schizophrenia is negatively correlated with severity of psychomotor poverty symptoms (taken from Liddle et al. 1992, with permission). Areas maximally implicated include bilateral prefrontal cortices. The labels VAC and VPC indicate a standard vertical reference plane passing through the anterior and posterior commissures (AC and PC), respectively.

examine the relationship between subsyndromes of schizophrenic symptomatology and resting state brain activity. With regard to the psychomotor poverty subsyndrome, which incorporates the symptom of avolition, they demonstrated an inverse correlation between symptom severity and prefrontal regional cerebral blood flow (an index of neuronal activity; fig. 10.5). Hence, the worse patients' psychomotor poverty (including avolition), the lower their prefrontal activity at rest. These data are congruent with PFC's implied role in the emergence of spontaneous behavior. However, in this case the inference is drawn from an association between a relative absence of PFC activation and an *absence* of action. Other studies have revealed congruent findings (e.g., Heckers et al. 1999).

Might such underactivity be reversible with treatment? This is clearly a legitimate target for therapeutic intervention, yet the evidence in schizophrenia is relatively limited. There have been studies demonstrating a reversal of "hypofrontality" in schizophrenia, in response to antipsychotic medication (e.g., Spence et al. 1998; Honey et al. 1999), but few have focused upon those most severely affected by negative symptomatology (although preliminary reports are beginning to appear; Spence, Green, et al. 2005). Using a novel wake-promoting agent (modafinil), we have begun to demonstrate temporary modulation of prefrontal function and cognitive performance (Spence, Green, et al. 2005). Indeed, Turner and colleagues (2004), in a nonneuroimaging study, demonstrated acute improvement in verbal working memory and attentional function on this drug.

To some extent, proof of concept (that prefrontal modulation impacts action performance) may be inferred from interventions in another neuropsychiatric disorder associated with poverty of action: Parkinson's disease (PD). While PD is clearly a different disorder from schizophrenia, characterized by tremor, rigidity, and bradykinesia, and also far better "understood" in terms of its pathophysiology, it may prove informative in the present context. One feature of advanced PD is the appearance of "on/off" phenomena, when the therapeutic effects of pharmacological treatments become less reliable and there emerge oscillations between excessive involuntary, abnormal movements and periods of stasis ("off") during which the subject cannot act (e.g., Starkstein and Merello 2002). In a study of patients with severe PD, manifesting "off" states, in which they were unable to act, Samuel and colleagues (1997) demonstrated that therapeutic pallidotomy (essentially, the introduction of a subcortical lesion to release excessive inhibition of PFC) was associated with increased frontal activation and a concomitant enhancement of motor performance. Jenkins et al. (1992) had demonstrated a similar effect in response to apomorphine (a dopamine D1/D2 agonist). Similarly, there is a literature on the use of dopamine agonists in the treatment of abulia (or lack of will) occurring in "frontal lobe" patients (e.g., Barrett 1991) and to enhance executive function post–head injury (McDowell et al. 1998).

The possibility that dopamine agonists might improve the negative syndrome of schizophrenia gave rise to trials of amphetamines, which met with mixed results (see Turner et al. 2004). The risk in schizophrenia is that dopamine agonists will exacerbate psychosis (which may also arise de novo when such treatments are applied in PD). Although the use of dopamine agonists has not been widely taken up in the treatment of avolition in schizophrenia, it is of interest that the most effective "atypical" antipsychotic, clozapine, releases dopamine in prefrontal cortex (Youngren et al. 1999). Also, third-generation antipsychotics, "dopamine stabilizers," offer a new means of modulating dopamine tone in vivo. It remains to be seen whether such therapies will substantially impact upon core negative symptoms (such as avolition).

Indeed, there are neuroimaging findings in people with schizophrenia that suggest that the scope for such improvement may be limited (e.g., Chua et al. 1997, below). So far, we have focused upon functional imaging studies, those that utilize PET or fMRI to examine *activity* in executive regions. But what of structure? What if the structure of executive brain regions were significantly altered in schizophrenia—might that not constrain functional recovery?

10.8   Structural Constraints: Prefrontal Gray Matter

Chua and colleagues (1997) studied 12 patients with schizophrenia, utilizing a within-group correlational design to examine the relationship between cortical *gray matter volume* and symptom profile in schizophrenia. This study is conceptually similar to that of Liddle and colleagues (1992), examining the *functional* correlates of the psychomotor poverty syndrome. In the later study, Chua and colleagues found that worse psychomotor poverty syndrome was associated with reduced prefrontal gray matter volume (particularly on the left) (fig. 10.6). Hence, not only does reduced spontaneous behavior exhibit a correlation with reduced *activity* in PFC, it also implies an underlying reduction in local gray matter. This was a small study (Chua et al. 1997); however,

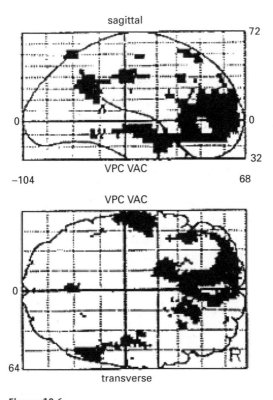

Figure 10.6
Areas where relative regional gray matter volume in people with schizophrenia is negatively correlated with severity of psychomotor poverty symptoms (taken from Chua et al. 1997, with permission). Areas maximally implicated include left prefrontal cortex. The labels VAC and VPC indicate a standard vertical reference plane passing through the anterior and posterior commissures (AC and PC), respectively.

its findings are congruent with others reporting a relationship between prefrontal structure and negative symptomatology (e.g., Gur et al. 1998; Wible et al. 2001; Sallet et al. 2003). Also, in a recent study from our lab, Farrow and colleagues (2005) examined the relationship between unconstrained motor activity in people with chronic schizophrenia (as measured over a day using an Actiwatch device) and the volume of specific PFC regions (DLPFC and ACC). They found a positive correlation between freely occurring ambulatory activity and volume of left ACC. This study does not elucidate the complexity of such motor behavior, merely its volume, but it does imply that specific executive structures may constrain freely undertaken behavior (at least in the disease state of schizophrenia). If correct, these and similar findings (e.g., Chua et al. 1997) may be a cause for some concern: for they seem to suggest that those who exhibit avolition do so as a consequence of the *structure* of their brains (admittedly, causation cannot be inferred from association, but nevertheless such a link is plausible). Also of concern are studies finding a progressive element to prefrontal volume reduction in schizophrenia (e.g., Gur et al. 1998; Madsen et al. 1999; Salokangas et al. 2002). While pharmacological interventions might modulate the hypoactivity of prefrontal cortex in this disorder (e.g., Spence, Green, et al. 1998, 2005; Honey et al. 1999), it is less clear how such therapies might ameliorate the effects of gross morphological disturbance.

10.9 Neural Plasticity

While the foregoing comments may seem rather pessimistic, they prompt a further empirical question: Are there strategies that might be applied to restore/induce greater prefrontal function/structure in people with schizophrenia? Such a question would be predicated on the belief that specific prefrontal regions are pivotal to voluntary behavior and that by improving their function and/or structure we would facilitate volition on the part of the subject/agent. This is clearly an ambitious proposal. Is there any evidence in its favor?

Several recent neuroimaging studies suggest that training undergone by humans in the course of their development and adulthood can impact upon the volume of specific cerebral structures. Two subject groups are particularly informative: taxi drivers and musicians.

In their studies of licensed London taxi drivers, Maguire and colleagues (2000) have demonstrated a relationship between "doing the knowledge" (acquiring a familiarity with traffic routes and regulations throughout London) and hippocampal volume. The hippocampus is known to be involved in spatial memory, and London taxi drivers certainly rely upon theirs. They have to learn all the streets in and around the city (a process that usually takes about 2 years; Maguire et al. 2000); they then continue to use this form of memory in their daily working lives. Such drivers exhibit larger posterior hippocampi than controls, a finding which in itself might imply either initial aptitude or some adaptation to the task. However, the volume of the right posterior hippocampus exhibits a linear relationship with duration of taxi driving. Hence, it seems as though the length of exposure to the mnemonic demands of driving a London taxi impacts upon the structure of a supporting brain region (in this case the hippocampus).

A less clear-cut example is provided by the literature concerning musicians' brains. A number of studies have demonstrated that professional musicians have larger motor cortices than controls, a finding which has left open the possibility that such differences may be inherited, not acquired. However, a study by Gaser and Schlaug (2003) demonstrates a relationship between length of musical practice and volume of motor and auditory cortices. Also, and this is particularly important for our purposes, it demonstrates that professional musicians exhibit larger left prefrontal foci (in the region of BA 46) when compared with amateurs and nonmusicians. This provides tantalizing evidence for a form of musical activity enhancing prefrontal structure; though, of course, we cannot extrapolate from this to either improved executive performance or specific therapies for schizophrenia. Nevertheless, it does prompt a hypothesis worthy of further empirical investigation: that specified activities might be used to impact prefrontal structure (in the hope that they would also impact function). In other words, that we might "grow" PFC.

Such a blunt proposal would be predicated on the belief that specific prefrontal regions are pivotal to voluntary behavior and that improving their function and/or structure would facilitate volition on the part of the subject/agent (it would also need to acknowledge that it is neural organizational complexity, rather than sheer volume, which is pivotal to successful outcome; Kolb and Gibb 2002).

A detailed account of the basic mechanisms supporting neural plasticity is beyond the scope of this chapter. The changes accompanying normal learning, especially involving motor cortex, have been clearly reviewed by Rioult-Pedotti and Donoghue (2003), those pertaining to PFC (primarily in animal models), by Kolb and Gibb (2002), and in the context of neurological disease, by Barker and Dunnett (1999).

In the acute setting, during new learning or immediately post–neurological insult, it seems likely that skill acquisition (or recovery) relies upon the mechanism of long-term potentiation (LTP). The latter occurs via the substrate of synapses of the long-range horizontal/lateral excitatory (mainly glutamatergic) projections running through layers II/III of motor cortex. The latter may cover relatively long distances and would serve to "couple" widespread cortical regions, in the context of new learning. Also, the patterns of functional reorganization seen with learning or recovery resemble these fibers' projection patterns (see Rioult-Pedotti and Donoghue 2003). "The appeal of LTP as a mechanism of learning and memory is that it is activity dependent and specific to the active synapses and their target neurons" (Rioult-Pedotti and Donoghue 2003, p. 6). While such learning implicates the voltage-dependent NMDA receptor, acting as "coincidence detector" between concomitant pre- (glutamatergic) and postsynaptic (depolarization) activity (thereby associating input from diverse cortical areas), this process appears to be held in check by local, GABA-mediated inhibition. Hence GABA antagonists may enhance, and GABA agonists (such as lorazepam) impede, LTP.

In the longer term, normal skill learning is associated with an increase in the number of synapses per neuron in motor cortex and cerebellum (Rioult-Pedotti and Donoghue 2003). Exposure to complex sensory environments is associated with increased synapses per neuron, increased spine density, and changes in spine morphology, in sensorimotor regions (Kolb and Gibb 2002; Rioult-Pedotti and Donoghue 2003). In animal models of PFC, exposure to a complex developmental environment is associated with increased dendritic spine density but not dendritic length (Kolb and Gibb 2002). However, dendritic length and spine density, within PFC, are both increased by dopamine, amphetamines, cocaine, and nicotine (Kolb and Gibb 2002). Neurotrophic factors have similar effects, while gonadal hormones exhibit a more complex influence, dependent upon gender and age of the organism (see Kolb and Gibb 2002). Hence, it may be seen that a number of processes and influences contribute to neural plasticity. With respect to the changes seen in the brains of humans (above), reflected in morphology, and large enough to be detected using MRI, it is likely that these reflect long-term changes in structure which may facilitate those behaviors required of the individuals concerned (taxi drivers and musicians). Conversely, reduced volume of PFC, as seen in schizophrenia, may reflect a long-term change in structure or a failure to develop normally (a neurodevelopmental origin), though we cannot exclude the role of atrophy occurring early in the psychotic process.

It is of note, in this regard, that at least one animal model of schizophrenia has demonstrated reduced synaptic density in PFC, in adulthood, consequent upon hippocampal insult in early development (Lipska et al. 2001). Hence, PFC is also susceptible to trophic influences arising in distal brain regions.

When a diseased system begins to fail it may first respond with compensation: essentially "working harder." Such changes accompany the early stages of PD, so that by the time patients actually present with motor impairment they have already lost 75 to 90 percent of their dopaminergic function in subcortical areas (Barker and Dunnett 1999). The implication is that there has been up-regulation of the remaining motor system, but that eventually, when functional reserve has been exceeded, motor disorder becomes manifest. As pathology progresses or is present for longer, other cerebral regions may take on the functions of one that is failing, a process termed "adaptation." Such adaptation may be seen in the cerebral reorganization seen in post-cerebrovascular accidents, but there is also a large literature relating to the relocation of sensory and motor functional representations following peripheral lesions. New synaptic connections may proliferate, or preexisting "silent synapses" may be activated (Barker and Dunnett 1999).

Hence, if we return to figure 10.1, there may be a great many distal (developmental) and more proximal (e.g., neurochemical) influences impacting upon frontal plasticity and, hence, action execution.

10.10 Executive Therapy: How to Avoid Automation?

In light of the above comments we have been interested in studying the executive system of a single subject scanned on multiple occasions, while he performed an executive task. The latter required him to modulate his behavior in time (through the generation of behavioral randomness as described in Hunter et al. 2003). He was allowed to move either his right index or middle fingers, at a time that he determined. He was required to be as random as possible, both in terms of finger selection and timing of movement. We wished to see how his prefrontal function might change over time (during successive scan sessions).

Our subject, S (for Sisyphus), is a 21-year-old healthy right-handed male, who volunteered to be scanned while performing the same task on six separate occasions over several months (here we present preliminary data from 4 sessions). S has a predicted IQ of 105 (National Adult Reading Test [NART]; Nelson and O'Connell 1978). He has no clinical history of neurological or psychiatric disorder and he provided written, informed consent to participate in the study, which was approved by the local Research Ethics Committees.

During each of the scanning sessions, S generated sequences of behavioral randomness. There were no differences in measures of his performance (in terms of randomness of selection or timing domains) across time. Analysis of fMRI data revealed activation of those regions seen in the Hunter et al. (2003, 2004) studies: PFC, SMA, and MC at the point of action, left DLPFC prior to it. However, over time, something interesting happened. S exhibited significantly greater activation of left BA 10, 6, and 4 with ensuing scan sessions, and he exhibited increasing deactivation of regions in right PFC (fig. 10.7). So, though his performance did not change, our subject exhibited salient changes in activation foci implicated in that performance. These data are, to a certain extent, consistent with the functional imaging data acquired during learning over shorter intervals (often within scan sessions; Passingham 1993; Jenkins et al. 1994), where subjects have gradually increased their activation of posterior regions as they learn the task. They also serve to highlight certain questions with regard to using executive tasks as cognitive remediation (below).

There is an intuitive appeal to trying to simultaneously probe and stimulate the human executive system over time through the repetition of an executive task. However, it is in the nature of such a process that it might also become increasingly automated over time. What would this look like? We suggest that it would involve maintenance (or improvement) of task performance levels (as is the case with S), while "lower" motor centers "take over" the execution of that index task. Hence, one would predict increasing activation of areas such as premotor and motor cortices (as seen in fig. 10.7). Hence, the potential automation of an executive task would undermine its use as a prefrontal "stimulant" since the latter would be required to intervene to a lesser degree (as the task became automated). However, if an executive task remained difficult or taxing to do, then it might resist automation. We have been interested in randomness generation for this reason. It is difficult to generate truly random sequences of behavior, and the development of a strategy, or failure to attend properly might both be revealed through the emergence of nonrandom response patterns. That randomness generation does to some extent "remain" an executive task for S is, we speculate, indicated by the increasing activation of left PFC over time (fig. 10.7). He seems to retain (and indeed increase) activation of relevant PFC regions, while also increasing the deactivation of those areas that would normally deactivate during the task (in this case right-sided, relatively inferior prefrontal regions; fig. 10.7). Thus, even though posterior motor regions activate more over time, the randomness task remains an "activator" of PFC (especially on the left; fig. 10.7).

Therefore, we seem to have a pattern of *functional* change (albeit in a single subject), which shares certain similarities with that *structural* change inferred from practicing musicians (above). While Gaser and Schlaug's (2003) musicians may have increased the volume of their left prefrontal and motor cortices over time, as a consequence of practice, S has increased the activation seen in similar areas (over a considerably shorter period of "practice") during randomness generation. There may be scope for further application of similar tasks in studies aimed at probing the response of PFC

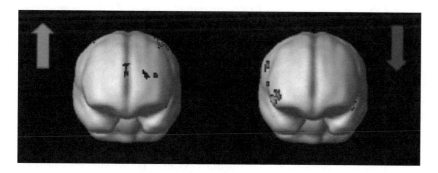

Figure 10.7
Changes in Sisyphus' brain over time on the two-finger version of the behavioral randomness task (Hunter et al. 2004). Over successive scan sessions, generation of random motor sequences elicits relatively greater activation in left prefrontal cortex (PFC), supplementary motor area, and motor cortex (left) and greater deactivation in right PFC foci (right). The figure shows statistical parametric maps thresholded for display purposes at $p < 0.05$. See plate 4.

in schizophrenia, helping to establish whether PFC (function/structure) might be enhanced through complex behavioral regimes in this disorder. As an aside, it may be worth noting that the task eliciting reversal of "hypofrontality" in people recovering from acute schizophrenia in the study by Spence et al. (1998) also required random-ness generation (with respect to paced movements of a joystick). Taken together, these findings suggest that there may be some scope for testing whether executive probes can be used to "overcome" prefrontal, structurally mediated, functional impairments.

10.11   Genetic Constraints: Dopamine Metabolism

If the prospect of a structural contribution to the emergence of avolition is a cause for concern (in view of its possible role in constraining functional recovery), another constraint is becoming increasingly well characterized: that of the subject's genotype. Space precludes a full review of the genetics of schizophrenia, but one example may serve to demonstrate emerging views of the genetics of executive function (and, by extension, volition).

Dopamine is a pivotal neurotransmitter in the physiology of volition. Deficits in dopaminergic transmission are most obvious in PD but are also believed to contribute to the pathophysiology of negative symptoms in schizophrenia (Mortimer and Spence 2001). It has been suggested that while the positive symptoms of the disorder (such as delusions and hallucinations) implicate subcortical dopaminergic excess, negative symptoms (such as avolition) implicate a cortical hypodopaminergic state (Abi-Dargham 2003). Pertinent to the levels of dopamine in the prefrontal cortex are the specific conditions of its metabolism. In prefrontal cortex, dopamine elimination is crucially dependent upon its catabolism by the enzyme catechol-O-methyltransferase (COMT) (this may be contrasted with the conditions pertaining subcortically, where there are additional means of dopamine elimination from the synaptic cleft). Factors which reduce the efficacy of COMT in metabolizing dopamine may be expected to lead to a relative enhancement in the latter's cortical activity (i.e., dopamine will become more "efficient"), while factors leading to dopamine's more rapid elimination will render the transmitter less efficient. In so-called knockout mice, which lack the gene that encodes COMT, cognitive performance is actually enhanced. In humans, the gene encoding COMT contains a common functional polymorphism (Val108/158Met) that has been found to influence cognitive performance in healthy people and those with schizophrenia (Egan et al. 2001). The COMT genotype is related, in an allele dosage manner, to performance on the Wisconsin Card Sorting Test, explaining 4.1 percent of the variance in the frequency of perseverative errors. Perse-veration, in this context, describes the continued performance of behaviors that are no longer contextually appropriate. The "Met" allele is associated with slower metab-olism of dopamine. Homozygotes for this allele made less perseverative errors than did homozygotes for the "Val" allele, with heterozygotes performing at intermediate

DEVELOPMENT   **ANATOMY**   **BEHAVIOR**

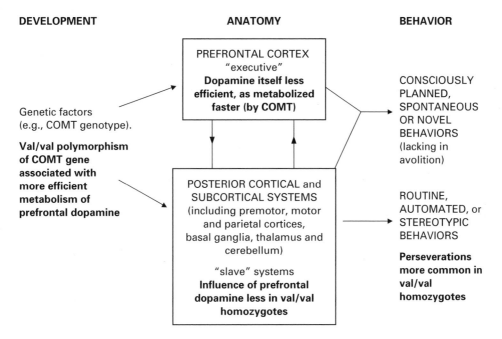

Figure 10.8
Schematic diagram illustrating the neural basis of behavioral control. Genetic factors (left, "Development"), such as the Val/Val polymorphism of the catechol-O-methyltransferase (COMT) geno-type lead to less efficient dopaminergic function in prefrontal systems (center, "Anatomy"). Hence, prefrontal modulation of "lower" centers is less efficient (center), and more stereotypical (perseverative) behaviors emerge during a test of executive function (right, "Behavior").

levels (Egan et al. 2001). Hence, if we return to our simplified cognitive schema described in figure 10.1, and adapted in figure 10.8, we can see that the contribution of a single gene ("Development," on the left of the figure) impacts upon prefrontal physiology (center figure) and hence volition ("Behavior," on the right of the figure). Met homozygotes will have more efficient PFC dopamine function and hence are less likely to perseverate (cf. Val homozygotes; fig. 10.8). Therefore, genetic characterization of prefrontal systems may have profound effects upon the way we come to think of "voluntary" behaviors in the future. Neural chemistry may impose a limit upon the envelope of possible responses emitted by the organism (person; Spence et al. 2002).

10.12 Ulysses and the "Response Space"

Finally, if we return to the case of Ulysses, let us consider his behaviors. We noted their extreme limitation manifest as stereotypical patterns: his always sitting in the same place, often rocking to and fro, engaging in only monosyllabic discourse. In terms of response probabilities, we can speculate that if Ulysses is in the TV room, then it is very likely he will be sitting in a certain chair; if he is sitting in that chair, he is very likely to be rocking to and fro; and he is unlikely to be speaking. What is obvious is that Ulysses's response parameters are very narrow; the behaviors he does perform he enacts frequently, but there are relatively few of them. If we think of them as constituting a response space (or "envelope"), a frequency distribution (as seen in fig. 10.9), we can imagine a hypothetical Gaussian curve, but one that is very narrow. We might speculate that Ulysses's range of behaviors will be considerably more constrained than those of his peers. What he lacks is behavioral diversity. Drawing on the functional and structural neuroimaging data that we have reviewed, we may posit that prefrontal cortex (especially left DLPFC) contributes to the "normal" process by which a range of behavior is elaborated (i.e., the Gaussian curve is spread across a larger range of potential behaviors; fig. 10.9). Indeed, this is the core finding of the Ganesan et al. (2005) study (above).

Tying together what we have described so far, we may posit that genetic and environmental factors act to determine the width of an individual's response envelope (Spence et al. 2002) but that, fortunately, most of us retain a range of possible behaviors in most environments (so that our limitations are not too obvious!). It is likely

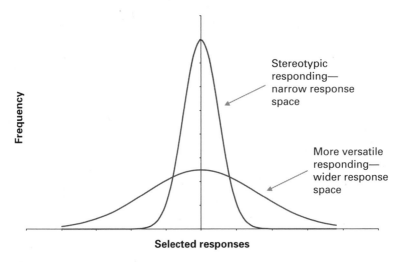

Figure 10.9
Notional response space for subject exhibiting stereotypical responses and another for a subject exhibiting a wider range of potential responses. A narrow Gaussian distribution implies a lack of variety in responses to a given environment. Such behavior will be more "predictable." The subject who varies his or her behavior within that environment is, accordingly, less predictable. See plate 5.

that response spaces vary between and within individuals over time and across environments but that, wherever we are, genetic factors play a role (as in the case of genetic polymorphisms for the COMT gene, above). However, should the environment prove stressful enough, then even the most constrained response space might yield a novel behavior (from the tails of the curve). Consider Ulysses's actions when he was taken to the rehabilitation ward. He didn't like it there, so he walked "home" to the acute ward. Then he resumed rocking on his chair.

Acknowledgments

Thanks to Mrs. Jean Woodhead and Mr. Chris Hobbs for assistance in preparation of this manuscript; to our colleagues in SCANLab for their contributions to the studies described, especially Drs. Mike Hunter, Tom Farrow, and Venkat Ganesan and Ms. C. Hughes. Thanks to the *British Journal of Psychiatry* for permission to reproduce images taken from Liddle et al. 1992 and Chua et al. 1997. Ulysses's name and demographic details have been adjusted to safeguard anonymity.

References

Abi-Dargham, A. 2003. Evidence from brain imaging studies for dopaminergic alterations in schizophrenia. In *Dopamine in the Pathophysiology and Treatment of Schizophrenia*, ed. S. Kapur and Y. Lecrubier, pp. 15–47. London: Martin Dunitz.

Andreasen, N. C. 1983. *Scale for the Assessment of Negative Symptoms (SANS)*. Iowa City: University of Iowa.

Aron, A. R., T. W. Robbins, and R. A. Poldrack. 2004. Inhibition and the right inferior frontal cortex. *Trends in Cognitive Sciences, 8*, 170–177.

Barker, R. A., and S. B. Dunnett. 1999. *Neural Repair, Transplantation, and Rehabilitation*. Hove: Psychology Press.

Barrett, K. 1991. Treating organic abulia with bromocriptine and lisuride: Four case studies. *Journal of Neurology, Neurosurgery, and Psychiatry, 54*, 718–721.

Blair, R. J. R. 2004. The roles of orbital frontal cortex in the modulation of antisocial behaviour. *Brain and Cognition, 55*, 198–208.

Blank, S. C., S. K. Scott, K. Murphy, E. Warburton, and R. J. Wise. 2002. Speech production: Wernicke, Broca, and beyond. *Brain, 125*, 1829–1838.

Bradshaw, J. L. 2001. *Developmental Disorders of the Frontostriatal System: Neuropsychological, Neuropsychiatric, and Evolutionary Perspectives*. Hove: Psychology Press.

Burgess, P. W., A. Quayle, and C. D. Frith. 2001. Brain regions involved in prospective memory as determined by positron emission tomography. *Neuropsychologia, 39*, 545–555.

Carter, C. S., T. S. Braver, D. M. Barch, M. M. Botvinick, D. Noll, and J. D. Cohen. 1998. Anterior cingulate cortex, error detection, and the online monitoring of performance. *Science, 280,* 747–749.

Chua, S. E., I. C. Wright, J.-B. Poline, P. F. Liddle, R. M. Murray, R. S. J. Frackowiak, K. J. Friston, and P. K. McGuire. 1997. Grey matter correlates of syndromes in schizophrenia: A semi-automated analysis of structural magnetic resonance images. *British Journal of Psychiatry, 170,* 406–410.

Desmond, J. E., J. D. E. Gabrieli, and G. H. Glover. 1998. Dissociation of frontal and cerebellar activity in a cognitive task: Evidence for dissociation between selection and search. *NeuroImage, 7,* 368–376.

de Zubicaray, G. I., J. B. Chalk, S. E. Rose, J. Semple, and G. A. Smith. 1997. Deficits on self-ordered tasks associated with hyperostosis frontalis interna. *Journal of Neurology, Neurosurgery, and Psychiatry, 63,* 309–314.

de Zubicaray, G. I., S. C. R. Williams, S. J. Wilson, S. E. Rose, M. J. Brammer, E. T. Bullmore, A. Simmons, J. B. Chalk, J. Semple, A. P. Brown, G. A. Smith, R. Ashton, and D. M. Doddrell. 1998. Prefrontal cortex involvement in selective letter generation: A functional magnetic resonance imaging study. *Cortex, 34,* 389–401.

Dolan, R. J., C. J. Bench, P. F. Liddle, K. J. Friston, C. D. Frith, P. M. Grasby, and R. S. J. Frackowiak. 1993. Dorsolateral prefrontal cortex dysfunction in the major psychoses: Symptom or disease specificity? *Journal of Neurology, Neurosurgery, and Psychiatry, 56,* 1290–1294.

Egan, M. F., T. E. Goldberg, B. S. Kolachana, J. H. Callicott, C. M. Mazzanti, R. E. Straub, D. Goldman, and D. R. Weinberger. 2001. Effect of COMT Val108/158Met genotype on frontal lobe function and risk for schizophrenia. *Proceedings of the National Academy of Sciences USA, 98,* 6917–6922.

Farrow, T. F. D., M. D. Hunter, R. J. D. Green, I. D. Wilkinson, and S. A. Spence. 2005. The structural correlates of unconstrained motor activity in people with schizophrenia. *British Journal of Psychiatry, 187,* 481–482.

Farrow, T. F., Y. Zheng, I. D. Wilkinson, S. A. Spence, J. F. Deakin, N. Tarrier, P. D. Griffiths, and P. W. Woodruff. 2001. Investigating the functional anatomy of empathy and forgiveness. *NeuroReport, 12,* 2433–2438.

Fletcher, P. C., T. Shallice, and R. J. Dolan. 2000. "Sculpting the response space": An account of left prefrontal activation at encoding. *NeuroImage, 12,* 404–417.

Frith, C. D., K. J. Friston, P. F. Liddle, and R. S. J. Frackowiak. 1991a. A PET study of word finding. *Neuropsychologia, 29,* 1137–1148.

Frith, C. D., K. J. Friston, P. F. Liddle, and R. S. J. Frackowiak. 1991b. Willed action and the prefrontal cortex in man: A study with PET. *Proceedings of the Royal Society of London, Series B, 244,* 241–246.

Frith, C. D., and U. Frith. 1999. Interacting minds: A biological basis. *Science*, *286*, 1692–1695.

Ganesan, V., R. D. Green, M. D. Hunter, I. D. Wilkinson, and S. A. Spence. 2005. Expanding the response space in chronic schizophrenia: The relevance of left prefrontal cortex. *NeuroImage*, *25*, 952–957.

Gaser, C., and G. Schlaug. 2003. Brain structures differ between musicians and non-musicians. *Journal of Neuroscience*, *23*, 9240–9245.

Goldberg, E. 2001. *The Executive Brain: Frontal Lobes and the Civilized Mind.* Oxford: Oxford University Press.

Goldman-Rakic, P. S. 1987. Motor control function of the prefrontal cortex. In *Motor Areas of the Cerebral Cortex: Ciba Foundation Symposium*, *132*, 187–200. Chichester: Wiley.

Goldman-Rakic, P. S., J. F. Bates, and M. V. Chafee. 1992. The prefrontal cortex and internally generated motor acts. *Current Opinion in Neurobiology*, *2*, 830–835.

Gur, R. E., P. Cowell, B. I. Turetsky, F. Gallacher, T. Cannon, W. Bilker, and R. C. Gur. 1998. A follow-up magnetic resonance imaging study of schizophrenia: Relationship of neuroanatomical changes to clinical and neurobehavioural measures. *Archives of General Psychiatry*, *55*, 145–152.

Heckers, S., D. Goff, D. L. Schacter, C. R. Savage, A. J. Fischman, N. M. Alpert, and S. L. Rauch. 1999. Functional imaging of memory retrieval in deficit vs. nondeficit schizophrenia. *Archives of General Psychiatry*, *56*, 1117–1123.

Honey, G. D., E. T. Bullmore, W. Soni, M. Varatheesan, S. C. R. Williams, and T. Sharma. 1999. Differences in frontal cortical activation by a working memory task after substitution of risperidone for typical antipsychotic drugs in patients with schizophrenia. *Proceedings of the National Academy of Sciences*, *96*, 13432–13437.

Hunter, M. D., T. F. D. Farrow, N. Papadakis, I. D. Wilkinson, P. W. R. Woodruff, and S. A. Spence. 2003. Approaching an ecologically valid functional anatomy of spontaneous "willed" action. *NeuroImage*, *20*, 1264–1269.

Hunter, M. D., R. D. J. Green, I. D. Wilkinson, and S. A. Spence. 2004. Spatial and temporal dissociation in prefrontal cortex during action execution. *NeuroImage*, *23*, 1186–1191.

Ingvar, D. H. 1994. The will of the brain: Cerebral correlates of wilful acts. *Journal of Theoretical Biology*, *171*, 7–12.

Jahanshahi, M., G. Dirnberger, R. Fuller, and C. D. Frith. 2000. The role of dorsolateral prefrontal cortex in random number generation: A study with positron emission tomography. *NeuroImage*, *12*, 713–725.

Jahanshahi, M., P. Profice, R. G. Brown, M. C. Ridding, G. Dirnberger, and J. C. Rothwell. 1998. The effects of transcranial magnetic stimulation over the dorsolateral prefrontal cortex on suppression of habitual counting during random number generation. *Brain*, *121*, 1533–1544.

Jenkins, I. H., D. J. Brooks, P. D. Nixon, and R. S. J. Frackowiak. 1994. Motor sequence learning: A study with positron emission tomography. *Journal of Neuroscience, 14*, 3775–3790.

Jenkins, I. H., W. Fernandez, E. D. Playford, A. J. Lees, R. S. Frackowiak, and R. E. Passingham. 1992. Impaired activation of the supplementary motor area in Parkinson's disease is reversed when akinesia is treated with apomorphine. *Annals of Neurology, 32*, 749–757.

Kolb, B., and R. Gibb. 2002. Frontal lobe plasticity and behaviour. In *Principles of Frontal Lobe Function*, ed. D. T. Stuss and R. T. Knight, pp. 541–556. Oxford: Oxford University Press.

Libet, B., C. A. Gleason, E. W. Wright, and D. K. Pearl. 1983. Time of conscious intention to act in relation to onset of cerebral activity. *Brain, 106*, 623–642.

Liddle, P. F., K. J. Friston, C. D. Frith, S. R. Hirsch, T. Jones, and R. S. J. Frackowiak. 1992. Patterns of cerebral blood flow in schizophrenia. *British Journal of Psychiatry, 160*, 179–186.

Lipska, B. K., B. Kolb, N. Halim, and D. R. Weinberger. 2001. Synaptic abnormalities in prefrontal cortex and nucleus accumbens of adult rats with neonatal hippocampal damage. *Schizophrenia Research, 49* (suppl.), 47.

Madsen, A. L., A. Karle, P. Rubin, M. Cortsen, H. S. Andersen, and R. Hemmingsen. 1999. Progressive atrophy of frontal lobes in first-episode schizophrenia: Interaction with clinical course and neuroleptic treatment. *Acta Psychiatrica Scandinavica, 100*, 367–374.

Maguire, E. A., D. G. Gadian, I. S. Johnsrude, C. D. Good, J. Ashburner, R. S. J. Frackowiak, and C. D. Frith. 2000. Navigation-related structural change in the hippocampi of taxi drivers. *Proceedings of the National Academy of Sciences, 97*, 4398–4403.

McDowell, S., J. Whyte, and M. D'Esposito. 1998. Differential effect of a dopaminergic agonist on prefrontal function in traumatic brain injury patients. *Brain, 121*, 1155–1164.

Milner, B. 1963. Effects of difference brain lesions on card sorting. *Archives of Neurology, 9*, 100–110.

Mortimer, A., and S. Spence. 2001. *Managing Negative Symptoms of Schizophrenia*. London: Science Press.

Nelson, H. E., and A. O'Connell. 1978. Dementia: The estimation of premorbid intelligence levels using the New Adult Reading Test. *Cortex, 14*, 234–244.

Passingham, R. 1993. *The Frontal Lobes and Voluntary Action*. Oxford: Oxford University Press.

Passingham, R. E. 1996. Attention to action. *Philosophical Transactions of the Royal Society of London, Series B, 351*, 1473–1479.

Paus, T. 2001. Primate anterior cingulate cortex: Where motor control, drive, and cognition interface. *Nature Reviews Neuroscience, 2*, 417–424.

Perret, E. 1974. The left frontal lobe of man and the suppression of habitual responses in verbal categorical behaviour. *Neuropsychologia, 12*, 323–330.

Petrides, M. 1996. Specialised systems for the procession of mnemonic information within the primate prefrontal cortex. *Philosophical Transactions of the Royal Society of London, Series B, 351*, 1455–1462.

Petrides, M., and B. Milner. 1982. Deficits on subject-ordered tasks after frontal- and temporal-lobe lesions in man. *Neuropsychologia, 20*, 249–262.

Rioult-Pedotti, M.-S., and J. P. Donoghue. 2003. The nature and mechanisms of plasticity. In *Plasticity in the Human Nervous System*, ed. S. Boniface and U. Ziemann, pp. 1–125. Cambridge: Cambridge University Press.

Sallet, P. C., H. Elkis, T. M. Alves, J. R. Oliveira, E. Sassi, C. Campi-de-Castro, G. F. Busatto, and W. F. Gattaz. 2003. Rightward cerebral asymmetry in subtypes of schizophrenia according to Leonhard's classification and to DSM-IV: A structural MRI study. *Psychiatry Research, Neuroimaging, 123*, 65–79.

Salokangas, R. K. R., T. Cannon, T. Van Erp, T. Ilonen, T. Taiminen, H. Karlsson, H. Lauerma, K. M. Leinonen, E. Wallenius, A. Kaljonen, E. Syvaelahti, H. Vilkman, A. Alanen, and J. Hietala. 2002. Structural magnetic resonance imaging in patients with first-episode schizophrenia, psychotic and severe non-psychotic depression and healthy controls. Results of the Schizophrenia and Affective Psychoses (SAP) project. *British Journal of Psychiatry, 181* (suppl. 43), s58–s65.

Samuel, M., A. O. Ceballos-Baumann, N. Turjanski, H. Boecker, A. Gorospe, G. Linazasoro, A. P. Holmes, M. R. DeLong, J. L. Vitek, D. G. T. Thomas, N. P. Quinn, J. A. Obeso, and D. J. Brooks. 1997. Pallidotomy in Parkinson's disease increases supplementary motor area and prefrontal activation during performance of volitional movements: An $H_2^{15}O$ PET study. *Brain, 120*, 1301–1313.

Shallice, T. 1988. *From Neuropsychology to Mental Structure*. Cambridge: Cambridge University Press.

Shallice, T. 2002. Fractionation of the supervisory system. In *Principles of Frontal Lobe Function*, ed. D. T. Stuss and R. T. Knight, pp. 261–277. Oxford: Oxford University Press.

Spence, S. A., D. J. Brooks, S. R. Hirsch, P. F. Liddle, J. Meehan, and P. M. Grasby. 1997. A PET study of voluntary movement in schizophrenic patients experiencing passivity phenomena (delusions of alien control). *Brain, 120*, 1997–2011.

Spence, S. A., T. F. D. Farrow, A. E. Herford, I. D. Wilkinson, Y. Zheng, and P. W. R. Woodruff. 2001. Behavioural and functional anatomical correlates of deception in humans. *NeuroReport, 12*, 2849–2853.

Spence, S. A., and C. D. Frith. 1999. Towards a functional anatomy of volition. *Journal of Consciousness Studies, 6*, 11–29.

Spence, S. A., R. D. J. Green, I. D. Wilkinson, and M. D. Hunter. 2005. Modafinil modulates anterior cingulate function in chronic schizophrenia. *British Journal of Psychiatry, 187*, 55–61.

Spence, S. A., S. R. Hirsch, J. D. Brooks, and P. M. Grasby. 1998. Prefrontal cortical activity in people with schizophrenia and control subjects: Evidence from positron emission tomography for remission of "hypofrontality" with recovery from acute schizophrenia. *British Journal of Psychiatry, 172*, 316–323.

Spence, S. A., M. D. Hunter, T. F. D. Farrow, R. D. J. Green, D. H. Leung, C. J. Hughes, and V. Ganesan. 2004. A cognitive neurobiological account of deception: Evidence from functional neuroimaging. *Philosophical Transactions of the Royal Society of London, Series B, 359*, 1755–1762.

Spence, S. A., M. D. Hunter, and G. Harpin. 2002. Neuroscience and the will. *Current Opinion in Psychiatry, 15*, 519–526.

Spence, S. A., P. F. Liddle, M. D. Stefan, J. S. E. Hellewell, K. J. Friston, C. D. Frith, et al. 2000. Functional anatomy of verbal fluency in people with schizophrenia and those at genetic risk: Focal dysfunction and distributed disconnectivity reappraised. *British Journal of Psychiatry, 176*, 52–60.

Starkstein, S. E., and M. Merello. 2002. *Psychiatric and Cognitive Disorders in Parkinson's Disease.* Cambridge: Cambridge University Press.

Stuss, D. T., and R. T. Knigh (eds.). 2002. *Principles of Frontal Lobe Function.* New York: Oxford University Press.

Turner, D. C., L. Clark, E. Pomarol-Clotet, P. McKenna, T. W. Robbins, and B. J. Sahakian. 2004. Modafinil improves cognition and attentional set shifting in patients with chronic schizophrenia. *Neuropsychopharmacology, 29*, 1363–1373.

Wegner, D. M. 2002. *The Illusion of Conscious Will.* Cambridge, Mass.: MIT Press.

Wible, C. G., J. Anderson, M. E. Shenton, A. Kricun, Y. Hirayasu, S. Tanaka, J. J. Levitt, B. F. O'Donnell, R. Kikinis, F. A. Jolesz, and R. W. McCarley. 2001. Prefrontal cortex, negative symptoms, and schizophrenia: An MRI study. *Psychiatry Research, Neuroimaging, 108*, 65–78.

Wise, R. J. S., J. Greene, C. Buchel, and S. K. Scott. 1999. Brain regions involved in articulation. *Lancet, 353*, 1057–1061.

Youngren, K. D., F. M. Inglis, P. J. Pivirotto, H. P. Jedema, C. W. Bradberry, P. S. Goldman-Rakic, R. H. Roth, and B. Moghaddam. 1999. Clozapine preferentially increases dopamine release in the rhesus monkey prefrontal cortex compared with the caudate nucleus. *Neuropsychopharmacology, 20*, 403–412.

11 Interpersonal Factors in the Disorders of Volition Associated with Schizophrenia

Chris Frith

11.1 Disorders of Volition in Schizophrenia

People with a diagnosis of schizophrenia display many different signs and symptoms. Currently the official definition of schizophrenia (*Diagnostic and Statistical Manual of Mental Disorders*, fourth ed.; *DSM-IV*; American Psychiatric Association 1994) requires that the patient manifest symptoms from at least two of the following four categories: (1) delusions (false beliefs), (2) hallucinations (false perceptions), (3) disorganization of speech or behavior, (4) negative symptoms including lack of volition. Thus, lack of volition, although a component of the disorder, is neither necessary nor sufficient for a diagnosis of schizophrenia. However, an abnormality of volition was very much a key feature in Kraepelin's original description of the disorder (Kraepelin 1896). He described dementia praecox as "a weakening of those very emotional activities which permanently form the mainspring of volition . . . the result . . . is loss of mastery over volition. . . ." That abnormal volition does not have a more important role in the *DSM-IV* definition of schizophrenia probably has more to do with the difficulty of reliably assessing this impairment rather than a lack of importance for the disorder.

The lack of volition associated with schizophrenia manifests itself as poverty in all domains: poverty of speech, poverty of action, and poverty of thought. In other words, such patients say and do very little. Poverty of speech can readily be assessed with a verbal fluency task. When asked to name all the animals he could think of, one patient with poverty of speech could only produce four names in three minutes (Allen et al. 1993). This difficulty is not due to a loss of knowledge. Rather, the problem reflects a difficulty in initiating actions.

After Kraepelin, probably the most important development in the description of schizophrenia was Schneider's categorization of first-rank symptoms (Schneider 1959). These are symptoms that are very rarely seen in any disorder other than schizophrenia. The first-rank symptoms include "passivity phenomena" or "made experiences." The patients report that some aspect of themselves is under the external control of another. Acts, emotions, and thoughts are experienced as being controlled by outside forces. Such symptoms include delusions of control (made acts) and thought insertion (made thoughts). These symptoms are also disorders of volition. More precisely, they are disorders in the experience of volition. This is made explicit in the instructions for conducting the Present State Examination (Wing et al. 1974) where delusions of control require the report that "the subject's will is replaced by that of some external agency."

11.2   Cognitive Neuropsychiatry

When we apply the methods of cognitive neuropsychology to psychiatric disorders, we do not aim to explain all the features of a diagnostic category such as schizophrenia. Our explanation is restricted to a particular symptom (e.g., delusions of control) or class of symptoms (e.g., passivity experiences). There are a great many symptoms associated with schizophrenia, but a series of cross-sectional, factor analytic studies suggest that they fall into three classes (e.g., Liddle 1987): (1) psychomotor poverty (the negative features of schizophrenia including poverty of action), (2) disorganization, and (3) reality distortion (delusions and hallucinations). These three classes define subgroups of symptoms rather than subgroups of patients. The three classes are independent in the sense that a patient with severe delusions is likely also to have hallucinations but may or may not show poverty or disorganization.

The lack of volition originally described by Kraepelin largely coincides with the symptom cluster now labeled psychomotor poverty. However, Schneider's passivity phenomena are only a subset of the cluster labeled reality distortion. Delusions of persecution, delusions of reference, and certain types of auditory hallucination would not be considered examples of passivity phenomena since there is no alteration in the patients' experience of their own will. The subtle differences in the mechanisms that underlie these different types of reality distortion are currently obscure. One of the earliest attempts to explain symptoms in cognitive terms (Frith 1987) was specifically concerned with, on the one hand, poverty of action, and on the other hand, passivity phenomena. Poverty of action was supposed to result from a failure to represent (be aware of) the goals of action. The patient did not initiate actions because he was not aware of any goal that he wanted to achieve. Passivity phenomena, such as delusions of control, were supposed to arise because the patient did not represent (was not aware of) the intentions in action derived to achieve particular goals. The patient was deficient in self-monitoring. He was aware of his goals but found the actions he made toward these goals unexpected and hence attributed them to some external force (see fig. 11.1).

Both difficulties were supposed to derive from a more basic problem with metarepresentation, that is with the representation of mental states such as desires and intentions (see contribution by Proust, this volume). Thus, lack of volition derived from a

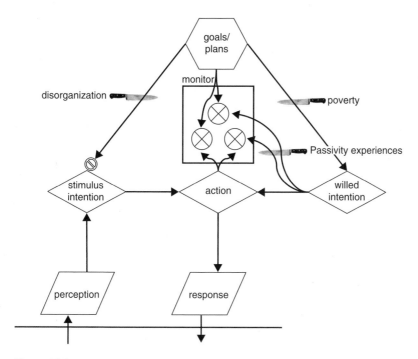

Figure 11.1
Simple flow diagram for the control and monitoring of action. Disorganized behavior results from a failure to inhibit inappropriate stimulus-driven acts. Poverty of will results from a failure to initiate willed acts. Passivity experiences result from a failure to monitor willed intentions (after Frith 1987).

failure to represent the patient's desires, while delusions of control derived from a failure to represent the patient's intentions.

11.3 Explaining Delusions of Control

11.3.1 Self-Monitoring

The self-monitoring deficit supposed to underlie delusions of control has been studied intensively in the last decade, and ideas about the nature of this deficit in the experience of volition have changed considerably. Several empirical studies have revealed subtle deficits in the motor control of patients experiencing passivity phenomena. Patients fail to make rapid, "central" error corrections (Frith and Done 1989; Turken et al. 2003). These are error corrections that depend upon the recognition that the wrong action has been initiated and so do not depend upon sensory feedback. The original idea was that such corrections require awareness of the intended action, which patients with delusions of control were not supposed to have. More recent formulations have emphasized the role of prediction, rather than awareness of intentions.

11.3.2 Forward Models

Sophisticated motor control systems depend upon various kinds of prediction (Miall and Wolpert 1996). The forward dynamic model predicts the future location of limbs in time and space on the basis of the intended motor commands (see fig. 11.2). It is this prediction that permits central error correction. We know in advance if our intended movement will end up in the wrong place. This model also enables us to make movements in our imagination that last the same time as the same movements made in reality. The timing of imaginary movements in patients with delusions of control does not show this pattern (Maruff et al. 2003; Danckert et al. 2002). The

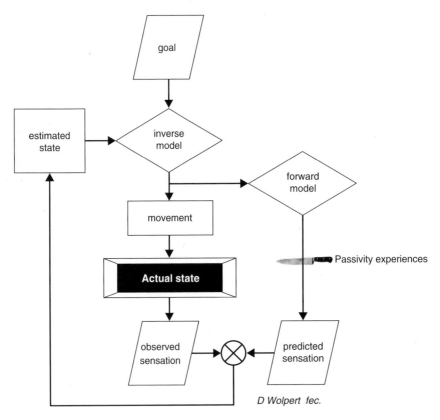

Figure 11.2
Simple flow diagram of the motor control system (after Miall and Wolpert 1996). Passivity experiences result from the failure to predict the consequences of actions.

forward dynamic model may also have a role in the self-recognition paradigms described by Jeannerod (this volume). If the hand we see is in fact that of someone else, then the precise timing and location of the movements will not be as predicted. Patients with delusions of control also have difficulty with this self-recognition paradigm (Franck et al. 2001).

The forward output model predicts the sensory consequences of the intended motor commands. This prediction makes it possible to attenuate our experience of these sensory consequences as when we tickle ourselves (Blakemore et al. 1998). Patients with delusions of control do not show this attenuation. They do not report attenuated tactile experience when tickling themselves (Blakemore et al. 2000), and they show overactivity in parietal cortex during voluntary actions (Spence et al. 1997; Farrer et al. 2004; see fig. 11.3).

Patients with delusions of control clearly have problems with predictions about their intended movements. This problem will certainly be sufficient to make them feel that they are not in control of their actions (Hohwy and Frith 2004). For example, the lack of attenuation of the sensory consequences of a movement will make an active movement feel like a passive one. However, this does not seem to be sufficient to explain

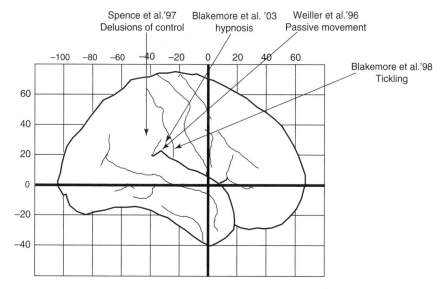

Figure 11.3

View of the right hemisphere of the brain in Talairach space. Arrows indicate the location of peak brain activity. Increased activity is seen in right parietal cortex during experience of delusions of control in patients making active movements and in healthy controls experiencing passive movements.

why they attribute their actions to another agent. Patients with parietal lesion also have problems recognizing their own movements (Sirigu et al. 1999) and with making movements in imagination (Sirigu et al. 1996), but they do not have delusions of control. Through hypnosis (Blakemore et al. 2003) or by distortion of feedback (Blakemore et al. 1999), we can interfere with the attenuation of sensory feedback in normal volunteers, but they don't report that another agent is controlling their actions. The feeling that one is not in control of one's actions is not sufficient for a delusion about agency.

11.3.3 Agency

Because of their subjective nature, symptoms such as delusions of control and thought insertion are difficult to pin down precisely (Mullins and Spence 2003). Recently, the distinction has been made between ownership and agency (Stephens and Graham 2000). In most cases patients recognize that the thoughts or actions are their own. What is lacking is a sense that they are controlling the thoughts or actions (the sense of agency). As Jeannerod points out (Jeannerod and Pacherie 2004), even in a normal state we can have a free-floating awareness of intentions or agency, that is, an awareness of agency that does not specify who the agent is. So how do we know who the agent is in relation to a particular action?

One possible source of this free-floating awareness of agency is the "intentional binding" recently described by Patrick Haggard (Haggard et al. 2002; see also this volume). Our awareness of the times of the events defining an intentional action are closer together than they are in reality. The moment of pressing the button is experienced as later, while the sound of the tone caused by this button press is experienced as earlier, pulling together in time the cause and its effect. With involuntary actions, this effect is reversed and the events seem to be further apart. However, this intentional binding also occurs when we observe the intentional actions of others (Wohlschläger et al. 2003). Furthermore, as long as the action has a consequence, this experience of intentional binding does not seem to be affected by the proprioceptive signals to which only the self has privileged access (Wohlschläger et al. 2003).

This system for experiencing intentionality has the advantage that it works just as well for others as for the self. It has the disadvantage that it does not specify who is performing the intentional act. As a result, we also need a "who" system. As Jeannerod points out in this volume, it is this who system that seems to be impaired in schizophrenic patients with delusions of control. Thus these delusions seems to depend upon two factors: first, the feeling of not being in control of one's actions that is caused by a failure of forward models in the motor system, and second, by the strong experience that the action is intentional that is caused by strong intentional binding (Haggard et al. 2003). If my arm makes an intentional movement that I am not in control of, then another agent must be involved.

We have yet to determine how these two problems are linked, as presumably they must be. However, it is clear that the disorders of the experience of will associated with schizophrenia cannot be explained simply through study of an individual motor control system. Agents only exist in a social context. We also need to study those mechanisms, crucial for social interactions, through which we recognized the intentions of others.

11.4 Explaining Defects of Will

11.4.1 Willed Action

Our actions lie on a continuum. At one extreme, there are reflex actions over which we have no control. We will kick our leg if our knee is tapped whether we like it or not. At the other extreme are spontaneous or willed actions that have no immediate external cause. Somewhere in between are the sorts of actions studied in reaction time tasks in which the subject is instructed to make a particular response whenever a particular stimulus occurs. These are stimulus-driven actions that can nevertheless be withheld at will. This distinction between willed and stimulus-driven acts is also found in the brain. Medial premotor areas (supplementary motor area; SMA; and pre-SMA) are involved in the generation of self-initiated actions (e.g., Thaler et al. 1995), while dorsal premotor areas are involved in the generation of stimulus-driven actions (e.g., Grafton et al. 1998). The poverty of speech and action shown by many patients in the chronic stage of schizophrenia also reflects this distinction. These patients can respond to questions, but rarely, if ever, initiate conversations or make spontaneous remarks. In other words, there is great reduction in self-initiated acts compared to stimulus-driven acts. The difficulty can be quantified in the performance of tasks in which the selection of the response to be made is underspecified. An obvious example is the verbal fluency task discussed above in which subjects have to find words beginning with A or names of animals (Milner 1964). Another widely used task with this property is the Wisconsin Card Sorting task (Milner 1963) in which the subject has to decide whether to use form, number, or color to select a response. Tasks with the minimum of response specification are probably the guessing tasks in which, for example, a subject has to guess the color of the next card in a shuffled pack. Confronted with such tasks, people typically produce a more or less random sequence of responses that resembles the sequence of the cards (probability matching; Goodnow 1955) even though guessing the same color every time would be just as successful.

Patients rated clinically as having poverty of action and other negative features produce stereotyped sequences of responses on the two-choice guessing task (Frith and Done 1983; Lyon et al. 1986). This behavior is not seen in patients with positive symptoms such as hallucinations, nor in patients with mild dementia.

Similar problems with these willed action tasks are also seen in patients with damage to prefrontal cortex, consistent with the observation from functional imaging studies that patients with schizophrenia, especially those with negative features, frequently show reduced activity in prefrontal cortex (Davidson and Heinrichs 2003; Rodriguez et al. 1997). Furthermore, brain imaging studies show that dorsolateral prefrontal cortex (DLPFC) is consistently activated during the performance of willed action tasks (Lau et al. 2004).

11.4.2 Deconstructing Willed Action

Do these observations imply that DLPFC is at the top of the hierarchy of control processes required for willed actions (see fig. 11.4) and therefore the site of the will? Andreas Roepstorff and I have argued (Roepstorff and Frith 2004) that this notion arises from a faulty analysis of the processes involved in performing willed action tasks. In particular we have argued that willed action tasks have an important social component. When Libet (Libet et al. 1983) told his subjects to lift their fingers "whenever they felt the urge to do so" (a typical willed action task), the subjects recognized that it would not be appropriate if they never had the urge. The most appropriate way to interpret this instruction is to lift your finger several times during the course of the experiment, but not to do this at regular intervals. In other words, you try to behave

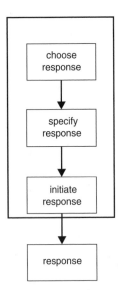

Figure 11.4
Simple flow diagram illustrating top-down control in a willed action task. What is at the top? (After Roepstorff and Frith 2004.)

like an independent agent by making responses at unpredictable moments. The same strategy is appropriate to the more common type of willed action task in which the subject chooses which response to make (e.g., moving a joystick in one of four directions) rather than when to respond. In this case the subject will try to produce a sequence of responses in which it is not obvious which one will be chosen next, that is, a random sequence. The apparently simple instruction "Choose whichever response you like" has to be unpacked into a much more complex script (Jack and Roepstorff 2002) concerning how to produce behavior that will be acceptable to the experimenter (see fig. 11.5).

This analysis explains why the pattern of brain activity associated with willed action is also observed when subjects are explicitly asked to produce random sequences of responses (Jahanshahi et al. 2000). The role of DLPFC in these tasks concerns the production of appropriate sequences, not the interpretation of the instructions. There is a correlation between activity in DLPFC and a measure of the randomness of the sequence, with low activity going with less randomness. Furthermore, when the task was made more difficulty by increasing the rate at which the numbers had to be

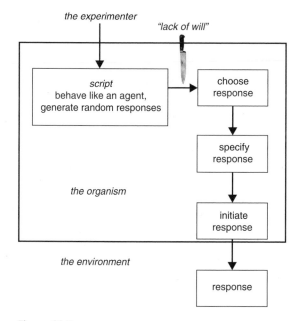

Figure 11.5
Simple flow diagram illustrating how performance in a willed action task depends upon a script implicitly agreed upon between subject and experimenter. Lack of will (i.e., poor performance of the task) results from a failure to select responses on the basis of this script. (After Roepstorff and Frith 2004.)

generated, subjects were able to produce responses at these high rates, but at the expense of producing less random sequences. This loss of randomness was associated with a reduction in DLPFC activity (Jahanshahi et al. 2000). In this situation subjects have to balance the incompatible requirements of responding at a high rate with selecting suitably random responses. This balancing act will engage the systems near the top of the hierarchy of executive control that are needed to resolve the competition for resources. DLPFC is clearly not at the top of this hierarchy since it is less active in the conflict situation. DLPFC seems to have a more restricted role in the selection of responses (Frith 2000), particularly when this selection is the focus of attention (Lau et al. 2004). In willed action and random generation tasks the role of DLPFC is to constrain the possible responses to a small subset suitable for the task. For example, if I have just given 4, I must avoid 3 or 5 since these are obvious counting sequences; I must also take account of my previous responses so as to avoid obvious rising or falling sequences. I must also give every number equally often. After applying all these constraints, I have very few options left, perhaps only two numbers, and it doesn't really matter which one I choose.

Thus, what makes a task a willed action task is not lack of constraint. The responses made in willed action tasks are just as constrained as responses made in stimulus-driven tasks. The difference concerns the source of the constraint. In willed action tasks, the experimenter does not explicitly specify the constraints. The subject has to work them out by inferring what the experiment has "in mind" when he says "Choose any response you like." So, in a sense, the responses are self-generated, since the subject applies the constraints himself, rather than simply doing what he is told.

11.4.3 Failure of Willed Action in Schizophrenia

Successful performance of a willed action task therefore depends upon (a) correctly working out the constraints the experimenter has in mind and (b) being able to apply these constraints. Both these processes are likely to be impaired in schizophrenia. These patients, particularly those with negative symptoms (and associated lack of will) have problems with "theory of mind" tasks (Frith 2004), which should lead to problems with working out what the experimenter has in mind. Such patients can also have problems in applying constraints, as do those who manifest disorganized behavior (Barch et al. 2003). In some cases of disorganization the lack of constraint can be so extreme that even the tendency to read print that most of us find completely automatic can fail, leading to abnormally good performance on the Stroop task (Jensterle et al. 2000).

In their computational account of these problems, Jonathan Cohen and his colleagues (e.g., Braver and Cohen 2000) suggest that the role of prefrontal cortex is to select and maintain context information related to current behavioral goals. It is this context information that applies the appropriate constraints to behavior. However, in all experiments, this context has a large social component. There is an implicit agreement that the subject will do what the experimenter wants. Willed action tasks are particularly problematic since "what the experimenter wants" is not fully specified. The problem that schizophrenic patients experience in using context to maintain appropriate behavior applies especially to social contexts. The patient no longer does what is appropriate in the social context. I have often finished an experimental session with a patient with the uncomfortable feeling that what the patient was doing was not quite what I intended. In the case of willed action tasks, their lack of random behavior can be seen not as a lack of will but as a failure to carry out what the experimenter had in mind.

Future research could determine whether patients have a general problem with maintaining context information or whether the problem is more specific to the social context. If poor performance on willed action tasks stems from failure to understand what the experimenter has in mind, then it should correlate with performance on theory of mind tasks. While there is some evidence that problems with "theory of mind" tasks are not associated with the executive processes concerned with planning or response inhibition (Langdon et al. 1997; Langdon and Coltheart 1999), there could still be a specific link between theory of mind problems and difficulties with response generation in willed action tasks.

I am not proposing that the defects of will should not be classified as executive dysfunctions. Rather, I am following Jonathan Cohen and others (Cohen et al. 1996) in suggesting that the unifying feature of executive tasks is that they require a mechanism whereby arbitrary constraints are applied determined by the context in which the task occurs. The novel idea is that in many situations these constraints are social. For this reason, fontal cortex has a crucial role to play in social interactions, and indeed prefrontal damage can impair performance on overtly social tasks (Rowe et al. 2001; Stuss et al. 2001).

11.5   Volition Is an Emergent Property of Social Interactions

I have suggested that two major features of schizophrenia, passivity experiences and lack of will, are in part social disorders. Passivity experiences involve a failure to recognize who is the agent of an action. Poverty of will (and disorganization) result from a failure to generate actions that are appropriate in the social context.

This proposal that we can only properly understand will and its disorders in a social context resolves certain difficulties. The idea of top-down control is critical for understanding cognitive processes such as selective attention and willed action. But this concept inevitably raises questions about the nature of the homunculus that is at the top in top-down control. This problem disappears if we stop trying to understand individuals and their brains in isolation.

Is volition the emergent property of a unitary system or the property of a controller that is separate from the system to be controlled? I would argue that, in terms of a single individual, volition is the property of a controller. However, if we think in terms of a system of two or more individuals interacting, then volition is an emergent property of this system determined by the constraints that individuals impose in one another.

References

Allen, H. A., P. F. Liddle, and C. D. Frith. 1993. Negative features, retrieval processes, and verbal fluency in schizophrenia. *British Journal of Psychiatry*, *163*, 769–775.

American Psychiatric Association. 1994. *Diagnostic and Statistical Manual of Mental Disorders* (4th ed.). Washington, D.C.: American Psychiatric Association.

Barch, D. M., C. S. Carter, A. W. MacDonald III, T. S. Braver, and J. D. Cohen. 2003. Context-processing deficits in schizophrenia: Diagnostic specificity, 4-week course, and relationships to clinical symptoms. *Journal of Abnormal Psychology*, *112*, 132–143.

Blakemore, S. J., C. D. Frith, and D. M. Wolpert. 1999. Spatio-temporal prediction modulates the perception of self-produced stimuli. *Journal of Cognitive Neuroscience*, *11*, 551–559.

Blakemore, S.-J., J. Smith, R. M. Steel, E. C. Johnstone, and C. D. Frith. 2000. The perception of self-produced sensory stimuli in patients with auditory hallucinations and passivity experiences: Evidence for a breakdown in self-monitoring. *Psychological Medicine*, *30*, 1131–1139.

Blakemore, S. J., D. A. Oakley, and C. D. Frith. 2003. Delusions of alien control in the normal brain. *Neuropsychologia*, *41*, 1058–1067.

Blakemore, S. J., D. M. Wolpert, and C. D. Frith. 1998. Central cancellation of self-produced tickle sensation. *Nature Neuroscience*, *1*, 635–640.

Braver, T. S., and J. D. Cohen. 2000. On the control of control: The role of dopamine in regulating prefrontal function and working memory. In *Control of Cognitive Processes: Attention and Performance XVIII*, ed. S. Monsell and J. Driver, pp. 713–737. Cambridge, Mass.: MIT Press.

Cohen, J. D., T. S. Braver, and R. C. O'Reilly. 1996. A computational approach to prefrontal cortex, cognitive control and schizophrenia: Recent developments and current challenges. *Philosophical Transactions of the Royal Society of London*, *351*, 1515–1527.

Danckert, J., Y. Rossetti, T. d'Amato, J. Dalery, and M. Saoud. 2002. Exploring imagined movements in patients with schizophrenia. *Neuroreport*, *13*, 605–609.

Davidson, L. L., and R. W. Heinrichs. 2003. Quantification of frontal and temporal lobe brain-imaging findings in schizophrenia: A meta-analysis. *Psychiatry Research*, *122*, 69–87.

Farrer, C., N. Franck, C. D. Frith, J. Decety, N. Georgieff, T. d'Amato, and M. Jeannerod. 2004. Neural correlates of action attribution in schizophrenia. *Psychiatry Research-Neuroimaging*, *131*, 31–44.

Franck, N., C. Farrer, N. Georgieff, M. Marie-Cardine, J. Dalery, T. d'Amato, and M. Jeannerod. 2001. Defective recognition of one's own actions in patients with schizophrenia. *American Journal of Psychiatry, 158*, 454–459.

Frith, C. D. 1987. The positive and negative symptoms of schizophrenia reflect impairments in the perception and initiation of action. *Psychological Medicine, 17*, 631–648.

Frith, C. D. 2000. The role of dorsolateral prefrontal cortex in the selection of action as revealed by functional imaging. In *Control of Cognitive Processes: Attention and Performance XVIII*, ed. S. Monsell and J. Driver, pp. 549–565. Cambridge Mass.: MIT Press.

Frith, C. D. 2004. Schizophrenia and theory of mind (editorial). *Psychological Medicine, 34*, 385–389.

Frith, C. D., and D. J. Done. 1983. Stereotyped responding by schizophrenic patients on a two-choice guessing task. *Psychological Medicine, 13*, 779–786.

Frith, C. D., and D. J. Done. 1989. Experiences of alien control in schizophrenia reflect a disorder in the central monitoring of action. *Psychological Medicine, 19*, 359–363.

Goodnow, J. J. 1955. Determinants of choice-distribution in two-choice situations. *American Journal of Psychology, 68*, 106–116.

Grafton, S. T., A. H. Fagg, and M. A. Arbib. 1998. Dorsal premotor cortex and conditional movement selection: A PET functional mapping study. *Journal of Neurophysiology, 79*, 1092–1097.

Haggard, P., S. Clark, and J. Kalogeras. 2002. Voluntary action and conscious awareness. *Nature Neuroscience, 5*, 382–385.

Haggard, P., F. Martin, M. Taylor-Clarke, M. Jeannerod, and N. Franck. 2003. Awareness of action in schizophrenia. *Neuroreport, 14*, 1081–1085.

Hohwy, J., and C. D. Frith. 2004. Can neuroscience explain consciousness? *Journal of Consciousness Studies, 11*, 180–198.

Jack, A. I., and A. Roepstorff. 2002. Introspection and cognitive brain mapping: From stimulus-response to script-report. *Trends in Cognitive Sciences, 6*, 333–339.

Jahanshahi, M., G. Dirnberger, R. Fuller, and C. D. Frith. 2000. The role of the dorsolateral prefrontal cortex in random number generation: A study with positron emission tomography. *NeuroImage, 12*, 713–725.

Jeannerod, M., and E. Pacherie. 2004. Agency, simulation, and self-identification. *Mind and Language, 19*, 113–146.

Jensterle, J., J. Mlakar, D. B. Vodusek, and C. D. Frith. 2000. Disorganisation in schizophrenia need not result from a failure to inhibit dominant response tendencies. *Cognitive Neuropsychiatry, 5*, 105–121.

Kraepelin, E. 1896. Dementia Praecox. Translated into English 1987, in *The Clinical Roots of the Schizophrenia Concept*, ed. J. Cutting and M. Shepherd, pp. 13–24. Cambridge: Cambridge University Press.

Langdon, R., and M. Coltheart. 1999. Mentalising, schizotypy, and schizophrenia. *Cognition, 71*, 43–71.

Langdon, R., P. T. Michie, P. B. Ward, N. McConaghy, S. V. Catts, and M. Coltheart. 1997. Defective self and/or other mentalising in schizophrenia: A cognitive neuropsychological approach. *Cognitive Neuropsychiatry, 2*, 167–193.

Lau, H. C., R. D. Rogers, N. Ramnani, and R. E. Passingham. 2004. Willed action and attention to the selection of action. *Neuroimage, 21*, 1407–1415.

Libet, B., C. A. Gleason, E. W. Wright, and D. K. Pearl. 1983. Time of conscious intention to act in relation to onset of cerebral activity (readiness-potential): The unconscious initiation of a freely voluntary act. *Brain, 106*, 623–642.

Liddle, P. F. 1987. The symptoms of chronic schizophrenia. A reexamination of the positive–negative dichotomy. *British Journal of Psychiatry, 151*, 145–151.

Lyon, N., B. Mejsholm, and M. Lyon. 1986. Stereotyped responding by schizophrenic outpatients: Cross-cultural confirmation of perseverative switching on a two-choice task. *Journal of Psychiatric Research, 20*, 137–150.

Maruff, P., P. Wilson, and J. Currie. 2003. Abnormalities of motor imagery associated with somatic passivity phenomena in schizophrenia. *Schizophrenia Research, 60*, 229–238.

Miall, R. C., and D. M. Wolpert. 1996. Forward models for physiological motor control. *Neural Networks, 9*, 1265–1279.

Milner, B. 1963. Effects of different brain lesions on card sorting. *Archives of Neurology, 9*, 90–100.

Milner, B. 1964. Some effects of frontal lobectomy in man. In *The Frontal Granular Cortex and Behavior*, ed. J. M. Warren and K. Akert, pp. 313–334. New York: McGraw-Hill.

Mullins, S., and S. A. Spence. 2003. Re-examining thought insertion—Semi-structured literature review and conceptual analysis. *British Journal of Psychiatry, 182*, 293–298.

Rodriguez, V. M., R. M. Andree, M. J. P. Castejon, R. G. Labrador, F. F. Navarrete, J. L. C. Delgado, and F. J. R. Vila. 1997. Cerebral perfusion correlates of negative symptomatology and parkinsonism in a sample of treatment-refractory schizophrenics: An exploratory 99mTc-HMPAO SPET study. *Schizophrenia Research, 25*, 11–20.

Roepstorff, A., and C. Frith. 2004. What's at the top in the top-down control of action? Script-sharing and "top-top" control of action in cognitive experiments. *Psychology Research, 68*, 189–198.

Rowe, A. D., P. R. Bullock, C. E. Polkey, and R. G. Morris. 2001. Theory of mind impairments and their relationship to executive functioning following frontal lobe excisions. *Brain, 124*, 600–616.

Schneider, K. 1959. *Clinical Psychopathology*. New York: Grune and Stratton.

Sirigu, A., E. Daprati, P. Pradat-Diehl, N. Franck, and M. Jeannerod. 1999. Perception of self-generated movement following left parietal lesion. *Brain, 122 (Pt 10)*, 1867–1874.

Sirigu, A., J. R. Duhamel, L. Cohen, B. Pillon, B. Dubois, and Y. Agid. 1996. The mental representation of hand movements after parietal cortex damage. *Science, 273*, 1564–1568.

Spence, S. A., D. J. Brooks, S. R. Hirsch, P. F. Liddle, J. Meehan, and P. M. Grasby. 1997. A PET study of voluntary movement in schizophrenic patients experiencing passivity phenomena (delusions of alien control). *Brain, 120*, 1997–2011.

Stephens, G. L., and G. Graham. 2000. *When Self-Consciousness Breaks: Alien Voices and Inserted Thoughts*. Cambridge, Mass.: MIT Press.

Stuss, D. T., G. G. Gallup, and M. P. Alexander. 2001. The frontal lobes are necessary for "theory of mind." *Brain, 124*, 279–286.

Thaler, D., Y. C. Chen, P. D. Nixon, C. E. Stern, and R. E. Passingham. 1995. The functions of the medial premotor cortex. I. Simple learned movements. *Experimental Brain Research, 102*, 445–460.

Turken, A. U., P. Vuilleumier, D. H. Mathalon, D. Swick, and J. M. Ford. 2003. Are impairments of action monitoring and executive control true dissociative dysfunctions in patients with schizophrenia? *American Journal of Psychiatry, 160*, 1881–1883.

Wing, J. K., J. E. Cooper, and N. Sartorius. 1974. *Description and Classification of Psychiatric Symptoms*. London: Cambridge University Press.

Wohlschläger, A., K. Engbert, P. Haggard, S. Clark, and J. Kalogeras. 2003. Intentionality as a constituting condition for the own self—and other selves. *Consciousness and Cognition, 12*, 708–716.

Wohlschläger, A., P. Haggard, S. Gesierich, and W. Prinz. 2003. The perceived time of self- and other-generated actions. *Psychological Science, 14*, 586–591.

III Disorders of Volition in Depression

12 Prefrontal and Anterior Cingulate Contributions to Volition in Depression

Jack B. Nitschke and Kristen L. Mackiewicz

The heterogeneity of symptoms in depression has been a critical confound in our attempts to understand and successfully treat individuals suffering from it. As a result, the etiology and pathophysiology of depression remain elusive. The cardinal features of sad mood and loss of interest or pleasure have not been particularly useful in elucidating our understanding of the disorder. Despite the advent of sophisticated techniques for imaging the brains of people with depression, the neuroimaging data accrued has not implicated a clear neural signature. Indeed, the lack of a clear consensus in the relevant neuroscience literature may reflect the symptom heterogeneity across individuals experiencing depression.

Viewing depression as a disorder of volition provides a promising line of inquiry for answering questions about the nature of depression. Volition is a multifaceted construct of high relevance to the dysfunction accompanying depression. Cognitive neuroscience research has uncovered the neural substrates of some of the key features of volition, which direct our attention to two brain territories in particular—the dorsolateral prefrontal cortex (DLPFC) and the anterior cingulate cortex (ACC), illustrated in figure 12.1. Neuroimaging and other neuropsychological investigations of depression have repeatedly reported abnormalities in those two cortical regions. This chapter reviews the neuroimaging findings demonstrating the recruitment of the DLPFC and ACC in functions central to volition as well as the large literature implicating those two structures in depression. A synthesis follows that highlights the importance of volition for understanding the phenomenology and neural circuitry of depression and points to innovative research designs to further probe how volition operates in depression.

12.1 Defining Volition and Its Relationship to Depression

In this chapter, "volition" is defined as the conscious implementation of an intention to act, either physically or mentally. Volition requires an individual to focus and properly allocate attention and resources for the initiation and implementation of a

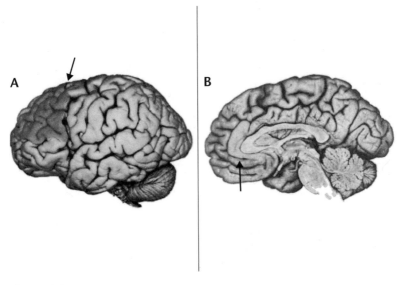

Figure 12.1
Key brain regions involved in volition and depression. (A) Dorsolateral prefrontal cortex (arrow).
(B) Anterior cingulate cortex shown (arrow). See plate 6.

definite action plan. Actual execution of the action is viewed as being beyond the
scope of volition. There are two crucial components involved in volition: the desire
to act and the formation and implementation of an action plan. The desire to act
demands that an individual wants to execute an action or action plan. This desire is
a conscious intention and subserves the formation of an action plan, similar to volitional ownership proposed by Metzinger (this volume) in his model of volition. It is
the underlying motivational force driving the implementation of an action plan and
therefore must be present before the formation of an action plan can even occur.

The second component focuses on an individual's ability to make a firm commitment to an action plan and organize the resources necessary to implement it. This
commitment entails taking all the prerequisite steps necessary to commence an action.
The fulfillment of such preparations central to the formation of a strategy for action
requires the coordination of multimodal resources. Individuals rely on environmental clues and various cognitive (e.g., memory retrieval) and affective processes (e.g.,
threat detection) to organize a representation of the relevant information, similar to
agency in Metzinger's model (this volume), and to generate a plausible strategy for
action. The implementation of an action plan requires an individual to appropriately
recruit and delegate both mental and physical resources in order to prepare for an
action.

Without the formation and implementation of a feasible action plan, it is unlikely an individual will execute an action. This is especially relevant to depression because many individuals suffering from depression often have a desire to act but lack the ability to implement an action plan. They fulfill the first component of volition—namely, desire—but are unable to execute the second component, formation and implementation of an action plan. Research by Hertel and colleagues provides direct empirical support for this contention. They have found that memory deficits in depressed participants are eliminated when they receive instructions prior to the start of a task to use specific organizational strategies requiring a memory-based action plan (for reviews, see Hertel 1994, 1997, 2000). Based on these and other data, Hertel posited a cognitive-initiative account that depressed individuals show diminished initiative in allocating available attentional resources for utilizing strategies that improve memory performance. This lack of initiative is highly pertinent to the compromised volition observed in depressed patients and suggests a deficit in the capacity to implement an action plan. Hertel and colleagues did not study individuals with very severe, treatment-refractory forms of depression, and people with this type of depression may lack both the desire to act and the ability to implement an action plan. Anatomical constraints, such as structural connectivity, limit the candidate brain regions that can provide the convergence and coordination required by volition. As illustrated in ensuing sections of this chapter, the DLPFC and ACC meet these anatomical criteria, perform functions of relevance to volition, and have been repeatedly implicated in research on depression.

12.2 DLPFC and Volition

Volition requires delicate balance and coordination between external sensory information and internal cognitive and affective processes. Cognitive control is the ability to synthesize information from the environment, usually gained through experience, with thoughts and affect to produce goal-oriented responses. Given the overlap between the functions of volition and cognitive control, cognitive control is a vital constituent of volition. The DLPFC serves a highly important executive role within the brain and subsequently is the main site of cognitive control in both humans and monkeys (Miller 2000; Miller and Cohen 2001; Koechlin et al. 2003; Badre and Wagner 2004; cf. Garavan et al. 2002). Recent neuroimaging data have demonstrated that tasks requiring high levels of cognitive control activate the DLPFC (Frith et al. 1991; Cohen et al. 1994, 1997; Baker et al. 1996; Smith and Jonides 1999; Banich et al. 2000; MacDonald et al. 2000). Given that cognitive control facilitates the culmination of sensory and motor information, the DLPFC is an appropriate gateway for directing cognitive control on account of its vast neural connections to virtually all sensory and motor systems and subcortical structures (Miller 2000).

A growing body of research has demonstrated that cognitive control in the DLPFC engages top-down processing, namely, behavior that is guided by affect, thoughts, and experience, as opposed to bottom-up processing, which is behavior directed by sensory stimulation (Cohen and Servan-Schreiber 1992; Passingham 1993; Wise et al. 1996; Miller 1999, 2000). Volition requires the engagement of top-down processing because of the effortful organization of resources implemented during the formation of an action plan. Furthermore, volition implies that an individual wants to eradicate established maladaptive behaviors and replace them with new responses to the same situation, event, or cognition. The DLPFC plays a critical role in acquiring novel behavioral responses corresponding to associations and respective neural connections that are weaker or less established than those for habitual responses. Rather than being fundamentally involved in automatic behaviors or the activation of established neural pathways, the DLPFC subserves the acquisition of new associations and the establishment and strengthening of new neural pathways driven by desired goals (Miller 2000; Miller and Cohen 2001). Based on the formation of new associations, the DLPFC is the likely sector of the prefrontal cortex (PFC) that derives rules used to direct ensuing behaviors (Dehaene and Changeux 1991; Miller 1999; Shimamura 2000). This aspect of cognitive control is absolutely critical to volition because it requires an individual to make attentional shifts and to implement novel actions. Such top-down processing aids in the organization and allocation of cognitive resources in order to successfully ignore competing alternatives and distractions.

Miller and Cohen (2001) have proposed a model of top-down processing in which the PFC represents goals and directs the utilization of resources necessary to achieve them. Integral to volition, goals are the crux of convergence between desire and the formation of an action plan. Goal-directed behavior is initiated and maintained through PFC biases, which are complex neural connections of varying strengths between areas of the PFC and other areas of cortex, such as the visual cortex, somatosensory cortex, thalamus, and basal ganglia. These pathways guide attentional shifts and goals based on established rules or patterns of behavior. Cues from the environment activate established neural pathways, and repeated activation strengthens the neural connections of these pathways. Goal-directed behavior requires the formation of new neural and behavioral associations. Activation of these new neural pathways in situations where they produce a desired behavior reinforces and strengthens the connections, perhaps via dopaminergic projections from the midbrain ventral tegmental area (Schultz et al. 1993; Mirenowicz and Schultz 1994, 1996; Montague et al. 1996; Schultz 1998; Miller and Cohen 2001). This plasticity of the PFC is crucial for the implementation of desired goal-oriented associations between a circumstance and new behavior.

An important aspect of the PFC's involvement in goal-oriented behaviors is its role in reward processing, consistent with the aforementioned links to the dopamine system. If goals were not rewarding, then we would not desire to pursue them or implement actions that would lead to subsequent goal attainment. Neurons in the PFC show increased activity as the quality and quantity of a reward increases, especially in response to behavioral changes (Miller 2000; Miller and Cohen 2001; Wallis and Miller 2003). By willfully changing behavior and establishing new behavioral trajectories, an individual can use the rewards reaped from these changes as a type of circular reinforcement for continued changes, an idea of obvious applicability in the psychotherapeutic treatment of depression.

Considering volition warrants an appreciation of the numerous subdivisions of the PFC. The emphasis in this chapter is on the DLPFC, which is primarily responsible for the constituents of volition outlined above, including the representation and selection of goals and the implementation of action plans and behavioral change. Indeed, the PFC findings for the recent elegant studies addressing cognitive control have a dorsolateral focus (Miller 2000; Miller and Cohen 2001; Koechlin et al. 2003; Badre and Wagner 2004; Kerns et al. 2004; Matsumoto and Tanaka 2004).

However, other sectors of the PFC may also contribute to the instantiation of volition. An impressive number of studies have reported dorsomedial PFC activation in a range of paradigms, suggesting a role in monitoring thoughts and emotions relating to the desired goals and plans for behavioral change (Gusnard and Raichle 2001). More ventral sectors of the medial PFC have been implicated in affective regulation processes (Morgan et al. 1993, 2003; Morgan and LeDoux 1995; Davidson et al. 2000b; Quirk et al. 2000; Milad and Quirk 2002; Pine 2003; but Gewirtz et al. 1997; Myers and Davis 2002) and may serve to dampen emotions that are not conducive with goals and initiating action plans. The established role of the ventrolateral PFC in response inhibition (Konishi et al. 1998a, 1998b, 1999; Garavan et al. 1999; Nielson et al. 2002; Aron et al. 2004) would be needed for inhibiting behavioral responses that contradict new goals. Directly below the ventrolateral PFC and lateral to the ventromedial PFC on the ventral surface of the frontal lobe, the orbitofrontal cortex (OFC) encodes the reward and punishment value of stimuli (Rolls 1999, 2000; Elliott et al. 2000; O'Doherty et al. 2001; Wallis and Miller 2003; Nitschke et al. 2004b, 2006). That information may reinforce or contradict one's goals, thereby enhancing or impeding subsequent initiation of an action plan. The varied functions performed by these other PFC sectors provide important information via direct connections with the DLPFC that is utilized by the DLPFC in the volitional processes of forming, coordinating, and implementing action plans (e.g., Wallis and Miller 2003).

In summary, the DLPFC subserves an executive role in cognitive control, which is exercised through top-down processing. Specifically, the DLPFC is a critical component in overriding established behaviors and creating new behavioral responses via neural associations. In addition, the DLPFC facilitates reward processing, especially in response to behavioral changes. These functions of the DLPFC overlap to a high degree with the constituent of volition corresponding to the formation and implementation of action plans. Although the emphasis in this chapter is on the DLPFC, other sectors of the PFC subserve specific functions required for volition.

12.3   DLPFC and Depression

As currently conceptualized, depression is comprised of a constellation of negative symptoms that result in reduced goal-directed behavior and decreased engagement in potentially rewarding activities. Such symptoms include a persistent depressed mood, a loss of interest or pleasure in activities that were once enjoyable, feelings of guilt and hopelessness, decreased movement and speech, slowness of action, reduced verbal and nonverbal expression, flat affect, and loss of drive (American Psychiatric Association 1994). Cognition is frequently disturbed in people with depression, particularly in the domain of maladaptive cognitive representations and processes (Beck 1967, 1987; Abramson et al. 1978, 1989; Blaney 1986; Nolen-Hoeksema 1987, 1990; Hertel 1994, 2000; Davis and Nolen-Hoeksema 2000; Hankin et al. 2001; Watkins 2002; Nitschke et al. 2004a), which may be fundamental to compromised volition. These cognitive aberrations and the demonstrated link between the DLPFC and cognitive control reviewed above suggest that depressed individuals should show abnormalities in this brain region.

Research examining the neural substrates of depression has identified aberrant activity patterns in the DLPFC during resting states. A number of positron-emission tomography (PET) and single photon emission computerized tomography (SPECT) studies have reported bilateral DLPFC decreases in blood flow and glucose metabolism (for reviews, see Dougherty and Rauch 1997; Heller and Nitschke 1997, 1998; Davidson and Henriques 2000; Davidson et al. 2002). Moreover, successful treatment is often accompanied by normalization of DLPFC activity (Bench et al. 1995; Buchsbaum et al. 1997; Mayberg et al. 1999, 2000, 2002; Kennedy et al. 2001; but see Brody et al. 1999; Martin et al. 2001; Goldapple et al. 2004). Early structural neuroimaging studies suggested that these functional findings might be accompanied by anatomical differences in the DLPFC (for a review, see Davidson et al. 2002). However, recent morphometric studies employing more sophisticated procedures for parceling of the frontal lobe into its constituent sectors indicated reduced volume in the OFC and ventromedial PFC but not in the DLPFC (for a review, see Davidson et al. in press).

Consistent with a general deficit in goal-oriented behavior, depressed individuals demonstrate impairments in different types of effortful processing, including memory (for reviews, see Hartlage et al. 1993; Burt et al. 1995; Heller and Nitschke 1997). In an elegant set of studies, Hertel and her colleagues have shown that memory deficits in depressed participants are eliminated when organizational strategies are provided prior to the start of a task (for reviews, see Hertel 1994, 1997, 2000). Her cognitive-initiative account posits that depressed individuals show diminished initiative in allocating available attentional resources for utilizing strategies that improve memory performance. As such, compromised memory performance in depressed people is not due to a lack of effort or insufficient cognitive resources but rather an inability to initiate or deploy organizing strategies. Consistent with Hertel's model, we recently found that depressed individuals did not show the association between DLPFC activity, as measured by electroencephalography (EEG), and memory performance observed for nondepressed controls (Nitschke et al. 2004a). In a PET study providing further support for Hertel's cognitive-initiative framework (1994, 2000), depressed patients showed less DLPFC blood flow bilaterally on a complex planning task than nonpsychiatric controls (Elliott et al. 1997). Similarly, patients with DLPFC lesions were impaired in using organization strategies during episodic memory tasks and benefited from instruction in the use of such strategies (Incisa della Rocchetta and Milner 1993; Gershberg and Shimamura 1995; see also Grafman and Krueger, this volume; Shallice, this volume; Burgess, Gilbert, Okuda, and Simons, this volume). Taken together, these data implicate the DLPFC in the impaired cognitive control, initiative, and volition characterizing depression, all of which are needed for selecting goals and implementing action plans.

Other cognitive characteristics of depression contribute less directly to avolition in depression. Depression is typically accompanied by a ruminative cognitive style characterized by automatic negative thoughts that interfere with other cognitive processes important for volition, such as cognitive control (Nolen-Hoeksema and Morrow 1993; Davis and Nolen-Hoeksema 2000; Watkins and Brown 2002). In research on cognitive biases for valenced information, depression is accompanied by better recall for negative material and worse recall for positive material (for reviews, see Blaney 1986; Watkins 2002). Such biases have been observed for explicit memory tasks and some conceptually driven implicit memory tasks, but not for perceptually driven implicit memory tasks. Two recent reports found that processing biases toward unpleasant stimuli in depression were associated with more right DLPFC activity (Elliott et al. 2002; Nitschke et al. 2004a). These right-sided findings are consistent with a large literature documenting asymmetric patterns of frontal activity (right greater than left) in depression (for reviews, see Heller and Nitschke 1997, 1998; Davidson and Henriques 2000; Davidson et al. 2002). Based on these and other data, we have proposed that right PFC mechanisms represent withdrawal-related negative emotions and threat perception (Nitschke and Heller 2002, 2005; see also Davidson et al. 2000a; Nitschke et al. 2006), which impede volitional processes such as the selection of goals and the implementation of action plans.

The diminished left DLPFC activity contributing to the asymmetry findings frequently observed in depression may be directly involved in avolition as well. Davidson has proposed that the left DLPFC is involved in goal-directed approach tendencies (for reviews, see Davidson 2000; Davidson et al. 2002, 2003b; see also Nitschke et al. 2004a; Urry et al. 2004). Accordingly, reduced left DLPFC activity in people with depression may explain their inability to override established behaviors and initiate new goal-directed behaviors. A recursive dysfunctional loop may ensue, with deficient approach tendencies leading to the preservation of negative affect and cognitions, which in turn hinder the willful formation and pursuit of action plans for desired behaviors.

In general, many of the negative symptoms and cognitive deficits associated with depression may be linked to DLPFC hypoactivity. In particular, memory impairment in depression stems from an inability to initiate organizational strategies, corresponding to reductions in DLPFC activity. Deficits in implementing organizational strategies parallel the formation and implementation of action plans apparent in volition. Links are also made between impaired volition and other cognitive abnormalities in depression, such as cognitive biases toward negative material. Moreover, the left and right DLPFC may contribute somewhat independently to volition, given their respective involvement in goal-directed approach and threat-related withdrawal tendencies.

12.4 ACC and Volition

Volition requires an individual to focus and allocate attention and energy, organize resources, and commit to an action plan. Furthermore, an individual must integrate clues from the environment with cognitive and affective processes in order to generate a plausible strategy for action. An important precursor of implementing an action plan is selecting a desired action from among competing alternatives. Conflict monitoring entails the mediation of internal and external incongruencies, thus informing the consequent selection of one action plan over another (Matsumoto and Tanaka 2004). Furthermore, conflict monitoring is central to detecting and subsequently responding to conditions that require increased cognitive control (Badre and Wagner 2004). Up-regulation of cognitive control is crucial for the volitional processes of successfully instituting and implementing new goal-directed behaviors in place of established behavior patterns. Providing evidence for the ACC as the "executor" in signaling this up-regulation of cognitive processes, numerous cognitive neuroscience reports have implicated the ACC in monitoring and detecting response conflict in information processing (Carter et al. 1998, 2000; Botvinick et al. 1999, 2001; Barch et al. 2000, 2001; MacDonald et al. 2000; Banich et al. 2001; Braver et al. 2001; Milham et al. 2001; van Veen and Carter 2002; Dehaene et al. 2003; Badre and Wagner 2004; Kerns et al. 2004).

This line of research indicates that the ACC detects cross talk relating to conflict and interference between different brain regions and subsequently issues a call for further processing and increased cognitive control to help resolve the conflict (Carter et al. 1998, 2000; Barch et al. 2001; Miller and Cohen 2001; Badre and Wagner 2004; Kerns et al. 2004). The primary center called upon is the DLPFC because of its involvement in maintaining necessary task demands and altering behavioral plans (Miller and Cohen 2001; Davidson et al. 2002). Research in this area has now documented interplay between the ACC and DLPFC (MacDonald et al. 2000; Botvinick et al. 2001; Badre and Wagner 2004; Kerns et al. 2004; Matsumoto and Tanaka 2004). Particularly noteworthy is the recent evidence of a direct relationship between ACC activity on high-conflict trials and subsequent DLPFC activity and behavioral adjustments (Kerns et al. 2004), supporting the claim that the ACC detects conflict and leads to the recruitment of the DLPFC in order to initiate cognitive control (Cohen et al. 2000; Botvinick et al. 2001; van Veen and Carter 2002; Kerns et al. 2004). However, causal ambiguity remains as to whether the cognitive control implemented by the DLPFC is a consequence of the conflict detected by the ACC or serves to prevent future conflicts (Matsumoto and Tanaka 2004). Nonetheless, these two key brain regions work together to orchestrate the implementation of volitional action plans. The plethora of neuroimaging reports finding DLPFC and ACC abnormalities in depressed patients suggest a disruption of this system that corresponds with the cognitive deficits that accompany depression (Hartlage et al. 1993; Hertel 1994, 2000; Heller and Nitschke 1997; Nitschke et al. 2004a).

As with the PFC, the ACC can be parceled into subdivisions serving distinct functions (Devinsky et al. 1995; Vogt et al. 1995; Mayberg 1997; Mayberg et al. 1999; Bush et al. 2000; Pizzagalli et al. 2001; Davidson et al. 2002; Nitschke et al. 2006). For example, a wealth of data point to the utility of a distinction between dorsal ACC as a cognitive sector and ventral ACC as an affective sector (Devinsky et al. 1995; Bush et al. 2000; Pizzagalli et al. 2001; Davidson et al. 2002). The aforementioned research on conflict monitoring has employed various cognitive paradigms and has consistently implicated the dorsal ACC. It is connected with the DLPFC, posterior cingulate, parietal cortex, and supplementary motor areas, which all play important roles in response selection and relevant cognitive processing (Davidson et al. 2002). As such, the dorsal ACC is of obvious relevance to the implementation of action plans required for volition.

Encompassing the rostral and ventral areas of the ACC, the affective sector may be instrumental in conflict monitoring for content that is affective in nature (Davidson et al. 2002; Nitschke et al. 2006). Implicated in the regulation of visceral and autonomic responses to stressful events, emotional expression, and social behavior (Davidson et al. 2002; Pine 2003), the ventral ACC is connected with a host of brain regions involved in emotion, such as the amygdala, nucleus accumbens, insula, periaqueductal gray, hypothalamus, and multiple sectors of the PFC, including the DLPFC (Pandya et al. 1981; Vogt and Pandya 1987; Devinsky et al. 1995). The ventral ACC likely performs functions similar to the dorsal ACC in detecting conflict and recruit-ing the DLPFC—either directly or via the dorsal ACC—for cognitive control. The primary difference between the two subdivisions of the ACC in this regard may be that the comparator in the ventral ACC fields affective input, such as signals repre-senting depressed mood or other unpleasant emotions. In addition to the up-regula-tion of cognitive control, volition requires down-regulation of unpleasant affect that interferes with goal-directed behavior. A growing body of evidence indicates that the ventral ACC and adjacent ventromedial PFC are directly responsible for these regula-tory functions via projections to the amygdala (Pine 2003; Milad and Quirk 2002; Davidson et al. 2000b) following from the detection of conflict involving emotion. The functions outlined here may be central to ACC involvement in various forms of normal and abnormal affective processing, including pain (Rainville et al. 1997; Ploghaus et al. 1999; Craig et al. 2000; Sawamoto et al. 2000; Craig 2003; Wager et al. 2004), aversion (Small et al. 2003; Nitschke et al. 2006), sad mood (Mayberg et al. 1999), major depressive disorder (Mayberg et al. 2000; Brody et al. 2001), obses-sive–compulsive disorder (Breiter et al. 1996; Rauch et al. 1997), simple phobia (Rauch et al. 1995), and posttraumatic stress disorder (Rauch et al. 1996; Shin et al. 1997). In fact, psychosurgical lesions of the ACC have been used as a means of treatment for patients with mood and anxiety disorders (for a review, see Binder and Iskandar 2000). Patients with ACC lesions are generally apathetic and unconcerned with significant events (Devinsky et al. 1995; Luu and Posner 2003), which may reflect an inability to detect conflict among competing response options.

In summary, the ACC is heavily involved in conflict monitoring, with the dorsal sector serving as a cognitive subdivision and the ventral sector as an affective subdi-vision. The ACC is responsible for detecting both internal cross talk and external con-flict and subsequently recruiting brain regions for assistance with resolving conflict and responding appropriately. For example, direct projections from the ACC to the DLPFC provide the call for the cognitive control and top-down processing needed for volition. Elements of volition executed by the ACC include selection of appropriate action plans from competing alternatives and the recruitment of neural components for the implementation of goal-directed behaviors.

12.5   ACC and Depression

Depression involves the disturbance of volitional processes dependent on the ACC, such as conflict monitoring and the selection of an action from among available alter-natives. There is sometimes a conflict between an individual's mood and the behav-ior expected in a particular role or social context. For example, depressed mood hampers goal setting and intentional action, yet demands of the environment may include expectations to act in specific ways. In an individual with normal levels of

ACC activity, the ACC would signal a call to other brain regions, particularly the DLPFC, to resolve the conflict and engage in the appropriate goal-directed behavior. However, in an individual with abnormally low levels of ACC activity, the conflict between one's mood and perceived expectations would not be effectively monitored, and thus the usual call for further processing would not be issued.

The data on ACC function in depression most consistently reveal a pattern of decreased activity in both dorsal and ventral regions of the ACC (Bench et al. 1992; Curran et al. 1993; Kumar et al. 1993; Mayberg et al. 1994, 2000; Ito et al. 1996; Drevets et al. 1997; George et al. 1997; Beauregard et al. 1998; Davidson et al. 2003a; Kumari et al. 2003). The majority of these findings were for the dorsal ACC (e.g., Bench et al. 1992; Mayberg et al. 1994; George et al. 1997), suggesting disturbances in cognitive function of relevance to conflict monitoring and the ensuing selection and implementation of action plans. Whereas the state of being depressed is associated with reduced dorsal ACC activity, remission has been characterized by increased activity in the same region (Bench et al. 1995; Buchsbaum et al. 1997; Mayberg et al. 1999, 2000, 2002; Kennedy et al. 2001; Goldapple et al. 2004).

Other studies on depression have reported ventral ACC hypoactivity (Ito et al. 1996; Drevets et al. 1997) and reduced ventral ACC responses to different tasks (Davidson et al. 2003a; Kumari et al. 2003; Bremner et al. 2004). Disengagement of the ventral ACC in depression may reflect hindered volitional processing related to detecting conflict between unpleasant emotions and desired goal states and to down-regulating such emotions. Indeed, depressed mood and feelings of failure often conflict with desires, goals, and societal expectations, as noted above. Hyperactivity in this area at baseline in eventual treatment responders (Wu et al. 1992, 1999; Ebert and Ebmeier 1996; Buchsbaum et al. 1997; Mayberg et al. 1997; Pizzagalli et al. 2001; Davidson et al. 2003a; see also Kumari et al. 2003) suggests that this important function of the ventral ACC is intact in a subgroup of depressed patients, with preserved volition perhaps playing a key role in treatment response. The rostral, pregenual aspect of the ventral ACC has been the locus identified in these treatment studies. Heavily connected with both dorsal and more ventral, subgenual sectors of the ACC (Pandya et al. 1981; Vogt and Pandya 1987; Devinsky et al. 1995), the rostral ACC is strategically located for facilitating the integration of affective and cognitive information (Mayberg et al. 1999; Pizzagalli et al. 2001).

In an influential model, Mayberg and colleagues (Mayberg 1997; Mayberg et al. 1999) have purported that the different regions of the ACC are responsible for the formation and eventual maintenance of some depressive symptoms. The dorsal region of the ACC is responsible for modulating cognitive symptoms, such as attentional and executive deficits, while the ventral region of the ACC is postulated to be involved in vegetative and somatic symptoms. Following from the recent evidence that the dorsal ACC signals the DLPFC when cognitive control is needed (Kerns et al. 2004;

Matsumoto and Tanaka 2004), the reduced dorsal ACC activity observed in depression might result in deactivation of the DLPFC and corresponding deficits in cognitive control, initiative, and executive function (Hertel 1994, 2000; Heller and Nitschke 1997; Davidson et al. 2002; Nitschke et al. 2004a).

Recent morphometric studies provide indications of structural differences in the ACC as well. Some reports have documented reductions in volume, glial cell density, and neuronal size (Drevets et al. 1997; Hirayasu et al. 1999; Cotter et al. 2001; Botteron et al. 2002; Ballmaier et al. 2004), whereas others have found no differences (Brambilla et al. 2002; Bremner et al. 2002). The contradictory findings in this nascent literature occurred in studies examining the entire ACC as well as those focusing on the ventral, subgenual sector, which has received particular attention as a result of the initial finding in this area reported by Drevets et al. (1997). If upheld in future research, reductions in the size of the ACC in depressed individuals may contribute importantly to compromised functioning in that area as it bears on volitional processing.

In sum, affective and cognitive deficits are closely linked with one another in depression, and the ACC is ideally situated anatomically to mediate this convergence. Optimal selection of action plans to be implemented depends upon the integration of relevant affective and cognitive information as well as the detection and resolution of conflict. The inability for depressed people to properly detect conflict and organize resources in order to respond may lead to decreased goal-oriented behavior and implementation of action plans; hence, volition is hampered because cognitive and affective information is not integrated into an organized plan of action. Interestingly, treatment studies have indicated that depressed patients with increased baseline activity in the rostral ACC, the region of the ACC implicated in the convergence of cognitive and affective information, demonstrate a better response to treatment.

12.6   DLPFC and ACC in Volition: Synthesis and Future Directions for Depression Research

In this chapter, we have outlined two constituent components in the neural circuitry of volition: the DLPFC and the ACC. These structures have distinct roles that contribute to the selection and implementation of action plans. Subserving cognitive control, the DLPFC is involved in the representation and selection of goals and in the implementation of action plans and behavioral change. The ACC has been implicated in monitoring conflict among external and internal cues, with the dorsal ACC modulating cognitive aspects and the ventral ACC more involved in affect. It plays a central role in signaling and recruiting additional brain regions, particularly the DLPFC, in order to resolve the conflict and initiate the appropriate action. Working in concert, these two key regions form the cornerstones of the neural signature of volition, especially with regard to the implementation of volitional action plans. The cascade of events that occur allow for the eventual selection of new goal-directed behaviors that override previously established behavior patterns.

The DLPFC and ACC hypoactivity observed in depressed individuals reflects the lack of volition that frequently accompanies depression. Avolition is a constituent of depression that is tightly linked to cognitive deficits in the organization and allocation of resources and attention. These cognitive deficits are highly affected by the functions of the DLPFC and the ACC and their respective roles in cognitive control and conflict monitoring. Deficient functioning of these two key regions leads to decreased goal setting and subsequent decreases in the formation of organizational strategies for action in people with depression.

An important line of inquiry is how the DLPFC and ACC with their respective roles in volition are linked to the broader circuitry and symptomatology of depression. A number of other brain areas have been implicated in depression including the hippocampus, amygdala, and parietal cortex (Heller and Nitschke 1997, 1998; Davidson et al. 2002, in press). As noted above, volition is likely crucial for the expression of other common symptoms of depression, such as psychomotor retardation and anhedonia. Finally, the emphasis on the brain instantiation of volition as it relates to depression may inform the heterogeneity in symptom expression that is so prominent in depression. For example, we have suggested that brain-based subtyping (e.g., PFC-based versus ACC-based depression subtypes) may prove to be superior to symptom-based subtyping in addressing heterogeneity (Davidson et al. 2002).

This chapter showcases volition as a symptom worthy of study in the depression literature. Further understanding of the operation of volition in depression will depend upon the utilization of novel paradigms in neuroimaging research that target specific symptoms and cognitive irregularities in depression. As this review demonstrates, the vast majority of neuroimaging studies conducted to date have concentrated on resting baseline data. In addition to potential confounds, such as falling asleep and the variability in mental processes engaged within and across research participants, little is known about the nature and meaning of a default mode of regional brain activity in the absence of a task (Gusnard and Raichle 2001; Raichle et al. 2001). Future research employing well-characterized paradigms employed in the literature on cognitive control and conflict monitoring reviewed here and tailored to include content pertinent to depression are particularly appealing, given the theoretical rationale for expecting compromised function in these domains among depressed individuals.

An appreciation of volition as a central feature of depression has implications for research on volition as well. Severe depression provides the opportunity to investigate avolition in an extreme form. As one manifestation of symptom heterogeneity in depression, affected individuals experience lack of volition to varying degrees, which may correspond to the replicated finding that a subgroup of depressed patients actually show increased ventral ACC activity prior to treatment and that the amount of pre-treatment ventral ACC activity is directly proportional to the degree of eventual treatment response. Thus, individuals with depression are an excellent research population for surveying individual differences in volition across a broad range of its expression.

Increased integration of depression and volition research may further inform the pathophysiology of the disorder and viable treatment options. Avolition as a symptom of depression could be directly attacked using biological or psychological interventions that target the DLPFC and the ACC and their respective functions in cognitive control and conflict monitoring. In addition, mental health care providers could capitalize on the preserved volition that exists in some patients, an issue that is not widely appreciated. In sum, serious consideration of volition could contribute significantly to mitigating the tremendous personal suffering and societal burden associated with depression.

Acknowledgments

We gratefully acknowledge the assistance of Krystal Cleven and Sid Sarinopoulos with preparation of this chapter. This chapter is reprinted here with permission from Elsevier. It also appears in M. Glabus (ed.), *International Review of Neurobiology: Neuroimaging (Part B)*.

Referencess

Abramson, L. Y., G. I. Metalsky, and L. B. Alloy. 1989. Hopelessness depression: A theory-based subtype of depression. *Psychological Review, 96,* 358–372.

Abramson, L. Y., M. E. Seligman, and J. D. Teasdale. 1978. Learned helplessness in humans: Critique and reformulation. *Journal of Abnormal Psychology, 87,* 49–74.

American Psychiatric Association. 1994. *Diagnostic and Statistical Manual of Mental Disorders,* 4th ed. Washington, D.C.: American Psychiatric Association.

Aron, A. R., T. W. Robbins, and R. A. Poldrack. 2004. Inhibition and the right inferior frontal cortex. *Trends in Cognitive Sciences, 8,* 170–177.

Badre, D., and A. D. Wagner. 2004. Selection, integration, and conflict monitoring: Assessing the nature and generality of prefrontal cognitive control mechanisms. *Neuron, 41,* 473–487.

Baker, S. C., R. D. Rogers, A. M. Owen, C. D. Frith, R. J. Dolan, R. S. Frackowiak, et al. 1996. Neural systems engaged by planning: A PET study of the Tower of London Task. *Neuropsychologia, 34,* 515–526.

Ballmaier, M., A. W. Toga, R. E. Blanton, E. R. Sowell, H. Lavretsky, J. Peterson, et al. 2004. Anterior cingulate, gyrus rectus, and orbitofrontal abnormalities in elderly depressed patients: An MRI-based parcellation of the prefrontal cortex. *American Journal of Psychiatry, 161,* 99–108.

Banich, M. T., M. P. Milham, R. Atchley, N. J. Cohen, A. Webb, T. Wszalek, et al. 2000. Prefrontal regions play a predominant role in imposing an attentional "set": Evidence from fMRI. *Cognitive Brain Research, 10,* 1–9.

Banich, M. T., M. P. Milham, R. Atchley, N. J. Cohen, A. Webb, T. Wszalek, et al. 2001. fMRI studies of the Stroop tasks reveal unique roles of anterior and posterior brain systems in attentional selection. *Journal of Cognitive Neuroscience, 12,* 988–1000.

Barch, D. M., T. S. Braver, E. Akbudak, T. E. Conturo, J. M. Ollinger, and A. Z. Snyder. 2001. Anterior cingulate cortex and response conflict: Effects of response modality and processing domain. *Cerebral Cortex, 11,* 837–848.

Barch, D. M., F. W. Sabb, D. C. Noll, and J. Jonides. 2000. The anterior cingulate cortex and response competition: Evidence from an fMRI study of overt verb generation. *Journal of Cognitive Neuroscience, 12,* 298–305.

Beauregard, M., J. Leroux, and K. S. Bergman. 1998. The functional neuroanatomy of major depression: An fMRI study using an emotional activation paradigm. *Neuroreport, 9,* 3253–3258.

Beck, A. T. 1967. *Depression.* New York: Hober Medical.

Beck, A. T. 1987. Cognitive models of depression. *Journal of Cognitive Psychotherapy, 1,* 5–37.

Bench, C. J., R. S. Frackowiak, and R. J. Dolan. 1995. Changes in regional cerebral blood flow on recovery from depression. *Psychological Medicine, 25,* 247–261.

Bench, C. J., K. J. Friston, and R. G. Brown. 1992. The anatomy of melancholia: Focal abnormalities of cerebral blood flow in major depression. *Psychological Medicine, 22,* 607–615.

Binder, D. K., and B. J. Iskandar. 2000. Modern neurosurgery for psychiatric disorders. *Neurosurgery, 47,* 9–21.

Blaney, P. H. 1986. Affect and memory: A review. *Psychological Bulletin, 99,* 229–246.

Botteron, K. N., M. E. Raichle, W. C. Drevets, A. C. Heath, and R. D. Todd. 2002. Volumetric reduction in left subgenual prefrontal cortex in early onset depression. *Biological Psychiatry, 51,* 342–344.

Botvinick, M. M., T. S. Braver, D. M. Barch, C. S. Carter, and J. C. Cohen. 2001. Conflict monitoring and cognitive control. *Psychological Review, 108,* 624–652.

Botvinick, M., L. E. Nystrom, K. Fissell, C. S. Carter, and J. D. Cohen. 1999. Conflict monitoring versus selection-for-action in anterior cingulate cortex. *Nature, 402,* 179–181.

Brambilla, P., M. A. Nicoletti, K. Harenski, and R. B. Sassi. 2002. Anatomical MRI study of subgenual prefrontal cortex in bipolar and unipolar subjects. *Neuropsychopharmacology, 27,* 792–799.

Braver, T. S., D. M. Barch, J. R. Gray, D. L. Molfese, and S. Avraham. 2001. Anterior cingulate cortex and response conflict: Effects of frequency, inhibition, and errors. *Cerebral Cortex, 11,* 825–836.

Breiter, H. C., S. L. Rauch, K. K. Kwong, J. R. Baker, R. M. Weisskoff, D. N. Kennedy, et al. 1996. Functional magnetic resonance imaging of symptom provocation in obsessive–compulsive disorder. *Archives of General Psychiatry*, *53*, 595–606.

Bremner, J. D., M. Vythilingam, E. Vermetten, A. Nazeer, J. Adil, S. Khan, et al. 2002. Reduced volume of orbitofrontal cortex in major depression. *Biological Psychiatry*, *51*, 273–279.

Bremner, J. D., M. Vythilingam, E. Vermetten, F. J. Vaccarino, and D. S. Charney. 2004. Deficits in hippocampal and anterior cingulate functioning during verbal declarative memory encoding in midlife major depression. *American Journal of Psychiatry*, *161*, 637–645.

Brody, A. L., S. Saxena, and M. A. Mandelkern. 2001. Brain metabolic changes associated with symptom factor improvement in major depressive disorder. *Biological Psychiatry*, *50*, 159–170.

Brody, A. L., S. Saxena, D. H. Silverman, S. Alborzian, L. A. Fairbanks, M. E. Phelps, et al. 1999. Brain metabolic changes in major depressive disorder from pre- to post-treatment with paroxetine. *Psychiatry Research*, *91*, 127–139.

Buchsbaum, M. S., J. Wu, B. V. Siegel, E. Hackett, M. Trenary, L. Abel, et al. 1997. Effect of sertraline on regional metabolic rate in patients with affective disorder. *Biological Psychiatry*, *41*, 15–22.

Burt, D. B., M. J. Zembar, and G. Niederehe. 1995. Depression and memory impairment: A meta-analysis of the association, its pattern, and specificity. *Psychological Bulletin*, *117*, 285–305.

Bush, G., P. Luu, and M. I. Posner. 2000. Cognitive and emotional influences in anterior cingulate cortex. *Trends in Cognitive Sciences*, *4*, 215–222.

Carter, C. S., T. S. Braver, D. M. Barch, M. M. Botvinick, D. Noll, and J. D. Cohen. 1998. Anterior cingulate cortex, error detection, and the on-line monitoring performance. *Science*, *280*, 747–749.

Carter, C. S., A. M. Macdonald, M. Botvinick, L. L. Ross, V. A. Stenger, D. Noll, et al. 2000. Parsing executive processes: Strategic vs. evaluative functions of the anterior cingulate cortex. *Proceedings of the National Academy of Sciences*, *97*, 1944–1948.

Cohen, J. D., M. Botvinick, and C. S. Carter. 2000. Anterior cingulate and prefrontal cortex: Who's in control? *Nature Neuroscience*, *3*, 421–423.

Cohen, J. D., S. D. Forman, T. S. Braver, B. J. Casey, D. Servan-Schreiber, and D. C. Noll. 1994. Activation of prefrontal cortex in a nonspatial working memory task with functional MRI. *Human Brain Mapping*, *1*, 293–304.

Cohen, J. D., W. M. Perlstein, T. S. Braver, L. E. Nystrom, D. C. Noll, J. Jonides, et al. 1997. Temporal dynamics of brain activation during a working memory task. *Nature*, *386*, 604–608.

Cohen, J. D., and D. Servan-Schreiber. 1992. Context, cortex, and dopamine: A connectionist approach to behavior and biology in schizophrenia. *Psychological Review*, *99*, 45–77.

Cotter, D., D. Mackay, S. Landau, R. Kerwin, and I. Everall. 2001. Reduced glial cell density and neuronal size in the anterior cingulate cortex in major depression. *Archives of General Psychiatry*, *58*, 545–553.

Craig, A. D. 2003. A new view of pain as a homeostatic emotion. *Trends in Neurosciences, 26,* 303–307.

Craig, A. D., K. Chen, D. Bandy, and E. M. Reiman. 2000. Thermosensory activation of insular cortex. *Nature Neuroscience, 3,* 184–190.

Curran, S. M., C. M. Murray, M. Van Beck, N. Dougall, R. E. O'Carrol, H. P. Austin, et al. 1993. A single photon emission computerized tomography study of regional brain function in elderly patients with major depressive disorder and with Alzheimer-type dementia. *British Journal of Psychiatry, 163,* 155–165.

Davidson, R. J. 2000. Affective style, psychopathology, and resilience: Brain mechanisms and plasticity. *American Psychologist, 55,* 1193–1214.

Davidson, R. J., and J. B. Henriques. 2000. Regional brain function in sadness and depression. In *The Neuropsychology of Emotion,* ed. J. C. Borod, pp. 269–297. New York: Oxford University Press.

Davidson, R. J., W. Irwin, M. J. Anderele, and N. H. Kalin. 2003a. The neural substrates of affective processing in depressed patients treated with venlafaxine. *American Journal of Psychiatry, 160,* 64–75.

Davidson, R. J., J. R. Marshall, A. J. Tomarken, and J. B. Henriques. 2000a. While a phobic waits: Regional brain electrical and autonomic activity in social phobics during anticipation of public speaking. *Biological Psychiatry, 47,* 85–95.

Davidson, R. J., D. Pizzagalli, and J. B. Nitschke. In press. Affect and depression: Perspectives from affective neuroscience. In *Cognitive and Affective Neuroscience of Psychopathology,* ed. D. M. Barch. New York: Oxford University Press.

Davidson, R. J., D. Pizzagalli, J. B. Nitschke, and N. H. Kalin. 2003b. Parsing the subcomponents of emotion and disorders of emotion: Perspectives from affective neuroscience. In *Handbook of Affective Sciences,* ed. R. J. Davidson, K. R. Scherer, and H. H. Goldsmith, pp. 8–24. New York: Oxford University Press.

Davidson, R. J., D. Pizzagalli, J. B. Nitschke, and K. Putnam. 2002. Depression: Perspectives from affective neuroscience. *Annual Review of Psychology, 53,* 545–574.

Davidson, R. J., K. M. Putnam, and C. L. Larson. 2000b. Dysfunction in the neural circuitry of emotion regulation—A possible prelude to violence. *Science, 289,* 591–594.

Davis, R. N., and S. Nolen-Hoeksema. 2000. Cognitive inflexibility among ruminators and non-ruminators. *Cognitive Therapy and Research, 24,* 699–711.

Dehaene, S., E. Artiges, L. Naccache, C. Martelli, A. Viard, F. Schurhoff, et al. 2003. Conscious and subliminal conflicts in normal subjects and patients with schizophrenia: The role of the anterior cingulate cortex. *Proceedings of the National Academy of Sciences, 100,* 13722–13727.

Dehaene, S., and J. P. Changeux. 1991. The Wisconsin Card Sort Test: Theoretical analysis and modeling in a neuronal network. *Cerebral Cortex, 1,* 62–79.

Devinsky, O., M. J. Morrel, and B. Vogt. 1995. Contributions of anterior cingulate cortex to behavior. *Brain, 118,* 279–306.

Dougherty, D., and S. L. Rauch. 1997. Neuroimaging and neurobiological models of depression. *Harvard Review of Psychiatry*, *5*, 138–159.

Drevets, W. C., J. L. Price, J. R. Simpson, R. D. Todd, T. Reich, M. Vannier, et al. 1997. Subgenual prefrontal cortex abnormalities in mood disorders. *Nature*, *386*, 824–827.

Ebert, D., and K. P. Ebmeier. 1996. The role of the cingulate gyrus in depression: From functional anatomy to neurochemistry. *Biological Psychiatry*, *39*, 1044–1050.

Elliott, R., R. J. Dolan, and C. D. Frith. 2000. Dissociable functions in the medial and lateral orbitofrontal cortex: Evidence from human neuroimaging studies. *Cerebral Cortex*, *10*, 308–317.

Elliott, R., C. D. Frith, and R. J. Dolan. 1997. Differential neural response to positive and negative feedback in planning and guessing tasks. *Neuropsychologia*, *35*, 1395–1404.

Elliott, R., J. S. Rubinsztein, B. J. Sahakian, and R. J. Dolan. 2002. The neural basis of mood congruent processing biases in depression. *Archives of General Psychiatry*, *59*, 597–604.

Frith, C. D., K. J. Friston, P. F. Liddle, and R. S. Frackowiak. 1991. Willed action and the prefrontal cortex in man: A study with PET. *Proceedings of the Royal Society of London: Series B*, *244*, 241–246.

Garavan, H., T. J. Ross, K. Murphy, R. T. Roche, and E. A. Stein. 2002. Dissociable executive functions in the dynamic control of behavior: Inhibition, error detection, and correction. *Neuroimage*, *17*, 1820–1829.

Garavan, H., T. J. Ross, and E. A. Stein. 1999. Right hemispheric dominance of inhibitory control: An event-related functional MRI study. *Proceedings of the National Academy of Sciences*, *96*, 8301–8306.

George, M. S., T. A. Ketter, P. I. Parekh, N. Rosinsky, H. A. Ring, P. J. Pazzaglia, et al. 1997. Blunted left cingulate activation in mood disorder subjects during a response interference task (the Stroop). *Journal of Neuropsychiatry and Clinical Neurosciences*, *9*, 55–63.

Gershberg, F. B., and A. P. Shimamura. 1995. Impaired use of organizational strategies in free recall following frontal lobe damage. *Neuropsychologia*, *33*, 1305–1333.

Gewirtz, J. C., W. A. Falls, and M. Davis. 1997. Normal conditioned inhibition and extinction of freezing and fear-potentiated startle following electrolytic lesions of medial prefrontal cortex in rats. *Behavioral Neuroscience*, *111*, 712–726.

Goldapple, K., Z. Segal, C. Garson, M. Lau, P. Bieling, S. Kennedy, et al. 2004. Modulation of cortical–limbic pathways in major depression: Treatment-specific effects of cognitive behavior therapy. *Archives of General Psychiatry*, *61*, 34–41.

Gusnard, D. A., and M. E. Raichle. 2001. Searching for a baseline: Functional imaging and the resting human brain. *Nature Reviews Neuroscience*, *2*, 685–694.

Hankin, B. L., L. Y. Abramson, and M. Siler. 2001. A prospective test of the hopelessness theory of depression in adolescence. *Cognitive Therapy and Research*, *25*, 607–632.

Hartlage, S., L. B. Alloy, and C. Vazquez. 1993. Automatic and effortful processing in depression. *Psychological Bulletin, 113*, 247–278.

Heller, W., and J. B. Nitschke. 1997. Regional brain activity in emotion: A framework for understanding cognition in depression. *Cognition and Emotion, 11*, 637–661.

Heller, W., and J. B. Nitschke. 1998. The puzzle of regional brain activity in depression and anxiety: The importance of subtypes and comorbidity. *Cognition and Emotion, 12*, 421–447.

Hertel, P. T. 1994. Depression and memory: Are impairments remediable through attentional control? *Current Directions in Psychological Science, 3*, 190–193.

Hertel, P. T. 1997. On the contribution of deficient cognitive control to memory impairment in depression. *Cognition and Emotion, 11*, 569–583.

Hertel, P. T. 2000. The cognitive-iniative account of depression-related impairments in memory. In *The Psychology of Learning and Motivation: Advances in Research and Theory*, ed. D. L. Medin, pp. 47–71. San Diego: Academic Press.

Hirayasu, Y., and M. E. Shenton. 1999. Subgenual cingulate cortex volume in first-episode psychosis. *American Journal of Psychiatry, 156*, 1091–1093.

Hirayasu, Y., M. E. Shenton, D. F. Salisbury, J. S. Kwon, C. G. Wible, I. A. Fischer, et al. 1999. Subgenual cingulate cortex volume in first-episode psychosis. *American Journal of Psychiatry, 156*, 1091–1093.

Incisa della Rocchetta, A., and B. Milner. 1993. Strategic search and retrieval inhibition: The role of the frontal lobes. *Neuropsychologia, 31*, 503–524.

Ito, H., R. Kawashima, S. Awata, S. Ono, K. Sato, R. Goto, et al. 1996. Hypoperfusion in the limbic system and prefrontal cortex in depression: SPECT with anatomic standardization technique. *Journal of Nuclear Medicine, 37*, 410–414.

Kennedy, S. H., K. R. Evans, S. Kruger, H. S. Mayberg, J. H. Meyer, S. McCann, et al. 2001. Changes in regional brain glucose metabolism measured with positron emission tomography after paroxetine treatment of major depression. *American Journal of Psychiatry, 158*, 899–905.

Kerns, J. G., J. D. Cohen, A. M. Macdonald, R. Y. Cho, V. A. Stenger, and C. S. Carter. 2004. Anterior cingulate conflict monitoring and adjustments in control. *Science, 303*, 1023–1026.

Koechlin, E., C. Ody, and F. Kouneiher. 2003. The architecture of cognitive control in the human prefrontal cortex. *Science, 302*, 1181–1185.

Konishi, S., K. Nakajima, I. Uchida, M. Kameyama, K. Nakahara, K. Sekihara, et al. 1998a. Transient activation of inferior prefrontal cortex during cognitive set shifting. *Nature Neuroscience, 1*, 80–84.

Konishi, S., K. Nakajima, I. Uchida, H. Kikyo, M. Kameyama, and Y. Miyashita. 1999. Common inhibitory mechanism in human inferior prefrontal cortex revealed by event-related functional MRI. *Brain, 122*, 981–991.

Konishi, S., K. Nakajima, I. Uchida, K. Sekihara, and Y. Miyashita. 1998b. No-go dominant brain activity in human inferior prefrontal cortex revealed by functional magnetic resonance imaging. *European Journal of Neuroscience, 10,* 1209–1213.

Kumar, A., A. Newberg, A. Alavi, J. Berlin, R. Smith, and M. Reivich. 1993. Regional cerebral glucose metabolism in late-life depression and Alzheimer disease: A preliminary positron emission tomography study. *Proceedings of the National Academy of Sciences, 90,* 7019–7023.

Kumari, V., M. T. Mitterschiffthaler, J. D. Teasdale, G. S. Malhi, R. G. Brown, V. Giampietro, et al. 2003. Neural abnormalities during cognitive generation of affect in treatment-resistant depression. *Biological Psychiatry, 54,* 777–791.

Luu, P., and M. I. Posner. 2003. Anterior cingulate cortex regulation of sympathetic activity. *Brain, 126,* 2119–2120.

MacDonald, A. W., J. D. Cohen, V. A. Stenger, and C. S. Carter. 2000. Dissociating the role of dorsolateral prefrontal cortex and anterior cingulate cortex in cognitive control. *Science, 288,* 1835–1838.

Martin, S. D., E. Martin, S. S. Rai, M. A. Richards, R. Royal, and C. Eng. 2001. Brain blood flow changes in depressed patients treated with interpersonal psychotherapy or venlafaxine hydrochloride. *Archives of General Psychiatry, 58,* 641–664.

Matsumoto, K., and K. Tanaka. 2004. Conflict and cognitive control. *Science, 303,* 969–970.

Mayberg, H. S. 1997. Limbic-cortical dysregulation: A proposed model of depression. *Journal of Neuropsychiatry and Clinical Neurosciences, 9,* 471–481.

Mayberg, H. S., S. K. Brannan, R. K. Mahurin, P. A. Jerabek, J. S. Brickman, J. L. Tekell, et al. 1997. Cingulate function in depression: A potential predictor of treatment response. *Neuroreport, 8,* 1057–1061.

Mayberg, H. S., S. K. Brannan, R. K. Mahurin, S. McGinnin, J. A. Silva, J. L. Tekell, et al. 2000. Regional metabolic effects of fluoxetine in major depression: Serial changes and relationship to clinical response. *Biological Psychiatry, 48,* 830–843.

Mayberg, H. S., P. L. Lewis, and W. Regenold. 1994. Paralimbic hypoperfusion in unipolar depression. *Journal of Nuclear Medicine, 35,* 929–934.

Mayberg, H., M. Liotti, S. Brannan, S. McGinnis, R. Mahurin, P. Jarabeck, et al. 1999. Reciprocal limbic–cortical function and negative mood: Converging PET findings in depression and normal sadness. *American Journal of Psychiatry, 156,* 675–682.

Mayberg, H. S., J. A. Silva, S. K. Brannan, J. L. Tekell, R. K. Mahurin, S. McGinnis, et al. 2002. The functional neuroanatomy of the placebo effect. *American Journal of Psychiatry, 159,* 728–737.

Milad, M. R., and G. J. Quirk. 2002. Neurons in medial prefrontal cortex signal memory for fear extinction. *Nature, 420,* 70–74.

Milham, M. P., M. T. Banich, A. Webb, V. Barad, N. J. Cohen, T. Wszalek, et al. 2001. The relative involvement of anterior cingulate and prefrontal cortex in attentional control depends on the nature of conflict. *Brain Research: Cognitive Brain Research*, *12*, 467–473.

Miller, E. K. 1999. The prefrontal cortex: Complex neural properties for complex behavior. *Neuron*, *22*, 15–17.

Miller, E. K. 2000. The prefrontal cortex and cognitive control. *Nature Reviews Neuroscience*, *1*, 59–65.

Miller, E. K., and J. D. Cohen. 2001. An integrative theory of prefrontal cortex function. *Annual Review of Neuroscience*, *24*, 167–202.

Mirenowicz, J., and W. Schultz. 1994. Importance of unpredictability for reward responses in primate dopamine neurons. *Journal of Neurophysiology*, *72*, 1024–1027.

Mirenowicz, J., and W. Schultz. 1996. Preferential activation of midbrain dopamine neurons by appetitive rather than aversive stimuli. *Nature*, *379*, 449–451.

Montague, P. R., P. Dayan, and T. J. Sejnowski. 1996. A framework for mesencephalic dopamine systems based on predictive Hebbian learning. *Journal of Neuroscience*, *16*, 1936–1947.

Morgan, M. A., and J. E. LeDoux. 1995. Differential contribution of dorsal and ventral medial prefrontal cortex to the acquisition and extinction of conditioned fear in rats. *Behavioral Neuroscience*, *109*, 681–688.

Morgan, M. A., L. M. Romanski, and J. E. LeDoux. 1993. Extinction of emotional learning: Contribution of medial prefrontal cortex. *Neuroscience Letters*, *163*, 109–113.

Morgan, M. A., J. Schulkin, and J. E. LeDoux. 2003. Ventral medial prefrontal cortex and emotional preservation: The memory for prior extinction training. *Behavioral Brain Research*, *146*, 121–130.

Myers, K. M., and M. Davis. 2002. Behavioral and neural analysis of extinction. *Neuron*, *36*, 567–584.

Nielson, K. A., S. A. Langenecker, and H. Garavan. 2002. Differences in the functional neuroanatomy of inhibitory control across the adult life span. *Psychology and Aging*, *17*, 56–71.

Nitschke, J. B., and W. Heller. 2002. The neuropsychology of anxiety disorders: Affect, cognition, and neural circuitry. In *Biological Psychiatry*, ed. H. D'Haenen, J. A. den Boer, and P. Wilner, pp. 975–988. Chichester: John Wiley and Sons.

Nitschke, J. B., and W. Heller. 2005. Distinguishing neural substrates of heterogeneity among anxiety disorders. *International Review of Neurobiology*, *67*, 1–42.

Nitschke, J. B., W. Heller, M. A. Etienne, and G. A. Miller. 2004a. Prefrontal cortex activation differentiates processes affecting memory in depression. *Biological Psychology*, *67*, 125–143.

Nitschke, J. B., E. E. Nelson, B. D. Rusch, A. S. Fox, T. R. Oakes, and R. J. Davidson. 2004b. Orbitofrontal cortex tracks positive mood in mothers viewing pictures of their infants. *Neuroimage*, *21*, 583–592.

Nitschke, J. B., I. C. Sarinopoulos, K. L. Mackiewicz, H. S. Schaefer, and R. J. Davidson. 2006. Functional neuroanatomy of oversion and its anticipation. *Neuroimage*, *29*, 106–116.

Nolen-Hoeksema, S. 1987. Sex differences in unipolar depression: Evidence and theory. *Psychological Bulletin*, *101*, 259–282.

Nolen-Hoeksema, S. 1990. *Sex Differences in Depression*. Stanford, Calif.: Stanford University Press.

Nolen-Hoeksema, S., and J. Morrow. 1993. Effects of rumination and distraction on naturally occurring depressed mood. *Cognition and Emotion*, *7*, 561–570.

O'Doherty, J., M. L. Kringelbach, E. T. Rolls, J. Hornak, and C. Andrews. 2001. Abstract reward and punishment representations in the human orbitofrontal cortex. *Nature Neuroscience*, *4*, 95–102.

Pandya, D. N., G. W. Van Hoesen, and M. M. Mesulam. 1981. Efferent connections of the cingulate gyrus in the rhesus monkey. *Experimental Brain Research*, *42*, 319–330.

Passingham, R. 1993. *The Frontal Lobes and Voluntary Action*. Oxford: Oxford University Press.

Pine, D. S. 2003. Developmental psychobiology and response to threats: Relevance to trauma in children and adolescents. *Biological Psychiatry*, *53*, 796–808.

Pizzagalli, D., R. D. Pascual-Marqui, J. B. Nitschke, T. R. Oakes, C. L. Larson, H. C. Abercrombie, et al. 2001. Anterior cingulate activity as a predictor of degree of treatment response in major depression: Evidence from brain electrical tomography analysis. *American Journal of Psychiatry*, *158*, 405–415.

Ploghaus, A., I. Tracey, J. S. Gati, S. Clare, R. S. Menon, P. M. Matthews, et al. 1999. Dissociating pain from its anticipation in the human brain. *Science*, *284*, 1979–1981.

Quirk, G. J., G. K. Russo, J. L. Barron, and K. Lebron. 2000. The role of ventromedial prefrontal cortex in the recovery of extinguished fear. *Journal of Neuroscience*, *20*, 6225–6231.

Raichle, M. E., A. M. MacLeod, A. Z. Snyder, W. J. Powers, D. A. Gusnard, and G. L. Shulman. 2001. A default model of brain function. *Proceedings of the National Academy of Sciences*, *98*, 676–682.

Rainville, P., G. H. Duncan, D. D. Price, B. Carrier, and M. C. Bushnell. 1997. Pain affect encoded in human anterior cingulate but not somatosensory cortex. *Science*, *277*, 968–971.

Rauch, S. L., C. R. Savage, N. M. Alpert, D. Dougherty, A. Kendrick, T. Curran, et al. 1997. Probing striatal function in obsessive–compulsive disorder: A PET study of implicit sequence learning. *Journal of Neuropsychiatry and Clinical Neurosciences*, *9*, 568–573.

Rauch, S. L., C. R. Savage, N. M. Alpert, E. C. Miguel, L. Baer, H. C. R. Breiter, et al. 1995. A positron emission tomographic study of simple phobic symptom provocation. *Archives of General Psychiatry*, *52*, 20–28.

Rauch, S. L., B. A. van der Kolk, R. E. Fisler, N. M. Alpert, S. P. Orr, C. R. Savage, et al. 1996. A symptom provocation study of posttraumatic stress disorder using positron emission tomography and script-driven imagery. *Archives of General Psychiatry, 53,* 380–387.

Rolls, E. T. 1999. *The Brain and Emotion.* New York: Oxford University Press.

Rolls, E. T. 2000. The orbital frontal cortex and reward. *Cerebral Cortex, 10,* 284–294.

Sawamoto, N., M. Honda, T. Okada, T. Hanakawa, M. Kanda, H. Fukuyama, et al. 2000. Expectation of pain enhances responses to nonpainful somatosensory stimulation in the anterior cingulate cortex and parietal operculum/posterior insula: An event-related functional magnetic resonance imaging study. *Journal of Neuroscience, 20,* 7438–7445.

Schultz, W. 1998. Predictive reward signal of dopamine neurons. *Journal of Neurophysiology, 80,* 1–27.

Schultz, W., P. Apicella, and T. Ljungberg. 1993. Responses of monkey dopamine neurons to reward and conditioned stimuli during successive steps of learning a delayed response task. *Journal of Neuroscience, 13,* 900–913.

Shimamura, A. P. 2000. The role of the prefrontal cortex in dynamic filtering. *Psychobiology, 28,* 156–167.

Shin, L. M., R. J. McNally, S. M. Kosslyn, W. L. Thompson, S. L. Rauch, N. M. Alpert, et al. 1997. A positron emission tomographic study of symptom provocation in PTSD. *Annals of the New York Academy of Sciences, 821,* 521–523.

Small, D. M., M. D. Gregory, Y. E. Mak, D. Gitelman, M. M. Mesulam, and T. Parrish. 2003. Dissociation of neural representation of intensity and affective valuation in human gestation. *Neuron, 39,* 701–711.

Smith, E. E., and J. Jonides. 1999. Storage and executive processes in the frontal lobes. *Science, 283,* 1657–1661.

Urry, H. L., J. B. Nitschke, I. Dolski, D. C. Jackson, K. M. Dalton, C. J. Mueller, et al. 2004. Making a life worth living: Neural correlates of well-being. *Psychological Science, 15,* 367–372.

Van Veen, V., and C. S. Carter. 2002. The anterior cingulate as a conflict monitor: fMRI and ERP studies. *Physiology and Behavior, 77,* 477–482.

Vogt, B. A., and D. N. Pandya. 1987. Cingulate cortex of the rhesus monkey: II. Cortical afferents. *Journal of Comparative Neurology, 262,* 271–289.

Vogt, B. A., E. A. Nimchinsky, L. J. Vogt, and P. R. Hof. 1995. Human cingulate cortex: Surface features, flat maps, and the cytoarchitecture. *Journal of Comparative Neurology, 359,* 490–506.

Wager, T. D., J. K. Rilling, E. E. Smith, A. Sokolik, K. L. Casey, R. J. Davidson, et al. 2004. Placebo-induced changes in fMRI in the anticipation and experience of pain. *Science, 303,* 1162–1167.

Wallis, J. D., and E. K. Miller. 2003. Neuronal activity in primate dorsolateral and orbital prefrontal cortex during performance of a reward preference task. *European Journal of Neuroscience, 18,* 2069–2081.

Watkins, E., and R. G. Brown. 2002. Rumination and executive function in depression: An experimental study. *Journal of Neurology, Neurosurgery, and Psychiatry, 72*, 400–402.

Watkins, P. C. 2002. Implicit memory bias in depression. *Cognition and Emotion, 16*, 381–402.

Wise, S. P., E. A. Murray, and C. R. Gerfen. 1996. The frontal-basal ganglia system in primates. *Critical Reviews of Neurobiology, 10*, 317–356.

Wu, J. C., M. S. Buchsbaum, J. C. Gillin, S. Cadwell, M. Wiegand, A. Najafi, et al. 1999. Prediction of antidepressant effects of sleep deprivation by metabolic rates in the ventral anterior cingulate and medial prefrontal cortex. *American Journal of Psychiatry, 156*, 1149–1158.

Wu, J. C., J. C. Gillin, M. S. Buchsbaum, T. Hershey, J. C. Johnson, and W. E. Bunney. 1992. Effect of sleep deprivation on brain metabolism of depressed patients. *American Journal of Psychiatry, 149*, 538–543.

13 Action Control and Its Failure in Clinical Depression: A Neurocognitive Theory

Werner X. Schneider

Clinical depression is a mind/brain disorder of major public interest. It is a serious disorder that affects within a lifetime more than 15 percent of the population in western societies (e.g., Comer 2001). A central feature of this disorder is a strongly reduced level of activity (e.g., American Psychiatric Association 2000) that is characterized by reduced approach actions toward stimuli normally perceived as rewarding and an increased avoidance behavior toward stimuli perceived as threatening (e.g., Lewinsohn, Antonuccio, Steinmetz, and Teri, 1984; Jacobson, Martell, and Dimidjian 2001; Kasch, Rottenberg, Arnow, and Gotlib 2002). In other words, the selection and execution of actions is fundamentally disturbed in clinical depression. If misregulation of action control is a central feature of depression, then an adequate explanation of how actions are normally selected, prepared, initiated, and terminated should be a decisive step in understanding this disorder. Following this line of reasoning in the first part of the chapter, a neurocognitive framework for action control is outlined along thirteen main hypotheses. "Neurocognitive framework" here simply means that, first, basic functions such as motor, perceptual, memory, or emotional processes are conceptualized as information processing by neurons in various, partly overlapping neural networks of the primate brain, and, secondly, that not only are behavioral data from normal human subjects taken into consideration but also data from human functional imaging, electroencephalograph (EEG) and single-cell recording (in monkeys), and neuropsychological lesion studies are considered (e.g., Kosslyn and Koenig 1992; Gazzaniga, Ivry, and Mangun 2002).

Basically, the action control framework presented here attempts to specify how goals compete, how a winner is selected, how this winner controls the preparation, initiation, and termination of motor actions, how the successful or erroneous outcome of an action is monitored and evaluated with respect to the intended goal, and how this evaluation modifies long-term memory contents. Furthermore, volitional processes that allow, in case of competing action tendencies, shielding of the current goal-directed action as well as executive processes for the execution of nonroutine activities will be introduced as central elements of action control. Finally, the role of a processing mode called "state analysis" and of chronic stress in changing the neuro-cognitive processes and structures of action control in the primate brain will be sketched.

Based on this goal-based action control theory, the second section of the chapter will offer steps toward a neurocognitive theory of clinical depression along ten main hypotheses. The basic idea put forward here is that depression arises as a chronic stress response due to repeated failures in pursuing important goals. As a consequence of this chronic failure, two main types of changes in the action controlling brain are assumed to occur, that is, short-term state-dependent changes (e.g., depressive mood) and long-term changes (e.g., generalized negative probability estimates of action outcomes), which should cause inactivity, reduced approach behavior, and increased avoidance behavior as well as deficient executive control and volitional processes.

13.1 Goal-based Action Control

Action control can be conceptualized at many different levels (e.g., from single neurons to social attitudes) and by various theoretical perspectives (e.g., from con-nectionist networks to the ecological approach). The "neurocognitive action control framework" advocated here uses four main research traditions from psychology and cognitive neuroscience as starting points. These four sources will be described below before the action control theory itself will be presented in the form of thirteen hypotheses.

The first source for conceptualizing action control originates from a research tradi-tion that can be called the "functional perspective on information processing" (e.g., Allport 1980; Heuer and Sanders 1987; Neumann 1987; Prinz 1987; Schneider 1995; Hommel, Müsseler, Aschersleben, and Prinz 2001). It assumes that basic neurocog-nitive operations such as perceptual, motor, memory, or attentional processes have evolved in order to allow efficient action control. In other words, an adequate con-ceptualization of these basic neurocognitive processes requires understanding their functions in the control of actions. Work in our own lab applied this functional per-spective on information processing to the experimental investigation of visual atten-tional processes. My colleagues and I asked what role visual attention processes might have in controlling simple actions such as saccadic eye movements (e.g., Deubel and Schneider 1996) or hand movements (e.g., Schiegg, Deubel, and Schneider 2003). One basic conclusion from this line of experimental research is that "selection-for-perception" processes and "selection-for-action" processes are coupled by one common attentional control mechanism (for recent overviews, see Schneider and Deubel 2002; Deubel and Schneider, in press).

The second source refers to the idea that goal states in the sense of reference states (e.g., Miller, Galanter, and Pribram 1960) or action outcome states (action effects; e.g.,

Duncan 1986; Prinz 1987; Hommel 1993) control the selection of motor actions. One variant of this goal-based action control approach is grounded within the functional view on information processing mentioned above, that is, the work by Prinz, Hommel, and colleagues (e.g., Prinz 1987, 1997; Hommel 1993; Hommel et al. 2001). Its most recent version, the "Theory of Event Coding" (TEC; Hommel et al. 2001), starts with the assumption that actions are controlled by their "effects" ("events"). Decisively, the "perceived event codes" and the "to-be-produced-event codes" (action effects) are claimed to be represented within a common representation medium. This "common coding" assumption (e.g., Prinz 1997) predicts an overlap of perceptual and action planning processes—a prediction that has been confirmed by a substantial number of experimental studies (see Hommel et al. 2001 for an overview).

Given this functional perspective on control, a guideline question is how effect- or goal-based processes are mediating the efficient control of actions in the human brain. Outside the functional view on information processing, this idea of goal-based control of motor actions has up to now not attracted a great deal of systematic research in cognitive neuroscience. The situation is beginning to change, and an increasing number of experimental and neural network studies have recently addressed the question how goal states are represented within different parts of the primate brain (e.g., prefrontal cortex; PFC) and how they may contribute to the control of action selection (e.g., Braver and Cohen 2000; Matsumoto and Tanaka 2004; Ramnani and Owen 2004; Schultz 2004). For simple actions such as saccadic eye movements, experimental and computational neurocognitive studies have now specified in considerable detail how the goal-based selection and execution of such actions may be carried out by neural computations in interacting cortical and subcortical areas (see, e.g., Glimcher 2003; Brown, Bullock, and Grossberg 2004).

The third source of the action control framework suggested here refers to the German tradition of human motivation and volition research that distinguishes action selection from action realization (for overviews, see, e.g., Ach 1935; Kuhl 1984; Heckhausen 1991). A first central assumption of this kind of approach is that two main factors for determining action selection are the value of an action, on the one hand—often expressed in terms of "incentives" or "emotional values"—and, on the other hand, the estimated probability that these actions lead to the intended goal state (see, e.g., Atkinson 1957; Weiner 1980; Heckhausen 1991). A second assumption is that action selection processes should be distinguished from action realization processes (for overviews, see, e.g., Ach 1935; Kuhl 1984; Heckhausen 1991). "Action selection" refers to motivational processes that choose one action tendency among several other tendencies. "Action realization" refers to volitional processes that allow initiation and continuation of a motor action in case of strongly competing action tendencies. Up to now, theories of motivation and volition in this tradition have mainly relied on the social science research approach, that is, for example, on verbal report data (e.g.,

Kuhl 1984; Carver and Scheier 1990; Heckhausen 1991; Grawe 2004; see also Cohen and Gollwitzer, this volume). Imaging, neuropsychological, and neurophysiological data, as well as the language of neural information processing, did not play a prominent role in this kind of approach—see, however, for instance, Goschke (2003), for a recent attempt in this direction, and, see, for instance, Adolphs (2003) for a brain science shift in social psychology in general.

Finally, the fourth source for conceptualizing action control draws on recent ideas and experimental work on "executive control" processes and their potential subdivision within the prefrontal cortex and other parts of the primate brain. A diverse set of functions have been investigated under the labels "executive control" or "cognitive control," including processes such as "planning in problem solving," "shifting the task set (intention)," "suppressing a prepotent response," and "error correction" (e.g., Norman and Shallice 1986; Miller and Cohen 2001; Monsell 1996). A central common feature of these executive functions is the idea that they are required in order to prepare and execute "nonroutine" actions (e.g., Norman and Shallice 1986), that is, actions that cannot be carried out by combining current environmental information with motor information retrieved from long-term memory (e.g., stored schemas of sensorimotor skills). Based on neuropsychological, single-cell, and imaging data, the prefrontal cortex has been suggested as a central site for implementing these executive control functions (for overviews, see, e.g., Passingham 1993; Fuster 1997; Schneider, Owen, and Duncan 2000). A lively debate is still going on concerning whether and which control functions may be carried out by different parts of the PFC (e.g., Duncan and Owen 2000; Grafman and Krueger, this volume; Owen, this volume; Burgess et al., this volume). Despite this debate, a theoretical framework on control—the "biased competition" approach—that is shared by many researchers (e.g., Norman and Shallice 1986; Desimone and Duncan 1995; Miller and Cohen 2001) assumes that executive PFC control processes modulate the competition of sensory-driven lower-order brain processes located in parts of the brain posterior to PFC.

The neurocognitive theory of goal-based action control proposed here not only relies on these four theoretical sources but also attempts to combine them in a new way. For instance, the functional view of information processing—the "cognitive side" of action control—will be linked with the social science research tradition on motivation and volition—the dynamic side of action control. Furthermore, the biased competition hypothesis from the executive control literature will be used to specify the common coding assumption of perceptual and motor processes. Moreover, beyond combining elements from these four sources, a few new suggestions about action control will be made, for instance, how mood states may arise due to long-term monitoring of action control outcomes and how these mood states may influence the current selection and execution of motor actions. The overall action control theory will be presented in the following sections in the form of thirteen hypotheses (13.1.1

to 13.1.14). These hypotheses are by far not meant as a complete theory of action control—the selection of questions and the issues addressed by the theory are heavily influenced by the aim to develop an action control account of clinical depression. This account will be specified in the second part of the chapter.

13.1.1 Actions Are Controlled by Goal States, and Goal States Refer to Representations of Action Outcomes

The most fundamental assumption of the action control framework proposed here is that actions are controlled by goal states (e.g., Miller, Galanter, and Pribram 1960; Powers 1973; Anderson 1983; Duncan 1986; Carver and Scheier 1990; Hommel et al. 2001; Grawe 2004; Matsumoto and Tanaka 2004). Here, the term "goal state" refers to a state or an event that has not yet occurred. More precisely, the content of a goal state represents the outcome (or effect) of an action (see, e.g., Duncan 1986; Prinz 1987; Hommel 1993; Grawe 2004). This implies that each action is carried out in order to achieve a certain effect or outcome—an outcome that is extracted by the perceptual system and stored as a goal state in reference to the action.

Goal states can refer not just to end states of actions but also to the results of ongoing actions (e.g., parts of the melody when playing piano) or the outcomes of complex events (for complex events and their potential structure, see Grafman and Krueger, this volume). In case of events, a dynamic variable is the reference value (goal state).

13.1.2 Goal States Are Intrinsically Linked to Motor Action Representations in the Form of "Goal–Action Episodes" (Common Coding Assumption)

What is the relationship between goal states and motor action representations? It is suggested here that they are always and intrinsically linked in the form of a "goal–action episode." In other words, it is claimed that representations of goals and actions do not exist in isolation but always as goal–action units, named here goal–action episodes. Every goal state should be connected to a corresponding (motor) action representation.[1] Many goal states can be realized by different motor actions. For instance, in football a "goal" can be shot by kicking the ball either via foot or via head. Importantly, it is suggested here that each combination of a goal state (e.g., shooting a "goal") with a motor action (e.g., foot or head kicking) is assumed to form an individual goal–action episode.

Even for highly overlearned and compatible actions such as reading, in which simple and direct links between stimuli (e.g., words) and motor actions (verbal responses) exist, individual actions or responses are assumed to be connected to the corresponding goal states, that is, representations of action outcomes. That is, in case of reading aloud, the verbal response to a word should be always connected to its intended sound pattern. This intrinsic link between "perceptual" goal states, on the one hand, and "motor" action processes, on the other hand, implements a version of the "common coding" approach to perception and action (e.g., Prinz 1987; Hommel et al. 2001) mentioned before as the second theoretical source. A new feature for this common coding approach is the assumption that goal–action episodes are selection units of competition for action control—see the next hypothesis, 13.1.3.

Goal–action episodes differ in respect to several dimensions (see also Grafman and Krueger, this volume). One dimension refers to the temporal domain of the goal states (e.g., Fuster 1997, 2001). In simple forms of goal pursuit, "goal states" refer to environmental stimuli that are always present during the pursuit (e.g., seeing, grasping, and eating a candy located directly in front of the actor). In more complex temporal forms, the goal stimuli are not all the time physically present and have to be maintained in working memory (e.g., imaging a special candy located somewhere in a drawer at home). Following Fuster (1997), pursuing temporally more distant goal states should require an involvement of PFC areas. A second dimension of goal states refers to the flexibility of the goal–action connection of episodes. Either the connection can be well-learned and stored in long-term memory (LTM) or, alternatively, the episode may take the form of a temporary connection (e.g., short-term memory) between the goal state and the representation of an action—"mental simulation" (and not real execution) of a possible action for goal state achievement may be used in this case for setting up the temporary connection. Such flexible connections allow the linking of new but not yet learned couplings of goal states and motor action processes in an ad hoc manner (e.g., for implementing instructions).

A third dimension of goal–action episodes refers to their content domain and complexity. Goal states can refer to very simple action outcomes such as the landing position of a saccadic eye movement or the results of complex social actions—see Grafman and Krueger (this volume) for a neuropsychologically based attempt to structure goal domains of different contents and complexities with respect to different prefrontal lobe areas. Analogous to this, motor action processes can have different levels of complexities, ranging from simple motor patterns for saccade generation to more complex motor action patterns involved in complex skills such as playing football (see, e.g., Rosenbaum 1991; Arbib 1990; Krakauer and Ghez 2000; Grafman and Krueger, this volume). For simple actions just a few motor brain areas are recruited, while more complex actions presuppose the activation of a wide-ranging network of motor areas (e.g., Krakauer and Ghez 2000). Importantly, the "action" part of an episode refers here only to medium and high levels of motor representations and not to low-level representations (e.g., muscle-specific motor patterns).

13.1.3   The Units That Compete for Action Control Are "Goal–Action Episodes," and Only One "Goal–Action Episode" at a Time Controls the Execution of an Action

As mentioned above, the neurocognitive theory of action control suggested here relies on the biased competition approach to the control of attention and executive functions within the brain (e.g., Phaf, van der Heijden, and Hudson 1990; Desimone and

Duncan 1995; Miller and Cohen 2001). In line with this approach, it is assumed that activated "goal–action episodes" compete for controlling the current action. Neither representations of goals in isolation nor of actions in isolation should compete but only units of individual goal–action episodes.

Competition is assumed to be regulated by the activation value (e.g., Cohen, Dunbar, and McClelland 1990; Phaf, van der Heijden, and Hudson 1990) of an episode—for factors that determine this value, see hypothesis 13.1.5. The winner of the competition is always one episode—see hypothesis 13.1.4. Competition between goal–action episodes is probably organized in a domain-specific way (see, e.g., Phaf, van der Heijden, and Hudson 1990). In line with Grafman and colleagues (e.g., Grafman and Krueger, this volume), it is assumed that complex goal–action episodes— which may be identical to Grafman and Krueger's (this volume) "structured event complex" (SEC) sequences—and also less complex "episodes" containing parts of SECs—are stored in prefrontal cortex. These sequences should also compete as goal–action episodes.[2]

Why is competition between episodes and the determination of one winner for controlling the execution of action necessary? The functional view of information processing suggested the following answer: Given that humans (and other primates) have a large repertoire of stored goals and corresponding actions, and given that internal (e.g., body-related) and external environmental stimuli often activate several goals simultaneously, it is important to prevent behavioral chaos—chaos that may, for instance, emerge from the simultaneous execution of incompatible actions. The behavioral chaos can be prevented by allowing only one goal–action episode at a time (e.g., Neumann 1987)—or "one list of goals" (Duncan 1986)[3] at a time—to control the execution of overt action (see, also, Norman and Shallice 1986). Here, this episode is called the "goal–action episode in charge." This capacity limitation of one episode in charge at a time refers only to the currently highest level of control. At lower levels of the goal–action episode hierarchy, several "subgoal–action episodes" might be simultaneously activated.

13.1.4 The Competition between Goal–Action Episodes Is Regulated on the Basis of Their Activation Values that, in Turn, Are Determined by Stored or Anticipated Emotional States, Importance, Urgency, and Action–Outcome Probability Estimates

External and internal stimuli usually activate several goals simultaneously that are stored in LTM. Which goal–action episode controls the current action and gets the status of the episode in charge? It is assumed that the episode with the highest activation value wins the competition. The selection principle is suggested to rely on the winner-takes-all principle of many connectionist models (e.g., Phaf, van der Heijden, and Hudson 1990; Cohen, Dunbar, and McClelland 1990). Given this winner-takes-all principle for competition resolution, the question arises of how the activation values of goal–action episodes are determined. In line with research on human motivation (see, e.g., Weiner 1980; Heckhausen 1991; Damasio 1996) it is assumed that four not necessarily exclusive variables determine the episode activation value, namely, emotional states stored in relationship to past attempts of the action to pursue the goal, importance of the goal–action episode, urgency of the goal–action episode, and the estimated probability that the action will be able to achieve the goal state; this list of factors is not meant to be complete.

First, in line with classical work on the psychology (e.g., Atkinson 1957; for an overview, see Weiner 1980) and neuroscience of motivation (e.g., Damasio 1996; Rolls 2000) it is assumed that competition and selection among goal–action episodes depends on stored emotional states associated in the past with successful or failed goal pursuit. "Emotions" may refer to the evaluation of the action outcome itself—for example, emotions of a pleasant or unpleasant kind. Furthermore, emotions may emerge as a consequence of successful or failed goal pursuit, that is, on the basis of the comparison between expected goal state (retrieved from memory or anticipated via mental simulation) and actual action outcome. Different kinds of emotions are probably computed in different brain areas such as amygdala or orbitofrontal cortex (e.g., LeDoux 2000; Rolls 2000).

Consistent with the dimension approach to emotion (for an overview, see, e.g., Gross 1999), it is assumed that emotions can be categorized as either of the positive (pleasant) or negative (unpleasant) type. It is assumed that these two types of emotions determine which kind of goal—desired or undesired—is generated (see also Gray 1990; Davidson et al. 2002) and which kind of episode is emerging. If in connection with an episode primarily positive emotions are stored, the goal state should be a desired state and the episode will be an approach episode. If in connection with an episode primarily negative emotions are stored, the goal state should be an undesired state and the episode will be an avoidance or withdrawal episode—a possible consequence may be a withdrawal action away from the goal object (e.g., Gray 1990; Davidson et al. 2002). A further function of emotion—besides tagging a goal state of an episode as a desired or undesired state—may be to influence the episode competition value via the strength of emotions. The strength of a conscious emotion (feeling) may be directly related to the competition value. The stronger a feeling evoked by a previous pursuit of a goal episode is, the higher the current competition value of this episode should be (see also Damasio 1996; Rolls 2000). Besides relying on stored information (LTM) about emotions associated with past goal pursuit, the mental simulation of a new action, more precisely, the mental simulation of the execution of an action not performed before, should also be able to anticipate possible emotions associated with successful or failing goal pursuit and should therefore be able to bias episode competition.

Second, it is assumed that goal competition depends on urgency and on importance of the goal state (see, e.g., Lewin 1926; Heckhausen and Kuhl 1985). Some goals such as the central representation of physiological needs (e.g., hunger, thirst, sex) have different degrees of urgency depending on the currently computed state of deprivation. The stronger the deprivation, the higher will be the urgency value of the corresponding goal. Another important factor in determining the urgency of an avoidance action is the expected occurrence of an undesired state. The closer the time of occurrence is, the more urgent should be the goal and the more urgent should be the initiation of an avoidance action.

"Importance" refers to a further class of factors determining the goal competition value. It is reasonable to assume that goals related to fundamental needs (e.g., hunger) should have a relatively high importance value. Social psychologists have long been claiming that goals in humans related to central aspects of the "self" (e.g., self-esteem; e.g., Crocker and Park 2004; Grawe 2004) have a high priority in action control. It is not claimed here that the variables of importance and urgency are completely separate from emotional processes—both variables may be connected to certain affective states. Currently, however, at least to my knowledge, no specific and empirically tested hypotheses about the relationship between importance, urgency, and emotions exist.

Third, a further factor that determines the competition value of an episode refers to action–outcome probability estimates (e.g., Weiner 1980; Heckhausen 1991). Probability estimates can be based on records of actual action executions of the past stored in LTM. They can also be derived from anticipation, that is, mental simulation, of the action execution. At least two kinds of probability estimates in relationship to goals and actions have to be distinguished (see Heckhausen 1991 for further options). First, the estimate can refer to the probability that a certain action is able to achieve the goal state—independent of a specific actor. Second, the estimate can refer to the availability of the required action to the actor—it reflects the action competence of the actor—similar to Bandura's (1977) concept of self-efficacy. The first probability to achieve goal X by action Y may be high—given knowledge of the actor about this relationship—but the second probability that the actor himself or herself is able to produce the action—either by LTM retrieval or by mental simulation—may be quite low.

How importance and probability estimates may be represented in the different areas of the primate brain has been investigated for "visual-saccadic decision making"—see, for example, Glimcher (2003) and Schultz (2004). Parietal and frontal areas at the cortical level, as well as parts of the basal ganglia (BSG; e.g., striatum) at the subcortical level, seem to be involved in this kind of computation.

13.1.5 When the Context for Initiation Is Perceived, a Go Signal Will Be Issued for Action Execution

Not every goal–action episode that wins the competition immediately causes the execution of corresponding motor processes and, therefore, an overt action. Humans are able to delay actions that have been completely prepared. Whether the motor action process of an episode is executed or not is a matter of context. Human action is characterized by a high degree of context dependence (e.g., Miller and Cohen 2001). Context can refer to spatial, temporal, and more complex, semantically defined conditions (see also Grafman and Kreuger, this volume). It is assumed that these context representations are part of goal–action episodes. This context dependency of human action and cognition is sometimes computationally modeled as control by "If condition X, then action Y" linkages, also called "conditional operations" (e.g., Newell and Simon 1972; Anderson 1983; Meyer and Kieras 1997). In our terminology, this means "If context X, then action Y." Such linkages have been found to be coded at the level of single neurons within the PFC (see, e.g., for an overview, Miller and Cohen 2001).

How might the action execution be controlled? A go signal controlled by the BSG is a very plausible suggestion given current evidence (e.g., Schulz 1999; DeLong 2000).[4] Once the context for initiation of a motor action process is detected, inhibition by BSG should be removed, that is, a go signal for the execution the goal–action episode, more precisely, for executing the motor action part of the episode, should be given.

How does the ability of human "prospective memory" (e.g., Burgess et al. 2003; Burgess et al., this volume) fit into this conception? For instance, think about Lewin's (1926) famous example of prospective memory "in action," namely, the intended action to put a recently written letter in a mailbox when such a mailbox is encountered on one's way home. Here, the current action (e.g., walking home) has to be briefly interrupted for performing the context-adequate action stored in prospective memory, namely, the action of putting a letter into a mailbox. In order to explain how processing works in such prospective memory examples, it is assumed that the perceived context information not only could lead to a go signal of a prepared and inhibited episode but may also deliver input to the goal–action episode competition system that may cause the replacement of the current episode by the context-defined episode. Structures involved in setting up and storing context for prospective action are probably the hippocampus (HC; e.g., Jeffery 2004) and maybe PFC area 10 (see Burgess et al. this volume, but also Ramnani and Owen 2004; Miller and Cohen 2001).

13.1.6 Persistence and Intensity of Action Execution as well as the Probability of a Goal–Action Episode Shift Depend on the Episode Competition Value

Persistence and intensity of motor action execution are important parameters in action control (e.g., Heckhausen 1991). If an action does not lead to immediate success, a decision has to be made in terms of persistence, that is, how often and how long attempts to achieve the goal via this action should be executed. It is assumed here that the goal–action episode competition value determines persistence (see also

Heckhausen 1991). The higher the competition value, the stronger the degree of persistence should be. Furthermore, the intensity of a motor action process execution should also depend on the competition value. The higher the competition value, the higher the intensity should be. Finally, the competition value should be related to the probability of a goal–action episode shift, that is, a change of the episode in charge (see, e.g., Goschke 2003). The lower the competition value of the current goal (e.g., due to low importance or urgency), the higher goal shift probability should be—see, for example, Monsell (1996) for an overview on the experimental literature on goal (task) shifting factors.

13.1.7 Executive Control Processes Are Called in Case of Action Failure, That Is, When the Action Did Not Produce the Intended Goal State and When the Probability Estimate for Being Successful by Repeating the Action Is Low

Sometimes, routine actions stored in LTM are not sufficient to achieve the intended goal state. As stated in the introduction to this section, executive control processes should be called in this case of nonroutine action (e.g., Norman and Shallice 1986). More precisely, it is suggested here that executive processes are called when the result of a simulated or actually executed motor action process is "negative," that is, the action of the winning episode was not able to achieve the goal state and the discrepancy between goal state and action outcome continues to exist. A second necessary condition for the call should be a low probability estimate that a repeated execution of the currently selected and failing action will be successful (see also Botvinick, Carter, Braver, Barch, and Cohen 2001 for a different concept of calling executive operations). If the probability is sufficiently high, persistence of the already selected action should occur. A further condition for triggering executive processes might be given when the rate of discrepancy reduction between current state and goal state (e.g., Miller, Galanter, and Pribram 1960) is too slow (e.g., Carver and Scheier 1990).

Which brain areas may be important for calling executive processes? Executive processes themselves are probably stored within the (lateral) PFC (see, e.g., Duncan and Owen 2000). The detection of the need to use executive processes—discrepancy detection—and the call of these processes is assumed to be carried out by the anterior cingulate cortex (ACC); for imaging, EEG, and other sources of empirical evidence, see, for example, Botvinick, et al. (2001), Paus (2001), and Holroyd and Coles (2002). For instance, the error-related negativity (ERN) in EEG recordings observed after action errors can be localized within the ACC (see, e.g., Holroyd and Coles 2002). ERN may not just reflect action failures (errors) but may also arise when executive operations are called, that is, when the actual or simulated action application was not successful and the probability estimate for a successful, repeated application of the same action is low; for a different view on executive control and the role of the ACC, see Botvinik et al. (2001).

13.1.8 If the Goal–Action Episode in Charge Is in Danger of Being Replaced by Competitors, Then Volitional Processes Located within the ACC Accomplish Shielding of the Episode in Charge

The term "volition" is sometimes used in the broad sense of the word, equating voli-tion with the control of "consciously-based" action (see, e.g., Grafman and Krueger, this volume). Here, the term should be used in the narrow sense (e.g., Ach 1935; Kuhl 1984; Heckhausen 1991), namely, that the currently pursued action (goal–action episode in charge) is in danger of being replaced by competing actions (episodes) that may be internally or externally cued[5] and that shielding processes are required for maintaining the current goal pursuit (see also Prinz, Dennett, and Sebanz, this volume). For instance, writing a paper during a beautiful summer day may be threat-ened by a friend asking (an external event) for company to go for an ice cream. Alternatively, an internal event such as a feeling of hunger might compete with writing a paper. Within the framework of the action control theory suggested here, these situations can be characterized as follows: The current goal–action episode competes with other externally or internally triggered episodes that have a higher current competition value. Without additional processes, the episode in charge would be replaced by another competing episode. Extra volitional processes are needed that temporarily support the current episode in charge with additional activation so that its overall activation is higher than the activation of the competitors.

This idea presupposes that the danger of replacement of the current episode in charge is detected and that this detection causes a call of volitional shielding processes (see also, e.g., Ach 1935; Kuhl 1984). The shielding process may work by supplying extra phasic activation to the goal in danger. This phasic activation should then increase the goal–action episode competition to a value sufficient for staying in charge. One way to implement this extra activation supply would be to instantiate a further temporary goal of high activation value that might correspond to the feeling of "will" and that sends activation to the episode in danger. A loop between this volitional goal episode and the episode in danger may be a possible mechanism for maintaining the increased phasic activation.

An experimental example of such a volitional situation is the Stroop task, in which the strong prepotent response tendency of word reading has to be suppressed and the weaker response tendency of color naming has to be executed for correct performance. Without the experimental instruction, subjects would read the word, but the tempo-rary goal of color naming prevents this and allows articulation of the color name. Viewed this way, the executive process of inhibiting a prepotent response (e.g., Miller and Cohen 2001) would be a volitional process (see below). Volitionally supported goal–action episodes should not be irreplaceable—otherwise, important environ-mental changes (e.g., a dangerous event) would not be able to replace the shielded goal (e.g., Goschke 2003). An experimental technique that measures the volitional capabilities of subjects is the "goal neglect" paradigm developed by Duncan and colleagues (e.g., Duncan et al. 1996). The task requires shifting occasionally from the currently executed main task to a less-often-performed secondary task. The call for the task shifting is given by an environmental signal. For correct performance, the task shifting set (including the signal) has to be maintained in prospective memory. Subjects with PFC damage or with a low G factor show "goal neglect," that is, they have problems in carrying out the task shift (see Duncan et al. 1996). Within the action control theory suggested here, goal neglect should arise due to volitional problems in maintaining the temporary supported goal episode of the secondary task.

Given the anatomical connections of the ACC with other action-control-related cortical and subcortical structures, and imaging data that ACC is activated in Stroop and other volitional tasks (for an overview, see e.g., Miller and Cohen 2001; Paus 2001), and findings that large ACC lesions can lead to akinetic mutism—a disorder of volitional action initiation (see, e.g., Bush, Luu, and Posner 2000; Paus 2001; Holroyd and Coles 2002)—this brain structure seems to be a reasonable candidate for calling and executing volitional control. Volitional processes are usually perceived as "effortful"; the same holds for most executive processes that are needed in case of nonroutine actions and should also be mediated by the ACC (see section 13.1.7). As stated above, volitional processes may refer to a subset of executive control processes (e.g., inhibition of prepotent response) that are called when the current goal–action episode is in danger of being replaced. This assumption fits with the last hypothesis in section 13.1.7 saying that the ACC should be involved in calling executive control processes. Thus, when effortful processing in the sense of executive or volitional processing is required for action control, the ACC should be the structure for calling and executing this type of processing.

13.1.9 Simulated or Real Outcomes of Actions Lead to the Generation of Emotional States, to Modifications of the LTM Connections between Goal–Action Episodes and Emotional States, and to Computations of Probability Estimates of Action–Outcome (Goal) Relationships

"Goal states" refers to the intended outcomes of an action associated with the goal–action episode. When the outcome of an action is perceived—due to either an actually executed or an anticipated (simulated) action—then a comparison between the goal state, (the intended action outcome) and actual action result should be made (e.g., Miller, Galanter, and Pribam 1960; Carver and Scheier 1990). Three kinds of events are important for action control as an outcome of this comparison process, namely, the generation of emotional states, LTM modifications of connections between goal–action episodes and emotional states, and the computation of action–outcome (goal) probability estimates.

First, depending on the result of this comparison, and influenced by context processing (e.g., attributions of action result; e.g., Weiner 1980; Heckhausen 1991), emotional states, more precisely, feelings (the conscious part of emotions), should arise. In case of success, that is, when a desired goal state is realized, positive feelings of pleasure or happiness may arise. When an undesired state is removed or avoided, positive feelings of relief should arise (see, e.g., Weiner 1980; Heckhausen 1991; Rolls 2000). The intensity of the feeling may be modulated by the importance and urgency of the goal pursuit. In case of a failure to achieve the goal state, negative emotions should arise—for example, anger or shame depending on context and further cognitive inference processes (see, e.g., Weiner 1980; Heckhausen 1991). A brain structure for computing emotional states based on the comparison between the intended (goal) state and the actual action outcome may be the ACC. As stated above in sections 13.1.7 and 13.1.8, the ACC is possibly involved in detecting discrepancies for calling executive and volitional processes, so it seems reasonable to suggest that the ACC may also be involved in detecting this emotion-generating discrepancy. The emotional subdivision of the ACC (e.g., Bush, Luu, and Posner 2000) may be the place for generating the comparison-based emotions that may actually be stored somewhere else in the cortex (e.g., amygdala or other limbic structures).

Second, the comparison between intended and actual action outcome should cause modifications of long-term connections between the goal–action episode and emotions. In general, connections between emotions and an episode should be adjusted according to the action result and its comparison-based emotional state. Connections of episodes to emotional states stored as results of previous actions may be weakened or strengthened depending on the congruency between expected and actual (or simulated) outcome states; connections to emotional states that arise for the first time as a result of an action may be stored as new connections between emotion and episode.

Third, probability estimates of action–outcome (action–goal state) relationships should be modified as a result of goal pursuit. If the action was successful, then an increase in the probability estimate that the action will lead to the goal state (intended outcome) should occur. In the case of failure, a decrease in the estimate should occur. Instead of modifying explicit representations of probability estimates, the connection between the goal state and action representations could also be modified as an implicit representation of probability estimates. For instance, an action failure could lead to a weakening of the goal–action connection within the episode.

Given the suggestion that the ACC computes the discrepancies for issuing comparison-based emotional states, it seems reasonable to assume that the ACC may initiate—in combination with the BSG—these LTM modifications of connections between goal states, action representations, and emotional states (e.g., Holroyd and Coles 2002) and may also initiate the probability estimate modifications.

13.1.10 "Metamonitoring" of Action Outcomes Generates Bias Signals for Episode Competition in the Form of "Probability Estimates of Action–Outcome Relationships" and Mood States

For efficient action control, it is necessary not just to monitor and store the outcomes of individual actions but also to metamonitor the results of the same action across repeated executions over a longer time scale. That metamonitoring plays a central role in action control has already been suggested by Carver and Scheier (1990, 1999), but they meant something different by this concept. They suggested that a low-level comparison process should compute the discrepancy between the goal state and the current action result, while a metacomparison process should detect the "speed" of discrepancy reduction during action execution. Here it is agreed with Carver and Scheier (1990, 1999) that such a metamonitoring process exists, but its function is conceptualized differently. It should not check the rate of discrepancy reduction for each individual action execution, but it should check the results of a repeated pursuit of the same goal–action episode at a longer time scale, that is, involving the stored results of several instances of pursuing the same goal.

Moreover, it is suggested here that metamonitoring leads to two major consequences. First, probability estimates of the action–outcome relationships (see section 13.1.9)—in the case of explicit representations called "beliefs"—should be produced or modified, and, second, "moods" should be generated. First, these beliefs should refer to the previously mentioned explicit (probably propositional) representations of probability estimates that an action leads to the achievement of the goal state of the episode. A major function of beliefs or implicit probability estimates is to bias episode competition. For instance, in the case of one goal and several possible actions for realizing the goal, competition between the corresponding episodes[6] should occur. A high probability of an action X for successful goal pursuit should increase the chance of the corresponding episode's being selected, while a low probability of another action Y should decrease it (see Glimcher 2003 for evidence of such processes in parietal cortex in saccadic decision making).

Second, high-level monitoring should generate not just beliefs, but also moods—affective states with longer durations than emotions that are characterized by brief durations (e.g., Gross 1999). Along the suggestions about comparison-based emotions of section 13.1.9, it is assumed that successful pursuit of the same goal–action episode on several occasions (over time), that is, successful and repeated discrepancy reduction between the goal state and the current state (Miller et al. 1960) by the same action, should lead to a positive, happy, optimistic mood. Repeated failure to reduce discrepancies should lead to an angry, hostile, or depressive mood dependent on attribution processes (see, e.g., Weiner 1980). A major function of mood is to bias the episode selection process. It is assumed here that mood states strengthen—in line with the congruency principle—emotions of the same type (positive or negative emotion)

during the episode competition and weaken emotions of the opposite type. Consequently, episodes containing mainly emotions of the same type as the current mood
will receive an activation increase of their competition value, and episodes containing mainly emotions of the opposite type will receive a reduction of the competition
value. For instance, in the case of a depressive mood, those avoidance episodes associated with negative emotions should get a higher competition weight as compared
to approach episodes with positive emotional values. Therefore, depressive mood
should increase the chance of withdrawal or avoidance behavior controlled by
episodes with negative emotional tags, and it should decrease the chance of approach
behavior controlled by episodes with positive emotional tags.

Goal pursuit might be monitored not only regarding a certain goal but also with
respect to a domain of goals (e.g., academic achievements). The results of such a
domain-wide metamonitoring process may be estimations of "own abilities," that is,
"self-related beliefs" (see, e.g., Heckhausen 1991). Verbally specified self-estimations
such as "I am a loser" may reflect the result of a generalized metamonitoring process
that refers to several important domains of life (e.g., personal relationships, professional career, faith, etc.). These generalized monitoring results should lead to generalized probability estimates.

13.1.11 Two Modes of Goal-based Action Control Are the "Goal Realization" versus "State Analysis" Mode for Goal Restructuring and Disengagement

A large part of the "mental life" of humans is concerned with the realization of a
certain goal (highest level of control) at a certain time. The goal–action episode in
charge often shifts during one day. Sometimes, "online acting" is interrupted by action
planning—but nevertheless, this planning process can also be done in the service of
the episode in charge. This mode of pursing one current goal–action episode at a time
is called "goal realization" mode here. If complex real-world problems have to be
tackled (see Grafman and Krueger, this volume), this goal pursuit mode implies
not only the execution of motor actions but also the implementation of executive
processes (e.g., mental simulation processes) for problem solving.

However, when repeated attempts in pursuing the current goal (e.g., via several different actions) do not generate the intended goal state and when no solution for pursuing the goal seems to be available to the organism, then a different mode of action
control will be called, namely, the "state analysis" mode (see also Kuhl 1984, 1994).[7]
The main function of the state analysis mode is to analyze the implication of a failure
of goal–action episode realization with respect to other stored and possibly important goals (e.g., self-esteem related goals; e.g., Crocker and Park 2004) and to allow
restructuring of the failing goal or other goals in terms of competition value and
goal compatibility. As part of this restructuring process "disengagement" of goals may

occur (e.g., Klinger 1975)—disengagement in the sense of reducing the ability of a goal and its episode to win the competition for action control. This LTM modification process could be realized by changing the stored emotional states associated with the goal episode—sometimes a difficult thing to accomplish given that fundamental needs may be connected to important goals (e.g., Klinger 1975; Grawe 2004).

What may be the calling condition for the state analysis mode? If a repeated failure to achieve an important goal—computed by the metamonitoring process—is detected and if executive mental simulation was not able to generate a solution to these failures, then the state analysis mode should be issued. Furthermore, "rumination" (e.g., Nolen-Hoeksema 2000; see section 13.2.7 below) should be one possible feature of state analysis after repeated failure. Moreover, humans should at one time either be in the goal realization or in the state analysis mode of action control.

13.1.12 A "Stress Response" Elicited by "Goal Pursuit in Danger" Leads to Increased Cortisol Output

A stressor is viewed here as a stimulus or event that activates a goal–action episode (in charge) that is characterized by high importance, high urgency, and low probability of successful goal pursuit. In other words, a stressful event activates an episode whose realization is in danger—the calling condition for executive and possibly volitional processes. Due to the action-outcome-related probability estimation, normal (routine) processing is expected to be insufficient for achieving the goal state. Extra effortful processing—either executive or volitional processes—should be mobilized in this case. In line with substantial evidence (for an overview, see McEwen 2002), it is assumed here that in the case of a stressful event what is initiated is not just effortful executive and volitional processing but also an increase of cortisol emission for delivering the extra energy for coping with the event—the cortisol level increase may be directly related to the degree of effortful processing.

What "stress" adds to the issue of estimated nonobtainment of important goals is the dimension of urgency. The goal pursuit cannot be delayed. In this case, it seems reasonable to assume that the degree of stressfulness of a goal–action episode in danger may depend on the goal competition value. Following section 13.1.4, the competition value should depend on how low the probability of achieving the goal by a certain action is—uncontrollability (e.g., Heckhausen 1991; Dickerson and Kemeny 2004)—and on how urgent and important the goal achievement is. The higher the urgency and importance are, and the lower the probability is, the higher the competition value of the goal would be, the more stressful an event should be, and the more cortisol should be emitted (see Dickerson and Kemeny 2004 for a recent meta-analysis of the role of uncontrollability in cortisol emission).

13.1.13 Chronically Stressful Events and, as a Consequence, a Chronically Increased Cortisol Level Can Damage Action-Control-Related Brain Structures (e.g., HC)

Chronically stressful events, that is, the repeated experience of goal pursuit in danger, causes a prolonged emission of cortisol and probably leads to a slower than normal return of free cortisol to baseline (e.g., McEwen 2002; Dickerson and Kemeny 2004). Consequently, over time, important brain structures for action control should be subject to a chronically high cortisol level, which is toxic for these structures. For the HC, such a damaging effect of chronically increased cortisol has been empirically confirmed (see, for overviews, McEwen 2002; Davidson et al. 2002); however, damage in HC can be reversed (e.g., McEwen 2002) if stressful events and cortisol level are reduced to a consistently normal level. Besides the HC, chronically increased cortisol may damage the ACC (which contains cortisol receptors) and parts of the PFC too—areas that are important in action control and whose functions are reduced in clinical depression (e.g., Davidson et al. 2002; Kempermann and Kronenberg 2003).

13.2 Clinical Depression as a Failure of Goal-based Action Control

In this chapter, the analysis of clinical depression is restricted to the primary type, that is, depression that is not a secondary consequence of another disorder such as Parkinson's disease or dementia, and to the unipolar type, that is, depression without mania (e.g., Comer 2001). In line with the neurocognitive framework, selected data from empirical depression research of the last decades that refer to all levels of the mind/brain system—ranging from experimentally measured behavioral deficits in humans and animals to brain activation and structural changes in specific cortical and subcortical areas (see, for recent overviews, e.g., Drevets 2001; Davidson, Pizzagalli, Nitschke, and Putman 2002; Gotlib and Hammen 2002; Nitschke and Mackiewicz, this volume) will be considered here.

The action control theory developed in the first section of this chapter will be used as the conceptual tool for understanding the mechanisms that cause and maintain the symptoms of depression. Along these lines of reasoning, depression is viewed as a disorder of action control characterized by an increased level of inactivity and avoidance behavior as well as a decreased level of approach behavior (see, e.g., Lewinsohn et al. 1984; Kasch et al. 2002). Such a point of view on depression has recently been put forward by R. J. Davidson and colleagues (e.g., Davidson and Irwin 1999; Davidson et al. 2002, 2003). Davidson's framework for understanding depression consists of two main sources. The first source is "affective neuroscience" (e.g., LeDoux 2000; Davidson and Irwin 1999) that aims to understand brain processes and representations of emotion regulation at the neurocognitive level. Structures of the primate brain such as PFC, the amygdala, the ACC, and the HC are suggested to play a central role in emotional processing. The second source refers to Gray's (e.g., 1990) distinction between two fundamental action systems, namely, a "behavioral approach system," mediating via positive affect approach toward reward stimuli, and a behavioral inhibition system, mediating via negative affect (e.g., anxiety) avoidance and withdrawal from aversive stimuli. Davidson and colleagues suggested that these two systems are lateralized in left and right PFC. Depression is assumed to be characterized by an underactive approach system and—if anxiety is comorbid—an overactive withdrawal system, a suggestion that has been confirmed by experimental studies (see, for overviews, e.g., Davidson and Irwin 1999; Davidson et al. 2002). Furthermore, Davidson et al. (2002) suggested new distinctions for decomposing depression into subtypes that will be described in sections 13.2.9 and 13.2.10.

Besides the above-described action control theory, Davidson's emotion regulation framework for understanding depression will be a major cornerstone of the neurocognitive theory specified below by ten main hypotheses. The second major theoretical idea that guides and constraints these ten hypotheses comes from a psychological approach to depression that describes this clinical disorder as a chronic misregulation of goal management. More precisely, it has been postulated that the perceived chronic nonattainment of important goals and the impossibility of disengagement from these goals leads to clinical depression (e.g., Klinger 1975; Kuhl and Helle 1986; Pyzcynski and Greenberg 1987; Carver and Scheier 1990). What is missing in these psychological formulations of depression is a description at the neurocognitive level that ascribes problems in goal management to dysfunctions in neural information processing of the brain. Steps in the direction of such a neurocognitive theory of depression will be made along the following ten main hypotheses.

13.2.1 Repeated Failures in Realizing Important Goals Are Perceived via Metamonitoring and Cause State-Dependent Changes of Action Control in Terms of Depressive Mood and of Negative Probability Estimates

Several psychological theories (e.g., Klinger 1975; Kuhl and Helle 1986; Pyzcynski and Greenberg 1987; Carver and Scheier 1990) have suggested that depression arises due to (short- and long-term) consequences of not being able to realize important goals. This perceived realization failure refers to unsuccessful action execution, that is, execution that was not able to achieve the goal state.

As stated in section 13.1.10, metamonitoring processes should evaluate the repeated attempts to pursue goals. In the case of repeated failures to achieve the intended action outcome, metamonitoring should initiate, first, the generation of negative action–outcome probability estimates—in the case of explicit representations called beliefs; see also Beck (1967) and Abramson, Alloy, Hankin, Haeffel, MacCoon, and Gibb (2002) for psychological theories that ascribe a central role to negative beliefs in causing and maintaining depression. As stated in previous sections, these action–outcome probability estimates can refer to the probability that the actor is able to perform the required action. Explicit probability estimates in the form of negative beliefs should be characterized by an estimated low probability of being able to successfully pursue the goal in question. Activated negative belief representations should send bias signals to the goal–action episode competition. The perception of repeated failures in pursuing important goals by metamonitoring processes should be sufficient to trigger the activation of such beliefs or implicit probability estimates.

Second, in cases of repeatedly perceived action control failures, metamonitoring should also cause the state-dependent initiation of an extended negative depressive mood state—a central characteristic of a unipolar mood disorder such as major depression (American Psychiatric Association 2000). Following section 13.1.10, depressive mood states should have a generalized effect in action control because they concern all activated goal episodes—see the next hypothesis. Third, the currently perceived goal pursuit failure by metamonitoring should also lead to the state analysis mode of action control that is characterized in this case by "rumination" (e.g., Nolen-Hoeksema 2000). A main function of state analysis and rumination is to allow the restructuring and disengagement of goals that seemed to be nonrealizable (e.g., Klinger 1975).

13.2.2   State-dependent Depressive Mood Causes a Reduction of Approach Actions and an Increase of Avoidance Behavior

How do activated negative beliefs, the state analysis mode, and the current depressive mood bias goal–action episode competition and selection in a short-term way? Following hypothesis 13.1.10, it is assumed that the goal–action episode selection is biased in a generalized way by negative depressive mood. More precisely, the congruency principle (section 13.1.10) predicts that negative mood should increase the value of all episodes primarily tagged with negative emotional states and should probably decrease the value of episodes primarily tagged with positive emotions. Consequently, during depressive mood, the episode value should be lower for approach goal–action episodes that are primarily tagged by positive emotional values (section 13.1.4)—these approach goals should therefore have a lower probability of winning the competition for action control compared to a state of nondepressive mood. This predicted feature of less approach behavior (see also Davidson et al. 2002) has, for instance, been confirmed for patients with major depression measured by self-reports of actions (Kasch, Rottenberg, Arnow, and Gotlib 2002). Furthermore, the increased impact of negative emotions by the depressive mood should increase the competition value of withdrawal- or avoidance-related goal–action episodes that are primarily tagged by negative emotions. Therefore, the probability of selecting avoidance episodes should be increased, and more avoidance actions should be issued. This second type of behavioral change has also been confirmed by the Kasch et al. (2002) study.[8] Moreover, a substantial reduction of this increased avoidance behavior of depressive patients is a central goal of cognitive-behavioral psychotherapies (e.g., Jacobson, Martell, and Dimidjian 2001).

13.2.3 State-dependent Depressive Mood and Negative (Low) Probability Estimates Cause Impaired Decision Making, as well as an Increase of Calls of Executive Control and Volitional Processes

Given the reduction of approach actions and the increase of avoidance actions, decision making in the sense of determining an episode competition winner should also be hampered by depressive mood. The episode activation value difference between competing approach goal–action episodes should be less due to their lower overall values. The opposite should be true for avoidance actions. Thus, on the one hand, decisions between approach goals should be harder to achieve. This reduced goal competition value in approach goals should also lead to less persistence and more interruptions or goal shifts (see hypothesis 13.1.6). In order to avoid goal–action episode shifts, volitional shielding processes have to be called (section 13.1.8). On the other hand, decisions between an avoidance goal–action episode and competing approach goal–action episodes should be easier to achieve due to the increased competition value of the avoidance episode. Persistence for avoidance episodes should also be increased, and goal shifts should be reduced. To my knowledge, there are no empirical data on these predictions distinguishing number, persistence, and shifts of approach and avoidance actions.

As stated in section 13.1.7, executive control processes should be called in the case of actual or anticipated action failure, that is, when the real or simulated action did not produce the intended goal state and when the probability estimate for being successful by repeating the action is low. Therefore, more executive processes should be called in case of depressive mood. How well these executive processes and volitional processes may work will be discussed in sections 13.2.9 and 13.2.10.

13.2.4 Modifications in LTM due to Repeated Failures in Realizing Important Goals: I. A Decrease in the Number of Stored Approach Episodes and an Increase in the Number of Stored Avoidance Episodes

A second, sustained consequence of repeated nonattainment of important goals refers to learning, that is, to modifications of specific LTM connections between emotional states and goal–action episodes. These connections should be modified according to the principles of "operant conditioning" and "reinforcement learning" (e.g., Bower and Hilgard 1981) so that selection of failing goal episodes will be less probable in the future. More precisely, after every failed goal pursuit, connections between the episode and negative emotions should be increased and connections to positive emotions should be decreased. For approach goal–action episodes, at some point in the learning history of repeated failures, these episodes may turn from desired into undesired, that is, into avoidance episodes. Consequently, the number of approach episodes should decrease during the course of depression while the number of avoidance episodes should increase (see, e.g., Jacobson et al. 2001; Kasch et al. 2002). In other words, the depressive state-dependent tendency to select less approach and more avoidance goal–action episodes (section 13.2.2) should be materialized in the form of a long-term correlate.

13.2.5 Modifications in LTM due to Repeated Failures in Realizing Important Goals: II. Decreased Persistence and Increased Switches of Approach Episodes in Charge

Similar to short-term changes, a long-term-based reduction of persistence of action execution and an increase of goal–action episode shifts should occur. Given that number and intensity of action execution calls depends on the goal competition value (hypothesis 13.1.6), persistence should be reduced due to chronically reduced competition values of approach episodes. These reduced competition values should also make a replacement of the current approach episode by competing goal–action episodes—episode shift—probable to a higher degree (see hypothesis 13.2.3). For avoidance episodes, the opposite pattern with respect to episode shift should hold. Current avoidance behavior should be harder to replace by competing approach episodes.

13.2.6 Modifications in LTM due to Repeated Failures in Realizing Important Goals: III. A Generalized Reduction of Probability Estimates (Negative Beliefs)

A further sustained consequence of repeated nonattainment of important goals refers to explicitly represented probability estimates of action–outcome relationships in the form of beliefs. First, due to learning of repeated failure, probability estimates for actions to lead to intended goal states (action outcomes) should be reduced (sections 13.1.9 and 13.2.1). Second, if several attempts to pursue the same goal by alternative actions—that is, several episodes containing the same goal but different actions—were unsuccessful, the probability that any kind of action for this goal is available for the actor should also be reduced. In other words, perceived "self-efficacy" (e.g., Bandura 1977) should be diminished (see hypothesis 13.1.9). Third, if several important goals of one action domain (e.g., the domain of interpersonal action abilities) could not be realized via different actions, a generalized probability estimate, a generalized belief, will emerge (see hypothesis 13.1.9, as well as, e.g., Beck 1967; Abramson et al. 2002). For instance, if several attempts to realize the fundamental goal of experiencing intimacy did not work over a longer time period, then a negative belief about this social action domain should be generated.

13.2.7 A Depressive Episode Triggered by a Stressful Event Is Maintained by an Increased Frequency of the "State Analysis Mode" and by Anticipated Negative Goal Pursuit Outcomes

As stated in sections 13.1.12 and 13.1.13, a stress response may arise when the organism perceives high importance and urgency but a low probability of goal pursuit. The cortisol emission should be strongly increased in this case. If the stressful event and the associated goal–action episode have been subject to repeatedly failing goal realization attempts in the past, the short- and long-term changes in action control (e.g., depressive mood, negative belief activation) specified before (sections 13.2.1–13.2.6) should occur. Important for clinical depression is the fact that depressive mood continues to exist, that is, a depressive episode emerges—despite the disappearance of the stressful event (or of other negative results of goal pursuit) or, in case of severe depression, even despite the presence of positive events. It is assumed here that this continuation of depressive mood beyond the stressor occurs because the state analysis mode of action control (including rumination) will be maintained or called with an increased frequency (compared to neutral or positive mood). The main reason for this maintenance or increased frequency of calls should be found in the long-term modifications of the action control system made by repeated failures to pursue important goals. A state analysis mode is initiated when actions for goal pursuit fail or when the failure is anticipated. This second case should be critical for the maintenance of depressive mood. Due to long-term modification in directions of generalized negative beliefs, that is, generalized low probability estimates (hypothesis 13.2.6) and due to an decreased competition value of approach goal–action episodes (hypothesis 13.2.5), the anticipation of action outcomes should suffer from generating an increased number of negative results. The anticipated negative results, in turn, should contribute via metamonitoring to the maintenance of the depressive mood.

13.2.8 Chronic Stress Causes HC Damage and Deficits in Context-guided Action, That Is, Leads to Reduced Execution of Routine Action and to Fewer Context-Triggered Episode in Charge Shifts

The activation of goal–action episodes with low probability for achieving important, urgent goals—that is, stressful events—should cause a prolonged emission of cortisol and probably a slower than normal return of free cortisol to baseline (see hypotheses 13.1.12 and 13.1.13). Consequently, over time, important brain structures for action control such as the HC, ACC, amygdala, or parts of PFC may be damaged by stress-induced, chronically increased cortisol. However, experimental evidence for the damaging effect of cortisol exists—to my knowledge—only for the HC (see, e.g., Davidson et al. 2003; McEwen 2002; Kempermann and Kronenberg 2003). As stated in section

13.1.5, the HC should be involved in prospective memory, that is, in setting up and retrieving the context conditions for action execution. Consequently, HC damage should lead to deficits in the context guidance (e.g. Davidson et al. 2002) of action execution. Context, in the sense of action triggers, may be less easily and less often retrieved. This, in turn, should lead to disturbances of context-guided daily routine actions that are characteristic for clinical depression (e.g., Jacobson et al. 2001). Consequently, the overall level of approach activity should decrease (e.g., Kasch et al. 2002). Furthermore, a switch of action in the direction of a context-induced goal–action episode—remember Lewin's (1926) mailbox example of section 13.1.5—should occur less often, and depressives should be stuck more often within the currently pursued goal–action episode.

13.2.9 In a First Phase of the Mood Disorder, Chronic Stress Should Lead to PFC Damage (ACC Still Intact) and to a Less Severe Form of Depression Characterized by Deficits in Executive and Volitional Processes and by Low-Probability Estimates for Successful Goal Pursuit

From functional and structural brain imaging studies, it is known that in individuals with depression, there is a reduction in not only the HC activation and HC volume but also the functioning of ACC, and of parts of the PFC (for an overview, see, e.g., Drevets 2001; Davidson et al. 2002). It is assumed here (see also Davidson et al. 2002) that HC and PFC damage occurs prior to the more far-reaching ACC damage as a first response to chronic stress and as a first phase of a less severe depressive disorder. Given that depressive mood and low probability estimates should lead to an increased call of the executive and volitional processes (see hypothesis 13.2.3), and given that executive and volitional processes may be located within PFC areas (see, e.g., Norman and Shallice 1986; Schneider, Owen, and Duncan 2000; Miller and Cohen 2001), PFC damage should cause problems in the efficiency of executive as well as volitional processes in depressives. For executive processes, this efficiency reduction has been empirically supported (see, e.g., Austin, Mitchell, and Goodwin 2001; Porter, Gallagher, Thompson, and Young 2003) but—to my knowledge—no data exist on the reduction of volitional processes.

Furthermore, if executive and volitional operations are not working properly in the service of goal pursuit, feedback about this failure (e.g., stored in LTM or simulated) should further decrease the probability estimates of a successful pursuit of goals in danger, that is, further decrease the probability estimates to respond appropriately to stressful events. This, in turn, should increase the stress response, that is, increased cortisol emission and further brain damage. More inactivity and less persistence should be further consequences.

13.2.10 In a Second Phase of the Mood Disorder, Chronic Stress Should Cause ACC Damage and a More Severe Form of Depression Characterized by Executive Control and Volitional Deficits as Well as Blunting of Emotions

If, within a second phase of the response to chronic stress, not only the HC and PFC but also the ACC are damaged, then a more severe form of clinical depression should arise. Given the suggested central functions of the ACC for action control (see hypotheses 13.1.7 and 13.1.8), namely, detecting the calling conditions of executive and volitional processes and initiating processes located within the PFC, severe deficits in goal-based action control should occur. Conditions for initiating executive and volitional processes should be detected and called less often in this second phase of the depressive disorder. Consequently, in the case of nonroutine actions that require executive control and in the case of goal pursuit in danger that requires volitional control, less and less successful action execution should be seen. Mainly, highly overlearned actions that do not rely on executive and volitional processes should be carried out. This description fits with a very severe form of depression that is characterized by a very high degree of inactivity (up to the level of stupor).

Davidson et al. (2002) suggested that an ACC subtype of depression exists that is characterized by a lack of "will to change." Within the theory suggested here, this lack of will to change should result from a strongly reduced ability of the damaged ACC to detect actual or anticipated failures in goal pursuit. If no failure is perceived, then no executive processes can be called, and consequently much fewer nonroutine actions will be executed.

Furthermore, blunting of affect in severe forms of depression (American Psychiatric Association 2000) should also be due to ACC dysfunction (Davidson et al. 2002). Discrepancies between the expected and real action outcomes should not be processed properly anymore, and therefore the resulting emotions (see section 13.1.9) should be much less intense.

13.2.11 Open Questions

The neurocognitive theory of depression developed up to now leaves many important questions without answers and is surely underspecified in many respects. For instance, the role of neuromodulators (e.g., serotonin or noradrenalin) in normal action control and the changes of these modulators in depression (see, e.g., Thase et al. 2002) and after recovery (e.g., by antidepressive medication) were not addressed here. The suggested capability of antidepressive medications, via the neuromodulatory changes they produce, to influence the repair process of damaged neural structures (see, e.g., Thase et al. 2002; McEwen 2002) may be of some interest here. Furthermore, the standard diagnostic distinction between a less severe and more chronic form of depression, called "dysthymia," and a more severe form of "major depressive disorder" (American Psychiatric Association 2000) has not been explicitly addressed here. A more detailed explanation of some classical symptoms of both forms of clinical depression (e.g., psychomotor slowing or agitation; American Psychiatric Association 2000) is also needed.

Overall, the neurocognitive theory about action control and about its failure in clinical depression outlined here should be viewed as a set of hypotheses that attempt to link often unconnected research domains (e.g., executive control and goal-based action control) and that attempt to fill the gap between basic experimental psychology and cognitive neuroscience, on the one hand, and empirical clinical research on depression on the other hand. Hopefully, some of these hypotheses will serve as a basis for future experimental research that will provide new insights into the neurocognitive processes and representations mediating goal-based action control and clinical depression.

Acknowledgments

I thank Heiner Deubel, Bernhard Hommel, Katharina Mahn, Natalie Sebanz, Robert Weiß, and especially Wolfgang Prinz for helpful comments.

Notes

1. In case of "covert actions" such as thinking and other inference processes, covert "motor" representations are assumed to be part of the goal-action episode.

2. This dynamic, competition-based part of action control theory is missing in Grafman's SEC framework and may deliver a useful supplement.

3. The idea of a "list of goals" (Duncan 1986) controlling the current action means in the framework advocated here that these goals are represented at a lower level and linked to one higher-level goal that won the competition against other goals.

4. See also Brown, Bullock, and Grossberg 2004 for an overview about evidence and specific computational suggestions about the role of BSG in saccade control.

5. Volitional processes should only be called when the danger of replacing the current goal exists and not when a new episode containing the same goal with a different action attempts to take control.

6. As stated in section 13.1.3, each combination of the same goal with a different action builds an individual episode.

7. The distinction between the state analysis and goal realization mode has some similarity to Kuhl's (1984, 1994) distinction between "action and state orientation." However, in contrast to Kuhl's (1994) theoretically complex distinction, a much simpler definition of goal realization versus state analysis is intended, namely, that the organism either pursues one goal or analyses the results of goal pursuit with respect to the overall goal structure.

8. However, in the Kasch et al. (2002) study, increased avoidance behavior for depressive patients did not—in contrast to increased approach actions—predict the course of depression.

References

Abramson, L. Y., L. B. Alloy, B. L. Hankin, G. J. Haeffel, D. G. MacCoon, and B. E. Gibb. 2002. Cognitive vulnerability–stress models of depression in a self-regulatory and psychobiological context. In *Handbook of Depression*, ed. I. H. Gotlib and C. L. Hammen, pp. 268–295. New York: Guilford Press.

Ach, N. 1935. Analyse des Willens. In *Handbuch der biologischen Arbeitsmethoden. Bd. VI*, ed. Abderhalden. Berlin: Urban and Schwarzenberg.

Adolphs, R. 2003. Cognitive neuroscience of human social behaviour. *Nature Reviews Neuroscience, 4*, 165–178.

Allport, D. A. 1980. Patterns and actions: Cognitive mechanisms are content-specific. In *Cognitive Psychology: New Directions*, ed. G. Claxton, pp. 26–64. London: Routledge and Kegan.

American Psychiatric Association. 2000. *Diagnostic and Statistical Manual of Mental Disorders*, 4th ed., text revision. Washington, D.C.: American Psychiatric Association.

Anderson, J. R. 1983. *The Architecture of Cognition*. Cambridge, Mass.: Harvard University Press.

Arbib, M. A. 1990. Programs, schemas, and neural networks for control of hand movements: Beyond the RS framework. In *Attention and Performance XIII: Motor Representation and Control*, ed. M. Jeannerod, pp. 111–138. Hillsdale, N.J.: Lawrence Erlbaum.

Atkinson, J. W. 1957. Motivational determinants of risk-taking behavior. *Psychological Review, 64*, 359–372.

Austin, M.-P., P. Mitchell, and G. M. Goodwin. 2001. Cognitive deficits in depression. *British Journal of Psychiatry, 178*, 200–206.

Bandura, A. 1977. Self-efficacy: Toward a unifying theory of behavioral change. *Psychological Review, 84*, 191–215.

Beck, A. T. 1967. *Depression: Clinical, Experimental, and Theoretical Aspects*. New York: Harper and Row.

Botvinick, M. M., C. S. Carter, T. Braver, D. M. Barch, and J. D. Cohen. 2001. Conflict monitoring and cognitive control. *Psychological Review, 108*, 624–652.

Bower, G. H., and E. R. Hilgard. 1981. *Theories of Learning*. Englewood Cliffs, N.J.: Prentice-Hall.

Braver, T. S., and J. D. Cohen. 2000. On the control of control: The role of dopamine in regulating prefrontal function: In *Attention and Performance XIIX*, ed. S. Monsell and J. Driver, pp. 713–737. Cambridge, Mass.: MIT Press.

Brown, J. W., D. Bullock, and S. Grossberg. 2004. How laminar frontal cortex and basal ganglia circuits interact to control planned and reactive saccades. *Neural Networks, 27*, 471–510.

Burgess, P. W., S. K. Scott, and C. D. Frith. 2003. The role of the rostral frontal cortex (Area 10) in prospective memory: A lateral versus medial dissociation. *Neuropsychologia, 41*, 906–918.

Bush, G., P. Luu, and M. I. Posner. 2000. Cognitive and emotional influences in anterior cingulate cortex. *Trends in Cognitive Sciences, 6*, 215–222.

Carver, C. S., and M. F. Scheier. 1990. Origins and functions of positive and negative affect: A control-process view. *Psychological Review, 97*, 19–35.

Carver, C. S., and M. F. Scheier. 1999. Stress, coping, and self-regulatory process. In *Handbook of Personality*, ed. L. A. Pervin and O. P. John, pp. 553–575. New York: Guilford Press.

Cohen, J. D., K. Dunbar, and J. L. McClelland. 1990. On the control of automatic processes: A parallel distributed processing account of the Stroop effect. *Psychological Review, 97*, 332–361.

Comer, R. J. 2001. *Abnormal Psychology*. New York: Worth Publisher.

Crocker, J., and L. E. Park. 2004. The costly pursuit of self-esteem. *Psychological Bulletin, 130*, 392–414.

Damasio, A. R. 1996. The somatic marker hypothesis and the possible functions of the prefrontal cortex. *Philosophical Transactions of the Royal Society of London: Biological Sciences, 351*, 1413–1420.

Davidson, R. J., and W. Irwin. 1999. The functional neuroanatomy of emotion and affective style. *Trends in Cognitive Science, 3*, 11–21.

Davidson, R. J., W. Irwin, M. J. Anderle, and N. H. Kalin. 2003. The neural substrates of affective processing in depressed patients treated with venlafaxine. *American Journal of Psychiatry, 160*, 64–75.

Davidson, R. J., D. Pizzagalli, J. B. Nitschke, and K. Putnam. 2002. Depression: Perspectives from affective neuroscience. *Annual Review of Psychology, 53*, 545–574.

DeLong, M. R. 2000. The basal ganglia. In *Principles of Neural Science*, ed. E. Kandel, J. H. Schwartz, and T. M. Jessell, pp. 853–867. New York: McGraw-Hill.

Desimone, R., and J. Duncan. 1995. Neural mechanisms of selective visual attention. *Annual Review of Neuroscience, 18*, 193–222.

Deubel, H., and W. X. Schneider. 1996. Saccade target selection and object recognition: Evidence for a common attentional mechanism. *Vision Research, 36*, 1827–1837.

Deubel, H., and W. X. Schneider. In press. Attentional selection in sequential movements, movements around an obstacle, and in grasping. In *Attention in Action*, ed. G. W. Humphreys and M. J. Riddoch. Hove: Psychology Press.

Dickerson, S. S., and M. E. Kemeny. 2004. Acute stressors and cortisol responses: A theoretical integration and synthesis of laboratory research. *Psychological Bulletin, 130*, 355–391.

Drevets, W. C. 2001. Neuroimaging and neuropathological studies of depression: Implications for the cognitive–emotional features of mood disorders. *Current Opinion in Neurobiology, 11*, 240–249.

Duncan, J. 1986. Disorganisation of behaviour after frontal lobe damage. *Cognitive Neuropsychology, 3*, 271–290.

Duncan, J., H. Emslie, P. Williams, R. Johnson, and C. Freer. 1996. Intelligence and the frontal lobe: The organisation of goal-directed behavior, *Cognitive Psychology, 30,* 257–303.

Duncan, J., and A. Owen. 2000. Common regions of the human prefrontal lobe recruited by diverse cognitive demands. *Trends in Neurosciences, 23,* 475–483.

Fuster, J. M. 1997. *The Prefrontal Cortex: Anatomy, Physiology, and Neuropsychology of the Frontal Lobe.* Philadelphia: Lippincott-Raven.

Fuster, J. M. 2001. The prefrontal cortex—An update: Time is of the essence. *Neuron, 30,* 319–333.

Gazzaniga, M. S., B. S. Ivry, and G. R. Mangun. 2002. *Cognitive Neuroscience: The Biology of Mind.* New York: W. W. Norton.

Glimcher, P. W. 2003. The neurobiology of visual saccadic decision making. *Annual Review of Neuroscience, 26,* 133–176.

Goschke, T. 2003. Voluntary action and cognitive control from a cognitive neuroscience perspective. In *Voluntary Action,* ed. S. Maasen, W. Prinz, and G. Roth, pp. 49–85. Oxford: Oxford University Press.

Gotlib, I. H., and C. L. Hammen, eds. 2002. *Handbook of Depression.* New York: Guilford Press.

Grawe, K. 2004. *Neuropsychotherapie.* Toronto: Hogrefe and Huber.

Gray, J. A. 1990. Brain systems that mediate both emotion and cognition. *Cognition and Emotion, 4,* 269–288.

Gross, J. J. 1999. Emotion and emotion regulation. In *Handbook of Personality,* ed. L. A. Pervin and O. P. John, pp. 525–551. New York: Guilford Press.

Heckhausen, H. 1991. *Motivation and Action.* Berlin: Springer.

Heckhausen, H., and J. Kuhl. 1985. From wishes to action: The dead ends and shorts cuts on the long way to action. In *Goal-Directed Behavior: The Concept of Action in Psychology,* ed. M. Frese and J. Sabini, pp. 134–159. Hillsdale, N.J.: Lawrence Erlbaum.

Heuer, H., and A. F. Sanders. 1987. *Perspectives on Perception and Action.* Hillsdale, N.J.: Lawrence Erlbaum.

Holroyd, C. B., and M. G. H. Coles. 2002. The neural basis of human error processing: Reinforcement learning, dopamine, and the error-related negativity. *Psychological Review, 109,* 679–709.

Hommel, B. 1993. Inverting the Simon effect by intention. *Psychological Research, 55,* 270–279.

Hommel, B., J. Müsseler, G. Aschersleben, and W. Prinz. 2001. The theory of event coding (TEC): A framework for perception and action planning. *Behavioral and Brain Science, 24,* 849–937.

Jacobson, N. S., C. R. Martell, and S. Dimidjian. 2001. Behavioral activation treatment for depression: Returning to contextual roots. *Clinical Psychology: Science and Practice, 8,* 255–270.

Jeffery, K. J. 2004. Remembrance of the future past. *Trends in Cognitive Sciences, 5*, 197–199.

Kasch, K. L., J. Rottenberg, B. A. Arnow, and I. H. Gotlib. 2002. Behavioral activation and inhibition systems and the severity and course of depression. *Journal of Abnormal Psychology, 111*, 589–597.

Kempermann, G., and G. Kronenberg. 2003. Depressed new neurons—Adult hippocampal neurogenesis and a cellular plasticity hypothesis of major depression. *Biological Psychiatry, 54*, 499–503.

Klinger, E. 1975. Consequences of commitment to and disengagement from incentives. *Psychological Review, 82*, 1–25.

Kosslyn, S. M., and O. Koenig. 1992. *Wet Mind: The New Cognitive Neuroscience.* New York: Free Press.

Krakauer, J., and C. Ghez. 2000. Voluntary movement. In *Principles of Neural Science*, ed. E. Kandel, J. H. Schwartz, and T. M. Jessell, pp. 756–781. New York: McGraw-Hill.

Kuhl, J. 1984. Volitional aspects of achievement motivation and learned helplessness: Toward a comprehensive theory of action control. In *Progress in Experimental Personality Research*, vol. 13, ed. B. A. Maher and W. B. Maher, pp. 99–171. Orlando: Academic Press.

Kuhl, J. 1994. A theory of action and state orientations. In *Volition and Personality*, ed. J. Kuhl and J. Beckmann, pp. 47–56. Göttingen: Hogrefe.

Kuhl, J., and P. Helle. 1986. Motivational and volitional determinants of depression: The degenerated-intention hypothesis. *Journal of Abnormal Psychology, 95*, 247–251.

LeDoux, J. 2000. Emotions circuits in the brain. *Annual Review of Neuroscience, 23*, 155–184.

Lewin, K. 1926. Untersuchungen zur Handlungs- und Affektpsychologie. II. Vorsatz, Wille und Bedürfnis. *Psychologische Forschung, 7*, 330–385.

Lewinsohn, P. M., D. O. Antonuccio, J. L. Steinmetz, and L. Teri. 1984. *The Coping with Depression Course.* Eugene, Ore.: Castalia.

Matsumoto, K., and K. Tanaka. 2004. The role of the medial prefrontal cortex in achieving goals. *Current Opinion in Neurobiology, 14*, 178–185.

McEwen, B. 2002. *The End of Stress as We Know It.* Washington, D.C.: Joseph Henry Press.

Meyer, D. E., and D. E. Kieras. 1997. A computational theory of executive cognitive processes and multiple-task performance: Part 1. Basic mechanisms. *Psychological Review, 104*, 3–65.

Miller, E. K., and J. D. Cohen. 2001. An integrative theory of prefrontal cortex function. *Annual Review of Neuroscience, 24*, 167–202.

Miller, G. A., E. Galanter, and K. H. Pribram. 1960. *Plans and the Structure of Behavior.* New York: Holt, Rinehart, and Winston.

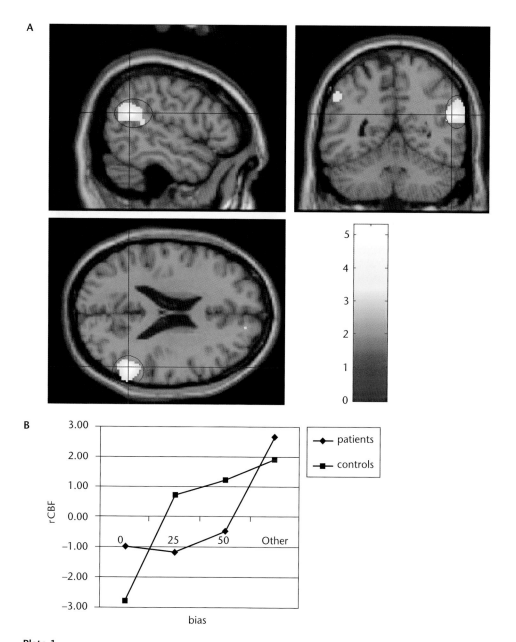

Plate 1

A. Activation of posterior parietal area 39 in subjects experiencing a mismatch between the movements they perform and the visual reafference of their movements. B. Amplitude of parietal activation for different degrees of mismatch. 0°, no mismatch; 25°, 50°, increasing mismatch; Other, complete mismatch. Subjects see the effect of movements performed by another agent. Squares: normal subjects. Note the progressive increase in parietal activation. Diamonds: schizophrenic patients. Note the poor correlation between activation and degree of mismatch. rCBF, regional cerebral blood flow. Data from Farrer et al. 2004.

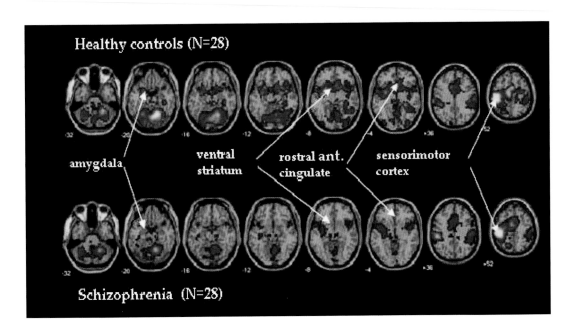

Healthy controls (N=28)

amygdala   ventral   rostral ant.   sensorimotor
            striatum   cingulate   cortex

Schizophrenia (N=28)

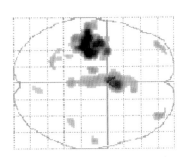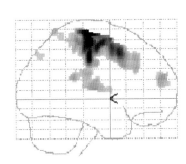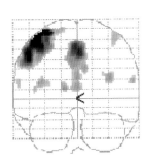

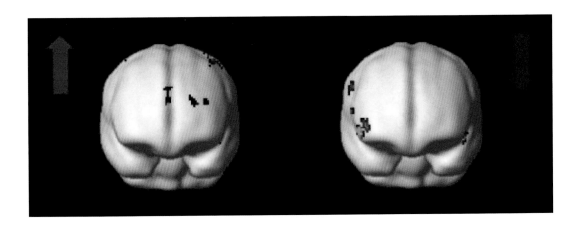

Plate 2

(opposite top) Functional magnetic resonance imaging study of auditory oddball target detection in 28 patients with schizophrenia and 28 healthy controls. Colored regions denote clusters of voxels in which activation was greater during processing of target stimuli than novel stimuli (cluster significance p < 0.05 corrected for multiple comparisons). The patients exhibit less activation than controls in the motivated attention system, especially in limbic/paralimbic areas (amygdala, ventral striatum, rostral anterior cingulate) despite a normal level of activity in sensorimotor cortex.

Plate 3

(opposite middle) Activations in subjects performing spontaneous actions using two fingers of the right hand. There is significantly greater activation of bilateral prefrontal, premotor supplementary motor area, and left motor cortices. The figure shows statistical parametric maps thresholded for display purposes at p < 0.05. Data reported in Hunter et al. 2003.

Plate 4

(opposite bottom) Changes in Sisyphus' brain over time on the two-finger version of the behavioral randomness task (Hunter et al. 2004). Over successive scan sessions, generation of random motor sequences elicits relatively greater activation in left prefrontal cortex (PFC), supplementary motor area (SMA), and motor cortex (left) and greater deactivation in right PFC foci (right). The figure shows statistical parametric maps thresholded for display purposes at p < 0.05.

Plate 5

(below) Notional response space for subject exhibiting stereotypical responses (blue line) and another exhibiting a wider range of potential responses (in red). A narrow Gaussian distribution implies a lack of variety in responses to a given environment. Such behavior will be more "predictable." The subject who varies his or her behavior within that environment is, accordingly, less predictable.

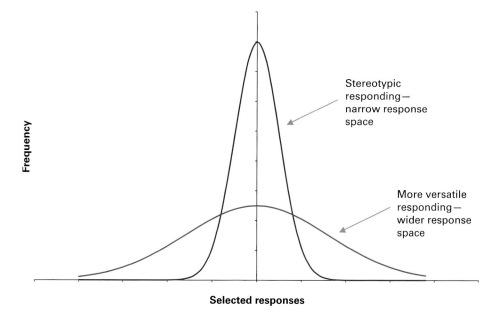

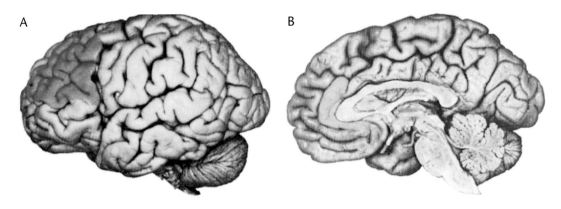

Plate 6
Key brain regions involved in volition and depression. (A) Dorsolateral prefrontal cortex shown in blue. (B) Anterior cingulate cortex shown in yellow.

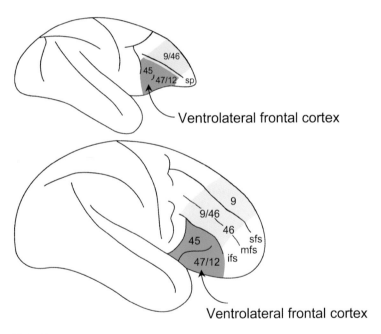

Plate 7
Schematic drawing of the lateral surface of the macaque brain (top) and the human brain (bottom), to indicate the location of the ventrolateral frontal cortex (Areas 45, 47, 12). Adapted from Petrides and Pandya 1994. sp, sulcus principalis; ifs, inferior frontal sulcus; mfs, middle frontal sulcus; sfs, superior frontal sulcus.

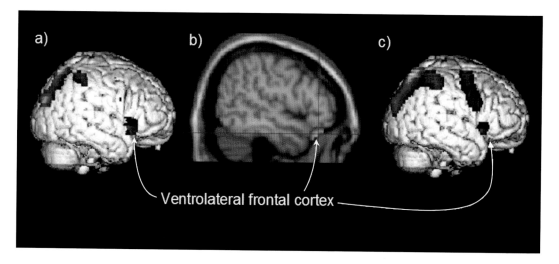

Plate 8

Regional cerebral blood flow maps from three independent positron-emission tomography studies activating an almost identical location within the midventrolateral frontal cortex. (a) Spatial span (adapted from Owen et al. 1996b), (b) digit span (adapted from Owen et al. 2000), and (c) spatial span (adapted from Owen et al. 1999). Right hemisphere only is shown.

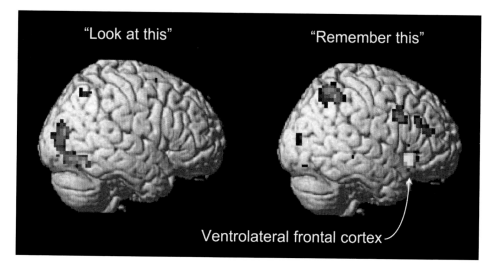

Plate 9

Event-related functional magnetic resonance imaging blood-oxygenation-level-dependent signal changes when volunteers are asked to either look at (left) or remember (right) a complex visual pattern. Signal change differs significantly in the midventrolateral frontal cortex. Right hemisphere only is shown. Adapted from Dove et al. 2001.

Monsell, S. 1996. Control of mental processes. In *Unsolved Mysteries of the Mind*, ed. V. Bruce, pp. 93–148. Stirling, U.K.: Lawrence Erlbaum.

Neumann, O. 1987. Beyond capacity: A functional view of attention. In *Perspectives on Perception and Action*, ed. H. Heuer and A. F. Sanders, pp. 361–394. Hillsdale, N.J.: Lawrence Erlbaum.

Newell, A., and H. A. Simon. 1972. *Human Problem Solving*. Englewood Cliffs, N.J.: Prentice Hall.

Nolen-Hoeksema, S. 2000. The role of rumination in depressive disorders and mixed anxiety/depressive symptoms. *Journal of Abnormal Psychology, 109*, 504–511.

Norman, D. A., and T. Shallice. 1986. Attention to action—Willed and automatic control of behavior. In *Consciousness and Self-regulation*, ed. R. J. Davidson, G. E. Schwartz, and D. Shapiro, pp. 1–18. New York: Plenum Press.

Passingham, R. E. 1993. *The Frontal Lobes and Voluntary Action*. Oxford: Oxford University Press.

Paus, T. 2001. Primate anterior cingulate cortex: Where motor control, drive, and cognition interface. *Nature Reviews Neuroscience, 2*, 417–424.

Phaf, R. H., A. H. van der Heijden, and P. T. Hudson. 1990. SLAM: A connectionist model for attention in visual selection tasks. *Cognitive Psychology, 22*, 273–341.

Porter, R. J., P. Gallagher, J. M. Thompson, and A. H. Young. 2003. Neurocognitive impairment in drug-free patients with major depressive disorder. *British Journal of Psychiatry, 182*, 214–220.

Powers, T. W. 1973. *Behavior: The Control of Perception*. New York: Aldine.

Prinz, W. 1987. Ideo-motor action. In *Perspectives on Perception and Action*, ed. H. Heuer and A. F. Sanders, pp. 361–394. Hillsdale, N.J.: Lawrence Erlbaum.

Prinz, W. 1997. Perception and action planning. *European Journal of Cognitive Psychology, 9*, 129–154.

Pyzcynski, T., and J. Greenberg. 1987. Self-regulatory preserveration, and the depressive self-focusing style after success and failure. *Psychological Bulletin, 102*, 122–138.

Ramnani, N., and A. M. Owen. 2004. Anterior prefrontal cortex: Insights into function from anatomy and neuroimaging. *Nature Reviews Neuroscience, 5*, 184–194.

Rolls, E. T. 2000. Precis of the brain and emotion. *Behavioral and Brain Science, 23*, 177–234.

Rosenbaum, D. A. 1991. *Human Motor Control*. San Diego: Academic Press.

Schiegg, A., H. Deubel, and W. X. Schneider. 2003. Attentional selection during preparation of prehension movements. *Visual Cognition, 10*, 409–431.

Schneider, W. X. 1995. VAM: A neuro-cognitive model for visual attention control of segmentation, object recognition, and space-based motor action. *Visual Cognition, 2*, 331–375.

Schneider, W. X., and H. Deubel. 2002. Selection-for-perception and selection-for-spatial-motor-action are coupled by visual attention: A review of recent findings and new evidence from stimulus-driven saccade control. In *Attention and Performance XIX: Common Mechanisms in Perception and Action*, ed. W. Prinz and B. Hommel, pp. 609–627. Oxford: Oxford University Press.

Schneider, W. X., A. M. Owen, and J. Duncan, eds. 2000. *Executive Control and the Frontal Lobe: Current Issues. Experimental Brain Research* (Special Issue), *133*, 1–138.

Schultz, W. 1999. The primate basal ganglia and the voluntary control of behaviour. *Journal of Consciousness Studies, 6*, 31–45.

Schultz, W. 2004. Neural coding of basic reward terms of animal learning Theory, microeconmics, and behavioral ecology. *Current Opinion in Neurobiology, 14*, 139–147.

Thase, M. E., R. Jindal, and R. H. Howland. 2002. Biological aspects of depression. In *Handbook of Depression*, ed. I. H. Gotlib and C. L. Hammen, pp. 192–219. New York: Guilford Press.

Weiner, B. 1980. *Human Motivation*. New York: Holt, Rinehart, and Winston.

14 The Cost of Pleasure: Effort and Cognition in Anhedonia and Depression

Roland Jouvent, Stéphanie Dubal, and Philippe Fossati

14.1 Introduction

Four domains appear to capture the core features of depression: affective, cognitive, motor, and circadian–somatic. The affective (i.e., loss of pleasure) and cognitive symptoms of depression may be considered to result from the impairment of a system underlying volition. This impairment may reflect both primary disorders of volitional operation and deficits in processes associated with the initiation of action and the allocation of attentional resources during cognitive effort. In this chapter we will emphasize the role of cognitive flexibility and the capacity to mobilize cognitive resources to explain deficits of cognitive control and emotional dysregulation in anhedonia and depression.

14.2 Volition and Depression

14.2.1 Executive Functions and Impaired Volition in Depression

Executive functions include a set of cognitive processes engaged in the integration of multimodal sensory input, generation of multiple response alternatives, planning abilities, and self-evaluation (Stuss and Benson 1984). It is now clearly established that the depressive state is associated with deficits of executive functions (for a review, see Fossati et al. 2002).

Major executive functions may depend on the effectiveness of more basic executive processes. In a recent study in normal subjects, Miyake et al. (2000) used latent variable analyses to determine to what extent different executive processes can be considered to be unitary (in the sense that they are reflections of the same underlying mechanism or ability) or nonunitary. These authors focused on three basic executive processes: shifting, inhibition, and updating. Factor analyses confirmed that these three executive processes, although moderately correlated with one another, are clearly separable and could contribute differently to the efficiency of more complex activities like planning and goal-directed behaviors.

Neuropsychological studies in depressed patients have demonstrated widespread executive deficits in depression with a negative impact on updating, shifting, and inhibition processes (Austin et al. 1999; Beats et al. 1996; Fossati et al. 2001; Harvey et al. 2004). Among the basic executive processes, the capacity to shift between tasks or mental sets is closely related to volition, allowing the subject to produce flexible and various behaviors in response to environmental demands. Several studies have identified specific deficits in tasks requiring set shifting processes in depression (Austin et al. 1999; Beats et al. 1996; Fossati et al. 2003; Franke et al. 1993; Merriam et al. 1999).

The Wisconsin Card Sorting Test (WCST), one of the tests most widely used in clinical neuropsychological practice to assess the shifting process within problem-solving capacities, requires subjects to sort cards according to criteria that must be inferred from feedback from the examiner. The WSCT evaluates both the ability to identify abstract categories and behavioral flexibility. Patients with depression produce fewer categories with this task and make more perseverative errors and responses (Merriam et al. 1999). One limitation of the WCST is that many sources of performance failure have been identified, that is, evaluating too many rules or hypotheses, neglecting the reward signal, or failing to alter behavior in response to feedback (Dehaene and Chaugeux 1991). It is therefore not easy to use the test to infer the exact nature of impairments.

Fossati et al. (2001) recently compared the performance of young and middle-aged inpatients with depression on two problem-solving tasks: the WCST and the California Card Sorting Test (CCST) to isolate cognitive processes underlying shifting and problem-solving impairments in depression. The CCST provides several different measures of concept generation, concept identification, and concept execution by asking subjects to sort three sets of six cards in three different sorting conditions: free, structured, and cued. Unlike the WCST, during the first condition of the CCST—concept generation—subjects must self-initiate the sorting process without feedback from the examiner.

Depressed patients display a specific deficit in concept generation but no major problems in concept identification or concept execution. Although there is a time limit for completion of the CCST, the deficit of depressed patients on the CCST is not related to cognitive speed. This suggests specific deficits in concept generation, believed to reflect both hypothesis-testing impairments and a loss of spontaneous cognitive flexibility in depression (Fossati et al. 1999).

"Cognitive flexibility" in this context refers to the capacity to adapt one's behavior to changing environmental circumstances. Eslinger and Grattan (1993) divided cognitive flexibility into spontaneous and reactive components. "Spontaneous cognitive flexibility" is closely related to initiation ability, mental slowing, and the capacity to generate diversity. "Reactive cognitive flexibility" refers to the capacity to change behaviors in response to the particular demands of a situation. Deficits on the WCST in depression are primarily related to difficulties in altering behavior in response to feedback (reactive cognitive flexibility; Channon 1996) or oversensitivity to negative feedback (Elliott et al. 1996). The reduced number of attempted sorts in the CCST also supports a deficit in spontaneous cognitive flexibility in depression and suggests a failure in self-initiated sorting and a difficulty in generating behavioral and cognitive diversity. Consistent with this interpretation, Kuhl and Helle (1986) proposed a degenerated intention hypothesis to explain the persistence of behaviors and affects in depression (see Schneider, this volume). According to this model, motivational state seems to be an intrinsic property of perseverance. Kuhl and Helle (1986) proposed that the perseverance of unrealistic intentional and motivational states (i.e., lack of goal flexibility) is common to all types of severe depression. Normal subjects give up on unattainable goals after a certain number of failed attempts; overmaintenance of unrealistic intentional states is associated with depression. The cognition linked to these unattainable goals (i.e., expectation of the object after object loss) and unrealistic intention could reduce the working memory capacity of depressed patients (Kuhl and Helle 1986; Schneider, this volume).

Hypothesis testing involves the ability to explore problem-solving alternatives. However, unlike cognitive flexibility, hypothesis testing also includes a risk-taking component as subjects test various solutions and evaluate them by analyzing the feedback obtained from the examiner. The fact that the percentage of correct sorts on the CCST does not differ between depressed subjects and controls suggests that patients adopt a conservative response (Fossati et al. 2001). Thus, the lack of volition in depression may partially reflect the tendency of depressed patients to be more conservative and to express behavior and action in which they have a high degree of confidence (Murphy et al. 1998).

Neuroimaging studies in normal controls have demonstrated that executive processes such as shifting, updating, and inhibition rely on a distributed cerebral network including the prefrontal, premotor, and parietal cortices. The dorsolateral part of the prefrontal cortex (DLPFC; Brodmann Areas 9/46) is commonly activated when subjects perform working memory tasks or card-sorting tests (Pochon et al. 2002; Nagahama et al. 1996). Likewise, normal spontaneous cognitive flexibility has been shown to be associated with the integrity of the DLPFC (Eslinger and Grattan 1993). DLPFC activity has been linked to psychomotor speed and executive functions in depressed patients (Dolan et al. 1992). Positron-emission tomography (PET)-based studies of blood flow and glucose metabolism in patients with primary depression generally report frontal abnormalities at rest (Baxter et al. 1989; George et al. 1994a; Mayberg 1994, 1997). The most robust and consistent finding is decreased frontal lobe function, although normal frontal and hyper frontal activity have also been reported (Brody et al. 2001; Drevets et al. 1992; see Nitschke and Mackiewicz, this volume). The frontal lobe includes the dorsolateral and ventral lateral prefrontal cortex (Brodmann Areas 9, 46, 10, 47) as well as the orbital frontal cortices (Brodmann Areas 10, 11). Findings are generally bilateral, although asymmetry has been described with predominantly left hypometabolism in the DLPFC.

What is the exact role of the DLPFC in volition and control of action? Frith (this volume) suggested that the DLPFC is activated when responses have to be selected without the help of any external cues. Frith called this "willed action." This interpretation of the role of the DLPFC is consistent with our findings of deficits of depressed patients in the first condition—free condition—of the CCST, when subjects have to self-initiate sorting without external cues (Fossati et al. 2001). Not all studies support the hypothesis that the DLPFC is involved in "willed action" (Hyder et al. 1997). Nathaniel-James and Frith (2002) argued that the most likely single cognitive function of the DLPFC is to specify a set of responses suitable for a given task and to bias these for selection (sculpting the response space). The DLFPC is involved in guiding complex behavior by defining the appropriate context of action (Nitschke and Mackiewicz, this volume). According to this view, dysfunction of the DLPFC would mainly result in deficits in the execution of actions adapted to specific contextual demands rather than global reduction of action.

An initiation deficit and psychomotor retardation have also been described in patients with prefrontal lesions. Disordered drive/motivation and apathy have been reported in patients with frontal trauma and lesions of the anterior cingulate (Dewinsky et al. 1995). In general, frontal damage that produces psychomotor retardation and apathy involves midline frontal structures and subcortical limbic-related pathways. Functional imaging studies in patients with primary depression have shown abnormal functions of these midline prefrontal structures including the dorsal and ventral (orbital) medial parts of the prefrontal cortex (see Mayberg and Fossati 2004) and anterior cingulate cortex (ACC). The affective component of the ACC (ventral part: Brodmann Areas 25, 33, and 24) has extensive connections with the amygdala and periaqueductal grey, and parts of it project into autonomic brainstem motor nuclei. The affective ACC is involved in autonomic regulation, monitoring of reward, and assigning emotional valence to internal and external stimuli (Nitschke and Mackiewicz, this volume). Abnormal activities in the ventral and dorsal ACC have been shown to be related to emotional dysregulation and abnormal reward processing as well as decision-making deficits and psychomotor slowing in depression (Drevets 2001).

Overall, these data suggest that several regions of the prefrontal cortex may support specific deficits in volition in depression; the dorsal (lateral) prefrontal cortices are associated with impairment in the execution and contextualization of goal-directed behaviors, and the ventral (medial) prefrontal cortex is associated with defective initiation, responses to reward, and drive.

14.2.2 Cognitive Resources and Volition: Toward a Functional Perspective of Depression

Since the seminal work of Hasher and Zacks (1979), it is believed that depression interferes with effortful processes (Weingartner 1987). From this point of view, normal individuals have limited cognitive resources (or limited capacity to process information) and mental operations may differ in the amount of attention or cognitive resources required. Automatic processes have the following characteristics: They might be accomplished in parallel, are not limited by short-term memory capacity, require little or no cognitive effort, require practice to develop, and are restricted to situations in which a given stimulus consistently involves the same response. In contrast, the characteristics of controlled processes include being accomplished in sequence, restricted by the short-term memory capacity, effortful, improved by minimal practice, and typical of situations in which there is no consistent mapping between stimulus and response (Hasher and Zacks 1979; Schneider et al. 1984).

Depression interferes with effortful cognitive processes, leaving intact automatic processes in several domains such as learning, memory, problem solving, reading, and speed processing (for a review, see Hartlage et al. 1993). Within the system of volition, the effortful deficit hypothesis in depression predicts impairments in actions requiring attentional and executive resources such as complex goal-directed behaviors (Schneider, this volume; see section 14.2.1 of this chapter).

Beyond the difficulty in precisely defining automatic and effortful tasks and the chicken/egg problem of applying the automatic/effortful distinction to the study of cognition in depression ("Is a cognitive task an 'effortful task' because of its impairment in depression?"), this approach also suggests that cognitive deficits and impairment in volition in depression are an "all or nothing" problem. Indeed, we can suggest that cognitive deficits and impairment of volition in depression result from the failure to maintain emotional and cognitive control in times of increased and sustained cognitive demands or somatic stress. According to this view, the deficits exhibited by depressed patients when faced with an effortful task are preceded by increasing effort to maintain a high level of performance. The progressive exhaustion of cognitive resources precedes the deficits, and the reduction of cognitive resources is a final by-product of the failure of depressed patients to adapt constantly to cognitive and emotional demands. Consequently, it is more important to test depressed patients with a cognitive task that they can perform than to show a deficit in a task that they cannot perform. Likewise, how depressed patients are doing provides more information about the pathophysiology of depression than what they are doing (see Partiot et al. 1994). Although the mechanisms mediating this "failure" to maintain cognitive and emotional control are not yet characterized, they are probably multifactorial; genetic vulnerability, affective temperament, developmental insults, and environmental stressors are all considered important contributors.

Recent behavioral and functional magnetic resonance imaging (fMRI) data support this hypothesis. For example, depressed patients with anhedonic features show deficits on continuous attentional tasks when compared to depressed patients with impulsive features (Dubal and Jouvent 2004). These deficits appear progressively during the task. This "time-on-task" (TOT) effect is consistent with previous findings on normal anhedonic subjects, suggesting that anhedonia is associated with a reduced capacity to maintain a sustained cognitive effort.

In a recent fMRI study (Harvey et al. 2005), we compared 10 depressed subjects and 10 normal controls on a verbal n-back task. The n-back task requires both maintenance of the n stimuli and updating of these stimuli each time a new stimulus occurs. The working memory load was manipulated across the experiment (1-, 2-, 3-back) to increase the cognitive demands. We a priori selected depressed patients with normal performance on the n-back task, and no difference between groups was found for both performance and reaction times (PTs) at each level of complexity. Both groups showed bilateral activation of DLPFC (Brodmann Areas 9/46), premotor and supplementary motor area (Brodmann Areas 6/8), Broca area, dorsal ACC, and parietal cortices during n-bask tasks. The activation levels of these regions were modulated by the complexity of the task. Within this n-back neural network, the DLPFC and dorsal ACC were more activated in depressed patients than in normal controls (see fig. 14.1; Harvey et al. 2005. Neuroimaging studies have shown a similar aberrant activation of the DLPFC in depressed patients (see Videbech et al. 2003; George et al. 1994b). For example, George et al. (1994b), using the Stroop task, observed a shift in brain activation to the left DLPFC—a region not normally recruited for this task in healthy subjects—associated with a blunting of an expected anterior cingulate increase in depressed patients.

The aberrant activation of the DLPFC and anterior cingulate associated with normal performance in depressed subjects may reflect several problems: (1) inefficiency of a task-related neural network reflecting difficulty in organizing neural activity; (2) structural brain abnormalities within the working memory network; and (3) an excess of subjective effort (volition) or task engagement (Harvey et al. 2005).

In healthy subjects, ACC activation may reflect the intentional amount of effort (volition) that a subject uses in a task. The ACC also contributes to cognition by detecting conflict and by monitoring error during information processing (Ridderinkhof et al. 2004). Carter et al. (1999) suggested that the ACC detects processing conflicts that may be associated with deteriorating performance during executive processes. It may be that during the n-back task, depressed patients need to monitor the putative errors and conflict more than controls and that this is reflected by greater activation of the ACC. The ACC has strong connections with the DLPFC. The activated ACC may signal to the brain the need for controlled processing, and the DLPFC would be critical for this form of controlled processing (see Schneider, this volume).

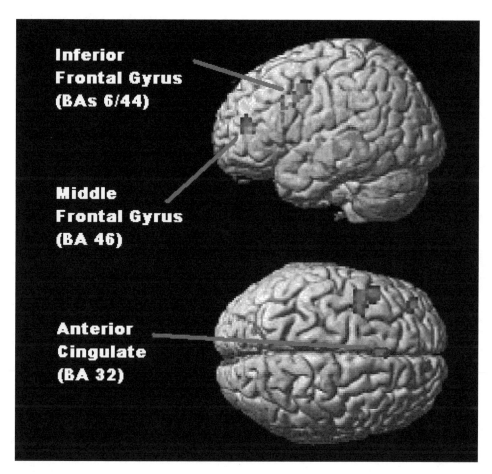

Figure 14.1

Comparisons of depressed and controls with the *n*-back task using functional magnetic resonance imaging. Depressed subjects showed greater activation than controls in the dorsolateral prefrontal cortex, ventrolateral prefrontal cortex, and dorsal anterior cingulate. *p* < .001, uncorrected.

14.3   Volition and Anhedonia

As for depression, these considerations may be applied to anhedonic healthy subjects. Anhedonia, a decrease in the capacity to experience pleasure, is a classic negative feature of various psychiatric disorders, such as depression and schizophrenia. Symptoms of emotional deficit, referred to as "negative symptoms," relate to the absence of a behavior, or function, normally expected to be present. From affective blunting to analgesia, emotional deficit corresponds to a limitation of the emotional tone and to a lack of ability to react to external stimuli that normally provoke a wide range of emotional responses. The concept of anhedonia related to the positive dimension of emotions was first introduced by Ribot in 1896 to describe the loss of capacity to experience pleasure. Anhedonia impairs the ability to relate with other people and weakens feelings of joy, affection, love, pride, and self-respect. Anhedonia may also be observed as a personality trait in healthy individuals and is associated with a greater risk of affective disorders and schizophrenia. The anhedonia dimension parallels specific negative symptoms in psychopathological states and relates to symptoms like social adjustment problems and attentional deficits. These symptoms are believed to fall on a continuum from relatively normal to personality disorders to full psychiatric states.

14.3.1   Attention and Anhedonia

Two main approaches have been used to study attention processing in anhedonic healthy subjects. The first one evaluates the resource allocation deficits that exist in anhedonic participants based on dual-task tests (Yee and Miller 1994) or event-related potential (ERP) studies (Miller 1986; Yee and Miller 1994). The second group of studies involves more specific explorations of attentional visual processing. Anhedonic participants have a number of difficulties maintaining conscious capacity-loading attention (Drewer and Shean 1993) and switching their attention (Wilkins and Venables 1992). Their performance on attention tasks suggests an abnormal mode of attention control (Jutai 1989) and reduced attention capacity (Simons and Russo 1987). In the early stages of information processing, anhedonic participants exhibit normal performances both in a target detection paradigm (Silverstein et al. 1992) and in the embedded figure test, a perceptual differentiation test (Shuldberg and London 1989). This suggests that pre-attentive visual information processing is preserved and is consistent with the idea that perceptual organization processes are intact in anhedonic subjects. Deficiencies in anhedonics appear when the task requires a higher level of attention.

We investigated the ability of anhedonic participants to focus their attention (Dubal et al. 2000). Focused attention concerns the ability of participants to reject irrelevant or distracting messages, implying that participants process only one input at a time (a classic example involving the need to ignore irrelevant inputs is a "cocktail party situation" in which a guest tries to listen to one conversation and ignore all others).

We measured focused attention abilities using the "Eriksen response competition task" (Eriksen and Eriksen 1974), which has been studied extensively (see Servan-Schreiber et al. 1998). ERPs were also measured during the experiment to index neural resource allocation as reflected by the P300 amplitude. The Eriksen task consists of a centrally presented target letter flanked by noise letters. The participants are required to detect the target letter and to ignore noise letters, which can be the same as the target letter (compatible condition) or different (incompatible condition), thereby causing interference. Anhedonic subjects were predicted to have lower P300 wave amplitudes than controls. The identity of the noise letters surrounding the central target affects task difficulty, producing larger interference in the incompatible than the compatible condition.

First-year college students were selected based on their physical anhedonia scale scores (anhedonic participants scored 2 standard deviations above the mean score of controls matched for age and gender). Although the performance of anhedonic subjects was in the normal range, they had lower P300 amplitudes and slower RTs than control participants. Previous studies with the Eriksen task indicated that incompatible distractors alter error rates, RTs, and P300 latency. The incompatible condition should trigger the incorrect response, thereby slowing information processing (Eriksen and Eriksen 1974). However, incompatibility had less effect on error rates and RTs in our anhedonic sample than in controls.

Eriksen and Eriksen (1974) demonstrated that participants are unable to ignore irrelevant inputs, that is, the noise letters, because the processing of noise letters is automatic and therefore causes interference. When noise letters are incompatible, they trigger the incorrect response (i.e., HHNHH triggers the H response, but not the N response). As shown by Eriksen and Eriksen, participants able to block out the distraction of the noise letters carried out controlled processing of these letters.

In our experiment, anhedonic participants appeared to treat noise letters in a more controlled way than did the controls, as shown by their slower RTs. The fact that anhedonic students had longer RTs than controls and the finding that their RTs and performances were less affected in the incompatible condition suggest that anhedonic participants use a different response strategy. They may have developed a more conservative response strategy.

The P300 amplitude is lower in anhedonic participants, particularly at parieto-occipital sites. Posterior P300 is considered to specify advanced cognitive factors and to reflect partially resource allocation to the task (Johnson 1986). Evidence of low P300 amplitude has been observed in subjects presenting physical anhedonia (Josiassen et al. 1985; Miller 1986; Simons 1982; Simons and Russo 1987; Yee and Miller 1994). The P300 findings reported in the literature are inconsistent, perhaps due to the differential effort required by different tasks. No P300 reduction has been found in studies of tasks requiring minimal controlled processes (Giese-Davis et al. 1993; Ward et al. 1984;

Yee et al. 1992). Miller et al. (1984) showed that task demand seems to determine the nature of observed electrocortical deficits: As the complexity of the task decreased, so did the difference between anhedonic and control participants. When participants process information in a more controlled way, fewer cognitive resources can be allocated to the task. A lower P300 amplitude is thus consistent with a more conservative response strategy in anhedonic subjects.

14.3.2 Automatic Versus Controlled Processes in Anhedonia

Anhedonic participants tend to use more controlled processes than nonanhedonic participants. The next step consisted in investigating automatic versus controlled processes in anhedonic participants.

Theoretically, a simple detection task requires less attention than a task requiring both the detection and the recognition of a stimulus. This latter task may require controlled processing, whereas the former task should be automatic. In this study, one task involved the detection of a stimulus, and the second task required more controlled processing, with both tasks being equal in physical complexity. The added complexity introduced into the second task determined the supplementary effort needed to complete it: To maintain the same level of performance in the more complex task, participants would have to allocate more attention. ERPs were measured during the experiment to evaluate the amplitude of the P300 wave.

Although anhedonic subjects performed within the normal range on both tasks, their P300 amplitude was lower than that of control participants in the effortful condition, and no differences in ERPs were observed in the simple condition. P300 amplitude increased from the simple to the effortful condition only in the controls.

Behavioral results validated the difference between the two tasks in terms of difficulty: error rates as well as RTs were higher in the effortful condition than in the simple condition. This effect was found in both groups, showing that anhedonic and control subjects were sensitive to the effortful nature of the task. The normal behavioral performance in anhedonic participants confirmed previous findings.

Differences between groups were found at the electrophysiological level for the P300 amplitude: The P300 amplitude was lower in anhedonic participants, particularly at the parieto-occipital sites. As already mentioned, the posterior P300 is considered to be specifically related to cognitive factors at a higher than basic level and may partially reflect resource allocation to the task (Johnson 1986).

The finding of a P300 amplitude reduction in anhedonic participants is not universal. We propose that this may be due to the effort required by the task. In studies using low-demand tasks, no P300 wave deficits were found in anhedonic individuals (Miller 1986). Miller also found a lower P300 amplitude among anhedonic participants. Our results confirmed this hypothesis, by showing that task difficulty had different effects in the index and control groups: The P300 amplitude for anhedonic participants was lower only in the effortful condition. By contrast, in the automatic task, the P300 amplitude was not smaller in the anhedonic group than in the control group. Moreover, the amplitude of the P300 wave increased from the simple to the difficult condition in controls, which is typically observed in the literature (Hoffman et al. 1985; Kramer et al. 1985; Strayer and Kramer 1990; Wickens et al. 1983).

The similarity of the P300 amplitude in the two groups in the simple condition, and the lower P300 amplitude in anhedonic participants than in controls in the effortful condition, confirms that anhedonia is related to difficulty in processing complex information. The electrophysiological correlates of information-processing deficits in anhedonic participants should be revealed by effortful tasks.

14.3.3 Sustained Attention and Anhedonia

The studies carried out to date suggest that anhedonic participants have depleted processing resources or difficulties in mobilizing or allocating processing resources. The ability to sustain attention is likely to modulate performance in tasks for which anhedonic participants have been reported to show deficits. As sustained attention is necessary for many of our cognitive tasks, we need to explore the ability of anhedonic groups to sustain attention before attributing the observed deficits to higher order cognitive functions (Rueckert and Grafman 1996).

We recently tested anhedonic participants using a TOT measure during the Eriksen task described above (Dubal and Jouvent 2004). Sustained attention has never been studied in anhedonic participants, but they perform normally on the continuous performance test (CPT; Simons and Russo 1987). The CPT measures the ability to detect and to respond to specified stimulus changes occurring infrequently and at random intervals over a prolonged period of time, while simultaneously inhibiting responses to extraneous stimuli (Rosvold et al. 1956). The CPT is designed to measure vigilance (Nuechterlein 1983), but if only the hit rate or sensitivity measure is considered, this test does not measure sustained attention over time (Van den Bosh et al. 1996). Vigilance levels indicate the ability to discriminate a signal from noise throughout a vigilance period. "Vigilance decrements" refer to the decrease in vigilance levels over the course of the test; this process is closely related to the concept of sustained attention, which implies sustained readiness to respond to task-relevant or signal stimuli over a period of time. If only overall detection rates are reported, with no analysis of trends over time on task, the results are more likely to reflect overall vigilance performance (Van den Bosh et al. 1996). As stressed by Nuechterlein et al. (1983), the decrease in sensitivity over the vigilance period is an index of a deficit in sustaining attention.

Sustained attention involves the continuous maintenance over time of alertness and receptivity to a particular set of stimuli or stimulus changes (Parasuraman and Davies 1984). Typically, it is assessed using tasks in which a target must be detected or discriminated from nontargets (Warm 1984) in a period lasting from minutes to an hour (Davies and Tune 1969; Parasuraman 1984). The vigilance decrement or decrement function, known as the TOT effect, is the degree to which performance declines over time; it may be plotted for detection or response latency. Depending on the task, the TOT effect involves an increase in RTs and in the proportion of targets missed, and there is often a similar increase in the number of false-positive errors (Mackworth 1948; Parasuraman and Davies 1984; Rueckert and Levy 1996). The TOT effect depends on many factors, including task parameters (event rate, stimulus type) and extrane-ous environmental stimuli (e.g., noise, temperature; Ballard 1996).

The dynamics of the response are not only important in sustained attention studies but have also been observed in various cognitive tasks. Matthysse et al. (1999) pro-posed a model for these intermittent lapses, known as "dialipsis," in the performance of schizophrenic patients. They observed that "schizophrenic patients are impaired in many behaviours, but they do not show deficit functioning all the time" (p. 131). Numerous examples of intraparticipant variability, outliers, and shapes of distributions have emphasized the role of the dynamics of the response in cognitive studies. In the present study, sustained attention was determined by task-induced changes (in accu-racy and RT) during the experiment. Anhedonic participants completed six blocks of hundred trials, with a 2-minute pause between each block. RTs were calculated each minute for each block, giving five measures for each block, and across successive blocks.

As illustrated in figure 14.2, we found that anhedonic participants' RTs increased with TOT, becoming longer from the first minute to the last minute of each block.

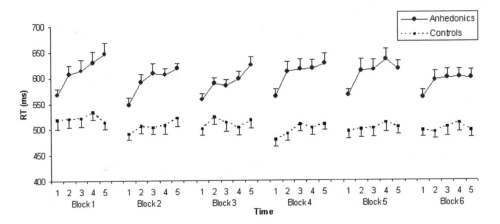

Figure 14.2
Mean reaction times (RTs) according to time on task. Subjects completed six blocks of 100 trials each. Each block lasted about five minutes. Blocks were separated by a 2-minute pause. The whole task lasted about 40 minutes.

However, no change in accuracy was found. It appears that anhedonic subjects have greater difficulty in maintaining rapidity over time but do so without sacrificing accuracy. There was no task repetition effect, as these effects did not vary between blocks. RT can only be measured if the participant is paying sufficient attention to respond to the task. The proportion of targets missed may be a more sensitive measure of the ability to sustain attention under most conditions (Parasuraman 1984). Therefore, our results may not reflect a pure sustained attention deficit. However, it should be borne in mind that our error rate was very low, and participants may have been responding at ceiling. Thus, before the hypothesis of a deficit in sustained attention is accepted, further tests are necessary with a more difficult task that would induce variability in performance.

How can a TOT effect on RT be related to cognitive processing of the task? According to Parasuraman, an increase in RT with TOT reflects a decrease in alertness (or arousal), whereas a decline in accuracy indicates a decline in vigilance (Parasuraman and Haxby 1993). An increase in RT in the context of declining performance suggests a process involving fatigue or task disengagement. In contrast, an increase in RT with maintenance of the level of performance suggests an integrated process of behavioral adaptation.

The adaptive behavior process hypothesis can be discussed in the light of incompatibility effects. Indeed, as expected, RTs and error rates were affected by incompatibility, although this effect did not vary with TOT. Error rates were particularly affected by incompatible conditions in the control group, similar to previous results obtained with the same procedure (Dubal et al. 2000). We suggested that these results reflect the participants' use of a more conservative response strategy.

One possible way of accounting for vigilance decrements involves distinguishing between controlled and automatic processes (Baddeley et al. 1999). As mentioned above, controlled strategies are very costly. If anhedonic participants use such strategies to approach this task, their attentional resources should be exhausted more rapidly than those of the controls, and this should be reflected by an increase in response time with time on task. Our results for block repetitions are consistent with this hypothesis.

The classical impairment of attention that accompanies anhedonia implies limitation of the ability to mobilize attentional processes, especially in high-demand situations. Our results are consistent with such a deficit in situations requiring effort and help to qualify the nature of the deficit. It may be that attentional resources are more rapidly exhausted rather than being limited.

14.4 Conclusions

Findings in depressed patients and anhedonic healthy subjects suggest impairment in the cognitive capacity of these subjects. Depressed patients and anhedonic patients recruit more cognitive resources than controls during cognitive effort. Repeating such cognitive effort may consume the cognitive and brain resources. The deficit of volition in depression and the "loss of pleasure" in anhedonia may partially reflect this exhaustion of cognitive resources.

At the brain level, foci of "network" dysfunction identified in the baseline depressed state should be considered as etiological abnormalities as well as sites of adaptive and maladaptive intrinsic compensatory processes. A given metabolic or brain activation pattern (assessed with PET scan or fMRI) is a combination of a "functional lesion" and an ongoing process of attempted self-correction or adaptation. From this perspective, the net regional activity is what accounts for the observed clinical symptoms. For instance, frontal hyperactivity could be seen as an exaggerated and maladaptive compensatory process, manifesting clinically as psychomotor agitation and rumination, the purpose of which is to override, at the cortical level, a persistent negative mood generated by abnormal chronic activity of limbic subcortical structures. In turn, frontal hypometabolism might reflect the failure to initiate or to maintain such a compensatory state with resulting apathy, anhedonia, and impaired executive functioning (see Mayberg and Fossati 2004).

References

Austin, M. P., P. Mitchell, K. Wilhelm, G. Parker, and I. Hickie. 1999. Cognitive function in depression: A distinct pattern of frontal impairment in melancolia. *Psychological Medicine, 29*, 73–85.

Baddeley, A., G. Cocchini, S. Della Sala, R. H. Logie, and H. Spinnler. 1999. Working memory and vigilance: Evidence from normal aging and Alzheimer's disease. *Brain and Cognition, 41*, 87–108.

Ballard, J. C. 1996. Computerized assessment of sustained attention: A review of factors affecting vigilance performance. *Journal of Clinical and Experimental Neuropsychology, 18*, 843–863.

Baxter, L. R. Jr., J. M. Schwartz, and M. E. Phelps. 1989. Reduction of prefrontal cortex glucose metabolism common to three types of depression. *Archives of General Psychiatry, 46*, 243–250.

Beats, B. C., B. J. Sahakian, and R. Levy. 1996. Cognitive performance in tests sensitive to frontal lobe dysfunction in the elderly depressed. *Psychological Medicine, 26*, 591–603.

Brody, A. L., S. Saxena, and M. A. Mandelkern. 2001. Brain metabolic changes associated with symptom factor improvement in major depressive disorder. *Biological Psychiatry, 50*, 171–178.

Carter, C. S., M. M. Botvinick, and J. D. Cohen. 1999. The contribution of the anterior cingulate cortex to executive processes in cognition. *Review of Neuroscience, 10*, 49–57.

Channon, S. 1996. Executive dysfunction in depression: The Wisconsin Card Sorting Test. *Journal of Affective Disorders, 39*, 107–114.

Davies, D. R., and G. S. Tune. 1969. *Human Vigilance Performance*. New York: Elsevier.

Dehaene, S., and J. P. Changeux. 1991. The Wisconsin Card Sorting Test: Theoretical analysis and modeling in neuronal network. *Cerebral Cortex*, *111*, 62–79.

Dewinsky, O., M. J. Marrell, and B. A. Vogt. 1995. Contributions of anterior cingulate cortex to behaviours. *Brain*, *118*, 279–306.

Dolan, R. J., C. J. Bench, R. G. Brown, K. J. Friston, and R. S. J. Frackowiack. 1992. Regional cerebral blood flow abnormalities in depressed patients with cognitive impairment. *Journal of Neurology, Neurosurgery, and Psychiatry*, *55*, 768–773.

Drevets, W. C. 2001. Neuroimaging and neuropathological studies of depression: Implications for the cognitive-emotional features of mood disorders. *Current Opinion in Neurobiology*, *11*, 240–249.

Drevets, W. C., T. O. Videen, and J. L. Price. 1992. A functional anatomical study of unipolar depression. *Journal of Neuroscience*, *12*, 3628–3641.

Drewer, H. B., and G. D. Shean. 1993. Reaction time crossover in schizotypal participants. *Journal of Nervous and Mental Disease*, *181*, 27–30.

Dubal, S., and R. Jouvent. 2004a. Loss of emotional fluency as a developmental phenotype. In *Emotional Development*, ed. J. Nadel and D. Muir, pp. 409–427. Oxford: Oxford University Press.

Dubal, S., and R. Jouvent. 2004b. Time-on-task effect in trait anhedonia. *European Psychiatry*, *19*, 285–291.

Dubal, S., A. Pierson, and R. Jouvent. 2000. Focused attention in anhedonia: A P3 study. *Psychophysiology*, *37*, 711–714.

Elliott, R., B. J. Sahakian, A. P. McKay, J. J. Herrod, T. W. Robbins, and E. S. Paykel. 1996. Neuropsychological impairments in unipolar depression: The influence of perceived failure on subsequent performance. *Psychological Medicine*, *26*, 975–989.

Eriksen, C. W., and B. A. Eriksen. 1974. Effects of noise letters upon the identification of a target letter in a nonsearch task. *Perception and Psychophysics*, *16*, 143–149.

Eslinger, P. J., and L. M. Grattan. 1993. Frontal lobe and frontal-striatal substrates for different forms of human cognitive flexibility. *Neuropsychologia*, *31*, 17–28.

Fossati, P., G. Amar, N. Raoux, A. M. Ergis, and J. F. Allilaire. 1999. Executive functioning and verbal memory in young patients with unipolar depression and schizophrenia. *Psychiatry Research*, *89*, 171–187.

Fossati, P., A. M. Ergis, and J. F. Allilaire. 2001. Problem-solving abilities in unipolar depressed patients: Comparison of performance on the modified version of Wisconsin and California sorting tests. *Psychiatry Research*, *104*, 145–156.

Fossati, P., A. M. Ergis, and J. F. Allilaire. 2002. Neuropsychologie des troubles des fonctions exécutives dans la dépression: une revue de la littérature. *L'encéphale*, *28*, 97–107.

Fossati, P., G. Le Bastard, A. M. Ergis, and J. F. Allilaire. 2003. Qualitative analysis of verbal fluency in depression. *Psychiatry Research*, *117*, 17–24.

Franke, P., W. Maier, J. Hardt, R. Frieboes, D. Lichtermann, and C. Hain. 1993. Assessment of frontal lobe functioning in schizophrenia and unipolar major depression. *Psychopathology, 26,* 76–84.

George, M. S., T. A. Ketter, and P. I. Parekh. 1994b. Regional brain activity when selecting a response despite interference: An H215O PET study of the Stroop and an emotional Stroop. *Human Brain Mapping, 1,* 194–209.

George, M. S., T. A. Ketter, and R. M. Post. 1994a. Prefrontal cortex dysfunction in clinical depression. *Depression, 2,* 59–72.

Giese-Davis, J. E, G. A. Miller, and R. A. Knight. 1993. Memory template comparison processes in anhedonia and dysthymia. *Psychophysiology, 30,* 646–656.

Hartlage, S., L. B. Alloy, C. Vazquez, and B. Dykman. 1993. Automatic and effortful processing in depression. *Psychological Bulletin, 113,* 247–278.

Harvey, P. O., P. Fossati, J. B. Pochon, R. Levy, G. Lebastard, S. Lehericy, et al. 2005. Cognitive control and brain resources in major depression: An fMRI study using the n-back task. *Neuroimage, 26,* 860–869.

Harvey, P. O., G. Le Bastard, J. B. Pochon, R. Levy, J. F. Allilaire, B. Dubois, and P. Fossati. 2004. Executive functions and updating of the contents of working memory in unipolar depression. *Journal of Psychiatric Research, 38,* 137–144.

Hasher, L., and R. T. Zacks. 1979. Automatic and effortful processes in memory. *Journal of Experimental Psychology: General, 108,* 356–389.

Hoffman, J. E., M. R. Houck, F. W. MacMillan, R. F. Simons, and L. C. Oatman. 1985. Event-related potentials elicited by automatic targets: A dual-task analysis. *Journal of Experimental Psychology: Human Perception and Performance, 11,* 50–61.

Hyder, F., E. A. Phelps, C. J. Wiggins, K. S. Labar, A. M. Blamire, and R. G. Shulman. 1997. "Willed action": A functional MRI study of the human prefrontal cortex during a sensorimotor task. *Proceedings National Academy of Sciences USA, 94,* 6989–6994.

Johnson, R. 1986. A triarchic model of P300 amplitude. *Psychophysiology, 23,* 367–384.

Josiassen, R., C. Shagass, R. Roemer, and J. Straumanis. 1985. Attention-related effects in somatosensory evoked potentials in college students at high risk for psychopathology. *Journal of Abnormal Psychology, 94,* 507–518.

Jutai, J. W. 1989. Spatial attention in hypothetically psychosis-prone college students. *Psychiatry Research, 27,* 207–215.

Kramer, A. F., C. D. Wickens, and E. Donchin. 1985. Processing of stimulus properties: Evidence for dual-task integrality. *Journal of Experimental Psychology: Human Perception and Performance, 11,* 393–408.

Kuhl, J., and P. Helle. 1986. Motivational and volitional determinants of depression: The degenerated-intention hypothesis. *Journal of Abnormal Psychology, 95,* 247–251.

Mackworth, N. H. 1948. The breakdown of vigilance during prolonged visual search. *Quarterly Journal of Experimental Psychology, 1*, 6–21.

Matthysse, S., D. L. Levy, Y. Wu, D. B. Rubin, and P. Holzman. 1999. Intermittent degradation in performance in schizophrenia. *Schizophrenia Research, 30*, 131–146.

Mayberg, H. S. 1994. Frontal lobe dysfunction in secondary depression. *Journal of Neuropsychiatry and Clinical Neurosciences, 6*, 428–442.

Mayberg, H. S. 1997. Limbic–cortical dysregulation: A proposed model of depression. *Journal of Neuropsychiatry and Clinical Neuroscience, 9*, 471–481.

Mayberg, H. S., and P. Fossati. 2004. Dysfunctional limbic–cortical circuits in major depression: A functional neuroimaging perspective. In *Cognitive and Affective Neuroscience of Psychopathology*, ed. D. M. Barch. Oxford: Oxford University Press.

Merriam, E. P., M. E. Thase, G. L. Haas, M. S. Keshavan, and A. Sweeney. 1999. Prefrontal cortical dysfunction in depression determined by Wisconsin Card Sorting Test performance. *American Journal of Psychiatry, 156*, 257–289.

Miller, G. A. 1986. Information processing deficits in anhedonia and perceptual aberration: A psychophysiological analysis. *Biological Psychiatry, 21*, 100–115.

Miller, G. A., R. F. Simons, and P. J. Lang. 1984. Electrocortical measures of information processing deficits in anhedonia. *Annals of the New York Academy of Sciences, 425*, 599–602.

Miyake, A., N. P. Friedman, M. J. Emerson, A. H. Witzki, A. Howerter, and T. D. Wager. 2000. The unity and diversity of executive functions and their contributions to complex "frontal lobe" tasks: A latent variable analysis. *Cognitive Psychology, 41*, 49–100.

Murphy, F. C., B. J. Sahakian, and R. E. O'Carrol. 1998. Cognitive impairment in depression: Psychological models and clinical issues. In *New Models for Depression: Advances in Biological Psychiatry*, vol. 19, ed. D. Ebert and K. P. Ebmeier, pp. 1–33. Karger: Basel.

Nagahama, Y., H. Fukuyama, H. Yamauchi, S. Matsuzaki, J. Konishi, H. Shibasaki, and J. Kimura. 1996. Cerebral activation during performance of a card sorting test. *Brain, 119*, 1667–1675.

Nathaniel-James, D. A., and C. D. Frith. 2002. The role of the dorsolateral prefrontal cortex: Evidence from the effects of contextual constraint in a sentence completion task. *Neuroimage, 16*, 1094–1102.

Nuechterlein, K. H. 1977. Reaction time and attention in schizophrenia: A critical evaluation of the data and theories. *Schizophrenia Bulletin, 3*, 373–428.

Nuechterlein, K. H. 1983. Signal detection in vigilance tasks and behavioral attributes among offspring of schizophrenic mothers and among hyperactive children. *Journal of Abnormal Psychology, 92*, 4–28.

Nuechterlein, K. H., R. Parasuraman, and Q. Jiang. 1983. Visual sustained attention: Image degradation produces rapid sensitivity decrement over time. *Science, 220*, 327–329.

Parasuraman, R. 1984. Sustained attention in detection and discrimination. In *Varieties of Attention*, ed. R. Parasuraman and D. R. Davies, pp. 243–289. New York: Academic Press.

Parasuraman, R., and D. R. Davies. 1984. In *Varieties of Attention*, ed. R. Parasuraman and D. R. Davies, pp. 12–23. New York: Academic Press.

Parasuraman, R., and J. V. Haxby. 1993. Attention and brain function in Alzheimer's disease. *Neuropsychology*, *7*, 242–272.

Partiot, A., A. Pierson, B. Renault, D. Widlocher, and R. Jouvent. 1994. Automatic information processing, the frontal system, and blunted affect: From clinical dimensions to cognitive processes toward a psychobiological explanation of temperament. *Encephale*, *20*, 511–519.

Pochon, J. B., R. Levy, P. Fossati, S. Lehericy, J. B. Poline, B. Pillon, D. Le Bihan, and B. Dubois. 2002. The neural system that bridges reward and cognition in humans: An fMRI study. *Proceedings of the National Academy of Sciences*, *16*, 5669–5674.

Ribot, T. 1896. *La psychologie des sentiments*, vol. 1, Alcan, 16th edition (1939). Paris: PUF, Bibliothèque de Philosophie Contemporaine.

Ridderinkhof, K. R., M. Ullsperger, E. A. Crone, and S. Nieuwenhuis. 2004. The role of the medial frontal cortex in cognitive control. *Science*, *306*, 443–447.

Rosvold, H. E., A. F. Mirsky, I. Sarason, E. D. Bransome, and L. H. A. Beck. 1956. Continuous performance test of brain damage. *Journal of Consulting and Clinical Psychology*, *20*, 343–350.

Rueckert, L., and J. Grafman. 1996. Sustained attention deficits in patients with right frontal lesions. *Neuropsychologia*, *34*, 953–963.

Rueckert, L., and J. Levy. 1996. Further evidence that the callosum is involved in sustaining attention. *Neuropsychologia*, *34*, 927–935.

Schneider, W., S. T. Dumais, and R. M. Shiffrin. 1984. Automatic and control processing and attention. In *Varieties of Attention*, ed. R. Parasuraman and D. R. Davies, pp. 1–27. New York: Academic Press.

Servan-Schreiber, D., C. S. Carter, R. M. Bruno, and J. D. Cohen. 1998. Dopamine and the mechanisms of cognition: Part II. D-amphetamine effects in human subjects performing a selective attention task. *Biological Psychiatry*, *15*, 723–729.

Shuldberg, D., and A. London. 1989. Psychological differentiation and schizotypal traits: Negative results with the Group Embedded Figures Test. *Perceptual and Motor Skills*, *68*, 1219–1226.

Silverstein, S. M., M. L. Raulin, E. A. Pristach, and J. R. Pomerantz. 1992. Perceptual organization and schizotypy. *Journal of Abnormal Psychology*, *101*, 265–270.

Simons, R. F. 1982. Physical anhedonia and future psychopathology: An electrocortical continuity? *Psychophysiology*, *19*, 433–441.

Simons, R. F., and K. R. Russo. 1987. Event-related potentials and continuous performance in participants with physical anhedonia or perceptual aberrations. *Journal of Psychophysiology*, *2*, 27–37.

Strayer, D. L., and A. F. Kramer. 1990. Attentional requirements of automatic and controlled processing. *Journal of Experimental Psychology: Learning, Memory, and Cognition, 16,* 67–82.

Stuss, D. T., and D. F. Benson. 1984. Neuropsychological studies of the frontal lobes. *Psychological Bulletin, 95,* 3–28.

Van den Bosch, R. J., R. P. Rombouts, and M. J. Van Asma. 1996. What determines continuous performance task performance? *Schizophrenia Bulletin, 22,* 643–651.

Videbech, P., B. Ravnkilde, S. Kristensen, A. Egander, K. Clemmensen, N. A. Rasmussen, A. Gjedde, and R. Rosenberg. 2003. The Danish PET/depression project: Poor verbal fluency performance despite normal prefrontal activation in patients with major depression. *Psychiatry Research, 123,* 49–63.

Ward, P. B., S. V. Catts, M. S. Armstrong, and N. McConaghy. 1984. P300 and psychiatric vulnerability in university students. *Annals of the New York Academy of Sciences, 425,* 645–652.

Warm, J. S. 1984. *Sustained Attention in Human Performance.* London: Wiley.

Weingartner, H. 1987. Automatic and effort-demanding cognitive processes in depression. In *Handbook for Clinical Memory Assessment,* ed. C. Poons, pp. 218–255.

Wickens, C. D., A. F. Kramer, L. Vanasse, and E. Donchin. 1983. The performance of concurrent tasks: A psychophysiological analysis of the reciprocity of information processing resources. *Science, 221,* 1080–1082.

Wilkins, S., and P. H. Venables. 1992. Disorder of attention in individuals with schizotypal personality. *Schizophrenia Bulletin, 18,* 717–723.

Yee, C. M., and G. A. Miller. 1994. A dual-task analysis of resource allocation in dysthymia and anhedonia. *Journal of Abnormal Psychology, 103,* 625–636.

Yee, C. M., P. J. Deldin, and G. A. Miller. 1992. Early processing stimulus in dysthymia and anhedonia. *Journal of Abnormal Psychology, 101,* 230–223.

IV Disorders of Volition in Patients with Prefrontal Lobe Damage

15 The Human Ventrolateral Frontal Cortex and Intended Action

Adrian M. Owen

15.1 Introduction

The idea that the frontal cortex is important for intended actions is not a new one, although the precise nature of this involvement has been neither behaviorally, nor anatomically, well specified (see Grafman and Krueger, this volume). As early as 1922, Bianchi suggested that the frontal lobes are involved in controlling behavior, while the neuropsychological literature throughout the last century is filled with descriptions of frontal lobe patients that imply an impairment of intended actions but lack testable, well-specified components. For example, terms such as "planning" (Owen et al. 1990; Shallice 1982, 1988), "temporal structuring of behavior" (Fuster 1997), "monitoring or manipulation in working memory" (Owen 1997; Petrides 1994), and the "control of behavior by context" (Cohen and Servan-Schreiber 1992) have often been used to describe the behavior of these patients. In this chapter, I will review recent evidence that suggests that the midventrolateral region of the frontal cortex, which in humans lies below the inferior frontal sulcus, is important for *intended action*, that is, any behavior (e.g., an action or a thought) that is consciously *willed* by the agent responsible for carrying out that behavior (see Prinz, Dennett, and Sebanz, this volume). Data from both neuropsychological investigations in patients and functional neuroimaging studies in healthy volunteers will be discussed, as will relevant evidence from lesion and electrophysiological studies in the macaque.

15.2 Neuropsychological Studies

In the last fifty years, numerous neuropsychological studies have reported, or implied, a dissociation between the performance of patients with frontal lobe damage on tests of recognition and recall (for a review, see Wheeler, Stuss, and Tulving 1995). For example, Owen et al. (1995) compared three groups of patients with frontal lobe excisions, temporal lobe removals, or unilateral amygdalo-hippocampectomy on a computerized battery of tasks designed to assess visuospatial short-term recognition memory and learning. In one delayed-matching-to-sample task, the patients were required to remember a complex visual pattern for up to 12 seconds and then to select that pattern from among three distractors. In the two posterior lesion groups, significant delay-dependent deficits were observed, while the frontal lobe group performed at an equivalent level to controls. Unlike the temporal lobe and amygdalo-hippocampectomy groups, the frontal lobe patients were also unimpaired at a pattern recognition memory task which required that they remember a series of twelve abstract color patterns and then select, from sequentially presented pairs of stimuli, those that had been seen previously. Like many so-called "recognition memory" tasks, both of these tests can be performed purely on the basis of judgments of relative familiarity or through the passive recollection of encoded information (Jacoby and Dallas 1981; Mandler 1980). Thus, on seeing a test stimulus, a subject may decide that it appears familiar but be unable specifically to recall having seen the stimulus before or any information about it or how and when it was encoded. Similar results have been reported throughout the neuropsychological literature; that is to say, compared to patients with damage to the medial temporal lobe region, patients with frontal lobe damage are relatively unimpaired on tests that can be solved using recognition memory (for a review, see Wheeler, Stuss, and Tulving 1995). Moreover, similar patterns of preserved function on tests of recognition memory have been reported in other patient groups who are often described in terms of their "frontal-like" behavior. For example, patients with Parkinson's disease (Owen et al. 1992) and schizophrenia (see Frith, this volume, and Spence and Parry, this volume) are unimpaired on the twelve-item pattern recognition memory test described above (Pantelis et al. 1997). This test is, however, highly sensitive to deficit in patients with dementia of the Alzheimer type, which is more commonly associated with temporal lobe dysfunction (Sahakian et al. 1988).

In contrast, profound deficits are often reported in patients with frontal lobe damage on memory tests which cannot be solved on the basis of familiarity judgments. For example, in one study the same three groups of patients with frontal lobe excisions, temporal lobe removals, or unilateral amygdalo-hippocampectomy were compared to healthy volunteers on a computerized spatial searching task (Owen et al. 1990, 1996a). This task is essentially a modification of a test used by Passingham (1985) to examine the effects of prefrontal cortex lesions in primates and is conceptually similar to the radial arm maze which has been used to assess working memory in rats (Olton 1982). Subjects were required to search through a number of colored boxes presented on the computer screen (by touching each one) in order to find blue "tokens" which were hidden inside. The object was to avoid those boxes in which a token had already been found. Clearly, like the visual memory tasks described above, this test places a significant load on memory, although unlike those tests, it cannot be solved using recognition memory alone. Each trial requires the active reorganization and manipulation of information within memory and the explicit (i.e., intentional) selection for later recall of some of the stimuli and the rejection of others. In fact, control subjects often adopt an explicit search strategy which involves retracing a systematic "route" and "editing" or "monitoring" those locations where tokens have been found previously, and, again, this behavior places demands on task performance which cannot be explained in terms of recognition memory alone (for discussion, see Owen et al. 1996a). Neurosurgical patients with frontal lobe damage were significantly impaired on this searching task and made more returns to boxes in which a token had previously been found even at the simplest levels of task difficulty (Owen et al. 1990, 1996a). In addition, these patients are less efficient in the use of the repetitive searching strategy described above, confirming that at least some of their memory impairment may arise secondarily from a more fundamental deficit in the use of explicit organizational strategies. In contrast, deficits in the temporal lobe group and the amygdalo-hippocampectomy group were only observed at the most difficult level of the task, and in neither group could this deficit be related to the inefficient use of an explicit searching strategy. "Frontal-like" deficits on this task have also been reported in patients with schizophrenia (Pantelis et al. 1997) and Parkinson's disease (Owen et al. 1992), even early in the course of the disease when clinical symptoms are relative mild and other aspects of cognition such as visual recognition memory remain unaffected.

Similar results are not difficult to find in the neuropsychological literature; that is to say, patients with frontal lobe damage are often impaired on tests that cannot be solved using recognition memory alone (for a review, see Wheeler, Stuss, and Tulving 1995). For example, Petrides and Milner (1982) reported that frontal lobe patients were significantly impaired on tests of verbal and visual "self-ordered pointing." In those tasks, patients were required to select each stimulus from an array without ever selecting the same stimulus twice. Clearly, on such tests recognition memory cannot be used because on every trial all of the stimuli have been seen before (on previous trials) and are, therefore, more or less equally familiar. In a more recent study, patients with frontal lobe excisions, temporal lobe removals, or unilateral amygdalo-hippocampectomy were compared to healthy volunteers on a task that required associations to be learned between up to eight visual patterns and a set of screen locations over a series of learning trials (Owen et al. 1995). Memory for the pattern–location associations was tested by presenting each pattern in the center of the screen, and the patients were required to select the appropriate location for each. Again, this task cannot be solved using recognition memory (which would be sufficient only to verify whether or not any particular shape or location had been used before and was therefore familiar), as the correct location for each pattern had to be generated or recalled from memory as and when required. Neurosurgical patients with frontal lobe damage were significantly impaired on this task, failing to select the appropriate location for each pattern (Owen et al. 1995). Moreover, similar deficits have been reported in other "frontal-like" populations, including patients with Parkinson's disease (Owen et al. 1993a).

While all of these tasks have their own unique requirements that may well contribute to the deficits observed in frontal lobe populations, they also have one thing in common; that is, unlike the recognition memory tasks described above, they all require an active and *intentional* search for a target item. In fact, in a review of neuropsychological studies carried out since 1984, Wheeler, Stuss, and Tulving (1995) reported that, while only 8% of these studies reported impairments in frontal lobe patients on tests of recognition, 80% reported significant impairments on tests of free recall. While few of the tasks described in detail above can strictly be described as tests of "free recall," they do nevertheless have requirements that are reminiscent of such tasks and, more importantly for this discussion, require the self-initiated, conscious (i.e., *intentional*) retrieval of remembered information in the absence of external cues.

Further consideration of the neuropsychological literature, however, makes it clear that any description of frontal lobe patients that focuses purely on memory is, at best, incomplete, as impairments have also been reported on tasks that have no clear mnemonic component at all (see Bechara, this volume). For example, deficits on the Wisconsin Card Sorting Test (Milner 1964; Nelson 1976; Drewe 1974; Robinson et al. 1980) and, more recently, on variants of the intra- and extradimensional set-shifting paradigm (Owen et al. 1991, 1993b) have been widely reported in both frontal lobe patients and in patients with "frontal-like" behavioral profiles (e.g., Owen et al. 1992; Pantelis et al. 1997). In fact, shifting deficits have even been reported in frontal lobe patients on much simpler tasks, including those where all that is required is a reversal of responding from one specific stimulus to another (e.g., Rolls et al. 1994; Rahman et al. 1999). While these tasks certainly have a memory component, this alone does not seem to account for the frontal lobe deficit (for discussion, see Owen et al. 1993b). On the other hand, all of these tasks require an intentional change or "switch" of attention that is not explicitly guided by an external cue. Similarly, disturbances of reasoning and planning (Milner 1964; Shallice 1982), the ability to regulate behavior according to instructions (Milner 1964; Luria 1966), and spatial orientation (Corkin 1965; Semmes et al. 1963) have all been reported after frontal lobe damage in humans (see also Grafman and Krueger, this volume). All of these tasks require explicit decisions and actions that are based on intentions and plans. Such evidence suggests that one important factor for understanding the functional relationship between the frontal lobe and more posterior association cortex may be the extent to which any behavior (e.g., an action or a thought) is under *intentional* control (see Prinz, Dennett, and Sebanz, this volume).

15.3   The Ventrolateral Frontal Cortex in Humans

The prefrontal cortex is cytoarchitectonically diverse, both in the human brain and in the macaque brain, and comprises a number of specific areas which have distinct patterns of connectivity with other brain regions (fig. 15.1). Until recently, direct investigation of the functional organization of cognitive processes within the human brain was limited to the sorts of comparisons described above, between groups of patients with damage to different cortical and/or subcortical regions (e.g., Petrides and Milner 1982; Owen et al. 1990, 1995, 1996a). In patient studies, it is not possible to establish which areas of the frontal cortex are involved in a given cognitive process with any degree of anatomical precision since the excisions are rarely confined to specific cytoarchitectonic areas. In recent years, however, functional neuroimaging techniques such as positron-emission tomography (PET) and functional magnetic resonance imaging (fMRI) have provided a unique opportunity for assessing the relationship between patterns of cortical and subcortical activation and different aspects of cognitive processing in healthy control volunteers. One area of the human frontal lobe which has been consistently activated in many different studies across a number of cognitive domains is the midventrolateral frontal cortex (for a review, see Owen, Lee, and Williams 2000). In the human brain, the midventrolateral frontal cortex (fig. 15.1) comprises the tissue below the inferior frontal sulcus and includes Cytoarchitectonic Areas 47/12 and 45

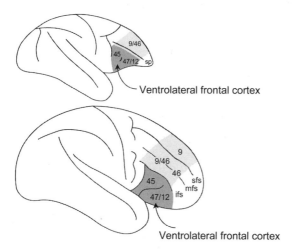

Figure 15.1
Schematic drawing of the lateral surface of the macaque brain (top) and the human brain (bottom), to indicate the location of the ventrolateral frontal cortex (Areas 45, 47, 12). Adapted from Petrides and Pandya 1994. sp, sulcus principalis; ifs, inferior frontal sulcus; mfs, middle frontal sulcus; sfs, superior frontal sulcus. See plate 7.

(Carmicheal and Price 1994; Petrides and Pandya 1994). Emphasis is usually placed on the connections between this region and the temporal lobe and ventral stream visual areas important for pattern and object vision (Webster et al. 1994; Carmicheal and Price 1995a, 1995b). It is now clear, however, that the ventrolateral prefrontal cortex is also interconnected with some dorsal stream parietal areas (Cavada and Goldman-Rakic 1989; Schall et al. 1995). The midventrolateral frontal cortex, therefore, constitutes the first level of interaction between several posterior cortical association regions and the entire lateral frontal cortex and, in this capacity, is anatomically well placed to play a fundamental role in facilitating interactions between the two.

Early functional neuroimaging studies that activated the midventrolateral frontal cortex in humans tended to emphasize the explicit retrieval of one, or a few, pieces of information and the sequencing of responses based directly on that stored information. For example, in one PET study (Jonides et al. 1993; see also Smith et al. 1995), healthy volunteers were required to remember the location of three simultaneously presented stimuli and then to decide whether or not a probe circle occupied one of those same three locations following a 3-second delay. Activation was observed in the midventrolateral frontal cortex, but not in more dorsal regions of the frontal lobe. More recently, activation has been reported in this same region during all sorts of cognitive tasks which make varying demands on mnemonic and attentional processes. For example, the midventrolateral frontal cortex has been activated in tasks that require the selection, comparison, and judgment of stimuli held in short-term and long-term memory (Petrides 1994) when spatial and nonspatial information is held "on-line" (Goldman-Rakic 1994; Courtney et al. 1997), during task switching (Dove et al. 2000), reversal learning (Cools et al. 2002), and stimulus selection (Rushworth et al. 1997), when the specification of retrieval cues is required (Dobbins et al. 2002), during the "elaboration encoding" of information into episodic memory (Henson et al. 1999; Wagner et al. 1998), and when judgments of word meaning are required (Kapur et al. 1994). While few of these studies set out specifically to investigate the functions of the ventrolateral frontal cortex, the combined results certainly suggest that this region responds to a variety of task demands across a number of stimulus modalities. In this sense, this region may be a good candidate for understanding how simple decisions, low-level plans, and other basic aspects of intended action are instantiated in the cerebral cortex.

15.4   The Ventrolateral Frontal Cortex in the Macaque

In the macaque, the midventrolateral frontal cortex lies below the sulcus principalis on the inferior convexity and comprises Areas 12 or 47/12 and 45 (Carmicheal and Price 1994; Petrides and Pandya 1994). Broadly speaking, the findings from lesion studies support the suggestion above, from human imaging studies, that this region makes a polymodal contribution to a variety of different cognitive tasks. For example, lesions of the ventrolateral frontal cortex, but not the more dorsal cortex surrounding the *sulcus principalis*, cause impairments in nonspatial delayed matching to sample for single items (Mishkin and Manning 1978; Passingham 1975), spatial and nonspatial delayed alternation (Mishkin et al. 1969), the learning of arbitrary stimulus–response associations (Gaffan 1994; Petrides 1994; Murray and Wise 1997), switching attention to behaviorally relevant aspects of the world (e.g., Dias et al. 1996), and even in object matching when the sample and the match are simultaneously present and there is no delay component (Rushworth et al. 1997). Thus, once a simultaneous version of a task has been relearned, the imposition of a delay between sample and match poses no more of a problem for a monkey with a ventrolateral frontal lesion than it does prior to surgery (Rushworth et al. 1997).

Electrophysiological data from the monkey also support a rather fundamental yet general role for this region in a variety of cognitive tasks. For example, Sakagami and Niki (1994) trained monkeys to make or withhold a response depending on which stimulus they were shown. On some blocks of trials, the relevant dimension of the stimulus was its color; on other trials, it was its position or shape. Ventrolateral neurons appeared to encode the stimulus dimension of current interest to the monkey. Similarly, Rao et al. (1997) identified neurons ventral to the principal sulcus that encoded either, or both, the location and the identity of stimuli presented in a novel delayed-response procedure. What was most remarkable about this finding was the apparent flexibility of some neurons to adapt as the emphasis of the task changed during its various stages. Thus, once a target object's identity was no longer relevant, many of the "what-and-where" cells no longer coded for object identity but switched to code for object location. This finding suggests that the response of ventrolateral prefrontal "memory cells" is flexible—that is, they can code different stimulus attributes at different times according to task demands. In other words, they will respond to a stimulus, irrespective of its modality, whenever there is an explicit requirement and an associated intention to do so. Finally, Li et al. (1997) taught monkeys a conditional response task and recorded from ventrolateral cells while they learned to associate each of the learned responses with a new cue. Ventrolateral neurons were particularly modulated during the process of learning the selection rule associated with each of the novel stimuli.

Flexible encoding of task-relevant variables within the ventrolateral frontal cortex is consistent with accounts of prefrontal function that emphasize its importance in switching and the top-down modulation of attention (e.g., Owen et al. 1991, 1993b; Knight 1994; Desimone and Duncan 1995; Dias et al. 1996). Compromising such a function would cause failure on a wide variety of tasks, but particularly those that require an *intended action*—that is, any behavior (e.g., an action or a thought), that derives from the subject's plans and *intentions*.

15.5   The Human Ventrolateral Frontal Cortex and Intended Action

Although many functional neuroimaging studies have activated the midventrolateral
frontal cortex in a variety of behavioral contexts, few have explicitly set out to investigate the role of this region directly. To address this issues, my colleagues and I
recently conducted a series of studies using PET and fMRI, employing spatial, visual,
and verbal stimuli in tasks that make differing demands on aspects of intended or
planned behavior (Owen et al. 1996b, 1999, 2000; Stern et al. 2000; Bor et al. 2003).
For example, one hypothesis tested was that frontal activation would be confined to
the midventrolateral region of the frontal cortex when the experimental task required
the subject to hold a sequence of five previously presented spatial locations in memory
and then to respond directly by touching those same locations following a delay
(Owen et al. 1996b, 1999). Thus, the emphasis of the task was on the explicit encoding of spatial information and the uncued recall of this information following a short
delay. During this task, a significant regional cerebral blood flow (rCBF) increase was
observed in ventrolateral Area 47 of the right hemisphere (fig. 15.2a). Similarly, in a
second task that required the volunteers to execute a fixed sequence of responses to
eight previously learned locations, ventrolateral frontal Area 47 was significantly
activated, bilaterally (Owen et al. 1996b). During both tasks, however, rCBF changes
within other frontal regions, including the dorsolateral frontal cortex, did not
approach significance. In a follow-up PET study, the five-item spatial span task was
used again but was compared with a variation on the widely used spatial "2-back" procedure (Owen et al. 1999). As predicted, during the spatial span task, which simply
required the uncued and intentional retrieval and reproduction of stored information,
a significant rCBF increase was observed in the midventrolateral prefrontal cortex (fig.
15.2b) at coordinates very similar to those reported previously (Owen et al. 1996b).

In a more recent PET study, a direct anologue of the spatial span task was employed
to investigate whether these findings could be extended to the verbal domain (Owen
et al. 2000). During one experimental task, subjects were required to hold a sequence
of five auditorily presented numbers in memory (e.g., 7, 3, 8, 2, 9) and then to respond
by (verbally) producing those numbers, in order, following a short delay (e.g., 7, 3, 8,
2, 9). Since the emphasis of this verbal working memory task was on the noncued,
active retrieval of remembered information from memory, it was predicted that the
midventrolateral but not the mid-dorsolateral prefrontal cortex would be activated. As
predicted, when the forward digits span task was compared to the control, significant
activation was observed in right midventrolateral Area 47 (fig. 15.2c) at coordinates
similar to those reported previously in studies of spatial span (Owen et al. 1996b, 1999;
see also Jonides et al. 1993; Smith et al. 1995).

These results confirm that the midventrolateral frontal cortex is important for tasks
in which volunteers are explicitly asked to encode or retrieve information or to make

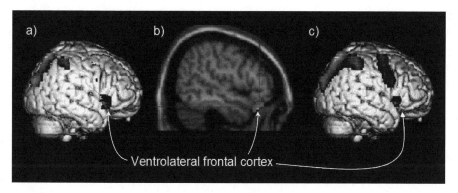

Figure 15.2
Regional cerebral blood flow maps from three independent positron-emission tomography studies activating an almost identical location within the midventrolateral frontal cortex. (a) spatial span (adapted from Owen et al., 1996b), (b) digit span (adapted from Owen et al., 2000), and (c) spatial span (adapted from Owen et al., 1999). Right hemisphere only is shown. See plate 8.

decisions about whether they have seen a particular stimulus before or not (Owen et al. 1996b, 2000; Petrides 1994), irrespective of the modality of the information being processed.

On the basis of PET activation data of this sort it is not, however, possible to attribute these findings unequivocally to any particular aspect of intended action on the part of the volunteer. PET activation studies, by their very nature, require "block" designs, usually of between 60 and 90 seconds duration, and throughout this period participants perform a cognitive or sensorimotor task of interest. Critically, however, the PET activation method does not allow for the decomposition of this lengthy acquisition time into more psychologically meaningful temporal units. Thus, the derived estimates of local cortical blood flow represent the total accumulative effect of all of those cognitive, motor, and perceptual processes taking place within the broad acquisition period. fMRI does not suffer the same limitations, and with event-related designs signal changes can be correlated with cognitive task performance on a trial-by-trial basis; in this way, differential time courses of activation within specific anatomical regions of interest may be examined and compared. Moreover, the increased effective power of high-field fMRI over PET activation studies means that such questions can be asked *within* an individual subject, allowing single-subject studies, group designs, or a mixture of the two to be implemented.

Recently, my colleagues and I used event-related fMRI to explicitly test the hypothesis that activity in the midventrolateral frontal cortex is specifically associated with intention to act, all other factors being held constant (Dove et al. 2001). Colorful stimuli, based on examples of abstract art, were presented, and volunteers were instructed on random trials either to just examine each piece ("incidental" encoding) or to try to remember it for later test ("intentional" encoding). Retrieval was examined by asking volunteers, on random trials, whether or not they remembered seeing specific pieces ("intentional" retrieval). In a fourth condition, designed to provide a control for these retrieval trials, volunteers were instructed to re-view stimuli that had been shown previously to elicit recognition ("incidental" re-viewing). Importantly, at the critical interval of each trial, that is, when the stimulus was presented, all sensory and motor factors were held constant across all conditions. The only difference between conditions was how the volunteer chose to implement an *intention* based on a prior instruction. As expected, intentional encoding led to significantly improved recall over incidental encoding, although, importantly, performance for incidentally encoded stimuli was significantly above chance. When incidental encoding was compared to the nonevents, significant increases in signal intensity were observed in the parahippocampal gyrus/hippocampus bilaterally. In contrast, no significant activity was observed in the midventrolateral frontal cortex. In contrast, when intentional encoding was compared to incidental encoding, significant signal intensity changes were observed in the midventrolateral frontal cortex but not in the parahippocampal gyrus/hippocampus. Thus, activity in the midventrolateral frontal cortex was specifically associated with the act of intentionally encoding stimuli, while nonintentional encoding (as indexed by later recognition performance) yielded no activity in this region. When incidental re-viewing and nonevents were compared, significant signal intensity changes were observed in the parahippocampal gyrus/hippocampus bilaterally, while no significant activity was observed in the midventrolateral frontal cortex. Given that performance on a later recognition task for these same stimuli was above chance, it is reasonable to assume that during these re-viewing periods the volunteers experienced some sense of familiarity with these stimuli, although one can also assume that this was relatively automatic (i.e., it could not be prevented by the volunteer) and was, therefore, in some sense *unintentional*. In contrast, when intentional retrieval was compared to incidental re-viewing, the midventrolateral frontal cortex was activated bilaterally (fig. 15.3), but no significant differences in activity were observed in the medial temporal lobe.

These results demonstrate that simply changing the task instructions at encoding and retrieval to encourage intentional processing produced significant bilateral increases in signal intensity in the midventrolateral frontal cortex in both conditions. On the other hand, when this region was examined during the corresponding incidental conditions, no significant activity was observed, although memory performance was still above chance. These findings suggest that the implementation of an intended act or plan to remember or recall may be the common factor that underlies activation of the midventrolateral frontal cortex during previous neuroimaging studies of memory (e.g., Jonides et al. 1993; Owen et al. 1996b, 1999, 2000; Smith et al. 1995;

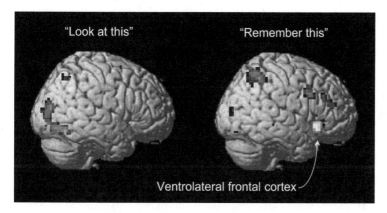

Figure 15.3
Event-related functional magnetic resonance imaging blood-oxygenation-level-dependent signal changes when volunteers are asked to either look at (left) or remember (right) a complex visual pattern. Signal change differs significantly in the midventrolateral frontal cortex. Right hemisphere only is shown. Adapted from Dove et al. (2001). See plate 9.

Henson et al. 1999; Wagner et al. 1998; Courtney et al. 1997). In the case of working memory tasks, this might correspond to the relatively straightforward mapping of stimuli to responses such as that which is assumed to occur in spatial and digit span tasks (e.g., Owen et al. 1996b, 1999), or even simple delayed-matching-to-sample paradigms (e.g., Elliott and Dolan 1999). In the case of long-term episodic memory (e.g., verbal paired associate learning), these "active" encoding and retrieval processes might correspond to the active mapping and implementation of a somewhat arbitrary learned response (e.g., a category exemplar) to a specific stimulus (e.g., a category name; e.g., Fletcher et al. 1998a, 1998b).

Damage to this area may also be responsible for the disproportionate impairment observed in patients with circumscribed excisions of the frontal cortex on tests that require recall (for a review, see Wheeler, Stuss, and Tulving 1995) and also for the similar pattern of deficits observed in other "frontal-like" populations of patients (Owen et al. 1992; Pantelis et al. 1997).

However, it is clear from the description of neuropsychological studies above that patients with frontal lobe damage are impaired on many tasks, some of which have no obvious mnemonic component at all (e.g., Milner 1964; Luria 1966; Corkin 1965; Semmes et al. 1963, Bechara, this volume; Grafman and Krueger, this volume). The question arises, therefore, whether an impairment of intended action might also be shown to be responsible for the deficits observed in those tasks.

In one recent study, event-related fMRI was used to examine frontal lobe activation in healthy human volunteers during performance of a probabilistic reversal learning task (Cools et al. 2002). Reversal learning involves the adaptation of behavior according to changes in stimulus–reward contingencies and places a relatively low load on memory. It is exemplified by visual discrimination tasks where subjects must learn to respond according to the opposite, previously irrelevant, stimulus–reward pairing. Reversal learning is disrupted following lesions of ventral prefrontal cortex in non-human primates (Iversen and Mishkin 1970; Dias et al. 1996). However, evidence of the same system being involved in reversal performance in humans is limited to two studies in patients with nonselective ventral prefrontal cortex damage (Rolls et al. 1994; Rahman et al. 1999). In the study by Cools et al. (2002), volunteers were required to respond to one of two stimuli according to probabilistic feedback; thus, switches in the correct response were uncued in the sense that they could not be determined based on the feedback received on any given trial (e.g., the trial immediately prior to a switch). A significant signal change was observed in the right ventrolateral prefrontal cortex on trials when subjects decided to stop responding to the previously relevant stimulus and shifted responding to the newly relevant stimulus. Moreover, the response on the final reversal error, prior to shifting, was not modulated by the number of preceding reversal errors, indicating that error-related activity does not simply accumulate in this network but rather corresponds precisely to the exact moment when volunteers *decided to make the shift*. These data indicate that intentional shifting of lower-level stimulus–reward associations is sufficient to activate the ventrolateral prefrontal cortex. The study also concurs well with other, human brain imaging studies that have emphasized a role for the right ventrolateral prefrontal cortex in behavioral inhibition (or intentional stopping) using, for example, go/no-go tasks (Garavan et al. 1999; Konishi et al. 1999).

15.6   Conclusions

The data from recent functional neuroimaging studies using event-related fMRI suggest that the midventrolateral frontal cortex in humans is important for intended action, that is, actions and thoughts that are consciously planned and implemented (see Prinz, Dennett, and Sebanz, this volume, for discussion). Thus, this region responds selectively when volunteers explicitly commit an item to memory and again when they attempt to recall that item following a delay. These data concur closely with neuropsychological studies in frontal lobe patients who are more impaired on tests of memory recall than on tests of recognition. However, two factors argue against a fundamental and specific role for this region in mnemonic processing. First, when volunteers are merely exposed to complex visual stimuli, in the absence of an explicit intention to encode, no activation is observed in the ventrolateral frontal cortex. However, subsequent recognition performance is above chance. Similarly, when volunteers are reexposed to familiar visual stimuli, no ventrolateral frontal activity is observed as long as there is no explicit instruction to verify whether the stimulus has been seen before or not. Second, activity in the midventrolateral frontal cortex has also been recorded during tasks that make relatively low demands on mnemonic processes but nevertheless require the initiation of an intended action (e.g., to shift responding from one stimulus to another) in the absence of an explicit external cue to do so. Shifting impairments, including deficits in simple reversal performance, have been widely reported in patients with frontal lobe damage.

The data from functional neuroimaging studies in healthy controls and from neuropsychological studies in patients also concurs in a broad sense with studies in nonhuman primates. Thus, both lesion and electrophysiological studies in the monkey have demonstrated that the ventrolateral frontal cortex is important for performance on a wide range of tasks that require the implementation of intended actions and plans.

While the data described above leave little doubt that, in both humans and nonhuman primates, the midventrolateral frontal cortex plays an important role in tasks that require *intention*, it is unlikely that this region is functionally exclusive in this regard. Thus, while strong reciprocal connections between this region and the temporal lobe ventral stream areas, as well as several parietal lobe dorsal stream areas, suggest that it is a crucial point of interaction between multiple posterior cortical association regions and the entire lateral frontal cortex, they also suggest that the midventrolateral frontal cortex is one component of a wider network responsible for the planning and initiation of complex actions. Indeed, Lau et al. (2004) argued recently that the supplementary motor area and the parietal cortex form a circuit underlying conscious intention, although whether the signal intensity changes observed in that study reflected the effects of attention on motor preparation, rather than conscious intention per se, is unclear (for discussion, see Haggard, this volume).

Finally, on the basis of the data described above, it seems likely that damage to the ventrolateral frontal cortex contributes significantly to the pattern of deficits seen in other groups of patients whose behavior appears to lack *intention*. Precisely how this translates into the parlance of clinical terminology is unclear, although it resonates well with many oft-used terms, including "diminution of spontaneous activity," "apathy and indifference," "stimulus-bound behaviour," "inertia," and "lacking volition." For example, elsewhere in this volume, schizophrenia has been described as a disorder of "volition" (Frith, this volume; Spence and Parry, this volume) and in terms of deficient "motivated attention" (Liddle, this volume). Similarly depression has been discussed both in terms of a failure of "action control" (Schneider, this volume) and a failure of "volition" (Nitschke and Mackiewicz, this volume). In both disorders, "frontal-like" cognitive abnormalities have been well described (e.g., Pantelis et al. 1997; Beats et al. 1996), although whether such deficits relate specifically to dysfunction of circuitry involving the midventrolateral frontal cortex and its apparent role in intended action remains a significant challenge for the future.

References

Beats, B. C., B. J. Sahakian, and R. Levy. 1996. Cognitive performance in tests sensitive to frontal lobe dysfunction in the elderly depressed. *Psychological Medicine, 26*, 591–603.

Bianchi, L. 1922. *The Mechanism of the Brain and the Function of the Frontal Lobes.* Edinburgh: Livingstone.

Bor, D., J. Duncan, and A. M. Owen. 2003. Encoding strategies dissociate prefrontal activity from working memory demand. *Neuron, 37*, 361–367.

Carmicheal, S. T., and J. L. Price. 1994. Architectonic subdivision of the orbital and medial prefrontal cortex in the macaque monkey. *Journal of Comparative Neurology, 346*, 366–402.

Carmicheal, S. T., and J. L. Price. 1995a. Sensory and premotor connections of the orbital and medial prefrontal cortex of macaque monkeys. *Journal of Comparative Neurology, 363*, 642–664.

Carmicheal, S. T., and J. L. Price. 1995b. Limbic connections of the orbital and medial prefrontal cortex in macaque monkeys. *Journal of Comparative Neurology, 363*, 615–641.

Cavada, C., and P. S. Goldman-Rakic. 1989. Posterior parietal cortex in rhesus monkey: II. Evidence for segregated corticocortical networks linking sensory and limbic areas with the frontal lobe. *Journal of Comparative Neurology, 287*, 422–445.

Cohen, J. D., and D. Servan-Schreiber. 1992. Context, cortex, and dopamine: A connectionist approach to behavior and biology in schizophrenia. *Psychology Review, 99*, 45–77.

Cools, R., L. Clark, A. M. Owen, and T. W. Robbins. 2002. Defining the neural mechanisms of probabilistic reversal learning using event-related functional magnetic resonance imaging. *Journal of Neuroscience, 22*, 4563–4567.

Corkin, S. 1965. Tactually-guided maze learning in man: Effects of unilateral cortical excisions and bilateral hippocampal lesions. *Neuropsychologia, 3*, 339–351.

Courtney, S. M., L. G. Ungerleider, K. K. Kell, and J. V. Haxby. 1997. Transient and sustained activity in a distributed system for human working memory. *Nature, 386*, 608–611.

Desimone, R., and J. Duncan. 1995. Neural mechanisms of selective visual attention. *Annual Review of Neuroscience, 18*, 193–222.

Dias, R., T. W. Robbins, and A. C. Roberts. 1996. Dissociation in prefrontal cortex of affective and attentional shifts. *Nature, 380*, 69.

Dobbins, I. G., H. Foley, D. L. Schacter, and A. D. Wagner. 2002. Executive control during episodic retrieval: Multiple prefrontal processes subserve source memory. *Neuron, 35*, 989–996.

Dove, A., S. Pollmann, T. Schubert, C. J. Wiggins, and D. Y. von Cramon. 2000. Prefrontal cortex activation in task switching: An event-related fMRI study. *Brain Research: Cognitive Brain Research, 9*, 103–109.

Dove, A., J. B. Rowe, M. Brett, and A. M. Owen. 2001. Neural correlates of passive and active encoding and retrieval: A 3T fMRI study. *Neuroimage, 13*, S660.

Drewe, E. A. 1974. The effect of type and area of brain lesion on Wisconsin Card Sorting Test performance. *Cortex*, *10*, 159–170.

Elliot, R., and R. J. Dolan. 1999. Differential neural responses during performance of matching and nonmatching to sample tasks at two delay intervals. *Journal of Neuroscience*, *19*, 5066–5073.

Fletcher, P., T. Shallice, and R. J. Dolan. 1998a. The functional roles of prefrontal cortex in episodic memory. I. Encoding. *Brain*, *121*, 1239–1248.

Fletcher, P., T. Shallice, C. D. Frith, R. S. J. Frackowiak, and R. J. Dolan. 1998b. The functional roles of prefrontal cortex in episodic memory: II. Retrieval. *Brain*, *121*, 1249–1256.

Fuster, J. M. 1997. *The Prefrontal Cortex: Anatomy, Physiology, and Neuropsychology of the Frontal Lobe*, 3rd ed. Philadelphia: Lippincott-Raven.

Gaffan, D. 1994. Interaction of the temporal lobe and frontal lobe in memory. In *Research and Perspectives in the Neurosciences, 3: Motor and Cognitive Functions of the Prefrontal Cortex*, ed. A.-M. Thierry, J. Glowinski, P. S. Goldman-Rakic, and Y. Christen, pp. 129–139. New York: Springer-Verlag.

Garavan H., T. Ross, and E. Stein. 1999. Right hemispheric dominance of inhibitoty control: An event-related functional MRI study. *Proceedings of the National Academy of Sciences USA*, *96*, 8301–8306.

Goldman-Rakic, P. S. 1994. The issue of memory in the study of prefrontal functions. In *Motor and Cognitive Functions of the Prefrontal Cortex*, ed. A. M. Thierry, J. Glowinski, P. S. Goldman-Rakic, and Y. Christen. Berlin: Springer-Verlag.

Henson, R. N., T. Shallice, and R. J. Dolan. 1999. Right prefrontal cortex and episodic memory retrieval: A functional MRI test of the monitoring hypothesis. *Brain*, *122 (Pt 7)*, 1367–1381.

Iversen S., and M. Mishkin. 1970. Perseverative interference in monkeys following selective lesions of the inferior prefrontal convexity. *Experimental Brain Research*, *11*, 376–386.

Jacoby, L. L., and M. Dallas. 1981. On the relationship between autobiographical memory and perceptual learning. *Journal of Experimental Psychology General*, *110*, 306–340.

Jonides, J., E. E. Smith, R. A. Koeppe, E. Awh, S. Minoshima, and M. A. Mintun. 1993. Spatial working memory in humans as revealed by PET. *Nature*, *363*, 623–625.

Kapur, S., F. I. M. Craik, E. Tulving, A. A. Wilson, S. Houle, and G. M. Brown. 1994. Neuro-anatomical correlates of encoding in episodic memory: Levels of processing effect. *Proceedings of the National Academy of Sciences USA*, *91*, 2008–2011.

Knight, R. T. 1994. Attention regulation and human prefrontal cortex. In *Motor and Cognitive Functions of the Prefrontal Cortex*, ed. A.-M. Thierry, J. Glowinski, P. S. Goldman-Rakic, and Y. Christen, pp. 161–173. Berlin: Springer-Verlag.

Konishi, S., K. Nakajima, I. Uchida, H. Kikyo, M. Kameyama, and Y. Miyashita. 1999. Common inhibitory mechanisms in human inferior prefrontal cortex revealed by event-related functional MRI. *Brain*, *122*, 981–991.

Lau, H. C., R. D. Rogers, P. Haggard, and R. E. Passingham. 2004. Attention to intention. *Science, 303*, 1208–1210.

Li, B.-M., M. Inase, T. Takashima, and T. Ijima. 1997. Potentiation of neuronal responses to well learned cues in the inferior prefrontal cortex during conditional visuomotor learning. *Society for Neuroscience Abstracts, 27*, 628.6.

Luria, A. R. 1966. *Higher Cortical Functions in Man.* New York: Basic Books.

Mandler, G. 1980. Recognizing: The judgement of previous occurrence. *Psychological Review, 87*, 252–271.

Milner, B. 1964. Some effects of frontal lobectomy in man. In *The Frontal Granular Cortex and Behaviour*, ed. J. M. Warren and K. Akert, pp. 313–331. New York: McGraw-Hill.

Mishkin, M., and F. J. Manning. 1978. Non-spatial memory after selective prefrontal lesions in monkeys. *Brain Research, 143*, 313–323.

Mishkin, M., B. Vest, M. Waxler, and H. E. Rosvold. 1969. A re-examination of the effects of frontal lesions on object alternation. *Neuropsychologia, 7*, 357–363.

Murray, E. A., and S. P. Wise. 1997. Role of orbitoventral prefrontal cortex in conditional motor learning. *Society for Neuroscience Abstracts, 27*, 12.1.

Nelson, H. E. 1976. A modified card sorting test sensitive to frontal lobe defects. *Cortex, 12*, 313–324.

Olton, D. S. 1982. Spatially organized behaviors of animals: Behavioural and neurological studies. In *Spatial Abilities*, ed. M. Potegal, pp. 325–360. New York: Academic Press.

Owen, A. M. 1997. The functional organization of working memory processes within human lateral frontal cortex: The contribution of functional neuroimaging. *European Journal of Neuroscience, 9*, 1329–1339.

Owen, A. M., M. Beksinska, M. James, P. N. Leigh, B. A. Summers, C. D. Marsden, N. P. Quinn, B. J. Sahakian, and T. W. Robbins. 1993a. Visuo-spatial memory deficits at different stages of Parkinson's disease. *Neuropsychologia, 31*, 627–644.

Owen, A. M., J. J. Downes, B. J. Sahakian, C. E. Polkey, and T. W. Robbins. 1990. Planning and spatial working memory following frontal lobe lesions in man. *Neuropsychologia, 28*, 1021–1034.

Owen, A. M., A. C. Evans, and M. Petrides. 1996b. Evidence for a two-stage model of spatial working memory processing within the lateral frontal cortex: A positron emission tomography study. *Cerebral Cortex, 6*, 31–38.

Owen, A. M., N. J. Herrod, D. K. Menon, J. C. Clark, S. P. M. J. Downey, T. A. Carpenter, P. S. Minhas, F. E. Turkheimer, E. J. Williams, T. W. Robbins, B. J. Sahakian, M. Petrides, and J. D. Pickard. 1999. Redefining the functional organisation of working memory processes within human lateral prefrontal cortex. *European Journal of Neuroscience, 11*, 567–574.

Owen, A. M., M. James, P. N. Leigh, B. A. Summers, N. P. Quinn, C. D. Marsden, and T. W. Robbins. 1992. Fronto-striatal cognitive deficits at different stages of Parkinson's disease. *Brain, 115,* 1727–1751.

Owen, A. M., A. C. H. Lee, and E. J. Williams. 2000. Dissociating aspects of verbal working memory within the human frontal lobe: Further evidence for a "process-specific" model of lateral frontal organization. *Psychobiology, 28,* 146–155.

Owen, A. M., R. G. Morris, B. J. Sahakian, C. E. Polkey, and T. W. Robbins. 1996a. Double dissociations of memory and executive functions in working memory tasks following frontal lobe excisions, temporal lobe excisions, or amygdalo-hippocampectomy in man. *Brain, 119,* 1597–1615.

Owen, A. M., A. C. Roberts, J. R. Hodges, B. A. Summers, C. E. Polkey, and T. W. Robbins. 1993b. Contrasting mechanisms of impaired attention: Set-shifting in patients with frontal lobe damage or Parkinson's disease. *Brain, 116,* 1159–1175.

Owen, A. M., A. C. Roberts, C. E. Polkey, B. J. Sahakian, and T. W. Robbins. 1991. Extra-dimensional versus intra-dimensional set shifting performance following frontal lobe excisions, temporal lobe excisions, or amygdalohippocampelectomy in man. *Neuropsychologia, 29,* 993–1006.

Owen, A. M., B. J. Sahakian, J. Semple, C. E. Polkey, and T. W. Robbins. 1995. Visuo-spatial short-term recognition memory and learning after temporal lobe excisions, frontal lobe excisions, or amygdalo-hippocampectomy in man. *Neuropsychologia, 33,* 1–24.

Pantelis, C., T. R. E. Barnes, H. E. Nelson, S. Tanner, L. Weatherley, A. M. Owen, and T. W. Robbins. 1997. Frontal-striatal cognitive deficits in patients with chronic schizophrenia. *Brain, 120,* 1823–1843.

Passingham, R. E. 1975. Delayed matching after selective prefrontal lesions in monkeys. *Brain Research, 92,* 89–102.

Passingham, R. E. 1985. Memory of monkeys (*Macaca mulatta*) with lesion in prefrontal cortex. *Behavioral Neuroscience, 99,* 2–21.

Petrides, M. 1994. Frontal lobes and working memory: Evidence from investigations of the effects of cortical excisions in nonhuman primates. In *Handbook of Neuropsychology,* vol. 9, ed. F. Boller and J. Grafman, pp. 59–81. Amsterdam: Elsevier Science.

Petrides, M., and B. Milner. 1982. Deficits on subject-ordered tasks after frontal- and temporal-lobe lesions in man. *Neuropsychologia, 20,* 249–262.

Petrides, M., and D. N. Pandya. 1994. Comparative architectonic analysis of the human and the macaque frontal cortex. In *Handbook of Neuropsychology,* vol. 9, ed. F. Boller and J. Grafman, pp. 17–58. Amsterdam: Elsevier Science.

Rahman, S., B. Sahakian, J. Hodges, R. Rogers, and T. Robbins. 1999. Specific cognitive deficits in mild frontal variant frontotemporal dementia. *Brain, 122,* 670–673.

Rao, S. R., G. Rainer, and E. K. Miller. 1997. Integration of what and where in the primate prefrontal cortex. *Science, 276*, 821–823.

Robinson, A. L., R. K. Heaton, R. A. W. Lehman, and D. W. Stilson. 1980. The utility of the Wisconsin Card Sorting Test in detecting and localising frontal lobe lesions. *Neuropsychologia, 48*, 605–614.

Rolls, E. T., J. Hornak, D. Wade, and J. McGrath. 1994. Emotion-related learing in patients with social and emotional changes associated with frontal lobe damage. *Journal of Neurology, Neurosurgery, and Psychiatry, 57*, 1518–1524.

Rushworth, M. F. S., P. D. Nixon, M. J. Eacott, and R. E. Passingham. 1997. Ventral prefrontal cortex is not essential for working memory. *Journal of Neuroscience, 17*, 4829–4838.

Sahakian, B. J., R. G. Morris, J. L. Evenden, A. Heald, R. Levy, M. Philpot, and T. W. Robbins. 1988. A comparative study of visuospatial memory and learning in Alzheimer-type dementia and Parkinson's disease. *Brain, 111*, 695–718.

Sakagami, M., and H. Niki. 1994. Encoding of behavioral significance of visual stimuli by primate prefrontal neurons: Relation to relevant task conditions. *Experimental Brain Research, 97*, 423–436.

Schall, J. D., A. Morel, D. J. King, and J. Bullier. 1995. Topography of visual cortex connections with frontal eye field in macaque: Convergence and segregation of processing streams. *Journal of Neuroscience, 15*, 4464–4487.

Semmes, J., S. Weinstein, L. Ghent, and H.-L. Tueber. 1963. Correlates of impaired orientation in personal and extrapersonal space. *Brain, 86*, 747–772.

Shallice, T. 1982. Specific impairments of planning. *Philosophical Transactions of the Royal Society of London B, Biological Sciences, 298*, 199–209.

Shallice, T. 1988. *From Neuropsychology to Mental Structure*. Cambridge: Cambridge University Press.

Smith, E. E., J. J. Jonides, R. A. Koeppe, E. Awh, E. H. Schumacher, and S. Minoshima. 1995. Spatial versus object working memory: PET investigations. *Journal of Cognitive Neuroscience, 7*, 337–356.

Stern, C. E., A. M. Owen, M. Petrides, R. B. Look, I. Tracey, and B. R. Rosen. 2000. Activity in ventrolateral and mid-dorsolateral prefrontal cortex during non-spatial visual working memory processing: Evidence from functional magnetic resonance imaging. *Neuroimage, 11*, 392–399.

Wagner, A. D., D. L. Schacter, M. Rotte, W. Koutstaal, A. Maril, A. M. Dale, B. Rosen, and R. L. Buckner. 1998. Building memories: Remembering and forgetting of verbal experiences as predicted by brain activity. *Science, 281*, 1188–1191.

Webster, M. J., J. Bachevalier, and L. G. Ungerleider. 1994. Connections of inferior temporal areas TEO and TE with parietal and frontal cortex in macaque monkeys. *Cerebral Cortex, 5*, 470–483.

Wheeler, M. A., D. T. Stuss, and E. Tulving. 1995. Frontal lobe damage produces episodic memory impairment. *Journal of International Neuropsychology Society, 1*, 525–536.

16 Volition and the Human Prefrontal Cortex

Jordan Grafman and Frank Krueger

16.1 Introduction

The American Heritage Dictionary of the English Language defines the word "volition" as the act or an instance of making a conscious choice or decision and describes it as synonymous with the concept of the "will" (Pickett 2000). According to Prinz, Dennett, and Sebanz (this volume), the act of making a conscious choice can be characterized in different ways. For example, volition can be described in terms of theories distinguishing between top-down and bottom-up control. Top-down theories claim that volitional activity should be modeled in an explicit and hierarchical fashion through a controller that is distinct from the action system. Bottom-up models, in contrast, tend to view volition as an emergent property, dedicated to action, of a unitary system.

In this chapter, we will distinguish between volition with versus without a direct executive (i.e., autonomous) component. Processes underlying volition without an executive component (volition-as-action) are often short-term, seemingly automatic, operations, whereas processes underlying volition with an executive component (volition-as-planning) are longer term operations requiring different degrees of autonomy. Autonomy, in our view, refers to independent judgments and behavior that is not controlled by others or by external stimuli.

We propose that the human prefrontal cortex (PFC) stores goal-oriented sets of actions—that is, structured event complexes (SECs)—which are activated when (volition-as-planning) trigger conditions are satisfied. The dissociation between internally controlled and externally controlled behavior suggests that these two types of behavior are mediated by two separate mental functions. Volition-as-planning utilizes motor control processes, but these processes are dependent upon the implementation of intentions that are based upon knowledge representations that have been acquired through prior learning. We claim, therefore, that only volition-as-planning requires the involvement of the PFC.

We will provide evidence for this claim by discussing three studies that show that patients with PFC lesions are impaired in their ability to develop and execute self-generated intentions, whereas their ability to decide to perform a simple action induced by others or elicited by situational cues remains relatively intact. The results of the first study indicate that patients with frontal lobe lesions have difficulty in addressing real-world planning problems with greater volition-as-planning deficits emerging as the planning problems extend into the future. The second study compares patients with right frontal lobe lesions to patients with parietal lobe lesions on a complex advice and decision-making task. The results show that only patients with PFC lesions have difficulty in advice taking and using foresight to make adequate volition-as-planning decisions. The last study, a case study, presents a patient with a right frontal lobe penetrating brain injury who lost his ability to make rational decisions in personal and social matters despite intact general cognitive decision-making ability, arguing for domain specificity in volition (for a somewhat opposing view, see the chapters by Frith and by Owen, this volume).

In each study, the results support our distinction between volition-as-action and volition-as-planning and the importance of considering autonomy rather than volition as the key component of the "will." Later in this chapter, we promote a testable and biologically plausible volitional framework that takes into account the different complexity of situations and different time scales of actions.

16.2   Study 1: Problems in Financial Planning

It has long been observed that patients with lesions in the PFC have difficulty deciding and solving problems in real-world, ill-structured situations, particularly when the situation includes planning and look-ahead components. The neuropsychological literature contains many compelling subjective case reports about the social, emotional, and cognitive consequences of lesions in the PFC (Harlow 1868; Penfield and Evans 1935; Rylander 1939). A study we conducted (Goel et al. 1997) provided more objective data on participants performing a real-world financial planning task.

Ten male patients (age range = 45–53 years) took part in the study. Eight of the patients (who were drawn from a Vietnam head injury population) received penetrating head injuries to their frontal lobes during their service in Vietnam in the late 1960s. One of the two other patients suffered a subarachnoid hemorrhage secondary to a right anterior communicating artery aneurysm, and the other one had neurosurgical intervention to relieve pressure due to a right frontal intracerebral hemorrhage. As determined by previous neurological and neuropsychological testing, all the patients had relatively intact language, motor, and sensory functions. Table 16.1 shows each patient's age, education, and cognitive profiles along with the size and laterality of lesions as determined by magnetic resonance imaging (MRI). For eight of the patients,

Table 16.1

Characteristics of patients with frontal lobe lesions and normal control subjects.

Characteristic	Normal subjects (*n* = 10)	Lesion in right hemisphere (*n* = 5)	Lesionin left hemisphere (*n* = 1)	Bilateral lesion(s) (*n* = 4)	All patients (*n* = 10)
Age (years)	43.50	49.67	44.00	45.00	47.23
Education (years)	15.21	15.40	15.00	12.50	14.10
WAIS–R (IQ)					
General	—	106.80	110.00	90.75	100.70
Verbal	—	110.80	109.00	91.00	102.70
Performance	—	99.60	111.00	90.25	97.00
WMS–R					
General	—	111.80	93.00	97.50	104.20
Verbal	—	120.75	96.00	97.75	107.78
Visual	—	105.00	92.00	98.25	100.56
WCST					
Categories	—	3.40	6.00	5.50	4.50
Perseveration	—	27.20	14.00	12.75	20.10
Picture arrangement	—	9.40	11.00	7.50	8.80
Word fluency	—	51.00	42.00	29.00	40.22
Tower of Hanoi	1,323.00	787.69	1,185.33	855.72	854.67
Volume loss (cc) (eight patients)	—	32.14	62.3	47.29	43.49

Note: WAIS–R = Wechsler Adult Intelligence Scale—revised; WMS–R = Wechsler Memory Scale—revised; WCST = Wisconsin Card Sorting Test.

figure 16.1 illustrates the extent of their lesions (as also determined by CT scan; Damasio and Damasio 1989). Ten normal volunteers were matched for age and education with the patients.

The planning task was taken from the real-life domain of household finance planning and management. The subjects were asked to help a young couple to achieve four specific goals: (1) balance their budget, (2) purchase a home within the next 2 years, (3) send their children to college in 15–20 years, and (4) have sufficient funds to retire in 35 years. The financial information about the couple was conveyed by way of an income statement and balance sheet. Subjects were asked to modify the couple's income and expenses and restructure their assets and liabilities to achieve the four main goals. All the patients understood and identified with the task because they had worked for a living, saved money, rented or bought a house, raised children, sent them to school, and were approaching retirement.

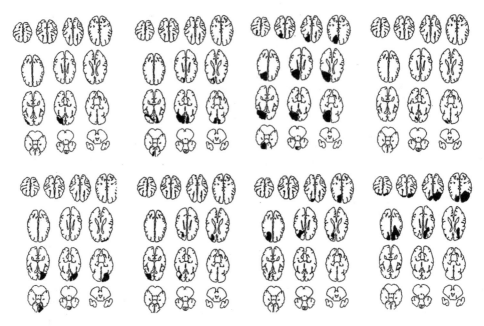

Figure 16.1
Location of lesions in eight patients, based on magnetic resonance imaging.

The task was presented as a "problem scenario." In videotaped sessions subjects were asked to talk aloud as they proceeded through the task and to vocalize the fragments of thoughts and ideas they might be attending to at that time. While time was not a critical factor, subjects were instructed to fully engage in the task. Since the information contained in the problem scenario was incomplete, they were also encouraged to ask as many questions as necessary. Experimenters answered any questions, but they did not initiate discussion or questions. The subjects had access to pen and paper, and the experimenters could help them in calculating their finances. Before subjects began generating a plan to manage the couple's finances, they were asked to answer specific questions designed to familiarize them with the already given financial information and goals of the couple.

The video recordings (plus written output) were analyzed with a methodology called "protocol analysis" (Ericsson and Simon 1984). Generally speaking, the subjects' verbalizations constituted the database and were interpreted in the context of an information-processing model we adapted (Ericsson and Simon 1984; Newell and Simon 1972; Simon 1961, 1978). The end result of the analyses is an explicit depiction of the cognitive processes engaged in by the subject during that problem-solving session. The explicit analysis and interpretation of the data begins with the transcription of the verbalizations. A three-level scheme was used to code the data (Goel 1994, 1995; Goel

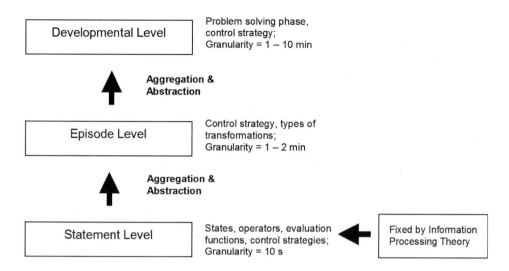

Figure 16.2
Specific categories used to code the verbalizations.

and Pirolli 1992). A general overview of the coding categories can be seen in figure 16.2. Each level of the scheme is associated with a different category and granularity, and provides insight into a different aspect of the subject's cognitive process.

At the statement level, protocols were aggregated into individual statements by using content cues, syntactic cues, and pauses representing single "thoughts" or ideas. The categories at this level included modes, sources, contents, and operators. The *statement level* gives a picture of cognitive processes at the granularity of a few seconds.

At the *episode level* statements were aggregated into episodes. Episodes are connected sequences of statements in the service of common goals/subgoals. The categories at this level are goals, subgoals, and strategies. The problem scenario contained four goals (stem negative cash flow/stabilize situation, purchase a house, send kids to college, and save for retirement) in which subjects can utilize three types of strategies (increasing income, decreasing expenditures, and reallocating assets) to achieve the goals/subgoals. Episodes are typically 1 to 2 minutes long.

At the *plan developmental* level, episodes were further aggregated into phases that have durations of 1 to 10 minutes. The planning phase contains problem structuring and problem solving. Problem structuring is a necessary prerequisite for the solution of problems; it involves generating information missing from the problem scenario. Problem solving generally was composed of several phases, starting with preliminary planning, passing through plan refinement, and ending with detailing of the plan. Preliminary plan statements result in the initial generation and exploration of ideas, refinement statements serve to elaborate and develop an idea, and detailing statements specify the final form of an idea. For the experiment it was common for subjects to return to an earlier phase as previously unnoticed aspects of their plan emerged.

Three research assistants who did not know the identity of the control subjects and patients coded the data. A recoding of 10 percent of the data by the first author resulted in a 92 percent rate of agreement.

Verbal protocols of the 10 patients and 10 control subjects were analyzed at three levels of granularity: statement, episode, and plan developmental level. At the statement level, the behavior of patients and control subjects was identical, indicating intact volition-as-action behavior. At the episodic level, the analysis provides a measure of the four explicit goals and three solution strategies pursued, which could be manipulated in various combinations to achieve the goals (table 16.2). Control subjects acknowledged all four goals and actively pursued a mean of 98 percent. Patients acknowledged (70%) and actively pursued fewer goals (58%). The control subjects were more successful than patients in utilizing each of these strategies (decreasing expenses, increasing income, and restructuring assets and liabilities). A number of patients focused exclusively on the decreasing expenses strategy. Only half the patients considered the "increasing income" strategy, and when patients did utilize the asset reallocation strategy, it tended to be at a superficial level.

The significant interaction in the number of statements that control subjects and patients devoted to the four goals can be seen in figure 16.3. Patients with frontal lobe lesions devoted more statements to the immediate goal (stabilize finances) and a decreasing number of statements to future goals, whereas normal control subjects devoted an equivalent number of statements to the three future goals (house, college, and retirement).

At the plan developmental level, the distribution of statements between problem structuring and problem solving was quite different for control subjects and patients (fig. 16.4). The patients used a significantly larger proportion of their statements (42%) than did control subjects (30%) on problem structuring. The control subjects used a

Table 16.2
Goal satisfaction and strategy utilization of the financial planning task.

	Controls	Patients
Goals		
Acknowledgment (%)	100	70
Active pursual (%)	95	58
Strategies		
Decrease expenses (%)	90	80
Increase income (%)	90	50
Reallocate assets (%)	100	80

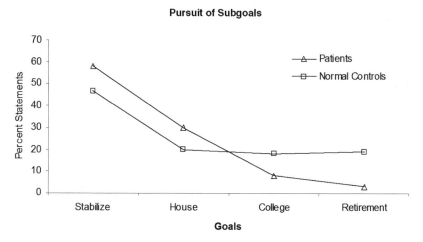

Figure 16.3

Percentage of statements which control subjects and patients devoted to each goal.

significantly larger proportion of their statements (59%) than did patients (47%) on the problem-solving phase, and this difference was significant.

Further significant differences occurred between control subjects and patients within the problem-solving phase (fig. 16.5). Patients spent most of their time on the preliminary plan (26%) and had less time left for refinement (14%) and detailing (7%), whereas control subjects distributed their statements approximately equally between preliminary planning (22%), refinement (19%), and detailing (18%).

Although this study indicated that patients with frontal lobe lesions are impaired when ask to solve real-world planning problems, it was quite clear that their volitional-as-action ability was relatively intact. First, patient performance was impoverished at a global level but not at the local level. At the statement level (granularity of seconds) their performance was indistinguishable from that of control subjects, that is, patients instantiated the same set of operators in the same sequence and with the same frequency as control subjects. But when performance was required to reflect their thinking over a scale of minutes to hours, differences between patients and controls began to emerge. Second, patients had difficulty in structuring and organizing their problem space. Once they began problem solving, patients had difficulty in allocating adequate effort to each problem-solving phase. Third, patients also had difficulty dealing with the fact that there were no right or wrong answers or an official termination point in this real-world planning problem. Fourth, patients found it problematic to generate their own feedback. They invariably terminated the session before the details were fleshed out and all the goals satisfied. Finally, patients did not take full advantage of the fact that constraints on real-world problems were negotiable. Patients tended to rely upon

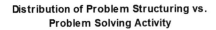

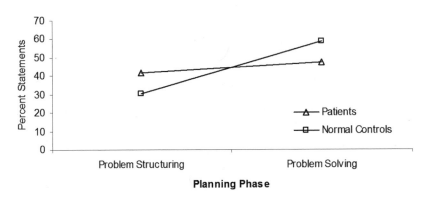

Figure 16.4

Percentage of statements which control subjects and patients devoted to problem structuring and solving.

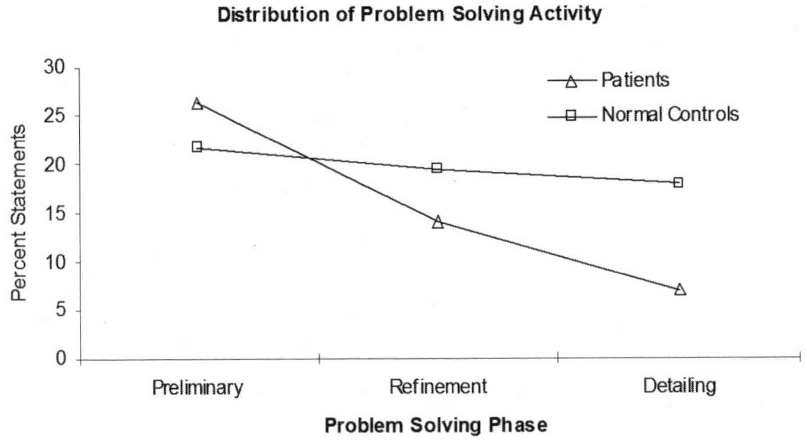

Distribution of Problem Solving Activity

Figure 16.5

Percentage of statements which control subjects and patients devoted to each phase of problem solving.

the stated problem space and did not seek alternative, unstated ways to modify it. They also retrieved episodes out of order and in a fragmentary way rather than linking them to the overall goal(s). In sum, the failures in this study are much more compatible with a relative loss of volition-as-planning compared to volition-as-action. The next study reports on whether patients with frontal lobe lesions are good at taking advice and recognizing whether the action they took was good or not.

16.3   Study 2: Deficits in Advice Taking

In a study with colleagues from the Basque region of Spain (Gomez-Beldarrain et al. 2004), we used a computerized task (designed by Harvey et al. 2000 and slightly modified for our study) to investigate the process of advice taking and decision making in patients with focal right PFC lesions and compared them to patients with focal parietal lobe lesions and controls.

Twenty patients (16 men and 4 women, age range = 32–60 years) with PFC lesions were included. Five had bilateral but predominantly right prefrontal lesions and 15 had strictly unilateral right prefrontal lesions (fig. 16.6). Frontal patients were divided into two groups, a dorsolateral (DL) group with 6 patients (Brodmann's areas [BA] 9, 46) and an orbitofrontal (OF) group with 14 patients (BA 10, 11, 12, 25, 32). In addition, 9 patients (4 men and 5 women, age range = 27–55 years) with parietal lobe lesions were studied. Six had undergone surgery for parietal meningiomas, and 3 had had strokes. Five patients had lesions in the left hemisphere, and 4 in the right hemisphere. Parietal lesions involved BA 7 and/or 31. Twenty healthy volunteers (11 men and 9 women, age range = 29–64) with a similar educational level as the patients were included.

In the decision-making task, participants were asked to regard themselves as the managing director of a firm that produces consumer products. To review the success of the products, the participants were asked to forecast how well they would sell over the next month by combining the estimates made by four of their female employees with their own estimate to produce their forecast. Altogether participants had to make decisions about 40 products. For each of the 40 trials, individual sales forecasts of the four advisors were presented on the computer screen for an unnamed product. Portraits of the advisors were arranged from left to right across the top of the computer screen. To avoid stereotypical responses, the advisors had the same face, but they could be distinguished by their names (Liz, Sue, Pam, and Fay), the different background color (red, blue, green, and yellow) for each face, and their position on the screen. For each participant, background color and advisor position were constant throughout the task but varied across participants.

Participants were instructed to produce the most accurate sales forecasts for the products. To accomplish this goal, participants were asked to make three decisions:

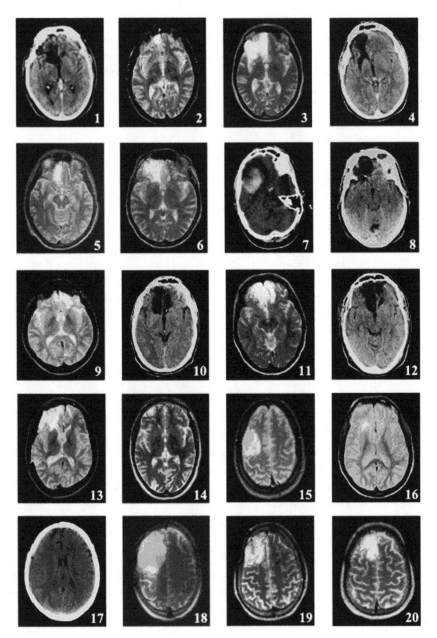

Figure 16.6
Lesions of the twenty frontal patients.

(1) rate their confidence in the accuracy of the four advisors' forecasts displayed in a box beneath the advisor's faces, (2) estimate the probability that the forecast they themselves would make would be accurate, and (3) make their own forecast by combining the judgments of the advisors with their own estimates. The assessment of the quality of each of the four forecasts was expressed by estimating the probability that each forecast would be accurate to within five units of the actual sales outcome. Participants gave their assessment in boxes with up–down arrows beneath each advisor's sales estimate. To avoid the effects of having a constant anchor, the initial value in the box varied between 0 and 100 percent across trials. At the end of the three decisions, the actual sales and the size of the error of the forecast for the product 1 month later were displayed on the screen. During the experiment, participants had to "learn" who the best advisor was in order to make more accurate forecasts. The task was designed so that the best advisor was Fay, followed by Liz, Sue, and Pam.

As expected, controls were able to both use and assess advice, that is, they systematically relied on the best advisors and assessed the best advisors as the best, and their ability to use advice was mediated by their ability to assess it. The controls learned the task very fast, within the first five trials, and committed fewer errors than the other groups. They were the most accurate in evaluating their performance on the task and were less overconfident than the patient groups.

The patients with frontal lobe lesions, on the other hand, made more errors in judgment and showed less cognitive command in the task than controls. They were inconsistent at using advice, and their forecasts were poor. By relying on different advisors to different degrees on different trials, patients with frontal lobe lesions used advice differently and more poorly than controls. They also relied more on the different perceptual characteristics of the advisors while performing the task. For instance, patients with frontal lobe lesions made comments like "Since it is springtime, I will rely on the green advisor."

Patients with OF lesions were the most impaired group in performing this task. They did not show a preference for relying on the worst advisor but were still unable to recognize the best advisor(s). OF patients progressively reduced their number of errors across the task, giving the impression that some degree of learning of the task was taking place. This learning was likely implicit since, when asked specifically, patients could still not identify the best advisor(s). In contrast, DL patients did not improve their performance over the task.

Patients with frontal lobe lesions tended to overestimate their performance on this task. Since accuracy in self-confidence requires the ability to monitor how well you are performing, this result suggested that patients with frontal lobe lesions were unable to monitor their own performance or the advice of others.

The performance of patients with parietal lobe lesions was significantly better than that of patients with frontal lobe lesions, but they still performed more poorly than controls. They were good at assessing advice, but not good at using advice. As with the frontal group, they were overconfident about their own performance.

Correlations between parameters of the decision-making task and selected neuropsychological tests requiring cognitive control also indicated differences between groups. Both frontal groups (DL and OF) performed poorly on the working memory (WM; *n*-back) and planning (Tower of Hanoi) tasks. Planning and WM are cognitively and anatomically distinct with the frontal pole mediating planning (Koechlin et al. 2000; Burgess, Gilbert, Okuda, and Simons, this volume) and DL cortex mediating WM (Cohen et al. 1997). The results show that impairments in decision making can occur in the absence of any WM impairment, but impairment in WM will exacerbate decision-making deficits. Overall, planning deficits were more predictive of performance on this task than WM deficits.

In addition, the patients' impairment in decision making was associated with larger frontal lobe lesions (Manes et al. 2002). The impact of the lesion volume on this task was minimal however, solely affecting the time taken to make the probability estimates, so that patients with larger lesions spent less time assessing advice.

In summary, right PFC lesions result in impaired decision making in tasks in which integrating information is important, and this correlates with the poor planning ability displayed by these same patients. The ability to both assess and use advice was impaired, and this compound deficit likely affects patients' ability to manage their daily affairs and to interact appropriately with others. As in the previous study, the patients exhibited volition-as-action behavior, as they could perform the task using frequently inappropriate strategies. Their lack of insight and reduced volition-as-planning (autonomy) behavior contributed to their choice of inappropriate strategies, leading to their overall poor performance.

The previous two studies highlight that patients with frontal lobe lesions can act and make decisions but that their decisions can be quite poor depending on the circumstances of the task. Next, we describe a patient who performed normally on cognitive tasks but had gross impairment in his social competence, social decision making, and social conduct. The case study emphasizes the role of volition-as-planning in interpreting the root cause of deficits in social behavior.

16.4 Study 3: Deficits in Rational Decisions in Social Matters

We had the opportunity to study (Dimitrov et al. 1999) a male patient named MGS, who was wounded in combat in Vietnam in August of 1968. He incurred a penetrating fracture of the right frontal skull with tissue damage to the right frontal lobe. MGS was unable to recall any episodes from one week prior to, and one week after, the injury but had clear recollection of events before and after that time period. He seemingly recovered fully, had a normal neurological examination, and was placed on active military duty in November 1968 as an instructor of army recruits in the United States.

After returning to active duty, MGS's personality and social behavior appeared to deteriorate. Because of ineptitude, he was demoted from the rank of sergeant to the rank of private first-class. Given his behavioral decline, MGS underwent another complete medical evaluation. His laboratory, physical, and neurological examinations were essentially normal again. Nevertheless, given the changes in his personality and behavior, MGS was recommended for permanent retirement from the army.

After his retirement, MGS's parents (with whom he stayed) reported "he was not like he used to be" and he met with "the lowest of the low." They observed unusual moodiness, sarcasm, bluntness of affect, lack of tact with others, remoteness of rapport, and social withdrawal. MGS was unable to handle any new jobs, to plan his daily activities, and to make and keep reputable friends. He had been married and divorced three times after his return from Vietnam. MGS showed questionable competency in handling large sums of money. In addition, his mother stated that "he possessed the experience and ethics of a 14-year-old" and had developed a big appetite for pornography.

At that time we studied MGS in 1998, he denied any neurological symptoms. He reported no other head injury beside his primary injury in Vietnam. MGS's neurological examination was once again normal, motor functions were normal, sensation was intact to all modalities, and his cranial nerves were intact including visual fields and extraocular muscles. The CT scan revealed evidence of a right frontal craniotomy with multiple surgical clips, anterior frontal encephalomalacia with compensatory enlargement of the right frontal horn, and no evidence of intracranial hemorrhage or extra-axial fluid collection. A precise lesion chart based on the CT scan was drawn (Damasio and Damasio 1989), and the topography of the lesion can be seen in figure 16.7. MGS's right frontal cortex lesion included mesial and polar frontal cortices (BA 8, 9, 10, 11, and 32) and the anterior segment of the anterior cingulate cortex (BA 24). His total lesion volume was estimated to be $31.97\,cm^3$ by summating the affected areas across each slice.

A broad-based clinical neuropsychological examination tested MGS's general cognitive and executive abilities and his emotional and social functioning. The neuropsychological evaluation indicated that MGS had preserved general cognitive, abstract thinking, and problem-solving abilities in contrast to gross impairment in his social competence, social decision making, and social conduct. In particular, MGS demonstrated diminished sensitivity to socially relevant stimuli and situational nuances, was abnormal in his attitude about sexual behavior, and had a diminished sense of responsibility.

In many respects, MGS's life is very similar to that of the famous 19th century patient Phineas Gage, who survived an injury from an iron rod that passed through

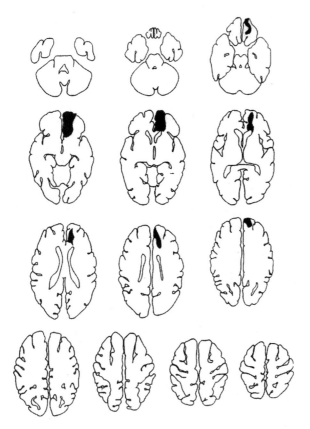

Figure 16.7
Lesion chart based on the CT scan of Patient MGS.

his brain (Damasio et al. 1994). Gage and MGS shared almost identical changes in personality and social conduct after their injury. In contrast with their relatively intact general cognitive abilities, their ability to make rational decisions in personal and social matters was compromised. This pattern of behavior has been described in other ventromedial frontal lesion patients (e.g., see Brickner 1934). It is well known now that the ventromedial frontal cortex subserves critical processes involved in the emotional and social regulation of behavior. As important for the topic of this volume, it is once again made clear that a focal lesion to the PFC does not automatically impair volition-as-action. In this case, the patient performed normally on many cognitive tasks—some of which required not only volition-as-action but also volition-as-planning behavior. It is clear, however, that while his volition-as-action social behavior was relatively unaffected, his volition-as-planning social behavior was very impaired. He was particularly drawn to the surface features of social stimuli, was satisfied by immediate gratification, and was submissive when asked to give money for no particular reason.

In sum, the prior two group studies and this case study make a compelling argument that patients with PFC lesions have impaired volition-as-planning. Perhaps the philosophical and psychological definition(s) of volitional behavior should be modified and made more precise.

16.5 A Modified Framework for Understanding Volitional Behavior

Based on our research studies and experience, we believe that any framework for understanding volitional behavior must take into account the kind of situation the subject is in, its complexity, and the time scale within which action is required. In addition, the framework should differentiate between volition-as-action and volition-as-planning as well as motoric action and cognitive intent. Finally, the framework should be testable and biologically plausible. The SEC framework fulfills the aforementioned criteria.

We (Grafman 1995, 1999, 2002; Wood and Grafman 2003) have proposed that certain aspects of episodic and semantic knowledge are represented in the form of SECs in the PFC (fig. 16.8). An SEC is a goal-oriented set of events that is structured in sequence and represents thematic knowledge, morals, abstractions, concepts, social rules, event features, event boundaries, and grammars. Aspects of SECs are independently represented but encoded and retrieved as an episode. SECs are composed of a set of differentiated representational forms that are stored in different regions of the PFC but activated in parallel to reproduce many of the elements contained in a typical episode in memory (Grafman 2002).

The SEC framework is consistent with what is known about the structure, connectivity, neurophysiology, and evolution of the PFC. The PFC occupies approximately one-third of the entire human cerebral cortex, and it is one of the latest cortices developed phylogenetically (Brodmann 1912; Jerison 1994). The proportion of cortical space devoted to the PFC (and Brodmann's Area 10 in particular) suggests that it may be the neurobiological substrate that supports some of our species' most distinctive cognitive abilities (e.g., thematic understanding, planning, and social intelligence). The PFC can be divided into ventromedial and dorsolateral regions. The ventromedial PFC (VMPFC) is well situated to support functions involving the integration of information about emotions, memory, and environmental stimuli since it has monosynaptic connections to both the limbic system and anterior prefrontal cortices. The dorsolateral PFC (DLPFC) supports the cognitive regulation of behavior and helps control our response to environmental stimuli. The current evidence from neuropsychological studies of brain-injured patients, lesion studies, and the application of neuroimaging techniques such as positron-emission tomography and functional magnetic

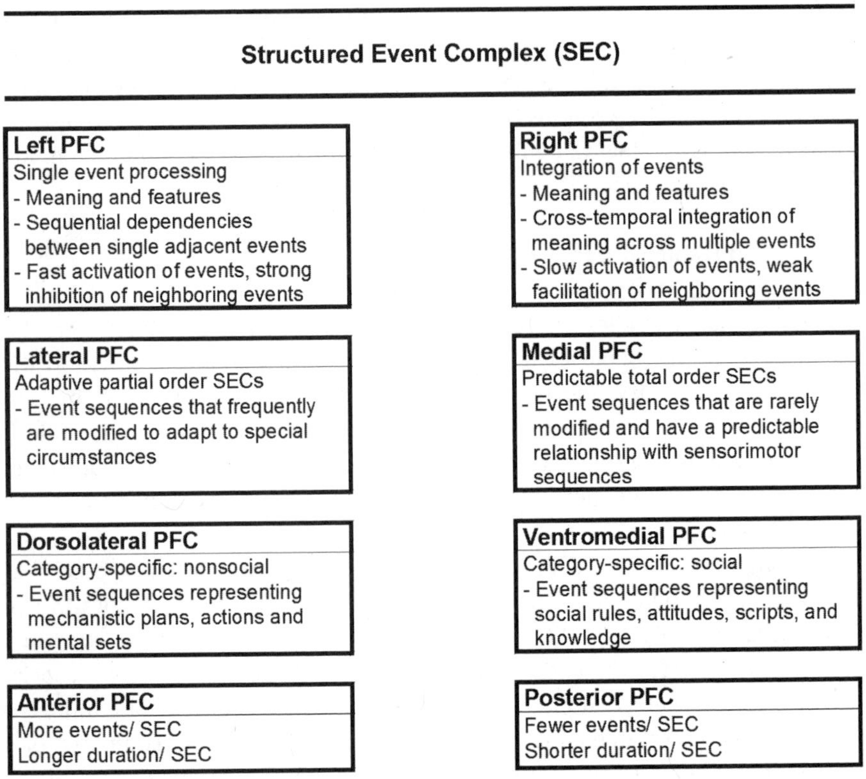

Structured Event Complex (SEC)

Left PFC	Right PFC
Single event processing - Meaning and features - Sequential dependencies between single adjacent events - Fast activation of events, strong inhibition of neighboring events	Integration of events - Meaning and features - Cross-temporal integration of meaning across multiple events - Slow activation of events, weak facilitation of neighboring events
Lateral PFC	**Medial PFC**
Adaptive partial order SECs - Event sequences that frequently are modified to adapt to special circumstances	Predictable total order SECs - Event sequences that are rarely modified and have a predictable relationship with sensorimotor sequences
Dorsolateral PFC	**Ventromedial PFC**
Category-specific: nonsocial - Event sequences representing mechanistic plans, actions and mental sets	Category-specific: social - Event sequences representing social rules, attitudes, scripts, and knowledge
Anterior PFC	**Posterior PFC**
More events/ SEC Longer duration/ SEC	Fewer events/ SEC Shorter duration/ SEC

Figure 16.8
Representational forms of the structured event complex (SEC) and their proposed localization within the prefrontal cortex (PFC).

resonance imaging (fMRI) support an SEC-type representational network. There is evidence for category specificity in that the VMPFC appears to be specialized for social knowledge processing (Dimitrov et al. 1999; Milne and Grafman 2001). Emotional and non-emotional SECs (Partiot et al. 1995) and social and nonsocial SECs are associated with different patterns of PFC activation (Wood et al. 2003). Consistent with this, impairment of social behavior is most evident after VMPFC damage, whereas impairment of reflective, mechanistic behavior is evident following DLPFC damage (Burgess et al. 2000; Goel and Grafman 2000). SECs appear to be selectively processed by anterior PFC regions (Koechlin et al. 1999, 2000, 2002). When the SEC is novel or multitasking is involved, anterior frontopolar PFC is recruited, but when SECs are overlearned, slightly more posterior frontomedial PFC is recruited (Koechlin et al. 2000). The PFC is a member of many extended brain circuits. There is evidence that the hippocampus and the PFC cooperate when the sequence of events has to be anticipated (Dreher et al. 2002). The amygdala and PFC cooperate when SECs are goal and reward oriented or emotionally relevant (Zalla et al. 2000). The basal ganglia, cerebellum, and PFC cooperate as well in the transfer of performance responsibilities between cognitive and visuomotor representations (Hallett and Grafman 1997; Koechlin et al. 2002).

Volitional behavior that is not simply driven by a compelling environmental stimulus must rely upon the activation and processing of information in the format of an SEC. In figure 16.9, the left column indicates the behaviors driven by autonomous intent, and the right column indicates behaviors driven by the environment. The center column illustrates that activities governed by the subject's intentions or environmental provocation are in various states of activation and inhibition in comparison to a baseline or homeostatic state. Volition-as-planning (autonomous) behavior is designed to inhibit environmental stimuli that are not relevant to the intentional activity, and environmental stimuli are designed to interfere with autonomous behavior when the person must adapt to unforeseen circumstances that interfere with autonomy. Furthermore, autonomous behavior is usually driven by long-term goals and desires, whereas environmental or stimulus-driven behavior is usually driven by perceptual saliency, emotion, and immediate rewards or punishment. Autonomous behavior is represented by SECs of various types that include plans, and these representations can be further subdivided into social and nonsocial plans and activities. Some of these social or nonsocial activities are quite routine and structured, whereas other activities require regular adaptation. Thus, while SECs are often predictable, occasionally persons may have to choose the next behavior from among competing choices. In that case, they may have to rearrange the order of to-be-carried-out activities or simultaneously engage in multiple activities to varying degrees of success. If they rearrange the events, they can be arranged into predictable and familiar sequences or could become a rather rare sequence. All of these choices are based on autonomous decision making.

The rightmost column of figure 16.9 reflects a sampling of the range of stimuli that occur in the environment or in reflective thought that may or may not be germane to the autonomous activity. For example, in the case of the intentional behavior of getting out of bed and preparing to leave for work in the morning, the environment could include relevant objects (e.g., alarm clock) or irrelevant objects (e.g., a crib). Representations of autonomous behavior will prime relevant objects before their appearance and inhibit irrelevant objects via attention mechanisms. With diminished autonomy (after frontal lobe lesions), persons will be more disrupted by task-irrelevant stimuli. Nevertheless, we claim that they can still make volition-as-action decisions in dealing with the task-irrelevant stimuli. Only massive lesions will truly block volition-as-action behavior, whereas smaller lesions (particularly in the PFC) will affect domain-specific volition-as-planning (autonomous) behavior.

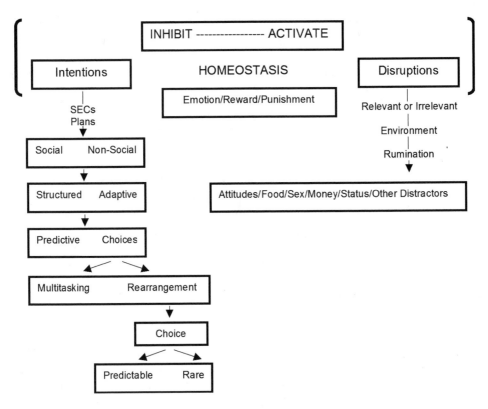

Figure 16.9
Volitional framework. SEC, structured event complex.

In addition, SEC representations can operate in real time but can also be compressed and translated into, for example, lists or heuristic knowledge (fig. 16.10). This enables SEC knowledge to be processed within WM and allows flexibility in altering volitional behavior. Volitional behavior is also influenced by emotional biases as reflected in the notion of somatic markers (see Bechara, this volume). Evidence has accumulated that places SECs, heuristics, and somatic markers at different levels of the central nervous system. Modulation of behaviors follows a top-down structure (partly based on the duration of the represented activity) with SECs modulating heuristics, which in turn modulate emotional processes. All this modulation can occur prior to action being initiated by the motor system. Note that volition, that is, choice followed by action, can be initiated by SECs, heuristic knowledge, or emotion in this framework.

We have argued that patients with PFC lesions have a diminished ability to perform self-generated intentional acts (volition-as-planning), whereas their ability to perform actions induced by others or elicited by situational cues (volition-as-action) remains

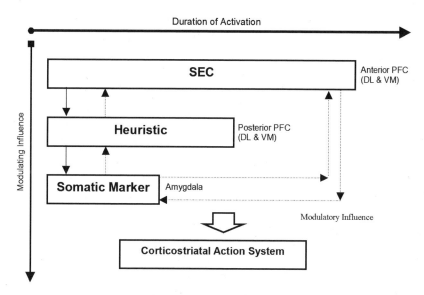

Figure 16.10

A simplified hierarchical control system. SEC, structured event complex; PFC, prefrontal cortex; DL, dorsolateral; VM, ventromedial.

intact. The characteristic deficits of patients with PFC lesions in the three studies described in this chapter can be explained and interpreted using the provided theoretical SEC framework. Our daily life involves extended sequences of actions that are both temporally and hierarchically organized. In order to execute these sequences in a coordinated manner, we must anticipate the future outcome of our current action. The SEC framework claims that such events and action sequences are represented in the form of SECs in the PFC. Each SEC is characterized by the specific duration and order of several events, which are linked into one overall thematic activity or plan to achieve a certain goal.

Our case study confirms the observation that patients with OR damage often have normal neurological and neuropsychological examinations but their ability to make rational decisions in personal and social matters is compromised. Thus, volition related to cognitive tasks may remain intact even when volition/autonomy-dependent social behavior is diminished—particularly when patients have to anticipate the consequences of their actions, be empathetic, or make social decisions about the future.

Volition-as-planning representations are stored throughout the PFC including VMPFC, although in that location they are directly linked to the autonomic nervous system as a part of a larger distributed network concerned with social behavior. Lesions in this part of the PFC can especially disable rapid automatic associative knowledge, causing patients to lose volition-as-planning abilities that help bias their rapid social decision making (i.e., a domain-specific deficit in autonomy). This deficit reflects a failure to retrieve social SECs (e.g., rules developed in childhood) and an inability to activate SECs previously experienced in association with specific social situations.

The SEC framework can also explain why patients with frontal lobe lesions have problems with adequately addressing future goals. In study 1, patients with PFC lesions spent a decreasing amount of time on future goals. Goals were temporally spaced into the future with a different time scale (stabilize situation now, buy a house in 1 to 2 years, send kids to collage in 15 years, and retire in 30 years). The greater the projection into the future, the less the projected situation will resemble the current situation. The SEC framework predicts that patient difficulty in retrieving information would increase as the task domain becomes more unfamiliar, because the strength of representation of large-scale knowledge structures such as an SEC is dependent on the frequency of exposure to these structures and the frequency of their activation. Hence, the patients should have more difficulty in processing low-frequency (unfamiliar) SECs compared with high-frequency (familiar) ones. In addition, our framework predicts that only SECs, of all the forms of cognitive representation, allow us to forecast and peer into the future, since SECs include yet-to-be-performed actions as part of their representational structure. As we have repeatedly claimed in this chapter, lesions to the PFC will damage the representation of SECs, and that should lead to diminished volition-as-planning.

For managing daily life activities, a plan is needed, which represents a blueprint of the future. The "goodness" of this plan cannot be determined until it is actually executed. It is self-determined and will be a function of how well someone is able to model the relevant parts of the world necessary to test the plan. The resulting information can then be used to modify and improve the plan. A judgment has to be made as to when we have satisfied the task requirements, because in planning many daily activities, there are often no right or wrong answers and no official termination points except for those imposed by the person. Patients with PFC lesions have poor judgment regarding the adequacy and completeness of a plan. They genuinely believe they have specified a complete plan when they stop.

Volitional behavior probably develops slowly throughout childhood and adolescence and does not mature until young adulthood in conjunction with the development of SECs. Volition-as-action behavior may mature at a faster rate than volition-as-planning behavior. One possibility is that the individual and paired events that make up primitive SECs (e.g., simple rules) develop early in childhood and only later expand into a large multi-event unit based on frequency of exposure to sequences of actions with adjacent events occurring together in time and in a typical temporal order. Based on repeated exposure to an SEC, the boundaries of that event series would become more firmly established, leading to a well-formatted SEC. Another possibility is that a fully formed SEC could be stored quite early in life but only in spare numbers. The growth in the SEC population would depend primarily on expanding life experience.

Both possibilities are consistent with the observation that the PFC undergoes relatively late development in the course of ontology by myelogenic and synaptogenic criteria (Conel 1939; Flechsig 1920; Huttenlocher 1990; Huttenlocher and Dabholkar 1997). Imaging studies also indicate that the PFC does not fully mature until adolescence and early adulthood (Chugani et al. 1987; Paus et al. 1999; Sowell et al. 1999).

Research on primates suggests that prefrontal lesions placed early in development do not affect performance on tasks presumably subserved by PFC until the monkey's PFC matures (Diamond 1991; Goldman-Rakic 1987, 1992). In addition, some human data are available that support this observation of the delayed effects of early prefrontal lesions in monkeys (e.g., Eslinger et al. 1992; Levin et al. 1994). Based on this evidence, it is impossible that a rich SEC cognitive architecture supporting mature autonomy could be developed until adolescence or adulthood, regardless of the richness of experience in childhood and volitional competence.

Children can engage in volitional behavior of all types, but their generation of rich autonomous behavior awaits adolescence and young adulthood. This observation supports the distinction between these two aspects of cognition and strongly suggests that the PFC is particularly important for the demonstration of volition-as-planning behavior (that we associate with a "will" based on reflective thought) but that volition-as-action behavior can occur even in the presence of an immature PFC.

16.6 Concluding Thoughts

In summary, almost all patients with focal frontal lobe lesions have relatively better volition-as-action than volition-as-planning behavior. This is not to deny that very large frontal lesions or advanced fronto-temporal dementias can lead to anergic, apathetic, and amotivational syndromes that dramatically reduce not only autonomy but volitional behavior across most domains (although there may be exceptions) and conditions.

Volition-as-planning behaviors are particularly impaired after focal frontal lobe lesions when choices are more ambiguous, the consequences are distant, the environment is especially compelling, and the cognitive domain that is affected by the lesion is particularly important for intentional behavior.

Since our research focus is on the functions of the PFC, we are left to conclude on the basis of our research studies that the investigation of behaviors associated with the concept of the "will" should be focused on a better understanding of what it means to have autonomous ideas and actions (i.e., volition-as-planning) rather than the more simple notion of volition only as a conscious decision, that is, "I will press this button, or I will go with you" (i.e., volition-as-action). In keeping with this approach, it might be wise to adapt a framework that recognizes a continuum of volitional ability that ranges from normal autonomous intentional choice behavior through selective and infrequent impairment of volition to an inability to demonstrate intention by choice and behavior.

Regardless of the approach to the study of volition that is adopted, we believe that it would be useful to determine whether there is just a general volitional syndrome or whether there are also domain-specific volitional failures as we suggested above. There is also a pressing need to develop at least generally agreed upon measures of volition, so that research across laboratories can be easily compared.

Finally, volitional deficits may be due to another impairment in a different cognitive process. For example, impaired strategic reflection, problems in counterfactual thinking, diminished plan development and/or execution, distractibility, and disinhibited social behavior can all lead to problems in volition-as-planning. If a framework for volition includes a hypothesized cognitive architecture, then the development of an assessment battery that includes tests that directly evaluate volitional ability as well as some of the other cognitive processes that can impact volitional behavior will be easier to build.

The concepts of will, volition, and autonomy, despite their historically shallow definitions, are important to think about, since they are "shorthand" for some of the key cognitive and social processes that define our humanity. Efforts, such as those described in this volume, to specify their underlying cognitive processes and architecture and how the brain represents such concepts will go a long way toward completing the agenda of cognitive neuroscience.

References

Brickner, R. M. 1934. *An Interpretation of Frontal Lobe Function Based upon the Study of a Case of Partial Bilateral Frontal Lobectomy.* New York: Association for Research in Nervous and Mental Disease.

Brodmann, K. 1912. Neue Ergebnisse ueber die vergleichende histologische Lokalisation der Grosshirnrinde mit besonderer Beruecksichtigung des Stirnhirns. *Anatomischer Anzeiger: Supplement, 41,* 157–216.

Burgess, P. W., E. Veitch, A. de Lacy Costello, and T. Shallice. 2000. The cognitive and neuroanatomical correlates of multitasking. *Neuropsychologia, 38,* 848–863.

Chugani, H. T., M. E. Phelps, and J. C. Mazziotta. 1987. Positron emission tomography study of human brain functional development. *Annals of Neurology, 22,* 487–497.

Cohen, J. D., W. M. Perlstein, T. S. Braver, L. E. Nystrom, D. C. Noll, J. Jonides, et al. 1997. Temporal dynamics of brain activation during a WM task. *Nature, 386,* 604–608.

Conel, J. L. 1939. *The Postnatal Development of the Human Cerebral Cortex*. Volumes 1–6. Cambridge, Mass.: Havard University Press.

Damasio, H., and A. R. Damasio. 1989. Lesion analysis in neuropsychology. New York: Oxford University Press.

Damasio, H., T. Grabowski, R. Frank, A. M. Galaburda, and A. R. Damasio. 1994. The return of Phineas Gage: Clues about the brain from the skull of a famous patient. *Science, 264*, 1102–1105.

Diamond, A. 1991. Guidelines for the study of brain–behavior relationships during development. In *Frontal Lobe Function and Dysfunction*, ed. H. S. Levin, A. Eisenberg, and A. L. Benton, pp. 339–380. New York: Oxford University Press.

Dimitrov, M., M. Phipps, T. Zahn, and J. Grafman. 1999. A thoroughly modern Gage. *Neurocase, 5*, 345–354.

Dreher, J. C., E. Koechlin, S. O. Ali, and J. Grafman. 2002. The roles of timing and task order during task switching. *Neuroimage, 17*, 95–109.

Ericsson, K. A., and H. A. Simon. 1984. *Protocol Analysis: Verbal Reports as Data*. Cambridge, Mass.: MIT Press.

Eslinger, P. J., L. M. Grattan, H. Damasio, and A. R. Damasio. 1992. Developmental consequences of childhood frontal lobe damage. *Archives of Neurology, 49*, 764–769.

Flechsig, P. 1920. *Anatomie des menschlichen Gehirns und Rueckenmarks auf myelogenetischer Grundlage*. Leipzig: Thieme.

Goel, V. 1994. A comparison of design and nondesign problem spaces. *Artificial Intelligence in Engineering, 9*.

Goel, V. 1995. *Sketches of Thought*. Cambridge, Mass.: MIT Press.

Goel V., and J. Grafman. 2000. Role of the right prefrontal cortex in ill-structured planning. *Cognitive Neuropsychology, 17*, 415–436.

Goel, V., J. Grafman, J. Tajik, S. Gana, and D. Danto. 1997. A study of the performance of patients with frontal lobe lesions in a financial planning task. *Brain, 120 (Pt 10)*, 1805–1822.

Goel, V., and P. Pirolli. 1992. The structure of design problem spaces. *Cognitive Science, 16*, 395–429.

Goldman-Rakic, P. S. 1987. *Circuitry of Primate Prefrontal Cortex and Regulation of Behavior by Representional Memory*. Washington, D.C.: American Physiological Society.

Goldman-Rakic, P. S. 1992. Working memory and the mind. *Scientific American, 267*, 110–117.

Gomez-Beldarrain, M., C. Harries, J. C. Garcia-Monco, E. Ballus, and J. Grafman. 2004. Patients with right frontal lesions are unable to assess and use advice to make predictive judgments. *Journal of Cognitive Neuroscience, 16*, 74–89.

Grafman, J. 1995. Similarities and distinctions among current models of prefrontal cortical functions. In *Structure and Functions of the Human Prefrontal Cortex*, ed. J. Grafman, K. J. Holyoak, and F. Boller, pp. 337–368. New York: New York Academy of Sciences.

Grafman, J. 1999. Experimental assessment of adult frontal lobe function. In *The Human Frontal Lobes: Functions and Disorders*, ed. B. L. Miller, and J. L. Cummings, pp. 321–344. New York: Guilford Press.

Grafman, J. 2002. The human prefrontal cortex has evolved to represent components of structured event complexes. In *Handbook of Neuropsychology*, vol. 7, ed. J. Grafman, pp. 157–174. Amsterdam: Elsevier.

Hallett, M., and J. Grafman. 1997. Executive function and motor skill learning. *International Review of Neurobiology, 41*, 297–323.

Harlow, J. M. 1868. Recovery after severe injury to the head. *Publications of the Massachusetts Medical Society, 2*, 327–346.

Harvey, N., C. Harries, and I. Fischer. 2000. Using advice and assessing its quality. *Organizational Behavior and Huamn Decision Processes, 81*, 252–273.

Huttenlocher, P. R. 1990. Morphometric study of human cerebral cortex development. *Neuropsychologia, 28*, 517–527.

Huttenlocher, P. R., and A. S. Dabholkar. 1997. Regional differences in synaptogenesis in human cerebral cortex. *Journal of Comparative Neurology, 387*, 167–178.

Jerison, H. L. 1994. Evoluation of the brain. In *Neuropsychology*, ed. D. W. Zaidel, pp. 53–81. San Diego: Academic.

Koechlin, E., G. Basso, P. Pietrini, S. Panzer, and J. Grafman. 1999. The role of the anterior prefrontal cortex in human cognition. *Nature, 399*, 148–151.

Koechlin, E., G. Corrado, P. Pietrini, and J. Grafman. 2000. Dissociating the role of the medial and lateral anterior prefrontal cortex in human planning. *Proceedings of the National Academy of Sciences USA, 97*, 7651–7656.

Koechlin, E., A. Danek, Y. Burnod, and J. Grafman. 2002. Medial prefrontal and subcortical mechanisms underlying the acquisition of motor and cognitive action sequences. *Neuron, 35*, 371–381.

Levin, H. S., M. A. Mendelsohn, J. M. Lilly, K. A. Flecher, S. B. Culhane, S. B. Chapman, et al. 1994. Tower of London performance in relation to magnetic resonance imaging following closed head injury in children. *Neurpsychology, 8*, 171–179.

Manes, F., B. Sahakian, L. Clark, R. Rogers, N. Antoun, M. Aitken, et al. 2002. Decision-making processes following damage to the prefrontal cortex. *Brain, 125*, 624–639.

Milne, E., and J. Grafman. 2001. Ventromedial prefrontal cortex lesions in humans eliminate implicit gender stereotyping. *Journal of Neuroscience, 21*, RC150 (1–6).

Newell, A., and H. A. Simon. 1972. *Human Problem Solving.* Englewood Cliffs, N.J.: Prentice-Hall.

Partiot, A., J. Grafman, N. Sadato, J. Wachs, and M. Hallett. 1995. Brain activation during the generation of non-emotional and emotional plans. *NeuroReport, 6,* 1397–1400.

Paus, T., A. Zijdenbos, K. Worsley, D. L. Collins, J. Blumenthal, J. N. Giedd, et al. 1999. Structural maturation of neural pathways in children and adolescents: In vivo study. *Science, 283,* 1908–1911.

Penfield, W., and J. Evans. 1935. The frontal lobe in man: A clinical study of maximum removals. *Brain, 58,* 115–133.

Pickett, J. P. 2000. *American Heritage Dictionary of the English Language.* 4th edition. Boston: Houghton Mifflin.

Rylander, G. 1939. Personality changes after operations on the frontal lobes. *Acta Psychiatrical et Neurologica, Supplement 20,* 1–327.

Simon, H. A. 1961. Human cognition and problem solving. University of California Medical School Symposium on "Control of the Mind," 1–8.

Simon, H. A. 1978. Information-processing theory of human problem solving. In *Handbook of Learning and Cognitive Processes,* vol. 5, ed. W. K. Estes, pp. 271–295. Hillsdale, N.J.: Lawrence Erlbaum.

Sowell, E. R., P. M. Thompson, C. J. Holmes, T. L. Jernigan, and A. W. Toga. 1999. In vivo evidence for post-adolescent brain maturation in frontal and striatal regions. *Nature Neuroscience, 2,* 859–861.

Tranel, D., and H. Damasio. 1994. Neuroanatomical correlates of electrodermal skin conductance responses. *Psychophysiology, 31,* 427–438.

Wood, J. N., and J. Grafman. 2003. Human prefrontal cortex: Processing and representational perspectives. *Nature Reviews Neuroscience, 4,* 139–147.

Wood, J. N., S. G. Romero, M. Makale, and J. Grafman. 2003. Category-specific representations of social and non-social knowledge in the human prefrontal cortex. *Journal of Cognitive Neuroscience, 15,* 236–248.

Zahn, T. P., J. Grafman, and D. Tranel. 1999. Frontal lobe lesions and electrodermal activity: Effects of significance. *Neuropsychologia, 37,* 1227–1241.

Zalla, T., E. Koechlin, P. Pietrini, G. Basso, P. Aquino, A. Sirigu, et al. 2000. Differential amygdala responses to winning and losing: A functional magnetic resonance imaging study in humans. *European Journal of Neuroscience, 12,* 1764–1770.

17 Rostral Prefrontal Brain Regions (Area 10): A Gateway between Inner Thought and the External World?

Paul W. Burgess, Sam J. Gilbert, Jiro Okuda, and Jon S. Simons

17.1 Introduction

This chapter reviews recent evidence from our laboratory (and others) that suggests that the most anterior parts of the frontal lobes of the brain support cognitive processes which are critical to complex volitional behavior in humans. We conclude by proposing a simple preliminary hypothesis about the role of this region in cognition.

17.2 Introduction to the Rostral Prefrontal Cortex

The part of the frontal lobes that is foremost in the brain has many names. The most common of these are "anterior prefrontal cortex," "the frontal pole," "frontopolar cortex," and "rostral prefrontal cortex" (rostral PFC). Of these, we favor the use of the term "rostral" since the term is equivalent to others that are used to denote regions of the brain (e.g., caudal, dorsal, lateral, medial, ventral). However, these terms all refer to a region which broadly corresponds to the cytoarchitectonic area known as Brodmann Area (BA) 10. There is very good reason for suspecting that this brain region plays a critical role in human cognition. For instance, it is large in humans: in volumetric terms probably the largest single architectonic region of the frontal lobes (Christoff et al. 2001), which themselves account for approximately 30 percent of the total cortical surface. Given that the brain may consume as much as 20 percent of the oxygen we extract from the air that we breathe (Raichle et al. 2001), there must be some evolutionary advantage to such a large brain region. Moreover, the rostral PFC regions are of unique proportional size in humans; they are for instance double the relative size in humans compared with chimpanzees (Semendeferi et al. 2001). And finally, this region is possibly the last to achieve myelination, and it has been argued that tardily myelinating areas engage in complex functions highly related to the organism's experience (Fuster 1997, p. 37). These are all good reasons to imagine that the rostral PFC may support cognitive processing which is especially important to humans.

However, until recently there has been very little evidence which might speak to the cognitive functions of this brain region.

17.3   Outline of the Arguments

Before outlining a potential theoretical resolution, this chapter seeks to explain why it is that we know so little and sets out the problems facing current theorists. In doing so, we will make the following points (for fuller exposition of the theoretical conclusion alone, readers are referred to Burgess, Simons, Dumontheil, and Gilbert, in press):

1. There are very few data concerning the putative functions of rostral PFC other than from functional imaging and a small number of human lesion studies.
2. Functional imaging data provide few constraints on theorizing because rostral PFC activation is found in such a wide variety of tasks.
3. Human lesion data rule out many aspects of the theories from functional imaging.
4. The most promising approach for functional imaging is therefore to start with the possible explanations emerging from lesion data.
5. Functional imaging studies that start from this base suggest that the role of rostral PFC is in the attentional control between stimulus-independent and stimulus-oriented thought.

Let us now consider these points in turn.

17.3.1   There Are Very Few Data Concerning the Putative Functions of Rostral PFC Other Than from Functional Imaging and a Small Number of Human Lesion Studies

There are many reasons why we know so little about the cognitive functions of rostral PFC. For instance, animal studies of this region are problematic: The very fact of the structural difference between humans and other animals creates doubt as to the transferability of findings from one species to another, and animal lesion studies of this region are in any case hindered by practical anatomical considerations. Other cognitive neuroscience methods also face limitations. For instance, electrophysiological methods do not presently have the required spatial resolution to separate subregions of the frontal lobes, and transcranial magnetic stimulation studies of certain aspects of rostral PFC (i.e., medial Area 10) may be difficult for anatomical reasons. Thus, virtually the only significant evidence one might call upon comes from two methods: functional imaging and human lesion studies. Human lesion studies are, however, difficult and costly: Area 10 lesions (e.g., tumors or strokes) are neither common nor do they typically produce "hard" neurological signs (such as hemiparesis, marked aphasia, etc.), and so unless they are the result of trauma, they are often not detected until they are large, affecting other brain regions in addition to Area 10. This then raises the question of which of the symptoms can be attributable specifically to the rostral aspect of the lesion, usually necessitating a group study using the overlapping lesion method. However, since there is no straightforward pathology–lesion site correspondence, the pattern will typically be made more difficult by issues of the effects of different pathologies. These issues are not insurmountable (see, e.g., Burgess et al. 2000; Burgess, Veitch, and Costello, submitted) but will necessitate careful and lengthy data collection and analysis, often taking several years. In this context, the functional imaging method, where data collection can be scheduled in advance and takes only a few hours, is understandably attractive to researchers.

17.3.2 Functional Imaging Data Provide Few Constraints on Theorizing because Rostral PFC Activation Is Found in Such a Wide Variety of Tasks

Functional brain imaging, principally positron-emission tomography (PET) and functional magnetic resonance imaging (fMRI), has shown that local hemodynamic (e.g., blood flow; blood oxygenation) changes occur in rostral PFC during the performance of a very wide variety of cognitive tasks (Grady 1999), from the simplest (e.g., conditioning paradigms; Blaxton et al. 1996) to highly complex tests involving memory and judgment (e.g., Burgess et al. 2001, 2003; Frith and Frith 2003; Koechlin et al. 1999) or problem solving (e.g., Christoff et al. 2001).

Indeed, one can find activation of the rostral PFC in just about any kind of task, for example, verbal episodic retrieval (Rugg et al. 1996; Tulving et al. 1996), nonverbal episodic retrieval (Roland and Gulyas 1995; Haxby et al. 1996), semantic memory (Martin et al. 1995; Jennings et al. 1997), language (Bottini et al. 1994; Klein et al. 1995), motor learning (Jenkins et al. 1994), shock/tone conditioning (Hugdahl et al. 1995), nonverbal working memory (Gold et al. 1996; Haxby et al. 1995), verbal working memory (Petrides et al. 1993), spatial memory (N. Burgess et al. 2001), auditory perception (Zatorre et al. 1996), object processing (Kosslyn et al. 1994, 1995), Tower of London Test (Baker et al. 1996), Wisconsin Card Sorting Test (Berman et al. 1995), reasoning tasks (Goel et al. 1997), and intelligence tests such as Raven's Progressive Matrices (Christoff et al. 2001; Prabhakaran et al. 1997).

Perhaps a meta-analysis of the tasks which most reliably produce rostral PFC activation would isolate the critical processing component in these tasks that this region supports? Grady (1999) provides just such an analysis. She reviewed 90 PET studies showing prefrontal regional cerebral blood flow (rCBF) changes and concluded that the most heavily represented function of BA 10 is episodic memory, on the grounds that most of the experiments reporting BA 10 activation were using episodic memory paradigms. This was a very useful and carefully conducted review. However, it didn't take into account the predominance of episodic memory investigations in functional imaging studies. If one takes this into account, a quite different picture emerges. Thus 37/90 (41%) of the studies that Grady considered in her review investigated episodic memory, and 47/90 (52%) of the studies she considered implicated BA 10. However, only 68 percent of the episodic memory studies were found to cause BA 10 activations, and just 25 (53%) of the paradigms that caused BA 10 activations were episodic memory ones. Furthermore, 7/90 of the studies that Grady considered were investigations of "working memory," and 6 of these (86%) showed BA 10 activation. And finally, 6/90 studies investigated conditioning or motor learning, and all 6 (100%) reported BA 10 activation. Thus, whatever role it is that BA 10 functions play in cognition, it is doubtful indeed that they are especially active when people are involved in episodic memory tasks. This is, of course, *not* to say that the processing BA 10 facilitates is unimportant to episodic memory (the findings are too consistent for this to be the case; see, e.g., Simons and Spiers 2003) but, rather, that whatever processing it supports is probably also used in many other types of situations.

On the need for convergent evidence from differing methods, this raises the issue of how one might progress in theorizing about the functions of BA 10, for example, by "narrowing down" the possibilities. One option is to rely upon converging evidence from different methods. Functional imaging as a method has some interesting properties as a way of developing and testing theories in cognitive neuroscience. However, it may be that it is not "equipotential" for all types of brain function, with the inferences getting harder as one attempts to evaluate more putatively "central" cognitive processes. This becomes especially important when one is trying to discover what is the function of a brain region rather than the brain regions that are involved in a particular function. A full examination of this issue is beyond this chapter. However, this is an important matter when trying to understand the scientific development of ideas about the functions of rostral PFC. What one would ideally like of a method in cognitive neuroscience in the current situation is that it can both "rule in" and "rule out" the involvement of a particular brain region in a particular function. However, functional imaging is essentially a correlative method, and therefore (in common with all correlative methods), invites inferential mistakes due to (among other possibilities) the influence of mediator variables and the like.

To illustrate this point, let us briefly consider how functional imaging might "rule in" the processes supported by a brain region in performing a particular task. Prima facie, a consistent relation between performance of task A and activation in brain region B suggests that region B supports processing important for task A performance. However, any "thought" will cause cerebral hemodynamic changes, whether they are strictly related to performance of the task or not. For the sake of argument, if we supposed that the function of rostral PFC is to support "stimulus-independent thought," one can begin to see how it might be easy to mistake activations associated with this for activations provoked by one's experimental task. Let us make this argument more concrete: Imagine that the principal information-processing role of the processes supported by brain region X is in facilitating daydreaming. If one were to devise a cognitive task (task Y) so easy and boring that subjects would sometimes daydream at the same time as performing it, one might easily find oneself suggesting on the basis of one's functional imaging data that region X is involved in performance of task Y. But if performance of task Y actually bears no necessary relation to daydreaming, this would be a false assumption. This is an especially relevant argument when one is investigating the functions of rostral PFC, since at least one study (McGuire et al. 1996) has indeed associated rostral activation with self-report of stimulus-independent thoughts (i.e., thoughts unrelated to the tasks subjects were instructed to perform or to their immediate sensory environment).

In this way, efforts to "rule in" a brain region on the basis of functional imaging data alone should be treated with caution, and the behavioral data from task performance requires close examination. But this is a relatively small problem compared with the difficulty of "ruling out" the involvement of a region in a particular task. This would likely rely upon a lack of significant activation in a brain region, and of course negative findings are not of equal power to positive ones for theorizing, since there will always be more reasons for not finding a statistically significant result than for finding one.

Compare the difficulty of these inferences for theorizing with the results one would attain from a lesion study. If damage to brain region X consistently causes severe impairment in task Y, then it is difficult to argue that brain region X does not support some process/system/pathway which is important to task Y (although this is not to say that it is a simple matter to determine what the exact processing contribution is). Similarly, if obliteration of brain region X consistently does *not* cause impairment in task Y, it is difficult to argue that that brain region plays some critical role in performance of that task. Thus, lesion studies, in theory, can both "rule in" and "rule out" the involvement of a brain region in performance of a particular task and, as a consequence, are potentially a much more powerful way of determining the functions of a brain region than functional imaging studies. A recent demonstration of this point is given by Bird et al. (2004), who describe a fascinating case study of a neurological patient who had suffered extensive damage to the medial rostral PFC bilaterally following a rare form of stroke. The areas damaged in this case included all those repeatedly implicated by functional imaging studies as critical for "theory of mind" tasks (i.e., those involving the attribution of mental states to other agents). However, their patient actually showed no impairment on a wide range of theory of mind tasks, although she was impaired on certain tests of executive function (most notably the Six Element Test and the Hayling Test, part 2 (Burgess et al. 1996; Burgess and Shallice 1996, 1997). Bird et al. (2004) rightly caution against the use of functional imaging as the sole method of establishing cognitive neuroanatomy. Bearing this in mind, we will now look at the theories of rostral PFC function that have emerged from functional imaging and then "test" these theories by considering the empirical evidence from lesion studies.

Perhaps because of the widespread findings of BA 10 involvement in functional imaging studies, theories of the possible function of this brain region predicated on these data tend to be quite general. For instance, one influential theory of the functions of *medial* rostral PFC is that it supports an "organized mode of brain function" that is present as a baseline or default state and attenuated during specific goal-directed behaviors (Gusnard et al. 2001; Raichle et al. 2001). This is argued to explain repeated findings by this group of medial rostral PFC "deactivations" when subjects are performing various cognitive tasks (compared with resting with one's eyes closed). This is referred to below as the "default mode hypothesis."

By contrast, other investigators have concerned themselves primarily with the functions of *lateral* Area 10. Christoff and Gabrieli (2000) have argued that "the frontopolar cortex is a functionally distinct prefrontal region that may be selectively involved in active processing, such as evaluation, monitoring or manipulation, performed on internally generated information" (p. 183). There is some broad agreement in framework here with the views of Koechlin and colleagues (e.g., Koechlin et al. 1999; Dreher et al. 2002; Koechlin, Ody, and Kouneihaer 2003). They maintain that (lateral) rostral PFC "selectively mediates the human ability to hold in mind goals while exploring and processing secondary goals" (Koechlin et al. 1999, p. 148), with the frontal lobes organized along a posterior to anterior axis as the task being performed becomes more endogenously guided (Dreher et al. 2002), with the highest level of this control being exerted by (lateral) rostral PFC according to the temporal episode in which the stimulus occurs (Koechlin, Ody, and Kouneihaer 2003). Koechlin was also one of the first people to demonstrate a possible medial-lateral dissociation in rostral PFC function, with a study that implicated medial rostral regions in situations where a subject encounters predictable sequences of stimuli, and lateral polar regions when the subject performed tasks in sequences contingent upon unpredictable events (Koechlin et al. 2000).

What predictions do these accounts make about the pattern of impairment that would be expected following rostral PFC lesions? If rostral PFC supports cognitive processes that are fundamental to a wide range of functions (e.g., the "default mode" hypothesis) or functions used in a wide range of conditions such as those involved in processing of internally generated information, it would be natural to expect that damage to this region in neurological patients should lead to marked cognitive impairment in many domains (e.g., problems with memory, language, perception, etc.). But what pattern actually occurs?

17.3.3 Human Lesion Data Rule Out Many Aspects of the Theories from Functional Imaging

The available evidence shows emphatically that it is *not* the case that patients with rostral lesions show deficits on a wide range of cognitive tasks. Consider, for instance,

Table 17.1

AP's Neuropsychological Test Performance.

Measure	Data Shallice and Burgess (1991)	Metzler and Parkin (2000)
Intellectual Functioning		
NART FSIQ	124	123
WAIS FSIQ	130	133[a]
PIQ	138	129
VIQ	124	128
Memory Tests		
Doors and People (%iles):		
Verbal Memory		99
Visual Memory		75
Recall		84
Recognition		98
AVLT (SS)		12
Recognition (SS)	10 (words) 14 (faces)	
Executive Function Tests		
FAS Verbal Fluency	70	56
WCST Categories	6	6
Perseverations	0	0
Cognitive Estimates	2	2
Stroop %ile	OK	100

[a]WAIS–R.

the case of AP from Shallice and Burgess (1991), who was called "NM" when he was investigated by Metzler and Parkin (2000). AP was involved in a serious road-traffic accident when he was in his early twenties, and sustained an open head injury, leading to virtually complete removal of the rostral PFC. But consider his performance on standard neuropsychological tests shown in table 17.1. This shows the results of both the Shallice/Burgess and Metzler/Parkin testing sessions, administered approximately 10 years apart. On standard neuropsychological measures of intellectual functioning, memory, and perception and even traditional tests of executive function, AP performs within the superior range.

This is not, however, to say that AP was unimpaired in other regards (Shallice and Burgess 1991; Metzler and Parkin 2000). The most noticeable of these impairments in everyday life was a marked multitasking problem. This manifested itself as tardiness and disorganization, the severity of which ensured that despite his excellent intellect and social skills, he never managed to make a return to work at the level he had enjoyed premorbidly. Shallice and Burgess (1991) invented two new tests of multi-tasking to assess these problems. One was a real-life multitasking test based around a shopping exercise (the "Multiple Errands Test"), and the second was a multitasking test for use in the laboratory or clinic (the "Six Elements Test"). Despite excellent general cognitive skills, AP and the other cases reported by Shallice and Burgess all performed these tasks below the 5 percent level compared with age- and IQ-matched controls.

There are now a number of cases reported in the literature of individuals who show similar everyday behavioral impairments (see Burgess 2000 for a review), and there is a remarkably consistent finding of involvement of Area 10 among them. For instance, in the six cases reviewed by Burgess, all had rostral PFC involvement of either the left or right hemispheres (or both). Moreover, all cases to whom the Shallice/Burgess multitasking tests have been administered have failed at least one of them. In addition to these cases, we might now also add that of Bird et al. (2004), described above, who failed the Six Elements Test.

Of course, anatomical–behavioral associations made on the grounds of data from single case studies should be treated with caution, since individual cases might be anatomically atypical (see Owen, this volume). However, two recent group human lesion studies also convincingly demonstrate that patients with rostral PFC damage do *not* necessarily have widespread cognitive deficits. Thus, Burgess et al. (2000) examined a series of 60 acute neurological patients (approximately three-quarters of whom were suffering from brain tumors) and 60 age- and IQ-matched healthy controls on a multitasking test called the Greenwich Test. In this test, subjects are presented with three different simple tasks and told that they have to attempt at least some of each of the tasks in 10 minutes, while following a set of rules. One of these rules relates to all subtests ("in all three tasks, completing a red item will gain you more points than completing an item of any other color"), and there are four task-specific rules (e.g., "in the tangled lines test you must not mark the paper other than to write your answers down"). Thus, this is a multitasking test where the majority of the variance in performance of the test comes from rule infractions rather than task-switching problems (see Burgess 2000 for a specification of the more general characteristics of a multitasking test). The Greenwich Test was administered in a form that allowed consideration of the relative contributions of task rule learning and remembering, planning, plan following, and remembering one's actions to overall multitasking performance. Specifically, before participants began the test, their ability to learn the task rules (by both spontaneous and cued recall) was measured; this measure was called "Learn." They were then asked how they intended to do the test, and a measure of the complexity and appropriateness of their plans was gained (a variable called "Plan"). The participants then performed the task itself, and by comparing what they did with what they had planned to do, a measure of "Plan Following" was made.

Multitasking performance (the number of task switches minus the number of rule breaks) was referred to as the test "Score." After these stages were finished, subjects were asked to recollect their own actions by describing in detail what they had done (variable name: "Recount"). Finally, delayed memory for the task rules was examined ("Remember").

If rostral aspects of the frontal lobes support processes which are critical to performance in many situations, one might expect that patients with lesions to this region would be impaired at all stages of this test, with perhaps the impairment profile reflecting the differing sensitivities of the measures (e.g., delayed memory would be worst, since delayed free recall measures are usually among the most sensitive to nonspecific neurological damage). However, this was not the case at all. Patients with left hemisphere rostral lesions, when compared with patients with lesions elsewhere, showed a significant multitasking impairment (i.e., the variable "Score") despite no significant impairment on remembering task rules (the "Remember" variable). Indeed, the left rostral prefrontal cases showed *no* significant impairment on any variable except the one reflecting multitasking performance. In other words, despite being able to learn the task rules, form a plan, remember their actions, and say what they should have done, they nevertheless showed a multitasking problem.

A further recent human group lesion study underlines these results (Burgess, Veitch, and Costello, submitted). In this study, a new version of the Burgess et al. (1996) Six Elements Test of multitasking was given to 69 acute neurological patients with circumscribed focal lesions and 60 healthy individuals, using the administration framework of Burgess et al. (2000). The Six Elements Test differs from the Greenwich Test in that the multitasking score reflects mainly voluntary time-based switching rather than rule following. Compared with other patients, those whose lesions involved the rostral prefrontal regions of the right hemisphere made significantly fewer voluntary task switches, attempted fewer subtasks, and spent far longer on individual subtasks. They did not, however, make a larger number of rule breaks (in contrast to the left rostral patients in the Burgess et al. 2000 study). As with the study of Burgess et al. (2000), these multitasking deficits could not be attributed to deficits in general intellectual functioning, rule knowledge, planning, or retrospective memory.

17.3.4 The Most Promising Approach for Functional Imaging Is Therefore to Start with the Possible Explanations Emerging from Lesion Data

In this laboratory we have therefore taken the constraints presented by human lesion data as a scientific starting point for our functional imaging studies. The multitasking failures in our patients clearly had as a root cause problems with prospective memory (i.e., failure to carry out a delayed intention), so the first step was to investigate the brain regions involved in prospective memory as indicated by functional imaging. In the first study, Burgess, Quayle, and Frith (2001) used PET to investigate rCBF changes in eight participants performing four different tasks, each under three conditions. The first condition (baseline) was subject paced and consisted of making judgments about two objects appearing together (e.g., which of two digits is the largest, or which of two letters comes nearer the start of the alphabet). The second condition consisted of the baseline task, but subjects were also told that if a particular combination of stimuli appeared (e.g., two vowels, two even numbers) they were to respond in a different way (press a particular key combination). However in this condition ("expectation"), none of these stimuli actually appeared. In the third condition, participants were given the same instructions and stimuli as in the first, except that the expected prospective memory stimuli did occur (after a delay, and on 20% of trials), and participants had the chance to respond to them ("execution" condition). In the terminology of prospective memory researchers, the last two conditions were "prospective memory" conditions in that they involved a delayed intention (see Burgess, Quayle, and Frith 2001 for an outline of the further characteristics of prospective memory tasks).

Burgess et al. (2001) considered the rCBF changes between conditions that were common across the four tasks. Relative to the baseline condition, rCBF increases were seen in the frontal pole (BA 10) bilaterally, right DLPFC (BA 45/46) and right inferior parietal regions (BA 7, 19, 39, 40), precuneus, plus decreases in left fronto-temporal regions (BA 38, 47 and insula) when the participants were expecting to see a stimulus, even though it did not occur. Further increases were seen in the thalamus when the intention cues were seen and acted upon, with a corresponding decrease in right dorsolateral PFC. It was concluded that at least some of the rCBF changes in the expectation condition were most likely associated with intention maintenance, with those in the execution condition associated with recognizing and responding to prospective memory cues. This result corresponded well with that of Okuda et al. (1998), who were the first to demonstrate a role for BA 10 in prospective memory using functional imaging.

Thus, there seems to be both within- and cross-method support for a role of BA 10 in prospective memory functions. And the Burgess, Quayle, and Frith (2001) study suggests that this role is material- and stimulus nonspecific, and probably involved more with maintenance rather than execution of the delayed intention.

However one possible explanation for the Burgess, Quayle, and Frith (2001) findings is that the activations seen in the expectation condition could be due to task difficulty or increased stimulus processing demands rather than anything to do with delayed intentions per se. This hypothesis was examined in a second PET experiment (Burgess, Scott, and Frith 2003). Three different tasks were administered under four conditions: baseline simple reaction time (RT), attention-demanding ongoing task only, ongoing task plus a delayed intention (unpracticed), ongoing task plus delayed intention (practiced). Under prospective memory conditions, Burgess et al. (2003)

found significant rCBF decreases in the superior medial aspects of the rostral PFC (BA 10) relative to the baseline or ongoing task only conditions. However, more lateral aspects of Area 10 (plus the mediodorsal thalamus) showed the opposite pattern, with rCBF increases in the prospective memory conditions relative to the other conditions. These patterns were broadly replicated over all three tasks. Since (a) both the medial and lateral rostral regions showed instances where rCBF was lower during a more effortful condition (as estimated by increased RTs and error rates) than in a less effortful one, and (b) there was no correlation between rCBF and RT durations or number of errors in these regions, a simple task difficulty explanation of the rCBF changes in the rostral aspects of the frontal lobes during prospective memory tasks was rejected. Instead, the favored explanation concentrated upon the particular processing demands made by these situations irrespective of the precise stimuli used or the exact nature of the intention, in particular the requirement to hold a thought in mind (i.e., stimulus-independent thought) while carrying out other operations on presented stimuli.

Significantly for the current account, there was good correspondence between the findings of this second PET study and the findings of the human group lesion study of Burgess et al. (2000). The left rostral region which showed significant decreases when a delayed intention was added to an ongoing task is (a subsection of) the same left rostral region which, when damaged, caused prospective memory impairments on the Greenwich Test of multitasking. This correspondence is shown in figure 17.1.

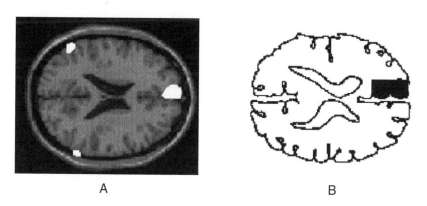

A   B

Figure 17.1
Comparison between the positron-emission tomography findings of Burgess, Scott, and Frith (2003) and the group lesion study of Burgess et al. (2000). Panel A shows the rostral prefrontal cortex (PFC) region which showed significant regional cerebral blood flow decrease in prospective memory conditions, and panel B shows the rostral PFC region which, when damaged, caused multitasking impairments on the Greenwich Test.

17.3.5 Functional Imaging Studies That Start from This Base Suggest That the Role of Rostral PFC Is in the Attentional Control between Stimulus-independent and Stimulus-oriented Thought: Introducing the "Gateway" Hypothesis of Rostral PFC

It is axiomatic of situations requiring prospective memory that there is a requirement to maintain a thought (or "internal representation") in the absence of external reminders (e.g., cues). Additionally, one is engaging in the ongoing task, which requires processing of externally presented stimuli. These are, of course, other requirements of multitasking, where one is "bearing in mind" that a task has to be performed (or returned to) while performing another task and may be using other internally maintained criteria (such a differing priorities) to determine behavior. And it would appear that rostral PFC is implicated in supporting processes critical to this behavior (see also Koechlin et al. 1999 for further evidence). But what exactly might this role be?

It is unlikely that rostral PFC is critical for all forms of stimulus-directed thought: Shallice and Burgess's (1991) three patients, all of whom had rostral PFC damage, performed ongoing tasks (e.g., arithmetic) as well as controls, and Bird et al.'s (2004) case similarly performed many tasks at a normal or near-normal level. So perhaps an explanation of their problems can be given by the opposing explanation from the functional imaging literature: that rostral PFC is involved in *stimulus-independent* thought, such as occurs in daydreaming, self-reflection, and other situations involving self-generated and maintained thought (e.g., McGuire et al. 1996; Christoff et al. 2001, 2003; Johnson et al. 2002; Zysset et al. 2002).

However, this explanation also fails as a good explanation of the pattern of cognitive deficits in lesion patients. Although a task such as mental arithmetic performed on a sum presented on a display undoubtedly involves processing externally presented material, it is equally true that the calculation itself must involve at least some "stimulus-independent thought" (i.e., the actual calculation itself) once past the early stages of visual processing and so forth. This would be even more the case with tasks with a large component of "internally generated thought" (cf. Christoff et al. 2001) such as theory of mind tasks. Thus, if the root of the rostral patients' problems were an incapacity for any form of stimulus-independent thought, they should again show cognitive impairment in a wide range of situations, and tasks involving judgment, theory of mind, and so forth, which have a large component of reflective thought, should be impaired. But they do not. Thus, a simple account in which rostral PFC is critical for all stimulus-independent thought can be rejected.

17.4 The Gateway Hypothesis

As we have seen, the idea which is at the center of most accounts of rostral PFC function is the notion of the contrast between stimulus-directed and stimulus-independent thought (e.g., Christoff and Gabrieli 2000; McGuire et al. 1996; Christoff et al. 2001, 2003; Koechlin et al. 1999; Frith and Frith 2003; Gusnard et al. 2001; Johnson et al. 2002; Zysset et al. 2002). As we have seen, absolute versions of this position (i.e., of the kind: rostral PFC supports all stimulus-independent thought) are unsupportable. However, one possible position that maintains this useful framework is to suggest that rostral PFC plays a role in the goal-directed *coordination* of both modes of thought without being directly responsible for the information transformations involved in either. A simple analogy might be a railway track switch-point, where we imagine the train as representing packets of information within the brain, and the tracks as the pathways that carry that information. The switch point will have no influence upon the train itself (i.e., does not effect an information transformation, aslo known as thought) but merely determines the direction of the flow. In this analogy, one "track" governed by the switch point may lead back to the specialist regions from which the information came, and another governs the flow of information to and from basic input/output systems (e.g., visual processing, motor effector systems, speech and language systems, etc.) via these central representations (see fig. 17.2 for a simple analogical representation of how such a system might operate). In a model of this type, there would be competition for activation of central representations between the two pathways (i.e., either input to central representations from more basic systems or reciprocal activation from currently active central representations), and much of cognition could occur naturally through this competition without influence from the processes supported by rostral PFC. It would only be either when one pathway has to be consistently biased or when there has to be rapid switching between the bias of the two that influence from the "switch point" would be needed. This biasing would typically occur in situations that were novel or where a specific demand for it has been determined (e.g., "I must pay special attention to . . ."; "I must think about . . .")—in other words, those situations which have been identified as requiring the operation of a "supervisory attentional system" (see Shallice and Burgess 1996 for details).

This account has some pleasing similarities with Raichle et al.'s default mode hypothesis. However, on the present account it is *not* the case that medial rostral PFC must be *deactivated* in order that goal-directed behavior may take place, as proposed by the default mode hypothesis. For instance, if one is asked to solve a series of arithmetic problems, we assume that the cognitive system effects its own bias between taking in information from the senses (e.g., basic visual and number processing systems) and internally generated thought (e.g., the products of step 1 of the sum being then operated on at step 2). Biasing from rostral PFC processes would only be required if an extra, novel requirement were added (e.g., "When you have done 20 sums, press key X") which requires maintaining the internal representation of the intention during the ongoing arithmetic task. Similarly, the state of conscious "rest,"

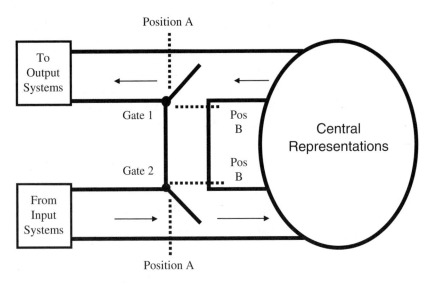

Figure 17.2
Stylized representation of the "Gateway Hypothesis, Version 1" of rostral prefrontal function. Rostral regions are hypothesized to bias the flow of information between basic systems and central representations. Gates are currently shown in a neutral position (bias freely determined by context). If both gates are at position A, stimulus-independent thought is favored. If both gates are at position B, full engagement with (external) stimuli is effected. Other combinations have further experiential correlates.

as investigated in functional neuroimaging studies, may involve continual selection between the various internal and external events that could serve as objects for further cognitive processing, in the absence of any specified task (Zuckerman, Albright, Marks, and Miller 1962). Or perhaps medial rostral PFC supports processes which are more active in conditions that require attending to the environment in the absence of stimuli (e.g., a general state of "preparedness"). Either account could explain the relatively high level of medial rostral PFC activity during the resting state.

In developing this account, we were mindful of the requirement in a first hypothesis to make the minimum of assumptions. The advantage of the current account is that it does not require the assumption that rostral PFC facilitates particular processing transformations, merely that it makes these possible by the simple action of directing the flow of the information between regions where transformations occur. Thus, it should be possible to observe rostral PFC activation associated with this function in a wide variety of tasks, involving many different types of information-processing transformations. This makes the hypothesis more readily testable.

17.5 Direct Empirical Support for the Gateway Hypothesis

In our laboratory, we recently conducted a series of experiments which lend support to this overall framework. These studies consistently find that areas of rostral PFC are involved in coordinating attention between externally presented and internally represented information. Thus Gilbert, Frith, and Burgess (2005) asked subjects either to perform three separate tasks that were provoked by stimuli presented to them visually or to do the same tasks "in their heads," while undergoing fMRI. In one task, subjects either tapped a response button in time with a visually presented clock or ignored the visual display (which now presented distracting information) and continued to tap at the same rate as before. The second task required subjects either to navigate around the edge of a visually presented shape or to imagine the same shape and continue navigating as before. In the third task, subjects performed a classification task on letters of the alphabet that followed a regular sequence. They either classified visually presented letters or mentally continued the sequence and classified the letters that they generated internally. Thus all three tasks alternated between phases where subjects attended to externally presented information and phases where they ignored this information and attended to internally represented information instead. We investigated both the sustained neural activity that differed between two phases, and transient activity at the point of a switch between these two phases. Consistently, across all three tasks, medial rostral PFC exhibited sustained activity that differed between the two phases, in all three cases showing greater activity when subjects attended to externally presented information. By contrast, right lateral rostral PFC exhibited transient activity when subjects switched between these phases, regardless of the direction of the switch. This dissociation between medial and lateral rostral PFC regions was confirmed statistically in all three tasks. Thus, the results of the study strongly support the hypothesis that rostral PFC supports selection between externally and internally oriented cognitive processes, and they suggest dissociable roles of medial and lateral rostral PFC in this selection process.

In a follow-up study (Gilbert, Simons, Frith, and Burgess, in press), we replicated the finding of greater medial rostral PFC activity during attention to externally presented versus internally represented information. In addition, we found that activity in this region was correlated on a trial-by-trial basis with faster RTs (i.e., there was a negative correlation) in a simple RT (SRT) baseline task. This finding is important for two reasons. First, it rules out an explanation of the activity we observe in medial rostral PFC in terms of "daydreaming" during simple tasks. If this were the case, greater medial rostral PFC activity (and hence the occurrence of daydreaming) would reflect disengagement from the baseline task and should show a positive correlation with RT. Second, this finding helps to constrain theorizing on the functional role of this brain region. By demonstrating that rostral medial PFC activity correlates with better performance in an SRT baseline task, we can point to a task requiring focused attention (in this case, focused attention toward intermittent visual targets) to which medial rostral PFC makes a functional contribution. Thus, contrary to the default mode hypothesis, it does not seem that any task requiring focused attention will lead to "deactivation" of this area. Rather, we propose that this region plays a specific role in particular types of focused attention tasks (i.e., deliberate biasing of attention toward externally presented or internally represented information), which it may also play during the state of conscious rest.

Evidence from our laboratory additionally suggests that rostral PFC is not only involved in selecting at the present moment between externally and internally oriented cognitive processing but is also involved in differentiating between memories of previous events that had an external or internal origin. Simons, Owen, Fletcher, and Burgess (in press) investigated an area of human cognition which previous studies have often (although inconsistently) associated with BA 10: the recollection of past events along with associated contextual information. Previously, it has not been clear how to account for the anomaly that some functional imaging experiments of contextual recollection observed activation in BA 10 (e.g., Rugg et al. 1999; Dobbins et al. 2002) whereas others did not (e.g., Nyberg et al. 1996; Henson et al. 1999). One possible explanation is that the studies which did find BA 10 activation involved recollecting which of two tasks was undertaken with target items ("task context"), whereas the other studies focused on externally derived features of context (e.g., recollecting the position on a monitor screen in which target items were presented: "position context"). Simons et al. investigated the possibility that BA 10 might be differentially involved in recollecting internally generated versus externally derived contextual information by contrasting directly the recollection of task context and position context within participants. They observed a functional dissociation within rostral prefrontal cortex, with lateral regions associated with recollection of both task- and position-based contextual details and a more medial region showing significantly greater activation during recollection of task context than position context. This lateral versus medial dissociation was apparent regardless of whether words or famous faces were being remembered, suggesting that the region is involved in central, stimulus-independent executive control processes and was unrelated to task difficulty as estimated by accuracy and RT. Thus, the results further support the view that the processes supported by rostral PFC involve mediating attentional engagement between internally generated and externally derived information, which is important for successful contextual recollection.

17.6   The Gateway Hypothesis and the Medial versus Lateral Rostral PFC Distinction

The results of these studies strongly support a role of rostral PFC in coordinating internally and externally oriented information. There is also strong evidence for functional dissociations between medial versus lateral rostral PFC across a number of tasks (see also Koechlin et al. 2000; Burgess et al. 2003). However, the precise operating dynamics of this system have yet to be determined. The difficulty of this task has been highlighted by two recent studies carried out by Jiro Okuda in this lab and at Tamagawa University in Tokyo, both of which concerned the distinction between time- and event-based prospective memory. In the first PET study, he contrasted a task involving voluntary uncued time-based delayed intentions (clasping your hands twice during a 30-second period while performing an ongoing task) with ones cued by an event (clasping hands to a specific cue while performing the same ongoing task). Okuda et al. (2002) found that contrasts involving the time-based intention (i.e., (time + event > ongoing task only; or time > ongoing only) were associated with increased activation in *lateral* left rostral PFC regions. However, in a second PET study, Okuda, Frith, and Burgess (2004) contrasted maintaining a time-based intention ("respond after time X," when a clock was visible while performing an ongoing task) with maintaining an event-based intention ("respond if you see cue X") while also performing an ongoing task. In this study, relative to the event-based condition, the time-based condition was associated with increases in *medial* Area 10. One possibility under the terms of the current framework is that the medial rostral activation reflects the difference in the *source* of the time information between the two experiments, with the first experiment relying upon self-generated estimates of time but the second using externally derived information (a clock). Thus, these intriguing findings clearly suggest future experimentation. It may well be that evidence from other methodologies may be yet again required to constrain the hypotheses that the fascinating functional imaging data provokes.

17.7   Summary

We have presented evidence concerning the functions of rostral PFC (principally frontopolar Area 10) which suggests that this area is critical for carrying out intended actions after a delay, which is one important form of volitional behavior. In neurological patients with rostral PFC damage, this deficit is particularly noticeable in situations requiring multitasking. These functions are common in everyday life (e.g., shopping, preparing a meal, etc.) so rostral PFC lesions can cause impairments which are very disabling, despite normal intellect, retrospective memory, and other cognitive abilities.

There also appears to be a potential dissociation in these impairments. People may quite independently show problems in carrying out delayed novel actions associated with particular events (e.g., "when X happens, do Y"), or problems with remembering after a delay all of the things they intended to do within a set time or "retrieval context." The involvement of rostral PFC (principally BA 10) in these kinds of "prospective memory" functions has also been confirmed by functional brain imaging. The results from this method suggest a dissociation between medial and lateral aspects of Area 10.

This chapter also presents a new information-processing hypothesis of rostral PFC function and some empirical supporting evidence. The framework makes a distinction between stimulus-oriented (i.e., provoked by, or directed toward) and stimulus-independent thought and suggests that rostral PFC acts as a "gateway" which biases the priority of information from each stream. The strength of this hypothesis is that it is a starting position (in other words, a description of a set of starting assumptions) which (a) makes the minimum number of assumptions (since the proposal is that rostral PFC is involved in cognitive processes that apply across a wide variety of task domains), (b) makes predictions that are more readily testable empirically than alternative theories, and (c) introduces a potentially unifying explanation of the previous findings involving both medial and lateral rostral PFC that is independent of "task difficulty."

If this account is correct, it makes interesting predictions about the potential involvement of this brain region in psychological or psychiatric disorders. Thus, one might suppose that some forms of dysfunction of a mechanism of this kind might lead to an inability to distinguish between one's thoughts and one's experiences, which could be a plausible account of hallucinatory phenomena in schizophrenia. Similarly, for instance, an account using this framework could be constructed for symptoms linked to unwanted (intrusive) thoughts. This speculation remains to be tested, however, and would have to compete with the excellent contrasting views described by, among others, Nitschke and Mackiewicz; Liddle; Frith; Jeannerod; Proust; and Spence and Parry in chapters in this volume.

Acknowledgments

Preparation of this chapter, and most of the work reported in it, was supported by Wellcome Trust Grant 061171 to Paul W. Burgess.

References

Baker, S. C., R. D. Rogers, A. M. Owen, C. D. Frith, R. J. Dolan, R. S. J. Frackowiak, and T. W. Robbins. 1996. Neural systems engaged by planning: A PET study of the Tower of London task. *Neuropsychologia, 34,* 515–526.

Berman, K. F., J. L. Ostrem, C. Randolph, J. Gold, T. E. Goldberg, R. Coppola, R. E. Carson, P. Herscovitch, and D. R. Weinberger. 1995. Physiological activation of a cortical network during performance of the Wisconsin Card Sorting Test: A positron emission tomography study. *Neuropsychologia, 33,* 1027–1046.

Bird, C. M., F. Castelli, O. Malik, U. Frith, and M. Husain. 2004. The impact of extensive medial frontal lobe damage on "Theory of Mind" and cognition. *Brain, 127,* 914–928.

Blaxton, T. A., T. A. Zeffiro, J. D. E. Gabrieli, S. Y. Bookheimer, M. C. Carrillo, W. H. Theodore, and J. F. Disterhoft. 1996. Functional mapping of human learning: A positron emission tomography activation study of eyeblink conditioning. *Journal of Neuroscience, 16,* 4032–4040.

Bottini, G., R. Corcoran, R. Sterzi, E. Paulesu, P. Schenone, P. Scarpa, R. S. J. Frackwoiak, and C. D. Frith. 1994. The role of the right hemisphere in the interpretation of figurative aspects of language. *Brain, 117,* 1241–1253.

Burgess, N., E. A. Maguire, H. J. Spirs, and J. O'Keefe. 2001. A temporoparietal and prefrontal network for retrieving the spatial context of lifelike events. *Neuroimage, 14,* 439–453.

Burgess, P. W. 2000. Strategy application disorder: The role of the frontal lobes in human multitasking. *Psychological Research, 63,* 279–288.

Burgess, P. W., N. Alderman, J. J. Evans, B. A. Wilson, H. Emslie, and T. Shallice. 1996. *The Modified Six Element Test.* Bury St. Edmunds, U.K.: Thames Valley Test.

Burgess, P. W., A. Quayle, and C. D. Frith. 2001. Brain regions involved in prospective memory as determined by positron emission tomography. *Neuropsychologia, 39,* 545–555.

Burgess, P. W., S. K. Scott, and C. D. Frith. 2003. The role of the rostral frontal cortex (Area 10) in prospective memory: A lateral versus medial dissociation. *Neuropsychologia, 41,* 906–918.

Burgess, P. W., and T. Shallice. 1996. Response suppression, initiation, and strategy use following frontal lobe lesions. *Neuropsychologia, 34,* 263–273.

Burgess, P. W., and T. Shallice. 1997. *The Hayling and Brixton Tests.* Bury St. Edmunds, U.K.: Thames Valley Test.

Burgess, P. W., J. S. Simons, I. Dumontheil, and S. J. Gilbert. In press. The gateway hypothesis of rostral PFC function. In *Speed, Control and Ageing: In Honour of Patrick Rabbitt,* ed. J. Duncan, L. Phillips, and P. McLeod. Oxford: Oxford University Press.

Burgess, P. W., E. Veitch, A. Costello, and T. Shallice. 2000. The cognitive and neuroanatomical correlates of multitasking. *Neuropsychologia, 38,* 848–863.

Burgess, P. W., E. Veitch, and J. Costello. Submitted. The role of the right rostral prefrontal cortex in multitasking: The Six Elements Test.

Christoff, K., and J. D. E. Gabrieli. 2000. The frontopolar cortex and human cognition: Evidence for a rostrocaudal hierarchical organization within the human prefrontal cortex. *Psychobiology, 28,* 168–186.

Christoff, K., V. Prabhakaran, J. Dorfman, Z. Zhao, J. K. Kroger, K. J. Holyoak, and J. D. E. Gabrieli. 2001. Rostrolateral prefrontal cortex involvement in relational integration during reasoning. *Neuroimage, 14,* 1136–1149.

Christoff, K., J. M. Ream, L. P. T. Geddes, and J. D. E. Gabrieli. 2003. Evaluating self-generated information: Anterior prefrontal contributions to human cognition. *Behavioral Neuroscience, 117,* 1161–1168.

Dobbins, I. G., H. Foley, D. L. Schacter, and A. D. Wagner. 2002. Executive control during episodic retrieval: Multiple prefrontal processes subserve source memory. *Neuron, 35,* 989–996.

Dreher, J.-C., E. Koechlin, S. O. Ali, and J. Grafman. 2002. The roles of timing and task order during task switching. *Neuroimage, 17,* 95–109.

Frith, U., and C. D. Frith. 2003. Development and neurophysiology of mentalizing. *Philosophical Transactions of the Royal Society of London B, 358(1431),* 459–473.

Fuster, J. M. 1997. *The Prefrontal Cortex: Anatomy, Physiology, and Neuropsychology of the Frontal Lobe.* Philadelphia: Lippincott-Raven.

Gilbert, S. J., C. D. Frith, and P. W. Burgess. 2005. Involvement of rostral prefrontal cortex in selection between stimulus-oriented and stimulus-independent thought. *European Journal of Neuroscience, 21,* 1423–1431.

Gilbert, S. J., J. S. Simons, C. D. Frith, and P. W. Burgess. In press. Performance-related activity in medial rostral PFC (Area 10) during low demand tasks. *Journal of Experimental Psychology: Human Perception and Performance.*

Goel, V., B. Gold, S. Kapur, and S. Houle. 1997. The seats of reason? An imaging study of deductive and inductive reasoning. *Neuroreport, 8,* 1305–1310.

Gold, J. M., K. F. Berman, C. Randolph, T. E. Goldberg, and D. R. Weinberger. 1996. PET validation of a novel prefrontal task: Delayed response alternation. *Neuropsychology, 10,* 3–10.

Grady, C. L. 1999. Neuroimaging and activation of the frontal lobes. In *The Human Frontal Lobes: Function and Disorders,* ed. B. L. Miller and J. L. Cummings, pp. 196–230. New York: Guilford Press.

Gusnard, D. A., E. Akbudak, G. L. Shulman, and M. E. Raichle. 2001. Medial prefrontal cortex and self-referential mental activity: Relation to a default mode of brain function. *Proceedings of the National Academy of Sciences, 98,* 4259–4264.

Haxby, J. V., L. G. Ungerleider, B. Horwitz, J. M. Maisog, S. I. Rapoport, and C. L. Grady. 1996. Storage and retrieval of new memories for faces in the intact human brain. *Proceedings of the National Academy of Sciences, 93,* 922–927.

Haxby, J. V., I. G. Ungerleider, B. Horwitz, S. I. Rapoport, and C. L. Grady. 1995. Hemispheric differences in neural systems for face working memory: A PET–rCBF study. *Human Brain Mapping, 3,* 68–82.

Henson, R. N. A., T. Shallice, and R. J. Dolan. 1999. Right prefrontal cortex and episodic memory retrieval: A functional MRI test of the monitoring hypothesis. *Brain, 122,* 1367–1381.

Hugdahl, K., A. Beradi, W. I. Thomson, S. M. Kosslyn, R. Macy, D. P. Baker, N. M. Alpert, and J. E. LeDoux. 1995. Brain mechanisms in human classical conditioning: A PET blood flow study. *Neuroreport, 6,* 1723–1728.

Jenkins, I. H., D. J. Brooks, P. D. Nixon, R. S. J. Frackowiak, and R. E. Passingham. 1994. Motor sequence learning: A study with positron emission tomography. *Journal of Neuroscience*, *14*, 3775–3790.

Jennings, J. M., A. R. McIntosh, S. Kapur, E. Tulving, and S. Houle. 1997. Cognitive subtractions may not add up: The interaction between semantic processing and response mode. *Neuroimage*, *5*, 229–239.

Johnson, S. C., L. C. Baxter, L. S. Wilder, J. G. Pipe, J. E. Heiserman, and G. P. Prigatano. 2002. Neural correlates of self-reflection. *Brain*, *125*, 1808–1814.

Klein, D., B. Milner, R. J. Zatorre, E. Meyer, and A. C. Evans. 1995. The neural substrates underlying word generation: A bilingual functional-imaging study. *Proceedings of the National Academy of Sciences*, *92*, 2899–2903.

Koechlin, E., G. Basso, P. Pietrini, S. Panzer, and J. Grafman. 1999. The role of the anterior prefrontal cortex in human cognition. *Nature*, *399*(6732), 148–151.

Koechlin, E., G. Corrado, P. Pietrini, and J. Grafman. 2000. Dissociating the role of the medial and lateral anterior prefrontal cortex in human planning. *Proceedings of the National Academy of Sciences*, *97*, 7651–7656.

Koechlin, E., C. Ody, and R. Kouneiher. 2003. The architecture of cognitive control in the human prefrontal cortex. *Science*, *302*, 1181–1185.

Kosslyn, S. M., N. M. Alpert, and W. L. Thompson. 1995. Identifying objects at different levels of hierarchy: A positron emission tomography study. *Human Brain Mapping*, *3*, 107–132.

Kosslyn, S. M., N. M. Alpert, W. L. Thompson, C. F. Chabris, S. L. Rauch, and A. K. Anderson. 1994. Identifying objects seen from different viewpoints: A PET investigation. *Brain*, *117*, 1055–1071.

Martin, A., J. V. Haxby, F. M. Lalonde, C. L. Wigges, and L. G. Ungerleider. 1995. Discrete cortical regions associated with knowledge of color and knowledge of action. *Science*, *270*, 102–105.

McGuire, P. K., E. Paulesu, R. S. J. Frackowiak, and C. D. Frith. 1996. Brain activity during stimulus independent thought. *NeuroReport*, *7*, 2095–2099.

Metzler, C., and A. J. Parkin. 2000. Reversed negative priming following frontal lobe lesions. *Neuropsychologia*, *38*, 363–379.

Nyberg, L., A. R. McIntosh, R. Cabeza, R. Habib, S. Houle, and E. Tulving. 1996. General and specific brain regions involved in encoding and retrieval of events: What, where, and when. *Proceedings of the National Academy of Sciences*, *93*, 11280–11285.

Okuda, J., C. D. Frith, and P. W. Burgess. 2004. Organisation of time- and event-based intentions in rostral prefrontal cortex. Abstract for the 10th Annual Meeting of the Organization for Human Brain Mapping, June 2004, Budapest, Hungary. Available on CD-ROM in *NeuroImage*, *22*.

Okuda, J., T. Fujii, H. Ohtake, T. Tsukiura, A. Umetsu, M. Suzuki, and A. Yamadori. 2002. Brain mechanisms underlying human prospective memory. In *Frontiers of Human Memory*, ed. A. Yamadori, R. Kawashima, T. Fujii, and K. Suzuki, pp. 79–96. Sendai: Tohoku University Press.

Okuda, J., T. Fujii, A. Yamadori, R. Kawashima, T. Tsukkiura, R. Fukatsu, K. Suzuki, M. Ito, and H. Fukuda. 1998. Participation of the prefrontal cortices in prospective memory: Evidence from a PET study in humans. *Neuroscience Letters*, *253*, 127–130.

Petrides, M., B. Alivisatos, E. Meyer, and A. C. Evans. 1993. Functional activation of the human frontal cortex during the performance of verbal memory tasks. *Proceedings of the National Academy of Sciences*, *90*, 878–882.

Prabhakaran, V., J. A. Smith, J. E. Desmond, G. H. Glover, and J. D. Gabrieli. 1997. Neural substrates of fluid reasoning: An fMRI study of neocortical activation during performance of the Raven's Progressive Matrices test. *Cognitive Psychology*, *33*, 43–63.

Raichle, M. E., A.-M. MacLeod, A. Z. Snyder, W. J. Powers, D. A. Gusnard, and G. L. Shulman. 2001. A default mode of brain function. *Proceedings of the National Academy of Sciences*, *98*, 676–682.

Roland, P. E., and B. Gulyas. 1995. Visual memory, visual imagery, and visual recognition of large field patterns by the human brain: Functional anatomy by positron emission tomography. *Cerebral Cortex*, *5*, 79–93.

Rugg, M. D., P. C. Fletcher, P. M. L. Chua, and R. J. Dolan. 1999. The role of the prefrontal cortex in recognition memory and memory for source: An fMRI study. *NeuroImage*, *10*, 520–529.

Rugg, M. D., P. C. Fletcher, C. D. Frith, R. S. J. Frackowiak, and R. J. Dolan. 1996. Differential activation of the prefrontal cortex in successful and unsuccessful memory retrieval. *Brain*, *119*, 2073–2084.

Semendeferi, K., E. Armstrong, A. Schleicher, K. Zilles, and G. W. Van Hoesen. 2001. Prefrontal cortex in humans and apes: A comparative study of Area 10. *American Journal of Physical Anthropology*, *114*, 224–241.

Shallice, T., and P. W. Burgess. 1991. Deficits in strategy application following frontal lobe damage in man. *Brain*, *114*, 727–741.

Shallice, T., and P. W. Burgess. 1996. The domain of supervisory processes and temporal organisation of behaviour. *Philosophical Transactions of the Royal Society of London B*, *351*, 1405–1412.

Simons, J. S., and H. J. Spiers. 2003. Prefrontal and medial temporal lobe interactions in long-term memory. *Nature Reviews Neuroscience*, *4*, 637–648.

Simons, J. S., A. M. Owen, P. C. Fletcher, and P. W. Burgess. In press. Anterior prefrontal cortex and the recollection of contextual information. *Neuropsychologia*.

Tulving, E., H. J. Markowitsch, F. I. M. Criak, R. Habib, and S. Houle. 1996. Novelty and familiarity activations in PET studies of memory encoding and retrieval. *Cerebral Cortex*, *6*, 71–79.

Zatorre, R. J., A. R. Halpern, D. W. Perry, E. Meyer, and A. C. Evans. 1996. Hearing in the mind's ear: A PET investigation of musical imagery and perception. *Journal of Cognitive Neuroscience, 8,* 29–46.

Zuckerman, M., R. J. Albright, C. S. Marks, and G. L. Miller. 1962. Stress and hallucinatory effects of perceptual isolation and confinement. *Psychological Monographs: General and Applied, 76,* 1–15.

Zysset, S., O. Huber, E. Ferstl, and D. Y. Von Cramon. 2002. The anterior frontomedian cortex and evaluative judgement: An fMRI study. *Neuroimage, 15,* 983–991.

V Disorders of Volition in Substance Abuse

18 Broken Willpower: Impaired Mechanisms of Decision Making and Impulse Control in Substance Abusers

Antoine Bechara

Reflexes and simple behaviors are the product of a deterministic relationship between a sensory input and a motor response output. However, complex behaviors, in which the relationship between sensory input and motor output is unpredictable, are the product of a process that Descartes called "the soul" and contemporary scientists may call "volition." The question is whether we can find a rich cognitive theory that rigorously describes the neural processes that connect sensation to thought to action and, thus, eliminate the need for Cartesian dualism. The present chapter discusses one such attempt. Prinz, Dennett, and Sebanz note that volition involves several varieties and suggest that when devising studies or ways to understand volition, it is helpful to make some useful distinctions among the different varieties (Prinz, Dennett, and Sebanz, this volume). Therefore, my discussion will address the neural mechanisms of "willpower," which I think is one specific form of volition. I will then assimilate my view with the views of other contributors to this volume.

Imagine yourself at a party during your first year in college, and you see your friends drinking, using drugs, and engaged in sexual activities. In the back of your mind, you hear the voice of your parents, warning you and asking you not to engage in such activities. What would you do? This is a hard decision, but you are the one who will ultimately decide, with a clear sense of deciding and exercising free will. Can a theory of the brain describe a process like this in neural terms? "Willpower," as defined by the Encarta World English Dictionary, is a combination of determination and self-discipline that enables somebody to do something despite the difficulties involved. This is the mechanism that enables one to endure sacrifices now in order to obtain benefits later. Otherwise, how would one accept the pain of surgery or the long, hard work in college? Why would someone resist temptations and delay gratifications? I will argue that these complex and apparently indeterminist behaviors are the product of a complex cognitive process subserved by two separate, but interacting, neural systems: (1) an *impulsive* neural system for signaling the pain or pleasure of the *immediate* prospects of an option and (2) a *reflective* neural system for signaling the pain or pleasure of the *future* prospects of an option. The final decision is determined by the relative strengths of the pain or pleasure signals associated with the immediate versus future outcomes. When the immediate prospect is unpleasant, but the future is more pleasant, then the positive signal from future prospects will override that from immediate prospects. This positive signal about the future forms the basis for enduring the pain of the present. This also occurs when both the immediate and future prospects are pleasant, but the future is even more pleasant. The stronger positive signal about the future forms the basis for delaying the gratification and resisting the more immediate temptation. If the signals triggered by thoughts about the future were relatively weak, then immediate prospects predominate, and decisions become biased toward short-term horizons. As suggested by Damasio (1994), "willpower is just another name for the idea of choosing according to long-term outcomes rather than short-term ones."

18.1 The Somatic Marker Framework: An Overview

The somatic marker framework provides a systems-level neuroanatomical and cognitive framework for decision making and for choosing according to long-term outcomes rather than short-term ones, and it suggests that the process of decision making depends in many important ways on neural substrates that regulate homeostasis, emotion, and feeling (Damasio 1994).

According to Damasio, there is an important distinction between *emotions* and *feelings* (Damasio 1994, 1999, 2003). The specific object or event that predictably causes an emotion is designated as an "emotionally competent stimulus." The responses toward the body proper enacted in a body state involve physiological modifications. These modifications range from changes in internal milieu and viscera that may not be perceptible to an external observer (e.g., endocrine release, heart rate) to changes in the musculoskeletal system that may be obvious to an external observer (e.g., posture, facial expression). The ensemble of all these enacted responses in the body proper and in the brain constitutes an *emotion*.

The responses aimed at the brain lead to (1) the central nervous system release of certain neurotransmitters (e.g., dopamine, serotonin, acetylcholine, noreadrenaline), (2) an active modification of the state of somatosensory maps such as those of the insular cortex, and (3) a modification of the transmission of signals from the body to somatosensory regions. The ensemble of signals as mapped in somatosensory regions of the brain itself provide the essential ingredients for what is ultimately perceived as a *feeling*, a phenomenon perceptible to the individual in whom they are enacted.

Thus *emotions* are what an outside observer can see, or at least can measure. *Feelings* are what the individual senses or subjectively experiences. Because the term "emotion" tends to mean different things to different people, we have used the term "somatic" to refer to the collection of body-related responses that hallmark an emotion. "Somatic" refers to the Greek word "soma," that is, body.

18.1.1 Induction of Somatic States

Somatic states can be induced from (1) primary inducers and (2) secondary inducers (Damasio 1995). *Primary inducers* are innate or learned stimuli that cause pleasurable or aversive states. Once present in the immediate environment, they automatically and obligatorily elicit a somatic response. Examples of primary inducers include the encounter of a fear object (e.g., a snake) or a stimulus predictive of a fear object. Primary inducers are also concepts that through learning have acquired automatic and obligatory properties to trigger somatic states, such as hearing that you have won a prize or that your life savings have been lost in a market crash (Bechara et al. 2003).

Secondary inducers, on the other hand, are entities generated by the recall of a personal or hypothetical emotional event, that is, "thoughts" and "memories" of the primary inducer, which when brought to working memory elicit a somatic state. An example is the somatic response elicited by the memory of encountering a snake or of losing a large sum of money. Imagining being attacked by a bear, winning an award, or losing a large sum of money is also an example of a secondary inducer (Bechara et al. 2003). It is important to note that the emotional (somatic) process associated with a secondary inducer is physiologically separate from the memory process. For instance, patients with frontal lobe lesions can remember the facts associated with an emotional event (e.g., the death of a loved one), but they fail to trigger the emotion associated with that memory. In other words, they possess the memory of the emotional event, but they lack the emotion of that memory (Bechara et al. 2003).

We see the amygdala as a critical substrate in the neural system necessary for triggering somatic states from primary inducers. By contrast, the ventromedial (VM) prefrontal cortex is a critical substrate in the neural system necessary for triggering somatic states from secondary inducers (Bechara et al. 2003).

18.1.2 Development of Somatic States

Evidence suggests that the normal development of secondary inducers is contingent upon the normal development of primary inducers, that is, if the processing of primary inducers were abnormal, then secondary inducer processing would be abnormal too. However, once secondary inducers have been acquired normally, the induction of somatic states by secondary inducers becomes less dependent on primary induction (Bechara et al. 2003). Besides the amygdala and VM prefrontal cortex, the physiological steps that lead to the normal development of somatic state representations include the somatosensory cortices. In brief, when the amygdala triggers somatic states from primary inducers, signals from these somatic states are relayed to the brain. This leads to the development of representations of these somatic states in brainstem nuclei (e.g., the parabrachial nucleus [PBN]), and in somatosensory cortices (e.g., insular/secondary somatosensory cortices [SII], primary somatosensory [SI] cortices, and cingulate cortices). After a somatic state has been triggered by a primary inducer and experienced at least once, a representation of this somatic state is formed. The subsequent presentation of a stimulus that evokes thoughts and memories about a specific primary inducer will then operate as a secondary inducer. Secondary inducers are presumed to reactivate the somatic state patterns belonging to a specific primary inducer and generate a fainter activation of the somatic state than if it were triggered by an actual primary inducer. For example, imagining the loss of a large sum of money (secondary inducer) reactivates the pattern of the somatic state belonging to an actual prior experience of money loss (primary inducer). However, the somatic state generated by imagining losing a large sun of money is usually fainter than one triggered by an actual experience of money loss.

Provided that somatic states associated with secondary inducers develop normally, generating somatic states from secondary inducers becomes dependent on cortical circuitry in which the VM cortex plays a critical role.

18.1.3 Somatic State Activation during Decision Making

During decision making, the activation of somatic states via the VM cortex may engage two chains of physiological events (fig. 18.1).

A. The "body loop" mechanism In one chain, the appropriate somatic state is actually reenacted in the body proper. This anatomical system is described as the "body loop" because it engages the body.

A large number of channels convey body information to the central nervous system (e.g., spinal cord, vagus nerve, humoral signals). Evidence suggests that the vagal route is especially critical (Martin et al. 2004). The enacted somatic state can then act at conscious or nonconscious level and influence activity in (1) regions involved in *body mapping*, that is, holding representations of somatic states that help generate *feelings*; (2) regions involved in the triggering of somatic states (e.g., amygdala and VM cortex), so that the threshold for triggering subsequent somatic states is increased or decreased; (3) regions involved in *working memory* (e.g., dorsolateral prefrontal cortex and other high-order association cortices), so that a particular representation is strengthened or weakened; the influence of somatic state signals on the contents displayed in working memory helps endorse or reject "objects" and "response options" (i.e., secondary inducers) brought to mind during the pondering of a decision, that is, they help *bias* the options and plans for action; and finally (4), somatic state signals influence activity in regions concerned with motor responses and behavioral actions (e.g., striatum and anterior cingulate/supplementary motor area; SMA). They interfere with response selection and thus render the occurrence of a given behavior more likely or less likely.

The conduit for the biasing action of somatic states on response selection is the release of neurotransmitters in the telencephalon (i.e., the cerebral cortex and the

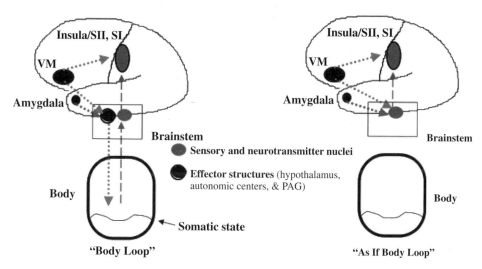

Figure 18.1

Simple illustrations of the "body loop" and "as-if body loop" chain of physiological events. VM, ventromedial. SI: primary somatosensory cortex. SII: secondary somatosensory cortex. PAG: periaqueductal gray matter.

diencephalon, which includes the basal ganglia and thalamus). The cell bodies of all major neurotransmitter systems—for example, dopamine (DA), serotonin (5–HT), noradrenaline (NA), and acetylcholine (Ach)—are located in the brainstem; the axon terminals of these neurotransmitter neurons synapse on cells and/or terminals all over the telencephalon. When somatic state signals are transmitted to the cell bodies of these neurotransmitter neurons, the signaling influences the neurotransmitter release at the terminals. In turn, these changes in neurotransmitter release will modulate synaptic activities of telencephalic neurons subserving behavior and cognition, thereby providing a mechanism for somatic states to exert a biasing effect on behaviors (e.g., selection of one response over another), feelings, and cognition.

B. The "as if body loop" mechanism   During the deliberation of decisions, the mental representation of a future event triggers a somatic state, no matter how faint, which may be consciously perceived as a good or bad feeling, or processed unconsciously (Damasio 1994; Overskeid 2000). When somatic states from primary or secondary inducers cannot be detected as changes in physiological parameters within the body proper, they can at least be detected as changes in the activity of different neurotransmitter systems. Indeed, the anatomy of these neurotransmitter systems is consistent with this notion, that is, there are multiple direct and indirect connections between the amygdala and the VM cortex, and the neurotransmitter nuclei within the brainstem (Nauta 1971; Blessing 1997). This chain of physiological events, which bypasses the body altogether, activates directly the insular/SII, SI cortices, and/or the brainstem nuclei holding covert representations of somatic states. In other words, instead of having somatic states expressed in the body, the activation of representations of somatic states in the brainstem and/or the cortex can induce changes in neurotransmitter release, without engaging the body. This anatomical system is described as the "as-if body loop" because the somatic state is not reenacted in the body. Although somatic signals are based on structures representing the body and its states, the somatic signals do not have to originate in the body in every instance. Somatic states can in fact be "simulated" intracerebrally in the "as-if body loop." The conditions that determine whether the body loop, or as-if-body loop, will be engaged are discussed elsewhere (Bechara and Damasio 2004).

18.2   A Neural Model for Willpower

The neural mechanisms involved in the development and activation of somatic states include several regions: (a) the VM cortex, (b) amygdala, (c) somatosensory cortices, (d) basal ganglia, anterior cingulate, brainstem nuclei, and the humeral and neural pathways that signal body states to the central nervous system. Based on the somatic marker framework, I propose that willpower is subserved by two separate, but interacting, neural systems (fig. 18.2).

18.2.1   An Impulsive System Triggers Somatic States from Primary Inducers
Exposure to primary inducers triggers somatic states via the amygdala system that are fast, automatic, and obligatory. Somatic states triggered by the amygdala are short-lived and habituate very quickly (Dolan et al. 1996; Buchel et al. 1998; LaBar et al. 1998). In other words, primary inducers trigger an emotion via the amygdala quickly, without much thought and effort. Thus, the amygdala constitutes a critical substrate in an impulsive neural system that biases decisions according to the immediate prospects of an option.

18.2.2   A Reflective System Triggers Somatic States from Secondary Inducers
Secondary inducers trigger somatic states via the VM cortex from perceived or recalled mental images. These somatic states may become conscious (i.e., perceived as a good or bad feeling) or remain nonconscious. While the amygdala is engaged in emotional situations requiring a rapid response, that is, "low-order" emotional reactions arising from relatively automatic processes (Berkowitz 1993; LeDoux 1996), the VM cortex is engaged in emotional situations driven by thoughts and reflection. Once this initial amygdala emotional response is over, "high-order" emotional reactions begin to arise from relatively more controlled, higher order processes involved in thinking, reason-

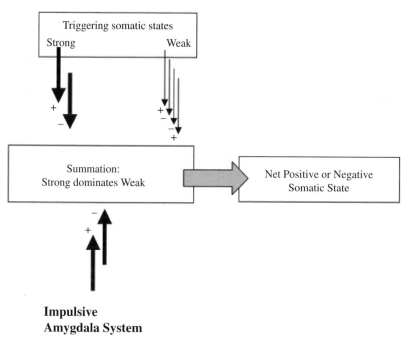

**Reflective
Orbitofrontal/Ventromedial
System**

**Impulsive
Amygdala System**

Figure 18.2
An illustration of the interaction of the reflective and impulsive systems in relation to their triggering of somatic states. The emergent net or overall somatic state plays a critical role in biasing decisions.

ing, and consciousness (Schneider and Shiffrin 1977). Unlike the amygdala response, which is sudden and habituates quickly, the VM response is deliberate, is slow, and lasts for a long time.

Thus, the prefrontal cortex, especially the VM part, helps predict the emotion of the future, thereby forecasting the consequences of one's own actions. However, the VM cortex is a relatively large region of the brain, and it has developed throughout evolution, so that not every part performs the same function. We have proposed a model suggesting that the mechanisms by which different "thoughts" or "mental representations" are coupled to somatic states via the VM region are based on hierarchical functional organization of the VM cortex in relation to *time* and *probability* (Bechara and Damasio 2004).

18.2.3   The Reflective System Controls the Impulsive System

Consistent with the proposal of how somatic states associated with secondary inducers develop, I suggest that, initially, the reflective system is poorly developed, and our
volition is perhaps dictated by our impulsive system—children tend to behave in a
manner in which they do what they feel like doing right now, without much thought
about the future. However, through learning and socialization, they learn to constrain
many desires and behaviors that conflict with social rules and lead to negative consequences. This is the first sign of the development of willpower and is an example
of how the reflective system gains control over the impulsive system. When the reflective system is damaged, then the impulsive system loses its restraint. Indeed, this is
what happens when areas of the VM cortex are damaged, as described in the case of
Phineas Gage, who became impatient of restraint or advice when it conflicted with
his desires (Damasio 1994).

However, it appears that there is more than one mechanism through which the
reflective system exerts control over the impulsive system. The functional evolution
of the prefrontal cortex appears to involve an incremental increase in its capacity to
access representations of events that occur in the more distant future. This enhanced
"futuristic" capacity coincides with the development of more rostral/anterior regions
of the VM cortex. Comparative studies of the frontal lobes in humans and nonhuman
primates have revealed that the major advancement in the size, complexity, and connectivity of the frontal lobes in humans relates primarily to BA 10, that is, the frontal
pole (Semendeferi et al. 2001) and not so much to the more posterior areas of the VM
cortex (Semendeferi et al. 2002). Perhaps this can explain the distinction between
two broad mechanisms of behavioral control: (1) Decision making, which reflects a
tendency to think about the consequences of a planned act before engaging in that
act. These consequences may occur in a more distant future, and perhaps there is a
low probability that they will occur. The critical neural region for this mechanism of
control is the more anterior region of the VM cortex, that is, the region involving the
frontal pole and BA 10 (Bechara 2004). (2) Impulse control reflects suppression or withholding of a prepotent act. The learning to quickly and automatically inhibit such a
prepotent act is due, in large part, to learning that the consequences will occur in the
near future and that there is a high probability that they will occur, that is, there is a
sort of immediate certainty. The critical neural region for this mechanism of control
is the more posterior region of the VM cortex, that is, those involving the anterior
cingulate (Bechara 2004).

Thus, decision making is one mechanism with a clear sense of deciding and exercising free will. It is generated by knowledge about facts and values, and it involves
conscious, slow, and effortful deliberation about consequences that may or may not
happen in a distant future. To give an example of a situation requiring decision
making, consider the situation of finding a briefcase with $100,000 in a dark alley.

The decision to take or not take the money may require some deliberation about the ethics, morality, and consequences of such an action. Impulse control, on the other hand, although it is willful, volitional, and conscious in nature, does not require as much deliberation and conscious effort to inhibit the response. Through learning, the control mechanism becomes much quicker and more automatic, not requiring much deliberation about consequences. An example of this quick and automatic mechanism of impulse control is finding a similar amount of $100,000 spread out on a table inside a bank. Normally, any thought, intention, or impulse to grab the money is inhibited automatically and effortlessly.

This distinction between the two mechanisms of control is supported by observations of patients with prefrontal lesions. Patients with bilateral VM lesions, especially those with lesions that spare the posterior VM region and involve only the more rostral/anterior areas, demonstrate deficits in somatic state activation and decision making that are selective for domains involving the remote future, that is, they have "myopia" for consequences that will occur in the far, as opposed to the more immediate, future (Damasio 1994). However, when the damage extends to more posterior areas of the VM region, that is, including the anterior cingulate, or to the lateral orbitofrontal area (inferior frontal gyrus), then in addition to poor decision making, there are problems in impulse control or response inhibition. When the damage is more extensive, then patients with unilateral or bilateral damage to the anterior cingulate and surrounding regions will present a condition known as akinetic mutism (more severe when the damage is bilateral). This indicates that the problem associated with damage to this region can go beyond simple impairments in response inhibition, and it may be due to damage to underlying white matter. However, in cases in which the damage is less extensive, this phenomenon involving "lack of response inhibition" may still be observed in such patients. For instance, in the frontal patients studied by Luria, among the important observations that were reported included examples such as asking the patient to draw a circle. However, once the patient drew the first one, he kept on drawing more and more circles, as if he was unable to stop, until the examiner stopped him (e.g., see Goldberg 2001 for a nice description of these patients). Many other patients with similar lesions exhibit signs of disinhibition or lack of impulse control: They may utter obscene and socially inappropriate words and phrases, or they may exhibit socially inappropriate behaviors, such as urinating in public (Fuster 1991).

18.2.4 The Control of the Reflective System Is Not Absolute

I suggest that the triggering of somatic states is the critical mechanism through which the reflective system controls the impulsive system. Once somatic states induced by primary and/or secondary inducers are triggered, an *overall positive* or *negative* somatic state emerges (see fig. 18.2). We have proposed that the mechanisms that determine the nature of this overall somatic state are consistent with the principles of natural selection, that is, survival of the fittest (Bechara and Damasio 2004). In other words, numerous and often conflicting somatic states may be triggered at the same time, but stronger ones gain selective advantage over weaker ones. With each "thought" brought to working memory, the strength of the somatic state triggered by that "thought" determines whether the same "thought" is likely to recur (i.e., will be brought back to memory so that it triggers another somatic state that reinforces the previous one), or whether that "thought" is likely to be eliminated. Thus, over the course of pondering a decision, positive and negative *somatic markers* that are strong are reinforced, while weak ones are eliminated. This process of elimination can be very fast. Ultimately, an overall, more dominant, somatic state emerges (a "gut feeling" or "a hunch," so to speak), which then provides signals to the telencephalon that modulate activity in neural structures involved in *biasing* decisions. In instances in which the somatic states that signal future outcomes are dominant, the reflective system exerts control over the impulsive system. However, this control is not absolute. In instances in which the somatic states signaling immediate prospects become stronger, the impulsive system can influence, modulate, or bias (consciously or unconsciously) activity within the reflective system, thus diminishing its power of control and causing a loss of willpower.

There may be a difference in the speed and number of neural steps through which different mechanisms within the reflective system exert their control. The processing of events (secondary inducers) that are near in time and/or highly probable (i.e., almost certain), depends on more posterior VM cortices. Events that are distant in time and less probable require more anterior VM cortices. Anatomically, the more caudal/posterior areas of the VM cortex (e.g., BA 25) are directly connected to brainstem structures for triggering and/or representing somatic states (e.g., autonomic, neurotransmitter, and sensory nuclei) and to cortical structures holding conscious representations of somatic states (i.e., "what it feels like") in insular/SII, SI cortices (Ongur and Price 2000). By contrast, the connections of more rostral/anterior areas of the VM cortex to neural structures involved in triggering and/or accessing representations of somatic states are more indirect. It follows that coupling of information (secondary inducers) to representations of somatic states via posterior VM cortices is relatively fast, effortless, and strong and is perhaps mediated through a shorter "as-if body loop" circuit. In contrast, coupling of secondary inducers to somatic states via anterior VM cortices is relatively slow, effortful, and weak and is perhaps mediated through a longer "body loop" circuit (see fig. 18.1). For example, walking into a bank and finding a million dollars on a table does not require triggering somatic states in the body (body loop) in order to suppress any impulse to take the money. The impulse is suppressed quickly and robustly. In contrast, finding a million dollars in a dark alley and deciding what to do with the money may engage the body loop.

18.3   The Loss of Willpower

I have proposed that choosing according to long-term outcomes rather than short-term ones requires that the somatic states triggered by the reflective system dominate those triggered by the impulsive system. Two broad types of conditions could alter this relationship and lead to loss of willpower: (1) a dysfunctional reflective system, which has lost its ability to process and trigger somatic states that signal future outcomes, and (2) a hyperactive impulsive system, which exaggerates the somatic states of immediate prospects. Addiction to drugs provides examples of disorders that affect each type of these two mechanisms.

Although VM cortex abnormalities have been observed in individuals with substance dependence (ISDs) for several years (Volkow et al. 1991; Stapleton et al. 1995; Childress et al. 1999; London et al. 2000; Volkow and Fowler 2000), very little attention was paid to the role of the prefrontal cortex in addiction. However, VM patients and ISDs show similar behaviors: (1) They often deny, or they are not aware, that they have a problem, and (2) when faced with a choice to pursue a course of action that brings an immediate reward, at the risk of incurring future negative consequences, including the loss of reputation, job, home, and family, they choose the immediate reward and ignore the future consequences. Because of this "myopia" for future consequences seen in VM patients and ISDs, the first attempt to establish a link between the two using strategies applied to the study of decision making in neurological patients was conducted by Grant and colleagues, who investigated the mechanisms of decision making in cocaine addicts using the Iowa Gambling Task (IGT) paradigm (Grant et al. 1997, 1999, 2000; Bartzokis et al. 2000). Since then, several groups have used similar strategies and found a relationship between substance abuse and poor decision making (Petry et al. 1998; Rogers et al. 1999; Mazas et al. 2000). We have also used strategies applied to the study of decision making in neurological patients and investigated the mechanisms of decision making and somatic state activation in ISDs. Studies have shown that the abnormal mechanisms of processing drug reward in ISDs generalize to other rewards, including monetary reward (Breiter and Rosen 1999; Breiter et al. 2001). Therefore, we predicted that the abnormalities of ISDs in processing somatic states would apply not only to drugs, but also to reward in general, such as the monetary reward used in the IGT paradigm.

18.3.1   Impaired Decision Making in Substance Abusers
We conducted experiments where we tested three groups of subjects: ISDs, normal controls, and VM patients on the IGT (Bechara et al. 1994, 2000). The task is carried out in real time, and it resembles real-world contingencies. It factors reward and punishment (i.e., winning and losing money) in such a way that it creates a conflict between an immediate, luring reward and a delayed, probabilistic punishment.

Therefore, the task engages the subject in a quest to make advantageous choices. As in real-life choices, the task offers choices that may be risky, and there is no obvious explanation of how, when, or what to choose. Each choice is full of uncertainty because a precise calculation or prediction of the outcome of a given choice is not possible.

In brief, the task involves four decks of cards. The goal in the task is to maximize profit on a loan of play money. Subjects are required to make a series of 100 card selections; however, they are not told ahead of time how many card selections they are going to make. Subjects can select one card at a time from any deck they choose, and they are absolutely free to switch from any deck to another at any time and as often as they wish. However, the subject's decision to select from one deck versus another is largely influenced by various schedules of immediate reward and future punishment. These schedules are preprogrammed and known to the examiner, but not to the subject. The detail of these schedules and the procedure to administer the task have been published elsewhere (Bechara et al. 1994, 2000). Briefly, almost every time the subject selects a card from deck A or deck B, the subject gets $100. Almost every time the subject selects deck C or deck D, the subject gets $50. However, in each of the four decks, subjects encounter unpredictable punishments or money loss. The punishment is set to be higher in the high-paying decks (A and B) and lower in the low-paying decks (C and D). In essence, decks A and B are disadvantageous because they cost more in the long run; decks C and D are advantageous because they result in an overall gain in the long term.

All ISDs met the Diagnostic and Statistical Manual of Mental Disorders (fourth ed.) criteria for dependence, with either alcohol or stimulants (methamphetamine or cocaine) as the primary substance of choice (Bechara et al. 2001; Bechara and Damasio 2002). The results revealed a significant impairment in the performance of ISDs relative to normal controls. A significantly high proportion of ISDs (63% vs. only 27% of normal controls) performed within the range of the VM patients, while the rest performed within the range of normal controls. Using the maximum score achieved by any of the VM patients as a cutoff score for impaired performance (below the cutoff score) and nonimpaired performance (above the cutoff score), the majority of normal controls and a minority of ISDs performed advantageously. Conversely, a majority of ISDs, all VM patients, and a minority of normal controls performed disadvantageously.

Measuring skin conductance response (SCR) activity of subjects after they received a reward or a punishment (Reward or Punishment SCRs), and before they made a choice (Anticipatory SCRs), revealed that a subgroup of ISDs was similar to VM patients. These ISDs triggered normal Reward and Punishment SCRs, but they failed to trigger SCRs (Anticipatory) when they pondered choices associated with high immediate gains, but also with more delayed and more severe losses (Bechara et al. 2002).

18.3.2 Impaired Impulse Control in Substance Abusers

In addition to decision making, my colleagues and I examined the integrity of the reflective system in ISDs by addressing their capacity to control impulses. In a preliminary study we assessed response inhibition using the stop-signal task. In the stop-signal paradigm, the participant performs a choice reaction time (RT) task requiring responses to left- and right-pointing arrows. Occasionally and unpredictably, the color of the arrows change, instructing participants to inhibit responses. The main dependent variables in this task are the and the estimate of the covert response to the stop signal, made by inferring the stop-signal reaction time (SSRT). Relative to normal controls, ISDs had significantly longer SSRTs, but shorter RTs, thus reflecting difficulties or impairments in impulse control.

In another preliminary study, we used a task-switch paradigm requiring participants to rapidly switch between two RT tasks, requiring left- or right-hand responses to squares and rectangles that could appear as local or global figures. The main dependent variable was the difference in RT between task repetition trials and task alternation trials. ISDs showed significantly larger switch costs than controls, while there was no difference in accuracy of responding.

Together, the results reflect disorders in the reflective system of ISD at both the level of decision making as well as the ability to control impulses. Of note, not all ISDs seem to exhibit both kinds of deficits. Some ISDs were impaired on the IGT but were normal on the stop-signal and switching tasks, or vice versa. This suggests that there is some degree of separation in the mechanisms by which the reflective system exerts control over the impulsive system.

18.3.3 Hypersensitivity to Reward in Substance Abusers

Emotional regulation, or "affective style" (Davidson and Irwin 1999), has been shown to play a significant role in decision making and impulse control. Emotional dysregulation, as may be reflected in hypersensitivity to reward or insensitivity to punishment, can interfere with decision making and impulse control. Anatomically, I suggest that the mechanism underlying this disorder of willpower, that is, poor capacity to resist temptation, relates to imbalanced activity between two systems: (1) a hyperactive impulsive system subserved by an amygdala-ventral striatal (nucleus accumbens) neural circuit, which exaggerates the processing of the incentive values of reward stimuli, and (2) a weak reflective system subserved by the prefrontal cortex for inhibiting and controlling activity within the impulsive system. In fact, it is possible to have a situation in which the reflective/prefrontal system is normal, but it is indirectly weakened by a hyperactive impulsive/amygdala system (e.g., trying to apply the car brakes while the other foot is pressing the accelerator).

We have suggested that many ISDs may suffer from a hyperactive amygdala system that exaggerates the processing of reward, which resulted in poor decision making as measured by their performance on the IGT (Bechara 2003). We have described this condition as "hypersensitivity to reward," in which a subgroup of ISDs expressed exaggerated responses to reward and relatively weak responses to punishment (Bechara 2003). Specifically, we used different versions of the IGT, where the contingencies were reversed, so that the punishment was immediate and the reward was delayed. On this variant task, VM patients chose according to immediate consequences, that is, preferred decks with low immediate cost but even smaller delayed gain, and avoided decks with higher immediate costs, but even larger delayed gains. Accordingly, we have described VM patients as insensitive to future consequences, positive or negative, so that their behavior is primarily guided by immediate prospects (Bechara et al. 2000). When testing ISDs on this variant task, only one subgroup performed like VM patients, and accordingly we have described this subgroup of ISDs as similar to VM patients in many respects. However, a separate subgroup of ISDs was different from VM patients. This subgroup behaved on the original and variant versions of the IGT in such a way that they were drawn to choices that yielded larger gains, irrespective of the losses that were encountered. This subgroup showed higher magnitude Reward SCRs and lower magnitude Punishment SCRs in comparison to normal controls. Furthermore, during the anticipation of a reward, this subgroup of ISDs showed higher Anticipatory SCRs, but this was not the case when they anticipated punishment (Bechara et al. 2002). On the basis of these behavioral and physiological results, we have described this subpopulation of ISDs as hypersensitive to reward, so that the presence or the prospect of receiving reward dominates their choice and behavior.

18.4 Discussion and Conclusion

To use Dennett's analogy, "A disordered will is not much like a broken computer. It is more like a society falling into anarchy" (Dennett, personal communication). I add that this is a society with a two-party system, with a certain balance of power between the two parties: an impulsive system that triggers somatic states that bias choices toward short-term outcomes and a reflective system that triggers somatic states that bias choices toward long-term outcomes. Through development, experiencing reward and punishment, and learning to respect social rules, the reflective system gains a slight control over the impulsive system by acquiring somatic markers that signal the stronger benefits and advantages (or dangers and disadvantages) of a long-term outcome when confronted with a choice that has a short-term outcome. This is what gives rise to the sense of having willpower. However, the control of the reflective system and the sense of willpower are not absolute. This control and willpower become weak whenever environmental (external) and/or homeostatic (internal) conditions enhance the somatic responses triggered by the impulsive system, thus shifting the balance of power in favor of immediate outcomes. A strong somatic state triggered via an impulsive system has the capacity to influence the nature of the net or overall somatic state that provides feedback for biasing decisions (see fig. 18.2). In order for somatic signals to exert a "biasing" effect on behavior and on "thought," they must act on appropriate neural systems. Both the striatum and the anterior cingulate play a role in this *biasing* function. We have suggested that at the level of the striatum, the biasing mechanism of behavioral response selection is nonconscious, that is, the subject learns to select a correct response, but without awareness of whether the response is right or wrong. At the level of the supracallosal sector of the anterior cingulate, and perhaps the adjacent supplementary motor area, the biasing mechanism of response selection is conscious, that is, there is "action with awareness of what is right or wrong"; the decisions are "voluntary" or "willful" and guided by knowledge, awareness, and premeditation. At the level of the lateral orbitofrontal and dorsolateral prefrontal region, the biasing mechanism of somatic states is conscious, but it is at the level of "thought" or "memory" and not the level of behavioral action. In other words, as individuals ponder several options and scenarios in their working memory, the biasing effect of somatic states is to endorse some options and reject other ones, that is, some thoughts become eliminated and some thoughts keep recurring in mind (fig. 18.3). Perhaps this mechanism can explain the attention bias discussed by Sayette (this volume) and shown in smokers responding to smoking cues.

I must note that this is not the only mechanism for a disordered will. Decision making depends on systems for memory, emotion, and feeling. During decision making, category events are brought to *working memory*, which includes several processes (Baddeley 1992). Maintaining an active representation of memory over a delay period involves the dorsolateral sector of the prefrontal cortex (Fuster 1996), and this function, in turn, is dependent on many cognitive resources mediated by multimodal and association cortices. Effector structures that mediate the emotional response (somatic states) are in the brainstem, whereas neural representations of feelings are thought to involve the insula, surrounding parietal cortices, and the cingulate (Damasio 1994). Thus, damage to the systems that impact emotion, feeling, and/or memory compromise the ability to make advantageous decisions. My studies have focused on disorders resulting from malfunctions of the systems underlying somatic state activation (i.e., those related to emotion and feeling). Some of the studies on schizophrenia, I suggest, address disorders of the will that arise from abnormalities related to the cognitive systems (e.g., working memory and its executive processes) that are necessary for the normal functioning of a reflective system (e.g., see Frith, this volume). Other disorders in schizophrenics discussed by Jeannerod (this volume) seem to relate to problems in the posterior parietal components of the reflective system (i.e., systems related to the representations of feelings). Damage to the prefrontal cortex

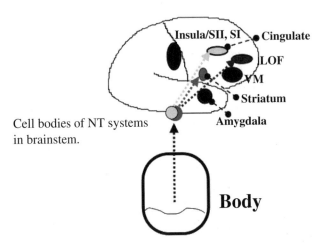

**Cell bodies of NT systems
in brainstem.**

Body

Figure 18.3
Illustration of three different levels at which somatic states can bias decisions via the release of neurotransmitters (NT). (1) Dopamine biases decisions covertly (perhaps through action in the striatum and anterior cingulate (BA 25 and lower 24, 32). (2) Serotonin biases decisions overtly (perhaps through action in the anterior cingulate and probably the adjacent supplementary motor area). (3) Somatic states also bias working memory in the lateral orbitofrontal and dorso-lateral regions of the prefrontal cortex (LOF). They help endorse or reject "thoughts," "options," or "scenarios" brought to mind during the pondering of decisions, that is, before their transla-tion into action. The neurotransmitter system that mediates this biasing function remains to be determined. VM: ventromedial. SI: primary somatosensory cortex. SII: secondary somatosensory cortex.

that is more extensive and extends posteriorly to include the cingulate is associated with increased complications: There is evidence of apathy in these frontal patients, and in extreme cases, the patient presents with abulia or akinetic mutism, such as the one discussed by Metzinger (this volume). Thus, the lack of drive and motivation described by Liddle (this volume) in schizophrenics may be explained by disorders of the reflective system, such as what occurs in patients with extensive prefrontal cortex damage.

The somatic marker framework (Damasio 1994), which is the basis of the neural model I have presented here, is consistent with the model developed by Shallice, Burgess, and their colleagues, which invokes the idea of marking various options with a value (Shallice and Burgess 1993). However, the nature of these markers is not spec-ified in the Shallice model, and it is implied that these markers are cognitive in nature. The notion of the somatic marker framework is that bioregulatory signals, including those that constitute feeling and emotion, provide the principal guide for decisions. Furthermore, I have suggested that the nature of these markers may be reduced further to specific neurotransmitters, such as dopamine and serotonin (see fig. 18.3).

Finally, Grafman and Krueger (this volume) proposed that frontal patients have "volition," but they lack "autonomy." Autonomy is defined in the Encarta World English Dictionary as "personal independence, and the capacity to make moral decisions and act on them." If one considers autonomy from a social perspective, then Grafman is correct: These patients cannot live independently in society because their choices cost them their employment and the financial resources needed for survival. If one considers autonomy from a biological perspective, then I suggest that the volition and autonomy described by Grafman are equivalent to the reflective and impulsive systems, respectively, which reverses the label of the deficit given by Grafman. Indeed, from a biological perspective, frontal patients possess a great deal of autonomy: They can eat, drink, dress, and mate independently. One can argue that they can even make moral decisions and act on them—whether they make good or bad decisions is a good question, but nonetheless they do express a moral opinion, and they do make decisions. Therefore, I argue that if these patients were left alone on an island with plenty of food, water, and shelter, they could be autonomous and survive perfectly well. They fail only when they have to fit into society. The reason for this failure is their lack of volition or the will to defer something immediate for something else that is better later on. These patients tend to say and do the first things that come into their mind without considering the social correctness or the future consequences of what they say or do. While much of their behavior becomes antisocial, they are unlikely to engage in activities that lead to physical harm to themselves or to others. Therefore, in a world where there are no social rules, frontal patients can have autonomy, because they possess the mechanisms that enable them to function impulsively and respond to immediate contingencies. Their problems emerge during volition or willpower, that is, when they have to obey certain social rules (i.e., inhibit some prepotent responses) or delay some immediate gratification for the sake of reaping better future outcomes. Their dysfunctional reflective system deprives them of that important capacity.

Acknowledgments

The studies described in this chapter were supported by National Institute on Drug Abuse Grants DA11779–02, DA12487–03, and DA16708, and by National Institute of Neurological Disorders and Stroke (NINDS) Grant NS19632–23.

References

Baddeley, A. 1992. Working Memory. *Science, 255,* 556–559.

Bartzokis, G., P. H. Lu, M. Beckson, R. Rapoport, S. Grant, E. J. Wiseman, and E. D. London. 2000. Abstinence from cocaine reduces high-risk responses on a gambling task. *Neuropsychopharmacology, 22,* 102–103.

Bechara, A. 2003. Risky business: Emotion, decision-making and addiction. *Journal of Gambling Studies, 19*, 23–51.

Bechara, A. 2004. Separate neural substrates underlie different mechanisms of performance monitoring and behavioral control. In *Errors, Conflicts, and the Brain: Current Opinions on Performance Monitoring*, ed. M. Ullsperger and M. Falkenstein, pp. 55–63. Dortmund, Germany: Max Plack Institute for Human Cognitive and Brain Sciences, Leipzig-Munchen.

Bechara, A., and A. Damasio. 2004. The somatic marker hypothesis: A neural theory of economic decision. *Games and Economic Behavior, 1*, 1–37.

Bechara, A., A. R. Damasio, H. Damasio, and S. W. Anderson. 1994. Insensitivity to future consequences following damage to human prefrontal cortex. *Cognition, 50*, 7–15.

Bechara, A., and H. Damasio. 2002. Decision-making and addiction: I. Impaired activation of somatic states in substance dependent individuals when pondering decisions with negative future consequences. *Neuropsychologia, 40*, 1675–1689.

Bechara, A., H. Damasio, and A. Damasio. 2003. The role of the amygdala in decision-making. In *The Amygdala in Brain Function: Basic and Clinical Approaches*, ed. P. Shinnick-Gallagher, A. Pitkanen, A. Shekhar, and L. Cahill, pp. 356–369. New York: Annals of the New York Academy of Science.

Bechara, A., S. Dolan, N. Denburg, A. Hindes, S. W. Anderson, and P. E. Nathan. 2001. Decision-making deficits, linked to a dysfunctional ventromedial prefrontal cortex, revealed in alcohol and stimulant abusers. *Neuropsychologia, 39*, 376–389.

Bechara, A., S. Dolan, and A. Hindes. 2002. Decision-making and addiction: II. Myopia for the future or hypersensitivity to reward? *Neuropsychologia, 40*, 1690–1705.

Bechara, A., D. Tranel, and H. Damasio. 2000. Characterization of the decision-making impairment of patients with bilateral lesions of the ventromedial prefrontal cortex. *Brain, 123*, 2189–2202.

Berkowitz, L. 1993. Towards a general theory of anger and emotional aggression: Implications of the cognitive-neoassociationistic perspective for the analysis of anger and other emotions. In *Advances in Social Cognition*, ed. R. S. Wyer and T. K. Srull, pp. 1–46. Hillsdale, N.J.: Lawrence Earlbaum.

Blessing, W. W. 1997. Anatomy of the lower brainstem. In *The Lower Brainstem and Bodily Homeostasis*, pp. 29–99. New York: Oxford University Press.

Breiter, H. C., and B. R. Rosen. 1999. Functional magnetic resonance imaging of brain reward circuitry in the human. In *Advancing from the Ventral Striatum to the Extended Amygdala*, pp. 523–547. New York: The New York Academy of Sciences.

Breiter, H. C., I. Aharon, D. Kahneman, A. Dale, and P. Shizgal. 2001. Functional imaging of neural responses to expectancy and experience of monetary gains and losses. *Neuron, 30*, 619–639.

Buchel, C., J. Morris, R. J. Dolan, and K. J. Friston. 1998. Brain systems mediating aversive conditioning: An event-related fMRI study. *Neuron, 20,* 947–957.

Childress, A. R., P. D. Mozley, W. McElgin, J. Fitzgerald, M. Reivich, and C. P. O'Brien. 1999. Limbic activation during cue-induced cocaine craving. *American Journal of Psychiatry, 156,* 11–18.

Damasio, A. R. 1994. *Descartes' Error: Emotion, Reason, and the Human Brain.* New York: Grosset/Putnam.

Damasio, A. R. 1995. Toward a neurobiology of emotion and feeling: Operational concepts and hypotheses. *Neuroscientist, 1,* 19–25.

Damasio, A. R. 1999. *The Feeling of What Happens: Body and Emotion in the Making of Consciousness.* New York: Harcourt Brace.

Damasio, A. R. 2003. *Looking for Spinoza: Joy, Sorrow, and the Feeling Brain.* New York: Harcourt.

Davidson, R. J., and W. Irwin. 1999. The functional neuroanatomy of emotion and affective style. *Trends in Cognitive Sciences, 3,* 11–21.

Dolan, R. J., P. Fletcher, J. Morris, N. Kapur, J. F. W. Deakin, and C. D. Frith. 1996. Neural activation during covert processing of positive emotional facial expressions. *Neuroimage, 4,* 194–200.

Fuster, J. M. 1991. The prefrontal cortex and its relation to behavior. In *Progress in Brain Research,* ed. G. Holstege, pp. 201–211. New York: Elsevier Science.

Fuster, J. M. 1996. *The Prefrontal Cortex: Anatomy, Physiology, and Neuropsychology of the Frontal Lobe,* 3rd edition. New York: Raven Press.

Goldberg, E. 2001. *The Executive Brain: Frontal Lobes and the Civilized Mind.* New York: Oxford University Press.

Grant, S., C. Contoreggi, and E. D. London. 1997. Drug abusers show impaired performance on a test of orbitofrontal function. *Society for Neuroscience Abstracts, 23,* 1943.

Grant, S., C. Contoreggi, and E. D. London. 2000. Drug abusers show impaired performance in a laboratory test of decision-making. *Neuropsychologia, 38,* 1180–1187.

Grant, S. J., K. R. Bonson, C. C. Contoreggi, and E. D. London. 1999. Activation of the ventromedial prefrontal cortex correlates with gambling task performance: A FDG–PET study. *Society for Neuroscience Abstracts, 25,* 1551.

LaBar, K. S., J. C. Gatenby, J. C. Gore, J. E. LeDoux, and E. A. Phelps. 1998. Human amygdala activation during conditioned fear acquisition and extinction: A mixed-trial fMRI study. *Neuron, 20,* 937–945.

LeDoux, J. 1996. *The Emotional Brain: The Mysterious Underpinnings of Emotional Life.* New York: Simon and Schuster.

London, E. D., M. Ernst, S. Grant, K. Bonson, and A. Weinstein. 2000. Orbitofrontal cortex and human drug abuse: Functional imaging. *Cerebral Cortex, 10,* 334–342.

Martin, C., N. Denburg, D. Tranel, M. Granner, and A. Bechara. 2004. The effects of vagal nerve stimulation on decision-making. *Cortex, 40*, 1–8.

Mazas, C. A., P. R. Finn, and J. E. Steinmetz. 2000. Decision making biases, antisocial personality, and early-onset alcoholism. *Alcoholism: Clinical and Experimental Research, 24*, 1036–1040.

Nauta, W. J. H. 1971. The problem of the frontal lobes: A reinterpretation. *Journal of Psychiatric Research, 8*, 167–187.

Ongur, D., and J. L. Price. 2000. The organization of networks within the orbital and medial prefrontal cortex of rats, monkeys, and humans. *Cerebral Cortex, 10*, 206–219.

Overskeid, G. 2000. The slave of passions: Experiencing problems and selecting solutions. *Review of General Psychology, 4*, 284–309.

Petry, N. M., W. K. Bickel, and M. Arnett. 1998. Shortened time horizons and insensitivity to future consequences in heroin addicts. *Addiction, 93*, 729–738.

Rogers, R. D., B. J. Everitt, A. Baldacchino, A. J. Blackshaw, R. Swainson, K. Wynne, N. B. Baker, J. Hunter, T. Carthy, E. Booker, M. London, J. F. W. Deakin, B. J. Sahakian, and T. W. Robbins. 1999. Dissociable deficits in the decision-making cognition of chronic amphetamine abusers, opiate abusers, patients with focal damage to prefrontal cortex, and tryptophan-depleted normal volunteers: Evidence for monoaminergic mechanisms. *Neuropsychopharmacology, 20*, 322–339.

Schneider, W., and R. J. Shiffrin. 1977. Controlled and automatic human information processing. *Psychological Review, 84*, 1–66.

Semendeferi, K., E. Armstrong, A. Schleicher, K. Zilles, and G. W. Van Hoesen. 2001. Prefrontal cortex in humans and apes: A comparative study of Area 10. *American Journal of Physical Anthropology, 114*, 224–241.

Semendeferi, K., A. Lu, N. Schenker, and H. Damasio. 2002. Humans and great apes share a large frontal cortex. *Nature Neuroscience, 5*, 272–276.

Shallice, T., and P. Burgess. 1993. Supervisory control of action and thought selection. In *Attention: Selection, Awareness, and Control*, ed. A. Baddeley and L. Weiskrantz, pp. 171–187. Oxford: Clarendon Press.

Stapleton, J. M., M. J. Morgan, R. L. Phillips, D. R. Wong, B. C. K. Yung, E. K. Shaya, R. F. Dannals, X. Liu, R. L. Grayson, and E. D. London. 1995. Cerebral glucose utilization in polysubstance abuse. *Neuropsychopharmacology, 13*, 22–31.

Volkow, N. D., and J. S. Fowler. 2000. Addiction, a disease of compulsion and drive: Involvement of the orbitofrontal cortex. *Cerebral Cortex, 10*, 318–325.

Volkow, N. D., J. S. Fowler, A. P. Wolf, R. Hitzemann, S. Dewey, B. Bendriem, R. Alpert, and A. Hoff. 1991. Changes in brain glucose metabolism in cocaine dependence and withdrawal. *American Journal of Psychiatry, 148*, 621–626.

19 Craving, Cognition, and the Self-Regulation of Cigarette Smoking

Michael A. Sayette

Cigarette smoking presents to the world perhaps its most serious public health challenge. For instance, in the United States, smoking remains the leading preventable cause of premature death (U.S. Department of Health and Human Services [USDHHS] 1989). Despite such alarming statistics, a large percentage of adults continue to smoke. More than 25 percent of American adults, for example, are smokers (Centers for Disease Control; CDC; 1996). It also is clear that quitting smoking reduces the chances of contracting a wide range of illnesses, including heart disease and various forms of cancer (USDHHS 1990). Unfortunately the majority of individuals attempting to quit will fail (Wetter et al. 1998).

One cannot help but wonder why so many people persist in a behavior that can kill them. Do smokers lack the free will to control their smoking? Not surprisingly, the role of free will in controlling smoking depends on how free will is conceptualized. On the one hand, the act of smoking requires the execution of a series of voluntary behaviors, so smokers would appear to have free will to control their smoking (Baumeister, Heatherton, and Tice 1994). Simply put, were a gun to be aimed at your head with the understanding that you would be shot if you lit a cigarette, you probably would abstain. On the other hand, the large number of people who remain smokers despite wanting, and perhaps trying, to quit suggests that nicotine addiction can foil many smokers' efforts at self-regulation (Sayette 2004). That is, using a group-level analysis, smoking appears to be beyond the control of a sizable number of people. Moreover, in many cases, relapse may occur without any awareness of what is happening. Tiffany (1990) noted that over many years of practice, a smoking routine (removing a cigarette from the pack, holding it, lighting it, taking an initial puff, etc.) becomes automatized, and consequently that "absent-minded relapses" can occur without smokers even realizing what they have done.

Because the role of free will in smoking is largely a function of how free will is defined, this chapter will not resolve the question of whether smokers lack free will to control their behavior. Instead, it will focus on the way that craving a cigarette may change a broad range of cognitive processes, which in turn create conditions under which the likelihood of smoking is increased. That is, rather than seeing craving as an irresistible impulse which completely overwhelms the capacity to reason, the chapter suggests a more nuanced approach in which craving is linked to a number of subtle shifts in perception and decision making that promote smoking. The main thrust will be to review studies of the effects of craving on several aspects of smoking-related cognition. This chapter will conclude with a discussion of the possible role of acquiescence in relapse.

19.1 Craving and Addiction

There has been extensive research investigating the relation between cigarette craving and tobacco addiction. Studies find that cigarette cravings predict relapse among smokers attempting to quit (Killen and Fortmann 1997). In a study of smokers attempting cessation, Shiffman and colleagues (1997) found that those with the most intense early morning cravings were the most likely to relapse. It also is possible that merely worrying about experiencing cravings can deter smokers from even trying to quit. These are just some of the reasons that craving continues to play a vital role in the study of addiction (see the special issue of *Addiction*, vol. *95*, 2000, devoted to craving).

Research recently has begun to focus on the mechanisms underlying the relation between craving and addiction (Sayette 1999). Specifically, there is interest in investigating just how craving a drug may facilitate or promote drug use. One research direction has been to examine the different ways in which drug craving may affect drug-related cognitive processes.

For the purpose of this chapter, "craving" is defined as an emotional state (or states) reflecting the activation of motivation (drug acquisitive) systems (see Baker, Morse, and Sherman 1987). In contrast to perspectives that associate craving with negative, but not positive, affect (e.g., Tiffany 1992), the current approach holds that cravings can be linked to either positive or negative emotional states (Baker et al. 1987; Sayette and Hufford 1995).

Manipulations of emotional states have been found to affect a range of cognitive processes, including attentional focus, memory, and problem solving (see Sayette 1999). Because cravings are emotional in nature, it may be useful to review studies that have provoked cigarette craving and then examined changes in smoking-related cognitions. Typically these studies involve providing smokers with smoking-related cues. Common cues include exposure to cigarettes (e.g., holding a lit cigarette), watching others smoke, and listening to tapes of smoking-related vignettes. Often these studies require smokers to abstain from smoking for at least several hours prior to cue exposure (see Sayette, Shiffman, Tiffany, Niaura, Martin, and Shadel 2000). Across numerous studies, it appears that during cue exposure, smokers tend to report high levels of cigarette craving, manifest a range of physiological responses, and enact behaviors linked to smoking (e.g., perform tasks to obtain cigarette puffs; Carter and Tiffany 1999; Sayette et al. 2000). In sum, it is well established that cue exposure studies provide a suitable paradigm for examining the effects of cigarette craving on cognitive processes related to smoking.

19.2   Attentional Processes

"Attention" refers to a variety of perceptual and cognitive processes having to do with limited resources or capacity (Shiffrin 1988). Because all possible information in the environment exceeds attentional capacity, organisms must select a subset of information for processing (Segal and Cloitre 1993). Researchers have used a number of tasks to examine the ways in which drug craving affects the stimuli that are attended to in the environment (Sayette 1999). Two of the most common are response time probes and emotional Stroop tasks.

Response time probes have been used by cognitive psychologists to identify the extent to which performance on a primary task draws on limited capacity resources (Wickens 1984). The aim is to measure the amount of cognitive capacity used during processing of a primary task by recording performance decrements on a secondary task. The longer the response latency to the probe, the more capacity is being consumed by the primary task (Wickens 1984). Studies have employed secondary response time probes to index the degree to which smoking cues affect limited-capacity attentional resources. These studies find that response latencies are greater during smoking cue exposure than during exposure to a control cue (e.g., Cepeda-Benito and Tiffany 1996; Juliano and Brandon 1998; Sayette and Hufford 1994; Sayette, Martin, Wertz, Shiffman, and Perrott 2001). Moreover, response time latencies tend to correlate with self-reported urge in studies that elicit strong cravings (see Sayette, Martin, et al. 2001).

Studies using response time probes reinforce what many smokers report, namely, that during craving, attention is easily captured by smoking cues. For instance, smokers may not notice the cigarette butts littering the sidewalk unless they are craving a cigarette. Researchers have labeled this attention-grabbing feature of drug cues "attentional bias."

Attentional bias has been measured using a number of methods including dot probe tasks (e.g., Mogg and Bradley 1998) and emotional Stroop tasks. This latter task requires participants to name the color of the letters of a stimulus word while ignoring word content. An increase in response time to stimulus words, relative to control words, indicates an attentional bias. Numerous studies reveal that negative affect-related words produce increased color naming interference in persons with emotional disorders (for review, see Williams, Mathews, and MacLeod 1996). Gross, Jarvik, and Rosenblatt (1993) used the emotional Stroop task to measure attentional bias in smokers. They found that abstinent smokers showed greater color naming interference when observing smoking-related words than control words. Other studies have generally replicated this pattern, with abstinent smokers showing greater effects than nonabstinent smokers (e.g., Waters and Feyerabend 2000; Wertz and Sayette 2001a). These studies suggest that individual differences in attentional bias toward smoking cues may contribute to addiction.

Recently, we examined the utility of an emotional Stroop task to predict smoking relapse (Waters et al. 2003). Smokers completed the emotional Stroop task on the initial day of a quit attempt. Smokers who showed the greatest attentional bias were most likely to resume smoking in the short term. That is, performance on the emotional Stroop predicted smoking lapses. This association remained even after statistically controlling for self-reported urges during the test session, suggesting that this task provided information pertaining to subsequent relapse that was not provided by traditional self-reported measures of smoking motivation (Waters et al. 2003).

In summary, research suggests that, while craving, smokers' attention shifts in a manner that makes smoking cues more salient. Furthermore, these shifts in attention, and the degree to which a smoker is vulnerable to this attentional bias, may predict smoking relapse. Though speculative, it may be that smoking cessation interventions aimed at reducing attentional bias would prove useful.

19.2.1 Selective Information Processing

Although it is established that smoking cues draw attention toward smoking-related information, it still must be shown that this attentional bias should promote drug use. It is possible, for instance, that selective focus by smokers on the unpleasant or negative features of smoking would serve only to "rub their noses in it" and repulse rather than entice them. Thus, it is important to examine the content of smoking-related information. Wise (1988) has posited that cravings draw upon past memories of reinforcing effects of the drug. Similarly, Baker et al. (1987) proposed the existence of urge networks containing information regarding the anticipated reinforcing consequences of drug use. Niaura, Rohsenow, Binkoff, Monti, Pedraza, and Abrams (1988) also suggest that drug cues trigger a series of responses which include positive outcome expectancies. Together, these theorists propose that while craving, expectancies concerning a drug's reinforcing properties are especially salient (Marlatt 1985; Sayette and Hufford 1997).

The enhanced salience of positive smoking-related information can be understood within the framework of motivated reasoning theory (Kunda 1990). According to this model, humans are guided by two types of motivation which are sometimes in conflict: motivation to process information accurately and motivation to arrive at desired conclusions. Consequently, people may modify their reasoning processes within limits to support the satisfaction of impulses and the execution of desired behaviors. These information-processing changes include biased generation and biased evaluation of information (Kunda 1987).

We examined the effects of smoking craving on both generation and evaluation processes. In the first study, smokers participated in two experimental sessions, once while deprived of nicotine and holding a lit cigarette (high crave) and once while non-deprived and holding a control cue (low crave; Sayette and Hufford 1997). During each session they were given 90 seconds to generate as many positive characteristics of smoking, and then 90 seconds to list as many negative characteristics, as they could. Results indicated that relative to the low-crave manipulation, the high-crave manipulation increased the number of positive, but not negative, characteristics of smoking.

In a subsequent study, we investigated the effects of cigarette craving on the evaluation of smoking-related outcomes (Sayette, Martin, et al. 2001). We hypothesized that craving would affect the evaluation of smoking outcomes provided on a smoking consequence questionnaire, such that participants who were experiencing stronger cravings would judge positive outcomes to be relatively more probable than would those experiencing weaker cravings.

Smokers were randomly assigned to nicotine-deprived or nondeprived conditions. Following the smoking cue exposure manipulation used in our prior research (e.g., Sayette and Hufford 1994), participants completed an abbreviated version of Copeland, Brandon, and Quinn's (1995) Smoking Consequences Questionnaire. (This abbreviated scale appears in Sayette, Martin, Hull, Wertz, and Perrott 2003.) An example of a negative item is "Smoking is taking years off my life." An example of a positive item is "I enjoy the taste sensations while smoking." For each item, participants rated on a 10-point scale the probability that they believed this consequence would occur. There was a trend, such that deprived smokers judged positive consequences to be more probable, relative to negative ones, than did nondeprived smokers. Subsequent research in our laboratory has found a significant effect of deprivation on this task, increasing our confidence in the reliability of the finding; (Sayette et al. in press). These data suggest that craving may distort the anticipated outcomes of smoking such that positive outcomes appear more likely than negative ones. This analysis is in accord with Marlatt (1985), who referred to bolstering tactics during craving, in which the probability of drug use outcomes are distorted in a way that enhances the attractiveness of drug use.

In addition to consideration of the advantages and disadvantages of smoking, other information may influence whether someone trying to quit will succumb to temptation and smoke. An important factor affecting decisions to smoke concerns the meaningfulness of specific high-risk situations for considering future behavior. Ainslie (1999, this volume) proposes that a smoker about to lapse will distinguish that particular moment from others in order to avoid the painful realization that the lapse may set a precedent for how to handle future temptations. If a smoker believes that smoking "just this once" is likely to precipitate a full-blown relapse, then there is pressure to resist smoking. If, however, indulging in the cigarette is viewed as a special circumstance, which does not signal a return to regular smoking, then the decision to smoke is more justifiable.

In summary, not only do smokers who are craving seem to bias attention toward smoking cues but they also appear to systematically bias the quality or content of the smoking-related information that is processed. Specifically, craving seems to enhance the salience and the estimated probability of occurrence of positive aspects of smoking, relative to negative ones. Moreover, the meaning of "having just one" may change while craving, such that a single smoking lapse no longer signals danger. These changes in information processing likely promote the probability of smoking (see also Baker, Piper, McCarthy, Majeskie, and Fiore, 2004).

These changes in smoking-related information processing that often accompany craving may have important practical implications (Sayette 1999). In the safety of the clinic, smokers trying to quit often are instructed to rationally consider the positive and negative features of smoking. This list typically is generated in a sterile clinical setting while smokers are not craving. Presumably, the balance between pros and cons will suggest to both the smoker motivated to quit and the clinician that the negative aspects of smoking predominate. Such a critical attitude toward smoking is likely to strengthen the smoker's motivation to remain abstinent. Indeed, studies often find that prior to quitting, smokers are overconfident that they will succeed (Gwaltney et al. 2001).

Unfortunately, many of the key moments that determine whether or not a smoker will relapse occur while smokers are neither in sterile environments nor when they are in neutral emotional states. In some cases high-risk moments are associated with strong cravings. While craving, the decision to smoke just one cigarette may not seem so foolish. Thus, a smoker may "rationally" choose to smoke, based on what might be an analysis of the pros and cons of smoking, the probability of particular smoking outcomes, the meaning of having a single cigarette for subsequent quitting, and so forth. (Alternatively, smokers may know they are making a mistake by having a cigarette but choose to do so anyway; Loewenstein 1999.) Once the cigarette is smoked and the craving is attenuated, however, the decision to smoke can be reexamined from the perspective of a neutral (i.e., noncraving) state of mind. Now the negative characteristics of smoking again hold sway, and the lapsed smoker is left to wonder how such a mistake was made. Without recognizing the powerful shifts in information processing occurring while craving, the smoker may conclude that the relapse reflects an immutable dispositional weakness.

This line of reasoning is consistent with Bechara's (this volume) view that control of the "impulsive" system (which signals the *immediate* hedonic prospects of an option) by the "reflective" system (which signals the *future* hedonic prospects of an option) is not absolute. There are instances in which the somatic states signaling immediate prospects, and mediated by the impulsive system, influence, modulate, or bias (consciously or unconsciously) activity within the reflective system, thus diminishing its power of control and causing a loss of willpower. According to Bechara, cigarette cues may acquire certain properties of triggering bottom-up, automatic, and involuntary somatic states through the amygdala, that is, primary induction. This bottom-up somatic bias can modulate or bias top-down, goal-driven attention resources and thus interferes with the attention shift from cigarette-related cues to cues unrelated to cigarettes, thus enhancing the likelihood of smoking.

19.3   Temporal Cognition

The research reviewed thus far suggests that craving can lead to systematic shifts across a range of cognitive processes. One other cognitive domain that may contribute to a failure to resist a smoking temptation is temporal cognition. Time perception can have a crucial impact on behavior and determines how individuals represent their environment. Time perception affects both attitudes and motivations (Zakay and Block 1997). Presumably time perception also could affect a smoker's motivation to resist a craving for a cigarette. Recently we investigated the effects of cigarette craving on two types of temporal cognition that may contribute to relapse: time perception and anticipated duration (Sayette et al. in press).

19.3.1   Time Perception

My colleagues and I tested whether craving would change the way in which smokers perceive the passing of time. Briefly, smokers were randomly assigned to high- or low-craving conditions using the same procedures described above (see Sayette, Martin, et al. 2001). All smokers next were informed that they could smoke in 2.5 minutes. They also were asked to indicate when 45 seconds and 90 seconds had elapsed. (There were no clocks or watches in the experimental room). High-urge smokers reported time to pass significantly more slowly than did low-urge smokers. Similarly, Klein, Corwin, and Stine (2003) found that smokers' estimations of a 45-second interval were slower when they were nicotine-deprived than when they were nondeprived (Klein et al. 2003). Taken together, these studies suggest that smokers who are craving find brief time periods to pass more slowly than do smokers who are not craving. Vohs and Schmeichel (2003) describe this experience of increased time perception during moments requiring sustained self-regulation as *extended now*: "The extended now state would likely narrow attention such that current feelings, thoughts, impulses, urges, and desires would be given extra weight, whereas distal (or even near-future) goals, ambitions, or plans would seem less consequential" (p. 219). Importantly, Vohs and Schmeichel found that increased time perceptions during moments requiring self-regulation led to diminished capacity for self-control during subsequent tasks. This change in time perception during craving suggests yet another cognitive mechanism to explain why craving may promote drug use.

19.3.2 Anticipated Urge Duration

In addition to measures of time perception, anticipated urge duration is an aspect of temporal cognition that has potential significance for understanding why craving may increase risk for drug lapses. Research finds that anticipated feelings associated with performing or inhibiting a behavior (e.g., regret) have influenced health-related behaviors, such as condom use (Norman and Conner 1995). Presumably, the estimated *duration* of an emotional state also may affect subsequent behavior. If we think that unpleasant feelings will soon pass, we may be better prepared to "tough it out."

There is evidence that moods tend to fluctuate and that even strong emotional states eventually diminish. Clinical research testing patients with bulimia, for example, finds that binge eating without subsequently purging will lead initially to extreme levels of anxiety, but within about a half hour, the anxiety begins to abate (e.g., Jansen 1998). Solomon and Corbit's (1974) opponent process model proposes that the experience of a particular mood may even trigger its opposite. With respect to cravings, research suggests that rather than being enduring, cravings tend to be momentary "pulsitile" states (Gawin 1991). Marlatt (1994) refers to cravings as ocean waves that build up to a peak state and then subside. Consistent with Marlatt's (1994) observation, data suggest that following peak craving levels, craving ratings begin to drop fairly quickly (Niaura et al. 1999; Sayette and Parrott 1999; Shiffman et al. 2003). It is unclear, however, whether smokers—at the moment they are craving—realize that their cravings may be short-lived.

We recently tested the hypothesis that smokers, while in a high-craving state, would overpredict the duration and intensity of their own future cravings over a 45-minute interval. Immediately following smoking cue exposure, smokers in the high-crave condition (the same participants used in the time perception study just described; Sayette et al. in press) were asked to estimate their future urges—if they were not permitted to smoke—at various times over a 45-minute interval. Results indicated that participants estimated that their urges would steadily rise over the entire 45-minute period. This expectation seems inconsistent with past studies that found smoking urges to begin to subside in less than 45 minutes (e.g., Niaura et al. 1999; Shiffman et al. 2003) and suggests that while craving, smokers may overestimate the duration and intensity of future cravings.

To further test our hypothesis that the smokers in our study who were craving were overpredicting the intensity and duration of their cravings over the next 45 minutes, we recruited a second sample of smokers. Nicotine-deprived smokers were exposed to the same smoking cue manipulation described earlier. These high-urge smokers then sat quietly in an experimental room devoid of distractions and rated their actual urges at the same intervals over 45 minutes as in the prior study. As expected, these smokers reported urges that differed significantly from the predicted urges provided by the initial group (Sayette et al., in press). Specifically, actual urge ratings did not rise over the 45-minute interval, providing evidence that smokers who are craving tend to overpredict the intensity and duration of their cravings. Such exaggerated perceptions of the persistence of craving may help to undermine efforts to quit.

Smokers who are in a craving state seem likely to overestimate the strength and duration of the craving episode. In contrast, smokers who are not craving may actually underpredict the power of future cravings. Loewenstein (1999) refers to the "cold-to-hot empathy gap" when observing that persons in an affectively neutral "cold" state often underestimate the impact of being in an affectively charged "hot" state on their own future behavior. Research seems to support this proposition, as across multiple domains people tend to be overly confident that they will be able to sustain health-promoting behaviors (Forsyth and Carey 1998). This overconfidence also has been found among people attempting to curb addictions (see Sayette 2004). My colleagues and I currently are testing whether smokers will underestimate how much they would value smoking a cigarette when they are craving. That is, while in a neutral state, we expect that smokers will tend to underpredict the intensity of their own future craving.

19.4 Acquiescence

When considering the role of free will in smoking, it is often assumed that the relapsing smoker wanted to remain abstinent. Baumeister et al. (1994) suggested, however, that in some cases "people actually [may] acquiesce in their own self-regulation failures" (p. 29). It may be that people sometimes, perhaps unconsciously, cooperate in their failure to exercise self-control. Accordingly, smokers occasionally may want to relax their level of self-awareness, which is likely to erode the monitoring necessary for successful self-regulation. Ainslie (1999) discusses such "sellouts" as occurring when short-term well-being supersedes the opportunity for a good long-term outcome.

I am unaware of research that provides a direct test of Baumeister et al.'s (1994) provocative notion of the role of acquiescence in drug use. Nevertheless, there are studies that provide indirect evidence that smokers may sometimes indulge their cravings (Sayette 2004).

One approach to the study of acquiescence is to examine the characteristics of cravings that precede drug use and the characteristics of cravings that do not precede drug use (i.e., when the temptations are resisted). Presumably, the former experiences are more likely than the latter to involve acquiescence. If a smoker is committed to quitting, then one might expect him or her to try to resist the urge. Through a number of possible mechanisms (conscious or unconscious), it would be useful for this smoker to exert self-control over, and attempt to suppress, the urge. In contrast, smokers who are disposed to acquiesce to their urge and smoke a cigarette would not be motivated to suppress their urge. As noted elsewhere (Sayette 2004): "Indeed, they might even wish to embellish their urge in order to justify drug use: 'I had no real choice but to smoke. Anyone with a craving as strong as mine would have smoked'" (p. 456).

We recently reviewed the drug cue exposure literature to test the hypothesis that addicts who perceived an opportunity to consume their drug would report stronger urges than would those who did not perceive the opportunity to use (Wertz and Sayette 2001b). Consistent with this hypothesis, we found that individuals who perceived an opportunity to use their drug reported significantly higher urges than did those who did not anticipate use (Wertz and Sayette 2001b). Indeed, this explanation may account for the counterintuitive finding that smokers report stronger urges during the days just prior to quitting than they do on the days immediately after quitting (Shiffman et al. 1997).

In addition to influencing the magnitude of craving, acquiescence may affect the emotional tone of a craving experience. In many cases the emotional experience associated with craving is that of frustration (e.g., Tiffany 1992). Yet smokers may experience positive affect when they expect to satisfy rather than resist an urge. The moments just prior to use and even the beginning of consumption may be particularly positive. One way to examine moment-to-moment fluctuations in emotional response is to analyze facial expressions.

Facial coding of expressive behavior can be conducted unobtrusively and can capture affect in real time (e.g., Ekman, Friesen, and Ancoli 1980). The most sophisticated and established system for assessing facial expression is the Facial Action Coding System (FACS; Ekman and Friesen 1978). FACS is an anatomically based system derived from 7,000 different expressions decomposed into 44 action units (AUs) that can be combined to describe all possible visible movements of the face. FACS has proven to be reliable and provides accurate and specific information across a range of emotional experiences (Ekman and Rosenberg, in press; Sayette, Cohn, Wertz, Perrott, and Parrott 2001). While facial expressions can serve a variety of purposes, it is clear that many are related to subjective affective experience, with particular AUs differentially reflecting affective valence (Ekman and Rosenberg 1997).

Studies using FACS indicate that manipulating instructions (i.e., informing smokers that they will or will not be able to smoke a lit cigarette) influences the probability of evincing expressions associated with either positive or negative affect (Sayette and Hufford 1995; Sayette, Wertz, Martin, Cohn, Perrott, and Hobel 2003). That is, under certain conditions, craving may be linked to positive affect (see also Carter and Tiffany 2001). Similarly, Zinser, Fiore, Davidson, and Baker (1999) used an electrophysiological assessment that suggested a pattern of activation related to approach motivation when smokers expected to smoke.

More recently, we reviewed brain imaging studies that examined drug cue reactivity. In particular, studies had examined neural activation in the prefrontal cortex. The two most investigated regions (orbital frontal cortex and dorsal lateral prefrontal cortex) have yielded inconsistent findings, with activation of these regions noted in only about half the studies (Wilson, Sayette, and Fiez 2004). When studies are organized according to treatment-seeking status, however, the pattern of findings is clarified. Half the studies recruited addicts who were seeking treatment, while the others used drug dependent persons not currently interested in treatment. Presumably, drug cue exposure occurred while subjects in the former group of studies were seeking abstinence, while subjects in the latter group were trying to avoid abstinence. Thus, the active users may have been more inclined than the treatment seekers to indulge their cravings. Analysis of this literature indicated that these two prefrontal regions were more likely to show activation in studies using active users than among studies using treatment seekers. This pattern is not altogether surprising, as activation of both orbital frontal cortex and dorsal lateral prefrontal cortex have been linked to reward expectancy during delay periods (see Wilson et al. 2004). Thus, though speculative, the neuroimaging literature also provides some indirect evidence that smokers may experience cravings differently when they are anticipating smoking a cigarette compared to when they are seeking to resist smoking.

Finally, research with the emotional Stroop task has examined the effects of perceived drug use opportunity on attentional bias (Wertz and Sayette 2001a). Nicotine-deprived smokers were told that they (a) would, (b) would not, or (c) might be able to smoke during the experiment. Participants then completed an emotional Stroop task, in which they were presented with smoking-related or unrelated words. As noted earlier, smokers demonstrated interference to the smoking words, relative to matched neutral words. Moreover, smoking opportunity affected the degree of interference, with those told they would be able to smoke during the study showing the most interference. Thus, data using the emotional Stroop task suggest that perceived smoking opportunity affects the salience of smoking-related stimuli among nicotine-deprived smokers.

In summary, data obtained from self-reported urge ratings, analysis of facial movement, brain imaging research, and emotional Stroop tasks suggest that craving may take different forms depending on whether one intends to resist or surrender to the temptation. All cravings are not created equal, and the context in which they occur exerts an important influence on their behavioral presentation and neurobiological underpinnings.

19.4.1 Savoring

If certain cravings—such as those experienced when one intends to indulge a craving and use the desired drug—can elicit positive affect, then it is possible that some of the perceived reward generally associated with drug use may actually precede drug consumption. Perspectives as disparate as neuroscience and economics have highlighted the power of anticipatory states. Recent animal studies find that dopamine is released during presentations of cues predictive of drug, food, and alcohol use (see Weiss et al. 2000). For instance, using Wistar rats, Weiss et al. (2000) report that anticipation of cocaine increased dopamine efflux in the nucleus accumbens and amygdyla, structures implicated in reward. Thus, craving itself may be rewarding, particularly to those who anticipate using the drug very soon.

Anticipating smoking a cigarette in the immediate future may be a rewarding experience when considered from an economic perspective. Loewenstein (1987) has described savoring as the "positive utility derived from anticipation of future consumption" (p. 667). In some instances, such as when children hoard their stash of Halloween candy rather than eating it, the anticipation may be more pleasurable than the actual consumption.

19.4.2 Acquiescence and Smoking Lapses

Relapse is often associated with poor use of coping skills (Shiffman 1982). Research has shown, for example, that 71 percent of smokers who mastered a set of coping skills during treatment, went on to quit smoking, but then subsequently relapsed, reported (after their initial lapse) using none of the skills that they had learned (Brandon, Tiffany, Obremski, and Baker 1990). The typical assumption is that poor use of coping skills contributed to the relapse. One implication of acquiescence is that poor coping may not cause lapses but rather may be a reflection of an intended lapse. That is, once individuals decide, perhaps unconsciously, that they are going to indulge their craving, then it stands to reason that they will fail to employ coping skills, even those skills they have mastered. From this perspective, coping sometimes may be a reflection of urges, such that mild urges provide opportunities for coping responses to be employed, while high urges, or at least urges associated with an intention to use, may to some extent preclude coping. (A less radical position is that intentions to smoke and coping resources are reciprocally linked, such that each can affect, and be affected by, the other.)

This alternative resembles Lazarus and Folkman's (1984) conception of stress and coping (Sayette 2004). Their three-stage appraisal model proposes that an experience of stress reflects a primary appraisal of loss, threat, or harm, coupled with a secondary appraisal of coping resources available to counter the stressor. A third "reappraisal" stage, which takes into account both the primary and secondary appraisals, ultimately determines the level of stress response. Importantly, these three appraisal processes blend together seamlessly.

In the context of craving, this model suggests that in an instant, an "urge appraisal" can emerge that actually is a function of (a) a primary appraisal of a desire to smoke,

(b) a secondary appraisal regarding whether or not one will acquiesce (i.e., cope with the urge by smoking a cigarette) or attempt to resist the desire to smoke, and (c) an urge reappraisal that may reveal a high urge along with weak efforts to cope (if the person were to acquiesce) or less intense urges accompanied by strong attempts to cope (if the person were to try to remain abstinent). Again, this model does not require that the secondary appraisal be subject to conscious awareness. At this point, of course, this application of the Lazarus and Folkman (1984) model is speculative and awaits empirical scrutiny. More generally, future research is needed to explore the possible role of acquiescence in self-regulation failure.

19.5   Conclusions

Advances in the study of cognition and emotion have led to an improved under-standing of how craving may affect decisions related to smoking. It is easy to imagine situations in which smokers who are craving may relapse despite knowing that it is a mistake (Loewenstein 1999). Nevertheless, it also is plausible that there are circum-stances in which smokers make decisions to smoke that appear rational at that moment. That is, craving may be linked with changes in cognitive processing that enhance the likelihood of smoking.

First, studies were reviewed showing cigarette craving to be linked to shifts in atten-tional bias. Consider the challenges awaiting smokers who have only just quit. When they walk down the street, there is much that reminds them of a cigarette. Certainly, bars or other obvious triggers will be noticed, but even ambiguous cues may remind them of their habit. "These ambiguous, yet ubiquitous, cues serve to activate well-practiced . . . smoking routines. . . . In essence, under certain conditions, the world can become one big temptation, requiring a vigilant effort to resist its allure" (Sayette 1999, pp. 277–278).

In addition to attentional bias, research linked craving to systematic bias in the processing of smoking-related information. Here, data examining the generation and evaluation of information related to smoking showed that smokers viewed smoking in a more favorable light while in a state of craving. These findings suggested that when craving, smokers attempting to consider the pros and cons of having a cigarette would not find smoking to be such a bad idea, and certainly not as foolish as they would have found it when considering smoking while in a neutral (low-craving) state of mind.

Finally, it was observed that craving led to changes in temporal cognition. Several types of changes in time perception were reviewed. While one is in a state of craving, time seems to slow down, thus extending these high-risk moments that require self-control (Vohs and Schmeichel, in press). At the same time, it appears that without smoking a cigarette, the craving will only intensify steadily. This apparent overprediction of the strength and duration of cravings likely contributes to the desperation often reported prior to relapse.

Together, these cognitive changes may increase the likelihood of smoking. If people in "cold" states tend to underestimate the strength of future emotional states (see Loewenstein 1999), then it may be that smokers underestimate the power of these craving-related changes in cognition. If people do underpredict the intensity of their own future craving, this would suggest that initial decisions to experiment with a drug, as well as decisions made by recovering addicts concerning the types of people, situations, and cues they expose themselves to, are distorted by biased expectations. Results from the Monitoring the Future longitudinal study (Johnston, O'Malley, and Bachman 1993), for example, suggest that high school students underestimate the chances of becoming addicted to cigarette smoking. In addition, it may be the individual's inability to recognize the effects of craving on cognitions related to smoking (i.e., to underestimate the motivational force of past or future cravings while in a non-craving state) that contributes to what Marlatt (1985) has labeled the "abstinence violation effect." The "abstinence violation effect" refers to a constellation of negative emotions and cognitions that follow an initial lapse. At a loss for why they lapsed, addicts attribute their drug use to immutable dispositional characteristics (e.g., "I just stopped thinking. Obviously, I just don't have what it takes to quit smoking"). This reaction associated with the abstinence violation effect may in part be caused by a failure to recognize the changes in cognitive and decision-making processes that have occurred while in a state of craving.

This chapter began with a question concerning the role of free will in smoking relapse. Although the act of smoking can be resisted under extreme conditions (e.g., a gun to the head), in most cases there is no gun to the head. The research discussed provides evidence that while craving, smokers likely experience the world differently, find different types of information to be salient, and experience time to pass in a different fashion than when in a more neutral state of mind. These changes in cognitive processing associated with cigarette craving may well enhance the probability that a smoker will smoke.

As noted at the outset of this chapter, whether or not this shift in the likelihood of smoking reflects a loss of free will is subject to debate and turns on one's definition of free will. Certainly these data suggest that craving alters how the will performs. Whether craving-induced changes in the functioning of free will qualifies as "disordered volition" is a more complicated question. In the introduction to this book, Prinz, Dennett, and Sebanz assert that the notion of disorder must be considered within the context of cultural and political influences. It is likely that the shifts in cognitive–motivational processes observed during cigarette cravings resemble those experienced when one is hungry or thirsty. In these latter domains, the shifts arguably are adaptive and can reflect healthy functioning. By the same token, not too many years ago smoking was viewed differently than it is today, and it would have seemed odd to consider the material reviewed in this chapter as reflecting disordered volition. Accordingly, as suggested by Prinz et al., research on craving-related processing may better be described as reflecting a *variety* than a *disorder* of volition.

Acknowledgments

Preparation of this chapter was supported in part by funding from the National Institute on Drug Abuse (R01 DA10605). I thank Tom Kirchner for comments on a draft of this chapter.

References

Ainslie, G. 1999. The dangers of willpower. In *Getting Hooked: Rationality and Addiction*, ed. J. Elster and O. Skog, pp. 65–92. Cambridge: Cambridge University Press.

Baker, T. B., E. Morse, and J. E. Sherman. 1987. The motivation to use drugs: A psychobiological analysis of urges. In *The Nebraska Symposium on Motivation: Alcohol Use and Abuse*, ed. C. Rivers, pp. 257–323. Lincoln: University of Nebraska Press.

Baker, T. B., M. E. Piper, D. E. McCarthy, M. R. Majeskie, and M. C. Fiore. 2004. Addiction motivation reformulated: An affective processing model of negative reinforcement. *Psychological Review*, *111*, 33–51.

Barlow, D. H. 1988. *Anxiety and Its Disorders: The Nature and Treatment of Anxiety and Panic*. New York: Guilford.

Baumeister, R. F., T. F. Heatherton, and D. M. Tice. 1994. *Losing Control: How and Why People Fail at Self-Regulation*. San Diego: Academic Press.

Brandon, T. H., S. T. Tiffany, K. M. Obremski, and T. B. Baker. 1990. Postcessation cigarette use: The process of relapse. *Addictive Behaviors*, *15*, 105–114.

Carter, B. L., and S. T. Tiffany. 1999. Meta-analysis of cue reactivity in addiction research. *Addiction*, *94*, 327–340.

Carter, B. L., and S. T. Tiffany. 2001. The cue-availability paradigm: Impact of cigarette availability on cue reactivity in smokers. *Experimental and Clinical Psychopharmacology*, *9*, 183–190.

Centers for Disease Control. 1996. Cigarette smoking among adults: United States, 1994. *Morbidity and Mortality Weekly Report*, *42*, 588–590.

Cepeda-Benito, A., and S. T. Tiffany. 1996. The use of a dual-task procedure for the assessment of cognitive effort associated with cigarette craving. *Psychopharmacology*, *127*, 155–163.

Copeland, A. L., T. H. Brandon, and E. P. Quinn. 1995. The Smoking Consequences Questionnaire—Adult: Measurement of smoking outcome expectancies of experienced smokers. *Psychological Assessment*, *7*, 484–494.

Ekman, P., and W. V. Friesen. 1978. *Facial Action Coding System*. Palo Alto, Calif.: Consulting Psychologists Press.

Ekman, P., W. V. Friesen, and S. Ancoli. 1980. Facial signs of emotional experience. *Journal of Personality and Social Psychology, 39*, 1125–1134.

Ekman, P., and E. L. Rosenberg, eds. 1997. *What the Face Reveals: Basic and Applied Studies of Spontaneous Expression Using the Facial Action Coding System (FACS)*. New York: Oxford University Press.

Ekman, P., and E. L. Rosenberg, eds. In press. *What the Face Reveals: Basic and Applied Studies of Spontaneous Expression Using the Facial Action Coding System (FACS)*, 2nd ed. New York: Oxford University Press.

Forsyth, A., and M. Carey. 1998. Measuring self-efficacy in the context of HIV risk reduction: Research challenges and recommendations. *Health Psychology, 17*, 559–568.

Gawin, F. H. 1991. Cocaine addiction: Psychology and neurophysiology. *Science, 251*, 1580–1586.

Gross, T., M. Jarvik, and M. Rosenblatt. 1993. Nicotine abstinence produces content-specific Stroop interference. *Psychopharmacology, 110*, 333–336.

Gwaltney, C. J., S. Shiffman, G. J. Norman, J. A. Paty, J. D. Kassel, and M. Gnys. 2001. Does smoking abstinence self-efficacy vary across situations? Identifying context-specificity within the Relapse Situation Efficacy Questionnaire. *Journal of Consulting and Clinical Psychology, 69*, 516–527.

Jansen, A. 1998. A learning model of binge eating: Cue reactivity and cue exposure. *Behaviour Research and Therapy, 36*, 257–272.

Johnston, L., P. O'Malley, and J. Bachman. 1993. *National Survey Results on Drug Use from the Monitoring the Future Study* [No. 93–3598]. Rockville, Md.: National Institute on Drug Abuse.

Juliano, L. M., and T. H. Brandon. 1998. Reactivity to instructed smoking availability and environmental cues: Evidence with urge and reaction time. *Experimental and Clinical Psychopharmacology, 6*, 45–53.

Killen, J. D., and S. P. Fortmann. 1997. Craving is associated with smoking relapse: Findings from three prospective studies. *Experimental and Clinical Psychopharmacology, 5*, 137–142.

Klein, L. C., E. J. Corwin, and M. M. Stine. 2003. Smoking abstinence impairs time estimation accuracy in cigarette smokers. *Psychopharmacology Bulletin, 37*, 90–95.

Kunda, Z. 1987. Motivated inference: Self-serving generation and evaluation of causal theories. *Journal of Personality and Social Psychology, 53*, 636–647.

Kunda, Z. 1990. The case for motivated reasoning. *Psychological Bulletin, 108*, 480–498.

Lazarus, R. S., and S. Folkman. 1984. *Stress, Appraisal, and Coping*. New York: Springer.

Loewenstein, G. 1987. Anticipation and the valuation of delayed consumption. *Economic Journal, 97*, 666–684.

Loewenstein, G. 1999. A visceral account of addiction. In *Getting Hooked: Rationality and Addiction*, ed. J. Elster and O. J. Skog, pp. 235–264. Cambridge: Cambridge University Press.

Marlatt, G. A. 1985. Cognitive factors in the relapse process. In *Relapse Prevention: Maintenance Strategies in the Treatment of Addictive Behaviors*, ed. G. A. Marlatt and J. R. Gordon, pp. 128–200. New York: Guilford.

Marlatt, G. A. 1994. Addiction, mindfulness, and acceptance. In *Acceptance and Change: Content and Context in Psychotherapy*, ed. S. C. Hayes, N. S. Jacobson, V. M. Follette, and M. J. Dougher, pp. 175–197. Reno, Nevada: Context Press.

Mogg, K., and B. P. Bradley. 1998. A cognitive-motivational analysis of anxiety. *Behaviour Research and Therapy*, 36, 809–848.

Niaura, R., D. B. Abrams, W. G. Shadel, D. J. Rohsenow, P. M. Monti, and A. D. Sirota. 1999. Cue exposure treatment for smoking relapse prevention: A controlled clinical trial. *Addiction*, 94, 629–770.

Niaura, R. S., D. J. Rohsenow, J. A. Binkoff, P. M. Monti, M. Pedraza, and D. B. Abrams. 1988. Relevance of cue reactivity to understanding alcohol and smoking relapse. *Journal of Abnormal Psychology*, 97, 133–152.

Norman, P., and M. Conner. 1995. The role of social cognition models in predicting health behaviours: Future directions. In *Predicting Health Behavior: Research and Practice with Social Cognition Models*, ed. M. Conner and P. Norman, pp. 197–225. Philadelphia: Open University Press.

Sayette, M. A. 1999. Cognitive theory and research. In *Psychological Theories of Drinking and Alcoholism*, 2nd ed., ed. K. Leonard and H. Blane, pp. 247–291. New York: Guilford.

Sayette, M. A. 2004. Self-regulatory failure and addiction. In *Handbook of Self-Regulation: Research, Theory, and Applications*, ed. R. F. Baumeister and K. D. Vohs, pp. 447–465. New York: Guilford.

Sayette, M. A., J. F. Cohn, J. M. Wertz, M. A. Perrott, and D. J. Parrott. 2001. A psychometric evaluation of the Facial Action Coding System for assessing spontaneous expression. *Journal of Nonverbal Behavior*, 25, 167–186.

Sayette, M. A., and M. R. Hufford. 1994. Effects of cue exposure and deprivation on cognitive resources in smokers. *Journal of Abnormal Psychology*, 103, 812–818.

Sayette, M. A., and M. R. Hufford. 1995. Urge and affect: A facial coding analysis of smokers. *Experimental and Clinical Psychopharmacology*, 3, 417–423.

Sayette, M. A., and M. R. Hufford. 1997. Effects of smoking urge on generation of smoking-related information. *Journal of Applied Social Psychology*, 27, 1395–1405.

Sayette, M. A., G. Loewenstein, T. R. Kirchner, and T. Travis. In press. Effects of smoking urge on temporal cognition. *Psychology of Addictive Behaviors*.

Sayette, M. A., C. S. Martin, J. G. Hull, J. M. Wertz, and M. A. Perrott. 2003. The effects of nicotine deprivation on craving response covariation in smokers. *Journal of Abnormal Psychology*, 112, 110–118.

Sayette, M. A., C. S. Martin, J. M. Wertz, S. Shiffman, and M. A. Perrott. 2001. A multidimensional analysis of cue-elicited craving in heavy smokers and tobacco chippers. *Addiction, 96,* 1419–1432.

Sayette, M. A., and D. J. Parrott. 1999. Effects of olfactory stimuli on urge reduction in smokers. *Experimental and Clinical Psychopharmacology, 7,* 151–159.

Sayette, M. A., S. Shiffman, S. T. Tiffany, R. S. Niaura, C. S. Martin, and W. G. Shadel. 2000. The measurement of drug craving. *Addiction, 95,* S189–S210.

Sayette, M. A., J. M. Wertz, C. S. Martin, J. F. Cohn, M. A. Perrott, and J. Hobel. 2003. Effects of smoking opportunity on cue-elicited urge: A facial coding analysis. *Experimental and Clinical Psychopharmacology, 11,* 218–227.

Segal, Z. V., and M. Cloitre. 1993. Methodologies for studying cognitive features of emotional disorder. In *Psychopathology and Cognition,* ed. K. S. Dobson and P. C. Kendall, pp. 19–50. San Diego: Academic.

Shiffman, S. 1982. Relapse following smoking cessation: A situational analysis. *Journal of Consulting and Clinical Psychology, 50,* 71–86.

Shiffman, S., J. B. Engberg, J. A. Paty, W. G. Perz, M. Gnys, J. D. Kassell, and M. Hickox. 1997. A day at a time: Predicting smoking lapse from daily urge. *Journal of Abnormal Psychology, 106,* 104–116.

Shiffman, S., W. G. Shadel, R. Niaura, M. A. Khayrallah, D. E. Jorenby, C. F. Ryan, et al. 2003. Efficacy of acute administration of nicotine gum in relief of cue-provoked cigarette craving. *Psychopharmacology, 166,* 345–350.

Shiffrin, R. M. 1988. Attention. In *Steven's Handbook of Experimental Psychology,* vol. 2: *Learning and Cognition,* ed. R. A. Atkinson, R. J. Herrnstein, G. Lindzey, and R. D. Luce, pp. 739–811. New York: Wiley.

Solomon, R. L. and J. D. Corbit. 1974. An opponent process theory of motivation: I. Temporal dynamics of affect. *Psychological Review, 81,* 119–145.

Tiffany, S. T. 1990. A cognitive model of drug urges and drug-use behavior: Role of automatic and nonautomatic processes. *Psychological Review, 97,* 147–168.

Tiffany, S. T. 1992. A critique of contemporary urge and craving research: Methodological, psychometric, and theoretical issues. *Advances in Behaviour Research and Therapy, 14,* 123–139.

U.S. Department of Health and Human Services. 1989. Reducing the health consequences of smoking: 25 years of progress: A report of the Surgeon General (DHHS publication no. CDC 89-8411). Washington, D.C.: U.S. Government Printing Office.

U.S. Department of Health and Human Services. 1990. The health benefits of smoking cessation: A report of the Surgeon General (DHHS publication no. CDC 90-8416). Washington, D.C.: U.S. Government Printing Office.

Vohs, K. D., and B. J. Schmichel. 2003. Self-regulation and the extended now: Controlling the self alters the subjective experience of time. *Journal of Personality and Social Psychology, 85,* 217–230.

Waters, A. J., and C. Feyerabend. 2000. Determinants and effects of attentional bias in smokers. *Psychology of Addictive Behaviors, 14* (2), 111–120.

Waters, A. J., S. Shiffman, M. A. Sayette, J. Paty, C. Gwaltney, and M. Balabanis. 2003. Attentional bias predicts outcome in smoking cessation. *Health Psychology, 22,* 378–387.

Weiss, F., C. S. Maldonado-Vlaar, L. H. Parsons, T. M. Kerr, D. L. Smith, and O. Ben-Shahar. 2000. Control of cocaine-seeking behavior by drug associated stimuli in rats: Effects on recovery of extinguished operant-responding and extracellular dopamine levels in amygdala and nucleus accumbens. *Proceedings of the National Academy of Sciences, 97,* 4321–4326.

Wertz, J. M., and M. A. Sayette. 2001a. Effects of smoking opportunity on attentional bias in smokers. *Psychology of Addictive Behaviors, 15,* 268–271.

Wertz, J. M., and M. A. Sayette. 2001b. A review of the effects of perceived drug use opportunity on self-reported urge. *Experimental and Clinical Psychopharmacology, 9,* 3–13.

Wetter, D. W., M. C. Fiore, E. R. Gritz, H. A. Lando, M. L. Stitzer, V. Hasselblad, and T. B. Baker. 1998. The agency for health care policy and research smoking cessation clinical practice guideline. *American Psychologist, 53,* 657–669.

Wickens, C. D. 1984. Processing resources in attention. In *Varieties of Attention,* ed. R. Parasuraman, R. Davis, and J. Beathy, pp. 63–102. New York: Academic.

Williams, J. M. G., A. Mathews, and C. MacLeod. 1996. The emotional Stroop task and psychopathology. *Psychological Bulletin, 120,* 3–24.

Wilson, S. J., M. A. Sayette, and J. A. Fiez. 2004. Prefrontal responses to drug cues: A neurocognitive analysis. *Nature Neuroscience, 7,* 211–214.

Wise, R. 1988. The neurobiology of craving: Implications for understanding and treatment of addiction. *Journal of Abnormal Psychology, 97,* 118–132.

Zakay, D., and R. A. Block. 1997. Temporal cognition. *Current Directions in Psychological Science, 6,* 12–16.

Zinser, M., M. Fiore, R. Davidson, and T. B. Baker. 1999. Manipulating smoking motivation: Impact on an electrophysiological index of approach motivation. *Journal of Abnormal Psychology, 108,* 240–254.

20 A Dynamic Model of the Will with an Application to Alcohol-Intoxicated Behavior

Jay G. Hull and Laurie B. Slone

Volition—The exercise of the will. (*The Oxford American Dictionary of Current English*, 1999)

Will—The faculty by which a person decides on and initiates action → (also willpower) control or restraint deliberately exerted → a desire or intention. (*The Concise Oxford Dictionary*, 1999)

Willpower—Control exercised by deliberate purpose over impulse; self-control. (*The Oxford American Dictionary of Current English*, 1999)

Willful—Willful neglect/murder, deliberate, intentional, intended, conscious, purposeful, premeditated, planned, calculated. (*The Oxford American Thesaurus of Current English*, 1990)

What is *volition* and what is the *will*? And when are they reflected in behavior? Is the will apparent when we act impulsively to attain that which we desire, like a *willful* child? Or, is it apparent when we restrain those impulses, choosing to forego a tempting dessert by sheer *willpower*? And what are the effects of external agents such as drugs and alcohol on the ability to exert one's will? In attempting to answer these questions, we think it is useful to adopt a systems theory approach. By doing so, we hope to clarify the many different ways in which "will" can be viewed and identify the specific manner in which alcohol can affect its operation.

20.1 A Dynamic Systems Model of Behavior

Elsewhere (Hull 2002), we have articulated a dynamic systems model of social behavior.[1] This model is formal in the sense that each of its propositions are expressed as mathematical equations that interact. The result is a true dynamic system that responds in qualitatively distinct ways to changing environmental circumstances. Rather than starting with a detailed description of the model, it will be useful to provide a general overview of its structure and the relation of its various aspects to questions of volition and the will.

20.1.1   Overview

The model is one of a general class of models that distinguish controlled from automatic behaviors (e.g., see Chaiken and Trope 1999). For us, this distinction of controlled versus automatic processes is fundamental to the distinction of volitional versus avolitional behavior. In addition to being "uncontrolled," automatic behavior is often held to be unintentional, nonconscious, and effortless. In contrast, controlled behavior is held to be intentional, conscious, and effortful (e.g., Bargh 1994). Note that in the definitions quoted earlier, key features of "will" included control, intentionality, consciousness, and "deliberate purpose over impulse" (e.g., effortfulness). We therefore propose that volition necessarily involves controlled processing.

Within the model, the primary features of controlled processing involve a set of linked processes that serve to override automatic behavior. This override involves the execution of a regulatory loop (e.g., Carver and Scheier 1981, 1998; Miller, Galanter, and Pribram 1960). Within this loop, (1) behaviors are perceived and coded into memory; (2) perceived acts are characterized as to their meaning through inference and elaboration processes; and (3) these now meaningful acts are compared to personal standards of behavior. Matches to these standards yield affective reactions but fail to trigger an override of current behavior. Mismatches to these standards also yield affective responses and motivation to control the current behavior in an attempt to reduce or avoid the mismatch discrepancy.[2] Motivated self-regulation takes place as action or inaction in service of plans adopted to achieve these approach/avoidance goals.

Viewed in this way, volitional behavior and the will can be associated with an override of automatic behavior that is based on personal standards. As such, volitional behavior appears controlled, intentional, and deliberate. In the absence of such an override, current behavior proceeds automatically.

If controlled processing is identified with volitional behavior, then factors that interfere with such processes can be argued to result in a "disorder of volition." Later, we will examine research on the specific behavioral effects of alcohol intoxication from this perspective. Before doing so, however, features of the model deserve closer scrutiny.

20.1.2   Automatic versus Controlled Behavior

As noted, the model begins by making a distinction between automatic and controlled behavior (e.g., Shiffrin and Schneider 1977). Automatic behavior follows from processes that link perception of a stimulus to a motor response system without engaging the comparison to standard process described above. For our purposes, it is important to note that these perceptual processes depend not simply on the properties of the stimulus but also on the accessibility and activation of preexisting representational structures (including what are traditionally viewed as cognitive and affective structures) and their associative interconnections as affected by experience. Similarly, the probability that an automatic action is executed is a function of the accessibility and activation of these representational structures and *their* linkages to motor sequences. One key set of associations concern the perception and response to contextual cues that signal potential reward or punishment for a specific motor sequence. Execution of this sequence constitutes one form of motivated (albeit automatic) approach/avoidance behavior. The accessibility of such sequences is governed in part by processes associated with classical and operant conditioning.

As noted earlier, controlled behavior as an override of current action (or inaction) follows from a process in which the stimulus is compared to an internal reference standard. We find it useful to conceptualize this controlled process in terms of distinct stages. These stages are not simply serial and unidirectional. Rather the model incorporates both serial and parallel processes and both "bottom-up" and "top-down" information flow. Although later stages are necessarily dependent for their content on early stage processes, it is also true that early stage processes are continually modified as a result of later stage processes in an integrated dynamic system (see Hull 2002 for details).

20.1.3 Perceptual System

As with automatic behavior, the first stage of controlled processing involves a perceptual system in which stimuli are processed to the extent that they are accorded sensory attention as moderated by accessible representational structures. Once again, such representational structures exist in multiple forms including what are traditionally viewed as cognitive as well as affective associations. Once perceived, a stimulus representation exists in short-term stores that decay at rates that are themselves affected by higher order processes (e.g., inferences) as well as lower order processes (e.g., the degree of sensory attention and activation of stimulus-relevant representations).

20.1.4 Inference System

Following this initial perceptual stage, information in some short-term stores is available for inference and elaboration. A key aspect of this inference stage involves the evaluation of the stimulus vis-à-vis relevant standards. These standards may be positive or negative in nature and can be conceptualized in terms of expectancies, norms, or goals depending on the nature of the stimulus being evaluated. Within any self-regulatory system, it is useful to conceptualize such standards as hierarchically organized according to level of abstraction (e.g., in terms of an individual movement; the place of that movement in a coordinated set of movements, or act; the meaning of that act within a social context; the implication of such a meaningful act for one's personal characteristics; the implication of those characteristics for one's enactment of a social role; the implications of those role enactments for one's sense of identity). The extent to which this "matching-to-standard" process occurs is in part a function of the activation of standard relevant knowledge located within this hierarchy. Similarly, the specific standard that is used is a function of its activation relative to other potentially applicable standards. "Matches" occur if the stimulus representation falls within a fuzzy set of acceptable representations. "Mismatches" occur if the stimulus falls outside this set. Mismatches typically evoke increased attention to the stimulus. In addition, both matches and mismatches yield distinct feeling states associated with affective responses. Depending on the nature of the expectancy that is matched or mismatched, this may be either positive or negative affect that, with invocation of specific attribution processes, can form the basis of a specific emotion. Furthermore, affective responses can combine to create mood states. Affect, mood, and emotion all decay over time at rates that are themselves a function of their activation intensity as well as the operation of other variables in the system.[3]

20.1.5   Regulation Motivation System

In addition to evoking a reallocation of sensory attention, mismatches yield both control-based affect and motivation to respond to the mismatch discrepancy. Degree of motivation is a function of the degree of violation, weighted by the importance of the standard being violated within a network of standards, as well as the intensity of the affective state that arises from the mismatch.

20.1.6   Behavioral Regulation System

Standard-relevant motivation can be directed toward either approaching the stimulus responsible for the mismatch sequence or toward avoiding it. The choice of approach (either active in the form of overt behavior or passive in the form of intentional inaction) or avoidance (either active avoidance such as escape or passive avoidance such as intentional neglect) is a break point such that subsequent affect, perception (sensory attention), cognition (inference, elaboration, evaluation), affect, and behavior are qualitatively different depending on whether motivation is channeled toward approach versus avoidance. This regulated approach/avoidance choice is a function of many factors including the accessibility of relevant plans and motor sequences. The relative accessibility of a particular plan over alternatives is in part a function of its perceived efficacy to reduce the mismatch discrepancy. Perceived efficacy is in turn a function of the size of the discrepancy mismatch, the availability of affirmational memories (memories of the effectiveness of a specific action as well as a general history of effective action), and the current affective state of the individual.

20.1.7   Learning

Enactment of an effective behavior increases the likelihood of the individual to respond in a similar fashion in response to the stimulus in the future by increasing the accessibility of both cognitive plans and motor sequences tagged as relevant to the situational context. Furthermore, effective action yields both specific and general representations of self as effective (i.e., affirmational memories). Finally, reducing mismatch discrepancies has ripple effects throughout the system, affecting such other factors as affect and affect decay, the weighting of standards within the hierarchical organization, and ultimately the necessity of controlled as opposed to automatic responses to similar future situational contexts.

20.2   Disorders of Volition

If volitional acts are associated with controlled as opposed to automatic processes, then circumstances that disrupt processes associated with the dynamics of control yield "disorders of volition." These disorders can occur either as failures to act where currently inactive or as failures to inhibit action where currently active or automatically impelled to act. As described, the control sequence is multifaceted, and hence "disordered wills" can occur as a consequence of disruptions at multiple points in the system. For example, volitional action can be impaired within the Perceptual System through disruptions of attention, encoding, and elaboration of a stimulus that is relevant to control standards. It can be impaired within the Inference System through disruption of the interpretation of the meaning of the stimulus, decreased activation or accessibility of relevant standards (e.g., impaired goal choice), or disruption of the mismatch recognition and the matching-to-standard process (e.g., reduced conflict recognition). In addition to disruption of these relatively "cold" cognitive systems, volition can be impaired through decrements in affective responses and their impact within a "hot" Regulation Motivation System. Within the Behavioral Regulation System, volition can be impaired through decreased accessibility or activation of discrepancy-relevant plans, decreased ability to switch from relatively ineffective to effective plans, or decrements in the perceived efficacy of those plans to reduce the discrepancy (e.g., yielding decreased determination). Finally, volition may be impaired as a consequence of decrements in the long-term registration of effective plans as relevant to specific contexts (i.e., lack of learning).

20.3   Alcohol Intoxication as a Disorder of Volition

In order to illustrate an application of this dynamic model to questions of volition, we consider the effects of alcohol intoxication on behavior. One might naturally assume that alcohol interferes with volitional behavior or will. After all, alcohol is popularly conceived as disinhibitory: People are assumed to behave in a variety of ways that they would not in a sober state.

In restricting ourselves to the impact of alcohol *intoxication* on disorders of volition, the reader should take note of multiple other ways in which alcohol may be related to volitional behavior. Elsewhere we provide a more complete review of each of these literatures (Hull and Slone 2004):

(a) Individuals who lack willpower or self-control are more likely to experience problem drinking and alcohol dependence (e.g., Adalbjarnardottir and Rafnsson 2001; Wills, DuHammel, and Vaccaro 1995).

(b) Environments that foster self-control decrease risk of alcohol dependence (e.g., Guo, Hawkins, Hill, and Abbott 2001; Wechsler, Lee, Gledhill-Hoyt, and Nelson 2001).

(c) Individuals who are addicted to alcohol are more likely to report uncontrollable urges to drink or craving when exposed to alcohol cues (i.e., alcohol availability cues impair "willpower"; e.g., Cooney, Litt, Morse, Bauer, and Gaupp 1997; Hussong, Hicks, Levy, and Curran 2001; Jansma, Breteler, Schippers, De Jong, and Van der Staak 2000; see Sayette, this volume, and Bechara, this volume, for similar points applied to smoking).

(d) Alcohol is usually consumed with the intent of achieving its positive social and psychological consequences (e.g., enhancing sociability and self-confidence; LaBouvie and Bates 2002; MacLean and Lecci 2000; Comeau, Stewart, and Loba 2001) as well as to blunt negative experiences (e.g., stress; Conger 1951, 1956). Far from impairing the will, then, alcohol consumption is usually a volitional act (although one might argue that this is less true once the individual becomes intoxicated). Whether or not one consumes alcohol is thus in part a consequence of whether one believes that drinking will advance one's intentions with respect to a chosen goal.

(e) Alcohol-related behavior is not simply a consequence of the intoxicated state but in part stems from the cognition that one has consumed alcohol (see Hull and Bond 1986 for a review). Having a handy excuse for inappropriate behavior, one is now free to engage in a variety of socially disapproved actions that one personally desires to enact. In other words, drinking becomes a vehicle for volitionally engaging in disapproved actions without accepting personal responsibility. Far from a disorder of volition, then, alcohol can serve as a facilitator of volition.

This list of observations makes clear that (a) volitionally impaired individuals may drink alcohol because they are volitionally impaired (drinking because of reduced willpower), and (b) volitionally unimpaired individuals may choose to drink alcohol because they are volitionally unimpaired (drinking as a willful act). Neither case concerns the hypothesis to which we turn next: Drinking alcohol makes individuals volitionally impaired (drinking yields a disorder of the will).

20.3.1 Empirical Literatures: Sex and Aggression

Two major literatures dedicated to questions regarding the impact of alcohol intoxication on disordered behavior involve disinhibited sexual activity and disinhibited aggression. If disordered volition is associated with engaging in action that one either would have not chosen or would have otherwise chosen to inhibit, then research on aggression and sex suggests that alcohol impairs the will.

There is little doubt that alcohol intoxication increases aggressive behavior (e.g., Wells, Graham, and West 2000). At the same time, this effect is subject to multiple qualifications (see Bushman and Cooper 1990; Hull and Bond 1986; Ito, Miller, and Pollock 1996). Specifically, it is not the case that alcohol is associated with increased aggression per se but rather that it is associated with increased aggression in response to provocation or threat (e.g., Taylor, Gammon, and Capasso 1976).

Similarly, there is no doubt that alcohol is associated with increased sexual behavior. However, once again, this effect is subject to multiple qualifications. Specifically, alcohol tends to be associated with indiscriminant and risky sex (e.g., intercourse with multiple partners over a short period of time; Graves 1995; Wechsler, Dowdall, Davenport, and Castillo 1995; sex with partners one just met; Testa and Collins 1997). For both sex and aggression, then, alcohol is perhaps best understood to interfere with the ability to control or override a situationally cued automatic response: aggression in response to provocation, sexual intercourse with an attractive but socially risky other.

20.3.2 Mechanisms

Several different mechanisms have been suggested to account for these effects. Each can be thought of in terms of processes delineated in the dynamics systems model presented earlier.

20.3.2.1 Perception   Several authors have argued that alcohol impairs attention and perception. Specifically, they have argued that alcohol narrows the perceptual field such that the intoxicated individual focuses on the most salient aspects of the situation (e.g., Taylor and Leonard 1983). For example, when cues that evoke aggression are dominant, the intoxicated individual is more likely than the sober individual to act aggressively (e.g., Taylor et al. 1976). Similar effects are observed with sexual behavior. Thus, intoxicated individuals perceive lower levels of risk and fewer negative consequences of unsafe sex than sober individuals (e.g., Fromme, D'Amico, and Katz 1999). Compared to sober women, intoxicated women see less risk and more benefits from actions that increase sexual vulnerability (Testa, Livingston, and Collins 2000) and less risk and higher relationship potential from attractive, sexually risky partners (Murphy, Monahan, and Miller 1998). Alcohol also appears to bias the perception of the other as sexually receptive: Compared to sober individuals, intoxicated individuals exaggerate the meaning of dating availability cues and ignore the meaning of ambiguous cues when making sexual judgments (e.g., Abbey, Zawachi, and McAuslan 2000), are slower to recognize the inappropriateness of a man's behavior in a date rape vignette, and are more likely to perceive the women in such a vignette as experiencing a higher level of arousal (Gross, Bennett, Sloan, Marx, and Juergens 2001).

20.3.2.2 Inference Others have argued that alcohol impairs cognitive mechanisms, particularly those that involve elaborative processing (e.g., Birnbaum, Johnson, Hartley, and Taylor 1980; Fillmore, Vogel-Sprott, and Gavrilescu 1999; Tracy and Bates 1999). A recent study by Curtin, Patrick, Lang, Cacioppo, and Birbaumer (2001) supports the notion that alcohol impairs recognition of the meaning of cues embedded in the situational context (see also Zeichner and Pihl 1979). Relative to sober individuals, intoxicated individuals in this experiment showed a decreased brain response associated with impaired cognitive processing of a threat cue (a P300 event related potential; ERP; in a divided attention task in which participants had been told the stimulus signaled shock; see Sommer and Leuthold 1998 for a review of related ERP findings).

20.3.2.3 Affect According to another account, alcohol blunts affective responses (e.g., anxiety) and as a consequence disinhibits behavior that may otherwise have been restrained. There are several accounts of how this might occur: either because alcohol decreases anxiety directly (Conger 1956), decreases anxiety indirectly via its impact on attention and/or cognition (e.g., Curtin et al. 2001), or decreases anxiety indirectly only when the meaning of stressful stimuli has not been sufficiently processed prior to intoxication (e.g., Sayette 1993, 1999).

20.3.2.4 Conflict detection and resolution Finally, several researchers have noted that alcohol is particularly likely to affect behavior when the situation involves conflicting cues (e.g., cues for action vs. cues for inaction/inhibition). According to some, it does so by biasing processing to focus on the most salient stimuli to the detriment of processing contradictory cues that are less salient (Steele and Southwick 1985). For example, with respect to the previously described research on sexual behavior, it would appear that alcohol had a greater impact on cues associated with negative rather than positive aspects of the target (diminished processing of sexual risk as opposed to attractiveness; Murphy et al. 1998; perception of sexual receptivity as opposed to unavailability; Abbey et al. 2000; Gross et al. 2001).

Some have attributed this pattern to the combined effects of alcohol on attention and cognition (termed "alcohol myopia" by Steele and Josephs 1990). More recently, some have argued that alcohol has direct effects on cognitive mechanisms responsible for processing and responding to conflict, per se. Thus, perceiving two stimuli is qualitatively distinct from perceiving conflict between those stimuli. As argued earlier, stimulus perception and elaboration mechanisms are distinct from the matching-to-standard mechanism. For example, perceiving a stimulus in a series is qualitatively distinct from recognizing that it does not fit a pattern of stimuli presented to that point (it violates an expectancy-based standard).

Diminished processing of conflict can most clearly be seen in studies specifically designed to investigate the role of alcohol intoxication in response to conflicted situations. For example, Cooper and Orcutt (1997) report that among sober men, conflict over sex is unrelated to the probability of sexual intercourse on the first date, whereas among intoxicated men, conflict over sex is associated with a fourfold increase in the probability of sexual intercourse.

Conceptually similar results have been observed in laboratory studies of intoxicated response to conflicting cues using go/no-go and go–stop paradigms. In a go/no-go paradigm, participants are told to respond with a behavior when a particular stimulus is presented (i.e., go), but to withhold the same response when an alternative stimulus is presented (i.e., no-go). In a go–stop paradigm, participants are told to respond to a target presentation (e.g., classify a target presented on a computer screen as a word or a nonword = go) unless the target is presented together with another cue (e.g., a noise burst = stop). Relative to sober control conditions, alcohol intoxication has little effect on responses in the absence of conflict (e.g., reaction times on go trials). On the other hand, alcohol substantially impairs performance on conflict trials (inhibition on stop trials; Mulvihill, Skilling, and Vogel-Sprott 1997). This effect seems to be unique to situations involving cues indicating both action and inaction. Thus, a manipulation that clarifies the situation by rewarding either correct responses *or* correct inhibitions (but not both) reduces the impact of intoxication (Fillmore and Vogel-Sprott 1999, 2000).

Recent research would seem to suggest that the effect of alcohol is not specific to response inhibition per se but rather follows from the inconsistency (mismatch) of the response signaled for the individual trial relative to the response signaled for most trials. For example, in a study by Marczinski and Fillmore (2003), if a majority of trials indicated action, alcohol impaired ability to inhibit responses on those trials that call for inaction; however, if a majority of trials called for inaction, alcohol impaired the ability to respond on those trials that call for action.

Consistent with the implication of this research, using a go/no-go paradigm, Marinkovic, Halgren, Klopp, and Maltzman (2000) found that among intoxicated individuals, motor preparation started *before* a decision could be reached as to whether the stimulus indicated a go or no-go response (as indicated by ERPs over motor cortex). In contrast, among sober individuals, a motor response was only begun after processing the cue indicative of a go trial. In other words, intoxicated individuals were set to respond, and this response was short-circuited if they completed processing of the no-go stimulus in time. In contrast, sober individuals waited to mobilize their response until they had processed a stimulus that signaled action.

A recent study by Curtin and Fairchild (2003) further suggests that intoxication impairs the *detection* of conflict per se (as opposed to the perception and encoding of the stimuli that happen to be in a conflicted relation to one another). This experiment involved a Stroop task in which participants were to name the color of words printed in various inks. The words could be congruent with the ink color (the word "red" in red ink) or incongruent (the word "red" in green ink). ERPs indicative of the detection of conflict and necessity for cognitive control (N450) as well as ERPs indicative of conflict resolution (NSW) were impaired by intoxication. The former response may be associated with the impact of alcohol on decreased activity in the anterior cingulate cortex (e.g., Ridderinkhof, de Vlugt, Bramlage, Spaan, Elton, Snel, and Band 2002) and the latter with its effect on decreased activity in the dorsolateral prefrontal cortex (e.g., Wendt and Risberg 2001). These brain structures have been implicated by many of the authors in the present volume (e.g., Spence; Frith; and Nitschke and Mackiewicz) as involved in volitional behavior.

20.3.3   Summary

On the basis of these studies, there appears to be support for several different mechanisms whereby alcohol affects behavior relative to sober controls. Specifically, these include attention/perception (Perceptual System), elaboration and conflict detection (Inference System), and conflict resolution (Behavior Regulation System). Each of these would appear to have specific implications for the association of alcohol intoxication with questions regarding volition and the will.

20.4   Dynamic Will

Insofar as the proposed dynamic system depends on a feedback-loop control system with basic elements of perception, cognition, and motor control, it shares much in common with other approaches taken in this volume: from the attention–cognition–motor control trichotomy discussed by Metzinger, to Proust's conceptualization of control theory as involving sensory monitoring and error feedback in a control loop, and Brown's model of goal-directed behavior specific to depression. In addition, the emphasis in the dynamic system of a control process override of automatic behavior echoes Frith's notion that volition involves suppression of stimulus-driven responses, Bechara's claim that the reflective system must be used to overcome the impulse system, and Sayette's notion of craving as a motivational state triggering multiple changes in cognitive processing that override resistance and promote drug use.

Beyond these general similarities of form (as a shared reliance on Good Old-Fashioned Artificial Intelligence; see Prinz, Dennett, and Sebanz, this volume), specific aspects of the system are relevant to processes viewed by others as central to volitional behavior. For example, Cohen and Gollwitzer's (this volume) contention that goals are differentially useful depending on their level of abstraction (i.e., implementation conceptualizations are more effective in guiding behavior than abstract goal conceptualizations) is consistent with our argument for the importance of conceiving standards as hierarchically arranged (see also Carver and Scheier 1981, 1998; Vallacher and Wegner 1987). Arguments by Spence, by Frith, and by Nitschke and Mackiewicz (each in this volume) that anterior cingulate cortex and dorsolateral prefrontal cortex are important to volitional behavior fits with our analysis of the impairment of processes associated with these structures as mediating the impact of alcohol intoxication on volitional action.

20.4.1 Theoretical puzzles and paradoxes

In addition to integrating a variety of perspectives represented in this volume, we also believe that conceiving volition in this way can serve to clarify long-standing questions regarding the nature of the will.

20.4.1.1 Factors not sufficient to define volitional behavior First, let us make clear that given the active role of the individual in the construction of perception, we regard both the individual (self) and the environment as jointly implied in both automatic and controlled behavior (e.g., Hull, Slone, Meteyer, and Matthews 2002). If controlled processing is a necessary feature of volitional behavior, it follows that involvement of the unique qualities of the individual (actions formed and informed by internal conditions) by itself is *not* sufficient to define volitional behavior.

Second, behavior guided through controlled regulation with respect to a standard (e.g., a goal) can become automated in service of that standard such that it no longer requires controlled processing (e.g., Shiffrin and Schneider 1977). Again, *if* controlled processing is a necessary feature of volitional behavior, it follows that goal-driven activity (actions in the service of needs, motives, desires, or goals) by itself is *not* sufficient to define volitional behavior. Third, both "hot motivation" and "cold cognition" may be involved in automatic behavior (cold cognition in the form of the encoding of cues; hot motivation in conditioned responses to stimuli indicating potential reward and punishment), and hence the hot/cold distinction is likewise not sufficient to distinguish volitional from avolitional behavior. Instead, we would argue that to the extent that volition involves the unique qualities of the individual, hot/cold processes, and goals as standards, it is only because they are *part of* a controlled process that necessarily involves comparison of current action to personal standards of behavior.

20.4.1.2 Volition and responsibility Finally, with respect to responsibility for one's actions (which typically assumes volition), the present approach simply assumes an ability to regulate one's behavior with respect to a standard through invocation of a controlled process. Responsibility for *choosing* to engage in one action as opposed to other potential actions assumes metacognitive controlled processes involved in the *regulated behavior of choosing* one's personal standard using a higher order standard concerning the morality of alternative standards. Codes of legal responsibility have qualities that follow this logic. This includes the McNaughten rule for criminal insanity (see Golding, Skeem, Roesch, and Zapf 1998) that a person be able to draw the inference that his or her behavior is right or wrong relative to a normative standard of conduct, and the American Law Institute's additional stipulation that one be able to regulate behavior based on this standard:

A person is not responsible for a criminal conduct if at the time of such conduct as a result of mental disorder or defect he lacks substantial capacity *either to appreciate* the criminality or wrongfulness of his conduct *or to conform* his conduct to the requirements of the law. (American Law Institute 1985, Section 4.01; emphasis added)

Note that such personal responsibility need not involve regulation to a personal standard, only recognition and disregard of the application of a societal standard.

20.4.1.3 Consciousness Questions of consciousness have not arisen in this discussion. As noted at the start of this chapter, consciousness is often included (together with intentionality and effortfulness) as a characteristic of controlled processing. Nonetheless, many have noted that these characteristics do not necessarily co-occur (e.g., Bargh and Chartrand 1999). Where they do not co-occur, we do not regard consciousness as necessary for characterizing an act as volitional. Quite the contrary, we see consciousness as frequently misinformed as to the actual causes of behavior including the involvement of volition (e.g., Wegner and Wenzlaff 1996). This does not negate the fact that consciousness of volition (e.g., as a phenomenal model of intentionality relations; see Metzinger, this volume) is an interesting problem in its own right.

20.5 Conclusion

We believe that the present analysis offers a definition of volitional action that is capable of clearly resolving sometimes confusing use of the terms "will" and "volition." Are children being willful when they act impulsively to attain that which they desire? No. Children may have desires and may act impulsively, but they only become "willful" when they recognize and reject a standard (e.g., your standard) as a guide for their behavior. Is the will involved when children restrain those impulses? Yes—and that is true whether they do so based on their own personal standards or societal standards, and whether they are aware or unaware of what they are doing or why.

Can the functioning of the will be impaired by external agents such as alcohol? Yes. We have noted multiple mechanisms involved in this effect as well as additional mechanisms that may be involved in other disorders of the will. As evidence that the impact of alcohol on the will has long been acknowledged by popular culture, we close as we opened with a common definition, this time of will-*less* creatures:

zom·bie (*noun*)
1 a will-less . . . human . . . capable only of automatic movement. . . .
3 a mixed drink made of several kinds of rum, liqueur, and fruit juice. (*Merriam-Webster's Collegiate Dictionary*, 1993)

Notes

1. Each of the postulates of the model is grounded in empirical research. Rather than reviewing this research and noting the specific similarities and differences between the account provided by this model and alternative models of self-knowledge and self-regulation (e.g., Carver and Scheier 1981, 1998; Duval and Wicklund 1972; Higgins 1987; Vallacher and Wegner 1987), we refer the interested reader to Hull 2002.

2. The model distinguishes positive and negative standards. Mismatches as undershooting a positive standard or overshooting a negative standard yield motivation to reduce the discrepancy (see Hull 2002 for details).

3. Within the system, positive and negative affect are distinct, independent, unipolar feeling states that follow as a consequence of match and mismatch processes. Mood is a bipolar combination of unipolar positive and negative affect. Emotions are feeling states that arise as a consequence of the application of specific cognitive labels to positive and negative affective states. When feeling states are subsequently paired with a specific mismatch discrepancy, they yield motivation to engage in behaviors that reduce the perceived discrepancy.

References

Abbey, A., T. Zawacki, and P. McAuslan. 2000. Alcohol's effects on sexual perception. *Journal of Studies on Alcohol*, *61*, 688–697.

Adalbjarnardottir, S., and F. D. Rafnsson. 2001. Perceived control in adolescent substance use: Concurrent and longitudinal analyses. *Psychology of Addictive Behaviors*, *15*, 25–32.

American Law Institute. 1985. Section 4.01.

Bargh, J. A. 1994. The four horsemen of automaticity: Awareness, intention, efficiency, and control in social cognition. In *Handbook of Social Cognition*, ed. R. S. J. Wyer and T. K. Srull, pp. 1–40. Hillsdale, N. J.: Lawrence Erlbaum.

Bargh, J. A., and T. L. Chartrand. 1999. The unbearable automaticity of being. *American Psychologist*, *54*, 462–479.

Birnbaum, I. M., M. K. Johnson, J. T. Hartley, and T. H. Taylor. 1980. Alcohol and elaborative schemas for sentences. *Journal of Experimental Psychology: Human Learning and Memory*, *6*, 293–300.

Bushman, B. J., and H. M. Cooper. 1990. Effects of alcohol on human aggression: An integrative research review. *Psychological Bulletin*, *107*, 341–354.

Carver, C. S., and M. F. Scheier. 1981. *Attention and Self-Regulation: A Control-Theory Approach to Human Behavior*. New York: Springer-Verlag.

Carver, C. S., and M. F. Scheier. 1998. *On the Self-Regulation of Behavior.* New York: Cambridge University Press.

Chaiken, S., and Y. Trope. 1999. *Dual-Process Theories in Social Psychology.* New York: Guilford Press.

Comeau, N., S. H. Stewart, and P. Loba. 2001. The relations of trait anxiety, anxiety sensitivity, and sensation seeking to adolescents' motivations for alcohol, cigarette, and marijuana use. *Addictive Behaviors, 26,* 803–825.

The Concise Oxford Dictionary. 1999. New York: Oxford University Press.

Conger, J. J. 1951. The effects of alcohol on conflict behavior in the albino rat. *Quarterly Journal of Studies on Alcohol, 12,* 1–29.

Conger, J. J. 1956. Alcoholism: Theory, problem, and challenge: II. Reinforcement theory and the dynamics of alcoholism. *Quarterly Journal of Studies on Alcohol, 17,* 296–305.

Cooney, N. L., M. D. Litt, P. A. Morse, L. O. Bauer, and L. Gaupp. 1997. Alcohol cue reactivity, negative-mood reactivity, and relapse in treated alcoholic men. *Journal of Abnormal Psychology, 106,* 243–250.

Cooper, M. L., and H. K. Orcutt. 1997. Drinking and sexual experience on first dates among adolescents. *Journal of Abnormal Psychology, 106,* 191–202.

Curtin, J. J., and B. A. Fairchild. 2003. Alcohol and cognitive control: Implications for regulation of behavior during response conflict. *Journal of Abnormal Psychology, 112,* 424–436.

Curtin, J. J., C. J. Patrick, A. R. Lang, J. T. Cacioppo, and N. Birbaumer. 2001. Alcohol affects emotion through cognition. *Psychological Science, 12,* 527–531.

Duval, S., and R. A. Wicklund. 1972. *A Theory of Objective Self-Awareness.* New York: Academic Press.

Fillmore, M. T., and M. Vogel-Sprott. 1999. An alcohol model of impaired inhibitory control and its treatment in humans. *Experimental and Clinical Psychopharmacology, 7,* 49–55.

Fillmore, M. T., and M. Vogel-Sprott. 2000. Response inhibition under alcohol: Effects of cognitive and motivational conflict. *Journal of Studies on Alcohol, 61,* 239–246.

Fillmore, M. T., M. Vogel-Sprott, and D. Gavrilescu. 1999. Alcohol effects on intentional behavior: Dissociating controlled and automatic influences. *Experimental and Clinical Psychopharmacology, 7,* 372–378.

Fromme, K., E. J. D'Amico, and E. C. Katz. 1999. Intoxicated sexual risk taking: An expectancy or cognitive impairment explanation? *Journal of Studies on Alcohol, 60,* 54–63.

Golding, S. L., J. L. Skeem, R. Roesch, and P. A. Zapf. 1998. The assessment of criminal responsibility: Current controversies. In *The Handbook of Forensic Psychology,* 2nd ed., ed. A. K. Hess and I. B. Weiner. New York: Wiley.

Graves, K. L. 1995. Risky sexual behavior and alcohol use among young adults: Results from a national survey. *American Journal of Health Promotion, 10,* 27–36.

Gross, A. M., T. Bennett, L. Sloan, B. P. Marx, and J. Juergens. 2001. The impact of alcohol and alcohol expectancies on male perception of female sexual arousal in a date rape analog. *Experimental and Clinical Psychopharmacology, 9,* 380–388.

Guo, J., J. D. Hawkins, K. G. Hill, and R. D. Abbott. 2001. Childhood and adolescent predictors of alcohol abuse and dependence in young adulthood. *Journal of Studies on Alcohol, 62,* 754–762.

Higgins, E. T. 1987. Self-discrepancy: A theory relating self and affect. *Psychological Review, 94,* 319–340.

Hull, J. G. 2002. Modeling the structure of self-knowledge and the dynamics of self-regulation. In *Self and Motivation: Emerging Psychological Perspectives,* vol. 2, ed. A. Tesser, D. Stapel, and J. Wood, pp. 173–203. Washington, D.C.: American Psychological Association.

Hull, J. G., and C. F. Bond. 1986. Social and behavioral consequences of alcohol consumption and expectancy: A meta-analysis. *Psychological Bulletin, 99,* 347–360.

Hull, J. G., and L. B. Slone. 2004. Self-regulatory failure and alcohol use. In *Handbook of Self-Regulation Research,* ed. R. F. Baumeister and K. D. Vohs, pp. 466–491. New York: Guilford Press.

Hull, J. G., L. B. Slone, K. B. Meteyer, and A. R. Matthews. 2002. The nonconsciousness of self-consciousness. *Journal of Personality and Social Psychology, 83,* 406–424.

Hussong, A. M., R. E. Hicks, S. A. Levy, and P. J. Curran. 2001. Specifying the relations between affect and heavy alcohol use among young adults. *Journal of Abnormal Psychology, 110,* 449–461.

Ito, T. A., N. Miller, and V. E. Pollock. 1996. Alcohol and aggression: A meta-analysis on the moderating effects of inhibitory cues, triggering events, and self-focused attention. *Psychological Bulletin, 120,* 60–82.

Jansma, A., M. H. M. Breteler, G. M. Schippers, C. A. J. De Jong, and C. P. F. Van Der Staak. 2000. No effect of negative mood on the alcohol cue reactivity of in-patient alcoholics. *Addictive Behaviors, 25,* 619–624.

Labouvie, E., and M. E. Bates. 2002. Reasons for alcohol use in young adulthood: Validation of a three-dimensional measure. *Journal of Studies on Alcohol, 63,* 145–155.

MacLean, M. G., and L. Lecci. 2000. A comparison of models of drinking motives in a university sample. *Psychology of Addictive Behaviors, 14,* 83–87.

Marczinski, C. A., and M. T. Fillmore. 2003. Preresponse cues reduce the impairing effects of alcohol on the execution and suppression of responses. *Experimental and Clinical Psychopharmacology, 11,* 110–117.

Marinkovic, K., E. Halgren, J. Klopp, and I. Maltzman. 2000. Alcohol effects on movement-related potentials: A measure of impulsivity? *Journal of Studies on Alcohol, 61,* 24–31.

Merriam-Webster's Collegiate Dictionary, 10th ed. 1993. Springfield, Mass.: Merriam-Webster.

Miller, G. A., E. Galanter, and K. H. Pribram. 1960. *Plans and the Structure of Behavior.* Oxford: Holt.

Mulvihill, L. E., T. A. Skilling, and M. Vogel-Sprott. 1997. Alcohol and the ability to inhibit behavior in men and women. *Journal of Studies on Alcohol, 58,* 600–605.

Murphy, S. T., J. L. Monahan, and L. C. Miller. 1998. Inference under the influence: The impact of alcohol and inhibition conflict on women's sexual decision making. *Personality and Social Psychology Bulletin, 24,* 517–528.

The Oxford American Dictionary of Current English. 1999. New York: Oxford University Press.

The Oxford American Thesaurus of Current English. 1990. Ed. Christine A. Lindberg. New York: Oxford University Press.

Ridderinkhof, K. R., Y. de Vlugt, A. Bramlage, M. Spaan, M. Elton, J. Snel, and G. P. H. Band. 2002. Alcohol consumption impairs detection of performance errors in mediofrontal cortex. *Science, 298,* 2209–2211.

Sayette, M. A. 1993. An appraisal-disruption model of alcohol's effects on stress responses in social drinkers. *Psychological Bulletin, 114,* 459–476.

Sayette, M. A. 1999. Cognitive theory and research. In *Psychological Theories of Drinking and Alcoholism,* 2nd ed., ed. K. E. Leonard and H. T. Blane, pp. 247–291. New York: Guilford Press.

Shiffrin, R. M., and W. Schneider. 1977. Controlled and automatic human information processing: II. Perceptual learning, automatic attending, and a general theory. *Psychological Review, 84,* 127–190.

Sommer, W., and H. Leuthold. 1998. Acute effects of alcohol revealed by event related potential. In *Nicotine, Caffeine, and Social Drinking: Behavior and Brain Function,* ed. J. Snell and M. Lorist, pp. 275–287. London: Harwood Academic.

Steele, C. M., and R. A. Josephs. 1990. Alcohol myopia: Its prized and dangerous effects. *American Psychologist, 45,* 921–933.

Steele, C. M., and L. Southwick. 1985. Alcohol and social behavior: I. The psychology of drunken excess. *Journal of Personality and Social Psychology, 48,* 18–34.

Taylor, S. P., C. B. Gammon, and D. R. Capasso. 1976. Aggression as a function of the interaction of alcohol and threat. *Journal of Personality and Social Psychology, 34,* 938–941.

Taylor, S. P., and K. E. Leonard. 1983. Alcohol and human aggression. In *Aggression: Theoretical and Empirical Reviews,* ed. R. G. Geen and E. I. Donnerstein, pp. 77–102. New York: Academic Press.

Testa, M., and R. L. Collins. 1997. Alcohol and risky sexual behavior: Event-based analyses among a sample of high-risk women. *Psychology of Addictive Behaviors, 11,* 190–201.

Testa, M., J. A. Livingston, and R. L. Collins. 2000. The role of women's alcohol consumption in evaluation of vulnerability to sexual aggression. *Experimental and Clinical Psychopharmacology, 8,* 185–191.

Tracy, J. I., and M. Bates. 1999. The selective effects of alcohol on automatic and effortful memory processes. *Neuropsychology, 13,* 282–290.

Vallacher, R. R., and D. M. Wegner. 1987. What do people think they're doing? Action identification and human behavior. *Psychological Review, 94,* 3–15.

Wechsler, H., G. W. Dowdall, A. Davenport, and S. Castillo. 1995. Correlates of college student binge drinking. *American Journal of Public Health, 85,* 921–926.

Wechsler, H., J. E. Lee, J. Gledhill-Hoyt, and T. F. Nelson. 2001. Alcohol use and problems at colleges banning alcohol: Results of a national survey. *Journal of Studies on Alcohol, 62,* 133–141.

Wegner, D. M., and R. M. Wenzlaff. 1996. Mental control. In *Social Psychology: Handbook of Basic Principles*, ed. E. T. Higgin and A. W. Kruglanski, pp. 466–492. New York: Guilford Press.

Wells, S., K. Graham, and P. West. 2000. Alcohol-related aggression in the general population. *Journal of Studies on Alcohol, 61,* 626–632.

Wendt, P. E., and J. Risberg. 2001. Ethanol reduces rCFB activation of left dorsolateral prefrontal cortex during a verbal fluency task. *Brain and Language, 77,* 197–215.

Wills, T. A., K. DuHamel, and D. Vaccaro. 1995. Activity and mood temperament as predictors of adolescent substance use: Test of a self-regulation mediational model. *Journal of Personality and Social Psychology, 68,* 901–916.

Zeichner, A., and R. O. Pihl. 1979. Effects of alcohol and behavior contingencies on human aggression. *Journal of Abnormal Psychology, 88,* 153–160.

List of Contributors

George Ainslie
Veterans Affairs Medical Center,
Coatesville, and Temple Medical College

Tim Bayne
Department of Philosophy, Macquarie
University, Sydney

Antoine Bechara
Institute for the Neurological Study of
Emotion, Decision Making, and
Creativity, University of Southern
California, and Department of
Neurology, University of Iowa

Paul W. Burgess
Institute of Cognitive Neuroscience and
Department of Psychology, University
College London

Anna-Lisa Cohen
Department of Psychology, New York
University

Daniel Dennett
Center for Cognitive Studies, Tufts
University

Stéphanie Dubal
CNRS UMR 7593, Laboratory for
Vulnerability, Adaptation and
Psychopathology, Hôpital de la
Salpêtrière, Paris

Philippe Fossati
CNRS UMR 7593, Laboratory for
Vulnerability, Adaptation and
Psychopathology, Hôpital de la
Salpêtrière, Paris

Chris Frith
University College London

Sam J. Gilbert
Institute of Cognitive Neuroscience and
Department of Psychology, University
College London

Peter Gollwitzer
Department of Psychology, New York
University, and Fachgruppe Psychologie,
University of Konstanz

Jordan Grafman
Cognitive Neuroscience Section,
National Institute of Neurological
Disorders and Stroke, National Institutes
of Health, Bethesda

Patrick Haggard
Institute of Cognitive Neuroscience,
University College London

Jay G. Hull
Department of Psychological and Brain
Sciences, Dartmouth College

Marc Jeannerod
Institut des Sciences Cognitives, Bron

Roland Jouvent
CNRS UMR 7593, Laboratory for
Vulnerability, Adaptation and
Psychopathology, Hôpital de la
Salpêtrière, Paris

Frank Krueger
Cognitive Neuroscience Section,
National Institute of Neurological
Disorders and Stroke, National Institutes
of Health, Bethesda

Neil Levy
Centre for Applied Philosophy and
Public Ethics, Department of
Philosophy, University of Melbourne

Peter F. Liddle
Division of Psychiatry, University of
Nottingham

Kristen L. Mackiewicz
Waisman Laboratory for Brain Imaging
and Behavior, Departments of Psychiatry
and Psychology, University of
Wisconsin, Madison

Thomas Metzinger
Philosophisches Seminar, Johannes-
Gutenberg University, Mainz

Jack B. Nitschke
Waisman Laboratory for Brain Imaging
and Behavior, Departments of Psychiatry
and Psychology, University of
Wisconsin, Madison

Jiro Okuda
Gene Analysis and Brain Activity
Imaging Laboratory, Tamagawa
University, Tokyo

Adrian M. Owen
Medical Research Council, Cognition
and Brain Sciences Unit, Cambridge

Chris Parry
Department of Academic Clinical
Psychiatry, University of Sheffield

Wolfgang Prinz
Department of Psychology, Max Planck
Institute for Human Cognitive and Brain
Sciences, Leipzig

Joëlle Proust
Institut Jean-Nicod, CNRS, Paris

Michael A. Sayette
Department of Psychology, University of
Pittsburgh

Werner X. Schneider
Neuro-cognitive Psychology, Ludwig-
Maximilians-University, Munich

Natalie Sebanz
Department of Psychology, Rutgers
University, Newark

Jon S. Simons
Institute of Cognitive Neuroscience and
Department of Psychology, University
College London

Laurie B. Slone
National Center for PTSD, Dartmouth
Medical School

Sean A. Spence
Department of Academic Clinical
Psychiatry, University of Sheffield

Author Index

Subject Index

Anterior cingulate cortex
  damaged by chronic stress, 285, 287, 288,
    292, 297–299
  and depression, 251, 253, 258–264
  and volition, 258
Apomorphine, 217
Appetite, 134, 139, 140
  and emotion, 127, 134, 138, 139, 143n1
Athymhormia, 175
Attention, 151, 155, 164, 332, 335, 341, 382,
    385, 387, 388
  selective, 107, 243
Attentional
  bias, 421, 422, 429, 431
  control between stimulus-independent and
    stimulus-oriented thought, 374, 384
  processes, 334, 421
  supervisory attentional system, 91, 385
Attribution
  of action, 179, 186, 187
  and action recognition, 179
  of agency, 103, 108, 109, 111
  factors of self-, 178
  mis-, 186, 188
  of representation, 183
  social, 88, 92, 99, 100, 108–110
Authorship, 87–89, 91, 99, 108, 112n22
  phenomenology of, 53, 56, 57
Automatic action control, 152, 153
Automatic activation of beliefs, 158
Automatic associative model, 162
Automaticity, 153
Automation, 153, 166, 222
Autonomy, 347, 348, 358, 363, 365–368
Avoidance
  action, 294, 295
  behavior, 275, 276, 290, 292, 294–296,
    300n8
  episode, 290, 294–296
Avolition, 207, 257
  schizophrenic, 207, 208, 214–217, 219,
    224
Awareness, 70–73, 80

Bargaining
  interpersonal, 135, 143
  intertemporal, 134, 135, 137, 139, 142, 143
Basal ganglia, 283, 284, 288
Behavior
  alcohol-intoxicated, 439
  automatic, 440, 441, 443, 445, 448, 449, 451
  intentional, 384, 385
  volitional, 373, 389
Biasing in substance abusers, 402–404, 407,
    411, 412
Binding mechanisms, 74–76
Brodmann Area 10, 373, 375, 376, 378, 382,
    383, 388. See also Rostral prefrontal
    cortex

Catechol-O-methyl transferase, 224
Central monitoring hypothesis of action
    recognition, 179
Central representations, 385
Choices, 137, 347
  bundling of, 128, 132
  principled, 129, 130
  rational choice theory, 119, 143
  resolute, 125, 127
Chronic stress, 276, 297–299
  damage of anterior cingulate cortex and,
    285, 287, 288, 292, 297–299
Cigarette(s)
  craving, 420, 421, 423, 425, 431, 432
  smoking, 420, 429, 432
  cues, 421–424, 426
  free will in, 419, 427, 432
  information processing in, 423, 424
  lapse of, 422–424, 430, 432
  quitting, 419, 424, 427, 428
  relapse into, 419, 420, 422, 424, 425, 427,
    428, 430–432
  -related cognition, 420
  -related information, 422, 424, 431
  savoring, 429, 430
  self-control in, 426–428, 431
  self-regulation of, 419, 426, 427, 431